Political Development:
A General Theory and
a Latin American Case Study

POLITICAL DEVELOPMENT:
A General Theory and a Latin American Case Study

Helio Jaguaribe

Instituto Universitário de Pesquisas do Rio de Janeiro

HARPER & ROW, PUBLISHERS
New York   Evanston   San Francisco   London

Political Development:
A General Theory and a Latin American Case Study

Copyright © 1973 by Helio Jaguaribe

Standard Book Number: 06-043262-4

Library of Congress Catalog Card Number: 72-86369

Contents

BOOK II
POLITICAL DEVELOPMENT

A. THE MEANING OF POLITICAL DEVELOPMENT

BOOK III
A LATIN AMERICAN CASE STUDY

A. THE MAIN STRUCTURAL CHARACTERISTICS
OF CONTEMPORARY LATIN AMERICA

Chapter 19
GENERAL DESCRIPTION AND TYPOLOGY

Chapter 20
A STRUCTURAL ANALYSIS

B. CAUSES OF LATIN AMERICAN UNDERDEVELOPMENT

Chapter 21
THE DUALISTIC SOCIETY

Tables and Charts

Preface

The present book is the end result of long research and study on the processes of both political and overall development of societies. A preliminary manifestation of these interests was a study of Brazilian nationalism and development (1958), a book which aroused at the time, to my amazement, a sharp controversy and is now out of print. A more elaborate work on that subject, but still a first approach, is my book on political and economic development, originally published in 1962. The updated and final version was published in the United States in 1968 and in Brazil the following year.

The present book expresses the results of a fuller development of that research and study. Its actual preparation, started in 1965, is connected with the courses I had been giving at Harvard, on political development and Latin American politics. I have been busy continuously in the five following years giving renewed and more developed versions of these courses at Stanford, M.I.T., the Fletcher School, El Colegio de México, and my Institute in Rio de Janeiro, and preparing and writing this book.

I feel strongly that the problems of political and overall development of societies must be viewed within a very broad perspective, involving many of the crucial theoretical questions of the social sciences and many of the crucial events in the history of mankind. This broad view is a *sine qua non* condition for the actual understanding of these problems. This feeling explains the wide framework of the book, its extended size, and the time demanded for its preparation.

A study like the present one, more than the result of one's own research and thought, expresses a confluence of the works and ideas of a wide constellation of scholars, past and present, who could not be listed here. I think the book itself will render a partial tribute, by the references and notes spread throughout it, to the men who have most deeply influenced me. Among those with whom I have maintained a close and frequent exchange of ideas, with a direct effect on this book, I would like to mention, particularly, with my cordial gratitude, Gabriel Almond, S. N. Eisenstadt, Samuel Huntington, Carl Friedrich, Karl Deutsch, Louis Hartz, Everett Hagen, Richard Fagen, Kalman Silvert, Frank Bonilla, Robert Packenham, Hayward Alker, Albert Hirschman, Paul Rosenstein-

Rodan, Raymond Vernon, Robert West, Paul Mandel, Alex Inkeles, Irving Louis Horowitz, John Johnson, Thomas Skidmore, John Wirth, Stephan Graubard, and Leo Gross, among my American colleagues. Among my Latin American colleagues, I would like to mention the late and always dearly remembered Jorge Ahumada, Osvaldo Sunkel, Claudio Véliz, José Medina Echavarría, Aldo Ferrer, Torcuato di Tella, Enrique Oteiza, Marcos Kaplan, Jorge Sabato, José Matos Mar, Julio Cotler, Eduardo Neira, Carlos Delgado, Luis Lander, J. A. Silva Michelena, Orlando Fals Borda, Victor Urquidi, Miguel Wionczek, Ivan Illich, Raúl Prebisch, Felipe Herrera, Gino Germani, Celso Furtado, Oscar Lorenzo Fernández, Romulo Almeida, Isaac Kerstenetsky, Israel Klabin, Candido Mendes, Fernando Henrique Cardoso, Octavio Ianni, Fernando Bastos de Avila, José Honório Rodrigues, and Celso Lafer.

Like most research, that which resulted in the present book would not have been possible without the active and generous assistance of many institutions and people. I am especially grateful to Harvard and Stanford Universities, the Massachusetts Institute of Technology, the Fletcher School of Law and Diplomacy of Tufts University, and my own Institute, which have given me particularly adequate working conditions, and to the Ford Foundation which, although not helping me directly, has been a major supporter of the programs on political and Latin American development at the preceding institutions. Personally, I am in great debt to Arthur Maass, former chairman of Harvard's Department of Government, the late and always missed Max Millikan, first director of the Center for International Studies of M.I.T., Ithiel de Sola Pool, former interim chairman of the Department of Political Science of the same Institute, John Johnson, chairman of Stanford University's Committee on Latin American Studies, Gabriel Almond, former chairman of the Department of Political Science of the same university, and Robert West, director of the program on developmental studies of Tufts University's Fletcher School. I am indebted to my dear friend Candido Mendes, director of my Institute, for his most generous and unflinching support, which, together with the most friendly assistance of Almir de Castro, created the very basic conditions that have made the present study possible.

I am thankful to Mr. Benjamin G. Varela, Mrs. Cynthia Harris, and Ms. Sandra Turner for their intelligent and skilled editing of my clumsy English. The awkward expressions still remaining in this book are not due to slips of their linguistic sensibility but to my concern for the preservation of certain technical meanings. I am also very grateful for the dedicated efforts of Misses Maria Helena Leme, Rosa Peña and my dear relative Maria Amalia Silva, who shared the heavy burden of typing the manuscript.

A long and time-consuming work like the present one brings about a multitude of inconveniences for the writer's family and could not be successfully carried out without their affectionate understanding and support. I am deeply thankful for the constant understanding and encouragement of my sons and of my wife Maria Lucia, to whom this book is dedicated with love.

Helio Jaguaribe

Introduction

Aims of this book

As the title indicates, the purpose of the present book is to present a general study of the political and the overall development of societies, particularly those of the Latin American countries. The whole is viewed from a broad political, anthropological, economic, and historico-sociological perspective, with an emphasis on a global and systemic approach to social processes. The polity is analytically distinguished from its corresponding society and from the other social subsystems, but it is always seen as being systemically interrelated with them. Social subsystems are analytical structures. Empirically, social processes are always societal processes—whatever the abstraction, scientifically legitimate and necessary, that may be used for the study of their political, cultural, economic, or participational aspects.

A global and systemic approach to the study of political development requires a previous analysis of those aspects and processes of the social system as a whole and of its subsystems that are most relevant for an understanding of structural changes, particularly changes of a developmental character, and especially the promotion of such changes by political means.

As far as political development itself is concerned, the main intention of this study is to reach an operationally valuable understanding of what sort of political and social phenomenon it is and of how it can be promoted. There is a decisive distinction between purely sociological and historical approaches to such a study, which are of a more descriptive character, in structural or in specific terms, respectively, and a political science (and policy-directed) approach to that same study, which is oriented toward understanding how the concerned processes actually occur and how can they be, if at all, deliberately and systematically promoted.

The present study gives a particular emphasis, on the one hand, to operational

1

developmental political models and on the other hand, to the operational analysis of political development, the discussion of the operational conditions for its achievement, and the study of the particular conditions presently resulting from the historical characteristics of our time. The primary intention of this book is to find out whether or not it is possible, in certain conditions and given the structural characteristics of a society, to determine an objectively optimal, or at least particularly fitting, recipe for the realistic and implementable (although not infallibly successful) promotion of the political and overall development of that society.

The same operational approach characterizes the Latin American case study in this book. It is not a study primarily interested in describing the current Latin American political systems and their comparative development. Other books should be consulted for that purpose, and there are already some good ones. (See the bibliography at the end of this book.) What the present book aims to do, as far as Latin America is concerned, is to determine, initially, whether it is possible to reach, at a higher level of generalization, an objective and precise explanation for the historically unremitting underdevelopment of the Latin American countries. On the assumption that that initial question can be conveniently answered, the fundamental purpose of this study is to find out whether it is possible to determine—by making appropriate use of the theory of political models—a set of developmental models specifically fitting the various types of Latin American countries, in such a way that the adequate adoption and implementation of the fitting model, given certain conditions, would actually tend to bring about the political and overall development of the concerned countries.

Organization of this study

This study has been divided into three main parts—Books I, II, and III.

Book I contains two sections. Section A is concerned with society and change. It tries, initially, to provide, in a very succinct way, a general view of society. First the main sociological assumptions, concepts, and theories adopted in this study are discussed, and then the processes of social change are analyzed—particularly the effects of structural changes in any of the social subsystems on the other subsystems and on the whole society.

Section B of Book I is devoted to a brief study of the polity. It tries to identify and to analyze the essential characteristics of the political system, including, in a schematic form, the views of the main classics. It discusses succinctly the key questions (ontogenetic and phylogenetic) concerning the formation of power and authority, in order to clarify the ways, conditions, and possibilities of promoting social change by authoritative decisions. It analyzes the main variables of the political system and their treatment for purposes of taxonomic classification, comparative politics, and the appraisal of levels of political development. The last part of this section is devoted to the study of nontrivial political change, discussing revolution and reform as ways of political change and of social change by political means, as well as the social content of revolution and reform.

Book II, containing three sections, is concerned with the study of political development. Section A initiates that study with an inquiry into the meaning of political development. It starts with a brief recapitulation of the sociopolitical findings and conclusions of the preceding chapters that are more immediately relevant for the discussion of the problems of political development. It continues with a critical survey of the current literature on the subject. And it concludes with my attempt, in accordance with the theoretical sociopolitical framework developed earlier, to formulate a comprehensive theory of political development and to relate that theory to the overall development of national societies through political means.

Section B of Book II is devoted to the study of political models. It starts with an analysis of representational models and their role in the social sciences. It leads to a theory of operational models, as ideal types with a voluntaristic element, for the promotion, in certain conditions, of the political development of certain societies and for the employment of political means for the overall national development of these societies. Then Chapters 12 and 13 analyze some typical historical cases of national development (Great Britain and the United States, France and Germany, Japan, Russia and China) and their implied models and more relevant characteristics and conditions. The study of these cases allows the determination of the essential factors and conditions contributing to the success of some and the failure of other societies. It is then possible, in the third part of Section B (Chapters 14 and 15) to arrive at a basic general typology of societal underdevelopment and to determine, in principle, given certain fundamental conditions, which political models fit certain typical cases of underdevelopment the best and are the most capable of promoting the national development of the concerned societies.

Section C, the last of Book II, is concerned with the study of the operations involved in, and the conditions required for, the successful promotion of the political and the overall development of certain societies. It starts with an operational analysis of the processes of development making and a discussion of the involved stages. It continues with a study of the general fundamental conditions necessary and, in principle, sufficient, for the successful achievement, in abstract terms, of a project of national development. This section concludes with an inquiry into the historical conditions of our time, these conditions being the ones in which all current developmental efforts will actually have to take place. The first part of that inquiry is oriented to provide a very brief indication of the main contemporary problems resulting from the technological dimension of our present life, including the deterioration of man's natural ecosystem. The second part gives a more extensive discussion of the international conditions that have come to prevail since World War II and the possibilities and constraints they present for the current developmental efforts of the third world; particular attention is given to the Latin American countries.

The last main part of this study, Book III, presents a case study of the political and national development of the Latin American countries. The same division into major sections of several chapters has been maintained. The first section of

Book III attempts initially to present a general description and typology of the Latin American countries. Then a structural analysis of these countries points out the basic common structural traits that, within their specific differences, configurate their underdevelopment.

Section B raises two fundamental questions concerning the underdevelopment of the Latin American countries and attempts to give an objective, precise, and operationally meaningful answer to these questions. The first question concerns the historical causes of Latin American underdevelopment up to 1930. The second question asks why, since the Latin American countries have acknowledged their underdevelopment in the last decades and have become officially committed to overcoming that situation, they have not succeeded in their efforts.

Section C of Book III, the last part of this study, is devoted to an analysis and discussion of the alternatives confronting the Latin American countries, currently and in the foreseeable future, and the prospective course they are likely to follow. It consists, essentially, in the identification and analysis of two basic alternatives: dependence or autonomy, vis-à-vis the United States, which is the hegemonic power of the region. The discussion leads to an analysis, in the first place, of the probable consequences of dependence, acknowledged to be the alternative currently in course, although not yet irreversible. In the second place, it leads to a critical discussion of the two possible ways for at least some of the Latin American countries to achieve autonomous development: the revolutionary and the reformist ways. That section and this book end with an attempt to appraise the trends and prospects confronting these countries, in terms of their own realities and vis-à-vis the United States, concluding with some critical estimates about these prospects.

Book I

SOCIETY, STRUCTURAL CHANGE, AND POLITY

A
Society and Change

1

A General View of Society

A GENERAL ANALYTICAL FRAMEWORK

Locating society

The problem of locating society in a general framework of reality, besides the
interest it presents from the point of view of the philosophy of knowledge, is
particularly relevant to the social sciences and the study of society because of
the question of the societal environment. What is included in the "social
system"—to use the Parsonian terminology—and what is its external environment? The answer to this question is not only essential for analyzing the boundary exchanges between society and its extrasocietal environment, but is also
decisive in the analytical determination of what is "social" and what the internal
components of the societal complex are.

The problem of locating society in a general framework of reality, however, is
far from being a simple one. In its broadest form the problem involves a double
difficulty: (1) the general ontologico-epistemological problem of what reality is
and how we can know it and (2) at the level of the social sciences, the problem
of what society is and how we can study it. As has been observed by Don Martindale (1960), the social sciences—which appeared in the middle of the nineteenth century as an answer to the sociohistorical needs of the Western European
societies of that time and as an attempt to bridge the gap between the humanities
and the physical sciences with a new "social science"—have inherited the ontologico-epistemological debate on the mind-matter relationship, both at the
general level of the theory of reality and the theory of knowledge and at the
specific level of the social sciences. At the latter level the question involves two
polarities. First is the ontological polarity between *holism*, or the view that
society is a system or whole that cannot be reduced to the sum of its parts, and
elementalism, or the belief that social reality is the aggregation of interacting
individuals. Second is the epistemological polarity between the *positivists*,

who believe that there is only one form of scientific knowledge of reality, the one of the natural sciences, and that the social sciences must work with the natural sciences and the *antipositivists,* who point out that the methods (or at least some of the methods) for the study of human reality are different from the ones that are convenient for the study of natural reality because natural reality is purely causal and objective and human reality is also intentional and has a meaning. The four theoretical possibilities emerging from these polarities represent an equal number of possible abstract types of social theory, which have, in fact, conditioned the actual development of social science, giving rise to several "schools" (basically twelve, according to Martindale) and their respective views on what society is and how it can be studied.

The analysis of these views would be beyond the scope of this book. What is necessary for our present purpose—the location of society in a general analytical framework of reality—is to realize, in the broadest form, how the four basic abstract types of social theory tend to view society, and to render explicit the general abstract type that was used as the perspective for this study.

The great distinction between positivists and antipositivists[1] is the acceptance by the former of a general scientific matrix that is appropriate for the empirical study of both nature and the cultural aspects of man, whereas the latter accept such a general matrix only at a higher philosophical level as a general theory of knowledge. At the level of empirical science, the antipositivists distinguish the natural sciences from the cultural ones. The result of these two views for the study of society is that the problem of locating society in a general analytical framework of reality is less important for the positivists than for the antipositivists. This is why Comte's classification of the sciences—following a continuum from mathematics as the most general and least complex to sociology as the least general and most complex—fell in desuetude among the positivists, who have come to regard the differences among sciences as mere expediencies for practical purposes of research. Accordingly, positivism does not properly acknowledge the existence of boundaries between society and environment. Comte saw society as comprehending the whole human race, including the dead. Modern positivists concede, as an empirical fact, that specific societies have limits, in terms of membership or of space and time, but they accept this fact in the same way they accept the individuality of living organisms and of specific physical bodies, such as a given stone or star. The laws regulating the motion of stones, stars, plants (tropism), and society are basically the same, even if the complexity of society conceals that fact under many other intervening laws of more restricted levels, such as the laws of tropism and psychological conditioning, which are ultimately reducible, in principle, to some of the general causal laws of nature.

As far as the question being discussed is concerned, the distinct views of the holists and the elementalists affect intrasocietal rather than extrasocietal exchanges. Elementalism understands social interaction as being, essentially, the result of some basic forms of interindividual relationships, which obtain a larger scale or greater complexity through an increase in number and the differentiation of the concerned individuals. Intrasocietal exchanges, therefore, must be explained by reduction to their elementary forms. Conversely, holists consider social interaction as happening according to various patterns, forming distinct social structures, and so being ununderstandable except as relationships and exchanges among subsystems of a system, or subparts of a whole. Even the simplest social relations between two individuals are submitted to social patterns, as those of kinship, barter, or games.

This rapid discussion of the basic abstract types of social theory requires still another brief comment concerning the two models of society—the equilibrium and the conflict ones. Whereas the four abstract types of social theory represent the mind-matter question at the ontological and epistemological levels, the equilibrium-conflict polarity expresses alternative views on what makes society an ongoing process. This polarity, therefore, concerns the specific level of the social sciences and is not intrinsically connected with trans-societal questions. The philosophical and sociological problems of the mind-matter question seem to be unanswerable in a conclusive way, or at least to have an answer that transcends its basic terms. The equilibrium-conflict polarity, however, seems to present a different picture. The simplest forms of this polarity—static equilibrium and single-factor conflict—are clearly being abandoned by its supporters in favor of more complex models, the dynamic equilibrium and the multifactor conflict models. This movement appears to indicate a tendency toward a synthesis, which has not yet been analytically formulated, but consists in a still more general unified equilibrium-conflict model. (See Chapter 4.)

The present study, as will become apparent, is based on a holistic point of view and an antipositivist (although strongly empirically oriented) approach, as far as the four basic abstract types of social science are concerned. However, since I believe that only a general unified equilibrium-conflict model contains the elements necessary for a full understanding of the societal processes, this study tries to obtain that perspective, using a multifactor conflict model as its central scheme and adjusting it to some of the essential requirements of the dynamic-equilibrium model.

The action system

The most comprehensive attempt, up to now, to locate society in a general analytical framework of reality is the one undertaken by Talcott Parsons, which he first published as *The Social System* (1951a) and then gradually refined to *Societies: Evolutionary and Comparative Perspectives* (1966). It was his acknowledgment of the need to understand society as a structured whole and to present typical relationships with its extrasocietal environment that led him to attempt to surpass the Weberean scheme of social action, which is oriented to the understanding of intrasocietal phenomena, not to the location of society in a general framework of reality.

Parsons' proposed scheme is based on a broad distinction among three levels of reality: transhuman, human, and infrahuman. The transhuman level is the one of "ultimate reality." As a sociologist, he is not concerned with studying or even with precisely defining that ultimate reality, which may be assumed to be a deity or the analytical locus of man's ultimate concerns. The human level includes four analytically distinct systems: (1) the cultural system, (2) the social system, (3) the personality system, and (4) the (human) organism system. The third level of reality includes the physical and organic environment of man. Table 1 gives a graphic indication of society's location according to Parsons and of the cybernetic relationship between the highest and the lowest levels.

As it can be seen, besides the concept of ultimate reality as transhuman, the Parsonian framework presents two other peculiar features. One is the assumption that, in analytical terms (not empirically), the human sphere is subdivided into subsystems. *Above* the level of society, or the social system, is a cultural system. Of the two, societies are the system with the highest degree of self-sufficiency. *Below* the level of society are the system of human personalities and the system of human organisms. Accordingly, individual men, as such, are not members of society, but stand below it as personalities and organisms. Society, analytically, is composed of the roles played by men, not of concrete men.

The second peculiar feature of this framework is the understanding of the relations between different levels of reality as occupying a distinct place in the cybernetic relationship. This relation, from top to bottom, is one of decreasing information and increasing energy and, in the opposite direction, of decreasing energy and increasing information. Higher levels control lower levels. Lower levels condition higher levels. Parsons seems to assume that, at an ontological level, this general principle presides over the total system of reality. At the level of social processes, this principle determines the relations between the cultural system and the social system, on the one hand, and between the social system and the subordinate systems of personalities and organisms on the other. Ultimately, then, the lower systems operate according to the "code" they are subject to, and the fulfillment of the code depends on the lower system's capacity to adapt to its environment, either by adjusting to the environment or by adjusting the environment to itself. Failure to adapt brings the dissolution of the system.

It is beyond the purpose of this study to develop or describe the Parsonian framework further or to criticize it. Whatever criticisms may be made of the

Table 1 *Parsons' trichotomic location of society*

Level	Cybernetic Relation	Analytical Type of Reality
I. Transhuman	High Information (Controls)	Ultimate Reality
II. Human		Cultural System Social System (Societies) Personality System Organism System
III. Infrahuman	High Energy (Conditions)	Physical-Organic Environment

general concept, it presents the undeniable advantage of giving the broadest meaningful framework for locating society and studying its boundary exchanges, which is the reason I have used it as a starting point for this study. Without attempting a critique of the scheme, however, I will suggest some modifications for its use as a frame of reference. These modifications concern both the general levels of reality and the analytical types of each level.

The adoption of a trichotomic ontological approach, regardless of the caution concerning the transhuman sphere and the deliberate avoidance of metaphysical excursions into the realm of ultimate reality, cannot conceal the fact that this ultimate reality is analytically distinct from the human reality—not simply in the sense that man may be analytically distinguished from his culture (this, in the Parsonian model, is expressed by the distinction between the cultural system and the social system), but in the sense that, for Parsons, human culture is analytically distinct from ultimate reality. Since the sphere of human culture, analytically, includes the sum total of all possible symbolic expression of man and his environment, assuming an ultimate reality above the level of the cultural systems implies the metaphysical postulate of its ontological existence beyond man and world. This assumption is obviously unwarranted from the point of view of the social sciences.

At the human level the Parsonian scheme seems to me to require a triple modification. The separation of the cultural system and the social system, even at an analytical level, seems to be unfounded and is necessitated by the acceptance of ultimate reality as an analytically distinct higher level. Culture can be seen, fundamentally, either as the abstract code of the symbolic medium of a society or as that medium itself, which exists in and through the actual symbolic exchanges among men. The first meaning is the one we use when we speak of the Hellenic culture as a system of intelligible symbols. The second, when we speak of the culture of a society as one of the planes of the societal process. In the first case, we have an analytically distinct system of referents, which have intrinsic meaning whether they are used or not; such a referent would be a book, which we can read or not and which can be written in a language known or unknown to us. The most general example of culture as a code is the one of civilization. It is preferable, for analytical purposes, to use the second meaning of culture at its most general level, calling it civilization. As an internal process of society consisting in actual symbolic exchanges, culture is one of the four structural planes of social interaction, together with the economic, the political, and the social (in a narrow sense, that is, social as expressing intrasocietal forms of sociation).

The second modification that the Parsonian model seems to require at the human level concerns the analytical distinction between personalities and organisms. It is not improper, analytically, to distinguish the personality system from the organic system in the human being. Neither would it be improper to stress that the personality system presents a triple analytical distinction among a superego, an ego, and an id. At that level of analysis, however, the distinction between id and organism would become improper. They would not be homologous. Opposition between organism and nonorganism, in man, expresses such polarities as the religious one between body and soul or the philosophical one between mind and matter. From the point of view of the "action system," the Freudian rather than the religious or even the philosophical analysis is the relevant one. But that level of analysis would be much more detailed than the one used for the other systems. Therefore the appropriate level for placing the human being between its societal condition and its natural environment seems to be the level of the human being itself.

A third modification concerns the humanized objects. Hegel understood the necessity of acknowledging, in the relation of man to his natural environment, the existence of an analytically intermediate sphere: the objective spirit. Today we would call this the sphere of "humanized objects." A tool or the material part of a work of art is neither nature, because it is transformed nature, nor qua a material object, culture. These items bear the imprint of culture. They are humanized objects. This analytical sphere includes all the representational objects, all the goods, and all the affective objects; these three kinds of objects form the repertory of meaningful objects.

At the nonhuman level of reality an analytical distinction must be made between living and nonliving nature, the former representing self-adaptive systems and the latter purely objective processes.

The result of these modifications can be seen in Table 2.

The social system

Having located society in a broad analytical framework of reality, we can now approach the social system in order to try to determine the locus of political processes.

Since we are not specifically concerned with the analysis of the social system in general, we can accept a broad definition of it, which would be endorsed by

Table 2 *Dichotomic location of society*

Level	Cybernetic Relation	Analytical Type of Reality
I. Human	High Information (Controls)	Civilization—system of fundamental meanings
		Societies—system of interaction
		Human Beings—system of action
		Humanized Objects—repertory of meaningful objects
II. Nonhuman	High Energy (Conditions)	Living Nature—system of adaptive processes
		Physical Nature—system of objective processes

most social theorists, as a *system of human interaction.* Such a system, whatever its dimensions, degree of complexity, and internal regime, will always consist in (1) a plurality of actors, (2) interacting to achieve ends, (3) through certain means (4) in certain conditions. This is almost the limit of analysis on which all types of social theory converge. When we proceed to determine the modes of interaction of these actors, the various theories and the polarity resulting from the equilibrium and conflict models introduce differences of view in one form or another.

It is probably still possible to keep the consensus of the students advancing Kingsley Davis' (1949, p. 30) theory concerning the universal functional necessities to be found in any society, including the nonhuman ones, because without any of them the society would cease to exist, as the following outline illustrates:

I. Maintenance of the population
   a. Provision of nutriment
   b. Protection against injury
   c. Reproduction of new organisms
II. Division of function among the population
III. Solidarity of the group
   a. Motivation of contact between members
   b. Motivation of mutual tolerance and resistance to outsiders
IV. Perpetuation of the social system

Considering the social system in its broadest form and essentially from the point of view of the cybernetic requirements necessary for any self-adjusting system to maintain itself and to reach its major goals, Parsons suggested that there are four distinct functions that any social system must perform: (1) pattern maintenance, (2) integration, (3) goal achievement, and (4) adaptation. In his general action system these four functions are performed, respectively, by the cultural system, the social system, the personality system, and the behavioral organism. The same functional requirements are present at any level of system complexity. Society itself, therefore, has (1) its pattern-maintenance functions, performed by the processes of cultural institutionalization through boundary exchanges with the suprasocietal cultural system, (2) its integrative functions, performed by the societal community, and (3 and 4) its goal-achievement and adaptation functions, performed intrasocietally by the polity and the economy, respectively.

As will be noted, the reservations formerly expressed concerning the Parsonian general action framework are applicable to Parsons' analysis of the essential functions of society. It seems, moreover, that his scheme is not easily compatible with nondisruptive structural change, since this kind of change brings about pattern changes and so requires pattern innovation, as well as pattern maintenance.

Transferring the general societal requirements indicated by Davis and Parsons to the level of human society and taking into account the peculiar (symbolic) nature of man, I suggest that the societal process presents four major analytically distinct systems of functions, which constitute the structural planes of society: the cultural, the social (in a strict sense), the political, and the economic. The cultural plane is the plane of symbolic interaction. Culture, as we have already observed, is both a code of the symbolic medium of a society and that medium itself. It is a *language,* expressing objects, persons, actions and relations, and is a *system of beliefs* about the world and man in the world, containing *factual beliefs, value beliefs,* and *normative beliefs.* Every social act is a cultural act, because it is expressed through symbols, just as every social act in the broad sense of the term is a social act in the narrow sense, because it expresses a certain relation of participation. So, although every social act has a cultural content, what is specifically cultural is what is immediately connected with the formulation and interpretation of symbols and their social allocation: what is what and what should be known and said or done by whom.

The social plane, in a strict sense, is the plane of participation, and therefore I suggest and will use the expressions *participational plane* and *participational system* to express the social interaction in a strict sense. The participation functions consist in the affective, evaluative and playful creation, modification, allocation, and extinction of actors, roles, and statuses in society. Every society is based on a certain regime of participation which defines who the members are and what their social situation is. This regime of participation involves three analytically distinct kinds of situations: kinship (including actual and potential sexual roles), generational, and status. While the creation of actors is the exclusive result of sexual intercourse (endo- and exogamic) between group members, the creation and allocation of roles and statuses by the participational system must be distinguished from analogous functions performed by other means, as the authoritative means, for instance. The political system creates and allocates roles and statuses by enforceable decisions. The economic system does the same by the exchange of commodities. At the participational plane the creation and allocation of roles and statuses is made by *affective* (as in the family), *evaluative* (as in status-giving or acknowledging), and *playful* (as in games) means.

The political plane is the plane of production and allocation of enforceable decisions. The political function consists, essentially, in the authoritative prescription of behaviors for the purposes of external defense and internal ordering. The latter activity is essentially centered on the conflicting attempts (1) to maintain and (2) to change the regimes of power and of participation and the correlated regime of property existing at any given moment. Political development, as we will see, is directly connected with the dialectics of the regime of participation.

The economic plane is the plane of production and allocation of commodities. To survive and to expand, any society needs to make use of commodities, basically obtainable from nature, but by forms that always involve the use of some means. The fact that commodities are never completely or immediately natural but must at least be gathered by some means and in some conditions is what introduces scarcity in economic relations and, according to the regime of participation prevailing in the society, differentiates the access to commodities among members.

Each of the structural planes is the locus of the production and allocation of some of the objects, or "goods," necessary for the satisfaction of societal needs. The cultural plane is the locus for factual, value, and normative beliefs; the participational plane, for actors, roles, and statuses; the political plane, for enforceable decisions; and the economic plane, for commodities. These goods, besides being directly exchangeable, tend to give rise to special media. These media are, primarily, instruments for the measurement and exchange of a specific type of goods, but they are also convenient, although in a less specific or appropriate way, for the exchange of goods of different kinds and even for the exchange of one medium for another. Since the words "goods" has a strong economic connotation, let us use the term "valuables" to express any of the objects, including symbolic objects, people, and services, produced at any of the four structural planes.

To begin with the most obvious case, economic valuables tend to be exchangeable by money. We can also see that the enforceable decisions, or commands, produced at the political plane constitute a political medium, as was so well observed originally by Talcott Parsons.[2] Parsons assumed, as a consequence, that "power" is a societal medium, exchangeable not only at the political level, as when two powerful men make a power deal, but also between boundaries—that is, an exchange can be made between the political system and another societal system. That is what occurs when power is exchanged for money, as when votes are purchased by politicians or a bureaucratic decision is bought by the rich, or in nondysfunctional behaviors, as when taxes are collected by the government.

The specific medium of the cultural plane, at the level on which the produced valuables are factual, value, and norm beliefs, is *culture*, which consists in a meaningful system of symbols. The specific medium of the participational plane, at the level on which actors, roles, and statuses are affectively, evaluatively, and playfully created and allocated, is *prestige*. Prestige is conferred and allocated, both ascriptively and competitively, in accordance with the prevailing regime of participation. Like all the other media, it is exchangeable both within the plane and between boundaries. High-status people give prestige to low-status people by accepting them into their group or by honoring them. Prestige can be exchanged for money, culture, and power. It is, however, a medium in itself, as people can have prestige without corresponding money, power, or culture.

The fact that the media can be used both for their primary purpose, the acquisition of valuables of the corresponding type, and, if not so adequately, for the acquisition of valuables of another type makes them essentially exchangeable. This implies the existence of another medium, a secondary medium, that reflects the possession of any other exchangeable medium. This secondary medium is *influence*. Influence should not be confused with prestige.[3] Prestige is a primary medium, obtainable directly as a result of basically ascriptive or consequential participational situations: prestige of high lineage, of seniority and old age, of parenthood, or of high rank. That is why some people and groups can be the richest in a society and have very low prestige, in spite of a certain correlation that tends to take place among possessors of media. Prestige, however, varies from one society to another, vis-à-vis other media. University professors and military officers, for instance, are evaluated differently in terms of prestige in culture-oriented and war-oriented societies. Conversely, influence is always the result of having exchangeable media and can only be reached through the acquisition of one of the primary media. Money brings influence because it is exchangeable, at the economic as well as at other planes. So is the case of prestige, culture, and power. A high degree of influence obtained, for instance, by much money does not necessarily bring high prestige.

Table 3 shows the planes, valuables, and media that have been discussed.

SOCIAL STRUCTURES

The consensus view

As we move from the general description of the social system to the analysis of its internal structures and processes, the differences between the equilibrium and the conflict models become more accentuated. The two views, of course, acknowledge that in any society we find both order and conflict. For the former, however, order is ultimately due to consensus on fundamental values, and conflict tends to be a marginal manifestation of deviance, whereas for the latter, order is the consequence of successful coercion, and conflict is the constant expression, in varying degrees of intensity and effectiveness, of the attempts of the ruled to overcome the rulers.

One of the best formulations of the consensus view is probably Kingsley Davis' (1949) theory on social regulation of the use of scarce means. Because man's

Table 3 *Societal planes, valuables, and media*

Structural Planes and Macrofunctions (Societal Subsystems)	Valuables	Media	
		PRIMARY	SECONDARY
1. Cultural: production and allocation of symbols of	Factual beliefs Value beliefs Norm beliefs Expressional symbols	Culture	Influence
2. Participational: affective, evaluative, and playful creation and allocation of	Actors Roles Statuses	Prestige	Influence
3. Political: production and allocation of	Commands	Power	Influence
4. Economic: production and allocation of	Commodities	Money	Influence

necessities are not immediately provided by nature, but must be obtained by the use of the proper means (technology) and because those are scarce, the use of means is always socially regulated according to a certain regime—the regime of property. Since that regime, however, is not likely to be equally observed by all the members and groups of society, due to the propensity of the less favored to change or violate it, its maintenance is always secured by norms sanctioned by the political system and enforceable by coercive means. This political system, however, is not arbitrary violence, but the sanctioning, supported by force, of the cultural values of the society, which have the consensus of the members. This consensus is what gives legitimacy to the norms and to their sanctioning by the political system.

Within that view Parsons (1966, p. 18) suggests a composition of society with four structural categories: (1) the normative order, including (a) values and (b) norms, and (2) the organized population, including (c) the collectivity and (d) the social roles. These categories are interrelated but independent variables. "Knowing the value pattern of a collectivity does not, for example, make it possible to deduce its role-composition." The cultural code, however, determines how basic social options tend to be viewed by members, according to a limited set (supposedly exhaustive) of dichotomic alternatives, the pattern variables. Initially understood as five, they have been lately expanded by Parsons to a set of six alternatives:

affectivity–affectivity neutrality
specificity–diffusion
universalism–particularism
quality–performance
self–orientation–collective orientation
instrumental–consummatory

Consensus provided by the common culture and leading to various typical forms of societies (notably achieving oriented versus ascriptive and universalists versus particularists) is the basis of norm observance and of the maintenance of the system, which always grants some flexibility for deviants but keeps them within tolerable limits.

The conflict view

Stressing the fact that conflict, not consensus, is the ultimate reality of social life and that social regulation is the product of coercion, the conflict view considers social structures as being determined by the situation of groups in society, not by values. Social structures consist, therefore, in regularities of relevant interests, which aggregate people and induce behaviors in accordance with the underlying social situation.

In the simpler terms of Marx's economistic (although not exclusively economistic)[4] model, social structures express the historical result of a coercively imposed division of labor in society. From that division results the private appropriation, by a minority, of the social means of production, imposing on the majority the contingency of selling their labor in exchange for wages that roughly correspond to the cost of their subsistence. The minority retains as profit or rent the plus value of the product. The two resulting classes, bourgeoisie and proletariat, with their less constant subclasses, are the basic structures of modern society, on which a superstructure of norms and values is built by the ruling class to legitimize its domination. The political system is the apparatus of coercion that maintains a social order based on the exploitation of the many by the few. And this is the reason the state was supposed to wither away once the class regime was abolished by the socialization of the means of production.

The generalization of Marx's hypothesis led in our times to a more complex conflict model in which, essentially, (1) social exploitation and alienation is not understood as being exclusively or even primarily economic, and (2) structural relationships are not supposed to be unidirectional from "infra-" to "superstructure," but pluridirectional, forming a circular process of interrelations among the four structural planes.

Using these premises, John Rex (1961) presented a new conflict model of the social process. The various factors differentiating members bring them, through various class and coalition groups, to a final conflict polarity, between those who ultimately want to preserve and those who ultimately want to change the existing order. Then, if the society is not segmented, either one of the factions wins, imposing its rule and its own legitimacy on the resulting order, or some sort of truce is finally reached. In the first case, the ruled tend to reorganize and to challenge the prevailing order and its legitimacy, reestablishing the conflict situation. In the second case, either the truce is broken, reestablishing the conflict situation, or the compromise is stabilized through the creation of a new order supported by a new legitimacy. With the new order, however, new forms of discrimination tend to appear, creating a new polarization, which will reestablish the dialectic of conflict at a new level.

Although a discussion of Rex's model is very tempting, it would digress into an area that is marginal to the central focus of this study. Let me just observe, as a suggestion of the kind of considerations that I think would be pertinent, that the cyclical reenactment of the conflict polarity, when new orders are created by a class supremacy or a class truce, may and has historically tended to present new and qualitatively different aspects. Since class conflict is the greatest evil for the contending factions short of having their interests undefended or unclaimed, technological progress, once made possible, permits—as has actually happened in history—the introduction of an increasing nonzero sum factor. Workers become consumers also; a middle class differentiates itself, grows, and becomes the largest and politically the most influential class in society; and self-optimizing for the bourgeoisie is no longer necessarily minimizing for the proletariat.[5]

Structural analysis

Whatever the factors are that determine their regularity, social structures, as "sets of patterned behaviors and interrelated roles," present various levels of depth. This level differentiation has been acknowledged by practically all social theorists. Much less clear, however, are the questions of how these different levels should be approached and along what lines their depth should be located and measured.

The first question, as we should expect, brings out the epistemological differences between such extremes as Lundberg's (1939) sense-data-approached behavior-events and Gurvitch's (1958) phenomenologically established *paliers de profondeur*. The second question, regardless of what means are employed in the approach to social structures, leads to a large variety of schemes of classification, levels of depth, and super- and subordination relationships. Although the resulting views are not reducible to a single system of classification, three major lines of differentiation are pointed out by most analysts. The first is the functional line, along which basic macro-functions, or field functions, in society are distinctly indicated. Thus, Parsons' subsystems of action are indicated along a functional line: the cultural system, for the pattern-maintenance function, the social system for the integration function, and so on. At the level of the social system, the same criteria differentiate the intrasocietal functions: the polity for goal attainment, the economy for adaptation and so forth. Many other analysts, starting from the level of the social system, consider such macrofunctions as the economic, political, and cultural ones as constituting an institutional level, to which the specific formal and informal organizations promoting political, economic, and cultural activities correspond at a lower level.

The second line of differentiation is the organizational one. Most writers understand that at a lower level the economic, political, and cultural institutions are represented by operating structures, organized or unorganized, oriented toward achieving economic, political, and cultural goals.

The third widely indicated line of structural differentiation is the one of social stratification. Whatever the factors are that originate them, classes, castes, and status levels are acknowledged by practically all theorists.

I suggest that these usually prevailing views can and should be integrated in a general picture of intrasocietal structures, although this picture will not necessarily comprehend all the views on the matter.

The proposed classification includes two dimensions and two levels. The dimensions are "horizontal" and "vertical." Horizontally, society presents four structural planes, which are the analytical loci of four societal macrofunctions: the *cultural, participational, political,* and *economic* ones. Each macrofunction of the social system is performed by one of four subsystems, the cultural, participational, political, and economic subsystems, which are themselves complex systems containing other subsystems. We will refer to these subsystems by the word "system" whenever they are considered in isolation or in such expressions as "societal systems." We will keep calling them "subsystems" in expressions mentioning or implying the term "social system."

Vertically, society presents two levels of depth, which are the "top" and the "bottom" levels of each structural plane and its respective societal system. The first level is the *situational* level, where the regime of stratification of each plane is analytically fixed: the *regime of values* for the cultural plane, of *participation* for the participational plane, of *power* for the political plane, and of *property* for the economic plane. For the society as a whole the situational level corresponds, analytically, to the site of the social regime. The second level is the *actional* level, where, analytically, human interaction actually takes place in each structural plane and where interplane exchanges are made for society as a whole.

The resulting picture can be seen in Table 4. As said formerly, the subsystems of the social system—cultural, participational, political, and economic—are themselves systems, each presenting a complex structure, variable with the general complexity of the particular society, and differentiated at the situational and the actional levels. Each of these systems is producer and allocator of some of the social valuables: (a) the cultural system: symbols of factual, value, and norm beliefs and expressional symbols, (b) the participational system: actors, roles, and statuses, (c) the political system: commands, and (d) the economic system: commodities. The valuables produced by the cultural system, or at the cultural plane, are symbols. At the participational plane, which is the social plane in its narrow sense, two different kinds of valuables are produced: (1) human beings who will become social actors and (2) social roles and statuses. Human beings can only result from the exo- or endogamic sexual intercourse of the members of society; roles and statuses are produced at the political plane by authoritative decision, at the economic plane by the production and exchange of commodities, and at the cultural plane by symbol making, explaining, or learning. The production and allocation of roles and statuses at the participational plane differ analytically from their production and allocation at the other three planes in that they are made and allocated by affective means (as in the family), evaluative means (as in statuses), and playful means (as in games). The valuables produced at the political plane are prescriptive behaviors, or commands, which provide for the authoritative maintenance or change of the existing social order. The social order, in turn, expresses in a coherent whole, the regimes of values, participation, power, and property. Elections, for instance, are a form of command that can introduce changes in the political system, which, in turn, can introduce changes in the other systems. Successful acts of "anti-order" violence, as in revolutions and coups, can also change the political system and, with it, the political, social, economic, and cultural orders. The actions of the state (political outputs) maintain the social order.[6]

The economic plane is the one at which elements extracted from nature are gathered, processed, and exchanged to suit human needs. The valuables produced are goods and services. Their allocation, however, is differentiated, in most cases, by social classes and, in a general way, according to the prevailing regime of participation.

In terms of value structures and effectivity structures, the horizontal articulation of the four planes provides a circular process of factual and value support.

Table 4 *Societal structural planes and macrofunctional systems*

Structural planes and macrofunctional systems / Levels of Depth	*Cultural*	*Participational*	*Political*	*Economic*
	System of production and allocation of symbols, factual beliefs, value beliefs, norm beliefs, and expressional symbols	System of affective, evaluative, and playful production and allocation of actors, roles, and statuses	System of production and allocation of enforceable commands	System of production and allocation of commodities
1. Situational Level Presenting a certain social order with differentiation among A. Upper B. Middle C. Lower strata	REGIME OF VALUES Supposing certain beliefs and based on a certain legitimizing regime of participation A. Symbol formulators and interpreters B. Symbol propagators C. Symbol consumers	REGIME OF PARTICIPATION Supposing, legitimized by, and inducing a certain regime of values and manifesting kinship, generational, and social status differentiation A. Upper status B. Middle status C. Lower status	REGIME OF POWER Supposing a certain regime of participation and of values and sanctioning accordingly a certain regime of property and the social order, in general A. Decision makers B. Decision implementers C. Ruled	REGIME OF PROPERTY Supposing a certain regime of participation and of values and sanctioned by a certain regime of power A. Controllers of means of production B. Managers and technicians C. Workers
2. Actional Level Formal and informal organizations	CHURCHES Legitimizing institutions Schools Research and symbol-propagating groups Religious, scientific, humanistic, and artistic groups	FAMILIES Generations Status institutions Play institutions Play groups Sport groups Companionship groups	STATE State powers and agencies Political parties and institutions Political groups	FIRMS Economic institutions Formal interest groups Informal economic groups

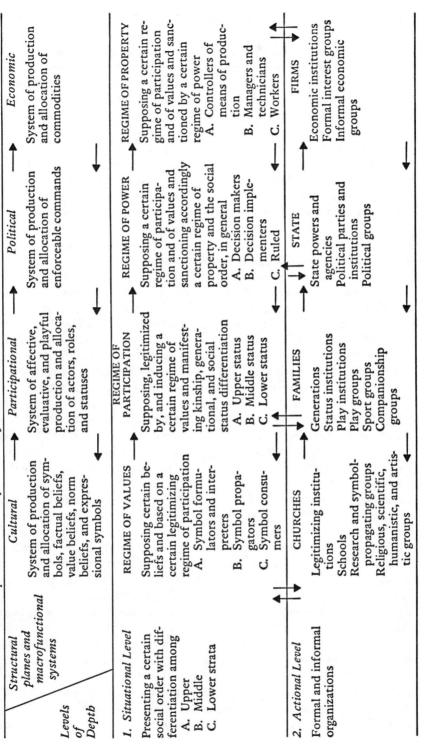

This is an extremely important aspect of the social structure, and it lies at the base of most of the theoretical controversies concerning society. Both the equilibrium model and the single-factor version of the conflict model started with the supposition that one of the planes was determining the other ones.

Marx, for instance, realizing (in a way that would later by developed for the psychological process by Freud) how much values, ethical norms, and laws are, functionally, a justification and protection of economic ("material," in his terminology) interests, concluded that this was because such values and norms are ideological rationalizations of those interests. It is existence that determines conscience, not vice versa. At the social level, the defense of interests leads, by ways individuals often do not realize, to their legitimization through religious, ethical, and legal means.

However, the theorists of the equilibrium model, taking into account the fact that a regime of property is always sanctioned by a regime of power and the latter by a regime of values, concluded that the values of a society and, therefore, its cultural system, are the determining factor of the social order.

Both models, as has been remarked, are acknowledged as being unsatisfactory. A dynamic element, structural change, has been introduced into the equilibrium model to explain aspects of social reality ignored by the homeostatic version. A multifactor, rather than a single-factor, explanation was adopted by the conflict model for similar reasons. It is not my intention to develop this discussion further. I just want to suggest again, in accordance with the view expressed in Table 4, which orients the present book, that the social sciences are moving in the direction of a synthesis between the *dynamic version of the equilibrium model* and the *multifactor version of the conflict one.*

In Table 4 the interrelation among the four structural planes and their respective systems is essentially determined by *a circular process of legitimation of factual situations by values ultimately induced by and from factual situations.* At any moment in any society the society has a certain cultural system, composed of symbolic factual beliefs (those real and ideal things that are believed in and how), value beliefs (those real and ideal things that are considered good or bad and how), norm beliefs (those behaviors that are acknowledged as the ones that should or should not be observed and how), and expressional symbols (the meanings of meaning and styles). This cultural system constitutes the guiding code of that society, which can only see and act in the world through its cultural medium. This guiding code results from a long (ultimately, since the origin of man) tradition of symbolizations formulated out of, and giving functional assistance to, life situations in given social contexts. Considering now the other aspect of the process—the factual one—we have that at any moment in any society its system of participation—which is the societal system of affective, evaluative, and playful production and allocation of actors, roles, and statuses—implies a certain regime of participation. People necessarily have parents and other relatives, who belong to different generations and who play different roles. So we have many other differentiating factors that bring about a certain regime of participation. Not randomly, but according to certain structures and norms, people are supposed to contribute to the social necessities and receive certain material and moral rewards. The way these participations and rewards are supposed to take place is fixed by the cultural system, in general, and specifically by the regime of values prevailing at any given moment, which legitimizes the existing regime of participation.

Within the general long-term process of values being induced by life situations and life situations being regulated by values, we have a closer circuit for the shorter-term process of the inducement of a regime of values by a regime of participation, which at the same time is legitimized by the regime of values. This process occurs because, given an existing cultural system, some values and norms are admissible and some are not, and the admissible ones limit the possible factual arrangements at the societal level. In other words, no regime of participation can (legitimately) violate the cultural system. Within the range of the admissible, however, the factual conditions of an existing regime of participation tend to coalesce into a certain line of values and norms that become the prevailing regime of values, legitimizing the regime of participation. In the shorter circular process the process of inducement can never be an overt manipulation of values (which is the situation of illegitimacy), and the process of legitimation cannot be an automatic confirmation of a preexisting state of affairs, but rather must be a configurative one which, although induced by a former state of affairs, modifies such former state of affairs while legitimizing it.

Given the broad and shorter circular processes of value inducement by factual situations and legitimation of factual situations by values, the two other societal subsystems, the political and the economic ones with their respective regimes, play an interrelated part. The political system, which is a specialized subsystem in that it is the social system for the authoritative prescription of behaviors (that is, for converting into enforceable ones the norms resulting from the regime of values and the interests resulting from the regime of participation), expresses such enforcement through a certain regime of power. The regime of power, expressing the regimes of values and of participation, sanctions the correlate regime of property and, in general, of social order. Only by a change of the regime of power is the regime of property, in particular, and the social order, in general, susceptible to change. The economic system, which is the societal subsystem for the production and allocation of commodities, in turn expresses, in a certain regime of property, the regime of participation existing under the sanctioning of the correlate regime of power.

NOTES

[1] The term "antipositivism," although widely used, has undoubtedly the disadvantage of all negative denominations. The various distinct positions covered by the general designation of antipositivism has hindered up to now the adoption of an affirmative denomination. "Perspectivism" might be a convenient label for these various tendencies.

[2] See particularly "The Political Aspect of Social Structure and Process" in David Easton, ed. (1966).

[3] Such is the case with Parsons, who among other writers, identifies prestige with influence and does not consider the existence of a medium of media.

[4] Marx and Engels conceptions on historical materialism, as systematically synthesized in the *Communist Manifesto* and in Marx's *Preface* to his *Critique of Political Economy* were, according to Engels in his last years, deliberately overemphasized for didactical purposes. See Engels' letters to Conrad Schmidt, Joseph Bloch, and Franz Mehring in Lewis S. Feuer, ed., *Marx and Engels: Basic Writings on Politics and Philosophy* (Anchor Books, New York, 1959).

[5] The qualitative changes introduced by cumulative societal development in interclass relations have not yet reached, in any society, the point of eliminating all class differences and ascriptive privileges. Such a result will probably never be obtained, since status differentiation, although predominantly competitive, tends to replace class stratification in highly developed societies.

[6] Although the state, as a state, is necessarily oriented for the sanctioning and maintaining of the social order, groups controlling strategic sectors of the state can use them for "superverting" that social order.

2

A General View of
Structural Change

MEANING OF STRUCTURAL CHANGE

Structure and process

A new interest in political development and in societal development in general
has brought about a new awareness of the problem of social change, particularly
of a structural character.[1] Most of the voluminous literature that has recently
appeared on the subject, however, has been directly aimed at the analysis of the
question either at the level of a given societal system (as the political system or
the economic system) or, in fewer cases, at the broader level of the social system
as a whole. Scarce, if any, consideration has been given to the problem of
structural change, in general, at the level of any possible system or, at least, any
empirically existing system.

The convenience, if not the necessity, of starting the analysis at the most
general relevant level results from the fact that only by clarifying the concepts
implied in the discussion and the general principles of structural change is it
possible to distinguish *what is specific in social change from what derives from
our conceptual framework of change or what is determined by general principles.*

Thus, we have to clarify the basic questions of what is meant by structural
change and how structural change tends to happen in observable empirical systems, in order to see if some general principles are inducible.

Our concepts of structural change involve our ideas on structure, process, and
change. The introductory purposes of the present discussion prevent any
thorough inquiry into this complex subject, which involves such different applications as the concept of structure in logic and mathematics, in physics or biology,
in psychology, or in social theory, as well as in semiotic and linguistic theories.
Taking this complexity into account in an implicit way, I will, for convenience,
present some basic definitions, which include all the relevant meanings for the
concepts to be analyzed, in order to provide a framework for empirical use.[2]

The fundamental ideas implied in our concept of structure are those referring to what determines or maintains (1) the shape or form and (2) the internal order of the constituent parts of something (real or symbolic). This could be expressed by the following proposition: *Structure is the form or pattern of relationships that determines and maintains the shape of something or the internal order of its constituent parts.*

That form or pattern of relationships always presents two characteristics. One results from the form or pattern itself—that is, from the form of the form and the pattern of the pattern, or the *typic* form of the structure, which can be defined by its general properties (as a triangle or an atom) or by the combination of general properties and constant peculiar features (the patriarchal family). The second characteristic, *capability,* refers to the intrinsic ability of the structure (inherent in its typic form) to maintain its own form or pattern. Rational structures (in the mind) are permanent and invariable (the traingle), whereas phenomenic structures can vary (with man's life as the implicit standard) from momentary occurrences to those of long-term duration (as in the solar system). In addition to these two constant characteristics, structures can also have two other characteristics. Symbolic structures have a *meaning*—that is, they refer to something else. These are the structures of cultural objects, as analytically distinguishable from the materials used for the symbolic expression. Intentional structures have a *function,* which is self-adjusting (by some sort of cybernetic feedback) and oriented toward a goal. These are the structures of biological, psychological, and social systems. These characteristics are outlined in Chart 1.

An important implication of the idea of structure is the idea of system. This idea is implied in the sense that whatever is structured becomes ipso facto a system (that is, a system is a structured whole with component parts).[3] Moreover, the idea of system is implied, not denotatively but connotatively, in that of structure in the sense that an analytically isolated structure besides containing an inherent system is also contained by a larger system from which it has been isolated. Finally, the idea of structure implies a general concept of reality: Reality is a

Chart 1 *General and particular characteristics of structures*

A. General characteristics of structures:	1. Typic form
	General properties and peculiar constant features
	2. Capability
	Intrinsic ability to maintain own form or pattern
B. Particular characteristics of certain structures; included in their typic form:	1. Meaning
	Reference to something else—occurs in symbolic structures
	2. Function
	Self-adjusting orientation to goal—occurs in biological, psychological, and social structures

system of systems, analytically reducible to one or several elementary parts and maintaining, among the various systems, analytically distinguishable levels of inclusiveness, which correspond to a scale of increasing intensity and decreasing extension.[4] This idea underlies the analytical framework of reality presented in Table 2.

Another important implication of the idea of structure is the idea of process. Regardless of what external system a structure is contained in and what internal system is formed by it, structures are the relatively permanent form or pattern of relationship shaping or ordering those things, whatever they are, that happen—that is, are processed—in accordance with the form or pattern. These processed things are processes vis-à-vis their structures. Structure and process are dichotomic concepts of reality manifesting what shapes or orders as opposed to what is shaped or ordered.[5]

What is shaped or ordered is determined by its respective structure either in a causal way (such as when water is shaped by the shape of a container or a chemical reaction, by the atomic structure of the components) or in (not exclusively) a purposive way, as in the case of intentional (conscious or not) processes, such as the biolocal or psychological ones. We can say, therefore, that in the most general form a process *is a sequence of events interconnected by a relationship of causality or finality.*

The structure-process relationship implies a superior and an inferior level. It is the relationship of an ordering principle and the occurrence that is ordered, of a shaping form to the matter that is shaped, and of a controlling norm to the event that is controlled. This two-level relationship can also mean, according to the application, the relationship of general to particular (as in symbolic structures) and of complex to simple (as in biological structures).

The structure-process concept enables us to understand the change concept. In its broadest application, change is the passage of something from one state to another, as compared to a standard state. The propensity of intuitive thinking, expressed in common language, to imply an Euclidean space, a Newtonian time, and an Aristotelian substance brings forth an idea of change loaded with such implications. Change appears to be the passage of a substance from one position to another, in absolute space or time, or the internal modification of a substance, either by alteration of its accidental attributes or by modification of its essence, in which case there is a change in the substance itself.

The structure-process concept permits another view of change, more compatible with modern philosophy and science,[6] without the necessity of shifting from common to conventional language. Whatever it is that actually changes and whatever its environment is, a change can be understood as processual or structural according to whether or not the passing from one state to another does or does not affect, analytically, the structure-process relationship. Let us take a simple example. Water flows through a pipe. In various senses, not only an empirical or ideal part of the water is changing position, vis-à-vis a point of reference along the pipe, but the whole system is changing. It changes not only in the Heraclitean sence of a constant dialectical flux of total reality, but also in the empirical sense that, among other things, microparts of the pipe are carried along with the water and that the whole system is affected by the general changes in the planet and by the general effects of entropy. All these changes, however, do not affect, analytically, the structure-process relationship existing between pipe and water. That relation will be affected only when, for instance, the incremental erosion of the pipe causes a hole and consequent leakage. We have, therefore, processual change before the leakage or structural change occurs. The same can be said of more complex examples, as, for instance, the structure of a cell and its processes in biology or the structure of a society and its activities in the social sciences.

The structure-process concept, combined with the already discussed concept of system, provides another important consequence for the understanding of change. This consequence is that, in a system, *what is structural at a lower or narrower level is processual at a higher or broader one.*[7] The logico-ontological explanation of that principle is that, while a system is accepted as the persisting ordination of its various levels of subsystems, a structural change at a lower or narrower subsystem—if the system as a whole is (analytically) supposed to persist—means that that change constitutes a process of the higher or broader subsystem that patterns the lower one. Let us take a biological example. A cell (structure) produces and orders certain intracellular functions (processes). The creation or destruction of a cell is, at the cell level, a structural change. At the level of the tissue and organ to which the cell belongs, however, it tends to be (not exclusively) a process of cell renovation. If we now consider, as a unit, the whole organism (structure) and its functions (processes), we see that the creation and destruction of organisms, their birth and death, are structural changes at the organism level. At the level of the species to which the organism belongs, however, they are a part of the demographic process. Creation and extinction of species are structural changes at the species level. At the biosphere level, however, they are part of the process of evolution.

As we see, the series can be extended indefinitely to such conceptual limits as (physically) the total universe or (ontologically) being as such. At that level we have a coincidence of structure and process. The structure of total universe, for instance, is its total process in the hypothetical sense of an exploding-expanding-contracting-exploding infinite series.

This new view of the structure-process idea leads us to a new distinction concerning structural change. Structural change within a system is a process of a higher or broader subsystem, vis-à-vis the subsystem shaped or patterned by the higher subsystem, when the change is compatible with the system as a whole. Some structural changes, however, involve (at least analytically) the destruction of the system. This is the case, for instance, with the creation and destruction of cells contrary to the principles ordering the process at a higher intrasystemic level, as happens when the cells are affected by a cancer. In this case, structural change at the cell level effects structural changes at the tissue and organ levels that are incompatible with the patterns of the organismal system as a whole, provoking its death. In a broader system, however, for example, in the species system, such structural change again becomes a process. In the broadest sense radical structural change is unthinkable, because it implies the conversion of being into nothingness. As was already remarked, at the concept limit, structure and process are the same,[8] as when one holds a cyclical view of existing reality as an expanding-contracting-expanding universe.

A final observation concerning structural change will clarify the distinction among its possible varieties. As was seen above, some structural changes are intra-systemic, when they are compatible with the overall system, and others are inter-systemic, when they imply the dissolution of a system in the context of a broader inclusive one. The most visible case of system dissolution is the analytical one. Structural changes incompatible with the system pattern produce the dissolution of the system at a certain level of its more elementary subsystems, which are "reinte-grated" as subsystems of another system. The typical example is the life cycle in which elementary subsystems, physicochemical compounds, integrated in the cells of an organism are disintegrated after its death and in a sense returned to the physicochemical system of the earth. What the process actually means, of course, is that physicochemical compounds, which are ceaselessly subjected to physico-chemical laws (in and outside organisms), may be integrated, as constituents of cells, by more complex laws, which ultimately constitute a special "form" of processing physicochemical reactions generating new ordering principles.

Besides analytical dissolution, systems may also be subject to synthetic disso-lution. In that case, the subsystem components do not disintegrate; only the level of the system's autonomy changes. Two cells combining in a reproduction process to form a new unit do not lose their subsystem components, but each ceases to be a unique autonomous cell in order to become fused in the new gen-erated specimen. The same can be seen at the level of societies fusing to form a larger one. The elements of continuity that the new system presents vis-à-vis its forming units cease to be an autonomous system. Whereas analytical dissolution of a system results in a loss of complexity and organization, synthetic dissolution creates a system of higher complexity and organization. In addition to the fusion of genetic cells to form a new specimen, another good example of the achieve-ment of a higher order is original biosynthesis, which brings physicochemical compounds to the higher level of organic life.

If we now turn our attention from the structural changes implying system dis-solution to those compatible with the maintenance of the system, that is, to intrasystemic structural changes, we will see that the division between analytical and synthetic processes can be retained. Analytical intrasystemic structural changes are those leading to the segmentation of a structure into two or more structures, either similar to the first one, as in normal cellular multiplication, or differentiated, as in the processes of mutation.

Intrasystemic structural changes by synthetic processes imply an increase or decrease in the complexity of a structure, brought about by differentiation (development) or simplification (regression). In the former case the structural change "develops" the capability of the structure, in terms of its intrinsic ability to perform its functions (for purposive structures), express its meaning (for sym-bolic ones), and maintain its own pattern. In the latter case (regression) the structure loses what it gains in the former.

Table 5 *Structural change*

Mode	*System Level* INTRASYSTEMIC		INTERSYSTEMIC
Analytical	Segmentation		Dissolution in lower elementary subsystem
	Similar units	Differentiated units	
Synthetic	Unification		Fusion
	Development (differentiation)	Regression (simplification)	

Table 5 shows graphically the various modalities of structural change discussed so far.

Social structures

The analysis of the general conceptual implications of structural change and of its meaning when applied, in principle, to any system affords an understanding of social structural change. Let us start with an application of the general concept of structure to the social case.

We saw that a structure is the form or pattern of relationship that determines and maintains the shape of something or the internal order of its constituent parts. Furthermore, we have accepted a widely adopted, broad definition of the social system as the system of human interaction. It follows, from these two basic concepts, that our idea of social structure involves a certain form or pattern of action determining, with some regularity, the orientation and characteristics of other social actions. Parsons (1966, p. 5) observed, in a general way, that "action consists of the structures and processes by which human beings form meaningful intentions and, more or less successfully, implement them in concrete situations." He also understood social structures (1961, p. 40) as sets of patterned behaviors and interrelated roles. It would be convenient, for the continuity of social research, to keep as much of these formulations as is compatible with our former analysis. We could do this by regarding social structure as the *form or pattern of action that determines and maintains the regularity and the characteristics of a set of behaviors and interrelated roles.*[9]

Rather than define action as a function of those structures that configurate it, however, as Parsons does, it is more relevant to consider the *manifestation of an actually implementable meaningful intention.* It is in this sense that a law can be a social structure. It manifests an actually implementable meaningful intention. When the intention cannot be implemented, as happens with some laws, either the law is supported by other factors determining behavior—such as social acknowledgment of the moral validity of the precepts expressed by the law or locally powerful groups whose interests coincide with the stipulations of the law—or the law simply ceases to be a social structure and does not determine actual behavior. Its manifested intentions are not actually implemented.

Social structures have the two general characteristics of any structure, typic form and capability, and the characteristics of intentional structures, function, and of the cultural ones—meaning. As "actions patterning actions," social structures are essentially intentional. They are oriented toward determining behaviors and the interrelated roles, and their systemic function is precisely that. On the other hand, while meaning is the specific characteristic of symbolic structures, social structures, as actions patterning actions, convey a meaning and so always require a symbolic medium, be it, as usually, explicit or implicit, oral or written language, or any other signal capable of symbolic expression.

Some more attention must now be given to the regularity aspect of social structure. In other empirical systems, as the physical one, the regularity of processes, vis-à-vis their determining structures, is subject to causal laws. Causal laws also operate in social processes in the sense of psychophysiological motivations. I eat because I am hungry. Moreover, of course, physical occurrences with social consequences, as birth or death or the products of technology, are causally determined. The leap from a natural order to a sociocultural order, however, brings with it the intervention of new forms and patterns of determination besides plain causality. Whatever these new intervening forms, or conditioning factors, may be, they are the result of the self-determination of the actors and the subjection of any actor to the physical, but intentionally and meaningfully oriented, activity of other actors.

The self-determination of actors presents two broad categories: rationally oriented and value-oriented. This was expressed by Max Weber (1944) in his distinction between actions that were *zweckrational*, that is, oriented according to the adequateness of means for the ends, and *wertrational*, that is oriented according to conscious beliefs in ethical values. Weber also distinguished two more categories of action: affective-oriented and traditional. Regardless of the indisputable convenience of taking the latter distinctions into account, the fact remains that, ultimately, affective and traditional action are forms (although mostly not conscious) of value-oriented action.

Rationally oriented action results from the inherently human (species given) propensity for rational pursuit (determined by the adequateness of means for the ends) of self-interest, either positive implementation of elected ends or negative prevention of unwanted effects. Value-oriented action results from the human propensity to observe norms that are understood as realizing desirable values or expressing moral obligations. Rationally oriented action is directly innate, although widely developed by socialization, whereas value-oriented action involves a more complex intervention of culturally transmitted values and norms, although man has an innate disposition for their acquisition.

A final aspect to consider is the physical disposability of any actor by means of the physically implemented intentions of others. Many social structures keep their regularity because of the positive combinations of rational orientations and value orientations. What gives the final effectiveness to social structures, however, and so maintains their regularity is the fact that uncomplying actors are subject to physical disposal by other ones in that they may be killed or physically deprived. Pyysical sanctions accompanying, in one way or another, all social structures cause most of the actors that would otherwise be inclined to disregard them to take them into account by a negative rational orientation. In other words, in the rational pursuit of self-interest actors are aware of the sanctions applicable when one's behaviors disregard certain social structures, and to prevent these sanctions, they observe the social structures. Some actors, however, may, for various reasons, disregard social structures even at the price of severe penalities. This eventuality is ultimately prevented by the physical disposal of uncomplying actors who, when convenient, can be removed from the stage of action by death or physical detention.

It must be understood, therefore, that all social structures, whatever their nature, can only be so when the sets of behaviors and interrelated roles patterned by them are regularly maintained, not only by rational or value inducements but also, at least ultimately, by the actual possibility of physical disposal of those who fail to comply. This is the case with social structures created by law. It is also the case with traditional social structures that are distinguishable from and not supported by legal provisions. Deviants from traditional social structure would be submitted, when their behaviors reached a certain degree of noncompliance, to the physical reaction of the community or of some of its members with the consent of the others. Contrary, therefore, to what is suggested by the equilibrium model, it is *not* the ultimate consensus that keeps the regularity of social structures, even if many or most of the structures may be supported by some sort of general agreement (See Chapter 4.)

The social process

We have already seen the location of society in a general analytical framework of reality (Table 2), the four societal structural planes, with the valuables produced and allocated to each of them, and the media of exchange of these valuables (Table 3), as well as the two vertical levels of society and their horizontal interrelations (Table 4). We have seen, further, what is meant by structural change in general and by social structure. We can now analyze how a social process takes place and how, in its course, structural social change is brought about.

To proceed to this new inquiry, we have to concern ourselves with three distinct aspects of the action process: (1) its depth level of performance, (2) its system location, and (3) its structure-process relationship.

As follows from our analysis of the societal subsystems, we see that every action, whatever its effects, is performed at the actional level. The actional level is (analytically) the depth level at which actors interact through formal or informal organizations. Some acts, as we will see, may affect the situational level of the actors, either by moving some of them up and moving the others down or by altering the patterns of social stratification. Some actions, on the other hand, may have important repercussions on any of the societal subsystems and, because of the reciprocal interrelation of these subsystems, may affect the whole social structure. Whatever effects they may cause, however, actions are always performed by individual actors and at the actional level.

From the point of view of their system location, social actions are always a relation, either (1) a relation between society and environment, (2) an intersystemic relation between different social subsystems, or (3) an intrasystemic relation within the same social subsystem. The first kind of relation involves another set of three alternatives: (1) actions of a symbolic nature between a society and the cultural code of its civilization, (2) actions of a social nature between different societies, and (3) actions of a physical nature involving the relations of a society and its natural environment.[10] What is relevant for our purpose is the fact that social action, or interaction, whatever its system location, always involves an exchange through one or several media of some valuables. Symbols are always exchanged in interaction, either primarily, as in cultural exchanges, or as a means for other purposes. Interaction of a participational nature, as pure socializing, involves prestige exchanges. Usually the interaction process is oriented toward money or power exchanges. The result of these exchanges *is always the production, extinction, modification, and allocation of symbols, actors, roles, statuses, commands, and commodities.* Thus, if we use an economic analogy, the full representation of these exchanges would present us with a kind of gross social total product. In growing societies such exchanges imply, in the last analysis, more knowledge, more values, more norms, more people, more roles and statuses, more commands and commodities. In declining societies the result would be some sort of reduction of the total available valuables.[11]

Whether the exchanges are in an increasing or in a decreasing direction, this total process, regardless of the intentions of the actors and their awareness of what is happening in their society, does not keep the same number of valuables or the same proportion of their distribution among members. Some people end up losing or winning more than others, which implies, immediately, upward and downward changes in the situational level of the actors. More than a simple change of the position of the actors with respect to unchanged sets of roles and statuses, however, the simple course of the social process tends to introduce changes in the actual form or pattern of such roles and statuses. If the upward tendency is predominant, for instance, more people can have more income, at the economic plane, or more education, at the cultural one. Power can also be more evenly distributed. In that case, not only actor *A* will be promoted, economically, from, say, a working-class position to a managerial one, but more people, in total, will become managers, creating new managerial roles and changing, even if slightly, the numerical relationship and some other consequential aspects of the social strata of that society.

Exchanges through the various social media, therefore, even when processed in accordance with the existing structures and in compliance with the existing social order (the prevailing regimes of values, participation, power, and property), bring out structural changes (1) at the actional level, by creation, extinction, and modification of valuables (symbols, actors, roles, statuses, commands, and commodities) and (2) at the situational level, by affecting their social allocation. This second level of structural change, in turn, can either be compatible with the existing order—the regimes of values, participation, power, and property—or affect it beyond its margin of tolerance. It may also be compatible or incompatible with the typic form of the societal subsystems, and it may or may not affect their capability.[12]

When structural changes affect (1) the formerly prevailing regimes of values, participation, power, or property at the situational level, and so, as a tendency, the social order as a whole or (2) the typic form or the capability, at the macrofunctional level, of any of the societal subsystems and so, as a tendency, of the social system as a whole, we have various kinds of social structural changes which will produce, according to their direction, either the development or the regression of the society in question.

DYNAMICS OF STRUCTURAL CHANGE

The process of change

Our former analysis of the social process and of the resulting social structural changes, whether deliberate or not, permits now the analysis of how such results are actually achieved.

The relevant factor, as we have seen, is whether or not the process of change, at any of the societal levels, is compatible with the regulating regime. We will call the changes that are compatible with their regulating regimes "incremental" and those that are not compatible "dialectical." Let us now analyze how each kind of change is processed.

Incremental changes, at the actional level of any of the social planes, *consist in the creation, extinction, or modification of social valuables in accordance with the respective regulating regimes.* This is what happens with most of the social processes. But the result of any cycle of exchanges, as we have seen, tends not only to increase or decrease the total of available valuables but, moreover, to change, even if only slightly, the former proportion of their allocation and the groups and actors to which they were allocated. We have, therefore, a distinction between incremental changes that affect the former allocation of valuables and those that do not. The latter are irrelevant for our purposes. Incremental changes affecting the former allocation of valuables, in turn, although resulting from processes that were, at the actional level, compatible with their regulating regime, can either affect the regime or have no effect on the regime, in which case they are not relevant for our analysis. The regime can be affected in one of two ways. The effect on the regime of incremental changes in the allocation of valuables can also be incremental, or the regime can be affected in a way incompatible with it, although by processes that were formerly incremental. In the latter case an incremental process of change is converted into a dialectical one. Such is the case of convertion of quantity into quality, so often referred to by Marx[13] and the conflict theorists.

Examples of such a case are innumerable and easily seen at any of the structural planes. Within the cultural system, for instance, we have the case of slight variations in the interpretation of a dogma which are compatible with the regime of values and with the cultural system in general until they start to be supported by too many people. At this point, the authority on the dogma may consider that the quantitative increase in new adepts of that interpretation has become dangerous and condemn the interpretation. This is how practically all heresies have been denounced in any dogma-centered church. So, for instance, the Albigenses (with their overemphasis on the spirit-flesh dichotomy) in the Christian history.[14] At the participational plane conversion of quantity into quality is a usual demographic phenomenon. The conversion can be kept incremental for an indefinite time when, for instance, the population growth keeps the same coefficient, which is what we are now considering. Dialectical changes in the demographic structure happen when there is a notable change in the coefficient of growth, due to improved sanitation, new immigration, and so forth.[15] At the moment when such a change occurs in the coefficient of growth, the regime of participation may be affected. People that were marginal can no longer be kept so, or the change in the quantitative composition of generations brings forth a sudden new pressure for more participation by younger people, as in the urban ghettos of the United States at the present time.

At the political plane incremental processes change into dialectical ones when new groups, which had been formed in accordance with the prevailing regime of power, become excessively important and come to pose—deliberately or not—a challenge to the rulers. This can happen as a consequence of changes of nonpolitical nature: the appearance of new classes, as the bourgeoisie with the commercial and industrial revolutions, or of new religious convictions, as with the Reformation. It can also happen as a result of a political process that was initially incremental. So is the case of political movements which, at a certain moment, shift from incremental growth to sudden importance, as the Christian Democrats, in Chile, at the succession of Jorge Alessandri by Eduardo Frei. It is also typical in strongly concentrated and authoritarian regimes, of the conversion of a subordinate follower, whose influence was growing incrementally in the past, into sudden principal leadership, as Stalin, vis-à-vis Lenin, or Cárdenas, vis-à-vis Calles.

Finally, at the economic plane incremental processes become dialectical ones when the gradual accumulation of wealth or of new technological means is suddenly bringing out new modes of production. Such was the case in fifteenth-century Italy when some merchants organized coordinated lines of craftsmen, multiplicating by many times the previous capacity for production, and bringing about an economic revolution that had repercussions in all the other planes of life.[16]

The conversion of an incremental process of change into a dialectical one submits it to a course of alternatives, which we will consider in the following analysis of dialectical change. First, however, we still have to consider the remaining alternative of incremental change: the incremental change of regime itself. As we have seen, an incremental change in the allocation of valuables that affects the regulating regime can also affect it in an incremental way. This happens when the typic form of the regime or the capability of its main structures are gradually changed. More often than not these two effects come together, although changes of the typic form can occur without capability modifications.

Incremental changes of typic form are the rule with most structures. Only the symbolic structures, as mental constructions, are by definition inalterable. These same structures, however, like cultural phenomena, are subject to this rule of incremental change, as seen with ordinary languages. We can say, therefore, that empirical structures are usually submitted to incremental change and that dialectical changes, as a starting form of change, are comparatively the exception.

At the cultural plane, an incremental change of the regime of values corresponds to the continuous process of circular determination between life situations and values. Changes in the regime of participation, more often than not of an incremental nature, induce corresponding changes in the regime of values, bringing about a constant process of incremental readjustment of legitimacy. So, to take an ancient and a modern example, the gradual urbanization of the former Greek tribes, from Homeric times to the emergence and consolidation of the polis system, incrementally changed the heroic ethos of the *Iliad* into the regime of values governing the Hellenic cities of the fifth century B.C. A similar phenomenon is seen in the various stages of Western civilization, as, for instance, in the transition from feudal to urban life in the late Middle Ages, the emergence, with the Renaissance, of a secular regime of values, and centuries later, the unfolding, during the Enlightenment, of modern ethics based on reason and liberty. The long-term process of secularization, in all its forms, represents that incremental change of the regime of values.[17]

At the participational plane the incremental change of the regime of participation is, once again, the general rule. Population growth tends to change the regime of participation by the sheer effect of decisive, if incremental, change in the size of organized groups. The same happens, at a much faster speed but still, more often than not, by incremental ways, in the process of urbanization. The general tendency is a shift of the regime of participation from gemeinschaft to gesellschaft models.

At the political plane, where dialectical changes are more common than in other planes, incremental changes of regime are still the rule. In spite of the many revolutions that bring dramatic dialectical adjustments between a regime of power and its social, cultural, and economic basis, regimes, whatever their origin, are always undergoing incremental change, by which power and legitimacy are readjusted to the changing aspects of society.[18] If most of these changes are performed by micro-adjustments, hardly perceived by ordinary men, their long-term effects are not less significant than those resulting from sudden dialectical movements, although the sudden or violent dialectical shake-ups are decisive guidelines for the processing of incremental political changes. Interesting examples, in that sense, are the democratization of the European political institutions after the French Revolution and their socialization after the Russian Revolution. England experienced, during the eighteenth century, an incremental political change generating out of Parliament a cabinet government by parliamentary delegation. That somehow intrinsic propensity for the democratization of power, initially controlled by the aristocracy, became increasingly bourgeois and middle class. On the Continent the reaction against Napoleon and the failure of the Francfort Parliament preserved the institutions of the *ancien régime*. In the course of the second half of the nineteenth century, however, incremental change finally achieved what the revolution of 1848–1849 had failed to do. A similar process would happen in our century with respect to the upgrading of the working class and the establishment of the welfare state. Social revolutions failed to change the bourgeois state in Western Europe. Since World War I and very rapidly since World War II, however, incremental changes have substantially adjusted the Western European countries to many of the aspirations of their lower strata.[19]

At the economic plane, once again, incremental change has been the rule, although, it is true, not at the higher level of control of the means of production. In this respect, political change, both incremental and dialectical, has been greater than economic change, either incremental or dialectical. Concentration of the control of the means of production appears to be greater today than in the time of Caesar, as the monopolistic capitalism of the great corporations has replaced the more diversified nineteenth-century capitalism of small firms. Socialism, far from the commune ideal of Marx, has brought about its own version of big corporations and bureaucratic ownership. What has changed in the regime of property has not been the control over production but the control over consumption. Today the multitudes in developed countries—which still represent, however, a small part of humanity—are enjoying an unparalleled abundance of consumption facilities. Most of that result was achieved through incremental change: The gradual, general development of most of the present, Western, developed societies, together with the gradual emergence of mass production, brought mass consumption.[20]

It is time now to shift our attention to dialectical change. As we have seen, dialectical change is structural change that is not compatible with its regulating regime. *At the actional level, dialectical change implies a form of creation, extinction, and modification of social valuables running against the prevailing regimes of values, participation, power, or property.* Such a change may or may not affect the former allocation of social valuables in an appreciable way. Killing a man or taking control of a firm without indemnification of its partners does not alter, noticeably, the former social allocation of valuables, even if one person is violently removed from society and some others are deprived of their assets. Such dialectical disruption of the social order is simple deviance, for which all societies have appropriate remedies which preserve the social order.[21] If, however, the slain man happened to have been the president of a state and the seized firm a large foreign oil company, the dialectical change would affect the social allocation of valuables and, more than that, the social order. *Dialectical changes affecting the social allocation of valuables always affect the regime that regulated those valuables,* which is why such dialectical changes are always subject to social repression. The repression, in minor cases, can be performed by the privately interested parties, with legal or traditional social support. In major cases the repression is carried out by a specialized social agency. At this point, dialectical changes have two alternative courses. If the repression is successful, the change (in the case of that specific occurrence) is stopped. Although deviance is a dialectical change that does not significantly affect the social allocation of valuables, rebellion does affect such allocation; but it can be successfully repressed by a competent social agency. If the regulating regime is unable to preserve or enforce its own rules and the repression is not successful, two new alternatives are opened. First, the change successfully brought about by the dialectical process may be incompatible with some formal aspects of the regulating regime *but not with the regime as such, or, at least, with the whole of the existing social order.* An example is the unlawful change of rules in which case the change is limited to the holding of the seized positions by the new incumbents. Second, the regime may be changed by the dialectical process that could not be repressed or controlled. In the last case, when the change of regime affects the typic form or the capability of the concerned societal subsystem, as usually occurs, *the whole social system tends to be affected in a corresponding way; and we have, according to the direction of the change, social development or social regression.*

Dialectical changes affecting the regime only partially, in ways ultimately compatible with the former social order, are limited to those changes that do not affect, in a noticeable way, the regime of participation and the regime of values. This is the typical case, at the political plane, of the illegal seizure of power by groups, as in many military coups, who are compatible with the ruling class and the formerly existing establishment. At the economic level, an analogous case is a violation of the regime of property that does not affect that regime in a general form but only in the particular application. For instance, frauds and corruption may be tolerated in periods of fast economic change, as in eighteenth-century Great Britain,[22] the United States after the Civil War (the robber barons), and most of the underdeveloped countries of today.

Dialectical changes affecting the regime and bringing about, along with the transformation of the social order, a change in the typic form and capability of a society are less common occurrences than simple deviance or incremental change. As has been said, most structural changes are incremental. This fact, however, among other factors, has misled certain schools of social thought to ignore macrodialectical changes. Although this kind of change cannot be taken as the only cause of historical change, as the former conflict theorists supposed, its paramount importance must be acknowledged. The charismatic revelation of new religions, as Christianity and Islam, the founding of new societies by people dramatically opposing their former ones, as the Puritan colonies in New England, the political revolutions overthrowing not only a group of leaders but a whole regime and its class basis, as the French and the Russian revolutions, and the revolutionary consequences of new technology, as the development of agriculture in the Neolithic period or the mechanization of production with the industrial revolution and, today, its automatization with cybernetics—these are events that, in various ways, have decisively changed the world. Moreover, such decisive occurrences have impelled and oriented the processes of incremental change, which, therefore, can only be understood in connection with the process of dialectical change.

Chart 2 gives a graphic representation of incremental and dialectical change.

The principle of congruence

The preceding analysis of the course of incremental and dialectical changes up to the level of affecting the typic form of any of the societal subsystems enables us now, shifting from the vertical to the horizontal process of change, to study the consequences of structural alteration in the regimes of values, participation, power, and property.

It is timely to remember, from the former analysis of structure and social structure, that we have defined the typic form of a structure as its general properties and peculiar constant features. We saw that in addition to their typic form, structures always have a certain capability, which is their intrinsic ability (given in the typic form) to maintain their own form or pattern. Social structures, moreover, present in their typic form a certain meaning, because of their necessary symbolic content or form, and a certain function, because of their necessary orientation toward a goal. From the point of view of their horizontal articulation, we saw that social structures are organized along four macrofunctional planes—the cultural, participational, political, and economic—and that a societal system corresponds to each of these planes. From the point of view of their vertical articulation, we saw that society as a whole and each of the structural planes present two levels of depth: At the top is the situational level. This level corresponds to the ordaining regime of each societal system (the regime of values, participation, power, and property) and, for the society as a whole, to its social order, which is the result and expression of the integration of the four regimes. At the bottom of each structural plane is the actional level, the analytical level where interaction actually takes place.

Let us now see the consequences of a change in the typic form of any of the societal systems. Such a change, as has already been stated, means that a system's regime has been altered in either an incremental or a dialectical way. The regimes of the societal systems are integrated in a social order, which, in a circular way, both results from each of these regimes and expresses them in an integrated form. The origin and foundation of this expressive-integrative circular process was analyzed in the first chapter of this book. It consists in the legitimation of factual situations by values ultimately induced by factual situations, within the general framework of the fundamental beliefs and expressional symbols provided by the cultural code of each society. Compatibility between the regime of values and the regime of participation is therefore necessary, although it can be submitted,

Chart 2 *Incremental and dialectical change*

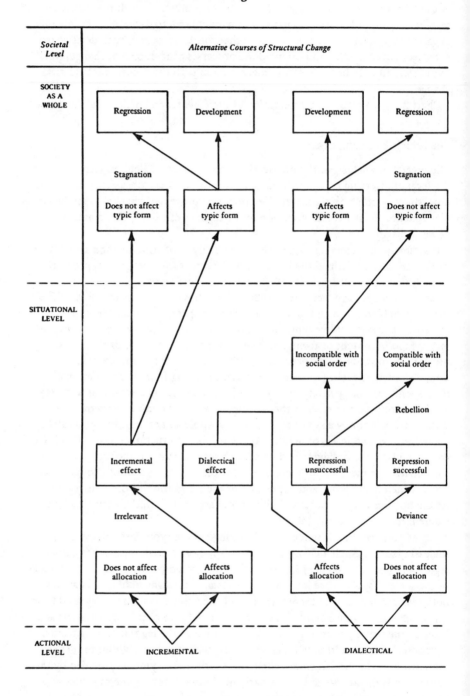

in the course of time, to adjustment crises, when structural change affects one of the two regimes. That compatibility results from the fact that, although the regime of participation is legitimized by the regime of values and, so, presents itself as if resulting from the sheer compliance of the former, regimes of values are induced by the factual situations of life, that is, by regimes of participation. This inducement, however, as has been seen, is never unilinear and deliberate. It is not purposefully obtained by manipulations and coercion, but results, in a nonconscious and nondeliberate way (for any actor), from the interaction between the preceding norms and the actual facts.

The circular correlation existing between the regimes of value and of participation involves the regimes of power and of property. The regime of power always reflects the cumulative effects of the prevailing regime of participation, which it consolidates, under the legitimation of the prevailing regime of values and the sanctioning of the prevailing regime of power.

A fundamental social principle originates with the circular process: the *principle of social congruence*. This principle can be formulated in the following way: *changes affecting the typic form of a societal system in a way that is incongruent with the typic form of the other systems either change the other systems to a form congruent with the new typic form of the former system or are not integrated in the social order; if the changes are not integrated, either the altered system regresses to its former typic form or the social system disintegrates.*

The principle of social congruence means that alterations, whatever their cause (extra- or intrasocietal), of the regime of values, for instance, either produce congruent adjustments in the regimes of participation, power, and property or do not last. In the latter case, as soon as the factor that caused the alteration ceases to exert its influence, as, for instance, a foreign invader imposing a new regime of participation, the former regime of participation is reestablished. If the factor imposing the new regime proves to be irreversible or lasts too long (for the capability of that society), and congruent readjustment in the other regimes does not take place, that society loses its integrating social order and disintegrates as a whole. The same process occurs if the change of regime takes place at the cultural, political, or economic planes.[23]

Let us examine some typical illustrations of this principle, with changes of typic form starting in each of the four societal systems.

The most typical example of original changes in the regime of values that produce congruent changes in the other regimes is the appearance of "totalitarian" religions such as Islam and, in a more complex way, Christianity. From 610, the year of the first communication of his divine revelations, to his death in 632, Muhammad succeeded in converting the Arab tribes of Medina and Mecca to the new faith, bringing about a completely new regime of participation.[24] From the tribal life based on kinship the Arabs were led to a tight association of believers in a suprafamilial religiopolitical community. The change was so deep that not only did it effect a complete readjustment of the other planes of Arab life to the religion-based new culture, but it immensely expanded the capability of the system, creating, with an integrated new Arab society, a new civilization. Similarly, Christianity succeeded in obtaining official recognition, after a long struggle with the social system of the Roman Empire, and finally became the religion of the state after the death of Julian. The greater complexity of both the Christian religion and the Roman world, compared to Islam and the Arab world, explains why the effects of the new value system on society were much less unilinear. Bringing over the Arabs from tribalism to Islam, Muhammad founded a new civilization in a couple of decades and created a new polity which would develop under the Caliphate. The much longer, more difficult, and complex expansion of Christianity took place within the most civilized part of the world, highly organized both at the cultural and the political levels. The new polities that Christianity would generate were to come much later, through the complex interaction between the new church and the invading barbarians. Before the collapse of the unified Roman Empire, however, the changes brought about by Christianity at the cultural plane had their counterparts at the other planes. These counterparts resulted, in large part, from a process of mutual adjustment. Christianity had to be thoroughly Hellenized, from Paul onward, to become acceptable at the cultural plane. Moreover, its otherworldly orientation and message had to be adjusted to the current participational, political, and economic requirements of the Roman society, somehow by a transference to liturgy and to postmortem expectations of many of such otherworldly claims. The Roman world was in turn deeply affected in all its planes by the new religion and its values, which humanized and accordingly changed the former regime of participation, incorporating the slaves and lower classes into the spiritual community, with many substantial practical consequences. Furthermore, the new system of values affected more directly and less compromisingly, although on a much smaller scale, the other subsystems of the Roman society by originating a strong and broad movement toward cenobitism and monasticism, mostly in the East after the Third century (St. Anthony, 250–356; St. Pachomius, 290–345). This movement of multitudes of ascetics, in various forms of monastical organization implies a radical adjustment to the new religion of the participational, political, and economic regimes.[25]

Changes in the regime of participation, more often than not by incremental ways, also produce congruent changes in the regime of values. The preceding examples mention the transition of the Greek tribes to the polis system and the consequent change of their regime of values from the Homeric ethos to the ideal of justice.[26] Similarly, the transition of the Western societies from feudal to urban life, during the Renaissance, changed the medieval Christian ethos into the modern secular one. Examples of the same phenomenon are innumerable. These examples do not occur only in processes of urbanization, leading from gemeinschaft to gesellschaft. The reverse is equally true, as in the disintegration of the Carolingian empire, when the fragmentation of the formerly unified political system led to the establishment of various kingdoms, which were almost only nominally coordinated by feudal links with a multitude of baronies.[27] The disappearance of imperial authority and the irrelevance of central authority in the various kingdoms brought about a new regime of participation, tightly linked to the parochial systems built around the feudal domains. Under these new circumstances the former "catholic" ethos generated by the Carolingian Renaissance and its revival of Universalism was changed into the chivalrous ethos of the eleventh and twelfth centuries, which so much contributed to the emergence of such diverse movements as the Cluniac order and the reform of the Church, the Crusades, and the development of the refined courtly culture of the troubadours.[28] In a different context, and independent of urbanizing or ruralizing processes, we can see how changes in the regime of participation introduced by new politico-legal arrangements, have corresponding cultural effects. In the case of the universalization of Roman citizenship, for instance, the gradual change of the former polis-based into a multipoleis empire (finally formalized by Caracalla's edict) led, much before the Christian influence, to the abandonment of the city cult and even of the Olympian one, which were replaced, at the civic level, by the cult of the emperor and, at the religious level, either by philosophy—among the cultivated sectors—or by the Euleusian Mysteries and Oriental religions.[29]

Changes in the regimes of values and of participation bring about corresponding political and economic changes. In all the examples we have been discussing, the alteration of the value-participational situations has caused politico-economic congruent effects, and changes originated at the political or economic planes have provoked cultural and participational counterparts. The relationships between the modes of production typical of feudal and capitalist societies and their respective cultural, participational, and political counterparts have been masterfully discussed by Marx, even if we today would reject his assumptions concerning the unilateral determination of the cultural and political effects of the economic factors. Events of a predominantly political nature, such as the Bolshevik revolution, whatever their ideological foundations, have caused radical economic and cultural changes. It is interesting to observe, in this connection, how the dogmatic view that economic changes produce their political counterpart but not vice versa has always been at odds with the course of events produced by the Russian Revolution.

In their essential theoretical aspects, the discussions between Mensheviks and Bolsheviks, between Plekanov and Lenin, and between Kautsky and Lenin or Rosa Luxemburg and Lenin, and finally the debate concerning Stalin and his theory of socialism in a single country[30] are all centered on the conflict between doctrinairian "truth" and empirical truth. The doctrinaires emphasized, successively, that a socialist revolution could not happen before the objective conditions (bourgeois capitalism) were ripe, that the political "superstructure" could not be used to change the economic infrastructure, that the dictatorship of the proletariat could not be replaced by the self-appointed rule of the party and its leaders, that socialism results from the international mobilization of the exploited proletariat and cannot be achieved in the bourgeois context of a single nation-state. Facts have proved the doctrinaires were wrong. Those who proved to be empirically right, however, whose goals were achieved in conditions reputedly impossible or through means considered inadequate, have not attempted to justify their ways by refuting the central thesis of their opponents but have pretended that their opponents' thesis was not applicable to what they were actually doing.

Another important question must still be discussed. We have seen how successful and enduring changes in any of the systems' regimes bring about corresponding changes in the other regimes in accordance with the principle of social congruence. We must now see how those changes that cannot be extended to the other planes are either regressive or disruptive.

The Ottoman and the Latin American societies provide both long-run and short-run examples of regressive processes due to the lack of congruent extension of change originating at one structural plane to the other planes. In long-run historical terms we see how the Ottoman Empire, after succeeding in extending its domain to the doors of Vienna and over the whole of North Africa, the Balkans and the Middle East, began to decline at the end of Suleiman's reign (1520–1566) and declined increasingly after the Enlightenment. The Ottoman Empire was essentially the result of a political tour de force. Built on the basis of total servile dedication to the sultan and legitimized on religious foundations, it was a society oriented entirely toward military power. The resulting theocratic-military state, frozen by its simplified form of Islam, was able to expand, keep control of the conquered areas, and successfully match Western resistance or counterattacks while its undeveloping cultural and economic system was maintained by rudimentary forms of organization and warfare. Its inability to achieve cultural and economic change, because of the double rigidity resulting from its regimes of value and of participation, proved, however, to be fatal in the long run, in spite of the enduring politico-military success of its military specialization. The failure to achieve at the other structural planes the same level of development obtained, in special terms, at the political plane brought the Ottoman experiment to final disaster.[31]

In Latin America a different form of highly successful specialization, this time at the economic plane, was responsible for a resulting failure. Specializing since the early colonial times in the production and exportation of primary goods, obtained from large-scale mining or plantations, based on slave labor and, later, on the payment of very low and partially nonmonetary subsistence wages, in conditions of practically unlimited natural resources and manpower, Latin American elites have been able, in a regime of very restrictive participation, to concentrate in their hands extraordinary wealth and power. In order to preserve their privileges these elites were led to establish a correspondingly restrictive regime of property and power, supported by a traditional regime of values. They succeeded in maintaining the system with minimal internal change until the early decades of this century. When, under the impact of the Great Depression of the 1930s and the internal exacerbation of its own contradictions, the system was suddenly brought to a collapse, the Latin American elites were confronted with the consequences of the nongeneralization to the other societal planes, on the one hand, and to the mass of their own people, on the other hand, of the former success of their economy. Suddenly faced with the need to develop, the

Latin American societies, in spite of the new opportunities created by, and partially realized through, the process of import substitution, had neither the cultural qualifications nor the sociopolitical conditions to take full advantage of and master new opportunities. The other societal systems, particularly the cultural and the political, were not prepared to follow, manage, and orient the opportunities for rapid economic development created by the import substitution process, and the large regional market of potentially 200 million consumers was actually reduced to less than 25 percent of that size because of the complete socioeconomic marginality of the masses. These two factors have been hindering the general process of development in Latin America in the decades since the Depression and World War II (See Chapters 19 and 20 for further details). Economic overspecialization in the Latin American case, like military overspecialization in the Ottoman case, engendered rigidities in the social system that hindered the development of the other subsystems and finally weakened the plane of the former successes, reducing the society to failure and stagnation.

If we shift from long-term to short-term events, the Ottoman and Latin American societies again supply interesting illustrations. One example is Mustafa Kemal and the Young Turks revolution. Roughly corresponding to the time of Lenin's revolution, Kemal's dramatic efforts toward the general development and modernization of Turkey were neither less seriously undertaken by the new Turkish elites nor lacking in radical means when such means were considered necessary. Lenin's revolution, however, although started at the political plane and promoted by political means, was oriented to the radical change of the regimes of participation and of property.

Kemal's revolution, although conceived, in a sense, in a broader framework than the Russian Revolution and implemented with no less throughness and consistency, failed to achieve the general national development that Atatürk aimed at and to reach the grade of irreversibility attained by Lenin's experiment. We will not attempt, even succinctly, to make a comparative analysis of the two revolutions, or to analyze the causes of the relative failure of the Turkish Revolution, which, of course, contributed to the distinct cultural characteristics of the Turkish society and to the substantially smaller extent of Turkey's human and natural resources. However, a decisive difference between the two revolutions was the fact that the Russian rural system was deeply and irreversibly changed by the Russian Revolution, whereas the Turkish Revolution only superficially affected the countryside.

The fact that both countries were agrarian societies at the time of their revolutions and, therefore, that their regimes of participation were predominantly determined by their rural regimes of property and of exploitation is the most important variable in the explanation of the final difference in the success and stability of the two revolutions. In both cases the revolution started at the political level, introduced decisive changes in the urban economic system, and deeply affected—in Turkey still more than in Russia—the cultural system. In Turkey, however, the basis of the rural system remained unchanged, whereas in Russia the new economic regime was ruthlessly extended to the rural system, which brought about a decisive and irreversible change in the regime of participation of the whole society, with congruent effects in its regime of power. The lack of such a change in Turkey preserved the conditions for a later return of traditional forces and tendencies, with the Democratic party, about a decade after the death of Mustafa Kemal. The subsequent return, with the coup of 1960, to many of Kemal's basic views has limited the effects of the Bayar-Menderes concessions to international capitalism, but the Turkish national capacity for capital accumulation and autonomous scientific and technological development has been seriously undermined, preventing the country from obtaining a self-sustained development.[32]

In some Latin American countries, such as Brazil and Argentina, vigorous economic changes have been promoted by some sectors of the cities and of the government since the crisis of the 1930s. These changes permitted the basic economic overcoming of the structural limitations inherited from the past. For diverse reasons, which will be studied in detail in the last part of this book, these two countries did not succeed in achieving the corresponding changes at the cultural, participational, and political planes. Most of their elites remained oriented toward conspicuous values and pseudo-Western styles unfitting for the process of development. The regime of participation was kept restrictive, marginalizing the vital sector, when not a substantial majority of the population. The political process did not become representative of the expectations and claims of the masses; nor was it effectively oriented for the promotion of national development. As a consequence, these countries have been dragged by regressive tendencies since the 1960s, their economic development has been led to a deadlock, and the general standards have declined to the level of their lower structural planes.

In these illustrations the noncongruent extension of a change of regime to the other structural planes brought about a regressive process, but consequences of a disruptive nature can also result. This tends to happen, as has been previously said, when factors that cause a change of typic form in one of the societal systems, but do not succeed in producing congruent changes in the other systems persist long enough to affect the social order. The most typical examples of such cases are those of superimposed political regimes that do not succeed in changing the regimes of value or of participation of the ruled societies. The Ottoman Empire is also a good example for the present hypothesis. In some areas the empire failed to Islamize the population. As soon as the coercive capability of the empire declined, these populations started striving for independence and finally succeeded in obtaining it, as happened with Greece. In Spain failure to change the preexisting feelings of nationhood and to introduce congruent adjustments in the former regime of participation was responsible for the country's failure from 1580 to 1640 to incorporate Portugal in her design of an all-Iberian monarchy. The Habsburgs also experienced similar failure when they did not succeed in adjusting the rising non-Germanic nationalities of the Austrian Empire to the Habsburg dynasty-centered system.[33] A recent example of such failure and of its disruptive effects can be found in the joint attempt of the Soviet Union and the East German Communist party to build a viable German Democratic Republic. Although the new political system built by the Communists in Eastern Europe was able to produce congruent effects in the other societal systems of these countries, which have obtained an increasing stability and autonomous and endogenous development, the German Democratic Republic experiment continues to be strictly dependent on the coercive apparatus of the party and the formidable Soviet garrison permanently stationed in East Germany.

Social and historical change

Our preceding discussion enables us now to comment briefly on the time dimension of social change and the relationship between such change and the other sorts of structural change occurring in the nonsocietal environment of society. The first point concerns the relationship between social change and historical change. The second point, to be treated subsequently, refers to the relationship between sociohistorical change and physical change, on the one hand, and biological change, that is, evolution, on the other hand.

The problem of the connections and distinctions between social and historical change is essentially one of analytical differentiation and conventional definition. Everything social is submitted to history, and everything historical (in a qualitative sense) is social. What we are concerned with is a clarification of a double concept. At one level we have the distinction between the subject matter of sociology, as the archetypical science of the "social," and history, as the discipline *par excellence* of the "historical." At another level we have the distinction between which social facts are historical and which are not.

The development of these two questions would pull us far away from our central theme onto the fields of the theory of history and of the philosophy of the social sciences. Let me just mention that the classic controversy, in that respect, centers on whether or not sociology should be purely nomothetic and, still more emphatically, whether or not history should be purely ideographic. Positivists tend to take the extreme position, considering that the social, as subject matter of sociology, is what is universal, structural-functional, and timeless in human interaction, and that the historical, as subject matter of history, is what is unique, individualized, time-seried, and nonrecurrent in human interaction. That extreme position tends to be much shaded by the dynamic (as opposed to the homeostatic) views of sociology, particularly among those having a dialectical or evolutionary approach, as well as, in history, by the structuralist views, requiring for the explanation of any event its location in its sociocultural framework. The result of this rapprochement would be the interdependence of the two disciplines whenever concrete events had to be studied. A history without sociology could not surpass the chronicle level and could not obtain the meaning of the narrated events by just considering their uniqueness, and the sociology of any concrete society could not understand the empirical reality of its type-described behaviors without considering their history.[34]

But although all concrete social events present, analytically, a certain uniqueness and specific individuality, they are not all equally historical. At the second level of our distinction we are differentiating events that are "relevant" from those that are not. Historical events are those that are historically relevant, which means, in a sense that is deeper than it looks, events that are relevant for the historian.[35] In trying to understand the past of any society or aspects of it, the historian selects, from among the multitude of knowable facts, those events that in his view have conditioned the subsequent course of that society or particular social aspect under his study. So, in an objective sense, to appear historically relevant means that an event presents accepted (by the historians) evidence of having conditioned later related events. Historical events are those considered as presenting some social relevance. This fact, however, gives evidence to the fact that all historical interpretation, whatever the objectivity of the historian's intent and method, implies an appraisal by the historian (so, a subjective one) of what has been influential on what. This is why, in my judgment, a purely positivistic view of history can never explain historical interpretation, because the model that would suit the positivist requirement—the so-called cover law explanation—does not fit that subjective reenactment of the past, as human interaction, that the historian is compelled to do in order to select the relevant from among the irrelevant events and conditions.[36]

Notwithstanding the inevitably subjective content of the historian's decision concerning the relevance of an event to his inquiry, its validity is subject to the objectivity of the intent and method with which the investigation is made. Ultimately, through objectively reliable data and inferences from these data, the social relevance of the event must be determined by the extent to which it may be judged as (1) having affected the social allocation of valuables and, eventually, the regime of a societal system, or the social regime, if not the typic form itself and the capability of one or more of the society's systems, or (2) having generated long-range effects on the concerned society, affecting one or several generations. The possible range of historical relevance presents a very large spectrum, from a minimum of creation, modification, or extinction of some valuables and their social allocation to a maximum of shaping the subsequent course of the history of a society, a whole civilization or even mankind.

The varying grades of relevance of historical events are at the origin of the division of history into periods. Historical periods are not random subdivisions of the historical process, although quite often the border line between distinct periods cannot be clearly traced in terms of unique events or dates.[37] Historians usually work with two basic units when delimiting periods: (1) *civilizations*, the largest unit, dividing the course of man's history into large sociocultural aggregates formed around a system of fundamental beliefs and (2) *epochs*, delimiting the distinct ontological-axiological forms through which the societies of a civilization have interpreted and lived their basic beliefs. Civilization implies a cultural code interconnected with an original regime of participation and conditioning original regimes of property and of power. In the course of time, however, changes may, and actually do, affect these regimes without necessarily replacing the basic beliefs with new ones, but by adjusting these beliefs to the new incoming regimes of values and participation. These changes generate successive epochs. In spite of the no less substantial changes, concomitantly occurring at the level of the regimes of property and power and in terms of the available technology of the concerned society, it is often more meaningful to identify and characterize succeeding epochs by their ontological-axiological views, that is, their life-style, than by more restrictive references to property and power regimes and to technological features. This can be seen if one considers Western civilization and its subdivision in terms of Romanesque, Gothic and Baroque epochs; these are expressions borrowed from the history of art, rather than political or economic characterizations.[38]

Historical anthropology has contributed to that situation by providing a general integrated view of the great periods in the development of mankind irrespective of particular civilizations and, of course, societies. After the gradual process of biocultural humanization of man and the resulting initial Paleolithic stage, a series of macro-revolutions, as has been observed by V. Gordon Childe (1964),[39] has affected all four structural planes of the majority of all existing societies, bringing about and diffusing the agricultural revolution of the Neolithic, the urban revolution of the fertile crescent, the humanistic revolution of the Hellenic civilization, and the technological revolution of modern times. The revolution of the subjective religions (Buddhism, Christianity, Islam), as well as the subjectivization of certain objective religions (Judaism by the late prophets and Hinduism by the gurus), which took place before the technological revolution, should be added to the list.[40]

These periods, however, are determined by large cultural-participational changes and do not consider the more gradual (in historical terms) changes that occur in any society within the framework of the life-style of an epoch but actually introduce irreversible elements of structural change. These shorter periods should be called "phases." While the succession of historical epochs is mainly determined by changes in the ontological-axiological views concerning their respective civilization, the succession of phases is due to the appearance and spreading of new operational means, affecting the social stratification and changing in a congruent way the regimes of property and power. *Phases are stages in the evolution of a society, occurring within a given epoch of a given civilization.* They result from innovations in technology and organization, and express the new social arrangement determined by these innovations. When the innovations are of a very radical nature and bring transcendent effects, which has happened only a few times in the evolution of mankind, the new phase reaches the highest level of societal change and becomes an anthropological revolution, as the agricultural revolution of the Neolithic. These, however, are very special cases. Usually, phases fit their epoch, introducing technological changes within it. The cultural readjustments, either gradual or sudden, forced upon an epoch by successive or major phase changes bring about ontological-axiological changes and generate a new epoch. Urbanization, in the archaic epoch of the Hellenic civilization, led to the cultural change from the epic values of Homer to the values of the polis of the classical period. A similar effect took place in Europe from the end of the Middle Ages to the Renaissance. Whatever their economic and political conditioning, however, religious reformulations, as the Reformation, or philosophical renewals, as the Enlightenment,[41] can become, irrespectively of technological innovations, the most relevant single factor in the generation of a new epoch. At a higher level new universal religions, whatever their sociohistorical conditioning, have been up to now the originators of new civilizations. Whether or not this will continue to follow now that the Western civilization has become the universal one and its fundamental beliefs have shifted from religious ones to a humanistic-operational belief in contingent rationality and liberty is a question open to speculation.

Social change and evolution

Let us now, taking into account the preceding analysis of historical change, consider the relationship between societal and nonsocietal change, particularly biological evolution.

Let us begin by reviewing our former study of the social process. We have seen that, whatever the purposes of the intervening actors, the social process consists in a creation, modification, exchange, and extinction of valuables, which, incrementally or dialectically, tend to affect their social allocation. The changes thus introduced in a society, either gradually or suddenly, have varying consequences. Technological innovations, whether original or spread by diffusion, introduce changes of phase. Successive or major changes of phase, as well as religious and philosophical reformulations, generate new epochs. New religions may generate new civilizations and transcendent technological innovations (as agriculture or industry), and new universal religions bring about anthropological revolutions and new macrostages in the cultural development of mankind.

Although we have analyzed the way in which these various changes occur, there are two relevant questions concerning their occurrence that still remain to be explained. The first concerns the conditions that cause such changes to take place. The second, the conditions that ensure the permanence of the results of these changes, once they have taken place. If it is true, as we have seen, that social processes affect valuables and their social allocation, why is it that in some cases the resulting consequences are socially relevant and lasting while in most cases they are not? What conditions contribute to or determine, the social relevance and the irreversibility of some results of social processes?

The social sciences are currently showing a tendency to answer these questions with a new, more refined, and broader formulation of the cultural evolutionary theory.[42] The first cultural evolutionists, such as Spencer and Tylor, apart from their differences, had in common a metaphysical propensity to an idealized view of evolution and progress. Evolution, as an empirical process, was subsumed in the idea of progress, as a moral concept. And as the cultural evolutionists tended to have their particular versions of what was or should be moral progress, they tended to interpret historical changes accordingly, introducing their own ideological bias in their interpretations. Although both Spencer and Tylor sustained that evolution is processed along many lines, their moral-progress orientation led them, finally, to a unilinear vision of cultural evolution that became increasingly at variance with empirical data.

The new cultural evolutionary theory, besides being supported by a far better formulated and empirically tested general evolutionary theory, particularly in reference to its biological foundations, presents, vis-à-vis the former one, two basic differences. The first concerns its nonmetaphysical character. Progress is not understood as a moral principle as far as evolution is concerned but as objectively comparable and measurable characteristics of the degree of adaptation and adaptability of any system to its environment. The second difference concerns the distinction between *specific evolution,* concerned with the various modes and means of adaptation, and *general evolution,* concerned with the conditions of adaptability.[43]

In its broader meaning, as Huxley and Lotka[44] have stressed, the empirical process of evolution represents an anti-entropy. While physical processes are submitted to a general law of energy degradation and randomization, those systems submitted to evolution, that is, the self-adjusting systems, follow the opposite direction. The general process of evolution consists in an increasingly efficient utilization of the earth's resources by self-adjusting systems for enhancing their command of their respective environment.

Evolution presents two distinct aspects: general and specific. General evolution is an overall tendency of self-adjusting systems to enhance their adaptability through stages of increasing capability for flexible and generic command of environments. Specific evolution is an increasingly specialized adaptation to a particular environment by a self-adjusting system; it is an adaptation through many lines and is oriented toward finding ecological conditions to which adaptation would be maximal and stable. Both processes exist with living systems and with cultural ones. Cultural evolution is the continuation, by new means, of biological evolution and is functionally homologous to it.

The distinction between general and specific evolution is both analytical and empirical.[45] Analytically, the distinction concerns the difference between adaptability and adaptation. Adaptability is a flexible and generic adjustment to environmental conditions through control over the environment. Increasing adaptability, therefore, means a passage from lesser to greater energy transformation, lower to higher levels of integration, and partial to all-around control. Adaptation is a specialized adjustment to a particular environment. Increasing adaptation is a narrowing of the relevant environment and is tendencially oriented toward finding an ecological niche perfectly and stably suited to the system's necessities and possibilities.

Empirically, the distinction between general and specific evolution consists in the fact that only specific evolution is a continuous phylogenetic, ramifying passage of living and cultural systems along many lines of adaptive modifications to particular environments. These various lines present, irrespective of their time occurrence, different levels of "evolutionary progress," that is, of adaptability. The higher the systems' ability to extract energy from the environment, store it, and use it for their own maintenance, expansion, self-development, and reproduction, the higher their level of general evolution is.

The difference between biological evolution and cultural evolution is that the former consists in physicochemical adjustments and the latter in symbolic ones. It should be stressed (something that cultural anthropologists are inclined to forget) that cultural evolution does not happen by itself, distinct from biological evolution, but always and necessarily occurs as a societal process. Culture is a dimension of society. Although a culture, as a system of symbols and meanings and the sum total of the expressions given to them, is methodologically and analytically separable from the society that has generated it (in a way analogous to the way honey is separable from the secreting bees), a culture by itself is not a self-adjusting system, although it is an adjustable one. Any cultural system has its systemic laws, in the sense that (1) it cannot be interpreted or even used capriciously by anybody, including the society that has generated it, and (2) it can be adapted and transformed along certain lines and according to certain rules. But only societies, as structured sets of human interactions, are actually self-adjusting systems.

Given these introductory indications about specific and general, and biological and cultural evolution, let us now approach the two questions proposed formerly and see how cultural evolutionary theory answers them.

The first question that is clarified by the evolutionary explanation is why some changes are lasting ones. The answer is given by the *principle of stability*. Adaptation is adjustment to the environment through varying levels of adaptability. Whatever the level of adaptability, once adaptation is reached, the resulting success establishes the change. In terms of cultural evolution, changes that increase the adaptation of a culture (and of the society bearing it) will be retained. Non-adapted cultures and their bearing societies will not survive their natural and societal environments. Only those achieving appropriate adaptation will survive, and they will do so to the extent that they keep their adaptive features. When cultures are acted upon by disturbing forces, therefore, they will, if necessary and they are capable, undergo specific changes to adjust themselves to these forces, but only to the extent necessary, still preserving unchanged their fundamental structure and character.[46]

The second point that is clarified by the evolutionary explanation is the question of what conditions cause changes. This question is answered by two evolutionary laws: the *law of cultural dominance* and the *law of evolutionary potential*.

The law of cultural dominance states that the cultural system that exploits the energy resources of a given environment most effectively will tend to spread in that environment at the expense of less effective systems. Cultural dominance, as evolution, may be specific or general. Specific dominance is the most successful specialization to an ecological niche. General dominance is the widest range of dominance. As far as culture is concerned, however, possible environments are much more limited than for life in general, since they are subject to the limitations of the human species. There are, because of that, few possibilities of cultural ecological niches. The remaining nomads and the Eskimos are the disappearing examples of specific dominance. Universal Western civilization is the example of general dominance. Its immense adaptability has imposed on all other cultures the dilemma of imitating it or disappearing. Cultural dominance, therefore, forces any other culture to adjust its own system to the dominant one, if the system permits adjustment and the social group is willing to do so, or to suffer extinction. The latter alternative occurs either because the society adhering to the lower culture is exterminated by the higher culture or because that society is forced to acculturate, that is, to take the culture of the dominant type in place of its former one and, therefore, disappear as a specific social system. The best modern example of the alternative of extinction through physical or cultural death is the case of the Indian cultures in the Americas. The best example of cultural adjustment to the dominant type is Japan, which has survived as a society because of the capability of her culture and the willingness of her societal community to make the necessary adjustment.[47]

The law of cultural dominance explains, as we have seen, why some cultural changes take place, either by the imposition of the dominant culture on lower ones or by the incorporation by the latter of the essential features of the former. The law of evolutionary potential completes the answer to the question of what conditions actually cause change by explaining how higher levels of adaptability, and therefore of dominance, are reached. This law expresses a dynamic consequence of the principle of stability. It states that the more specialized and adapted a form is, in a given evolutionary stage, the smaller is its potential for passing to a higher one. The fact expressed by this law results from the dialectic contradiction peculiar to the phenomenon of evolution. Empirically, evolution proceeds by adaptation, the propensity to achieve the necessary adjustment to the environment by specialization. Quantitatively, however, such specialization is a limitation, preventing adjustment to the environment through higher adaptability. The species, at the biological plane, and the societies, at the cultural one, that succeed in securing a perfect adaptation to a given environment lose their capability to increase their general adaptability. On the contrary, the systems that have remained more flexible—at the price of having less adjustment to their environment and so less security for a certain period of their history—are capable of higher adaptability if they can overcome the challenges of their former situation. For cultures these challenges are the former dominant cultures. As Sahlins and Service (1965, p. 95) have so well observed, the "dominance which higher species may exert over lower species tends to be the most effective inhibitor of any potential that may reside in an unspecialized species."

As these authors have also realized (1965, p. 99), the best previous formulation of that principle was made by Trotsky (1950, vol. 1, pp. 16–17), when he observed that the comparatively inferior stage of development of Russia would be a favorable asset once the new conditions created by the revolution permitted her to develop and pushed her forward. "The privilege of backwardness" consists in the fact that the backward culture that survives the risks of (1) external extinction and (2) internal disruption has a greater evolutionary potential precisely because, being less specialized in and committed to specific forms, she is freer to adopt the most effective ones at the highest evolutionary level then obtainable.[48]

The application of this law to cultural development presents a double set of twofold conditions. For intrasocietal conditions, it follows, first, that promoters of change, more often than not, are individuals and groups who are less committed to the former social order and less specialized for predominance under it. These are the various "generalist entrepreneurs," at any of the four societal structural planes (cultural, participational, political, and economic), as opposed to well-settled people and specialized performers. Second, it follows, as stressed by Don Martindale (1962), that phases of sociohistoric innovation are more favorable to evolutionary progress than phases that are characterized by the consolidation or preservation of acquired advantages.

For extrasocietal conditions, it follows, first, that less-integrated and institutionalized societies, that is, less-developed ones, are more capable, if they survive their external and internal challenges, of reaching higher levels of development. Second, it follows that new lands and areas that are in the process of original occupation and settlement constitute a more favorable condition for the sociocultural development of a society than areas that were the site of older civilizations.

The United States in the nineteenth century and up to the recent past provides a very good illustration of these conditions. Less specialized than the European countries, having the advantage of new lands, and not having suffered severe external and internal challenges, that society was able to reach the highest level of development in the middle of the twentieth century. The fact, however, so perceptively pointed out by Service (Sahlins and Service, 1965, chap. 5), that in the years since World War II there have been strong tendencies in the United States to impose, by all means, a freezing of the world situation and to consider any change at variance with her own system to be a subversion of a status quo which she has converted into a moral principle is indicative of excessive cultural specialization. It shows the existence in the United States of a propensity torward converting her general dominance into a specific one, which will result in a decreasing of her evolutionary potential.[49]

NOTES

[1] For further reading see the bibliography at the end of this book.

[2] On the subject see particularly the comprehensive discussion in Jean Viet (1967). See also *Centre International de Synthèse* (1957), S. F. Nadel (1957), Jean Piaget (1949 and 1950), Roger Bastide, ed. (1962), and Lucien Goldmann (1969).

[3] See Anatol Rapoport's definition of system: "System as (1) something consisting of a set (finite and infinite) of entities (2) among which a set of relations is specified, so that (3) deductions are possible from some relations to others as from the relations among the entities to the behavior or the history of the system." *International Encyclopedia of the Social Sciences* (1968, vol. 15, p. 453).

[4] On the systemic interrelationship of reality, see Ernst Cassirer (1953a particularly chap. 4, sect. 6).

[5] See Piaget (1967, pp. 167 ff).

[6] See, for instance, Alfred North Whitehead on changeless substances (1938, p. 131).

[7] Higher and broader level and lower and narrower level are references to the relative levels of intensity and cybernetic control of any system of systems, as indicated in Table 2.

[8] See, in this respect, Whitehead's conception of the interrelatedness of macro- and micro-processes. For instance, he states: "There are two species of process, macroscopic process and microscopic process. The macroscopic process is the transition from attained actuality to actuality in attainment; while the microscopic process is the conversion of conditions which are merely real into determinate actuality" (1929, p. 247).

[9] As has been indicated by Don Martindale (1962, particularly chaps. 1 and 19), although there are different views about the causes of structural social change, the various basic sociological models of society show that there is an underlying consensus among most writers, concerning the concept of social structure. Basically this underlying concept is in agreement with the view presented in this book. In this respect see also, for instance, Marx's and Max Weber's concepts of the social relations *Wage Labor and Capital* for the former and *Economy and Society,* 1944, vol. I, pp. 24–25 for the latter), Alfred Reginald Radcliffe-Brown's (1952) views on structure and function.

[10] See Kingsley Davis' classification of social acts as (1) technical, (2) economic, (3) political, and (4) cultural (1949, chap. 5). Martindale (1962, chap. 2) distinguishes three forms of social action: (1) socialization (transformation of "natural" man into social man), (2) mastery of nature, and (3) social control.

[11] The foregoing generalization has been proposed by Parsons, although in a less specified way, in several of his analyses of the social process. See, for instance, Talcott Parsons, (1959, pp. 16 ff. and 1966-a, pp. 20–21).

[12] See Parsons' (1951), p. 481 ff.) similar distinction between changes *within* the system and *of* the system. The same view is shared by Marx, who always differentiated the changes of the forces of production compatible with the economic relation of production from those that are not and that will ultimately bring about the change of the latter. See, for instance, his Preface to the *Critique of Politic Economy*

[13] See particularly *Capital,* I, XI.

[14] See Friedrich Heer (1968, vol. I, chap. 7).

[15] Such was the case of small European villages suddenly turned into large towns as a result of the industrial revolution in the nineteenth century. See, for example, Werner Sombart (1946, vol. I, chap. 24).

[16] On the general aspects of the Renaissance bourgeoisie, see Alfred von Martin (1946) and on sixteenth-century merchants, see Pierre Jeannin (1969).

[17] On the process of the formation of the social city and its ethical effects, see Werner Jaeger (1945, vol. I, chap. 6); see also Gustave Glotz (1968, Introduction, and part II, chap. 1). On the process of urbanization in the Middle Ages, see Henri Pirenne (1947, chap. 2); see also Johannes Bühler (1946, pp. 201 ff.). On the later stage of the process of secularization in the eighteenth century, see Paul Hazard (1946, vol. I, chaps. III and V); see also Bernhard Groethuysen (1943, pp. 73 ff. and 172 ff.).

[18] On the capability of political systems to preserve their typic forms while undergoing continuous incremental changes, see Bernard Barber's study (1957) on comparative social stratification.

[19] See Reinhard Bendix (1964). On German incremental democratic socialization since Bismarck, see Peter Gay's study (1962) on Bernstein and his influence.

[20] On the characteristics of contemporary capitalism and the effects of mass consumption or democratic regulation on capital concentration, see John Strachey (1956). For the historical development of capitalism, see Maurice Dobb (1967, part I). On the Soviet present economic system, see Harry Schwartz (1968). On the stratification of contemporary Soviet society, see Alex Inkeles (1968, chap. 3).

[21] See Parsons (1951-a, chap. 7, particularly pp. 249–251 and 297 ff.).

[22] See Ronald Wraith and Edgar Simpkins (1963).

[23] The principle of congruence is a universally valid generalization about the internal structure of the social system, and the character of the interdependence among its four

major subsystems. It expresses the general conditions under which structural changes occurring in a societal system will or will not affect the whole society and will or will not be stable in the societal system in which it initially took place. As formulated in this book, the principle of congruence represents, in terms of social theory, an overcoming of certain limitations, already discussed, of the static equilibrium and the single-factor conflict models of society. The principle of congruence expresses the same underlying principle but in an extended and circular way, that was expressed by Marx in his discussion of the relationship between infrastructural and superstructural changes. Not only the economic system, as Marx thought, but also the cultural, political, and participational ones are the possible analytical loci of infrastructural changes that may condition the whole society. Conceived, hypothically, as the only rational formulation for the structural, interdependent, mutual adjustment among the subsystems of the social system, the principle of congruence is empirically confirmed by both historical and current observation.

[24] On Muhammad and the formation of Islam, see Francesco Gabrieli (1968). For a general history of Islam see Carl Brockelmann (1960).

[25] On the influence of Christianity on the making of a new society, see Christopher Dawson (1960 and 1958). See also Henry O. Taylor (1958), M. L. W. Laistner (1967), and Charles N. Cochrane (1949).

[26] See particularly Jaeger (1945, vol. I, book 1).

[27] Western feudalism, whose origins go back to Merovingian times, changed in political and social character with the dissolution of the Carolingian empire. From an expedient used to assure, if loosely, the unity of the empire, it became a self-standing institution, in which private control of lands and fields, not public appointment, were the source of political power. See F. L. Ganshof (1961); see also Heinrich Fichtenau (1964) for the Carolingian empire.

[28] See particularly Bühler (1946, chap. 3) for his views on the transition from the Low to the High Middle Ages, from the age of *senectus* to the age of *juventus*. See also William J. Brandt (1966, p. 140 ff.).

[29] See Mikhail Rostovzeff (1960, chaps. 15 and 22) and Albert Grenier (1969, first part, chap. 4 and third part, chap. 5).

[30] About these discussions, see G. V. Plekhanov (1922–1927), Lenin, *The Tasks of the Proletariat in Our Revolution* (April Thesis), Karl Kautsky (1964), Lenin, *The Proletarian Revolution and Kautsky, the Renegade*, Rosa Luxemburg (1922), Lenin *What Is to Be Done?*, Stalin, *Problems of Leninism.*

[31] See Arnold Toynbee (1934–1961, vol. III, pp. 22 ff.) and Brockelmann (1960, chap. 2).

[32] See the studies of Peter F. Sugar, Dankwart A. Rustow, Arif T. Payasliouglu, among others, in Robert E. Ward and Rustow, eds. (1964). See also Benoist-Méchin (1954) and Toynbee (1934–1961, vol. VIII, pp. 263 ff.).

[33] See Karl W. Deutsch (1966, particularly chap. 4), on nationalism and communication.

[34] There are many good recent studies on the subject. See, for instance, Patrick Gardiner, ed. (1964), William H. Dray, ed. (1966), W. B. Gallie (1968), and Ronald H. Nash (1969).

[35] See particularly Jan Huizinga (1946) and Edward H. Carr (1963).

[36] See Gallie (1968).

[37] See Wilhelm Bauer (1957, chap. 5), Toynbee (1934–1961, vol. I, pp. 17 ff.), Alfred Kroeber (1962 and 1966), Philip Bagby (1963), Huizinga (1946, pp. 71 ff.), and the studies of Alfred Cordoliani (pp. 37–51) and Guy Beaujouan (pp. 52–67) in Charles Samaran, ed. (1961).

[38] See Kroeber, (1963-c).

[39] See V. Gordon Childe (1953 and 1964).

[40] For a sociological analysis of the new elements introduced by religion, see Salomon Reinach (1960). On the sociohistorical effects of prophets on ancient Israel and gurus on India, see Martindale (1962).

[41] "Enlightenment"—both in its usual historical concrete meaning, referring to the new intellectual outlook that emerged in the West during the eighteenth century, and in its

abstract and formal meaning, referring to any historical period of rationalization according to transempirical and trans-circumstantial norms—always implies a correlate situation at the participational, political, and economic planes. It is for understanding and operating such situations that an enlightenment was required.

[42] Of the original contributors to the new multilinear, empirically based, and complex cultural and social evolutionism, special mention should be made of the German historian and philosopher Erich Kahler (see particularly, 1961), the American anthropologist Leslie A. White (1949), and the English archeologist Childe (1953). A comprehensive effort to integrate sociocultural neoevolutionism into the systematic body of sociology has been successfully undertaken, with the revision of his former homeostatic views, by Parsons, in his later works (particularly 1961 and 1966). An important development of his original views on cultural evolution has been given by Kahler in his article *Culture and Evolution* (1967b).

[43] See Sahlins and Service, eds. (1965).

[44] Cited by Marshall D. Sahlins and Elman R. Service, eds. (1965, pp. 8–9).

[45] The following analysis summarizes the essential points of Sahlins and Service (1965, chap. 2).

[46] See Sahlins and Service, 1965, (chap. 3).

[47] Toynbee's dichotomic typology of Herodianism and Zealotism corresponds, loosely, to these same effects of cultural dominance. See (1934–1961, vol. VIII, pp. 580 ff.).

[48] See George Novack (1966) on these observations. See also a critical discussion of Marxist theories in Marek (1969).

[49] See Chapter 18 on imperial trends in the United States, and for alternatives and possible developments, see Chapter 27, particularly the second section.

B
The Polity

3

Political Action
and Political Plane

WHAT IS THE POLITICAL?

Basic concepts

Political theory, as the study of the polity, presents a still greater variety of views than the study of society as a whole, because political science, as a discipline, has to face the same problems as sociology plus the conflict, or at least an aggravated form of the conflict, between the ethical and the factual approaches to its subject matter.

This conflict comes from the origin (and character) of political thinking. It can be seen in Greece in the opposition between Socrates and the Sophists, and later between the Stoics and the Epicureans. It continues throughout the centuries: John of Salisbury and St. Thomas Aquinas, Locke and Hobbes, Kant and Hume, Hegel and Marx, neo-Kantians and neopositivists.

The different views facing political students, however, afford a wide margin of agreement concerning the elements with which the political is concerned. We saw in Chapter 1 that the political, as one of the four macrofunctions of society, deals with the production and allocation of commands through a special medium, which is power. This concept is and has been widely accepted by political theorists. An analysis of that concept, supported by both past and contemporary literature, would indicate that six basic elements constitute the constant and universal content of the political, as shown in Table 6.

Practically all political theorists, past and present, would agree with this table of "political elements." Their differences of opinion would arise concerning the nature and meaning of some of these elements. The dispute would center around two questions: (1) What are "power" and "validity," and how and to what extent does the former depend on the latter? (2) Who are the "rulers," how are they selected, and how and where is one to draw the line separating them from the "ruled."

Table 6 *Constant elements of the political*

Description	Elements
1. The political is normative and always implies the prescription of a behavior	1. Command
2. by one or more decision makers;	2. Ruler
3. the prescription is addressed to decision obeyers;	3. Ruled
4. it is supported by the physical capacity to enforce compliance	4. Power
5. with the implementable threat of some penalty	5. Sanction
6. and is founded on some justifying principle.	6. Validity

This dispute, which is both historical and current, has led to various alternative conceptions of the political process involving a variety of basic political views, philosophic assumptions, and evaluative biases. The dispute, however, can be reduced to a definable set of alternatives, each of which implies certain political views, philosophic assumptions, and evaluative biases. This reduction can be obtained by combining an analytical investigation of the various concepts with an historico-comparative study of the positions adopted, explicitly or implicitly, by the major political writers.

An extensive research of the dispute would be beyond the scope of this book. It is important, however, for our general view of the polity to understand what the major points of the controversy are, and how the present terms have evolved. Therefore, I will restrict myself to the most relevant aspects of the discussion: the nature and meaning of power and validity, and their mutual relationship. For that purpose I will consider validity as whatever principle or condition beyond sheer enforcement, if there is such principle, that makes the ruler and his decisions objects that the ruled feel obligated to comply with. Without pretending to exhaust the analytical possibilities or to cover all the formulations ever given, I present the most relevant alternatives of the power and validity question in Table 7.

Table 7 *Alternative concepts of power and validity*

1. *Power and Authority*

    1.1 POWER: ability to issue enforceable decisions (commands)

        Consists in the actual and sufficiently stable control of exclusive or substantially superior means of physical coercion in a society, inducing (authority) the regular and acknowledged compliance from the members insofar as:

        1.1.1 power is sufficiently valid (*ethical view, deistic assumption, optimistic bias*).

1.1.2   power is sufficiently effective (*factual view, naturalistic assumption, pessimistic bias*).

1.2   SOCIAL ENFORCEABILITY: conditions that generate power

A.   In the formation of society, social enforceability results from:

1.2.A.1   man's natural sociability (*man's sociality assumption*).
1.2.A.2   a social contract (*man's completeness assumption*).

   a.   Social status is preferred to the natural status for mutual cooperation: positive convenience (*optimistic bias*).
   b.   Social status is preferred to the natural status for the settling of wars with everybody against everybody: negative convenience (*pessimistic bias*).

B.   In the formation of power in society, social enforceability results from:

1.2.B.1   the natural disposition of some to command and others to obey (*natural harmony view, inegalitarian bias*).

   a.   command of the best (*ethical view*)
   b.   command of the fittest (*factual view*)

1.2.B.2   delegation by ruled to ruler (*social harmony view*).

   a.   delegation by notables (*authoritarian bias*)
   b.   delegation by the people (*liberal bias*)
   c.   original (mythical or symbolic) and once-and-for-all delegation (*traditional view, limited authoritarian bias*)

1.2.B.3   the successful manipulation of media and valuables, in ascriptive or competitive conditions (*conflict view*).

2. *Validity*

2.1   OF THE RULER'S RULING

2.1.1   Intrinsic competence and virtue of the ruler (*harmonic view, authoritarian bias*)

2.1.1.1   acknowledged by:

   a.   the capable ones (*ethical view*).
   b.   the people (*factual view*).

2.1.1.2   founded on original pact of permanent delegation, by notables or the people (*traditional view, man's completeness assumption, authoritarian bias*).

2.1.1.3   manifested by self-assertion confirmed by performance: hero consecrated by his deeds, enlightened tyrant (*factual view, inegalitarian bias*).

2.1.2   Delegation by specific mandate from: (*contractualistic view*)

2.1.2.1   notables (*authoritarian bias*).
2.1.2.2   the people (*liberal bias*).

Table 7 *Alternative concepts of power and validity* (continued)

2.1.3   Delegation by the divinity (*theocratic view, deistic assumption, authoritarian bias*).

2.1.4   Resulting from sheer (or principally) political success in power manipulation: validity as the counterpart of stable power, self-generated by the regular enforcement of authority (*factual* and *conflict views*).

2.2 OF THE DECISION TO BE OBEYED

2.2.1   Intrinsic validity, acknowledged by qualified or general consensus, founded on: (*harmonic view, authoritarian bias*)

2.2.1.1   the virtue of the decision or of the order it represents (*ethical view*).
2.2.2.2   the utility of the decision or of the order it represents (*factual view*).

2.2.2   Expression of, or conformity with, God's transcendent will (*theocratic view, deistic assumption, authoritarian bias*).

2.2.3   Accordance with the rules of natural law (*speculative* and *institutional views, deistic assumption, liberal bias*).

2.2.4   Positive legality: act of the competent authority in accordance with the competent law (*empirical* and *institutional views, liberal bias*).

2.2.5   Absoluteness of the authority founded on accepted legitimacy, traditional and/or divinely granted (*absolutistic, traditional,* or *idealistic views, deistic assumption, authoritarian bias*).

2.2.6   Consequence and expression of stable and successful ability to enforce compliance (*factual* and *conflict views, naturalistic assumption, egalitarian bias*).

*The decimal code in this table will be used in this section and in the following tables to indicate these concepts.

Table 7 presents, in the form of itemized alternatives, the main analytical and historical conceptions concerning some aspects of power: (1.1) whether or not power depends on its validity in order to induce regular and acknowledged compliance, (1.2.A) whether society is natural or contractual, (1.2.B) and whether the social formation of power results from (1.2.B.1) some natural disposition of man to command or to obey, (1.2.B.2) some delegation from the ruled to the ruler, or (1.2.B.3) successful manipulation. It presents also the main alternatives concerning validity, that is, that which induces the ruled to acknowledge the fulfillment of the commands of the authorities as a moral or legal obligation. Concerning the validity of the ruler, we have (2.1) that his competence to rule (2.1.1) is considered an intrinsic attribute (2.1.1.1) because of his virtue or fitness, (2.1.1.2) because of an original delegation by the ruled, or (2.1.1.3) because his deeds reveal and confirm the legitimacy of his claims to intrinsic right to rule, (2.1.2) that his competence was actually delegated by the ruled, (2.1.3) that his right to rule was divinely granted, or (2.1.4) that validity is the socialized internalization of the acknowledgment of the ruler's authority purely because of its regular effective enforcement.

Major political implications

Implied in these various alternative conceptions, expressing different ways of observing and interpreting the facts of political life, are several conditioning factors. We can differentiate three major types: (1) basic political views, (2) immediate philosophic assumptions, and (3) interfering evaluative biases. First, let us consider basic political views. As we saw in Chapter 1, there is a circular relationship among society's four structural planes, particularly between the cultural and the participational ones. Values are induced from life situations, and life situations are commanded by values. This circularity brings some theorists to emphasize the ethical content of authority (norms command behaviors) to the point that, as with Plato, political science is understood as the study of justice (the norm of social harmony) and its societal requirements. Others see the factual content of power (interests condition norms) as the ultimate foundation of authority. Other basic political views also condition the angle from which political facts are seen, and the interpretation by which they are explained. Thus, political science is understood as a speculative or as an empirical discipline, as being concerned with the systematization of tradition or the building of new forms, as depicting a theocratic or a secular process, and so forth.

Second, implied in a theorist's concept are his immediate philosophic assumptions. He may see man as a creation of the divinity or as an evolutionary product of nature. He may understand man's nature as intrinsically social or, on the contrary, he may understand society as resulting, historically or transcendentally, from a pact among preexisting individuals. The distinction between basic political views and immediate philosophic assumptions is largely a matter of convention, since most basic views express or reflect some philosophical ideas. I am taking a broad conception of the former and a narrow concept of the latter, limiting the group of philosophical assumptions to the deistic versus the naturalistic assumptions and man's sociality versus his relative completeness.

Third, implied in any theorist's concept are his evaluative biases. These biases, as has been shown by the sociology of knowledge, are simply unavoidable. They result from situational (as class and status) and personal (as personality and biography) conditions as well as from one's philosophical assumptions and basic political views. Although man is the proper study of man, any study of man, whether the approach be humanistic or scientific, is always in some degree subjectively appraised (regardless of what the adopted methodological criteria are), because the human qua human is not purely factual but also intentional, that is, value-oriented and value-loaded. In the present discussion only some very restricted sets of values have been considered: those interfering directly in the choice of political perspectives and explanations. Such interference can be detected from analytical inference and historical occurrence. Such sets of values are the optimistic-pessimistic disjunction, the authoritarian (unlimited or limited) and liberal, and the inegalitarian and egalitarian disjunctions.

Systematizing the basic political views, the philosophic assumptions, and the evaluative biases implied in the alternatives concerning power and validity presented in Table 7, we have the picture shown in Table 8. (These implications have already been indicated in Table 7 within parentheses.)

Although influenced, in different ways and to different extents, by the situational and personal conditions of the individual thinkers, these views, assumptions, and biases have a systematic relationship with one another and with the sets of alternative political conceptions. In other words, some basic political views also imply some philosophic assumptions and evaluative biases and vice versa, and at the same time, some views, assumptions, and biases imply some political conceptions and vice versa. This may be seen in Table 9.

The study of the several positions adopted by the classic political theorists from the Greeks to our times[1] becomes more significant if we not only give due consideration to the historical approach—that is, the understanding of these writers and their ideas in terms of their chronological development and within the context of their societies and their situational and personal conditions—but also consider these theorists in terms of the possible, more relevant analytical alternatives they were (consciously or not) confronted with. These alternatives are the ones itemized in Table 7. As has been mentioned, although this table is a first attempt which further research should improve and correct, it is neither a random aggregation of items nor the sheer expression of this writer's own views.

Table 8 *Implications of political conceptions*

Basic Views (V)		Philosophic Assumptions (A)		Evaluative Biases (B)	
V1a	Ethical	A1a	Deistic	B1a	Optimistic
V1b	Factual	A1b	Naturalistic	B1b	Pessimistic
V2a	Speculative	A2a	Man's sociality	B2a	Authoritarian
V2b	Empirical	A2b	Man's completeness	B2ab	Limited authoritarian
V3a	Traditional			B2b	Liberal
V3b	Institutional				
V4a	Theocratic			B3a	Inegalitarian
V4b	Secular			B3b	Egalitarian
V5a	Absolutist				
V5b	Contractual				
V6a	Harmonic				
	a1–Natural Harmony				
	a2–Social Harmony				
V6b	Conflictive				

It is a highly generalized representation of the main, alternative, analytical concepts of power and validity derived from the principal ideas of political classics, according to a representative sample of thirty major writers.

If we now confront these thirty major political theorists with the sets of alternatives contained in that table, we will have, in addition to the usual historical information about and interpretation of these writers, a comparative propositional analysis of their political conceptions. This analysis is presented in Tables 10, 11, and 12. Table 10 classifies these political classics according to their explicit or implicit positions concerning the analytical alternatives. Table 11 reverses the picture, by listing the classic writers and showing what alternatives each of them has adopted. Table 12 presents the implied (acknowledged or not) basic political views, philosophic assumptions, and evaluative biases of the same historical writers.

Comparative analysis

A quick comparative look at Tables 10, 11, and 12 shows that some tendencies and trends are easily discernible. With respect to the relationship between power and validity, it can be seen from Tables 10 and 11 that most writers have emphasized the dependence of power on the validity, and only a scattered few have contended that regular and acknowledged compliance to power is obtained whenever power is sufficiently effective. With respect to the formation of society, we see that the concept of the natural sociability of man has prevailed both in antiquity and among modern writers, whereas the Renaissance writers and the early liberals leaned toward the idea of social contract. Relative to the formation of power in society, we see that the ancient and the Renaissance authors saw in the formation of power a natural disposition of some men to lead and most to follow, that early and late liberals stressed the hypothesis of delegation, and that a few scattered writers understood power accumulation as the product of successful political manipulation. Regarding the validity of the ruler's ruling, we can observe that in antiquity, validity was seen mainly as expressing the intrinsic merits of the ruler, that the medieval and Reformation writers stressed God's will, that the early and late liberals made the ruler's validity dependent on delegation by the people, and that sheer political success was considered the reason for validity by a few writers: the Sophists, Machiavelli, and Marx. Validity of the decisions was attributed mainly to their intrinsic merits by ancient writers, to God's will by the early Christians and the Reformation writers, but particularly to their legal support, either in the speculative terms of natural law or in the positivist terms of current legality, by the counter-Reformation and the liberal authors. A few authors—the Sophists, Machiavelli, Hobbes, and Marx—made validity of the decisions dependent on successful enforcement.

If we move to Table 12 and compare the basic political views, the philosophic assumptions, and the evaluative biases of the classics in our sample, we find that, up to the middle of the nineteenth century, some of these items were influenced

Table 9 *Views, assumptions, and biases and political conceptions**

Basic Political Views	Philosophic Assumptions				
	NO IMPLICATIONS	A1a DEISTIC	A1b NATURALISTIC	A2a MAN'S SOCIALITY	A2b MAN'S COMPLETENESS
V1a - Ethical	2.1.1.1.a 2.2.1.1	1.1.1	1.1.2		
V1b - Factual	1.1.2–2.1.1.1.b 2.1.1.3–2.1.4 2.2.1.2		2.2.6		
V2a - Speculative		2.2.3 2.2.5			
V2b - Empirical	2.2.4				
V3a Traditional	1.2.B.2.c	2.2.5			2.1.1.2
V3b - Institutional	2.2.4	2.2.3			
V4a - Theocratic		2.1.3 2.2.2			
V4b - Secular					
V5a - Absolutist		2.2.5			
V5b - Contractual	2.1.2.1 2.1.2.2				
V6a - Harmony	2.2.1				
V6a1 - Natural Harmony					
V6a2 - Social Harmony	1.2.B.2.a 1.2.B.2.b				
V6b - Conflictive	1.2.B.3 2.1.4		2.2.6		
No implications				1.2.A.1	

*The code numbers in the body of this table refer to alternative political concepts given in Table 7. The code numbers for the basic political views, philosophic, assumptions, and evaluative biases refer to those in Table 8.

Evaluative Biases

NO IMPLICATIONS	B1a OPTIMISTIC	B1b PESSIMISTIC	B2a AUTHORITARIAN	B2ab LIMITED AUTHORITARIAN	B2b LIBERAL	B3a INEGALITARIAN	B3b EGALITARIAN
2.1.1.1.a	1.1.1		2.2.1.1				
2.1.1.1.b 2.1.4		1.1.2	2.2.1.2			2.1.1.3	2.2.6
					2.2.3		
					2.2.4		
			2.1.1.2 2.2.5	1.2.B.2.c			
					2.2.3 2.2.4		
			2.1.3 2.2.2				
			2.2.5				
			2.1.2.1		2.1.2.2		
			2.1.1 2.2.1				
						1.2.B.1	
			1.2.B.2.a				
2.1.4					1.2.B.2.b		2.2.6
	1.2.A.2.a	1.2.A.2.b					

Table 10 *Classification of political classics according to the analytical political alternatives of Table 7*

1. Power

1.1 Control of means of physical coercion inducing regular propensity of ruled to obey insofar as the power is:

1.1.1 Sufficiently valid	1.1.2 Sufficiently effective
(Plato),* Aristotle, later Stoics (St. Ambrosius), (St. Augustine) (John of Salisbury), St. Thomas Aquinas Jean Bodin, (Locke) (Montesquieu), (Rousseau), (Kant) (Fichte)	Sophists, (Epicureans) Machiavelli Hobbes (Hume) Marx

1.2 Social enforceability

A. In the formation of society

1.2.A.1 Man's natural sociability	1.2.A.2 Social contract	
	1.2.A.2.a Positive convenience	1.2.A.2.b Negative convenience
(Sophists), Plato, *Aristotle,*** later Stoics John of Salisbury, St. Thomas John of Paris, Montesquieu, Kant *Hume,* (Fichte), (Hegel) *Marx*	*Epicureans* (St. Augustine) Marsilio de Padua Machiavelli Mariana, Suarez Bodin, *Locke, Rousseau*	*Hobbes*

B. In the formation of power in society

1.2.B.1 Natural disposition to command or obey	1.2.B.2 Delegation, actual or original, from ruled to ruler	1.2.B.3 Successful political manipulation
Plato (a),[†] *Aristotle* (a), later Stoics (a) John of Salisbury (a) St. Thomas (b) and Machiavelli (b) Montesquieu (a and b) Hume (b), Hegel (b)	John of Paris (c) Marsilio de Padua (c) Mariana (b), Suarez (b) Locke (b), Rousseau (b) Kant (b), Fichte (b)	Sophists *Hobbes* *Marx*

2. Validity

2.1 Of the ruler's ruling

2.1.1 Intrinsic competence and virtue			2.1.2 Delegation by mandate of		2.1.3 Delegation by divinity	2.1.4 Sheer political success
2.1.1.1 By acknowledgment	2.1.1.2 By original pact	2.1.1.3 By self-assertion	2.1.2.1 Notables	2.1.2.2 The people		
Plato (a) Aristotle (a) later Stoics (b) Montesquieu (a) (2.1.2.2)[‡] (Hegel–b)[§]	(John of Paris) (Marsilio) Vindiciae Hobbes	(Epicureans) (St. Augustine)	Marsilio [2.1.2.2][88]	*St. Thomas* (2.1.3) *Marsilio* (2.1.2.1) Occam *Mariana* *Suarez* *Bodin* *Locke* Montesquieu [2.1.1.1.a] Kant (Fichte)	*St. Ambrosius* *J. of Salisbury* St. Thomas [2.1.2.2] Egidio Colonna Luther Calvin *Pierre du Bellay*	Sophists *Machiavelli* (Hume) *Marx*

Table 10 *Classification of political classics according to the analytical political alternatives of Table 7 (continued)*

2.2 Of decisions to be obeyed

2.2.1 Intrinsic validity		2.2.2 God's will	2.2.3 Accordance with natural law	2.2.4 Legality	2.2.5 Absoluteness of authority	2.2.6 Successful enforcement
2.2.1.1 Virtue	2.2.1.2 Utility					
Plato Aristotle later Stoics (2.2.3) *Rousseau* (Fichte) (Hegel)	*Epicureans* *Machiavelli* [2.2.6] Hobbes (2.2.6) Hume Marx [2.2.6]	*St. Ambrosius* *St. Augustine* *J. of Salisbury* *Egidio Colonna* Luther Calvin	L. Stoics [2.2.1] St. Thomas (2.2.4) *J. of Paris* Marsilio [2.2.4] Vindiciae Mariana [2.2.4] Suarez [2.2.4] Bodin [2.2.4] Locke [2.2.4] Montesquieu (2.2.4) Kant [2.2.4]	St. Thomas [2.2.3] Marsilio (2.2.3) (Occam) *Mariana* (2.2.3) *Suarez* (2.2.3) *Bodin* (2.2.3) Locke (2.2.3) Montesquieu [2.2.3] Kant (2.2.3)	*Pierre du Bellay*	Sophists *Machiavelli* (2.2.1.2) Hobbes (2.2.1.2) *Marx*

*Parentheses indicate that the writer's position is more implicit than explicit.

**Italics indicate that the position is particularly relevant for this writer.

†The code letters (a) and (b) refer to the subdivisions in Table 7.

‡Table 7 code numbers enclosed in parentheses indicate that the writer also follows, complementarily, the position indicated by that number.

§Parentheses enclosing both the writer and "a" or "b" indicate that the writer's position is more implicit than explicit and follows subdivision (a) or (b) of Table 7.

§§Table 7 code numbers enclosed in brackets indicate that the writer's position is complementary. His most important position is the one indicated by the bracketed number.

Table 11 *Political alternatives and classic thought*

Writers	1.1.1	1.1.2	1.2.A.1	1.2.A.2.a	1.2.A.2.b	1.2.B.1	1.2.B.2	1.2.B.3	2.1.1.1	2.1.1.2
1. Sophists		x	+						x	
2. Plato	÷		x			(xa)			xa	
3. Aristotle	(x)		(x)			+a			xa	
4. Epicureans		+		(x)						
5. Later Stoics	x		x			xa			xb	
6. St. Ambrosius	÷									
7. St. Augustine	+			+						
8. J. of Salisbury	+		+			+a				
9. St. Thomas	x		(x)			(xb)				
10. E. Colonna										
11. J. of Paris				x			xc			+
12. Marsilio				x			+c			+
13. Occam										
14. Machiavelli		x				xb				
15. Luther										
16. Calvin										
17. Vindiciae										x
18. Mariana			(x)				(xb)			
19. Suarez			x				xb			
20. P. du Bellay										
21. Jean Bodin	x		x				xc			
22. Hobbes		x			(x)			(x)		x
23. Locke	+			(x)			xb			
24. Montesquieu	+		x			+ab			xa	
25. Rousseau	+			(x)			(xb)			
26. Kant	+		(x)				(xb)			
27. Hume		+	(x)			xb				
28. Fichte	+		+				+b			
29. Hegel			+			+b			+b	
30. Marx		x	(x)					(x)		

Symbols: + indicates that the writer's position is implicit rather than explicit.
     x indicates that the writer's position is explicit.
    (x) indicates that the writer's position is explicit, and the political alternative is particularly relevant for this writer.

2.1.1.3	2.1.2.1	2.1.2.2	2.1.3	2.1.4	2.2.1.1	2.2.1.2	2.2.2	2.2.3	2.2.4	2.2.5	2.2.6
			x								
					(x)						
					x						
+						(x)					
					x						
		(x)					(x)	÷			
							(x)				
+							(x)				
		x	÷					(x)	÷		
		x									
	÷	x					x	(x)			
		x						÷	x		
			(x)			÷			+		(x)
		x					x				
		x					x				
							x	÷	(x)		
		(x)						÷	(x)		
		(x)	(x)							(x)	
		(x)				÷		÷	(x)		x
		(x)						÷	x		
		(x)	(x)					÷	x		
		x				(x)					
	+		+	+							
				+		÷					
			(x)			÷					(x)

÷ indicates that the alternative is complementary to the writer's view.
a, b, and c indicate qualifications of the writer's view, according to the subdivisions in Table 7.

Table 12 *Assumptions, biases of the classics, and implied views*

Writers	Philosophic Assumptions				Evaluative Biases						
	A1a	A1b	A2a	A2b	B1a	B1b	B2a	B2ab	B2b	B3a	B3b
1. Sophists		x	+			x			+		x
2. Plato	(x)		x		x		(x)			(x)	
3. Aristotle	x		(x)		x			+		+	
4. Epicureans		+			(x)				+		
5. Stoics		+	x		+			+			x
6. St. Ambrosius	(x)				+		(x)				
7. St. Augustine	(x)				+		(x)				
8. J. of Salisbury	(x)		+		+		(x)				
9. St. Thomas	(x)		(x)		x			+			+
10. E. Colonna	x					x					
11. J. of Paris	(x)		x		x			x			
12. Marsilio	x				x			x			+
13. Occam	x								x		+
14. Machiavelli		(x)				x				+	
15. Luther	x						(x)			+	
16. Calvin	x						(x)			+	
17. Vindiciae	x			x				x			
18. Mariana	x				(x)				(x)		
19. Suarez	x				x				x		
20. P. du Bellay	(x)						(x)				
21. J. Bodin	x				x			x			
22. Hobbes		x		x		(x)		x			x
23. Locke	x				(x)				(x)		+
24. Montesquieu	+		x		+				(x)		+
25. Rousseau	x			(x)	(x)				(x)		x
26. Kant	x		(x)		+				(x)		x
27. Hume		x	(x)			+			x		x
28. Fichte	x		+		+				x		+
29. Hegel	x		+					+			
30. Marx		(x)	(x)						(x)		(x)

Symbols: +   indicates that the writer's position is implicit rather than explicit.
          x   indicates that the writer's position is explicit.

					Basic Views								
V1a	V1b	V2a	V2b	V3a	V3b	V4a	V4b	V5a	V5b	V6a	V6a1	V6a2	V6b
	x	x											x
(x)	x									(x)			
(x)	x	x								(x)			
	+	x											
(x)	x	x								+			
+		x				(x)							
+		x				(x)							
+		x				(x)							
x	(x)	(x)			(x)	(x)				x			
		x				x							
		x	+				x					x	
		x	+		(x)		x					x	
			+		x								
	(x)						(x)						x
						(x)				x			
						(x)				x			
		x		+	x							x	
		x			x	+						(x)	
		x			x	+						x	
		x	x		(x)			(x)					
x		x	+	+	(x)	+						x	
	(x)						x						(x)
+			x		(x)							x	
+	x	x			(x)						x		
x					x							(x)	
+		x			(x)					x			
	x		x		x		x						+
+					x								
+	+	x			x					+			
	(x)				x		(x)						(x)

(x) indicates that the writer's position is explicit, and the view, assumption, or bias is particularly relevant for this writer.

little by the course of time. The ethical and speculative views, the deistic assumption, and the optimistic bias, for instance, have been noticeably predominant. Others, however, were manifestly affected by the times. The institutional view has obviously prevailed since the *Vindiciae contra Tyrannos*. The assumption of man's sociality, stronger in antiquity, becomes again the prevailing one from Kant's time onward. The liberal and the egalitarian biases, less influential after antiquity than their opposing biases, become dominant from Locke onward.

Present-day understanding of the political field reflects the tendencies of the past. Our understanding is, as a whole, marked by the increasing influence of the factual, empirical, institutional, and secular views, rather than the ethical, speculative, traditional, and theocratic ones. The philosophic assumptions are naturalistic and on the side of man's natural sociability. There is a frank predominance (independent of what actually happens in the societies of today) of the liberal, rather than the authoritarian, and of the egalitarian, rather than the inegalitarian, biases. And so the current tendencies are a continuation of the Sophists, Machiavelli, Hobbes, and Hume much more than of Plato, Bodin, Locke, and Rousseau. Underlying this common trend, we find today a widely accepted and deep-seated distinction, among political theorists, between "political philosophy," as a moral discipline concerned with ethical values in political processes (whatever the epistemological conditions are under which such inquiry is considered meaningful or not),[2] and "political science," as an empirical discipline concerned with "the study of the shaping and sharing of power," to use Lasswell and Kaplan's definition (1952, p. 14). Thus, if we use a revised formulation of Easton (1965a) it can be said still more concisely that the political is understood as *the authoritative allocation of valuables*.[3]

These circumstances have substantially increased the area and extent of the consensus among political scholars concerning the object and the nature of their discipline. As far as the discipline's object is concerned, most political scientists, if not all, would agree that the political involves both constraint and deliberate compliance. As Karl Deutsch (1963, p. 242) has said, "politics involves the steering or manipulation of human behavior by a combination of threat of enforcement with habits of compliance." Political institutions are characterized, therefore, by the combination of these two elements which makes enforcement legitimate. The state, as Max Weber (1944, vol. 1, I, p. 217) has observed, "should be understood [as] a political institute of continuous activity and insofar as its administrative staff keeps successfully the claim to the legitimate monopoly of physical coercion for the maintenance of the existing order."

This combination occurs because social ordering, in general, is both a social necessity and one that could not be achieved without some form of ruling (as the equilibrium theorists have stressed) and because, in any particular order or decision, some alternative solution might be found (as the conflict theorists have noted) if different value or interest premises were adopted. And this is so (1) because of the systemic functional aspect of politics so well stressed by Parsons, who observed that political structures [and we could read, more broadly, the political process] are concerned with originating collective action for the attainment of collectively significant goals, either territorially or functionally defined, and (2) because, although representing a societal necessity, the political process also necessarily involves power manipulation, since social aims are always seen and formulated according to the situational interests and values of somebody. That is why, as Jouvenel (1963, pp. 54–55) puts it, *"politique [est] tout effort systématique accompli en quelque endroit que se soit du champ social, pour entrainer d'autres hommes à la poursuite de quelque dessein choisi par l'auteur."* [4]

As far as the nature of political science is concerned, there is also widespread agreement that it has a double character, involving a body of verifiable knowledge and a dimension (smaller or larger, according to differing views) of subjective appraisal—which does not mean arbitrary appraisal. As Duverger (1964b, pp. 18–19) has explained, politics is a science to the extent (limited for Duverger) to which it allows objective observation and measurement and the formulation of verifiable propositions, and it is an art to the extent (larger for Duverger) to which its data and hypotheses are conditioned by the situation and personality of the observer and depend on his assumptions, values, and skills.

In spite of this increased and increasing agreement among political scientists, at a moment when the discipline is acknowledgedly approaching (within its limits of verifiability) scientific maturity, there are still major points of disagreement. They result from the above-indicated "art" content of politics. "There is no totally objective image of politics because there is no politics totally objective" (Duverger, 1964b, p. 19). As a result, as was also pointed out by Duverger, political processes are viewed differently by the oppressed groups and the ruling groups, by the rulers and the ruled.

Within this generally accepted dichotomy between the art and science of politics, there are two general theoretical lines that divide political scientists. The first results from the large divisions in social theory, which have already been discussed sufficiently for the purposes of the present study in Chapter 1. The second is relevant to political science and continues the discussion of the relationship between power and validity. It opposes those who consider that power depends, to some extent (larger or smaller), on the social acknowledgment of its rightness, that is, nonarbitrary validity, and those who consider that regular compliance to power is determined only by its effectiveness.

This is basically the question on which Socrates and his disciples opposed the Sophists. Although the Socratics of today would be, in political science, of the Aristotelian rather than of the Platonic brand and would consider the moral concerns of the Nichomaedean ethics alien to their discipline, they would still make a distinction between compliance due to the effectiveness of power and compliance assured by the legitimacy of the authority and the rightfulness of the law.

C. Friedrich (1965, p. 201), one of the leading representatives of the emphasis on validity, stresses that it is an error "to base the law upon an act of will alone." Friedrich distinguishes legality, which is simply the accordance of a decision with its legal system and so, ultimately, with power, from legitimacy, which requires intrinsic rightfulness. "An order is legitimate when it is recognized as rightful; its legality is provided by its having a basis in positive law" (p. 202). That is why "Hitler's rule was legal, but it was not legitimate; it had a basis in law, but none in right and justice" (pp. 202–203). If it is so that the validity of decisions depends on their basic justice, the validity of rulers depends on their authority, which for Friedrich is something more than power effectiveness. Authority, Friedrich emphasizes, is "auctoritas," which means augmentation—ultimately, the augmentation of a ruler's capacity for making decisions according to his and their reasonableness. "In conclusion, we might say the authority of law rests upon its reasonableness—that is to say, its justice— that the legitimacy of a constitution, a statute, or a decision rests upon its rightfulness, and that its legality rests upon its accord with the positive laws. The same may be said of the 'bearers' of authority, legitimacy, and legality, the rulers or sovereigns" (p. 205).[5]

Unlike the ancient supporters of the thesis of validity, however, Friedrich and the modern writers do not assume this validity has an objective permanent content. Since Stammler it has been accepted that the criteria of rightfulness are cultural, presenting variable contents and forms although keeping at a formal and abstract level the character of the Kantian categorical imperative.

Contrary to Friedrich and the thesis of validity, the supporters of the thesis of effectiveness stress that regular and acknowledged compliance with the decisions of the rulers depends on the effectiveness of their power, although by that one should not understand crude coercion. Hart (1965), one of the leading representatives of this position, makes very clear the qualifications concerning the necessity of some voluntary cooperation for the very possibility of the existence of a system of coercion. "But the dichotomy of law based merely on power and law which is accepted as morally binding is not exhaustive. Not only may vast numbers be coerced by laws which they do not regard as morally binding, but it is not even true that those who do accept the system voluntarily must conceive of themselves as morally bound to do so" (p. 198). Unlike Friedrich, who distinguishes legality from legitimacy, Hart distinguishes primary from secondary laws or decisions (pp. 113 ff.). Primary laws establish the substantive system of prescriptions for the ruled. Secondary laws establish the rules of recognition (that is, of validity), of change (how laws are to be modified and created), and of adjudication (who decides what). Validity is determined by the secondary laws. Validity, therefore, is for Hart the equivalent of legality for Friedrich. Friedrich's concept of legitimacy is for Hart a moral concept, which, although influencing political behavior (in the sense that the propensity to comply increases or decreases according to the ruled's convictions concerning the morality of immorality of the laws), is in itself alien to the obligatory character of legal rules. If the officials who have to enforce the laws are willing to do so, iniquitous laws will be enforced, and so compliance to them is not dependent on their moral content.

Just as the current doctrines of validity give a much larger place than the ancient ones to the effectiveness of power and, within broad formal limits, to the cultural and historically variable character of the foundations of validity, so the present doctrines of effectiveness, such as Hart's, are willing to accept, at variance with old sophistry or pre–World War II positivism, a minimum of moral content. This moral content is concerned with the attendance to basic human needs, at least for the officials, and is a requirement of power, in addition to sheer coercion, to which any self-sustained political system must give place (1965, chap. 9).

This narrower gap brings contemporary political scientists to the common admission of an inverse correlation between coercion and social allegiance. As Dahl (1963, pp. 19 and 31) puts it, if authority is defined as legitimate power, there is a relation between resource cost and authority: The less the authority (of the leaders or rules) is, the more resources are required for enforcement.

Another relevant variation is that in nontraditional societies[6] power and validity are determined by their degree of social integration, which results from the existing regime of participation. The more integrated a society is, the more it will demand validity from its rulers and laws, and the more it will tend to refine its conceptions of rightfulness and equity. Poorly integrated, not typically traditional, societies, subject to highly discriminative regimes of participation will be concerned much less with validity and much more with the effectiveness of power, because the privileged strata or groups will be ready to support any rule preserving the status quo against the assault of the underprivileged. It is for this reason that military regimes and dictatorships are able to win and to keep power in unintegrated societies (usually during their transitional stage toward higher development) without any legitimacy or even pretense to it, as Franco in Spain, Castello Branco in Brazil, or Ongania in Argentina.

POLITICAL ACTION

"Nonpolitical" politics

The comparative study of structures and organizations, at the biological as well as the sociological level, provides empirical evidence for the analytical principle that the more independent the subsystems of a system are, the more they tend to accumulate general systemic functions of their own in addition to the specialized functions they perform for and within the system. For instance, cells, which are rather independent subsystems of any organic system, perform several general systemic functions at their own level (as nutrition, growth, self-defense), and organs and tissues, which are less independent as subsystems, have only specialized functions. At the level of the social system, whose subsystems are still more independent than the biological ones, this principle is still more apparent. Such is the case with political activities and the political function.

In Chapter 1 we saw that society is a system of four major systems: cultural, participational, economic, and political. Although, as will be analyzed later, politics is the specific societal function of the political system, or polity, political action also takes place in the other societal systems both at the situational and at the actional levels. That means, on the one hand, that politics plays a part in the forming and the functioning of the three nonpolitical societal regimes—the regimes of values, participation, and property—and, on the other hand, that political action also takes place in the nonpolitical planes, at their actional level.[7] There is "nonpolitical" politics in churches, in families and associations, in business firms, and the specific sorts of interaction taking place at the actional level of the nonpolitical planes—that is, in religious and cultural, affective and recreational, and economic activities—also have a political content.

The political, as we have seen, is the authoritative allocation of valuables. It is functionally originated by the necessity of coordinating collective action for the attainment of collective goals (Parsons, 1966a, p. 13). Whenever, therefore, human interaction takes place, in any societal system, goal-achieving activities imply political action.

There are two aspects to nonpolitical politics, which we can call the external and the internal aspects. The external aspect involves the situational level of the concerned activity; that is, it is a part of the shaping and operating of the respective regime, be it cultural, participational, or economic. The internal aspect is concerned with the extent to which—and there is always some extent in any goal-oriented interaction—valuables are authoritatively allocated.

Let us consider some examples. Religious activities, which are a modality of the cultural ones and so are functionally performed at the societal level of the cultural system, present an external and an internal political aspect. The external aspect is concerned with the use of church authority, vis-à-vis other societal institutions, for attaining certain goals. The most typical example is the pressure on governments to make political decisions on matters of dogma against heresy. Although heresies are problems of doctrinal conviction and so have to be dealt with primarily at the level of ideas and symbols, which is typically cultural, churches have always, in different forms and to different extents, complemented their efforts in doctrinal persuasion with political pressure. Not rarely, as in the case of the Crusades and the Inquisition, political pressures have outweighed the work of persuasion in the attainment of the desired goals. Pressures on businessmen for fund raising and on intellectuals for ideological support are other examples of ecclesiastic external nonpolitical politics.

In the case of churches the internal aspect of nonpolitical politics is concerned with their domestic affairs and the allocation of church authority. The most obvious example of such politics is the election of a pope in the Catholic Church, but in less dramatic terms internal politics is a constant activity of any church.

The same is applicable to any nonpolitical institution or organization. External and internal politics in business have been extensively studied and even often exaggerated by crude economic views. Politics in nonpolitical associations, as professional[8] or recreational ones, are also well known. So are politics in armies. Armies, however, as agencies of legalized violence, are part of the political system, and their external politics cannot be called nonpolitical politics but, rather, are typical examples of political action. What belongs to the nonpolitical category is the nonofficial internal politicking for promotions and facilities. Politics also exist in the family. There is, to start with, a political aspect in sexual relations, at its biological level and more so at its human and culturalized one. Sexual relations are not a perfectly balanced relationship for higher species and so imply a coercion-compliance factor, which is still more politicized for humans by its cultural context, both in the patriarchal institutions of tribal societies and in the patriarchal residues of modern ones. In addition, families have external and internal nonpolitical politics in their interfamily relationships, as in neighborhood cooperation for the protection of children, and in the interaction of familial roles, as in alliances of some brothers against others or against their father.

Let us consider, now, the distinction between nonpolitical and political politics. The distinction first formulated by Aristotle in a criticism to Plato, is, in general terms, more analytical than empirical. Political politics, that is, politics at the level of the social system as one of the macrofunctions of society and consisting in the authoritative allocation of valuables, is characterized by its systemic generality, its binding autonomy, and its enforceable superordinating authority. In the first place, nonpolitical politics never consists in acts affecting, in any general form, the social system, but in explicit or tacit transactions between nonpolitical organizations, between actors, or between a nonpolitical organization or actor and a political one, which bind the parties only by links (formal or informal) of a contractual nature. In the second place, nonpolitical politics has a dependent, not an autonomous, binding capacity. The decisions thus generated do not in themselves bind the parties, except in moral terms; as far as they are binding in any legal sense, their binding capacity is derived from the legal system authoritatively sanctioned by the political power. In the third place, the enforceable authority found in nonpolitical politics is ultimately subordinated to the forms of authority and enforceability of the political system. Both forms of politics are concerned with interactional goal attainment. The goals in nonpolitical politics, which are of cultural, participational, and economic character, are end-goals, to be achieved *inter-partes*, or in subordination to the rules of the concerned society, whereas the goals of political politics are means-goals, consisting in the production and allocation of rules and decisions or in the obtention of power, to be achieved *super-partes*, or for the superordination of the society.

Although these distinctions are analytically clear and are also very clear in modern societies, they may not be so, empirically, in societies in which the macrofunctions of the four structural planes are not sufficiently differentiated. The legal system, as Hart has stressed,[9] does not differentiate the secondary laws regulating recognition, change, and adjudication from the primary laws; moral and legal obligations are fused in the same normative tradition; and religious and secular, as well as public and familial, authority are largely overlapping. Even in later stages, in patrimonial societies, there is no clear distinction between the public sphere and the private sphere of the notables, which explains the contractual character of the feudal political system and the public implications (in feudal societies) of some nonpolitical institutions and organizations, particularly religious institutions or the households of princes and notables.

The political process

Political politics, as has been said, is characterized by its systemic generality, binding autonomy, and enforceable superordinating authority. These characteristics deserve a brief elaboration. On the one hand, all of them result from the fact that the political function, as one of the four macrofunctions of a social system, is related to society as a whole and constitutes its goal-attainment function. On the other hand, these characteristics express the *external discreteness* and *internal unity* inherent in the process of power.

Let us first make clear what is meant by each of the three characteristics. Systemic generality means that even if the political process of a given society is subdivided by territorial and functional divisions, it is a general process that applies to all interactions involving the authoritative allocation of valuables, and it is a unified process because it is in itself a system whose parts are related to one another in a basically compatible way under a unifying principle of compatibility. Territorial and functional divisions, in any political system, are subsystems with varying degrees of autonomy. Empirically, they often present some contradictions, but ultimately they are subject to basic integrating rules and patterns and to higher coordinating norms and authority. Binding autonomy means that the obligations resulting from the political process—laws and decisions—are binding by themselves, because they are externally enforceable and internally conducive to compliance. Enforceable superordinating authority means that in a given society political decisions and authority prevail over any other decisions or authority as far as commands are concerned.

We will soon discuss how these characteristics may be temporarily, sometimes for long periods, or permanently affected by external aggression or internal disruption. Let us now take them as typical characteristics of the political process of any society. As was said above, these three characteristics express the external discreteness and internal unity inherent in the process of power. It is the process of power that, externally, separates societies from each other. Societies may be differentiated by many distinctive features or circumstances of cultural, ethnic, geographic, or economic nature, and yet peoples presenting diverse features may remain united in a single society, as in multicultural and multiethnic Switzerland or the Soviet Union, or in the geographically discontinuous United States. What separates societies from one another is their respective processes of power which make each society an individual and distinct one, vis-à-vis any other society, by submitting it to its own system of commands, internally unified and externally distinct from any other.[10] When these two characteristics do not exist, we can only speak of different societies in a limited sense, particularly in a sociocultural sense, as when distinct regional populations of a country (for example, New Englanders and Texans or Castillians and Andalusians) are said to be different societies. Conversely, a too loose or nominal political bond of super-subordination between peoples who are actually regulated by autonomous political systems, as was the case with the Holy Roman Empire and several of its nominally subordinated kingdoms, or between two authorities, as the pope and the emperor, does not really make one society out of the several societies involved, because such a bond becomes a symbolic and ritual one, changing its political character to a cultural one and losing with that change its capability for self-enforcement.

These essential features of the political process were well understood by Bodin and led him to his theory of sovereignty, although he confused the autonomy and the uniqueness of the political system of a society with the absoluteness of the ruler and, to some extent, with the monarchical form of government.[11] It should also be remarked that discreteness, as the external characteristic of the political system of an individual society, has a broader meaning than "sovereignty." Sovereign societies are those whose external discreteness is assured by formal independence, that is, nonsubordination to any other society's political system; such independence presents variable degrees of effective international autonomy. In itself, discreteness does not imply independence, as will be seen, although formal independence is the most complete form of formal discreteness, and self-maintained international autonomy is the most complete form of self-maintained societal individuality.

As has already been advanced, the two typical characteristics of the political system of a society—external discreteness and internal unity—can be temporarily, even for rather long periods of time, or permanently affected by disturbing factors. External discreteness may disappear under the superior power of an alien aggressor, as is constantly happening in history. In such cases the defeated society no longer has its own political system but is subject to a political power generated by, and representing, a different society. This fact, by itself, is not enough to suppress the individuality of the vanquished society. When, for whatever reasons (the enemy's purpose being only temporary occupation of the defeated country, as with the Allies in Germany after World War II, or the enemy's inability to keep permanent control, as with Napoleon in Spain), submission to the enemy does not destroy the objective and subjective conditions for autonomous government in the defeated country, her capacity to survive as an individual society drives her to rebuild her own independent political system as soon as the enemy is led voluntarily or forcefully to accept the system. It also happens, however, that in different conditions the vanquished society is either destroyed by her conqueror, as Carthage was by Rome, or is incorporated into the victor's society. The form of the incorporation may vary from egalitarian fusion into a larger society, as in the processes that brought about modern metropolitan France, Spain, and many other countries, to a society with an inegalitarian constitution, as in Sparta and many other ancient kingdoms where the dominated society formed the inferior classes and the conquering one the privileged strata.

Another case occurs when the vanquished society is neither exterminated nor incorporated, even at a lower social level, into the victor's society, but is reduced to a colonial status. Such a case can be defined as a political regime that maintains the individuality of the dominated society, at least in the sense that the nationals of the dominated society remain under its jurisdiction, but subordinates the political system of the colonial society to the political system of the metro-politan one. The suppression of the external independence of the political system of the colony is a permanent feature. It does not, however, mix the political systems of the two societies or dissolve the boundaries of the colonial society vis-à-vis other societies. The colonial society is maintained as an individual one, even if the reasons are for the spoils. The metropolitan society, for instance, may have all the advantages of control and command over the colonial society without giving its people the advantages of belonging, even at lower social levels, to the metropolitan one. The political system of the colonial society is maintained by the metropolitan one and functions not for the colonial society's general external protection but as a mechanism for her oppression and contain-ment for the benefit of the metropolitan society, while internally it keeps the usual functions of all political systems: the authoritative (if unfair) allocation of valuables. Discreteness without independence is thereby assured.

The ostensive inequity of formal colonial regimes has contributed, along with other factors, to their disappearance in the contemporary world. Since World War II most colonial systems have been changed formally into more liberal ar-rangements, chiefly following the Commonwealth model. Often in the process the nonindependent discreteness of the colonial political systems was changed, either because discreteness was actually suppressed in order to integrate the colonial peoples more equitably into a comprehensive imperial state or, more often, because the way to formal independence was opened to the colonies.

Even a brief discussion of the fascinating question of the "decolonization" of the world and of the replacement of formal colonial ties with informal but more effective neocolonial ones, as well as with the increasing and expanding forms of satellitism, would take us too far from our central concern. Let me just remark, with respect to the question of discreteness, that neocolonialism and satellitism, although representing more effective forms of domination, are also more clearly preserving the discreteness of the concerned societies, because the deliberate concession or the maintenance of their formal independence is a fundamental part of the strategy of contemporary imperialism.

The second typical characteristic of political systems, their internal unity, can also be temporarily, for shorter or longer periods, or permanently affected by disturbances resulting because the incumbent has lost his authority or the polit-ical system has lost its capacity for enforcement and its ability to obtain support. This happens either when coups or revolutions disrupt the capacity of the incum-bent authorities to impose, in accordance with the legal system, compliance to their decisions throughout the society or when the political system itself loses its unity or even its effectivity and validity. The first case is by far the more frequent.

A coup may be defined as the total or partial use of the subsystem of enforce-ment of a political system to change either the incumbent authorities or the legal rules or part of the rules, under conditions that violate these legal rules. Some coups are made by the incumbent authorities themselves in order to change the legal rules, in violation of these rules, as in the case of Napoleon's coup of

18 Brumaire. Some are made by subordinate agents, usually military chiefs controlling the army, against the incumbent authorities, as in the case of the overthrow of President Arturo Frondizi in Argentina in 1962. Political revolutions, on the other hand, may be defined[12] as all ways of changing the political system, ousting the incumbent authorities, or modifying legal rules in violation of these rules through the use of coercion or the threat of its use, the ability to use coercion resulting from the mobilization of enough people in a society to prevent the incumbent authorities from imposing compliance to their decisions over the society or relevant parts of it. Coups and revolutions directed against the incumbent authorities may eventually be repressed, and those with the support of the higher executive authorities may be defeated by the counteraction of the authorities who remain loyal to the legal rules (which also means the political regime) or by popular resistence. In any case, for a longer or shorter period of time, larger or smaller sections of the society, usually involving parts of its territory, are subtracted from the command of the incumbent authorities and/or submitted to rules violating the legal ones, with the consequent interruption of the unity of the political system. Often these interruptions are short in time, affecting only a few sections of the political system, as some military units, or smaller parts of the territory. Sometimes, however, even if they are not finally successful, these breaches in the unity of the political system are long and deep, and they actually divide the society into two independent political systems that compete to reunify the divided society under their respective rule. Crane Brinton (1965), in his classic study of revolutions, called this division the duality of power and authority. It tends to happen in all major revolutions: king versus Parliament in the English, king versus the Assembly in the French, and the Duma versus the Council of the Soviets in the Russian Revolution.

Coups and revolutions may also be successful, in which case, after a long or short period of struggle or indecision, a new power is established, new authorities enforced, and eventually, a new legal system or a new social regime comes into being.

What happens in all these situations is that the unity of the political system is actually severed, for a short or long time, and the duality of power and authority is not followed by its reunification, under the former rulers or the new ones. We cannot, however, speak of the interruption of the unity of a society, during a period of political dualism, when the competing segments of the formerly unified political system are trying to reestablish unity under their respective rule, and the other societal functions are performed in view of a unique society within what remains of the general societal framework. Since the social system is not an organism, like the biological system, but an organization, it can endure a unity crisis much longer than a living being, and furthermore, it can resume unity after long periods of effective segmentation. This is the case when a country reannexes, a long time later, parts of its population and territory that had been incorporated into another one, as in Alsace and Lorraine, which France lost in 1870 to Prussia and regained from Germany in 1919, or when revolutions cause long territorial divisions, as in the American Civil War.

Social unity, however, is not always or often regained after the breaking down of the unity of the political system. The breaking down of the political unity is particularly serious when it takes place at the level of the political system itself, and not only in terms of the incumbent authorities' loss of the capacity for enforcement. It is also particularly serious when it results in territorial division and the formation in each part of a new political system. The disintegration of the political system means that the goal-achieving function of a society is out of work. There are no general binding commands (laws); nor are there centers of decision (authorities) with the ability to obtain compliance and enforce it with the help of physical means of coercion. The resulting state is anomie, usually followed by virtual anarchy. Under such conditions the survival of the society, as a collective organization, is in serious danger. Such situations lead to two alternatives: either (1) a center of power is formed within the anomic society and succeeds in obtaining support, and with it authority, for extending its rule over the whole social body or (2) the society is submitted to segmentation, giving birth to two or more separate societies, or is incorporated into one or more alien societies. In the first case, the former society survives under the new regime. The best historical example is the affirmation and consolidation of Soviet power after the breakdown of Czarist Russia. In the second case, new societies gradually emerge out of the various parts of the former one and fall under the varying influence of other alien societies, as was the case of the Barbarian kingdoms. The most dramatic example is the dissolution of the Roman Empire.

Permanent dissolution of the former unity of a society also results, as a consequence of the subdivision of its political system, from the congruent adjustment of the other structural planes to the succeeding political systems. This dissolution takes place either when one division of the political culture causes the sucession and is able, after the sucession, to consolidate a new society or when effective political segmentation or unification is successfully followed by the congruent adjustment of the cultural, participational, and economic planes of the new social unit or units to its or their new political condition. The former case is historically more frequent. It reflects, in general, the existence of a cultural cleavage in the former society, as in the case of ethnocultural minorities (Irish in the United Kingdom, Slavs in the Austro-Hungarian Empire) who were striving for autonomy and obtained it through sucession and independence. The second case is the one in which successful fusions or annexations are achieved, as in the successful unifications of Germany and of Italy and in the successful annexation by the Soviet Union of Lithuania, Latvia, and Estonia.

Some theoretically interesting cases, in this respect, have resulted from the settlement of World War II: the new frontiers of Poland and the subdivision of Germany. There are many indications that the former will be a stable and successful incorporation of displaced lands and peoples into their new countries: parts of Germany into Poland and of Poland into the Soviet Union. The final destiny of the two Germanies is still doubtful, since, on the one hand, the political system of the German Democratic Republic seems, many years later, to be excessively dependent on Soviet support, and on the other hand, the Federal

German Republic and its Western allies do not seem to be able to find a realistic way of reunifying Germany.

THE POLITICAL PLANE

Horizontal dimension

As we have seen, the political may be briefly understood as the authoritative allocation of valuables through political action. This allocation of valuables can be of two kinds, both consisting in interactional goal attainment. The goals of nonpolitical politics, of a cultural, participational, and economic character, are end-goals for the actors, whose achievements are subordinate to the enforceable rules and decisions of the authorities of the concerned society. The goals of political politics are means-goals and consist in the production and allocation of enforceable rules and decisions, as well as in obtaining and exercising power and authority that are superordinate to the concerned society, that is, the power and authority to prescribe what is to be done, how, when, where, and by whom. Nonpolitical politics is an *inter-partes* deal, binding only the concerned parties and doing so with a binding capacity derived from the jurisdiction of superordinating authorities. Political politics is a *super-partes* process, with an autonomous binding capacity, which brings about the creation and the exercise of enforceable superordinate authority.

As we have seen in Chapter 1, the political function, consisting for the whole of society in the production and allocation of commands, is one of the four societal macrofunctions which takes place, analytically, in one of the corresponding structural planes of society: the political plane. As we saw, each of the structural planes is the analytical locus of the production and allocation of some of the societal valuables, which are primarily measurable and exchangeable through a specific medium and, secondarily, through influence, the medium of media. The specific medium for commands, the valuables produced and allocated at the political plane, is power, whereas culture, prestige, and money are the specific media of the cultural, participational, and economic planes, respectively. The macrofunctions whose analytical loci are at each one of the structural planes form a subsystem of the social system at the societal level; at their respective levels, each of them is a system, that is, a structural whole with component parts.

We have therefore, in analytical terms, that the four societal macrofunctions—cultural, political, participational, and economic functions—are, in terms of their analytical location, processed at their respective structural planes, and, in terms of their analytical structure, are four subsystems of the social system, each of which is in itself a system: the cultural, participational, political, and economic systems.

Vertically, the four planes present two levels of depth. At the situational level, that is, the level that determines the relative positions of roles in each plane, the four planes are the analytical loci of the macrofunctional regimes: of value, participation, power, and property. Taken together at that level they are the analytical locus of the social regime. At the actional level, that is, the level where human interaction actually takes place, they are the analytical loci of the production, modification, exchange, and extinction of their respective valuables and respective media and of the exchange of valuables and media between the boundaries of the four structural planes.

This brief review permits us now to begin the analysis of the more relevant characteristics of the political plane. From our previous observation concerning the structural planes and the corresponding systems, we have, with respect to politics, that the political plane is the analytical locus of the production and allocation of commands in a society, and the political system is, analytically, the structured whole by which these functions are performed. Together they form the polity, which is the political dimension of society—that is, society analytically considered—as the locus where politics is made and the system that makes politics.

In the present discussion we will briefly cover the main characteristics of the political plane. As we have seen, structural planes present a double dimension: horizontally, they are the interconnecting loci of the macrofunctions of society; vertically, they present the situational and actional levels mentioned above. These two dimensions bring us to two distinct aspects of the political process, according to whether we view the process horizontally or vertically.

Considered in its horizontal dimension the political process is the process of securing the external defense of society and its internal ordering by means of enforceable decisions. These two functions correspond, as we have seen in the preceding section, to the external discreteness and internal unity peculiar to the process of power. Horizontally, the political process is the societal exercise of power. The various requirements for the preservation of the societal boundaries vis-à-vis its external environment can be inferred from the external defense of society. It is not only a defense against the aggression of other societies; it is also a defense against nature, that is, it is the normative aspect of collective action for adaptation to the natural environment. And it is a defense against alien cultures, that is, it is the normative aspect of collective action for preserving the societal cultural identity, with or without deliberate incorporation of alien cultural traits.

The internal ordering of society presents two aspects. The first, internal political statics, concerns the normative preservation and coordination of the other structural planes. By normative means the cultural, participational, and economic planes are kept in adequate condition for the fulfillment of their societal macrofunctions. Such is the case when, expressly or implicitly, a society uses normative means to interfere in its cultural, social, and economic affairs, which even the most laissez-faire societies do to a large extent. The second aspect, internal political dynamics, is the actual making of goal-oriented decisions. By normative means the authorities provide for the attainment of collective goals.

In both external defense and internal ordering of a society the political process manifests and puts to use the amount and the sort of power that the society has been able to generate. On the one hand, societal power generation is conditioned by the capability of the society's political system. Developed and modern political systems generate increasingly more concentrated power than underdeveloped and traditional ones. On the other hand, power generation corresponds, within limits, to the societal needs. Challenged societies generate increasingly more concentrated power than peacefully existing ones. This correspondence, however, is often unbalanced, with a consequent excess or deficit of power.

Excess of power, channeled for defense purposes, leads societies to overreact to external challenges, as sometimes happens in the initial phase in the formation of empires. The Roman Empire is the classic example of such overreaction. To the almost fatal challenge of the Carthaginian invasion, the Romans responded by counterattacking overseas, in Spain, Sicily, and Africa and, as an unplanned result, started their own process of empire building. There is a striking similitude, despite the different historical and technological conditions of our days, between the Roman case and the American response to the postwar challenge of Stalinist Russia, which brought the United States much beyond the balancing of that challenge to a Roman-like world expansion of her military, political, and economic influence. (See Chapters 18 and 27.)

Excess of power can also be channeled in the internal ordering of a society, bringing about a predominance of the political system over the rest of the societal activities, as happens in revolutionary or counterrevolutionary times. The external and internal orientation of the excess of power of a society tend, moreover, to go together and to be mutually induced. Entering into a systematic imperial career broke the equilibrium reached by the Roman society in the third century B.C. and brought to an end its internal democracy. Conversely, the power surplus generated by the English, French, and Russian revolutions brought about the British maritime expansion, the Napoleonic conquests, and the Russian-based Third International.

Failure to generate enough power, however, either for external defense or for internal ordering, causes the decay and dissolution of the concerned society, as the Ottoman and the Austro-Hungarian empires so well illustrate in modern times.

Vertical dimension

Let us now turn to the vertical dimension of the political process. Whereas horizontally politics consists in the external defense and internal ordering of society, that is, in the societal exercise of power, assuming its existence, its processes, and its double characteristic of external discreteness and internal unity, vertically the political process consists in the complex sets of interactions bringing out the relationships between power and validity, on the one hand, and the political actors, on the other one. This process, therefore, is essentially related to the societal formation of power and validity, its exercise by and allocation among the intervening actors, and the various situations resulting thereof.

In the following paragraphs I will give, initially, a succinct description of the main elements and alternatives involved in the complex process of vertical politics. Subsequently, I will proceed to a brief analysis of the political process at the situational level and then to a brief analysis of that process at the actional level.

As we have seen in the first section of this chapter, the basic elements of the political process are contained in the fundamental relation among (1) commands, (2) rulers, (3) ruled, (4) power, (5) sanction, and (6) validity. Each of these basic elements present considerable complexity. For the present purpose it will suffice to clarify a few points concerning commands, rulers, and validity. By commands we mean (1) the legal order (itself a system of primary and secondary laws) as a whole and its regulation of the conditions of validity of power and its regulation of the use of power by the authorities (constitutional aspect); (2) the several specific laws and their regime of application (ordinary legislation aspect); and (3) the enforceable decisions of the authorities (administrative and judicial aspects). By rulers we actually mean those who have power and claim or strive to have authority as well as those who may try to become rulers, although when the latter are specifically mentioned, they are called pretenders. By validity we mean the value quality of power or of a ruler consisting, on the one hand, in legality, that is, widely acknowledged conformity with the legal order, and, on the other hand, in legitimacy, that is, widely acknowledged conformity with the prevailing regime of values. Whenever these two aspects of validity do not coincide, the applicable one will be specifically designated.

As was said earlier, the vertical process of politics is essentially related to the societal formation of power and validity, its exercise by, and allocation among, the intervening actors and the situations resulting thereof. We will subsequently study this process at the situational and at the actional levels. What is relevant now is the fact that, whatever the alternative courses that may be followed by the political process, the process always includes some combination of the basic political elements. The combination is always related to, and centered around, the various alternatives by which power, as the medium of political interaction, is available and used.

The various alternative combinations are the *power variables* and present a limited set of dichotomic possibilities which may be found in, and are constitutive of, any political process. Although it would be interesting to study the power variables in more detail and to see how they necessarily occur in any political process, it will suffice for our present purpose to list the more relevant pairs of power variables, as has been done in Table 13.

Power and authority

We can now move to the study of the political process at the situational level. The situational level is the analytical locus of the macrofunctional regimes; in the political plane this regime is the regime of power. The regime of power determines, in accordance with the regimes of values and participation, which

Table 13 *Power variables*

1a	(power)	creation	1b (power)	extinction
2a		maintenance	2b	disruption or exhaustion
3a		obtaining	3b	losing
4a		gain	4b	loss or cost
5a		conservation	5b	transformation
6a		accumulation	6b	allocation
7a		centralization*	7b	decentralization*
8a		saving	8b	expenditure
9a		investment	9b	consumption
10a		validation	10b	invalidation
11a		concentration**	11b	diffusion**
12a		liquidity	12b	nonliquidity
13a		mobilization	13b	immobilization
14a		generality	14b	particularity
15a		convertibility	15b	inconvertibility
16a		exchange†	16b	transaction‡
17a		usability	17b	unusability
18a		autonomy	18b	heteronomy
19a		endogeny	19b	exogeny
20a		increase	20b	decrease
21a		flexibility	21b	rigidity
22a		development	22b	decay
23a		stability	23b	instability
24a		superordination	24b	subordination

*in the political plane
**in the whole society
†for other medium
‡for other form of power

social groups and persons can have power, under what general conditions, and for what general purposes, and accordingly it sanctions—and receives support from—a certain regime of property as well as, in a general way, the social regime of the concerned society.

The regime of power is analytically distinct from the political regime and the structure of authority. The political regime is based, explicitly or implicitly, on the regime of power, which determines who may and who may not hold power, how they may hold it, and what for. The structure of authority, although connected with and influenced by the political regime and so, ultimately, the regime of power, has a fixed pattern of its own, which is independent of whether political participation is broad or restrictive.

Let us first consider the regime of power and the political regime.

Societies with a restrictive regime of power, as Classical Athens, can have a democratic political regime for those admitted to full citizenship. This distinction between the regime of power and the political was first understood by Marx, who denounced the bourgeois democratic government as sheer executive committees of their social class. Even today this distinction is not yet altogether understood. Most of the monotonous stereotypes involved in the mutual cold war accusations between the "free world" and the "classless societies" result from the former's ignorance of the distinction between the regime of power and the political regime and from the latter's unwarranted assumption that a supposedly broad regime of power implies a supposedly democratic political regime.

The regime of power, as has been said, expresses the regimes of values and participation of a given society. And these, as we saw in Chapter 1, are circularly interrelated: The values of a society, within the general framework of its culture, are induced from its life situations; and its way of life, within the general conditions of its natural environment and its capacity to adjust to it, is governed by its values. The role of the regime of power is to preserve the equilibrium of that value-factual situation, which constitutes the nucleus of the social regime of the society. In simple societies, especially before the differentiation of the secondary laws from the primary ones, there is a direct correspondence between the regime of power and the political regime. Those having higher levels of participation and of power are the authorities of the society. Once, however, the increasing complexity of a society brings about the differentiation between primary and secondary laws, converts the legal order into a defined set of rules and forces, and brings about an increasing specialization in social roles, including the governmental ones, a specific political regime is also brought about, defining the structure and functions of the government, how the authorities are to be selected, and how they are to proceed. At that moment the analytical distinction between the two regimes becomes empirically observable. The society will always have a certain regime of power, expressing its regimes of values and of participation and sanctioning, and being supported by, its regime of property. According to the regime of power, some people will be considered citizens, some will not; some will have certain privileges, some will not, and so forth. The regime of power may be, to a greater or smaller extent, acknowledged and regulated by the formal political regime, but it will always, whatever the regulations, shape and condition the political regime. The political regime may be broad, tending to open political participation to all of those admitted by the regime of power, or it may be restrictive, tending to be more or less discriminative concerning the rights and duties of the citizens. Whatever the character of the political regime, the structure of authority has its own invariable basic features, derived from the intrinsic characteristics of power, as a medium, and of decision making, as a political activity.

These basic characteristics of the structure of authority have been long misunderstood because of the already mentioned confusion between the political regime and the regime of power. The classic Aristotelian differentiation between government by one, by few, and by many or most of the citizens, which applies to the political regime, has obscured the permanent characteristics of the structure of authority. These have only become clear through contemporary political science, as a consequence of the functionalist approach and the systems analysis method.[13]

Briefly, it can be said that, whatever the regime of power and the political regime may be, the structure of authority in a society invariably presents three distinct levels of power relationship. At the higher level are always a few decision makers. At an intermediary level are several decision implementers. At the bottom are the many decision compliers. As soon as the political regime becomes distinct from the regime of power, another differentiation takes place, at the two higher levels, between those formally invested with the authority of being "in office," as we say today, from those wanting to have authority or striving for office. This is expressed graphically in Table 14.

Both authorities and pretenders have some means, which they have to use within given conditions. Some of these means are common in nature, as culture, prestige, money, and influence, although they are usually unevenly distributed among the authorities and pretenders. The authorities also have power and validity. Sometimes those having power have little validity and are only acknowledged as rulers. A minimum of validity, however, as we have seen in the preceding section, must be kept by the rulers, at least vis-à-vis their officials. The pretenders, however, have some power, in the sense that they make decisions that their militants and their supporters comply with, although their power is not general, autonomous, or superordinate.

There is an active exchange of valuables and media between the three levels of the structure of authority. Basically, those at the highest level give parcels of the media and some of the valuables they control, including symbolic valuables and promises for the future, to those at the middle level in exchange for their services. And those at the highest level also supply, according to whether they are in or out of office, means and strategic and tactic calculations, media and valuables for instrumenting their action to the middle level. The decision implementers receive from the higher echelon media and valuables for their own consumption and for their instrumental use and, in exchange, give them services for the implementation of their decisions. The implementers, as officials, supply the decision compliers with services of a general (public services) or a particular nature (favors) and impose on them the regulative and extractive decisions of the authorities, thus collecting media and valuables to refill the stock of the rulers. As militants, the decision implementers play particularly with those

Table 14 *Structure of authority*

Level	In Office	Out of Office
1. Decision Makers (few)	(A) Authorities or Rulers	(P) Pretenders
2. Decision Implementers (several)	(O) Officials	(M) Militants
3. Decision Compliers (many)	(R) Ruled: 1. Supporters of A or P 2. Opposers to A or P 3. Indifferent	

among the ruled who are dissatisfied with the authorities, bringing to them and propagandizing the pretenders' promises to promote, if given power, allegedly better alternative policies and conditions. Within the very limited possibilities of voluntary acceptance of regulation and extraction, the militants also perform extractive and regulative services for the pretenders.

From the higher echelons the ruled receive public services and favors, regulations for their current activities and extractions from their activities, and symbolic valuables in the form of justifications and glorifications of the status quo or, conversely, of criticisms of it and promises of change. To the higher echelons they give support or opposition, and with that, they do or do not supply the means and conditions for organized power and legitimate authority, ultimately keeping the rulers in power or forcing them out and bringing the pretenders in. Figure 1 presents a graphic representation of this flux.

What is peculiar to the structure of authority is that its basic features are independent of the political regime and the regime of power, whereas the latter, as we have seen, determines the political regime, which is nothing more than a partial manifestation, with strong ideological colorations and (conscious or not) falsifications, in legal terms, of the prevailing regime of power. Sometimes such explication may be rather unfaithful, as tends to happen in societies whose political culture gives to the laws the character of a desirable but remote ideal, rather than the character of strictly operational rules. In such societies, always of an oligarchical and highly ascriptive character, the political regime often pretends to establish a democratic and competitive rule, in contradiction with the regime of power. The result is that the political regime is not observed (and is not really supposed to be observed) whenever its functioning leads to consequences incompatible with the regime of power.

The basic features of the structure of authority, however, are not affected by the regime of power and the political regime. The regime of power may be very broad and all-inclusive, and the political regime may express that feature. This will not change the structure of authority, according to which few will be the decision makers, several, the decision implementers, and many, the decision compliers. The regime of power and the structure of authority will be made compatible by various formal or informal processes of delegation. In most democratic political regimes these delegations involve, notably: (1) a distinction between the potential sovereignty of the people and the actual power and authority of the few executive rulers, their power and authority being provided by direct electoral delegation (the powers of the American president) or by subsequent parliamentary delegation (the powers of the British prime minister); (2) a distinction between the broad, but not totally or directly self-implementable, authority of collective governing bodies, such as parliaments and large executive cabinets, and the more limited but direct authority of the few executive officers who, in the name of the people and of the large governing bodies, actually make decisions or implement them.

This does not mean, however, that all regimes of power are ultimately the same. The distinction between oligarchical and democratic regimes of power

Figure 1 *The Flux of Power*

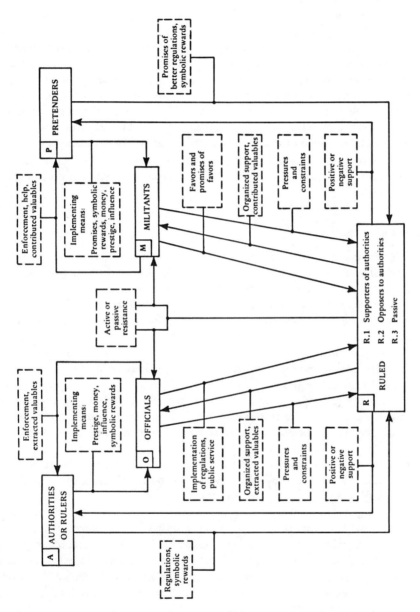

does not consist in the latter having many and the former few decision makers. The decision makers are always few in both cases. Rather the distinction lies in the fact that in democratic regimes of power the decision makers are accountable to a large number of citizens whom they have to satisfy, even if by manipulative means, whereas in oligarchical regimes of power they are accountable to themselves or a few more pairs.

The principle is also true in reverse. Even if the political regime overstresses the importance of the supreme ruler and pretends that the decision implementers have no status of their own but are, as much as the rest of the people, unconditional subjects of an absolute ruler, as was the case, for instance, in the Ottoman Empire, the fact remains that the power of the ruler is determined by the performing capacity of his implementation apparatus and therefore depends on an intermediary layer of officials. This layer can sometimes be rather thin, as in the case of Stalin's Russia (the top party echelons and the secret police), but it still exists as a socially and politically distinct group, vis-à-vis both the ruler and the ruled.

The use of power

It is now finally possible to make a rapid analysis of the political process at the actional level, where power is actually exercised. At this level the political process presents two relevant aspects. The first concerns the process of power and manifests the ways in which the power variables, listed in Table 13, are dealt with by the power actors, within the limitations of their conditions and means. The second aspect concerns the relationship between the authorities and the legal order that establishes the political regime (within the existing regime of power) and regulates accordingly the conditions for the exercise of power by the authorities.

As has been stressed by some contemporary political analysts, the fundamental principle concerning the process of power is that power is a medium and, as such, a resource that can be used only at a certain cost for obtaining (or not) certain results, which may or may not pay off the cost. This general principle, which has been clearly stated by writers like Parsons and Dahl, becomes more understandable if we use our previous analysis of the power variables, the structure of authority, and the resulting power flux.

At any given moment the authorities, wishing to reach some goal by political means, that is, by normative prescription, will find that the corresponding commands will involve the mobilization of the implementers at a certain cost, in exchange for achieving, in larger or lesser accordance with their design, a certain result. Let us suppose the authorities wish to balance the budget, and, concluding that the expenses cannot be curtailed further, they decide to increase the taxes. It can follow that because of the amount of the increase and its nature, it neither causes great resistance among the taxpayers nor overloads the tax collectors, and so produces the desired effect of balancing the budget. But, of course, various other alternatives are possible: There may be stubborn resistance from the public, excessive stress on the collecting services, unexpected depressive effects on the whole of the economy due to an excessive reduction of demand, and so forth. The problem for the authorities, therefore, is always to see, on the one hand, if the adopted measure was technically correct (was the budget balanced without economic disturbances?) and, on the other hand, whether the political cost of the decision (in terms of both the reaction of the public and the impact on the collecting services) was balanced by the results obtained. In political terms, then, the power cost of a decision can be larger than its power gains, or it can reduce the power autonomy of the authorities for the next move. The simple legitimate use of power is not by itself enough to secure its maintenance. Power is a medium like money and as such is subject to the equivalent phenomena of saving, investment, consumption, gain and loss, and so forth, as indicated in Table 13. Legitimate authorities brought down to power bankruptcy will lose, with their effectivity, not only their capacity for enforcing compliance by coercive means but even their own legitimacy.

The second aspect of the political process at the actional level concerns the relationship between the authorities and the legal order. Authorities can be chosen according to the existing political regime, in accordance with the prevailing regime of power, and can successfully rule accordingly. There are, however, many alternatives to this hypothesis. Pretenders may successfully take over power in violation of the legal order. The authorities may violate the legal order in order to perpetuate themselves in power. Or the legal order may be used by the authorities in ways that are not compatible with the regime of power. What is at stake at one level in these various situations is the relationship between power and validity, already discussed in the opening section of this chapter. At a deeper level, what is at stake is whether the authorities or the pretenders are able to influence their society to the point of introducing changes of some consequence in the regime of power, causing, according to the principle of congruence, the corresponding changes in the regimes of participation and values. All sorts of issues are possible and have historically occurred. Whatever the issues happen to be, they will always manifest (1) the conformity of the political regime to the regime of power, (2) the final obtention of a minimum of validity by those succeeding in keeping stable power, and (3) the final loss of power by those unable to obtain a minimum of validity.

NOTES

[1] See the basic bibliographic list on the history of political thought at the end of this book.

[2] Political philosophy in the sense above should not be confused with the philosophy of political science, as a branch of the philosophy of social sciences, itself, a part of the philosophy of sciences.

[3] See David Easton's statement (1965a, p. 59): "A political system, therefore, will be identified as a set of interactions, abstracted from the totality of social behavior, through which values are authoritatively allocated for a society." My revised version tries to correct the idealistic implications and bias of the above proposition, saying "valuables" instead of

"values." Not only and not primarily values are allocated in politics, but goods and services, roles and statuses, and actually everything. This means, according to what was discussed in Chapter 1, that what is allocated are valuables.

[4] "Politics is every systematic effort promoted at any place of the social field in order to lead other men to pursue designs chosen by the promoter."

[5] On the same subject, see Robert Dahl (1963, pp. 19 ff.)

[6] Traditional societies can rest on validity concepts compatible with highly discriminatory rules, as the old caste system in India.

[7] The same principle applies to the other structural planes of society and their functions.

[8] A classic example is the obstacle the veto of the American Medical Association has long been to medical programs.

[9] See H. L. A. Hart (1965), particularly chaps. 3 and 5.

[10] As will be discussed further, the essential feature of external discreteness is not independence, which brings additional features, but the fact that a political system is not conclusive vis-à-vis any other system, although it is all-inclusive for its own society.

[11] See J. W. Allen (1960) pp. 394 ff.

[12] Under the influence of Marx some writers reserve the concept "revolution" for movements changing not only the political system, but also the social regime. In my opinion, however, such a concept should be a "social revolution."

[13] Pareto's elite and Michel's iron law of oligarchy were important anticipations, but they were still affected by the lack of distinction between the regime of power, the political regime, and the structure of authority, which is why, when these writers found the oligarchical feature of the structure of authority, they thought it reduced democracy to an illusion.

4

Participation and Power

THE SOCIAL GROUP

The concept of group

We will continue the study of the polity in the present section by analyzing the basis and origins of the power process and structure as they are found, currently, in the elementary forms of association existing in any society and, historically and anthropologically, in primitive groups. The combined and comparative study of the elementary forms of power as they appear, sociologically, in the social group and, historico-anthropologically, in primitive societies, is indispensable for the systems analysis of the polity.

The *social group* has been defined in the sociological literature primarily in terms of two main alternative variables: the form of communication and the form of sociability. Charles H. Cooley (1909) and Ferdinand Tönnies (1947) gave the classic formulations of these two alternatives. Cooley stressed the difference between primary groups, characterized by a face-to-face communication, and the groups, not named by him but later called secondary groups, characterized by remote contact. Tönnies (1947) and after him Durkheim (1967) pointed out the difference between the deeper and all-pervasive bonds of community (Durkheim's "mechanical solidarity") and the more superficial and contractual links of society (Durkheim's "organic solidarity"). Modern writers have, in part, accepted these alternative variables and, following one of the alternatives, have added enrichments and qualifications, as Kingsley Davis (1949) did in the line of Cooley and as Georges Gurvitch (1958, 2nd Section, chap. III) did in the line of Tönnies, or they have introduced more complex models, as Robert MacIver and Charles Page (1962) did.

I think myself that if the various forms that social groups can assume are to be understood, more than one line of variables are required for their characterization. Besides the two essential variables indicated above and several others of less generic importance, two others have to be included in any classificatory scheme: the origin of group associations (whether they are transmitted, by birth or lineage, or individually acquired) and the purposes, deliberate or not, of the association (consummatory or instrumental). Tables 15 and 16 present the suggested variables of characterization and a classification of typical groups.

In accordance with the preceding view a group can be broadly defined as *the association of two or more individuals who, in given conditions, maintain a relatively stable pattern of relationship, objectively identifiable and subjectively presenting a minimum acknowledgment of participation.*[1]

That broad form comprehends all types of groups. There are six major elements that are characteristic of it: (1) A group is always the association of two (dyad) or more individuals. Groups with remote communication could, theoretically, be as large as the whole population of the world, if conditions giving a purpose to their association, as a worldwide danger, should eventually arise. (2) Group association is always determined by certain conditions. There are no unconditional groups. These conditions include conditions of place, as territorial contiguity for a village group, conditions of time, as ephemeral, enduring, or constant conditions for the group association, conditions of origin, as being the children of given parents, and various other kinds of conditions including those of occasional or circumstantial nature. Occasional and circumstantial conditions are the ones that determine the nondeliberate formation of instrumental groups of the society kind, as, for instance, when passengers are on a bus or plane that is subsequently damaged. Under normal conditions these passengers do not form a group, in the sense of *an association objectively identifiable presenting a minimum of acknowledgment of participation.* Each passenger behaves individually, vis-à-vis the others, and feels himself only connected with the bus or plane as a passenger on a vehicle operated by some people in behalf of some company. If, however, the bus gets stuck in a place without easy rescuing facilities or if the plane suffers an accident and is forced into an emergency landing, the passengers

Table 15 *Group characterization*

Variable	Model	Type of Group
Communication	Direct	Primary groups
	Remote	Secondary groups
Sociability	Community	We-centered groups
	Society	Ego-centered groups
Origin	Transmitted	In-born groups
	Acquired	Out-born groups
Finality (purpose)	Consummatory	Associations existing for their own sake
	Instrumental	Associations existing for other purposes

will be brought, by that occasional and circumstantial condition, to form a self-helping association (or, in certain cultural conditions, a praying group), objectively identifiable by its specificity (passengers of bus or plane in such place at such time) and subjectively compelled to acknowledge, whatever their reciprocal personal feelings, that they participate in that specific group. (3) While the conditions determining or predominantly influencing the group association persist, the relationship of the members of the group to the group remain relatively stable, within the pattern of the group. (4) Groups are always teleologically oriented even if the finality, or purpose, is just the consummatory purpose of reciprocal socializing or if the purpose is nondeliberate, as occurs with some transmitted groups (child in family) or occasional groups (passengers of damaged vehicle as members of ad-hoc self-helping group). This teleological nature of groups derives from its associational character and is reinforced by its minimum amount of self-conscious content. The socially more important groups are those containing, at least negatively, an element of deliberation. That deliberation is an overt one in nonoccasional acquired groups, as in the elective forms of the husband-wife dyad, the contractual groups, and those formed by adhesion. Negatively deliberate groups are those in which membership was transmitted by kinship or territoriality but from which members could separate themselves by an act of will, such as repudiation or a change of territory and/or of citizenship. Both historically and currently the kin and the territorially originated bonds of association have been the ones that bring about the socially more important groups. (5) A group association is objectively identifiable, in the sense that the sheer subjective feeling, on the part of some individuals, of belonging to a certain group will not engender the supposed group or, for that matter, any group at all if the feeling is not supported by objectively identifiable forms of association. Groups are associations empirically existing as such and can only be so if the group members reciprocally interact, which means that they act in and by ways transcending their own individual subjectivity through direct or remote forms of communication with each other. (6) But groups are not sheer objective collectivities, as, for instance, a street crowd or the passengers of the above-mentioned bus or plane before trouble forces their acknowledged participation in some common enterprise. Groups result from, and express, their members' "grouping" behavior and intention.

Participation and sociation

The group association brings out a double relationship: the relationship of participation between each individual member and the group as a collectivity (a formal or informal moral person) and the relationship of sociation, or social relationship, among the individual members. As Gurvitch (1958, vol. I, pp. 174–175 and 186–187) has observed, in spite of the voluminous studies dedicated to the group, the terms of relationship that characterize its internal sociability have usually been reduced to the social relations among individuals. In the dyad the relationships of participation and sociation are coextensive. In

Table 16 *Classification of relevant typical groups*

	Direct		
TRANSMITTED		**ACQUIRED**	
Consummatory	*Instrumental*	*Consummatory*	*Instrumental*
Family Bands	Phratries	Love dyad	Village
Lineage groups	Local sodalities	Friends	Resid. groups
Traditional club	Village Traditional school	Club	Church Cultural groups
Traditional friends	Traditional church		Gang
	Traditional cooperatives		Cooperatives
	Traditional firms		
Friends	Cooperatives	Friends	Residential groups
Club	Firm	Club	Ad-hoc groups Schools Institutes Church Art groups Gang Cooperatives Firm Union

	Remote		
TRANSMITTED		**ACQUIRED**	
Consummatory	*Instrumental*	*Consummatory*	*Instrumental*
Clan	Other sodalities	-	-
Tribe	Traditional church		
Nation	Traditional pressure groups		
Club	City	Club	City
	School		Residential groups
	State		Interest associations
	Firm		School
			University
			Church
			Cultural associations
			Party
			State
			International organization
			Firm
			Corporation
			Union
			Professional associations

small groups members may be subjectively unaware of the distinction between the relationship of participation and the social relationship. The distinction exists analytically, however, whenever more than two people are involved in the group, and it tends to be very clear in large groups.

The relationship of participation expresses and determines the form and degree of group membership. It is the founding relation of the group association, and it may be the only one existing, in an actual form, for some group members. Such is the case, for instance, for certain members of professional or recreational groups, who may be highly interested in enjoying professional privileges or, in the case of clubs, in enjoying the privileges of membership, such as swimming pools and restaurants, and even in enjoying the prestige eventually conferred by membership without actually engaging in any social relationship with the other members.

The relationship of participation determines, in the first place, the form of inclusion in the group, establishing the distinction between members and non-members, full members and restricted ones (active or passive, independent or dependent, free or not free), permanent members and occasional or conditional members. In the second place, the relationship establishes the degree of each member's contribution and his acquisition of group duties and rights, thus determining the status of each class of members. All large groups present, at least informally, a minimum or basic status differentiation. In political groups and in nonpolitical ones (in which internal politics become especially important for members), the status differentiation tends to present the same pyramidal feature as the structure of authority: a few high status members, several medium status, and many low status ones. The pattern of the various forms and degrees of participation in a group constitutes its regime of participation.

The relationship of sociation is founded on the relationship of participation but varies according to status stratification, ingroup and outgroup roles, and individual personalities. For many groups and many individual members there is often a correlation between both types of relationship: high participation status is connected with high sociation status. This is not true of all groups and does not fit all roles and status situations. In society at large some roles and conditions, as entertainers, women, and young people, for instance, tend in several groups to provide higher sociation than participation status. Other social roles and conditions, as, for instance, guardians, priests, and elders, tend to enjoy a lower sociation than participation status. Leadership roles tend to be high in both sociation and participation status, and unskilled working roles, low in both. And in most groups but particularly in acquired consummatory ones, individual personalities are highly influential in the sociation status of group members.

The conditional and teleological characteristics of groups have very important consequences for the group association, for they determine its statics and its dynamics. The principles of group statics and group dynamics are related to the conditions under which or due to which the group came to be formed and to the group's finality, or purpose, deliberate or not.

Group statics

The principle of group statics can be formulated as the principle of maintenance of a group's teleology and regime of participation. *Groups tend to pursue the same purposes and to maintain the same regime of participation as long as the internal and external conditions that have been relevant in the determination of these purposes and the regime of participation persist.* Let us illustrate that principle with examples. A nuclear family is centered around a husband-wife dyad. If external and internal conditions do not change significantly, (that is, if the unity of the dyad is not disturbed by the challenge of competing affinities, forceful separation of the family members, or drastic changes in its conditions of subsistence), the group will persist as a family unit, rearing the young children and fulfilling the other activities that in their sociocultural context families are supposed to do. A production cooperative of peasants will keep its unity, purposes, and internal structure, and notably its regime of participation, as long as natural and social conditions do not, externally, disrupt its conditions of production and marketing and, internally, the members keep the same interests, and membership rotation, due to the death or retirement of old members and admittance of younger ones, does not disrupt the internal balance of interests and power. At a larger scale the same is applicable to a state.

An important consequence of the principle of group statics is the functional, if informal, organization of groups for the performance of their explicit or implicit, deliberate or nondeliberate finalities. This important aspect of all group associations has been well understood by the equilibrium theorists (former or current ones) and given elaborate treatment by such writers as Parsons and Kingsley Davis. However, these writers did not establish the derivation of the functional features of groups from their statics. This functional aspect of groups consists, in the first place, in the fact that, given the principle of statics, the behaviors performed to achieve the explicit or implicit finalities of the group become a sufficiently stable set of interrelated typical behaviors to provide for their formal or informal institutionalization in various roles. Given the group finalities and its regime of participation, the roles and typical behaviors resulting from them allow the systemic achievement of the concerned goals. In the second place, this role-based systemic achievement of goals provides for formal or informal coordination of the involved roles, which gives rise to the role (formal or informal) of group leader, or authority.

We come here to the source of the political process, of authority, and ultimately, of power. Essentially, in its simplest functional manifestation, *authority is the role, formal or informal, of coordinating the roles and activities oriented toward the achievement of collective goals and toward the maintenance of the existing regime of participation and the implied regime of values.* The demand for coordination for the achievement of goals and the maintenance of the group's regime of participation (derived from the group statics) provides group support and sanction for the authority's decisions, independent of any other condition, insofar as these decisions, because of their simplicity and directness, are immediately understood and accepted as reasonably convenient for their ostensive purpose. This is the case of what should be called *self-validating commands.* In its simplest forms authority is always and necessarily followed by compliance and implies the propensity for group enforcement. Group enforcement, independent of organization and other conditions, provides a minimum of coercion and reward. In this informal way *the coercive ability, and therefore the power, implied in the minimal forms of authority consists in the actual or virtual preparedness of the group to impose some moral or physical penalties on transgressors or deviants.* In some groups these penalties can affect the life or liberty of transgressors or deviants, as is the case with politically autonomous groups. On the other hand, *the informal rewards implied in the minimal forms of authority consist in the actual or virtual preparedness of the group to grant some moral or material benefits to those who are considered to have made special contributions to the pursuit of the group's purposes or the maintaining of the regime of participation.* The usual moral rewards for group services include the maintenance of successful leaders in leadership roles, the conferring of these roles on skilled and active group members, institutionalizing these roles, and surrounding them with an aura of respect.

As long as the group statics is maintained, opposition to the leader is repressed as transgression or deviance insofar as the leader's commands are understood by the group as representing reasonable requirements for goal achievement and for the maintenance of the regime of participation, that is, as long as the commands remain self-validating. The institutionalization of the authority role enlarges, in a corresponding way, the limits to its self-validation. As progress is made toward more complex and organized forms of authority, however, as in the state, the principle of self-validation ceases to be applicable. Validation in that case is provided by the group's regime of values and, in more elaborated form, as has been discussed in Chapter 3, by the secondary laws.

Opposition to the leader and leadership competition cease to be automatically a transgression or deviance when the decisions of the leader cease to be self-validating, either because of the complexity of the matter to be decided or because the leader, willingly or not, appears to have broken the balance between command and required coordination.[2] In that case the regime of values determines the extent and conditions of opposition and leadership competition that are acceptable within the limits of the regime of participation and the implicit regime of power. Opposition or competition that is not compatible with these limits will not be tolerated as long as the group statics is maintained. Once group statics is broken, either the limits will be correspondingly enlarged or the group unity will be disrupted.

Group dynamics

And so we can now consider the principle of group dynamics. The principle of group dynamics can be formulated as the principle of change in a group's teleology or in its regime of participation. *Changes in the external or internal conditions that have been relevant for the determination of a group's purposes or of its regime of participation tend either to bring about corresponding adjustments in the group's purposes or regime of participation or to disrupt the group association.*

Noncontrollable changes in the external conditions of a group will affect, beyond some limits, the group's capacity for pursuing or fulfilling its former purposes. According to the nature of these purposes and the character of the group, either the group will want to, and will be able to, effect some changes in its purposes or, obviously, the group association will have to be discontinued (in some cases, because of the physical elimination of the former members). A fishing group, for instance, of riverside inhabitants cannot keep its former purposes if the river becomes inhospitable to fish. The members can decide to preserve their association by transforming the group into a boat club, or they can dissolve their association because they lack the facilities and disperse to pursue other hobbies. If these riverside inhabitants, however, were a primitive fishing community, they would be confronted with a much more severe challenge. In that case their own survival would be at stake. In order to procure their food, they would be obliged to move to another fishing site, to use boats to fish in the ocean or farther up the river, to become hunters and food-gatherers, or, eventually, to incorporate or invent agricultural techniques. In all of these cases the external change either forces a corresponding adjustment of the purposes of the groups or of their ways of achieving their former purposes, or suppresses the group association.

Internal changes (often caused by external ones but also resulting for other reasons) that bring about the disruption of the former equilibrium between the various classes and strata of members will affect the former regime of participation in a corresponding way. In Chapter 2 we saw the cases and examples of dialectic change, both by dialectic and by initially incremental processes. Whatever the cause and the process, dialectical changes can break down the former regime of participation. When the group is confronted with such a change, either a new regime of participation is established, peacefully or otherwise, within the group, keeping an appropriate balance between the strengths of the various strata and their terms of participation, or the group association is disrupted. A change in the conditions affecting the group's purposes or its regime of participation creates a gap in the enforceability of some commands or even in the validity of the existing authority, creating expectations of different commands or authority. When a change of allegiance substantially affects the functions of coercion and reward, a corresponding change takes place in the process of political enforcement. In that case a new authority or new forms of authority take the place of the former one, reestablishing the correspondence between the regime of participation, collective purposes, and the internal ordering of the group. When the change of allegiance is not powerful enough to affect the functions of coercion and reward, adjustment to the new conditions proves to be compatible with the preservation of the former authority, which comes out strengthened, if somehow modified, and the dissenters are penalized accordingly.

As can be seen, the static principle of the group contains the basis of the formation and operation of political authority, and the dynamic principle contains the basis of the process of revolution and counterrevolution.

PRIMITIVE AUTHORITY

Formation of the tribe

Let us complement the sociological analysis of the social group by focusing on the formation of authority with an historico-anthropological approach. The study of the origin of human societies and civilizations, as well as the research on the forms of social control and intergroup ordering of contemporary primitive societies, provide a decisive explanation of the essence and the elementary forms of the polity.

The first objective explanation of the formation of the polity and of political authority was presented by Sir Henry Maine (1861) and remains, in its basic lines, valid today: The polity and ultimately the state resulted from a transference of jurisdiction from kinship bonds to territorial ones. In more elaborate form and with a wealth of prehistorical and anthropological information that was not available a century ago, contemporary writers have shown how, after the early Paleolithic social life was regulated on a familistic basis, according to rigid norms controlling marriage, residence, the relationships of sub- and superordination within the extended family, the regime of cooperation or conflict among families, and the various other relevant situations of social life. As was said by MacIver (1949, p. 23–24), whose studies on the origin of the state are still a classic, "the same necessities that create the family create also regulation. . . . The existence of the family requires the regulation of sex, the regulation of property, and the regulation of youth. If we briefly examine what is involved in these three types of regulation we shall see why the family is everywhere the matrix of government." Increasing complexity in interfamily, originally egalitarian, relationships, due to growth in size and diversification of primitive societies, and other factors, notably warfare, made kin-based regulations and authority insufficient and provided for the formation, through hereditary lines, of territorially based forms of authority. As MacIver puts it to show the transition from nondiversified to diversified societies: "For the most part it is only when the community extends and grows more complex that the specific assignment of men and groups to higher and lower orders comes into effect. It is only then that ruling and subject classes appear. It is only then that government becomes formalized, and for the reasons already offered the practice of war gave a strong impetus toward this transformation" (p. 37).

More recent historical and anthropological studies, although confirming Maine's territorial theory, which was accepted and developed by contemporary political science, have shown that the transition from kin-based to territorially based jurisdiction was, and is, a far more complicated and longer process than was believed until a few years ago. If, using the more recent information, we try to give a general picture of the process of the formation of the polity since the origin of man, we can say that basically it has consisted, through the course of millennia, in the gradual solving, by successive stages, of four main difficulties concerning the terms of participation in the primary groups. These difficulties can be briefly and successively given, always with reference to primary groups, as: (1) intragroup cooperation, (2) intragroup regulation, (3) intergroup ordering, and (4) supergroup government.

The problem and the process of intragroup cooperation is coextensive with the problem and the process of the humanization of the Hominidae. This process took place, in the late Pliocene and early Pleistocene, in the band life of the Hominidae family. It can be described as a double process of adaptation. On the one hand, there was adaptation to the external environment of band life: physical and living nature, with its preys and predators, and other competing bands of Hominidae. Through natural selection the species most able to realize and take advantage of the natural properties of things have been given the premium of survival and general dominance. Thus were formed, from common ancestors, the great apes, or man apes, as the Oreopithecus and the Australopithecus, first makers of rudimentary pebble tools, and the various species of *Homo erectus*, or Pithecanthropus, first makers of fire and predecessor of *Homo sapiens*.[3] On the other hand, there was adaptation to the social life of the group. Prehuman life, as has been so well discussed by Service (1967), was characterized by a purely passive social life, which has continued to characterize the great apes. Individuals lived in small bands, including, under the despotism of a dominant male, two or more generations of subdominant males and females. There was no sharing of food and no cooperation for the obtention of food in prehuman conditions. The dominant male would control all the available food, and only after he was satisfied would subdominant males and females, according to their pecking order, feed themselves. Social life, within any band, included cooperation only for the defense of the natural territory.

The process of humanization of the hominids consisted basically in the development of a capacity for cooperation and for sharing, through the formation of the nuclear family, within the band. Biological conditions in the hominids, contrary to what continues to happen with the apes (Dobzhansky, 1965b, p. 197), favored the emergence of the nuclear family by allowing female receptability all year round. At the same time, toolmaking provided a much greater hunting capability and required more than an individual approach to the capture of big game. Interindividual cooperation began with the division of labor between male and female in the mating dyad (Service, 1967, pp. 39 ff). This division of labor stabilized the mating dyad, incorporating into it, in a nuclear family, the mother-children dyad. Speaking capability and symbolic communication in general, genetically given with the emergence of the genus *Homo*, was actually implemented as the result of the necessities of intrafamilial cooperation. And so the first and the greatest leap in the evolutionary course of the hominids, their overcoming of crude egotism and their humanization through cooperation and communication, was achieved with the triple process including toolmaking, symbolic communication, and the formation of the nuclear family.

As a sequel to the formation of nuclear families, mankind solved the second difficulty, intragroup regulation, in the early Paleolithic. The solution consisted, basically, in the rise of mating rules and the consequent conversion of sexual intercourse into the social institution of marriage. These rules established certain sexual taboos, the exogamic norms, the formation of lineages, and the adoption of residential rules. Lineages, predominantly agnatic, and residence, predominantly virilocal, gave rise to a system of intragroup regulation affecting not only the institutions regulating the nuclear family, marriage and the rearing of the children, but also the social life of Paleolithic communities, including in a band several families of the same lineage as well as other lineages with which they were allied and would exchange women in marriage. The lineage system provided, besides the basis for marriage, an economic unity, with the common ownership of goods and territory, and cooperative hunting and food-gathering. It also provided the nucleus of a political system by establishing a blood solidarity among the members and with it egalitarian duties and rights for mutual helping, revenge of wrongs, and collective regulation of the band life.[4]

The third major difficulty to be overcome, intergroup ordering, emerged out of the lineage system in a way analogous to the rise of this system from the nuclear family. The development was preceded by an increase in the size and complexity of the interacting groups. Within a lineage the functional requirements of hunting and fighting gave rise to the brotherhood of cooperative males. Voluntary associations, or sodalities, for ceremonial or other purposes, associated kin people from different residences, usually of the same sex and age group. Clans also appeared. These were based on lineages linked by a more remote or mythical common ancestor, but, like sodalities, the members were without common residence and committed to specific purposes. These developments, going beyond the smaller residential unit of the band and other primary groups, led to the formation of secondary groups, or tribes. Unlike bands, which are associations of nuclear families, tribes are associations of much larger segments of people, maintaining the most varied kinship relationships. The formation of tribes, besides being the result of the more complex relationships among people brought about by nonresidential sodalities and clans, was decisively conditioned by one of the most revolutionary events of human evolution: the agricultural revolution and the practice of taming and breeding animals. The agricultural revolution changed the life of primitive man in a very deep way, bringing him, according to the well-known expression of Childe, from Paleolithic savagery to Neolithic barbarism.[5] Among the various and profound changes caused by the agricultural and pastoral revolution, the most relevant was the substantial increase in the food supply and its relative stability. Wandering bands could become sedentary groups, settled around their crops and livestock. This situation strongly reinforced the propensity to form larger tribes to replace the former small groups of hunters and food-gatherers. But it also accentuated the necessity for coordinating the various associated groups of lineages in a way that sheer family regulation could not do. Tribal society gave birth to a more complex form of intergroup ordering. On the one hand, this ordering was based on several coordinating devices or practices, such as elders' councils and, along functional lines of integration, on a large increase in the number of sodalities: magic-ceremonial ones, secret clubs, young warriors phratries, and so forth. On the other hand, particularly for warfare purposes, charismatic leaders, who were selected by consensus because of their fighting prowess, assured the defense of the tribe. The tribe, however, remained a loose egalitarian collectivity, very poorly coordinated, because of the noninstitutional form of its leadership and the nonexistence of an authority above and beyond the lineage level. Because of the absence of a superlineage authority that could settle internal disputes along with a lineage solidarity that included all of one's kindred and the practice of lineage revenge for wrongs, disruptive internal conflicts and fights were maintained, presenting a constant risk to the tribes' external defense and a serious disturbance to their farming.[6]

Formation of the polity

The transition from intergroup ordering, based on a contractual coordination of lineages, to a supergroup authority, invested with the institutional capacity for making binding decisions for all the members of the community, whatever their familistic groups, constituted the last step in the gradual formation of the polity. It was also one of the greatest difficulties to overcome, perhaps second only to the transition to intragroup cooperation. Not only did man take a long time to pass through the previous stages, but the transition to supergroup authority was not reached in a single and direct leap. Rather, as Service has so well shown (1967), supergroup authority was arrived at through an intermediary level, the chiefdom level. The great innovation of chiefdoms, vis-à-vis the tribal societies, was the creation of a redistribution system, under the superfamilistic authority of an hereditary chief. Tribal societies were unspecialized egalitarian associations of kinsmen bonded by their respective lineages. Chiefdoms were inegalitarian societies in which, besides the hereditary chief, there was an aristocracy of the chief's relatives and eventually of other notables,[7] who enjoyed a differential regime of participation, under rules supervised by the redistribution chief.

In addition to the conditions that created the necessity, in tribal societies, for a more convenient form of interlineage regulation, the emergence of chiefdoms in the late Neolithic expressed the effects of the increasing mobility of goods and people and of the corresponding gradual accumulation of wealth. The settlement of people in villages around their major crops spurred an increasing exchange of goods among areas of different ecology, permitted, along with the creation of food reserves, the formation of nonagricultural classes of craftsmen, traders, magicians, and warriors, and stimulated economic specialization among the communities, according to ecological conditions. Some people became pastoral and were led to abandon the sedentary life of the village for a seminomadic following of their cattle. Some became hillsmen. In the frontiers between

Neolithic peoples and those keeping their former Paleolithic ways of life, some people became herdsmen or hillsmen without passing through the phase of the agricultural village. In addition to their role in the Neolithic exchange of goods, these herdsmen and hill dwellers played a still more important political role, because they developed a tendency toward war and leadership, which led, in various ways, to the origin of several original kingdoms. In the increasing process of differentiation that characterized the late Neolithic and the emergence of the early kingdoms, the agricultural villager contributed to the formation of the peasantry of the old civilizations. Before this development, however, Neolithic differentiation led to a corresponding differentiation in the regime of participation of the people within a community. In a general way, the agricultural revolution increased the importance of women, who were the primitive farmers,[8] and correspondingly, of matrilineal lineages and uxorilocal residence. The development of pastoralism, however, shifted patrilineages, virilocalism, and economic predominance back again to the men. Within these general trends, economic and political differentiations took place among lineages and nuclear families in the late Neolithic, the chiefdoms being characterized by their unequal regimes of participation.

In spite of that differentiation and of the creation of hereditary chiefs, who supervised the system of redistribution and accumulated priestly functions, chiefdoms were not able to reach a supergroup system of government because they lacked a coercive apparatus. Enforcement of laws and traditions and of the decisions of the chief depended on the collective sanction of the community. This was due to the fact that chiefdoms had not completely or properly overcome the basic lineage bondage. The lineage and the nuclear family of the hereditary chief had become differentiated from the common ones and were surrounded by taboo, sacredness, and magic power, to which was ultimately attributed the chief's authority, transmissible, as magic powers were supposed to be, by heredity. The emergence of a sacralized lineage, which came to be associated with the mythical origins of the tribe, did not annul, however, the other lineages and the other family bonds. Enforcement, therefore, was limited by the jurisdictional autonomy of each lineage and could only be achieved with the consent of the concerned lineage or, ultimately, by the general pressure of the rest of the community.[9]

Historically, the next step in the development of a supergroup government is associated with the urban revolution and the creation of the early kingdoms with which the original civilizations appeared and developed. This process, so well elucidated by the studies of Gordon Childe (1951 and 1964), can be summarized in four major steps. First, it was originally a very localized process, which started in the valleys of the Fertile Crescent (the Nile and the Mesopotamic rivers), the Indus Valley, and the Yellow River Valley (in addition to the unconnected beginnings of the pre-Columbian civilizations) and was only later spread, by expansion or diffusion, to other sites and communities. This geo-ecological limitation of the origins of civilization stresses the overwhelming importance that artificial irrigation and the social requirements for its control have played in the development of civilization.

Second, the emergence, with the early kingdoms, of a supergroup government depended on the previous accumulation of wealth and the economic diversification of the late Neolithic. As the study of contemporary chiefdoms has revealed, one of the causes of the weakness of chiefdoms is that the chiefs have to support their magical prestige with a distribution of gifts which tends to overtax their meager revenues. In the historical process, aside from the cases of conquest, it was usually after the heads of villages and families of noble lineage succeeded in becoming patrimonial lords that they obtained the economic ability to maintain for their personal service a group of followers and courtiers who could be used as implementers of their decisions.

Third, the composition of a body of followers and decision implementers who were loyal exclusively to a chief was dependent on the increased personal mobility of the late Neolithic. For many reasons, varying from voluntary or forced migration of people to outside their kin circles and their convertion into clients of the chiefs of their adopted communities to the military conquest of agricultural communities by groups of herdsmen or hillsmen, either the former or the new chiefs were able to make use of followers and dependents who were not subject because of familistic bonds to any of the other lineages and families of the community. These people could use, without moral and social restrictions, the violence necessary for the imposition of authority and the implementation of the chief's decisions.

Fourth, there was a profound transformation of religious and magic beliefs and practices, which led to the rise of religions oriented toward the collective protection of the communities, their territory, and their means of subsistence. These religions were understood as being directly dependent on the magic powers of the royal chiefs, when the chiefs were not themselves, as in Egypt, deemed to be incarnations of the protective god. With the agricultural revolution the chaotic animistic-demoniac vision of the Paleolithic bands was succeeded by more structured magico-religious beliefs, oriented toward the propitiation of fertility and associated with the idea of immortality. In the place of, or superimposed on, the former totemic and familistic spirits, divinities, mostly female, who were coextensive with and represented and controlled natural phenomena, emerged to form the Neolithic pantheon. As the sown grain dies to have a rebirth with the next crop, so the dead could be rescued for an afterlife by propitiating rites that appeased the divinities. The rise of the early kingdoms is connected with the emergence, in the place of the natural and chthonic divinities, of gods who were associated with a given people and place, representatives and controllers of the natural elements and of immortality, and accessible to, or identified with, the king.[10]

In two typical examples of the emergence of transfamilistic supergroup governments, the early cities of Mesopotamia and Egypt, we see this interdependence of the development of a new religious myth and of the new city-states. In Mesopotamia the new polity was initially founded on, and around, the temples, and the authority of the priests preceded the emergence of the king, who appeared as a result of the necessity for an executive coordination of the religious-civilian complex. The king's own early title, Ishakku, meaning the tenant farmer of the gods, expressed the dependence of his authority and power on his religious functions. The gods themselves were deemed to be the lords of the land, which was managed in their behalf.[11] In Egypt, where the authority of the kings preceded the authority of the priests, who never became autonomous rulers, the early unification of the cities and subsequently of the Lower and Higher lands under the same king brought about the deification of the pharaoh, who was the dispenser of immortality and lived, himself, in the cycle of the eternal renewal of life, appearing incarnate as Horus and becoming Osiris again after his earthly life.[12]

AUTHORITY AND POWER

Ontogenetic and phylogenetic synthesis

The previous analysis of current groups and the survey of the development of primitive groups and of the gradual emergence within them of the elementary forms of authority and power make it possible for us to return now to the political sociology of the group. Comparing our former analytical generalizations with the historical course of the process, we can see how much the latter has corresponded to the former, and we can extract from this comparison our final conclusions concerning the essential features, both analytical and empirical, of the role of authority and the process of power.

It is convenient for this purpose to summarize the main findings of our analysis of the social group, which can be done in terms of three major points: (1) characterization of the social group, (2) the principle of group statics, and (3) the principle of group dynamics.

Concerning the characterization of the group, we have seen, after discussing the more relevant variables determining the group and the classifications resulting thereof, that by "group" we mean the association of two or more individuals who, in given conditions, maintain a relatively stable pattern of relationship, objectively identifiable and subjectively involving a minimum acknowledgment of participation. We saw that there are six major characteristic elements in any group: (1) the association of two or more individuals, (2) the determination of the group by certain conditions, (3) the correspondence between the persistence of these conditions and the persistence of the relationship of the members of the group with the group, (4) the teleological nature of groups, (5) the objective identifiability of groups, and (6) the existence of a minimum of acknowledgment of participation in the group by the members. Finally we observed that the group brings out a double relationship: (1) the relationship of participation, or the relationship of the group members with the group, according to a certain regime of participation, and (2) the relationship of sociation, or the relationship of the members of the group with each other.

We have formulated the principle of group statics in the following way: Goups tend to pursue the same purposes and to maintain the same regime of participation as long as the internal and external conditions that have been relevant in the determination of these purposes and the regime of participation persist. One of the major consequences of group statics is the existence in any group of a functional requirement for authority, which tends to be filled by the appearance of a role, formal or informal, that coordinates roles and activities oriented toward the achievement of collective goals and the maintenance of the existing regime of participation, with its implied regime of values. We observed also that in its simplest forms (self-validating commands) authority is always and necessarily followed by compliance, due to the actual or virtual readiness of the group to enforce self-validating commands by imposing some moral or physical penalties on transgressors or deviants.

Finally, we formulated the principle of group dynamics by stating that changes in the external or internal conditions that have been relevant in the determination of the purposes of a group or of its regime of participation tend to bring about either a corresponding adjustment in the group's purposes or regime of participation or the disruption of the group association. We saw that this change can be external, in the natural or social environment of the group, or internal, involving the quantitative or qualitative conditions affecting its regime of participation. We observed then that once changes affecting the group's regime of participation take place, either the existing functions of coercion and reward are enough to preserve the existing authority, albeit in a changed form, or the former authority or form of authority is changed, in a way corresponding to the resulting regime of participation.

It is also convenient for the clarity of our subsequent discussion to summarize the main findings of our historico-anthropological survey of primitive groups. We can condense these findings in two points: (1) the successive difficulties concerning the terms of participation in the primary primitive groups and the corresponding successive stages in which these difficulties were solved and (2) the four major aspects of the transition from the third stage of intergroup ordering to the last one of supergroup government.

The difficulties concerning the terms of participation in the primary primitive groups and the successive stages of their solution were enumerated as follows: (1) intergroup cooperation: the overcoming of closed biological egoism and the development of the ability to share valuables (originally food) and cooperate for the satisfaction of mutual interests, (2) intragroup regulation: institutionalization of family and kinship, (3) intergroup ordering: organization of multifamily societies, (4) supergroup government: institutionalization of a superfamilistic or territorial authority and of a centralized system of enforcement.

The four major aspects of the transition from the third stage, of a contractual intergroup ordering of society, to the last one, of a supergroup government, can be indicated as follows: (1) formation, through the accumulation of wealth, of patrimonial dominations, economically capable of financing a group of followers, (2) increase in the mobility of people and goods, generating, besides conquest by warlike peoples, professional differentiation in the communities and among communities, migrations to non-kin groups, and formation of clients who depend on chiefs of adopted communities, without kinship bonds to other lineages, (3) existence of natural conditions especially favorable to large and permanent organized settlements of people, and (4) emergence of new religious beliefs, based on territorial and pantribal gods believed to be leading and protecting the community directly or to be doing so through the intermediation of the king's magic powers, which were considered hereditarily transmissible.

This review of the main analytical and historical aspects of social groups and the elementary forms of authority points out very clearly the correspondence between an ontogenetic and a phylogenetic approach. The current characteristics of the group, as expressed in our definition and in the enumeration of its six major component elements, can also be found in the primitive group. Let us note only that the acknowledgment of belonging to a group is perfectly observable among nonhuman groups, and the meaningfulness acquired by symbolic communication in the most primitive forms of human interaction stresses the subjective content of the earliest Paleolithic bands.

The principle of group statics is entirely supported by prehistoric and anthropological evidence. As long as external conditions (chiefly the climate and the state of the other communities) and the internal conditions (the number of interacting people and their roles and skills) persisted, the Paleolithic bands also persisted unchanged. The very slow cultural evolution of the Paleolithic, the faster pace of the Neolithic, and the much faster rhythm of the early civilizations correspond to the relative duration of these phases. The same is true when the relatively static early civilizations are compared with the Hellenic or the Western civilizations. The functional basis of authority is also confirmed by the evolution of its early forms. Before the Neolithic differentiation of the terms of participation along occupational and status lines, which generated a corresponding differentiation in the regime of participation and in the resulting forms of authority, authority was noninstitutionalized and coextensive with lineage and familistic roles. Corresponding to the pre-differentiated forms of society were forms of collective enforcement by the whole community or by lineage, in support of the self-validating commands of charismatic leaders or traditional elders.

The principle of group dynamics is also confirmed empirically by the available historico-anthropological evidence. The four stages in the development of the relationship of participation represent fundamental changes in the pattern of relationships of primitive groups due to corresponding changes in their external and internal conditions. The first and most important of all these changes, the humanization of the hominids, was due, as has been stressed, to the triple process which began with the central behavioral innovation of food sharing in the mating dyad and led to toolmaking and symbolic communication. Similarly, intragroup regulation was due to exogamy and kinship solidarity; intragroup ordering, to the contractual arrangements of the sodalities, combined with the coordination provided by the self-validating commands of noninstitutionalized charismatic leaders.

It is particularly important, for the understanding of the elementary forms of authority and power, to analyze the process of transition from the third stage, intergroup ordering, to supergroup government, the fourth and last stage. This transition, as we have seen, was essentially a change from an *inter-partes* contractual arrangement to a *super-partes* authoritarian disposition. Tribal societies were egalitarian ones, in which the institutionalized differentiation of statuses corresponded to sex and age groups. Chiefdoms, the intermediary stage, were differentiated societies. They presented the distinction between (1) the hereditary chief, his family, and his lineage and (2) the commoners. They also manifested various other differentiations resulting from the growing social complexity that arose out of the agricultural revolution: the increase of trade, the economic specializations in and among communities, and the occupational differentiation between magicians and warriors. What prevented chiefdoms from having a centralized system of enforcement was the fact that legitimate coercion was still dependent on kinship bonds and general consensus. Overcoming the familistic barrier and obtaining a supergroup validity proved to be a very difficult and complex achievement, which required two distinct and cumulative conditions.

One of these two conditions was of an operational nature and consisted in the formation of social groups unconnected by kinship bonds to the other lineages of a community. We have seen that these groups originated in two different ways. In some cases, they were formed by migrants from other communities, who joined their adopted community as clients of the local chiefs, on whom they depended entirely and to whom they were linked by exclusive bonds of loyalty, in a relationship which, following the general rule of lineal transmission, became hereditary. Once the criteria of validity were adjusted to correspond with the new sociocultural conditions emerging with the copper age and the urban revolution, this clientele system permitted the formation of a body of implementers of the decisions of the authority. In other cases, groups that were not bonded by kin relationships to other lineages of the community originated through the conquest of peasant communities by warlike bands of herdsmen or hillsmen. In such cases, the intruders were not dependent clients of the local chiefs but became a governing aristocracy, and the military authority of the conquerors' chiefs was institutionalized and sacralized, according to religious beliefs that will be subsequently considered. In both cases, the authority of the chief acquired conditions for the systematic and institutionalized implementation of decisions. If we remember our study in Chapter 3 of the structure of authority, we can see that this development was tantamount to completing and putting into operation the system of authority in the social system. As we then saw (particularly in Figure 1), the input-output flux of commands from the ruler to the ruled and supports from the ruled to the ruler is processed by the mediation of the officials, who implement the decisions, perform public services, and extract the revenues.

The other of the two cumulative conditions was of an axiological nature and consisted in the formation of a religious foundation for the validity of the ruler. The cultural development of the original sexual taboos that led to exogamic practices brought about the formation of the family system and provided the basis for the institutional organization of primitive societies up to the tribal level. Further sociocultural development in the process of the organization of the polity, as we have seen, could no longer be provided by the values of the familistic system. Superfamilistic authority needed superfamilistic validity. The foundation for this new validity was provided by the new religious beliefs that came to be shaped along with the transition from Neolithic conditions to the beginning of urbanization.

As we have seen in the two examples of Mesopotamia and Egypt, either priestly corporations, in the name of the new gods, or the deified kings, as incarnations of the god, were able to establish a sacred system in which the magic of propitiating and obtaining the benevolence of the gods supported both the orderly functioning of the polity and the orderly functioning of the natural elements. Civilization, in its origins, is essentially a sacred and teleological closed system of manipulative propitiation of the gods, by the hereditarily transmitted magic powers of priests or godly kings, for preserving the physical and the moral order, social and individual life, and the otherworldly immortality of souls.

Founding beliefs of the polity

Although there are several fascinating aspects to the founding beliefs of the polity, I will restrict myself, for the purposes of this book, to briefly comment on three of them: (1) the coextensiveness of factual and value beliefs and hence, as far as authority is concerned, of validity and power, (2) the coexistence of two unconnected systems of causality, and (3) some correspondences between the origin of the polity and differing explanatory theories.

First, the coextensiveness of factual and value beliefs, as was shown by Lucien Lévy-Bruhl (1921), is one of the well-known characteristics of primitive thought. It lies on a pansubstantialism that envisages all occurrences, physical and moral, as produced by a supernatural activating entity. As has already been noted, this way of thinking passed from Paleolithic demonistic animism to the Neolithic female divinities and then to the great gods of the earlier religions. As Frankfort (1956) observed, the Egyptian vision of reality presented a cosubstantialist continuum from Nun, the undifferentiated abysmal waters, to the gods that emerged from these waters, to nature, and to man. It was as if there were an eternal divine substance that took all states and forms, without net boundaries and in a way that permitted inconsistent manifestations, although various of these forms, those corresponding to the gods and to regular natural and moral phenomena, were permanent. The inherent properties of these permanent forms were the causes of both natural and moral occurrences. Hence the regulation of social affairs by inherent qualities, including the magical hereditary powers of priests and divine kings.

The religious foundation of the validity of the rulers, based on their magic capability for assuring the willingness of the gods to preserve the natural and the social order, was not a political stratagem of priests and kings. On the contrary, it was the emergence and development of these religious beliefs that permitted, given other objective conditions (as, particularly, the formation of an intermediary stratum of officials), the political evolution to supergroup authority and power. And it was because of the nature of these beliefs, which attributed the same divine causation to facts and values and held that these facts and values were kept in good order by the magical mediation of the rulers, that the authority to rule was coextensive with the power to do so. The magical vision of reality of the earlier civilizations prevented them, at the same time, from distinguishing political validity from political power and allegiance from enforcement. This does not mean that force was not used to overthrow, through revolution or conquest, a legitimate ruler. As we will see momentarily, these civilizations had two unconnected systems of causality. Revolutions and conquests, however, were always the expression of a belief in the inherent magical powers and therefore authority of a certain leader. If the revolution was successful, it just proved the superiority of the winner's magical powers over the defeated chief.

The second aspect that I will make a brief reference to concerns the two unconnected systems of causality. The earlier civilizations retained, along with other forms of primitive thought, an unconnected dualism in their causal explanation. There was an everyday understanding of causality, which was used in a topical and pragmatic form for daily instrumental purposes. This was the commonsense homo faber adjustment of means to ends, resulting from the observed relationships of dependence of consequents to antecedents, which afforded the making, use, and improvement of tools and the development of all sorts of skills, including engineering, medical, and military ones. And there was a metaphysical causality, of a magico-religious nature, which provided the ultimate explanation for everything, including commonsense causality, but which was not related to the former by any empirically observable or analytically consistent relationship. Generals relied, as today, on the weapons of their armies, the number of their soldiers, and other objectively effective factors for winning battles. But victory was provided by the gods, because of the greater magical strength of the priests and the king of the winners. In addition to the religious foundations of ancient authority, this double system of causality provides another illustration of the principle discussed at the end of Chapter 1: the mutual dependence of the regime of participation and the regime of values. The differentiation of Neolithic society, in the process of transition to civilization, established a new regime of participation, with the king and the high priests at the top, the officials in the middle, and the peasants at the bottom. The regime of values followed a concomitant and interrelated course, with the emergence and development of beliefs centered around the magico-religious causality of the gods and the magical means to propitiate them.

The third aspect which I would like to comment on concerns the comparison of our historico-anthropological survey of the formation of primitive authority and some differing theories on the nature and origin of the polity. It is not my purpose to review, even very briefly, all the theories discussed at the beginning of Chapter 3. I just want to refer, in the first place, to the differing views of the equilibrium and functionalist theories, on the one hand, and the conflict theories, on the other hand. In the second place, I will make a comment on the contractualist's theories and controversies concerning the state of nature.

As we studied more extensively in Chapter 3, the central opposition between equilibrium theorists and functionalists, on the one hand, and conflict theorists, on the other hand, lies in the fact that the former understand authority as a functional requirement of any social system, providing its goal-achieving function, whereas the conflict theories stress the domination of the ruled by the rulers as the basic fact of any political system. It is interesting to observe that our analysis of the group association and the subsequent survey of the formation of authority in the primitive groups support both views as being partially true. Our analytical discussion of authority in the social group led us to the same conclusion as the functionalists. And the historico-anthropological survey showed that original authority was based on self-validating commands. With the transition from intergroup ordering to supergroup government, authority was no longer based on self-validating commands but was believed to be conferred either by the divine nature of the king or by his sacred magical powers which gave him the capacity to provide divine protection. Confirming the conflict view, however, we have seen that as soon as a superfamilistic association that is, a real polity, was achieved, the former equality of tribal societies was suppressed, and in its place rose a deeply differentiated society, whose top members had a divine or quasi-divine nature and whose lower strata had neither rights nor even an ontological reality of their own, because their souls were not inherently immortal but would only become so by the sheer dispensation of the godly king. This partial reconciliation of these two opposing views confirms my former statement on this question that only a higher synthesis, leading to a conflict-functionalist model, can give an adequate representation to the phenomenon of society.

A last word should be said now about the contractualists' theories and controversies concerning the state of nature. The point in question is, in the first place, whether man precedes society, as the various contractualist theories would suggest, or whether society precedes or is coeval with man. Putting aside terminological tautologies (human society cannot, by definition, precede the existence of human beings), we have seen how, anthropologically, the hominids evolved into humanity within the prehuman society of the primates' bands. In a sense, therefore, later bio-anthropological evidence confirmed the view of Aristotle and of those who supported the natural sociability of man. It is interesting to note, however, that both Rousseau's intuition of a precontractual *état naturel*, characterized by equality, in contrast to socially imposed inequalities, and Hobbes' state of presocial universal war, in contrast to the authoritatively imposed order of society, correspond to salient characteristics of the transition from the pre-authoritative arrangements of the stage of intergroup ordering to the authority-based stage of supergroup government. In fact, societies without a centralized enforceable authority were, on the one hand, egalitarian societies, while, on the other hand, they were constantly ravaged by intergroup warfare because of the nonexistence of a proper political jurisdiction.

NOTES

[1] See Gurvitch's (1958, vol. I, p. 187) definition: "Le groupe est une unité collective réelle, mais partielle, directement observable et fondée sur des attitudes collectives continues et actives, ayant une oeuvre commune à accomplir, unités d'attitudes, d'oeuvres et de conduite qui constitue un cadre social structurable, tendant vers une cohésion relative des manifestations de la sociabilité." (The group is a real collective unity, but partial, directly observable and founded on active and continued collective behaviors, having a common work to accomplish, unities of behavior, works and behaviors that constitute a structurable social framework, tending toward a relative cohesion of the manifestations of sociability.) MacIver and Page's (1962, p. 14) definition: "By a group we mean any collection of social beings who enter into distinctive social relationship with one another." And, subsequently, their remark: "A group, then, as we understand it, involves reciprocity between its members."

[2] Commands are functionally indispensable in any collective goal-achieving action, but most situations and actions allow alternative methods of coordination, which severely limits the possibilities for self-validation.

[3] See Theodosius Dobzhansky (1965b, pp. 162 ff.).

[4] See Jacquetta Hawkes (1963), particularly chap. 5 of *Prehistory*. See also Elman R. Service, 1967, pp. 34 ff.

[5] See V. Gordon Childe (1951, pp. 59 ff.) and (1942, chaps. 2 and 3).

[6] See Service (1967, pp. 110 ff.).

[7] Primitive societies probably had, like contemporary primitives, migrations of nobles from their original chiefdom to other villages interested, for prestige reasons, in having a noble. See Lucy Mair (1966, pp. 125 ff.). See also, I. Schapera (1967) and E. A. Haebel (1967).

[8] See Childe, (1951, pp. 59 ff.).

[9] See Service (1967, pp. 143 ff.) and Mair (1966, pp. 61 ff.).

[10] See Henri Frankfort *et al.* (1956, pp. 11 ff.).

[11] See Thorkild Jacobsen, "Mesopotamia," in Frankfort *et al.* (1966).

[12] See Frankfort *et al.* (1956, pp. 71 ff.) and Frankfort (1961, pp. 30 ff.).

5

Systems Analysis

INTRASOCIETAL EXCHANGES

Problems

We can now approach the last part of our general view of the polity, outlining it as a societal subsystem which receives certain basic inputs from the other societal subsystems and provides them with its own basic outputs and, at the same time, is itself a system within a flux of internal inputs and outputs. With this systems-analysis approach, already adopted in our attempt to obtain a general view of society in Chapter 1, we will use two reference parameters for our present inquiry: the systems analysis of society as a whole and the systems analysis of that societal subsystem that is the political system.

The first point, concerning the polity as a societal subsystem, brings us back to the study of societal interchanges and to our former discussion of the main views presented on the subject, notably the relevant contribution of Talcott Parsons. The second point leads us to the systems analysis of the polity, which represents one of the most if not the most salient feature of contemporary political analysis, and hence to the discussion of the pioneer views of David Easton (1953, 1965a and 1965b) and of their elaboration by Gabriel Almond and G. B. Powell, Jr. (1966).

Let us first consider the process of social interchange and the position of the polity within it. For this it is advisable to briefly recapitulate the findings in Chapter 1. As we saw, society consists of four structural planes: the cultural, participational, political, and economic. Each plane is the analytical locus of a subsystem of the whole, and each subsystem is in itself a complex system with its own subsystems. Each of the structural planes is analytically the locus of production and allocation of some of the basic societal valuables. At the cultural plane the corresponding subsystem produces and allocates beliefs (factual, value, and norm beliefs) and symbols. At the participational plane actors, roles, and statuses are produced and allocated in affective, evaluative, or playful ways. At the political plane commands are produced and allocated, and at the economic plane, commodities. A specific medium corresponds to each of these classes of basic valuables, both for their evaluation and for their exchange. Culture, prestige, power, and money are, respectively, the specific media for the cultural, participational, political, and economic planes. There is, moreover, a fifth medium, influence, a secondary medium, which is a medium of media and is a consequence of the interchangeability of valuables of different planes and, therefore, of the different media.

We have also seen that society presents two dimensions. Horizontally, it is a system of the four subsystems referred to above. Vertically, it has two levels of depth: (1) the situational level, which is the analytical locus, for each subsystem, of its respective regime and, for society as a whole, of the social regime and (2) the actional level, which is, analytically, the locus where social interaction actually takes place. Each subsystem supplies the others with its valuables and demands valuables from them (boundary exchanges). At the same time, there is, in each subsystem, a constant interrelation between the structure of its respective regime and the current process of exchanging valuables (vertical exchanges). Although the subsystem's regime regulates its processes of exchange, these processes, as has been discussed in chapter 2, incrementally or dialectically affect and change the regime. Because of the principle of congruence, which interrelates the four structural planes, changes in the regime of one of the subsystems affect the other subsystems. Either the changes produce a congruent change in the other subsystems, or the changed regime suffers a regression to its former state. Otherwise, as a third alternative, the society's integration breaks down.

What concerns us now are the boundary exchanges between subsystems, particularly with reference to the polity. According to our recapitulation, the polity supplies commands to the other subsystems in the form of the various decisions of the authorities or, in periods of trouble, in the form of competing injunctions for supreme command. In exchange, the polity receives from the other subsystems their respective basic valuables: actors, roles, and statuses from the participational one; beliefs and symbols from the cultural one; commodities from the economy. These exchanges are in terms of both the basic valuables and their respective media: exchanges of money, power, culture, or prestige for each other. And they are exchanges both of actual valuables or media and of commitments concerning their future availability, as in the case of credit with economic exchanges. The concept and the practice of credit is also applicable, although not with the same accuracy (due to the more qualitative than quantitative nature of the concerned valuables), to the exchange of commitments concerning power, culture, and prestige. Alliances and treaties of mutual defense, both between parties of the same country or between countries, are typical examples of political credit. Social credit consists in claimable expectations of prestige or deference due either to ascribed situations, as that of heir of a social position, or to various forms of exchange, within the participational plane or between boundaries. Typical cases of exchanges within the participational are obligations resulting from favors and gifts; by granting a favor, the donor obtains a social credit, which is payable by deference or by gifts and favors in return. Social credit obtained through exchanges between boundaries is the usual form of upward participational mobility available to people who come from low prestige situations but have a greater wealth of other media. It is through such exchanges that successful or newly important politicians, functionaires, intellectuals, or businessmen who come from lower classes, or statuses, usually open up the way to their admission into exclusive higher class circles. Social credit is accumulated in exchange for power, money, or culture and is later used to consolidate the ascending actor in a higher status position.

Similarly, cultural credit consists in the obtention of relatively claimable expectations of a cultural status or performance, either by intercultural or by boundary exchanges. The most usual form of intercultural exchanges with claimable cultural expectations, among poets and musicians, for instance, consists in the reciting or playing of the work of an author by another author of the same relative cultural status. Cultural credit, like economic credit, follows the estimated solvency of the bearer. Reputedly rich people have financial credit in a way similar to the way reputedly cultured people have cultural credit. This explains the large audiences for famous artists or lecturers, the fast selling of books by famous writers, and so forth. Exchanges between boundaries are as usual with cultural credit as they are with social credit, the most common case being the exchanges between men who are influential because of their money, prestige, and power and culturally influential people, in a Maecenas-poet sort of relationship.

Societal interchange

This circular understanding of societal interchanges and its application to the polity, both in its boundary exchanges and in its internal fluxes, is principally due to the contribution of Talcott Parsons. We have already discussed Parsons' general views and his conception of society in Chapter 1. We will now make a brief critical reference to Parsons' ideas on the polity in order to see to what extent they fit what has been studied up to now.

Parsons' political studies, spread in part throughout his sociological writings, are contained particularly in his more recent papers[1] and in his contribution to Easton's anthology *Varieties of Political Theory* (1966). His views are essentially an application of his conception of the four basic subsystems (pattern-maintenance, integrative, adaptive, and goal-achievement) to the position and functions of the polity (goal-achievement subsystem) in society. The polity receives resources from the economy (adaptive subsystem) and provides mobilization. It receives support from the integrative subsystem and provides political decisions. It receives legitimation from the pattern-maintenance subsystem and provides codification. Ultimately, these exchanges imply exchanges of media, according to a value principle and a coordinating standard, by which factors and products supplied by each of the subsystems are controlled by the others. (See Table 17 for Parsons' table of the media as sanctions.)

It would be alien to the nature of the present study to attempt a detailed or systematic appraisal of Parsons' views on the boundary exchanges of the polity. Let me just make some basic comments in order to make clear what aspects of the Parsonian scheme have been retained or changed in the picture presented in this book and why. The first point to be stressed, of course, refers to the kind of subsystems Parsons adopted. That matter has already been discussed in Chapter 1. Parsons' subsystems are analytically justified at a high level of abstraction. As he contends, the structural functions performed by his subsystems are the necessary functions of any integrated self-adjustable system. Although it is useful, for studies dealing with diverse levels of reality, to keep the most abstract categories representative of such levels, it is more convenient, for empirical studies of a specific level of reality, as human societies, for instance, to use the categories that are immediately applicable to that particular level. It is advantageous to call the four structural functions or planes of society by their specific societal functions—cultural, participational, political, and economic—rather than to use the too abstract general categories of any possible self-adjustable system.

The second point I would like to consider briefly concerns Parsons' view on the media interchange between the polity and the other subsystems. As far as the media are concerned, it has already been explained that culture and prestige are considered the media corresponding to cultural and participational exchanges. Influence is not a primary but a secondary medium, resulting from the control and exchangeability of any other primary media. As far as value principles are concerned, it seems that integrity and effectiveness are not sufficiently representative of their respective value systems. Integrity is the value principle of action values. Action values, however, do not exhaust the cultural system, which contains beliefs and symbols unconcerned with integrity. What is common to all beliefs that deserve to be believed in and to all symbols that are meaningful is validity. The same kind of limitation is applicable to effectiveness. Effectiveness is also the characteristic of several nonpolitical relationships, as the physical ones submitted to the law of causality. And many political relationships are not submitted to effectiveness, as those concerning ineffective acts or situations: the breaking down of a law or of the legal order, or, conversely, the adjustment of a behavior to its legal norm in spite of the material ineffectiveness of the behavior. The value principle of power results from its compulsory character, whether effective or not, and so, the value principle is compulsoriness. As far as coordination standards are concerned, consensus seems to be a particular case of participational coordination. In various regimes of participation the negatively discriminated classes, although keeping their group membership, do actually oppose the regime, in spite of maintaining enough solidarity with the system. Consensus, therefore, is not always the coordination standard of solidarity, since a statute can be preserved in spite of dissension. Statutory status, therefore, should be acknowledged as the coordination standard.

A final observation, concerning Parsons' view of the interchange of media,

Table 17 Parsons' table of the media as sanctions

Media in Hierarchical Control	Components of Media and Interchange Reciprocals		Messages (Sanctions)				Types of Sanction and of Effect
	Codes		Source		Destination		
	VALUE PRINCIPLE	COORDINATION STANDARD	FACTORS CONTROLLED		PRODUCTS CONTROLLED		
Commitments L*	Integrity	Pattern Consistency	Wages	A	Consumer's demand	A	Negative intentional (activation of commitments)
			Justification of loyalties	I	Claims to loyalties	I	
Influence I*	Solidarity	Consensus	Commitments to valued association	L	Commitment to common values	L	Positive intentional (persuasion)
			Policy decisions	G	Political support	G	
Power G*	Effectiveness	Sovereignty	Interest demands	I	Leadership responsibility	I	Negative situational (securing compliance)
			Control of productivity	A	Control of fluid resources	A	
Money A*	Utility	Solvency	Capital	G	Commitment of services	G	Positive situational (inducement)
			Labor	L	Expectation of goods	L	

*The symbols L, I, G, and A, in Parsons' Table refer, respectively, to Pattern Maintenance (laws of cultural and motivational commitments), Integrative Subsystem, Goal-Attainment Subsystem, and Adaptive Subsystem.

SOURCE: Talcott Parsons, "The Political Aspect of Social Structure," p. 111, Fig. 3, in David Easton (ed.) *Varieties of Political Theory* (Englewood Cliffs, N.J.: Prentice-Hall, 1966).

refers to the necessity of correlating each medium with the essential or basic functions that it permits the exchange of. For that purpose, as will be seen later, I suggest a different flux of functions and a distinct classification of the respective types of sanction.

It is possible, now, to pass on to the direct analysis of societal interchanges and to present an alternative picture of the process.

At the most general level this picture presents us with a double flux of exchanges from each of the subsystems to the other subsystems, including the basic valuables of each system and their respective media. Figure 2 gives a graphic representation of the interchanges.

Figure 2 *Flux of Societal Interchanges*

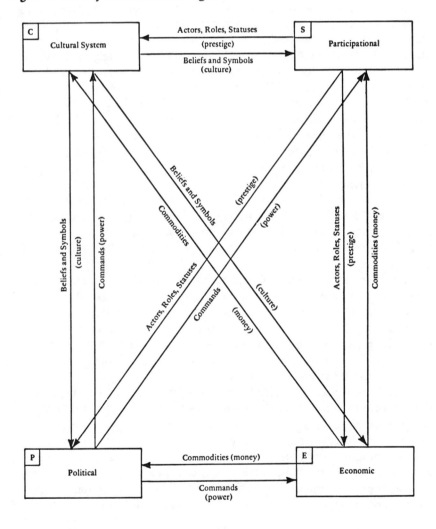

The four sets of basic valuables and their respective media, plus the implicit content of influence carried by each medium, interchanged as shown in Figure 2, comprehend essentially those valuables indispensable for the working of the other subsystems, although, in a general way, they include all the kinds of valuables produced in each subsystem. In other words, although the input-output flow of intrasocietal exchanges includes, in principle, all the available valuables, it is a process oriented for the exchange between boundaries of the essential valuables each subsystem needs from the others to perform its societal functions. So, the boundary exchanges between the cultural subsystem and the participational one consist, essentially, in the input to the former of formulators and propagators of beliefs and symbols, as well as of believers (cultural actors), and the output to the latter of integrative values. Boundary exchanges between the cultural subsystem and the polity consist, essentially, in the input to the former of value enforcement and the output to the latter of legitimity. Between the cultural and the economic subsystems, the interchange consists in the input to the former of installational and operative facilities and the output to the latter of institutionalization and scientific-technological (or magico-religious) orientation. The participational subsystem receives integrative values from the cultural subsystem and supplies it with formulators, propagators, and believers. The inputs from the political subsystem to the participational are internal order and external defense; the outputs from the participational to the political subsystem are decision makers, implementers, and the ruled (political actors). Consumption facilities are the inputs from the economic subsystem to the participational, and controllers, managers, and workers (economic actors) are the output from the participational subsystem to the economic one. The polity's input from the cultural subsystem is legitimity, and its output to the cultural subsystem is value enforcement. Finally, the interchanges between the economy and the polity comprehend inputs to the former of legal order and public services and output from the former of solvency. These interchanges are graphically represented in Table 18.

These interchanges fill a basic functional need of each of the receiving subsystems, while transferring from each of the subsystems the essential valuables produced therein. As was sharply pointed out by Parsons (in Easton, 1966, pp. 110 ff. and Fig. 3), these between boundary exchanges are subject to a specific value principle and coordination standard and provide a particular type of sanction or effect. Introducing the previously mentioned changes, we have the picture represented graphically in Table 19.

This table is sufficiently clear to be understood without additional explanations. I will just comment very briefly on the demanded and supplied functions and the types of sanction and effects provided by each of the media and their corresponding valuables, plus, in each case, the implicit content of influence. The cultural subsystem needs the function of performance to display and personify its beliefs and symbols, and that function is filled by cultural actors provided by the participational subsystem. It needs enforcement for some of its fundamental values, provided by power. And operative means, obtainable by

Table 18 *Inputs and outputs in the societal interchange of essential valuables*

Outputs ↑ Inputs ↓ Subsystems

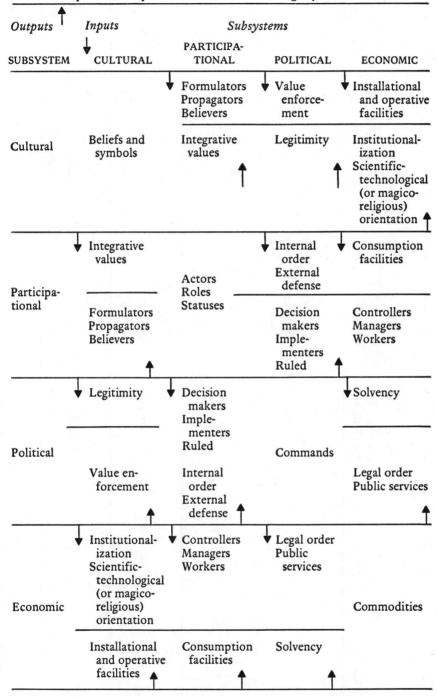

SUBSYSTEM	CULTURAL	PARTICIPATIONAL	POLITICAL	ECONOMIC
Cultural		↓ Formulators Propagators Believers	↓ Value enforcement	↓ Installational and operative facilities
	Beliefs and symbols	Integrative values ↑	Legitimity	Institutionalization Scientific-technological (or magico-religious) orientation ↑
Participational	↓ Integrative values		↓ Internal order External defense	↓ Consumption facilities
	———————	Actors Roles Statuses	———————	
	Formulators Propagators Believers ↑		Decision makers Implementers Ruled ↑	Controllers Managers Workers
Political	↓ Legitimity	↓ Decision makers Implementers Ruled		↓ Solvency
	———————		Commands	———————
	Value enforcement ↑	Internal order External defense ↑		Legal order Public services ↑
Economic	↓ Institutionalization Scientific-technological (or magico-religious) orientation	↓ Controllers Managers Workers	↓ Legal order Public services	
	———————			Commodities
	Installational and operative facilities ↑	Consumption facilities ↑	Solvency ↑	

Table 19 *Societal interchange of basic functions*

Subsystems and Media	Codes		Functions		Types of Sanction and of Effect
Implied Values and Exchanged Services	VALUE PRINCIPLE	COORDINATION STANDARD	DEMANDED	SUPPLIED	
			From	*To*	
Culture (influence) C	Validity	Consistency	Performance S Enforcement P Operability E	Respectability S Legitimacy P Rationalization E	Validation
Prestige (influence) S	Solidarity	Statutory status	Respectability C Security P Subsistence E	Performance C Support P Labor E	Integration
Power (influence) P	Compulsoriness	Sovereignty	Legitimacy C Support S Solvency E	Enforcement C Security S Order E	Ordination
Money (influence) E	Utility	Solvency	Rationalization C Labor S Order P	Operability C Subsistence S Solvency P	Utilization

money. The participational subsystem, in order to preserve its statutory standard, needs respectability, which is obtained from culture, security, which is provided by power, and means of subsistence, which is obtainable with money. To maintain compulsoriness, which is dependent on sovereignty, the polity requires legitimacy from culture, support from the participational subsystem, and financial solvency. Finally solvency is a standard requiring rationalization[2] from culture for its relationship with the natural and human environment. It is dependent on labor to make commodities, and on order to coordinate action and preserve its results. In these interchanges of basic functions each of the subsystems, by its specific medium and valuables, and implied influence, brings to the social system the types of sanction and effect indicated in Table 19: cultural validation, social integration, political ordination, and economic utilization.

THE POLITICAL SYSTEM

Easton's views

The introduction of the category of system in political science is the most recent manifestation of the expansion of the structural views in the social sciences. David Easton, "the first political scientist to analyze politics in explicit system terms,"[3] made the pioneering contribution in three successive books. Concerning these works, Easton said:[4] *The Political System* (1953) "sought to present the case for general theory in political science. The second, *A Framework for Political Analysis* (1965), laid out the major categories in terms of which it has seemed to me that such a theory might be developed. In the present book [*A Systems Analysis of Political Life* (1965)], the task will be to put that structure of concepts to work and, in doing so, to elaborate them further so that they can be more readily applied to empirical situations."

Easton understands the political system "as those interactions through which values are authoritatively allocated for a society" (1965b, p. 21).

The political system is an open and self-adjustable system that works within an environment. This environment is twofold: (1) the intrasocietal environment, including the ecological, the biological, the personality, and the social system and (2) the extrasocietal environment, including the international political, the international ecological, and the international social systems.

Easton points out two of the salient features of the political system. On the one hand, it is a system of processes of exchanges and transactions. Exchanges are bilateral between the system and the environment. Transactions move from one direction to another within the political system. On the other hand, this system is subject to disturbances and stresses, which can disrupt its equilibrium, requiring compensatory reactions within the system in order to prevent its fragmentation. Disturbances are influences from the environment. They can be favorable, or they can strain the system. Stresses are internal effects resulting from the pushing of essential variables beyond their critical range.

The components of the political system are (1) inputs, (2) conversions of demands, and (3) outputs. Inputs include (1) demands and (2) supports. Demands are formulated expectations addressed to the authorities. Although in any political system at any moment there are innumerable wants and expectations, most of them do not achieve the social level of effective formulation. Once they do, they become demands. Demands are possible sources of stress to a system. Volume stress results when the number of demands exceeds the system's capacity for processing. Content stress can be caused by the lack of available time for processing the demands. Demands can also cause stress because of their complexity and the difficulty of attending to them, because they conflict with the system or its prevailing features, and because they drain the system's limited resources.

Supports, oriented toward certain political objects, are the second kind of input to a political system. They can be positive or negative, attitudinal or active, overt or covert. They express positive and negative reactions of the political community toward certain objects. These objects are the authorities, the regime, and the political community itself. The authorities include the upper and the lower strata of those making and implementing political decisions. The regime includes values, norms, and the system of authority.

The process of conversion consists in the ways by which the political system uses its resources, including supports, to refuse, to satisfy, or to modify the demands addressed to the authorities. Basically, demands addressed to the authorities are treated in four different ways. (1) Some demands are met directly, either positively or negatively, as, for instance, jobs given or refused. (2) Most of them are converted first into a general demand and given a general solution with the making of a general rule. The general ruling, however, is sometimes preceded (3) by the conversion of demands into issues of general interest, so that they reach the importance required for a general ruling, as in the case of civil rights. Sometimes, (4) demands are reduced first and later converted into general issues, as welfare expectations.

The usual way of meeting demands is by their reduction. There are three forms of reduction. The first, collection and combination, consists in putting together similar or comparable demands and giving them a general treatment. The second is intrasystemic gatekeeping. Between the political system and the other societal systems and, internally, between the various subsystems of the political systems, there are gates, and passage through these gates depends on the fulfillment of certain requirements controlled by gatekeepers. Courts and parliaments are such intrasystemic gates, controlled by judges and deputies. The various departments and offices of the administration are other gates, with their gatekeepers. In this method of reduction the demands are submitted to the requirements necessary for passage through the convenient gates with the result that those demands that are incompatible with the system or its resources are obstructed. Finally, the third method of reduction is issue formulation. As has been anticipated, it consists in upgrading the level of importance of the demands, on the initiative of the authorities (Medicare) or of sectors of the political community (civil rights), so that the demands acquire general significance and become amenable to (positive or negative) solution through the adoption of general rules.

The conversion process can, in itself, bring about an erosion of support, because of (1) failure to meet the demands of important members of the political community, (2) failure to anticipate (and to meet) relevant demands, or (3) inappropriateness of the authorities' decisions. Failures cause cleavages in attitudes and conflicts among groups, which are dangerous to the integrity of the system. Political systems have three ways of meeting the erosion of their support: (1) direct reduction of cleavages, (2) building reservoirs of support, and (3) rewarding supporters. Direct reduction of cleavages can be achieved either by a structural change in the political system, making the system more flexible or differentiating it, or by the suppression through repressive means of the minority sectors causing the cleavage. Building reservoirs of support (the most important of the three) involves the use of political credit and leads to diffuse support. Rewarding supporters is to allocate direct incentives to followers of the authority and the regime, at the expense of the political system.

Easton distinguishes three sources of diffuse support: ideologies, structural reasons, and personal qualities. He envisages two objects for such support: the regime and the authorities. Ideologies can be of two kinds: partisan, based on a set of preferred policies, and legitimating, consisting of a set of founding values. Structural reasons concern the legality and legitimacy of the regime and thus benefit the incumbent authorities. Personal qualities, such as charismatic appeal, bring support to the authorities and thus to the regime they represent.

Outputs, the third general component of the political system, are the acts with which the authorities, by the process of conversion, try to meet the demands of the political community, including those generated by the authorities themselves. Outputs are essentially of two kinds: authoritative and associated. The former are binding decisions of various modalities from general laws to executive and judicial decisions on particular cases. Associated outputs are not directly binding but have a referential function. They consist in policies, rationales, and commitments by which the authorities define their objectives and propose a course of action or try to justify their objectives or to obtain support for them or for the regime or for themselves.

Considered from another point of view, outputs represent the reaction of the authorities to the strains on the political system created by stresses or cleavages due to certain demands or by disturbances from the environment. The authorities react either to reestablish the former stage of equilibrium or to obtain a new equilibrium by means of structural adjustments. A double feedback takes place in the process. One is the feedback of information that the authorities use to check and correct the effectiveness of their outputs. The other is the feedback of the outcome of their outputs and the effect on the political community, on the inputs to the political system, and on its environment, adapting the system to the circumstances or changing the circumstances so they are more favorable to the system.

This very brief exposition of Easton's theories, mainly drawn from *A Systems*

Analysis of Political Life (1965b) but taking into account his previous work, is enough both for an understanding of their central points and for an evaluation of the importance of his contribution to the construction of a valuable paradigm for political science. Following the general lines of Parsons' structuralism and of his systems analysis, Easton designed a general framework which is a representative model of the political system and filled it with a comprehensive set of categories for the description and understanding of empirical processes. The fact that further studies, particularly Almond and Powell's *Comparative Politics* (1966), have brought about an enlargement and a modification of some of Easton's categories and their analytical development without changing his basic framework is a confirmation of the soundness of Easton's model.

It is not my purpose to present, even succinctly, a critique of Easton's theoretical framework. I will give a very condensed indication of Almond and Powell's further development of the systems analysis of the polity, and in conclusion, as an overall appraisal of the state of the science, I will formulate some remarks on the contribution of these writers. For the sake of permitting an easy comparison between Easton's and Almond's formulations, I will follow the same line of exposition for Almond that was adopted for Easton: (1) the political system, (2) inputs, (3) conversions, and (4) outputs.

Almond's views

Although their basic view of the political system is the same, Almond rejects Easton's innovational definition (authoritative allocation of values) of the system. Almond sticks to Max Weber's view and considers that the distinctive feature of the polity is the monopoly, controlled by the authorities, of the legitimate use of physical coercion. Almond, like Easton, considers the political system an open self-adjustable system surrounded by an intra- and an extra-societal environment. Almond elaborates more on the components of the political system. He distinguishes the content of the system from its functional aspects. The content components are: (1) political structures, (2) political culture, and (3) political actors. The political structure is the set of interrelated roles existing in any polity. The political culture, one of Almond's most important conceptual contributions, is understood as the underlying propensities of the system. It includes a triple set of orientations: (1) cognitive orientations, including what people believe the polity is, (2) affective orientations, including the feelings of the various sectors of the polity about the system and its elements, and (3) evaluative orientations, including the judgments and opinions about the political objects. The way people understand the polity and their position in it brings about three modes of participation: (1) the parochial, those who are only aware of and concerned with their immediate local social context, (2) the subject, those who are aware of the polity as a whole but consider themselves submitted to the will and guidance of the sovereign authority, and (3) the participants, those who understand the whole of the polity and consider themselves full active members of it. Almond points out that the political culture can vary along a scale from low to high degrees of integration. The higher degrees correspond to a very homogeneous and continuous political culture, both throughout the polity's territory and along its various strata and sectors. The lower degrees correspond to unintegrated political cultures, which are segmented both territorially and sectorially and present various conflicting subcultures as one passes from one region or sector to another one. The political actors, the third component of the political system, play, in various modalities of adjustment and conflict reflected in the political culture, the roles provided by the political structure.

Almond considers three major aspects from the functional point of view: (1) the system's capability, (2) the conversion process, and (3) the system's maintenance and adaptation. The system's capability comprehends its structural facilities for performing its major functions. These functions are: (1) regulative, concerning the system's capacity to order its own political community, (2) extractive, concerning its capacity to levy taxes and obtain services from the community, (3) distributive, concerning its capacity to transfer valuables from sectors, groups, and people to other sectors, groups, and people, and (4) responsive, concerning the extent to which the system can actually process its demands and formulate convenient symbolic outputs.

The conversion process includes the modalities by which inputs are attended to. Here we have another important contribution from Almond, which, clarifying Easton's ideas about the process of conversion, linked the new functional vision of the discipline with the view of the classics. As Almond pointed out, the process of conversion is twofold: On the one hand, there are the various operations by which demands are processed so that they will be attendable. On the other hand, there are the typical modalities by which attendable demands are actually attended to by the authorities. We will see that point again when we treat the process of conversion specifically.

The third functional aspect of the political system, maintenance and adaptation, is performed through (1) political socialization, by which social roles are taught, in various ways, to the members of the community and (2) political recruitment, by which roles are filled.

The structural and the functional aspects mentioned above provide an objective parameter to compare distinct political systems. Systems are more developed or less developed according to: (1) whether they have more or less differentiated and specialized structures and roles, including a more or less secularized political culture, and (2) whether these structures and roles are more or less autonomous or subordinated to each other. This point is another significant contribution made by Almond. On the one hand, he introduced a dynamic variable in comparative political analysis, comparing systems in terms of the degree of their development, and, on the other hand, he overcame subjective or ethnocentric yardsticks of judgment, providing objective and relatively admeasurable criteria for this purpose. In Chapters 8 and 9 we will discuss this sort of problem in detail.

Concerning the inputs of the political system, Almond follows Easton's framework more closely. He adopts the same dual division between demands and supports, and his understanding of both is similar to Easton's. Since Almond obtained a more structured view of the functions of the system, he correspondingly distinguished four kinds of demands: (1) those for allocation of goods and services, as wages or education, (2) those for regulation of behaviors, as public safety, (3) those for political participation, as voting, and (4) those for communication, as obtaining and issuing information and opinions. Almond also adopts a fourfold distinction for supports: (1) material supports, as taxes, (2) supports for obedience, as to the law, (3) participatory supports, as voting, and (4) deference supports, as respecting the authorities and official symbols such as a country's flag.

In their chapter on conversion, Almond and Powell maintained Easton's framework but enlarged it both conceptually and analytically. To start with, as was mentioned, Almond gave a new formulation to the process of conversion, seeing in it, on the one hand, the typical ways in which most demands are given conditions of attendability and, on the other hand, the typical ways in which they are actually attended to by the authorities. This process is expressed in the following set of conversion functions: (1) interest articulation, (2) interest aggregation, (3) rule making, (4) rule application, (5) rule adjudication, and (6) communication.

Interest articulation is the function by which actors and groups wishing to give to their wants and expectations starting conditions of attendability formulate and address them to the authorities in ways compatible with their purpose. Interest articulation involves, essentially: (1) interest groups, from self-representation to institutions, (2) channels of communication, from physical demonstration to mass media, and (3) styles of communication, including several typical alternatives.

Interest aggregation is equivalent to Easton's reduction: conversion of several demands into a general one that can be taken care of by a general decision. In this respect Almond stresses: (1) the agencies of aggregation for the public, which are political parties, and the bureaucracies of the authorities, (2) the styles of aggregation, which are (a) pragmatic bargaining, (b) absolute value orientation, and (c) traditionalism, and (3) the fact that conversion leads to stress in societies in which all demands are formulated in political terms and brought to the political system because of the inoperance of other intrasocietal systems, which is the usual case in underdeveloped countries.

The three subsequent functions (rule making, rule application, and rule adjudication) are the classic functions of government: legislative, executive, and judicial. Like all modern writers, Almond points out the importance of bureaucracies in the performance of governmental functions, not only in the executive branch but in the other ones as well. Following Merle Fainsod (1963), he distinguishes five types of bureaucracies: (1) representative, (2) party-state, (3) military-dominated, (4) ruler-dominated (as in ancient empires), and (5) ruling bureaucracies.

The sixth and last of the conversion functions is communication. Almond stresses three aspects of the subject: (1) the types of communication, (2) the degree of autonomy, which correlates positively with the neutrality and the effectivity of the media, and (3) the decisive influence of political communication on all other aspects of the polity.

Let us now take the last of the four major points in our comparative study of Easton's and Almond's systems analysis: Easton differentiated the outputs according to whether they are binding decisions or rationalizations, whereas Almond took a more analytical course, classifying the outputs in functional terms. He explicitly points out: (1) extractions, (2) regulations, (3) allocations, and (4) symbolic outputs (Easton's rationalizations). Although not expressly included in his classification, a sixth type of outputs, responses, should be added to the list, in the context of Almond's analysis.

Easton concludes his analysis with a study of the feedback concerning the impact of the authorities' decisions on the polity and its environment and the flux of information to the authorities about the outcome of their decisions. Almond is interested in obtaining a final comparative classification of the various types of political systems, affording the measurement of their relative levels of political development. His two major variables, as has been mentioned, are (1) structural differentiation and cultural secularization and (2) subsystem autonomy. His analysis brings about a general classification of political systems and a table of their comparative development.

Almond's classification of political systems (1966, p. 217) distinguishes the following major types:

I. Primitive	a) Primitive bands
	b) Segmentary systems (Nuer)
	c) Pyramidal systems (Ashanti)
II. Traditional	a) Patrimonial (Ouagadougou)
	b) Centralized bureaucracies (ancient empires)
	c) Feudal (twelfth-century France)
III. Modern	a) Secularized city-state (Athens)
	b) Mobilized modern systems
	b.1) Democratic systems (Britain)
	b.2) Authoritarian systems (U.S.S.R.)
	c) Premobilized modern systems (Ghana)

A brief critical discussion

This rapid synthesis of Easton's and Almond's major views on the political system allows some final comments on the matter. In making these comments, I will follow the same points considered formerly: (1) the political system, (2) inputs, (3) conversion, and (4) outputs.

It has already been stated that Easton's merit was the introduction of systems analysis in political science and the creation of a general framework of universal application for the analysis of all kinds of political systems. And it has been also mentioned that the subsequent contribution of Almond and Powell, while confirming the validity of Easton's framework, enlarged it both conceptually and analytically, giving, at the same time, a sort of condensed critical appraisal of the present state of the knowledge on the polity.

While keeping the same basic understanding of the political system, Almond did not retain Easton's dynamic definition of it as the system of authoritative allocation of values. He preferred, instead, to stick to the Weberian conception of a monopoly of the legitimate use of physical coercion. Now, what is interesting in Easton's definition is precisely his attempt to define the polity from the general point of view of the social system, particularizing the specific difference of the political by the *authoritative* way in which its process of allocation is performed. Almond's return to the Weberian concept of the legitimate monopoly of the means of physical coercion, besides missing the systemic articulation of the polity in the whole of society, has the disadvantage of assuming that a particular case—monopoly of the legitimate use of violence—defines the political genus. Illegitimate and conflicting (nonmonopolistic) use of violence, however, are also empirical occurrences of political systems which cannot be excluded from any definition. It is not acceptable, on the other hand, to limit the political, as Easton does, to the realm of values, which are not even, primarily, of political extraction, but of a cultural one. What is political in the political system is the way it works, as a social system, by authoritative decisions, in the same way that affective decisions are typical of the participational system. Political allocations, however, are not only or primarily of values, but of any other valuables and, ultimately, are not concerned with values, as such, although dealing with values, but with objective behaviors, whatever the value judgment of the actors may be.

Another aspect of Easton's and Almond's conceptions of the political system that deserves comment is the excessive autonomy they give to it. It is, of course, very clear in both concepts that the political system is an analytical system, and the social collectivity is the empirical reality in which the political system can be analytically isolated. But once this is admitted, the political system is treated as if it were equivalent to empirical systems, and the other societal subsystems are considered as a part of the political system's total environment, like the natural environment and alien societies. This implies a reification of the political system and conceals the structural interdependence that the four subsystems of society continuously keep among themselves. Almond, in a certain sense, is aware of the necessity to bridge the space between the polity and the other societal subsystems. His concept of the political culture introduces cultural elements in the polity, and his concepts of political socialization and political recruitment connect the political subsystem to the participational one. Political culture, however, is understood as being independent of the cultural system, rather than the political aspect of the cultural system. Whatever aspect of society we consider, we always see men interacting through social roles. The analytically indispensable distinction of each of the four planes of society requires our concomitant understanding of their structural interdependence and the constant flux of exchanges among them. This, I believe, was clearly pointed out in the first part of this chapter.

Concerning the inputs of the political system, which both Easton and Almond divide into demands and supports, it seems advisable to stress the distinction, not considered by them, between the "positional" and the "actional" form of inputs. Positional inputs are formulations of demands and of agreements or disagreements with political objects that are not followed by any sustained effort to promote their handling by the authorities. Actional inputs are demands sustained by pressure for their realization, tendentiously containing actual or virtual sanctions, as is typical in the action of pressure groups; and they are also manifestations of support of, or opposition to, some political object under conditions implying an actual or virtual tendency to attempt the organized implementation of such support or opposition. Besides its analytical significance, this distinction is essential for the characterization of political mobilization, which is itself a prerequisite, as will be seen in Chapter 9 of political development. Chart 3 presents this distinction.

The processes of conversion have been particularly well studied by these two writers. Some remarks would be appropriate about Almond's distinction between the types of value content in the political culture. He considers three typical forms: (1) pragmatic, (2) absolute value-oriented, and (3) traditional. The distinction is both empirically and analytically pertinent. Almond sees in this differentiation one major cause of the differences among political parties, bureaucracies, and processes of political transaction and of conversion. Pragmatic political cultures lead to objective confrontations of interest and issues, allowing the possibility of rational policies and reasonable compromises. Traditional political cultures are unaware of alternatives and of rational criteria and so have little capacity for self-improvement and self-development. Absolute value-oriented political cultures have a dogmatic approach, which neither allows for the rational appraisal of issues and conditions nor permits reasonable compromises.

Chart 3 *Inputs*

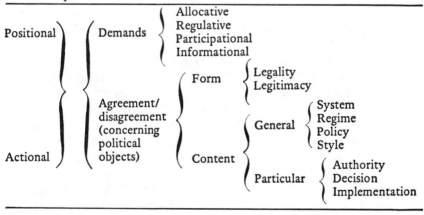

Although these typical features cannot be objected to in several respects (including, for instance, the fact that the appointed consequence of each type is tautologically contained in its description), they carry an ethnocentric bias, which must be pointed out. Higher cultural values and goals may or may not be susceptible to meaningful comparative judgments. This is a philosophical question, which in itself transcends the domain of political science. But, whatever the philosophical soundness of civilizations and cultures stressing the necessity of subordinating individual and collective life to certain absolute values, as in the Western culture in its (effective) Christian epochs, the political system of societies commanded by such a principle, like their goal-attainment system, cannot but manifest the same value orientation in their political culture. It would be inconsistent to suggest that a pragmatic political culture (supposing it could actually occur) would be more rational, in the context of such a dogmatic civilization, than a political culture adjusted to the general culture of the concerned society.

A second point concerning the ethnocentric bias of Almond's classification has to do with the relationship between the type of political culture and the degree of integration of the concerned society. Almond has observed very well that conflicting political subcultures express unintegrated societies. Now, a pragmatic political culture, besides being the result of cultural secularization as Almond has stressed, is also the result of the basic uniformity of value orientations of a society due to its higher integration and development. This being the case, the pragmatic approach tends to require the prerequisite of a relatively high integration and development; for societies lacking high integration and development, a political culture capable of generating development and integration cannot be of the pragmatic type but must assume the promotion of societal development as an ultimate goal and value.

I will now make a final comment concerning the question of outputs. Almond and Powell made a valuable contribution to Easton's theory of outputs, not only by elaborating it and adjusting it to a general functional view of the political system, but also by providing objective and roughly quantifiable criteria for comparing different systems and their relative degree of development. The two variables proposed by Almond, (1) structural differentiation and cultural secularization and (2) subsystems autonomy (which are actually three variables), would allow such comparisons.

Once again, I believe, we have a theoretical framework that is analytically consistent and can be used empirically with profit, but it has serious limitations because it is implicitly constructed from the point of view of developed societies currently presenting a high degree of subsystems autonomy. The limitations of that framework can be intuitively felt when one considers the uneasiness with which the comparative degree of development of Soviet Russia is evaluated in Almond and Powell's study. That matter will be discussed at length in Chapter 8, which deals with political development. For now, however, it can be stressed that the trouble with the indicators of political development adopted by Almond is that they do not permit the indispensable distinction between general and specific political development. Comparing political systems in terms of their political development actually implies two distinct admeasurements. One concerns the general degree of development of a polity, as far as it can be conveniently defined in empirically verifiable terms, compared to other polities. The other distinct admeasurement consists in comparing the specific fitness of a political system for the promotion, acceleration, or preservation of the overall development of the concerned society to other alternative political models *for the same society*, given the structural conditions of that society. The distinction between these two admeasurements expresses another distinction between political development as the political aspect of the overall development of a society and political development as a political condition and process for developing a society. In order to admeasure specific political development, it is essential to identify and quantify those aspects of the political system that are structurally and functionally conducive to the overall development of the concerned society. Subsystems autonomy, for instance, can in certain conditions be a negative factor or even an obstacle for developmental purposes.

COMPARATIVE POLITICS

A basic model for comparative analysis

Political systems have always been compared. Since political systems are the goal-achieving system of a society, the understanding of their structural and operational characteristics requires a functional approach, which evaluates the way in which they perform their goal-achieving activity, and such an evaluation cannot be done properly unless a political system is compared to other political systems. In this as in so many other areas, Aristotle, in his comparative study of constitutions and polities, was the pioneer of scientifically oriented comparative politics.

Whatever the relative merits of former attempts at comparative politics, however, that important branch of political science could not go beyond the existing limits of the discipline as a whole. Only after the introduction of systems analysis in political science did it become possible to make use of an objective set of relevant, empirically based, variables and categories, which provide a significant model of any political system and so permit the actual comparison of political systems. This basic political model, as has already been mentioned and will be considered in detail in Chapter 9, is also the analytical instrument permitting an objective and comparative evaluation of political development.

Almond and Powell (1966) and Eisenstadt (1964) have provided two distinct, but ultimately similar, schemes for an objective and general comparison of political systems. Almond speaks of two (but actually uses three) macrovariables: (1.a) structural differentiation, (1.b) cultural secularization, and (2) subsystems autonomy. Considering the most important typical forms of political systems, he analyzed, according to a classification that will be given later, whether they were comparatively low or high in the above-mentioned variables, and so he obtained a table (1966, p. 308) of systems showing their comparative degrees of structural differentiation, cultural secularization, and subsystem autonomy.

Eisenstadt uses three macrovariables: (1) structural differentiation, (2) political goals of rulers, and (3) type of legitimation. A closer analysis reveals that the variable of political goals includes, basically, the same data and aspects as Almond's subsystem autonomy, and Eisenstadt's types of legitimation roughly corresponds to Almond's cultural secularization.

These proposed schemes have the advantage of providing a general and objective set of significant variables for comparative politics, by using some of the same variables and categories adopted for the individual analysis of each system. That very advantage, however, points out, I would suggest, the necessity of using the same set of macrovariables for the two purposes. The set of variables required, and actually used by Almond and other writers, for the individual analysis of a political system is much more comprehensive than the above set proposed for comparative politics. In addition to the three macrovariables included in that scheme, others are just as necessary both for the description and understanding of an individual system and for comparing systems to each other.

I suggest that the relevant variables for systems analysis and for comparative politics, including comparative development, are reducible to eight macrovariables, classifiable in three sets of macrovariables, as indicated in Table 20. The first set of macrovariables, the operational variables, includes those macrovariables corresponding to the structural conditions determining the operational capacity of the political system and, as far as it is dependent on political action, of the society as a whole. The first of the macrovariables included in this set, roughly corresponding to Almond's secularization, concerns the extent to which the political system operates at a lower or higher level of rationality (rational orientation). The second macrovariable concerns the larger or smaller structural differentiation (1) of the political system vis-à-vis the other societies, (2) of the political system in its own society, vis-à-vis the other societal systems, and

---

Table 20 *Systems macrovariables*

1. *Operational Variables*

   A. Rational orientation
   B. Structural differentiation
   C. Level of capability

2. *Participational Variables*

   D. Political mobilization
   E. Political integration
   F. Political representation

3. *Directional Variables*

   G. Political superordination
   H. Development orientation

---

(3) within the political system itself, of its own subsystems. The third macro-variable of that set concerns the system's level of capability (1) for adapting itself and its society to their respective environments, (2) for adapting its environment to its own requirements, and (3) for self-adjustment to adaptive and developmental change.

The second set of macrovariables, the participational variables, includes the macrovariables concerning the smaller or larger participation of the members in the system, in terms of political mobilization, political integration, and political representation.

The directional variables, the third set of macrovariables, are directional in two senses. The first sense is the system's political superordination and the extent to which the political system is superordinate to the other societal systems. The second sense concerns the orientation of the system, its regime, and its authorities toward more or less modernization and more or less institutionalization and so, altogether, toward more or less political development.

This final aspect of this set of macrovariables is extremely important and will be considered in detail in Book II, which is devoted to the analysis of political development. Let us now only note, in the first place, that the first set of macrovariables, the operational variables, includes those variables that determine the higher or lower degree of modernization of a political system, and that the second set of macrovariables, the participational variables, includes those that determine the degree of institutionalization of a polity, which results from its higher or lower degree of political mobilization, political integration, and political representation. In the second place, let us note, reserving the discussion of the problem for Book II, that what should be properly considered as political development is the cumulative process of political modernization and political institutionalization. The third set of macrovariables, the directional variables, indicates —whatever the level of political development of a political system may be at any given phase of its history—the current trend of the system's course toward more or less modernization, more or less institutionalization, and consequently, toward more or less political development.

The eight macrovariables in Table 20 present various quantitative and qualitative variations. These variations result, positively or negatively, and to different comparative degrees, in several other variables, which can be used to analyze and compare systems. Table 21 presents, synthetically, a general scheme of these possible variations and of the resulting variables. This table represents an attempt to provide a basic model for systems comparative analyses, which can be filled, in each case, with concrete data obtainable by empirical research.

Although Table 21 is self-explanatory, some clarifications may still be necessary.

Set I, operational variables, contains the macrovariables concerned with the operational capacity of the system. As has already been indicated, macrovariable A, rational orientation, includes both the rationality of the decisions, in terms of the way information is collected, processed, and used, and the rationality of decision implementation. According to the quantitative and qualitative variations of

Table 21 *Basic model for systems comparative analyses*

Macrovariables	Quantitative and Qualitative Variation	Resulting Variables +/−
I. Operational Variables (indicating extent of modernization)		
A. RATIONAL ORIENTATION		
1. Decision rationality	Extent, accuracy, and rational use of information	
	Degree of consistency of decisions	
2. Implementing rationality	Degree of consistency of action	
	Degree of control of results	Secularization
	Degree of achievement self-awareness	Controllability (control and self-control)
B. STRUCTURAL DIFFERENTIATION		
1. Intersocietal	Degree of intersocietal differentiation and self-determination	Independence
2. Intrasocietal	Degree of intrasocietal differentiation and self-determination	Autonomy
3. Intrasystem	Degree of subsystem structural differentiation	Complexity
	Degree of subsystem functional autonomy	Subsystem autonomy
C. CAPABILITY		
1. For adapting to environment		
Intersocietal capability	Degree of intersocietal capability for self-preservation	Societal (national) viability
Intrasystem capability	Degree of subsystems' and roles' functional performance	Dependability

2. For adapting environment to system		
Intrasocietal capability	Degree of intrasocietal capacity for enforcement of commands	Effectiveness
Regulative capability		Penetration
Extractive capability		Obtention of resources
Accumulative capability		Saving of resources
Allocation capability		Redistributive power
Symbolic capability		Responsiveness
3. For adaptive and developmental change		
Of system	Degree of structural and institutional adjustment of system to adaptive and developmental change	Adaptability
Of regime	Degree of structural and institutional adjustment of regime to adaptive and developmental change	Flexibility

II. *Participational Variables* (indicating extent of institutionalization)

  D. POLITICAL MOBILIZATION

1. Social mobilization	Degree and accuracy of members' social awareness	Socialization
2. Political socialization	Degree, accuracy, and congruence of members' participation in the political culture	Politicalization
3. Political participation	Extent of membership and degree of participation	Participation
4. Political franchise	Extent, scope, and freedom of franchise	Political equality
5. Political engagement	Degree of commitment to current or alternative regime or authorities	Political commitment

Table 21 *Basic model for systems comparative analyses* (continued)

Macrovariables	Quantitative and Qualitative Variation	Resulting Variables +/-
E. POLITICAL INTEGRATION		
1. Into the society (nation)	Degree of societal (national) integration of discrete groups	Societal (national) integration
2. Into the political system	Degree of compatibility, mutually and with system, of political commitments	Value integration
3. Into the social order	Degree of support of the social order	Mass-elite integration
F. POLITICAL REPRESENTATION		
1. Representativeness	Degree of actual correspondence between authorities and policies and the will of the members of the polity	Legitimacy of the authorities
2. Stability	Degree of noncoercive compatibility of current political process with the system and regime	Legitimacy of the regime
3. Civility	Degree of unenforced socialization and internalization of system, regime, and policies	Legitimacy of the system
III. *Directional Variables* (indicating political orientation)		
G. POLITICAL SUPERORDINATION		
1. On economic affairs	Degree and scope of political intervention in economic affairs and state management of business firms and activities	Economic "statization"*
2. On social affairs	Degree and scope of political intervention in participational relationships and state management of participational associations and activities	Social statization

3. On cultural affairs	Degree and scope of political intervention in cultural affairs and state management of cultural associations and activities	Cultural statization*
H. DEVELOPMENT ORIENTATION		
1. Toward modernization	Extent and scope of authorities' actual orientation toward modernization	Modernizing commitment
2. Toward institutionalization	Extent and scope of authorities' actual orientation toward institutionalization	Institutionalizing commitment

*Control by the state.

the more relevant aspects of these two processes, the system will manifest greater or lesser secularization and controllability.

Structural differentiation presents three main aspects: the intersocietal, intrasocietal, and intrasystemic ones. What is at stake in intersocietal differentiation is the degree of differentiation and self-determination of the political system and the society to which it belongs vis-à-vis other societies and their political system. This variation gives the degree of independence of the system. What varies in intrasocietal differentiation is the degree of differentiation and self-determination of the political system vis-à-vis the other (cultural, participational, economic) systems of the same society. Accordingly, the concerned polity will have more or less autonomy. Within the political system itself, the intrasystemic aspects include: (1) the degree of structural differentiation of the subsystems, which indicates the system's lower or higher complexity, and (2) the degree of functional autonomy of the subsystems, which indicates the system's lower or higher subsystem autonomy.

Macrovariable C, capability, is concerned with three distinct aspects of the system's adaptation. The first aspect is the capacity of the system and its society to adapt to their respective environments. Intersocietally, the environments are the other political systems and their societies. Depending on the capacity of the system and its society for self-preservation in that environment, they will have more or less societal viability, which in the conditions of our time means having more or less national viability. Intrasystemically, the polity's capability for adapting to its societal environment, the other systems of the same society, depends on the degree of functional performance by its subsystems and related roles. Functional performance gives the measure of the dependability of the political system.

The second aspect of the system's capability is its capacity to adjust the environment to its own requirements. This means, in other words, the extent to which the polity is able to perform its basic functions. The result is the polity's level of effectiveness. As we have seen from our system analysis of the polity, these functions are its regulative, extractive, accumulative, allocative, and symbolic ones, which indicate, respectively, the degree of its penetration, obtention of resources, saving of resources, redistributive power, and responsiveness.

The third aspect of the polity's capability is the capability of the system and the regime to adapt themselves to change. The degree of the structural and institutional adjustment of the system to adaptive and developmental change indicates its adaptability. The degree of structural and institutional adjustment of the regime to adaptive and developmental change indicates its flexibility.

The next set of macrovariables includes the participational variables. Macrovariable D, political mobilization, has five aspects, which are explained sufficiently in Table 21. They correspond to increasingly deeper levels of involvement in the polity by its members.

Macrovariable E, political integration, concerns the integration of discrete groups into society (the nation in the modern world), the degree of compatibility of the various political commitments mutually and with the system, and the degree of support that the members give to the social order, which includes, as we know, the regimes of value, participation, power, and property. Depending on the extent of these several forms of integration, the system will have a lower or higher societal integration, value integration, and mass-elite integration.

Macrovariable F, political representation, expresses the various levels and degrees of adjustment of groups and members to the political system, its regime, and its authorities.

Whereas the set of operational variables corresponds to the lower or higher level of modernization of the polity, indicating its capacity for rational and autonomous action, the set of participational variables corresponds to the system's lower or higher level of institutionalization, indicating the internal adjustment of the system's members, groups, subsystems and institutions, mutually and with the system and its society. As the degree of institutionalization of a system increases, so does its degree of consensus, and the internal necessity for and actual use of coercion decreases. Within limits, as will be seen in Book II, the levels of modernization and institutionalization may vary independently. Fascist systems, as in Nazi Germany, can have a high level of modernization and a low level of institutionalization, and primitive systems have the highest level of institutionalization and the lowest of modernization.

The third set of macrovariables, the directional variables, corresponds to those variables that indicate the system's orientation in its intrasocietal relationships and in its trend toward higher or lower levels of political development. Macrovariable G, political superordination, expresses the triple relationship of super-subordination of the polity vis-à-vis the other societal systems. Depending on that relationship, the system presents lower or higher economic statization, social statization, and cultural statization. Macrovariable H, development orientation, expresses the extent and scope of the authorities' actual orientation toward modernization and institutionalization. This orientation results in weaker or stronger modernizing commitments and institutionalizing commitments.

Typology of systems and regimes

The possible variations indicated in Table 21 bring about considerable differentiations among systems. Although these variations fluctuate along a continuum of innumerable possible, and empirically occurring, intermediate positions, between a maximum and a minimum, they tend to maintain some typological features, which are empirically observable and so can be classified. In Table 22 an attempt is made to present a classification of general types of political systems and political regimes. This classification is based on observable typologically differentiated graduations of the most relevant variables resulting from the eight macrovariables.

Table 22 deserves some clarification in addition to that already given in its notes. For the moment the operational variables do not require further comment. Thus let us turn to the participational variables. With respect to macrovariable D, political mobilization, we might note initially, that with slight

Table 22 *General types of political systems and regimes*

Variables	Degree		Types
I. Operational Variables			
A. RATIONAL ORIENTATION			
Secularization	Low	A.1	Primitive (Australian)
Controllability	Medium	A.2	Traditional (Inca)
	High	A.3	Modern (Britain)
B. STRUCTURAL DIFFERENTIATION			
Independence	Low	B.1	Mono-simple (Nyakundi) (no intrasocietal autonomy, no complexity)
Autonomy	Medium	B.2	Pluri-simple (Inca) (some intrasocietal autonomy, no complexity)
Complexity		B.3	Pluri-segmented (feudal) (some intrasocietal autonomy with segmented political unity)
Subsystem autonomy		B.4	Mono-complex (city-state) (little intrasocietal autonomy [city as sacred] but complexity)
	High	B.5	Pluri-complex-centralized (U.S.S.R.) (intrasocietal autonomy, complexity, little sub-system autonomy)
		B.6	Pluri-complex-decentralized (U.S.A.) (intrasocietal autonomy, complexity, subsystem autonomy)
C. CAPABILITY			
Viability	Low	C.1	Ineffective (Australians) (unadaptable, inflexible)
Dependability	Medium	C.2	Subeffective (Colombia) (some adaptability, low flexibility)
Effectiveness		C.3	Effective undependable (U.A.R.) (adaptable, some flexibility, little dependability)
Adaptability	High	C.4	Effective dependable (Britain) (adaptable and flexible)
Flexibility			

II. *Participational Variables*

D. POLITICAL MOBILIZATION	Low	D.1	Prepolitical immobilized (Australians)
Socialization		D.2	Parochial immobilized (feudal) (parochial participation)
Politicalization	Medium	D.3	Premobilized (India) (subject participation)
Participation	High	D.4	Mobilized (Britain) (citizen participation)
Political equality			
Political commitment			
E. POLITICAL INTEGRATION*	Low	E.1	Unintegrated (feudal) (segmented integration)
Societal integration	Medium	E.2	Semi-integrated (Inca) (societal integration)
Value integration		E.3	Quasi-integrated (Britain) (societal and value integration)
Mass-elite integration	High	E.4	Fully integrated (primitives) (societal, value, and mass-elite integration)
F. POLITICAL REPRESENTATION	Low	F.1	Autocratic (czar) (self-referred)
Legitimacy of authorities	Medium	F.2	Authoritarian (feudal) (elite-referred)
Legitimacy of regime		F.3	Plebiscitary (Britain) (mass-referred)
Legitimacy of system	High	F.4	Consensual (primitives, Sweden?) (all-referred)

III. *Directional Variables*

G. POLITICAL SUPERORDINATION	Low	G.1	Precapitalist (primitive, feudal)
		G.2	Free capitalist (nineteenth-century Britain)
Economic statization	Medium	G.3	Regulated capitalism (U.S.A.)
Social statization		G.4	Welfare capitalism (Britain)
Cultural statization		G.5	Welfare socialism (Sweden?)
	High	G.6	Ordinated capitalism (Nazism)
		G.7	Ordinated socialism (E. Germany)
		G.8	State capitalism (U.A.R.)
		G.9	Developmental socialism (U.S.S.R.)

Table 22 *General types of political systems and regimes* (continued)

Variables	Degree				Types
H. DEVELOPMENT ORIENTATION**					
Modernization					
Institutionalization					
Speed for change or antichange					
ORDER	MODERNI-ZATION	INSTITUTION-ALIZATION	SPEED	DEGREE	TYPES
H0.1 Immovable	None	None	None	(0)	H-1 Primitive and traditional (change not conceived)
H0.2 Conservative	Low	None	None	(1)	H-2 Conservative traditional (Metternich) (historical conservatism)
	Low	Low	Low	(3)	H-3 Modern conservative (Churchill) (historical liberals)
H0.3 Conservative modernizer	High	Low	Medium	(6)	H-4 Conservative modernizer (Bismarck, Japan's Meiji) (modernization within former institutionalization)
	High	Low	Low	(5)	H-5 Revolutionary conservative (Ulbricht) (conservatism of revolutionary regimes)

Category					Type
H0.4 Reactionary	None	None	Medium	(2)	H–6 Reactionary traditionalist (Guatemala's Castillo Armas) (militant antidevelopment)
	High	None	Medium	(5)	H–7 Reactionary modernizer (Franco) (modernization with contention of institutionalization)
H0.5 Developmental	High	Medium	Low	(6)	H–8 Modern liberal (J. Kennedy) (development by incremental and bargaining ways)
	High	Medium	High	(8)	H–9 Radical developmentalist (Nasser) (development by rapid state action)
	High	High	High	(9)	H–10 Revolutionary developmentalist (Lenin) (development by revolution)
	High	High	Medium	(8)	H–11 Welfare developmentalist (Myrdal) (development with and for liberty)

*Myron Weiner's concept of integration [in Claude Welch, ed. (1967)] adopted: (1) societal (national) integration, which concerns integration of discrete societal groups and implies political commitment to the society, (2) territorial integration, which concerns imposition of central control over territory and implies regulative capability, (3) mass-elite integration, which involves ruler-ruled and mass-elite integration and implies support of the social order, (4) value integration, which concerns minimum functional consensus, by unifying procedures and style, and implies support of a given regime, and (5) integrative behavior, which concerns the capacity for providing for organizational requirements, and implies dependability.

**Although the order and types of systems and regimes indicated have a general and universal meaning, they have been considered particularly for modern times (post-French Revolution), and their application to preceding historical periods, notably to the Classical world, would require certain qualifications.

adjustment Almond's concepts of the parochial, the subject, and the citizen forms of participation provide a convenient gauge for admeasuring the low, medium, and high degrees of political mobilization.

Macrovariable E, political integration, has been used in three of the five meanings analyzed by Weiner for political integration. The four resulting degrees of integration express, of course, distinct realities when applied to simple primitive polities and to complex modern ones. That is why it can be said that fully integrated modern complex polities still do not exist. Quasi-integrated polities expressing, in addition to the more common societal (or national) integration, a significant degree of value integration, that is, of basic compatibility among the ideological expectations of the major groups of the polity, are still very few. They represent the more successful cases of societal development. This stage of development has clearly been reached by Sweden, which appears to be on the way to becoming in the not too distant future a fully integrated polity. Great Britain could be appointed as a typical middle-level example of quasi-integration.

Macrovariable F, political representation, presents the variations of regime that were classified for the first time by Aristotle. His distinction between "sane" and "corrupt" forms, however, should not be retained for that variable. Ultimately, these forms express lower or higher degrees of political integration. The classic concept of democracy, as the regime where authority is controlled or conferred by the many and accountable to them, should be differentiated into two varieties: plebiscitary and consensual. The former implies a quasi-integrated polity, and the latter requires a fully integrated one.

In the set of directional variables the first macrovariable, political superordination, required a more refined typology than the one currently in use. The essential point in question is the kind of relationship prevailing between the political and the other societal systems, particularly the economic. Precapitalism, capitalism, and socialism are excessively simplified categories. Other relevant types have to be considered. The proposed typology contains nine categories, representing distinct degrees of political superordination. Precapitalism, used as a single category for the purpose of analyzing modern political systems, includes both the primitive and the feudal forms of precapitalism. Free capitalism is the typical regime that prevailed in nineteenth-century Britain and which has been retained today by several underdeveloped countries with a low degree of independence.[5] Regulated capitalism is an intermediary form between free capitalism and welfare capitalism. In such a regime state intervention in nonpolitical affairs aims, primarily, to preserve the regime's conditions of operability. There is not so much a decisive purpose to suppress or compensate for the inequalities inevitably generated by competition among unequals as to reduce its effects to tolerable levels, as much for the general benefit of the society as for the particular defense of the regime itself. Welfare capitalism, even when labeled socialist, is a regime in which inequalities are not suppressed and the market economy is basically retained, while its excesses are deliberately corrected and the political system provides compensatory devices for the masses. Welfare socialism, although not yet existing as an empirical reality, is a political model characterized by the socialization of opportunities, the basic equalization of relevant conditions, and the maximization of personal and social liberty, although not implying, necessarily, the statization of the means of production. As already mentioned, Sweden seems to be proceeding in that direction. Ordinated capitalism and ordinated socialism are two new categories suggested for the characterization of regimes in which there is a complete superordination of the political system over the other systems, without the guidance and restraint of an effective developmental orientation. Ordinated capitalism is suggested for the condition of privately owned systems of production and ordinated socialism for publicly owned systems of production. The best examples are Nazi Germany for ordinated capitalism and the German Democratic Republic for ordinated socialism. The ordinated features of the German Democratic Republic are not its Stalinist remains but its absence of any developmental commitment. Stalin's Soviet Russia was not an ordinated socialism but a developmental one, if for no other reason, because the regime was actually guided by a purpose and effectively performed policies oriented (whatever their relative merits) not only toward the country's modernization but also toward its increasing institutionalization, which could be brought to overt light under Stalin's successors. East Germany, however, has been consistently kept as an intransitive socialist barracks, whose ultimate destination is alien to the individual and social personality of the East Germans.

State capitalism is a form of strong political superordination over the other societal systems characterized, on the one hand, by the nonformal suppression of the private appropriation of the means of production and, on the other hand, by its radical and actually implemented commitment toward societal development. Nasser's regime is the most typical example of such a model today. Developmental socialism is a still more radical form of political superordination, in which the means of production are formally transferred to the ownership and control of the state and the actual commitment to societal development is the supreme rule of the regime. The Soviet Union was the first example of such a regime, which is typical of China and Cuba today and, with some qualifications, of the East European popular democracies.

Some comments are also required concerning the relationships of the macrovariables among themselves. Both the relationships between the sets and those within each set must be studied. As has been remarked, there is, in some respects, a lack of correlation between the sets. A polity can present a high level of modernization and a low level of institutionalization (Nazi Germany) and vice-versa (primitive systems). Trends toward development, however, can be positive or negative at different levels of modernization, but not at different levels of institutionalization. In the latter case higher institutionalization prevents, as a rule, negative developmental trends. The relationship between modernization and institutionalization, with the implied positive or negative developmental direction, is no less applicable when we pass from primitive or traditional to modern polities. In modern polities increasing institutionalization requires increasing modernization, although modernization, by itself, is not a sufficient condition for institutionalization.

Within their respective sets the macrovariables follow an order of decreasing generality. Concerning the operational variables, we have that the level of rational orientation determines, in a general way, the level of structural differentiation. Primitive and traditional polities have less autonomy, are simpler, and have less subsystem autonomy than modern ones. Accordingly, polities of lower autonomy, complexity, and subsystem autonomy have lower degrees of capability than those with higher structural differentiation levels.

In the set of the participational variables, we also see that for modern polities the degree of political mobilization conditions the subsequent macrovariables. Premobilized polities tend to be semi-integrated, whereas the quasi-integrated ones have a high degree of political mobilization. Accordingly, higher levels of political integration lead to higher degrees of political representation. Only fully integrated polities can be consensual. Plebiscitary polities are always more integrated than authoritarian ones.

A different kind of relationship exists between the first and the second directional variables. The correlation between the quantitative and qualitative increase in political superordination is not a homogeneous one. Although low levels of political superordination do not allow a qualitatively high level of politico-juridical regulation of the polity, very high grades of political superordination bring the suppression of any form of autonomy of the other societal systems. This brings about a totalitarian regime which, regardless of its functional necessity, is not compatible with high qualitative levels of politico-juridical regulation.

Accordingly, the relationship between political superordination and development orientation is that the highest degree of development orientation, welfare development, requires medium levels of political superordination. Low levels of political superordination, however, tend to generate low levels of development orientation. At high levels there is also a correlation between state capitalism and developmental socialism, and between radical developmentalism and revolutionary developmentalism.

Another relevant aspect of Table 22 is that it provides the basis for a general classification of political systems and regimes. As is well known, the classic categories for classifying regimes, based on Aristotle, have been substantially enlarged and readjusted by modern writers in order to take into account more complex variables than just the number of those the authorities are accountable to. Along with some other noteworthy attempts, the classifications proposed by Almond and by Apter may be considered among the most representative of the new political taxonomy.

Almond, using as a basis his set of three macrovariables (secularization, structural differentiation, and subsystem autonomy), proposed a classification in which he initially distinguishes (1) primitive, (2) traditional, and (3) modern systems. The latter are divided in three groups as shown in Table 23.

Apter's classification of political regimes is based on two variables: (1) the regime of values and (2) type of authority. Concerning the regime of values, Apter points out the distinction between "consummatory" and "instrumental" regimes of values. The former views the social collectivity as sacred, in itself or

Table 23 *Almond's classification of political systems*

A. *Secularized City-State*

   Limited differentiation—Athens

B. *Mobilized Modern Systems*

   High differentiation and secularization

   1. Democratic systems
       (Subsystem autonomy and participant culture)

       a. High subsystem autonomy—Britain
       b. Limited subsystem autonomy—Fourth Republic of France
       c. Low subsystem autonomy—Mexico

   2. Authoritarian Systems
       (Subsystem control and subject-participant culture)

       a. Radical totalitarianism—U.S.S.R.
       b. Conservative totalitarianism—Nazi Germany
       c. Conservative authoritarianism—Spain
       d. Modernizing authoritarianism—Brazil

C. *Premobilized Modern Systems*

   Limited differentiation and secularization

   1. Premobilized authoritarianism—Ghana
   2. Premobilized democracies—Nigeria prior to 1966

---

in its transcendental meaning, whereas the latter has a secular view of the collectivity and tends to see the individual as the bearer of supreme value. Concerning the type of authority, Apter opposes the "hierarchical" to the "pyramidal" forms. The former type of authority expresses a rigid differentiation from higher to lower levels, as in military organizations, and implies an intrinsic right to command by the bearer of higher authority. The latter form of authority is more functionally oriented, as in a hospital, and implies some rules of accountability to which the exercise of authority is subordinated. By combining these two variables, Apter produced the basic types of political regimes, as shown in Chart 4.

These two systems of classification have obvious merits. Almond's classification is based on a typology of political systems qualified by a typology of political regimes. Apter's classification is a typology of types of authority. Almond's classification has the advantage of keeping a clear conceptual distinction between political systems and political regimes, but although it provides a valuable taxonomy for the classification of political systems, it is less elaborate in its taxonomy of regimes. Apter does not differentiate between political systems and political regimes but provides an original and valuable characterization and typology of forms of authority, that is, of political regimes.

I will try to combine the advantages of both contributions in the broader

Chart 4 *Apter's classification of political regimes*

Values	Authority		
	Hierarchical		Pyramidal
Consummatory (sacred)	A. Sacred-collectivity		D. Theocracies
Instrumental (secular)	C. Progressive-oligarchy		B. Secular-libertarian

TYPES	SUB-TYPES
A. Sacred collectivity	Mobilization system
B. Secular-libertarian	Reconciliation system
C. Progressive oligarchy	Neo-mercantilist societies
	Military oligarchy (tendentiously transitional)
D. Theocracy	Modernizing autocracies

framework already provided by Table 22, keeping the indispensable differentiation between political systems (macrovariables A, B, C, D, and E of Table 22) and political regimes (macrovariables F, G, and H). Initially, however, some terminological and conceptual changes have to be made in Apter's types of authority. The terms "mobilization system" and "reconciliation system" should be changed to "mobilization regime" and "reconciliation regime" to prevent confusion between political systems and political regimes. Conceptually, I suggest that the other elements of Apter's classification be adjusted so that they are based on the same principles as the mobilization and reconciliation regimes. As a matter of fact, as will be seen more clearly in Table 24, these two regimes are functions of the macrovariable G, political superordination. The reconciliation regime is a genus of which the species are the various types of regimes characterized by a medium degree of superordination of the political system over the other systems. The mobilization regime implies the highest degree of political superordination. Apter's inclusion of "military oligarchy" and "modernizing autocracies" in the typology mixes concepts of political representation into a frame of political superordination and is not compatible with the regulating principles of his typology. Instead, in addition to the two regimes already mentioned, two others should also be included: "conservation regime" and "ordination regime." The conservation regime corresponds to very low levels of political superordination, as in precapitalist regimes. The ordination regime comes between the reconciliation regime, which has a lower degree of political superordination, and the mobilization regime, which has a higher degree of political superordination, and corresponds to what Apter calls "neo-mercantilist society."

We can now proceed to try to combine, within the framework of Table 22, the advantages of Almond's and Apter's taxonomic attempts. The purpose, as we remember, is to provide a model for the classification of political systems and political regimes that keeps the conceptual distinction between the two and is applicable to any polity, although particularly to the modern ones.

Table 22 provides a comprehensive system of categories and variables, which is good for both comparative politics and taxonomic purposes. That table, however, is excessively comprehensive for the current classification of political systems and does not contain some of the indications required for the comparative analysis of political regimes. The first point to consider, therefore, is the selection of the essential macrovariables for the current classification of political systems. The macrovariables to start with, as can be deduced from our preceding analysis of Table 22, are the first of the two first sets: rational orientation (A) and political mobilization (D). As we have seen, these macrovariables condition the possible variations of the subsequent ones, of their respective sets. Given the difference between "classic modern" (Athens) and "recent modern" (United States) polities, macrovariable B, structural differentiation, must be taken into account if the taxonomic system is to have general validity. Of the directional variables, macrovariable G, political superordination, is enough for the characterization of the political regimes in most cases. A complete characterization, however, requires the inclusion of macrovariable H, development orientation, in order to clarify those cases in which the regime of superordination presents more than one developmental orientation. Table 24 presents the model in question, indicating, in parentheses, the variable combinations that might correspond to each of the macrovariables subsequent to A, political orientation.

The model of Table 24 is constructed for general use and is applicable to all sorts of polities from the most primitive to the most developed. For practical classificatory purposes, however, primitive and traditional systems may be identified and differentiated more simply, because of the relatively few varieties to be considered. So, instead of unnecessarily utilizing all the discriminative categories of that model for such systems, we may classify them by using macrovariable A, rational orientation, combined with more detailed specifications for macrovariable G, political superordination. For this purpose we need a more detailed presentation of the part of the model concerning the political regimes, as shown in Table 25.

For most current uses, the specification of subtypes is not necessary for regimes of types G.1 and H.1. For historical analyses or comparisons, however, such a specification becomes indispensable. Table 26 presents the varieties of subtypes for regimes G.1 and H.1 and, at the same time, all the general correlations between the macrovariables G and H.

To conclude our classificatory attempts, we can now present a general list of political systems, using the typologies and categories of the former tables. (See Table 27.)

Table 24 *Model for the classification of political systems and regimes*

(*SYSTEMS*)

1. A. *Rational Orientation*

    A.1   Primitive
    A.2   Traditional
    A.3   Modern

2. B. *Structural Differentiation*

    B.1   Mono-simple (A.1)
    B.2   Pluri-simple (A.2)
    B.3   Pluri-segmented (A.2)
    B.4   Mono-complex (A.3)
    B.5   Pluri-complex-centralized (A.3)
    B.6   Pluri-complex-decentralized (A.3)

3. D. *Political Mobilization*

    D.1   Prepolitical immobilized (A.1, B.1) (A.2, B.2) (A.2, B.3)
    D.2   Parochial immobilized (A.2, B.2) (A.2, B.3)
    D.3   Premobilized (A.3, B.4) (A.3, B.5) (A.3, B.6)
    D.4   Mobilized (A.3, B.5) (A.3, B.6)

(*REGIMES*)

4. H. *Development Orientation*

    H0.1   Immovable (A.1, B.1, D.1) (A.2, B.2, D.1) (A.2, B.2, D.2)
    H0.2   Conservative (A.2, B.5, D.2) (A.2, B.5, D.3) (A.2, B.6, D.3)
    H0.3   Conservative modernizer (A.2, B.5, D.2) (A.2, B.5, D.3)
           (A.2, B.6, D.3)
    H0.4   Reactionary (A.2, B.5, D.3) (A.3, B.5, D.3)
    H0.5   Developmental (A.2, B.5, D.3) (A.3, B.5, D.4) (A.3, B.6, D.4)

5. G. *Political Superordination*

    G.1   Precapitalist (H0.1)
    G.2   Free capitalist (H0.2) (H0.4)
    G.3   Regulated capitalist (H0.3) (H0.5)
    G.4   Welfare capitalist (H0.5)
    G.5   Welfare socialist (H0.5)
    G.6   Ordinated capitalist (H0.4)
    G.7   Ordinated socialist (H0.2)
    G.8   State capitalist (H0.5)
    G.9   Developmental socialist (H0.5)

Table 25 *Detailed model for the classification of political regimes*

Variables	Societal and Political Characteristics					Types of Regime
	SOURCE AND ACCOUNTABILITY OF AUTHORITY	ORIENTATION OF RULE				
		To Polity	To Ruler			
F. Political Representation	One	Monarchy	Tyranny			F.1 Autocratic
	Few	Aristocracy	Oligarchy			F.2 Authoritarian
	Many	Democracy	Mobocracy			F.3 Plebiscitary
	All	Democracy	—			F.4 Consensual
				GS. SOCIETAL CHARACTER	GP. POLITICAL CHARACTER	
G. Political Superordination				GS.1 Patrimonial regimes	GP.1 Conservation regime	G.1 Precapitalist
				GS.2 Civil regimes	GP.2 Reconciliation regime	G.2 Free capitalist
						G.3 Regulated capitalist
						G.4 Welfare capitalist
						G.5 Welfare socialist
				GS.3 Totalitarian regimes	GP.3 Ordination regime	G.6 Ordinated capitalist
						G.7 Ordinated socialist
						G.8 State capitalist
					GP.4 Mobilization regime	G.9 Developmental socialism
H. Development Orientation	HO.1 Immovable					H.1 Primitive and traditional
	HO.2 Conservative					H.2 Conservative traditionalist
						H.3 Modern conservative
	HO.3 Conservative modernizing	Conservative modernizing				H.4 Conservative modernizing
						H.5 Revolutionary conservative
	HO.4 Reactionary					H.6 Reactionary traditionalist
						H.7 Reactionary modernizing
	HO.5 Developmental					H.8 Modern liberal
						H.9 Radical developmentalist
						H.10 Revolutionary developmentalist
						H.11 Welfare radical

Table 26 *Correlations between macrovariables G and H*

G. Political Superordination		H. Development Orientation		Varieties of Regimes
POLITICAL CHARACTER	TYPE OF REGIME	POLITICAL CHARACTER	TYPE OF REGIME	
GP.1 Conservation regime	G.1 Precapitalism	H0.1 Immovable	H.1 Primitive and traditional	(A.1 Primitive) 1. Band (Australians) 2. Tribe (Iroquois) 3. Chiefdom (Caribbeans) (A.2 Traditional) 1. Patrimonial systems (Nyakundi) 2. Nomad or conquest empires (Mongols) 3. Centralized historical bureaucracies (Egypt) 4. Feudal (Chou China) 5. Theocracies (Mesopotamian temple-states)
		H0.1 and H0.2 Conservative	H.1 and Conservative traditionalist	6. Autocracies (Czarist Russia) 7. Oligarchies (Sparta)
GP.2 Reconciliation regime	G.2 Free capitalism	H0.2 Conservative	H.3 Modern conservative	(A.3 Modern) 1. Nineteenth-century Western bourgeois democracies 2. Consular oligarchies (Central America)
		H0.4 Reactionary	H.6 Reactionary traditionalist	1. Traditional oligarchies (Guatemala's Castillo Armas)

	G	HO	H	Examples
	G.3 Regulated capitalism	HO.2 Conservative	H.3 Modern conservative	1. Conservative regimes in present Western democracies (Churchill)
		HO.5 Developmental	H.8 Modern liberalism	1. Plebiscitary democracies (United States' J. Kennedy) 2. Authoritarian democracies (de Gaulle) 3. National capitalism (Mexico)
	G.4 Welfare capitalism			1. Plebiscitary democracies (Wilson's Great Britain)
	G.5 Welfare socialism		H.11 Welfare radicalism	1. Tendentiously, Nordic Socialism
GP.3 Ordination regime	G.6 Ordinated capitalism	HO.3 Conservative modernizing	H.4 Conservative modernizing	1. Modernizing autocracies (Iran) 2. Modernizing elites (Meiji clans)
		HO.4 Reactionary	H.6 Reactionary traditionalism	1. Tutelary militarism (Greece's Junta) 2. Praetorian regimes (So. Vietnam)
			H.7 Reactionary modernizing	1. Fascism, Falangism (Franco) 2. Colonial-Fascism (Castello Branco)
	G.7 Ordinated socialism	HO.2 Conservative	H.5 Revolutionary conservativism	1. Conservative socialism (Ulbricht)
	G.8 State capitalism	HO.5 Developmental	H.9 Radical developmentalism	1. State capitalism (Nasser)
GP.4 Mobilization regime	G.9 Developmental socialism	HO.5 Developmental	H.10 Revolutionary developmentalism	1. Developmental socialism (Lenin)

Table 27 *General list of political systems*

1.　　(A.1)　*Primitive Systems*

　　　　　　1.　Band (Australians, Tasmanians, the Ona)
　　　　　　2.　Tribe (Iroquois, Bororo, Nuer)
　　　　　　3.　Chiefdom (Caribbeans, the Volga Kalmuk, Ashanti)

2.　　(A.2)　*Traditional Systems*

　　　　　　1.　Patrimonial systems (Nyakundi, Mandari, early Egyptian)
　　　　　　2.　Nomad or conquest empires (Mongols, first caliphs)
　　　　　　3.　Centralized bureaucracies* (Egyptian, Babylonian, Inca, Aztec, Chinese Han to Ch'ing, Achaemenid and Sassanid, Gupta, Maurya, Mogul, Hellenistic and Roman empires, Byzantium, Carolingian empire, European monarchies (sixteenth to eighteenth centuries), colonial empires (sixteenth to twentieth centuries)
　　　　　　4.　Feudal systems (Chou China, Western, Japanese Shogunate)
　　　　　　5.　Theocracies (Mesopotamian temple-states, first caliphs, Teutonic states, Tibet)
　　　　　　6.　Autocracies (Czarist Russia, Saudi Arabia, Kuwait, Nepal)
　　　　　　7.　Oligarchies (Sparta, Etruscan cities, Carthage, Haiti)

3.　　(A.3)　*Modern Systems*

3.1　　(D.3)　PREMOBILIZED SYSTEMS

3.1.1　　　(H0.5)　Developmental

3.1.1.1　　　　　(GP.3)　Ordination regime

　　　　　　1.　State capitalism (U.A.R., Syria, MNR Bolivia, Nkrumah's Ghana, Cárdenas' Mexico)
　　　　　　2.　Modernizing elites (Japan Meiji, Iraq, Jordan, Bismarck's Germany)
　　　　　　3.　Modernizing autocracies (Iran, Ethiopia)

3.1.1.2　　　　　(GP.2)　Reconciliation regime

　　　　　　1.　National capitalism (India, Kubitschek's Brazil)

3.1.2　　　(H0.2)　Conservative

3.1.2.1　　　　　(GP.2)　Reconciliation regime

　　　　　　1.　Consular oligarchies (Central America, Dominican Republic, Ecuador, Thailand)

3.1.3　　　(H0.4)　Reactionary

3.1.3.1　　　　　(GP.3)　Ordination Regime

　　　　　　1.　Praetorian regimes (South Vietnam, South Korea, Taiwan, Paraguay)
　　　　　　2.　Tutelary military (Indonesia, Portugal, Turkey, Greece, Ghana)

3.2　　(D.4)　MOBILIZED SYSTEMS

3.2.1　　　(B.4)　Mono-complex

　　　　　　1.　Classic secularized city-state (Athens, Republican Rome)

3.2.2	(B.5)	Pluri-complex centralized
	(GP.3)	Ordination regime

1. Ordinated capitalism (Fascist regimes, Falangism, colonial fascism: Hitler, Franco, Castello Branco)
2. Ordinated socialism (German Democratic Republic)

3.2.2.2	(GP.4)	Mobilization regime

1. Developmental socialism (U.S.S.R., Chinese Popular Republic, Cuba)

3.2.3	(B.6)	Pluri-complex decentralized
3.2.3.1	(GP.2)	Reconciliation regime

1. National capitalism (Mexico, Venezuela, Chile)
2. Authoritarian democracy (France, Germany, Japan)
3. Plebiscitary democracy (U.S.A., Britain, Nordic countries)
4. Consensual democracy (tendentiously, Sweden)

*The list of traditional centralized bureaucracies is based on Eisenstadt's list (1963).

NOTES

[1] "On the Concept of Influence," *Public Opinion Quarterly*, XXVII (1963), 37–62; "On the Concept of Political Power," *Proceedings of the American Philosophical Society*, CVII, No. 3 (1963), 232–262; "Evolutionary Universals in Society," *American Sociological Review*, XXIX (June, 1964), 339–357.

[2] Rationalization is used here in Mannheim's sense, as the function of providing credibility and justification. It can be performed by magic means. But it is subject, as any social function, to the requirement of effectivity, which is the reason why, historically, magic thought has been replaced by rational thought for the purpose of validation.

[3] See Gabriel Almond and G. Bingham Powell, Jr. (1966, p. 25).

[4] David Easton (1965b, Preface, p. VII).

[5] Following Guerreiro Ramos, I will use the term "consular bourgeois" for the free capitalist-oriented bourgeois of underdeveloped countries that act as "consular" representatives of the metropolitan bourgeois of developed countries.

6

Political Change: Revolution and Reform

WAYS TO ACHIEVE POLITICAL CHANGE

Means and contents

To conclude our overview of the polity, we still need to obtain a better understanding of the process of political change insofar as it affects, in a relatively lasting form, the regimes of the social system and its subsystems, their basic structures, and their modes of operation.

The broadest and most general aspects of this process have already been considered in our analysis in Chapter 2 of the dynamics of structural change. As we have seen, the crucial question about social change is whether or not it is compatible with its regulating regime. First, we have changes of an incremental character, which are by far the most usual. Some of these changes, when they affect the typic form of their regulating regime, may reach a high level of relevance and produce developmental or regressive effects at the level of any of the social subsystems and, ultimately, of the society as a whole. Second, we have changes of a dialectical character. Such changes, when they do not regress, may affect the typic form of their regulating regime and, likewise, produce developmental or regressive effects. In terms of the political system those dialectical and incremental changes that achieve a high level of relevancy, immediately affecting the typic form either (1) of the regime of power or of the political regime or (2) of the regime of participation usually correspond to political revolutions or to coups, in the first case, and to reforms, in the second.[1]

As will be discussed further, it is indispensable to distinguish, in political changes immediately affecting the regime of power, the political regime, or the regime of participation, the *means and ways* by which such changes are carried out from the *social nature* of their content. This is particularly important for differentiating the two meanings of both revolution and reform, which are considered, on the one hand, as ways of introducing changes and, on the other hand, as the social nature of the content of a given change. This distinction is not necessary for the concept of coup, which refers exclusively to a way of seizing and using political power, without any reference to matters of content.

Revolution as a way of change

In strict political terms, as was seen in Chapter 3, revolution is a process of changing or trying to change the political system, ousting the incumbent authorities, or modifying their rules, in violation of these rules, by means of the threat or use of the capacity for coercion resulting from the mobilization of enough people in a society to prevent the incumbent authorities from imposing over the society or relevant parts of it the compliance with their decisions. Like the coup d'état, it is a process of introducing political change through violence and in violation of the political regime. Different from the coup d'état, however, the coercive element used in revolutions to violate the former rules and to suppress the incumbent authorities' capacity for enforcement is not the use of the former subsystem of enforcement, but the mobilization of enough people, in the society, to neutralize or actually defeat that former subsystem of coercion. The key aspect of a revolution, as a process, is the formation of another subsystem of coercion, independent from and opposed to the former one and capable of keeping or putting it out of action. Because of that, revolutions, even if they do not alter the regulating regimes of the other social subsystems—as is seldom the case—do necessarily change the former regime of power. Conversely, coups may, and frequently do, keep and reinforce the former regime of power but, whether or not they affect the regulating regimes of the other social subsystems, they tend to impose a political regime more adjusted to the actual realities of power.

Revolutions, because of their dramatic character and their often far-reaching consequences, have been widely studied by political analysts, if along rather diverse lines, from Aristotle to our time. With his usual perceptiveness, Aristotle understood that revolutions—to express it in the terminology of the present study—either (1) manifest an attempt to change a society's regime of participation by changing its regime of power, its political regime, and the authorities supporting the regime of power, or (2) are simple forceful attempts on the part of pretenders primarily aspiring to seize power, to change the incumbent authorities.[2]

In this view of Aristotle's the distinction between revolutions as political processes and revolutions as a certain kind of change in the content of a social regime is already implied. That distinction was stressed by Marx, for whom revolutions, compared to elections and other institutional forms of transference of power, were only relevant insofar as they would change the relations of production. For Marx the causes of revolutions lie in the contradiction between evolving forces of production and petrified relations of production, with their corresponding superstructural institutions. He saw the contradiction, inherent in capitalism, between the increasing pauperization of the masses and the increasing concentration of wealth among a decreasing number of capitalists as the cause of the inevitable revolutionary overthrow of capitalism.[3]

A general discussion of the phenomenon of revolution and of the literature on the subject would take us too far from the central scope of this book. What we need for an understanding of the problems of political development and of the models of its deliberate promotion, including the case study of Latin America, is to become aware of the ways in which revolutions and reforms can be carried out, as political means of change, and to differentiate this process from the social nature of the content of each. Since the available literature on revolution, in spite of the controversies still existing on so many aspects of the question, provides much more information that the literature on reform, I will restrict myself to some essential comments on revolution and develop the discussion of reform a little more, including in the discussion appropriate references to and comparisons with revolutionary change. Moreover, as will be seen in the last part of this book, the conditions in Latin America practically exclude, currently and in the foreseeable future, the possibility of change by revolutionary ways. It is of the utmost importance, therefore, for Latin American studies, to analyze more closely the potential for change by reformist ways.

Given the above distinction between revolutionary ways and revolutionary contents of change, what we need to clarify for the purpose of the present study is, ultimately, three main questions: (1) The first question is of an instrumental and operational character. What are the typical forms, if there are any, that revolutionary processes can take for overthrowing incumbent authorities and superseding the former regime of power and political regime. (2) What, if any, connections exist between the types of revolutions and the types of revolutionary change in terms of the content envisaged by the revolutionists or of the changes ultimately produced? (3) What characterizes the revolutionary content of a social change?

Although the first question concerns a very central aspect of revolutions, that is, the typology of the revolutionary processes as they have occurred in the course of history and are likely to continue to occur, it has only been systematically approached in recent times. The excessive concern, inherited from the classics, with the typology of governments has, in a way, obfuscated the typology of revolutions, as if the latter could be considered within the same category as the former. Moreover, the Marxian influence, which led to an underrating of the importance of revolutions as political means of change because of its emphasis on the content of, or conditions for, social revolutions, also contributed to the delay in the construction of an empirical typology of revolutionary processes. Along with some other contemporary efforts, I believe the analyses of Chalmers Johnson and his typology of revolutions[4] deserve attention and provide a convenient framework for the characterization of revolutionary processes. Later use will be made in this book of Chalmers Johnson's typology, particularly in the discussion of the relationship between types of underdeveloped societies and political models of development. (See Chapters 14 and 15.)

The second question, concerning the connection between types of revolutions and types of desired revolutionary change, will be part of the general topic of Book II, particularly Chapters 14 and 15, and will not be discussed here for that reason. As will be seen, I suggest that there is a structural interdependence between certain typical situations of underdevelopment and (1) the kind of political model appropriate for overcoming these situations and (2) the political ways in which this model can be implanted and implemented. In some cases that way is of a transactional character and can be achieved through reformist means. In some other cases a coup d'état is indispensable for the implantation of the required model. And in still other cases the required model can only be adopted by revolutionary ways.

The third question, concerning the main characteristics of social changes with a revolutionary content, will be succinctly discussed in the final part of this chapter in conjunction with the discussion of the characteristics of social changes with a reformist content. This discussion will be preceded by a brief analysis of the reformist way of change.

Reform as a way of change

As has been observed, revolutions, as a means of change, are characterized by the formation of a subsystem of coercion independent from, and opposed to, the one formerly existing in the concerned political system. The victory of a revolution, in military as well as in political terms, consists in the neutralization or defeat of the former subsystem of coercion, which supported the status quo and the incumbent authorities, by the new coercive subsystem, which supports the revolution, with the consequent forceful ousting of the former authorities and the transfer of power and authority to the leaders of the revolution. Different from revolution but also implying the achievement of its goals by forceful means, the coup d'état, as has also been formerly mentioned, requires the use, partial or total, of the former subsystem of coercion to change the incumbent authorities or, at least, the political regime. As a political means of change, reform implies the basic maintenance of the former coercive apparatus and excludes any drastic change in the composition of the incumbent authorities. *As a political means of change, reform consists in a reorientation of policies affecting the regime of participation of a society, fundamentally in the sense of enlarging that regime; this reorientation results from a decision of the ruler or of the prevailing members of the ruling group, and it is based on the former regime of power and is in basic accordance with the former political regime.*

Considered as a political means of change, reform includes three essential features. First, the process of change concerns policies and their supporting or required political structures and regulating institutions, rather than incumbent authorities. In autocratic regimes, such as Russia under Peter the Great or Catherine II, the reforming decisions are made and carried out by the autocrat himself. In nonautocratic regimes the reformers are the same group that formerly controlled the decision-making process of the concerned policy, although eventually some of the members of the ruling group are changed. Within the limits of the concept, the change of authorities can go as far as including the transference of office from one group or clique to another within the same general ruling circle, such as the change in the English Parliament, in 1830, from Tory to Whig rule for the promotion, in agreement with King William IV and popular demand, of the reformist policies that culminated in the Reform Bill of 1832. Japan's Meiji restoration, although presenting many features of a change by reform, is distinctively associated with elements of revolution, because of the neutralization (and partial defeat) of the Shogun's coercive capability by the parallel, competing, and superior armed strength of the Western clans. Reforms are acts of policy reorientation or innovation that are taken by the former authorities, although with some eventual change in the composition of the governing group. They are acts taken on the initiative of and are the will of the governing group itself, or at least of the governing circle, whatever the motivations inducing this group to act may be. If, therefore, as in the Meiji case the behavior of the former authority is determined by elements of coercion, such as forcing the resignation of the Shogun, we cannot speak of reform as a means of change, even if the resulting changes are of a reformist nature. (See Chapter 12 on the Meiji case.)

Second, in reform as a way of change, what is changed is the former regime of participation, not, at least initially, the regime of power and the political regime. Those may change later, in one way or another, as a result of the reform. Such is usually the consequence of participation enlargements. Unlike revolutions, however, which produce at least immediate changes in the regime of power, and coups, which produce at least immediate changes in the political regime, reforms are based on the former regime of power and are performed in basic accordance with the former political regime. It is not by changing the former subsystem of coercion or by violating the basic principles of the former political regime, but by using these, if adapted somehow, that changes are achieved through reform. The powers of the enlightened despots of eighteenth-century Europe and their political regime were not changed, nor were the power and the political regime of the English Parliament and Cabinet with the enactment of the Reform Bills of 1832 and 1867. What was changed was the former regime of participation, as in, for instance, the extension of participation in local affairs to the local gentry by Catherine the Great in the Reform of 1775 or the suppression of the rotten boroughs and extension of political participation to the ten-pound householders and the tenant farmers by the English Reform Bill of 1832.

Third, when reform is the means of change, the changes introduced in the regime of participation are fundamentally for its enlargement, encompassing more than the immediate power capability of the favored strata or sectors. Whether the reformers' motivations are of an idealistic or a realistic character, one of the essential traits of their action is the extension of the former regime of participation beyond the range of the immediate political capacity for imposition to the beneficiaries of the reform. *It is in that sense that reform, as a political means of change, always means, on the one hand, the enlarging of the regime of participation and, on the other hand, the providing of this enlargement by an enlightened act of liberality, even if for reasons of self-interest, on the part of the ruling group and the social strata it belongs to.* When we speak of reactionary reforms, therefore, we are not using the concept of reform in the sense in which it expresses a means of political change, but, as will be discussed later, in a sense related to the social nature of the content of certain changes. Such changes, however, precisely because of their social nature, have to be adopted through nonreformist ways. This is so because the only way in which changes in the regime of participation can be achieved without immediately changing the regime of power and the political regime is through voluntary acts of enfranchisement practiced by the authorities and supported by the ruling strata as well as by the beneficiaries of the change. Should a change keep its meaning of enlarging the regime of participation but not its character of being voluntarily practiced by the authorities, its achievement would require a corresponding change (by violence) of the regime of power. And should a change keep its character of being voluntarily practiced by the authorities but bring about restrictions in the regime of participation, curtailing rights and privileges formerly enjoyed by certain social strata or sectors, it would imply a change of the political regime.

Another relevant aspect of reform, as a political means of change, is related to the factors that determine reform. Consisting in a reorientation of policies rather than in a change of authorities and the corresponding regimes, changes by way of reforms are the expression of decisive factors that induce the rulers, against some of the short-term interests of the social strata they belong to, if not against some of their own personal interests, to act in a certain way. There are essentially two kinds of factors. *One is the occurrence of a change in the values and ideas of the rulers*, usually reflecting a corresponding change of mind in the social strata they belong to. Such a change occurs, for instance, when new religions, such as Christianity or Islam, convert broad sectors of a society to a new and more comprehensive view of the world and to new and more humane values.[5] Such a change also happens as a consequence of cultural changes marking the transition from one historical epoch to another, as occurred in the Western civilization with the Renaissance and, with still greater political effects, with the Enlightenment.[6] The other kind of factor that can induce the rulers to make reforms *is the existence of important new circumstances in their society or its environment* that put the survival of the society or its social regime, or the situational interests of the rulers or of their social strata, in jeopardy. Such was the case with the Meiji reformers, who were confronted with the Western challenge, or less dramatically, with Disraeli's conservatives, who, confronted with the risk of their political marginalization, took the initiative for the Reform Bill of 1867. Reforms ensuing from the change of values and ideas of the ruling group and strata are of a *transformative* character. An understanding of the risks created by new circumstances stimulates reforms of an *adaptive* character. Historically, it is not unusual for the two kinds of factors to appear intermixed. A new sensibility enhances an understanding on the part of the political elite of the potential challenge contained in given situations and induces the rulers to take the initiative for reforms while they are still capable of shaping them.

Modalities of reforms

A final comment is required about the process of reform. It concerns the way in which reforms are carried out, both historically and analytically. Because reforms are acts of enlightened liberalization adopted by the rulers of a polity—whatever the ultimate selfishness of their motivations—reforms express the characteristics of the rule. If we set aside nonessential details of the regimes of power and their institutional forms, what is relevant, in ultimate accordance with the Aristotelian classification of political regimes, is the determination of whether, in any specific case, power is accountable only to the supreme ruler, to an oligarchical circle, or to a large part of the people. In the two first cases the modalities of reform will be, respectively, autocratic and oligarchic. In the last case reforms affect the relation between the active and the passive, the inside and the outside, the enfranchised and the disenfranchised sectors of the people. Essentially, in this case reform means the incorporation of some or all of those who are disestablished or disenfranchised into the established or enfranchised sector of people. Whatever the extent of democracy actually existing in the concerned society, the decision will be taken, as has been seen in Chapter 3, by a small group of decision makers, acting under the influence of the existing relationship between the enfranchised and disenfranchised sectors of the people.

In such a situation, reforms tend to follow one of two typical alternatives. In one case the pressures for the reform are pushed by speakers, mostly radical intelligentsia, representing the disenfranchised sector. These speakers usually enjoy, personally, a higher status than their constituency and de facto, if not de jure, belong to the ruling strata, which is one of the conditions making it possible that they will be given attendance. In the other case the drive for reform is represented by speakers, mostly progressive intelligentsia, who are usually full and active members of the inner social or political circle of their society, but who claim the necessity for a liberal act giving some or all of those in the disenfranchised or marginal sectors of the people active social membership.[7]

There are, therefore—in agreement with Chalmers Johnson's six modalities of revolution—four typical modalities of political change by way of reform: (1) the *autocratic*, (2) the *oligarchic*, (3) the *radical*, and (4) the *progressive*. Although, as will be seen, there is a certain relation between the social nature of the content of reforms and the way in which they are carried out, these four modalities refer to reform as a political means of change, independent of their content.

Today interest in the autocratic modality is primarily historical. The most typical expression of this modality was the enlightened despotism of the eighteenth century. Under the influence of the philosophes and of the enlightened ideas of the time, such rulers as Catherine II of Russia, Frederick II of Prussia, Gustavus III of Sweden, Joseph II and Leopold II of Austria, Charles III of Spain, and Joseph I of Portugal carried out intensive transformative reform programs. To a certain extent the modernizing reforms made in Iran by Riza Shah Pahlavi, founder of the new Pahlavi dynasty, and by his son, the Shah Mohammed Riza Pahlavi, are contemporary versions of autocratic reform.

Oligarchic reform is more common. This is due not only to the fact that autocratic forms of power are less usual than oligarchic ones, but also to the fact that ruling oligarchies, which have little accountability to their masses, are more likely to be led by emergencies to adaptive reforms than to transformative reforms. The classical cases of the reforms of Solon and Cleisthenes in Athens and of the Roman reforms of the fifth and fourth centuries B.C., extending to the plebs' increasing participation in the affairs of the republic, are typical examples of the enlightened self-interest of a ruling class, which takes the initiative of making reforms in order to prevent social revolutions and to increase the functionality of the social system. Particularly interesting for our time are the technical reforms adopted by modernizing but conservative agents of the oligarchy, such as the cameralists in eighteenth-century Germany and Austria or the *Científicos* in Mexico's Porfiriate. They were a sort of ancestor of the contemporary conservative technocrats, such as those currently managing most of the Latin American countries. Interested, primarily, in increasing the capability and the efficiency of their societies, not in enlarging popular participation, and representing the ruling oligarchy without strictly belonging to it, both old and new technocrats attempt to achieve modernization without institutionalization,[8] and both fail equally. The German liberal revolution of 1848, the Mexican revolution from 1910 to 1940, and the current revolutionary agitation throughout Latin America are indications of the ultimate sterility of all forms of technocratic reform when unaccompanied by a corresponding enlargement of the regime of participation.

Radical and progressive reformism

The third and fourth modalities of reform, the radical and the progressive, are the two most important ones, historically as well as analytically. Historically, they have been associated with the great European liberal reforms of the eighteenth and nineteenth centuries and with the great socialist and welfare reforms of the late nineteenth century and of the current century, as well as with other reforms. Analytically, the radical and the progressive ways of reform are compatible with the complexity of modern mass societies, in which autocratic or oligarchic ways of reform have become either impossible or basically dysfunctional, rendering them useless as a means of developmental change.

Typically, in both radical and progressive ways of reform there is an interclass broker action by an effort of intellectual and emotional persuasion. In one case this brokerage is exercised by radical intelligentsia, representing a vanguard group—as such already admitted to the ruling circle—from a growing and emerging new class, which is still disenfranchised or marginalized. The best historical example of this type of reform is the Enlightenment. The Enlightened philosophes were, as a rule, members of the *tiers état*, who had, however, because of their talent and the prestige that was given in their time to higher learning and intellectual superiority, gained effective admission, if not actual social parity, to the highest ruling circles and groups. From Montesquieu to Rousseau what they did, ultimately, was to persuade the aristocracy and the political rulers of their time that the rationality already admitted as the regulating principle of the physical world and of the natural sciences was also the regulating principle of social affairs and of the competent understanding and management of these affairs. There were natural social and moral laws as well as natural physical laws. To understand these laws and to act accordingly was an imperative of rationality and a condition for objective success and subjective happiness. The acknowledgment of man's natural rights and the democratic implications of this acknowledgment were, therefore, imperatives of reason, just as the understanding of Newton's gravitational laws was.[9] Completing this intellectual appeal with an emotional picture of man's inherent natural goodness, only perverted by society, and recoverable by education, the philosophes carried out the most successful work of persuasion ever performed with the use of reason. It is true that between the enlightenment of ideas and the actual change in institutions, there were not only reforms adopted through acts of persuasion but the powerful and all-pervasive influence of the French Revolution. That notwithstanding, it is indispensable to take into account the large extent to which reformist change has actually taken place, both in areas not directly affected by the French Revolution, such as England and North America, and in areas, including France, where the forces of the revolution were finally smashed by military defeat and the work of persuasion achieved by the philosophes was ultimately reasserted. And it is still more important to acknowledge the extent, which is usually so underrated, to which the French Revolution itself was an expression of the persuasive work of the philosophes, who motivated the *tiers état* to fight for their equality and who deprived the nobility of their belief in the legitimacy of their privileges. As was well understood by Napoleon, the *ancien régime* had and kept for a long time the military capability to destroy the organized forces of the Revolution, but just did not have the resolve to use it because of an inner lack of conviction concerning its own cause.[10]

In another typical historical case of interclass broker mediation by intellectual and emotional persuasion, this persuasion is exerted by a progressive middle-class intelligentsia. This intelligentsia is represented, in the first place, by the Fabians and, in the second place, by the several Continental reformist versions of socialism, directly or indirectly related to the revisionism of Eduard Bernstein. Although the two movements are not completely parallel, there are important analogies between the changes that the philosophes caused in the ideas and values of the ruling circles, bringing about the liberal reforms of the eighteenth and nineteenth centuries, and the new intellectual and emotional outlook promoted in Europe by the progressive intelligentsia from the end of the past century to the middle of the current one. Like the philosophes of the Enlightenment, the progressive intellectuals had access to the ruling circle of their societies. They were not, however, as a rule, well-educated members of the class they sponsored —the working class—but understanding and unbiased members of the middle class, which, along with the bourgeoisie and the remainders of the former upper class, formed part of the new ruling cluster, the new Establishment. As in the case of the liberal reforms, the Russian Revolution and socialist revolutions in other parts of the world have exerted, directly and particularly in an indirect and latent form, a powerful and all-pervasive influence in the promotion of social change.

Unlike the radical intelligentsia, however, who could draw their central ideas directly from a continuous intellectual legacy, running from Locke to Montesquieu, to Rousseau, to Condorcet, and to John Stuart Mill, the progressive intelligentsia had a more complex relationship with the Marxian legacy, because of the several ways and modes in which they tended to accept most of his criticisms of capitalist society. They tended to convert his historically inevitable revolutionary predicament into the evolutionary or transactional way peculiar to revisionism and social reformism.[11] The purpose of this brief analysis is not to attempt any comparative assessment of revolutionary and reformist socialism. Its aim is just to indicate how progressive reformism, independent of its merits and fallacies, has been historically rather efficient[12] in a way comparable, if at a lower level of achievement, to the efficiency of the earlier radical reformism. Nineteenth-century Western liberal democracy was the final result of radical reformism, not omitting the direct and indirect contributions of the French Revolution, and the twentieth-century Western welfare state is the final result of progressive reformism, not omitting the direct and indirect contributions of the Russian Revolution and the subsequent manifestations of revolutionary socialism.

CONTENTS OF POLITICAL CHANGES

The content variables

Radical and progressive reformism, in addition to providing historical cases of successful change, continue to be prototypes of current and future possible ways of change. Considered as such, they should not be expected, of course, to maintain the same content they have manifested in the historical cases discussed formerly. As has already been mentioned and as will be discussed in more detail, reforms, as political means of change, are distinct from the social nature of the changes achieved by reformist ways. Radical reformism, as a way of change, is not in any way inherently connected with the demo-liberal content that it manifested in the eighteenth and nineteenth centuries. Likewise, progressive reformism, as a way of change, does not necessarily imply Fabianism or revisionist socialism. As ways of change radicalism and progressivism imply only a process of interclass broker exerting intellectual and emotional persuasion, undertaken, respectively, (1) by an intelligentsia belonging to an emerging class and representing its claims for more or full participation and (2) by an intelligentsia belonging to the ruling cluster but advocating the rights and participational claims of a deprived class or sector, which is prevented from higher or full participation in the concerned society.

It is possible now to consider, very succinctly, the content aspect of reforms. First, we must distinguish between the social nature of the content of reforms as means of change and the "reformist" content of a given change. In the latter sense "reformist" is not a qualification that implies the adoption of the change in question by means of reform. Rather it expresses a value judgment, stressing the mild and implicitly insufficient character of a certain change, in contrast with what one thinks that change should have been. Reformist changes, in that sense, could have been adopted by the way of a reform as well as by the way of a political revolution or a coup. The social nature of the content of a reform, however, refers to the social meaning of a change achieved by way of reform. In this sense, the nature of the change can be quite nonreformist.

The social nature of changes, regardless of whatever means they may have been achieved by, is determined by the form and the extent to which they affect the social regime of a given society and the regimes of each of the social subsystems, as well as by the relevant structural and functional aspects of these subsystems, including the composition of the elites and the relations between these elites and the subelites and masses. The ways in which any changes can affect the social regime and the regime, structures, and functions of the social subsystem are determined by two variables: (1) a *directional variable*, concerning the developmental or regressive character of the change and (2) a *depth variable*, concerning the systemic level at which the change is produced.

As will be seen in Chapter 9, the direction taken by social changes presents a developmental or a regressive character, depending ultimately on whether they increase or decrease the potential rationality of the social system or of its subsystems, and, accordingly, the adaptation and adaptability of these systems to their environments. Decreases in the potential rationality of a system, as an organization for achieving its ends in given conditions, imply the decrease of the adaptability of that system to its environment. Usually, in the case of society and polity, this decrease in adaptability results from the dysfunctionalities of the elite. (See Chapter 13.) Along the directional variable, therefore, social changes, whatever the way in which they may have been achieved, present a developmental or regressive character, identifiable and admeasurable according to the criteria indicated in Chapter 5, particularly in Tables 22 and 25. As will be seen in Book II, developmental changes increase the modernization and institutionalization of the system; regressive changes have the opposite effect.

Concerning the systemic depth at which a change takes place, both in the social regime and in the regulating regimes of each of the four social subsystems, we have, as a result of our preceding analyses of the social system and the polity, that there are three basic modalities of change. With the first and deepest modality the potential rationality of the system is increased or decreased *by a change in its regime*. With the second, less deep, modality the potential rationality of the system's regime is increased or decreased *by a change in its basic structures*. With the third and least deep modality the potential rationality of the basic structures of a system, under a given regime, is increased or decreased *by their improved or worsened operation*.

The social character of a change can be determined and measured by combining its directional determination and admeasurement with the determination and admeasurement of its systemic depth. Let us suppose we have, at the deepest systemic level, changes that increase or decrease the potential rationality of a polity and its society by changing the regimes of power and of participation of that society, causing corresponding changes in its regime of value, congruent adjustments in its regime of property, and congruent changes in the social regime as a whole. In terms of the main actors of that society, a counterelite successfully neutralizes or defeats the former subsystem of coercion and takes the place of the former elite, causing similar and congruent changes at the level of the subelite. That sort of change characterizes a political revolution with revolutionary social consequences. If the directional orientation of that revolution is a developmental one, bringing about an elimination of most of the barriers that were preventing the masses from a fair opportunity for social advancement, imposing functional criteria for the selection and behavior of incumbents with subelite and elite roles, and generally promoting the modernization and institutionalization of all the planes of that society, we have the typical example of a development revolution.

Suppose, however, that an equally deep social change takes place but with a regressive directional orientation. Instead of being led by a developmental counterelite, the successful political revolution is led by a dysfunctional circle of old oligarchs, who had been removed from power by popular elections but who have been able, by combining their former control of the army with the mobilization of an irresponsible lumpen proletariat, to form a powerful rebel army, to defeat the army loyal to the democratic government, and to oust the former authorities. In such a case, we would have not only a political revolution but also a social one. Since the concept of revolution, because of the influence of Marx, has acquired a positive connotation,[13] inducing people to forget that regressive changes can also take place at a very deep systemic level, it seems as if such an "antirevolutionary revolution" might be empirically impossible or should not be acknowledged as presenting the characteristics of a social revolution. Actually, the hypothesis of a regressive revolution is analytically pertinent, and such revolutions have, if not too often, empirically occurred in history. Examples include Sulla's suppression of the popular institutions and franchises at the end of the republican period in Rome and the oligarchy-plus-CIA-plus-lumpen revolution that overthrew Mossadegh and the Iranian national-populist regime in 1953.

Revolutionary, radical, and progressive change

Whether or not regressive revolutions should be called by a different name to distinguish them from developmental ones[14] is something that should not worry us now. What is important to observe is that, regardless of whether changes are developmental or regressive, if they present the character of a social revolution at the societal level, they cannot be achieved, at least not directly and immediately, by the way of reform. It can be said in that sense that *if society is considered as a whole, the nature of the social content of changes achieved by way of reforms cannot be revolutionary*. If, however, we consider only the participational plane and assume that immediate substantial change is not concomitantly affecting the regime of power and, basically, the political regime, the social content of changes by reformist ways can be of a revolutionary character as far as the regime of participation is concerned. The classic reforms of Solon and Cleisthenes, mentioned formerly, as well as such drastic and deep changes in the regime of participation as those resulting from the abolition of serfdom by Alexander II or of slavery in Brazil by princess Izabel, have a revolutionary content. This content, however, is only revolutionary at a strictly participational plane, without bringing about, immediately, a corresponding change in the regime of power. In the long run, however, because of the principle of congruence, reforms of revolutionary content at the participational plane provoke deep societal readjustments, either of a developmental or of a regressive character, as has occurred in Russia and in Brazil.

The second modality of change, in terms of systemic depth, consists in increases or decreases of the potential rationality of a regime through improvement or deterioration of the functionality of its basic structures. At that level we have, assuming a developmental direction, a kind of change whose main aspects are: (1) removal of dysfunctional incumbents at the elite and subelite levels and their replacement with functional actors, (2) enlargement and clearing of the main social channels of circulation and communication, (3) increase of the mobility and flexibility required for the performance of any relevant role in all social subsystems, and (4) increase of the functionality of all major structures of the system, with corresponding institutional adjustments. This kind of change includes the character of a reform (enlargement of the regime of participation) and has been often called *radical*. I suggest that we retain that expression for its designation. *Radicalism consists, precisely, in putting a regime, with functional adaptations, into its potentially best structural and operational conditions.* If, however, instead of a developmental direction, changes at that systemic level of depth take a regressive direction, so that the system's structures, main roles, and actors are oriented toward maximizing the restricted advantages of the ruling class and group, we have, instead of a reform, a counterreform, and instead of a radical, a *reactionary* social change.

The third and least deep modality of change, in terms of systemic depth, consists in increases or decreases of the actual rationality of a system through the improved or worsened operation of its basic structures. Assuming a developmental direction, we have in that case: (1) transfer of leadership and of relevant roles from incumbents to more capable and usually younger actors, chosen from among alternative members of the same former strata and circles, eventually of the same former groups, and (2) adjustment of the institutions and instrumental structures to the new policies and styles.

This sort of change characterizes what is usually understood as *progressive reforms*. In terms of the social nature of their content, independent of the ways in which they are adopted, progressive reforms differ from radical ones in the sense that they are oriented less toward the general restructuring of a system than toward the optimization of *its existing structures, through their improved operation because of better men and better policies*, under the same basic regulating principles as those of the existing regime. Progressivism, in that sense, is not the appanage of the so-called progressive parties as was claimed, for instance, by the Whigs and nineteenth-century liberals. Modern "conservative" parties, which are willing to bid for popular support and to exercise power by popular consent and delegation, are capable of being progressive, as Disraeli was the first to prove.

At the same systemic level of depth but in a direction opposed to societal development, we have that kind of antiprogressive change, or counterreform, that should technically be called *regressive*. Its main feature consists in the use of basic structures and roles, under the regulating principles of the existing social regime, for the restricted advantages of the ruling class, circle, and group. Unlike reactionary changes, in which there is an ideological militancy in favor of socially dysfunctional principles and goals, *regressive changes*, usually introduced by oligarchic counterreforms, *are of a pragmatic nature and achieve their purposes more by actual practice than by the overt postulation of their aims.*

NOTES

[1] Other dialectical political changes, such as foreign occupation or incremental changes, as in the case of urbanization, may also affect the regime of power and participation with congruent effects on the social regime, but their discussion would be alien to the purposes of our present study.

[2] See Aristotle, *Politics*, Book V, chap. 1.

[3] See Marx's Preface to the *Critique of Political Economy*. See also, on the subject, Franz Marek (1969).

[4] See Chalmers Johnson (1964 and 1966). Johnson's typology differentiates six phyla: Jacquerie, millenarian rebellion, anarchistic rebellion, Jacobin communist revolution, conspiratorial coup d'état, and militarized mass insurrection. On the technique of the coup d'état, see Curzio Malaparte's classic (1948) and Edward Luttwak (1969). On revolutions and political development, see Samuel Huntington (1968, chap. 5, particularly pp. 308 ff.)

[5] On conversion as a sociopsychological phenomenon, see the excellent study of A. D. Nock (1963). On relations between religion and reform, see Robert N. Bellah, ed. (1965).

[6] On cultural historical change, see particularly Alfred Weber (1943) and Erich Kahler (1961).

[7] Although in both cases radical or progressive intelligentsia are the speakers for reform, the decision concerning the reform, whatever the intellectual and emotional influence exerted by the intellectuals, is made by the rulers and expresses, as has been said, an act of enlightened liberality on their part.

On the strategy of reform implementation, in either a case-by-case or an all-inclusive approach, see Huntington (1968, pp. 344 ff.).

[8] On the meaning of these two concepts, see Chapters 8 and 9.

[9] See Ernst Cassirer (1943, particularly chap. 6). See also Harold J. Laski (1946, particularly chap. 3) and Paul Hazard (1946, particularly chaps. 3 and 4); Albert Salomon (1963, particularly chap. 4); and Peter Gay (1966–1969, chap 1).

[10] It should not be forgotten that, in addition to its lack of conviction, the traditional characteristics of the *ancien régime* and its low general level of capability severely limited its means of action in the process of confronting the newly mobilized masses.

[11] On evolutionary socialism see Eduard Bernstein (1963). See also Leopold Labedz, ed. (1962). On the Fabians' history and influence see Margaret Cole (1964); see also *Fabian Essays* by Bernard Shaw *et al.* (1948).

[12] On Bernstein's impact, see Peter Gay (1962). On the Second International see James Joll (1966).

[13] An interesting and illustrative example of Marx's influence on terminology can be seen in the fact that the Brazilian generals in their conservative and obsessively anti-Marxist coup of 1964 felt the necessity, for propaganda purposes, of labeling the coup a revolution.

[14] Some authors have used the expression "antirevolution" to designate regressive revolutions. That word, however, should be reserved for indicating attempts to contain or reverse a revolutionary process. The word "counter-revolution," however, could be used to convey the notion of a revolutionary change of dysfunctional character.

Book II
POLITICAL DEVELOPMENT

A

The Meaning of
Political Development

7

Retrospective Survey

We reach now, with the study of political development proper, the core of our inquiry. The subject of Book II will be grouped around three major questions concerning: (1) the meaning of political development: what should be understood by political development? (2) the models for the promotion of political development: how can it be purposefully promoted, under what conditions, and with what foreseeable results? and (3) the process of political development: how does it occur in a society?

Society and social change

It is advisable, before we start this study, to make a brief survey of the position we have reached up to now. Putting aside the Introduction because of its special character, we have that in the preceding chapters a systematic effort was made to approach the problem of political development from its most general premises. So we started our inquiry studying the social system, locating it in its general environment and observing that, analytically, it comprehends four subsystems: the cultural, participational, political, and economic ones. Each subsystem is a structural plane of society, the analytical locus of the performance of a societal macrofunction, and each subsystem presents two levels of depth. At the top we have the situational level, which is the analytical level of the respective regime for each of the structural planes and of the social regime for the whole of society. At the bottom we have the actional level, where, analytically, social interaction actually takes place. Each of these four subsystems is itself a complex system, producing and exchanging valuables and media. Given the interdependence of these subsystems and their functional autonomy, we have seen that society is based on a special reciprocal inducement between life situations and value beliefs. The regime of participation and the regime of values of any society are reciprocally conditioned. It is not true, therefore, as suggested by the equilibrium and functionalist views, that values determine society. And it is also not true, as proposed by the unilinear conflict theorists, that societies are determined by their "material" conditions or, more broadly, that existential conditions determine the cultural conditions. Existential conditions and culture are reciprocally conditioned. And so a multifactor conflict view must be combined with a dynamic functionalist view to produce an adequate model of society.

The next step in our approach was the study of structural change. Political development, whatever form it may take, is a type of social structural change, which is itself a case of structural change in general. We started our analysis by trying to understand, in their broadest meaning, what structure and process are, and we have been led to see social structures as patterned sets of behaviors and social processes as the production, extinction, modification, and exchange of valuables and their media. Social structural change is incremental or dialectical, producing development or regression, besides periods of stagnation. When it happens in and to society, it is subject to the principle of congruence. Structural change in one of the social subsystems either provokes congruent changes in the other ones, does not last, or causes the disruption of the system. Historical changes are relevant social changes, understood as those changes that condition or directly influence (as can be ascertained by historiographic methods) the subsequent course of a society. Social changes are subject to the laws of cultural evolution, which continue, by other means, natural evolution. Following Sahlins and Service, we stressed the major aspects and consequences of cultural evolution: the distinction between general and specific evolution, the principle of stability (changes increasing social adaptation are retained), and the laws of cultural dominance and of evolutionary potential, all of them fundamental for explaining why certain social changes are relevant and durable or irreversible.

Political action

Coming nearer to our present subject matter, we devoted special attention to the general study of the polity. We tried initially to understand political action and the political plane. Relevant for our present inquiry were our findings of the six basic elements of the political realm, the distinction between nonpolitical politics (*inter-partes* and end-oriented) and political politics (*super-partes* and means-oriented), and the characteristics of the polity: external discreteness and internal unity. We observed the two dimensions of the political process: Horizontally the process is concerned with external defense and internal ordering; vertically, with the relationship between power and validity, on the one hand, and the political actors, on the other hand, according to the possible combinations admitted by the power variables. We concluded our study of political action with the comparative analysis of the regime of power, the political regime, and the structure of authority, observing how the structure of authority is independent of the political regime and always presents a patterned relationship between a few decision makers, some decision implementers, and several decision compliers.

Participation and power

We continued our analysis by studying the problems of participation and power, concerning ourselves with the social group and the primitive groups. This brought us to some basic findings in the field of the political sociology of the group: the principles of group statics and group dynamics, which show the correlation between stability and change of the group and between stability and change of the relevant internal and external conditions that have influenced its formation or its finality. With this analysis we found the functional source of political authority, which is, ultimately, the self-validating commands for the achievement of collective goals. The analysis of primitive groups and primitive authority showed the successive stages of the social humanization of man and revealed, in the transition from the (third) stage of intergroup ordering to the (fourth) stage of supergroup government, the particular importance of the emergence of new religions in the formation of the first civilizations. And this analysis confirmed, from a phylogenetic perspective, our findings in the ontogenetic study of the social group. Although the social origin of authority, both historically and analytically, is consensual, based on the functional requirements of self-validating commands, its institutionalization and operationalization is both historically and analytically dependent on, and inducive to class differentiation and discrimination and tends, sociopolitically, to engender and aggravate such effects.

Intrasocietal exchange

Chapter 5 was devoted to a systems analysis of the polity. There the problems that are more closely connected with, or relevant to, our present inquiry were treated. The first item considered in that chapter was concerned with intrasocietal exchanges. There, it will be remembered, starting with a revised version of Parsons' theories on the exchanges between the polity and the other social subsystems, we were led to find the flux of basic societal interchanges. The polity exchanges commands for (1) beliefs and symbols from the cultural plane, (2) actors, roles, and statuses from the participational plane, and (3) commodities from the economic plane. When these exchanges are put into an input-output table, as was done in Table 18, they imply an exchange (1) of value enforcement for legitimacy with the cultural system, (2) of internal order and external defense for political actors, as decision makers, decision implementers, and decision compliers, with the participational system, and (3) of legal order and public services for solvency with the economy. A last analysis of these interchanges enabled the establishment, in basic accordance with Parsons, of their implied values and exchanged services (Table 19).

The political system

The subsequent item in Chapter 5 focused on the input-conversion-output processes of the political system and discussed Easton's and Almond's contributions.

What is most relevant for our present inquiry is the final critique of Almond's criteria for the classification of political systems. The merit of Almond's approach, as was often remarked, is that it provides the same basic framework for systems analysis, comparative analysis, and development analysis. It is limited, however: His sets of variables are not comprehensive enough for the purpose, and his insistence on univocally correlating subsystem autonomy with political development brings about a deformation of reality, hindering his understanding of developmental socialism and other political models based on a strong promotional action of a centralized state. It is necessary, as was stressed, to distinguish general from specific political development. This question, which will be studied in detail in Chapter 9, is extremely relevant for the understanding of those processes of societal development that, given the structural conditions of a society, can only start by a political development oriented toward overall development of the society as a whole through political means.

Comparative politics

The last item of Chapter 5 is the most relevant of all for our present inquiry. The critical discussion of the current models for comparative politics, notably the taxonomic schemes proposed by Almond and by Eisenstadt, brought us a suggested alternative model, constructed so that it is as good for the representation of any polity as for taxonomic and comparative purposes and including, particularly, the representation, admeasurement, and comparison of different levels of political development. This model is based on three sets of macrovariables: (1) operational variables (indicating the extent of modernization), including (A) rational orientation, (B) structural differentiation, and (C) capability, (2) participational variables (indicating the extent of institutionalization), comprehending (D) political mobilization, (E) political integration, and (F) political representation, and (3) directional variables (indicating political orientation), including (G) political superordination and (H) development orientation. These sets of macrovariables provide the basis for several distinct tables, with distinct applications, including systems, individual, and comparative analyses; classification of general types of political systems and regimes; and comparative admeasurement of political development.

   The study of political development, as we have seen, started when social scientists became aware that economic development, the first form of social development to be scientifically analyzed, was not explainable without recourse to noneconomic factors and conditions, and that it should not be accepted as the only form of social development. Once the specificity of political development was understood, the next step was to point out the major analytical features of political development, which, as we will see in detail in the next chapter, has been done gradually, up to now, although not in an uncontroversial way. A third step is now in process, which consists in obtaining a general model of the polity that is both descriptive and comparative. On the basis of such a model we started to advance, in Chapter 5, a theory of political development, which will be treated at length in Chapter 9 and according to which: (1) the variables for the characterization and admeasurement of political development are the same as those required for a systems analysis of the polity, for a taxonomy of systems, and for a comparison of distinct polities; (2) political development is a political direction, in the same way that general evolution, of which political development is a social aspect, is a direction of self-adjusting systems and entropy is a direction of physical systems—in the latter case in the sense of thermodynamic degradation; (3) political development, as a process, is political modernization *plus* political institutionalization.

Ways of political change

Our last endeavor in Book I was to study the ways and contents of relevant political change. We saw the necessity of distinguishing the means and ways by which relevant political changes can be introduced, variously affecting the political system and its regulating regime, from the social content of such changes. Concerning the ways in which changes are made, we saw the difference between (1) revolution, which involves the neutralization or defeat of the former subsystem of coercion through the mobilization of enough social forces and enough people to achieve that result, (2) the coup d'état, in which the former subsystem of coercion is used in ways that are not compatible with the former political regime, and (3) reform, in which the political regime and the former regime of power are basically preserved, and changes involving an enlargement of the comprehensiveness of the political system are brought about by an act of enlightened liberality (even if self-interested) on the part of the ruling group or circle.

Concerning the ways in which reforms can be undertaken we saw that there is an important difference between radical and progressive reforms. In the case of radical reforms the promoters, although accepted by the ruling circle, do not belong to this circle, but rather to the ascending social stratum that will benefit from the reform. In the case of progressive reforms, considered as a way of change, the promoters are themselves members, if particularly enlightened and socially concerned ones, of the ruling circle, and their initiative is oriented toward benefiting a lower social stratum distinct from their own.

Contents of political change

As far as their social content is concerned, political changes may have a revolutionary or a reformist character. What is in question, however, is not, directly and primarily, the ways and means by which these changes can be introduced, but the social nature of the achieved changes. Revolutionary changes—of both a developmental and a regressive character—are those, in terms of content, that immediately and directly change the former regime of power, usually with congruent effects on the regimes of participation and of property. Reformist changes, in terms of content, are differentiated into (1) radical or reactionary changes and (2) progressive or regressive changes.

This time, however, the question is not whether the change promoters belong or do not belong to the ruling circle, but the depth of the social level of the achieved changes. Changes of a radical or of a reactionary content are those that affect, either developmentally or regressively, the basic structures of the social system and the polity, although they are fundamentally compatible with the former regime of power. Changes of a progressive or regressive character are those affecting only, functionally or dysfunctionally, the operation of the former structures, including changes involving the use of functionally more capable or less capable men.

8

Review of the Literature

A systematization of basic views

As Samuel Huntington (1965) observed in his valuable contribution to the study of political development, "definitions of political development are legion." The matter is relevant for much more than reasons of formal purity. The concept itself of political development—not only the logical accuracy or the verbal elegance of its definition—is not clear and is subject to conflicting interpretations. And if it is true that political scientists have already reached a large area of agreement concerning the phenomenon of political development, it seems also to be true that it is presently possible for them to obtain a much clearer and more precise understanding of it by starting with that area of agreement.

I will try to contribute to such an understanding by attempting to present a comprehensive theory of political development, the succinct enunciation of which was advanced in Book I. First, I will briefly review the current ideas on the subject and will try to locate the various views in a broader framework, constructed in accordance with the theory to be analytically discussed.

Huntington,[1] who attempted a similar task, also felt the necessity for establishing some criteria for the discussion of the various views and proposed definitions of political development. He stressed the necessity, on the one hand, of giving a functional treatment to the concept, so that it might be useful for political analysis and, on the other hand, of preserving the necessary universality for it. Modernity, which is one of the requirements of political development that analysts usually indicate, is often understood in the concrete sense of modern history. Premodern systems, therefore, must be conceptually understood as underdeveloped. This brings about, most obviously, a double limitation. For one thing, it leads to a factually incorrect statement: Pericles' Athens was not an underdeveloped polity, either with respect to contemporary Greek or Persian political systems or even with respect to historically more modern systems such as Western feudalism or present-day Haiti. For another thing, it deprives the concept of a functional meaning. Development becomes an effect related to a certain historical period, not a functional characteristic of a polity, subject to qualitative and quantitative admeasurement and comparison.

As has already been advanced, the theory of political development suggested in this book defines political development as political modernization plus political institutionalization. Both terms are used in a functional way. Modernization and institutionalization are the general denominations given to certain levels and trends of the operational and participational variables discussed in Chapter 5. Furthermore, according to this theory, political development includes three aspects: (1) development of the capabilities of the political system, (2) development of the contribution of the political system to the overall development of the society, and (3) development of the responsiveness of the political system, with the qualitative and quantitative increase of its representativeness, legitimacy, and serviceability. We will use these concepts as a broad frame of reference for the location of the various current views on political development to be discussed. This comparison will help us to proceed in Chapter 9 to the discussion of the theory of political development proposed by this writer.

Making the same review, Huntington observed that the category or requirement of modernity, either in a naive historically situated meaning or in a functional and historically abstract sense, is the most usual characteristic of political development in the literature on the subject. Several writers even prefer the term "political modernization" to "political development" and use them interchangeably. In a more analytical way Huntington states that four characteristics of political development are referred to most commonly: (1) rationalization, (2) national integration, (3) democratization, and (4) participation.

Lucian Pye (1966b) carries out an exhaustive enumeration and analysis of the major meanings of political development, including all those that can be found in the literature and those that can legitimately be considered with reference to the subject, and obtains a list of ten principal meanings. These meanings and his own criticisms or comments are succinctly summarized in Table 28.

Pye's ten major meanings and his own additional personal conclusions, as well as the more representative views found in the literature on the subject, can be grouped according to six central interpretations. Using the frame of reference given in Table 28, we have the interpretations of political development shown in Chart 5.

Political development as political modernization

The understanding of political development as political modernization, typically supported by the writers of the first group in Chart 5, differs considerably, according to the various meanings given to modernization. Bendix (1964) sees modernization both in the sense of an historically situated process and in a functional sociocultural sense. In terms of an historically situated process,

Table 28 *Pye's major meanings of political development*

Political development is understood as:

1. the political prerequisite of economic development.

   (Pye's comment: The view is insufficient, since economic growth has taken place in distinct political systems and regimes.)

2. the politics of industrial societies.

   (P.: The view is inappropriate as a political criterion.)

3. political modernization.

   (P.: Political modernization is considered as being equal to Westernization. Pye opposes the view in the name of cultural relativism.)

4. the operation of the nation-state.

   (P.: This is the view attributed to Kalman Silvert. Pye agrees in part but considers it insufficient. In addition to nationalism, citizenship is required.)

5. administrative and legal development.

   (P.: This is the colonialist view. Citizenship training and popular participation are missing.)

6. mass mobilization and participation.

   (P.: This is a partial view. Public order is not considered.)

7. democracy building.

   (P.: This view is a value concept. Pye objects on methodological grounds.)

8. stability and orderly change.

   (P.: This is a middle-class view. Order is less important than getting things done.)

9. mobilization and power.

   (P.: This is understood in the sense of increasing political capability. Pye agrees in large part.)

10. one aspect of a multidimensional process of social change.

    (P.: This is Millikan's view. Pye basically agrees; political development is intimately associated with the other aspects of social and economic change.)

---

modernization designates, basically, the transformation of the Western societies since the eighteenth century and, under the influence of that process, the transformation of other societies, such as the Russian with the enlightened czars and the Communists, the Japanese with the Meiji restoration, and the contemporary

Chart 5 *Basic interpretations of political development*

I. Political modernization:	Bendix, Pye's number 3, Packenham, Eisenstadt, Almond
II. Political institutionalization:	Deutsch, Pye's number 6, Huntington
III. Development of the capability of the political system:	Diamant, Pye's number 9, in part Almond and Apter, and Organski.
IV. Development of the contribution of the political system to the overall development of society:	Pye's numbers 1, 2, 4, 5, 8, and in part 10
V. Development of the responsiveness of the political system:	Pye's number 7
VI. Political modernization plus political institutionalization:	Pye's own conclusion, in part Weiner, Horowitz, and Apter

societies gradually or suddenly emerging from traditionalism. Socioculturally, this process has been, and continues to be, marked by the conversion of the master-servant relationship into one of employer-employee. The evolution of the guilds, in the European case, the generalization of elementary education, and the adoption of a broad political franchise have been the principal factors commanding the process of modernization.

Pye's meaning number 3, considering political development as political modernization, takes the latter concept as being practically identical to Westernization. He is then inclined to consider that meaning as being affected by Western ethnocentrism. Once what is Western and what is modern become almost coextensive, there is no other way to measure political development except to assume that its level increases or decreases according to its larger or smaller incorporation of Western institutions and traits, a view opposed by Pye in the name of cultural relativism. Packenham (1966b) takes a functional view of modernization and, with some qualifications, identifies political development with it. Political development, in his own definition, is "the will and the capacity to cope with and generate continuing transformation toward modernization while maintaining basic individual freedom."

Eisenstadt (1964 and 1966) considers the process of modernization in both historical and functional terms. Functionally, political modernization consists in (1964): (1) the development of highly differentiated political structures, (2) the growing extension of central government activities, and (3) the weakening of traditional elites. Essential to that process (1966) is (a) a structural diversity and differentiation, and continuous structural change, resulting in the impingement of broader groups on the center and (b) the ability of the emerging structures to deal with continual change, bringing about sustained growth. Historically, this process has involved two phases. The first was the phase of limited modernization, which took place in the Western countries in the eighteenth and nineteenth centuries. It consisted, ultimately, in the incorporation of the middle classes into the centers of decision and of better conditions of life, together with a process of secularization and of technological development. The second phase, which has been occurring since the nineteenth century, is the phase of mass modernization, by which the broad masses are being incorporated. The process has been comparatively easy when the first phase preceded the second, and the two waves of incorporation could be gradual. When the process of political modernization starts late and begins with the second phase, serious stresses affect the political system, which may break down. This happens (1964) because of the incapacity of the system to solve new conflicts when the level of articulation is excessively higher or lower than the level of aggregation and conversion and (1966) because of the overlapping of demands, instead of their discreteness and successiveness. Consequently, there is either (1) the establishment of a relatively stagnating, regressive regime, at a lower level of differentiation and responsiveness, or (2) the development of a more flexible and modern society, as in the cases of Russia and Mexico.

The views of Almond (1966) on political development are the most systematic in the literature up to now. As has been observed, Almond has the merit of having successfully combined, in a higher synthesis, Easton's systems approach with a developmental view. He has thus obtained a set of variables that are as appropriate for the individual analysis of a political system as for the classification of systems and their synchronic or diachronic comparative study. (See Chapter 5.) In accordance with these variables Almond understands political development as a cumulative process of increasing (1) role differentiation, including (A) specialization of roles and subsystems, (B) flexibilization of resources, (C) rationalization of functions, and (D) creation of resources, (2) subsystem autonomy, and (3) secularization.[2]

Structural (role) differentiation and secularization are parallel processes, since they represent, for Almond, the two variables of modernization. Subsystem autonomy, however, is unrelated to the former variables, so that some systems may have a high subsystem autonomy at a low level of modernity, as in the feudal systems, and other systems may achieve high levels of modernity while keeping a low level of subsystem autonomy, as in the Communist systems. This permits Almond to construct a table for several significant systems, presenting their comparative levels of structural differentiation and secularization, on the one hand, and of subsystem autonomy on the other, as can be seen in Table 29.

Political development, for Almond, results from changes in the political system due either to inputs from the international system, notably threats of external aggression, or to internal factors, as increasing pressures from the masses forcing appropriate responses from the elites—or leading to a change of elites—or centralizing policies established on the initiative of elites who are trying to increase the capability of the system. The most typical result of political development

Table 29 *Almond's table of political development*

	Low	Medium	High
Modern systems (Differentiated political infrastructures)	Radical totalitarian		High autonomy democratic
	Conservative totalitarian	Modernizing authoritarian	Limited autonomy democratic
		Conservative authoritarian	Low autonomy democratic
	Premobilized authoritarian	Premobilized democratic	
Traditional systems (Differentiated governmental structures)		Bureaucratic empires	
	Patrimonial systems		Feudal systems
Primitive systems (Low differentiation and secularization)		Pyramidal systems	
	Primitive bands		Segmentary systems

Increasing structural differentiation and cultural secularization (vertical axis, increasing upward)

Increasing subsystem autonomy (horizontal axis) →

Source: Almond, op. cit. pg. 308.

is an increase in the capabilities of the system: its regulative, extractive, distributive, responsive, and symbolic potentiality.

Analytically, political development follows a succession of four main stages: (1) state building, corresponding to an increase in the penetration and integration of the system, (2) nation building, bringing about an increasing loyalty and commitment to the system, (3) participation enlargement, increasing and widening the inclusiveness of members in the system, and (4) distribution expansion, leading to the reallocation of resources and their more even distribution.[3]

Almond finally points out that the process of political development is subject to five basic conditions and varies according to them. The first condition is whether the process presents, empirically, a succession or a cumulation of its analytical stages. Successiveness favors and cumulativeness hinders the prospects of successful development. A second condition is whether there is a larger or smaller availability of mobilizable resources for the extractive and distributive functions of the political system, with correspondingly better or worse chances of development. A third condition is whether or not there is a concomitant development of the other systems of the society. Excessive dependence on the political system, due to the stagnation of the other ones, causes stresses in the former and can bring about its breakdown. A fourth condition is the former level of capability of the developing system, which will be more or less likely to achieve successful development according to its previous higher or lower capability level. Finally, a fifth condition is the response of the political elites to challenge. Creative elites tend to respond to challenges to their interests by developing the system, whereas stagnant elites respond to such challenges by trying to suppress demands by coercive means and so overtax their resources without increasing the capability of the system.[4]

Political development as political institutionalization

The second group of writers, according to the classification in Chart 5, includes those understanding political development as political institutionalization. Once again with this group of analysts, we have a large variety of interpretations, this time of the meaning of institutionalization. In the classification itself, the term is based on the meaning presented in Chapter 5. The referents of political institutionalization are the participational variables represented by macrovariables (D) political mobilization, (E) political integration, and (F) political representation. Former writers, however, as will be seen, tend to use only one of these three macrovariables or parts thereof.

Deutsch (1961), in the broader frame of the process of societal modernization, equates political development with political mobilization and considers social mobilization as the general condition of political mobilization. The latter results from the exposure, in the process of social mobilization, to political structures, values, and issues. For him social mobilization is "the process in which major clusters of old social, economic, and psychological commitments are eroded or broken and people become available for new patterns of socialization and behavior" (p. 206). This process is admeasurable by certain referents, of an economic, social, cultural, and political nature, as the per capita GNP or the percentage of literacy, of urban population, of party affiliation, and so forth.

Pye's meaning number 6 of political development, as mass mobilization and participation, is close to Deutsch's view but carries a distinct connotation. The process, for Deutsch, is essentially a social phenomenon, which presents a political aspect. Pye's meaning is essentially political and results from deliberate efforts to convert parochial people into active participants, mobilized by an ideological motivation, a mass party, and charismatic leaders. According to Pye, this view of political development is typical in former colonial countries and, in general, in countries that were formerly submitted to unpopular traditional governments and expresses the awakening of these countries to self-government and mass politics. Pye himself contends, however, that this meaning is insufficient and that political development, besides mass mobilization and participation, requires the establishment and preservation of public order.

Huntington (1965 and 1968), the most noteworthy theoretician of the institutionalization view, has a distinct and somehow more restricted interpretation of institutionalization. Deutsch and Pye's meaning number 6 see particularly, in the process of institutionalization, the social and political movements striving to build new institutions or acquiring new institutional participation, but Huntington's focus is on the sociopolitical institutions as such, as a complex of structures and norms regulating the polity and the whole of society. Political development, for Huntington, is "the institutionalization of political organizations and procedures" (1965, p. 393). This institutionalization is characterized by the direction and the level presented in four major dichotomic variables: (1) adaptability-rigidity, (2) complexity-simplicity, (3) autonomy-subordination, and (4) coherence-disunity. Institutionalization and so political development take place when the political process goes in the direction of the first pole of each dichotomy, and they are admeasurable by the level reached in that direction.

The dichotomic variables present several relevant aspects, and the analysis of these permits an objective appraisal of the overall tendency of an institution according to each of these variables. So to determine the adaptability-rigidity tendency and level of an institution, one should check (1) its chronology (a longer existence is a proof of adaptability), (2) the number of successive generations that have been able to operate or control the institution (regular leadership succession is a proof of adaptability), and (3) its functional adaptation to new conditions (direct expression of adaptability). To determine the tendency and level of complexity-simplicity, one should check (1) the function differentiation and (2) the function articulation of an institution. The autonomy-subordination tendency and level of a system is determined by the degree of (1) its distinctness from other institutions, (2) the specificity of its jurisdiction, and (3) its self-determination. The coherence-disunity tendency and level can be verified by a measure of the consensus and internal unity prevailing in the organization.

An important corollary of Huntington's institutional view, duly stressed by him, is his theory on the negative effects of excessive mobilization. Mobilization becomes "excessive," for a given organization or institution (1968, pp. 86 ff.), when it brings the participation of more people than those who have internalized the values of the system. In other words, when the process of political mobilization and participation exceeds the process of political socialization, the concerned political system is submitted to unmanageable stresses and begins to decay. Political development, therefore, implies both political institutionalization and the containment of excessive political mobilization and participation. One facet is oriented toward the creation and consolidation of institutions. The other toward the slowing down of mobilization, particularly through the institutionalization of stages of admittance of the masses to the centers of decision, so that a balance will be kept between participation in the system and adjustment to it. For both functions Huntington considers the political party the most relevant instrument.

Political development as one of the three aspects of our frame of reference

Points III, IV, and V of Chart 5 correspond to the three aspects of political development referred to in the frame of reference presented on page 198. Some writers consider that political development is identical, or largely corresponds, to one of these aspects. Let us briefly review these interpretations.

Initially, we have the understanding of political development as the development of the capability of the political system (point III in Chart 5). This view is close to the interpretation of political development as political modernization. As we have seen in Chapter 5 and Tables 21 and 22, the operational variables, which correspond to the referent of the extent of modernization, include macrovariables (A) rational orientation, (B) structural differentiation, and (C) capability. Although capability is only one of the macrovariables whose level increases or decreases according to increasing or decreasing modernization, it happens that the final and most expressive result of increasing modernization is the increasing capability of the political system. This is the reason why writers like Almond, who have stressed the aspects of political development related to modernization, are inclined to view the development of the capability of a polity as being almost identical to its political development.

Diamant's (1964) definition of political development uses that conception. "In its most general form," he says, "political development is a process by which a political system acquires an increased capacity to sustain successfully and continuously new types of goals and demands and the creation of new types of organizations" (p. 92). That view is also expressly endorsed by Organski (1965), whose important contribution to the study of the stages of political development will be discussed later in this book. (See Chapter 16.) Organski defines political development as "increasing governmental efficiency in utilizing the human and material resources of the nation for national goals" (p. 7). Pye's meaning number 9 follows the same line. "This point of view," Pye observes, "leads to the concept that political systems can be evaluated in terms of the level or degree of absolute power which the system is able to mobilize" (p. 43). According to the same writer, who personally accepts that view to a large extent, it has the advantage of permitting admeasurement through the use of Deutsch's indicators. Apter's (1965) understanding of political development as the "proliferation and integration of functional roles in a community," although implying a much broader context, is also connected with the capability view.

Another aspect of political development, the contribution of the political system to the overall development of society (point IV of Chart 5), corresponds to most of the meanings given to political development in Pye's list, including numbers 1, 2, 4, 5, 8 and, in part, 10, as can be seen in the chart.

The third aspect used in our frame of reference (point V of chart 5) is political development as the development of the responsiveness of the political system, which corresponds to Pye's meaning number 7: political development as democracy building. This view, which Pye endorses axiologically but objects to as a factual definition because of its value content, has been the prevailing view among Western writers for a long time. Political development has been considered as being a process of imitation of the political structures and procedures typical to the Western democracies, and the democratic content of the Western industrial societies has been uncritically or ideologically exaggerated by the mechanical identification of democracy with the formal machinery of elections and parliaments. As Almond pointed out in his remarks concerning the recent evolution of political science (1966, p. 5), the new conditions of the world after World War II forced a new intellectual approach to politics, and political systems started to be studied in empirical terms.

Political development as political modernization plus political institutionalization

In the terms of the theory proposed in this book, which will be critically discussed in the next chapter, the understanding of political development as political modernization plus political institutionalization is a novel formulation. But although the responsibility for it should be borne by the present writer, that theory, like most new theories, is not an arbitrary discovery or a fully new invention. Rather it results from the trends of former investigations, and many of its elements were already present in previous formulations. Leaving the theoretical discussions on that respect for the next chapter, I will just stress the extent to which the views of some writers concerning the meaning of political development, although expressed in different terms and, particularly, based on different categories, fall within the same conceptual frame or come close to it. This is largely true of Pye's own conclusion and of the views of Apter; it is partially true of the interpretations of Weiner and Horowitz.

Weiner (1965) made an important contribution to the study of political development, clarifying and classifying the five meanings implied in the concept of political integration. In that same study he advanced an interpretation of political development as the process that brings about: (1) the expansion of the functions of the political system, (2) the new level of political integration required because of this expansion, and (3) the capacity of the political system to cope with these new problems of integration (p. 533). This view, as can be seen, combines requirements of political modernization, such as the expanding functions of the political system and its increasing capability, with requirements of institutionalization, such as new levels of political integration.

Irving Horowitz (1969a) sees development as a broader concept comprehending both modernization and industrialization, as distinct and sometimes conflicting constituent elements. Modernization is related to the urban style of life and implies the functional rationalization of this life-style. But it is essentially a posture for the consumption of ideas and commodities. Industrialization, in the process of development, is that aspect of development related not only to the technology of mechanized production but also to the decisions, concerning the regimes of savings and investment, at a certain consumption cost, that make mechanized production possible. Although not formally mentioned in Horowitz's formulation, it is clear enough that his view of the requirements of industrialization are related to the participational variables and the process of political institutionalization.

Lucian Pye (1966b), reviewing critically his ten meanings of political development, presents his conclusions, and those of his fellow members of the Comparative Politics committee,[5] on the "development syndrome." According to these writers, the process of political development is characterized by the increase of three major features, the cumulative growth of which constitutes the development syndrome: (1) equality, (2) capacity (meaning political capability), and (3) differentiation and specialization. Although these writers have not used the concepts and the terms we have used in our frame of reference, their understanding of political development clearly associates the features of the process of political modernization—increase in the capacity (capability) of the system and in the differentiation and specialization of subsystems and roles—with at least one of the relevant aspects of the process of political institutionalization: the increase in equality. And by equality they meant: (1) some extent—larger or smaller—of participation, (2) the universality of law, or legal equality, and (3) recruitment for political office according to achievement standards, rather than the ascriptive standards of traditional societies.

With Apter (1965) we have, finally, the formal distinction between political modernization and political development. Apter stresses the functional aspect of modernization, in general, and political modernization, in particular. For him modernization is essentially an increase in the rationality and liberty of the decision-making process, with the correlated adjustment of structures and procedures. Development is a broader concept, which he does not clearly elaborate, but which he implies is an integrated quantitative and qualitative structural growth. He considers development as the most general case and modernization as a particular one. Development "results from the proliferation and integration of functional roles in a community" (p. 67). Modernization, as a particular case of development, involves the increase of three main features: (1) innovation without disruption, (2) differentiation and flexibilization of social structures, and (3) a social framework for providing skills. Implied in this distinction is another process, in addition to the process of modernization which, combined with modernization, results in the overall process of development. In Apter's concept this additional process is one of social integration and functional participation. These processes, as we have seen, are an essential part of the process of political institutionalization.

NOTES

[1] See Samuel Huntington (1965). His views on the subject were subsequently expanded to cover other topics (particularly in 1966a and 1966b) and finally integrated into a book-length work (1968).

[2] Almond distinguishes, according to his own terminology and conceptual framework, political modernization, which would include role differentiation, in its structural aspect, and secularization, in its cultural aspect, from the broader concept of political development, which includes, additionally, subsystem autonomy. However, according to the frame of reference adopted in this book, as explained in Chapter 5 and as will be discussed further in the next chapter, the referents of political modernization also include subsystem autonomy, which is one of the variables of the macrovariable (B) structural differentiation. This is,

incidentally, the reason why Almond's views are discussed in the group of writers who consider political development as political modernization.

[3] The problems concerning the stages of political development are discussed in Chapter 16.

[4] The conditions for political development are discussed in Chapter 17.

[5] The Committee on Comparative Politics of the Social Science Research Council, organized in 1960, has maintained continued research and has prepared a series of seven volumes of Studies in Political Development, six of which had been published in 1968. Starting under the chairmanship of Gabriel Almond, who was succeeded by Lucian Pye in 1965, the Committee also included the following scholars: Leonard Binder, R. Taylor Cole, James Coleman, Herbert Hyman, Joseph LaPalombara, Sidney Verba, Robert Ward, Myron Weiner, and the late Sigmund Neumann.

9

A Comprehensive Theory
of Political Development

Propositional formulation

I can now present and discuss in detail the theory of political development about which I have made some very brief comments. I will initially state in a succinct propositional form the central theses of the theory, concerning the meaning and scope of political development, and subsequently will discuss each of them, analyzing their foundations and comparing them critically with the views of other writers, which have been studied in the preceding chapter.

I. *The variables of political development*
   The variables for the characterization and admeasurement of political development are the same as those required for a systems analysis of the polity, for a general taxonomy of political systems, and for the synchronic and diachronic comparison of distinct political systems.

II. *Political development as a political direction*
   Political development is a political direction, just as general evolution, of which it is a social aspect, is a direction of self-adjusting systems and entropy is a direction of physical systems, in the latter case in the sense of thermodynamic degradation.

III. *Political development as a process*
   Political development as a process is political modernization plus political institutionalization (PD = M + I). Political modernization is the process of increasing the operational variables of a polity—which comprehend macrovariables (A) rational orientation, (B) structural differentiation, and (C) capability—with the consequent increasing of the resulting variables indicated in Table 21. Political institutionalization is the process of increasing the participational variables of a polity—which comprehend macrovariables (D) political mobilization, (E) political integration, and (F) political representation—with the

207

consequent increasing of the resulting variables also indicated in Table 21.

IV. *The three aspects of political development*

1. Development of the capability of the political system, which corresponds to the development of the effectiveness of the polity as a subsystem of the social system

2. Development of the contribution of the political system to the overall development of the concerned society, which corresponds to the development of the whole society by political means

3. Development of the responsiveness of the political system, increasing its representativeness, legitimacy, and serviceability, which corresponds to the development of political consensus and of social consensus by political ways.

The first thesis, concerning the variables of political development, expresses the fact that political development is an occurrence of the polity characterized by certain structural changes of the political system. The foundation of that thesis is of an analytical nature. Once we understand the political system as a certain structural plane of society, as well as a subsystem of the social system, characterized by the fact that it is, analytically, as a plane, the locus, and as a subsystem, the structural pattern of interactions resulting in the authoritative allocation of valuables, we have that the variables for characterizing and admeasuring that sort of structural change that is political development must necessarily be the same variables as those required in systems analysis for characterizing the political system and for admeasuring its occurrences. This reasoning also explains why the variables required for the general classification of political systems and for their synchronic and diachronic comparison are also the same.

In other words, a systems approach implies the acknowledgment that some structural variables are setting the pattern for the functioning of the system, that these variables are identifiable through the empirical observation of the system, and that they can be objectively characterized and objectively admeasured by the use of appropriate indicators. Given these empirically verifiable assumptions and conditions, we have the necessity for using the same variables for the characterization and admeasurement of the observable structural occurrences of the system, such as its development. And being political systems characterized by these observable sets of variables, their classification and comparison require the use of the same indicators.

As was formerly mentioned, Almond was the first political scientist to adopt the same sets of variables for the three purposes of systems analysis, political taxonomy, and comparative politics. His table of variables, however, is not sufficiently comprehensive, because he expects to include all the relevant features while using only some—in my terminology—of the operational variables. As was discussed in Chapter 5, the basic model for comparative systems analysis also requires the participational and the directional variables. Moreover, the set of operational variables required for that purpose needs to include more variables than there are in Almond's typology, and a distinction needs to be made between the macrovariables and their content, on the one hand, and the resulting variables, on the other hand. The resulting variables are the ones whose increase or decrease is to be measured.

The second thesis, concerning political development as a political direction, is also founded on analytical principles. A direction is the sense of a movement or change. As a structural change of the political system, political development should necessarily have a certain direction. Structural changes, in general, as we have seen in Chapter 2, are analytical or synthetic, and they occur intrasystemically or intersystemically. Analytic change, intrasystemically, is segmentation; intersystemically, it is dissolution. Synthetic change, intrasystemically, is unification; intersystemically, it is fusion. Unification, in turn, is either differentiation or simplification, resulting, respectively, in the development or regression of the concerned system. We have, then, that political development, as a form of intrasystemic synthetic structural change, is a process of structural differentiation. That means, analytically, that the direction is from the less to the more complex and from a smaller to a larger number of component units and subsystems. That direction is a political direction because the structural differentiation is a political one and the more complex and numerous units and subsystems resulting from the differentiation are political units and subsystems.

Directions, however, can be arbitrary, as in conventional rules, like traffic regulations, or necessary, when the rules are the patterns of the system, as in astronomical movements and, in general, in effects subordinated to the laws of causality. Directions can also be reversible, when the movement is (by hypothesis) of an unchanging body from one point to another, as when a car on a road goes from south to north or vice-versa, and irreversible, when what is concerned is a structural change of simplification or of differentiation. The latter is the case of political development, which is a species of the genus development and the social expression of a broader process, the general process of evolution. (See Chapter 2.) That sort of irreversibility does not mean, however, that processes of political development cannot be stopped and that developing polities cannot be submitted to regressive trends. What it means is that a change of direction, from differentiation to simplification, means necessarily a change of process, from development to regression.

The understanding of political development as an irreversible (but not unalterable) political direction is common, although not in that explicit way, among the writers who view political development as a structural political change, as most do. This is particularly true of those included in group VI of Chart 5, notably Apter, of those in group I, notably Eisenstadt and Almond, and of some of those in group II, as Huntington. The understanding of political direction as a social aspect of general evolution is associated with the reformulation of cultural evolution undertaken by Leslie White (1959) and his anthropological school and, in sociology, by Parsons (1966a).

The third thesis, stating that the process of political development is political modernization plus political institutionalization, is founded on both analytical and empirically deducted principles. It is founded on analytical principles in the sense that the statement PD = M + I is formally true when the concepts of M and I are meaningfully compatible and taken together form a meaningful concept coextensive with the concept of PD. It is founded on empirically deducted principles in the sense that the concepts of modernization (M) and institutionalization (I) are generalizations of certain characteristics of a political system, that are observable and admeasurable whenever one correlates the increase or decrease of the component variables of certain macrovariables (see Table 21) with the increase or decrease of certain resulting variables.

Let us give an example of this last statement. Macrovariable (A) political orientation contains: (1) the variables of decision rationality, meaning, and admeasurable by, (1.1) the extent, accuracy, and rational use of information by the concerned political system and (1.2) the degree of consistency of decisions, (2) the variables of implementing rationality, meaning, and admeasurable by, (2.1) the degree of consistency of action, (2.2) the degree of control of results, and (2.3) the degree of achievement self-awareness. Increases in these variables, that is, increases in (1) decision rationality and (2) implementing rationality, results, in terms empirically observable and admeasurable and according to an empirically verified correlation, in more secularization and controllability. If we define political modernization (M) as a process increasing, along with other features, the secularization and the controllability of a political system, we have that an increase of macrovariable (A) rational orientation brings out political modernization (if other things remain equal).

Political modernization plus political institutionalization

Given this formal explanation, we can now analyze the third thesis in a little more detail. An understanding of the statement that PD equals M plus I requires a better understanding of its two component terms. Modernization, as we have seen in Chapter 5, is the adopted designation[1] for the political process bringing about an increase in the resulting variables of the first set of macrovariables, the operational variables, including (A) rational orientation, (B) structural differentiation, and (C) capability. The effect of these increments is an increasing command, by the political system, over its environment and its decreasing dependence on casual favorable circumstances. In evolutionary terms this effect expresses a higher control and use of the sources of energy and of utilizable resources for the system's ends, that is, an evolutionary advance.

Institutionalization, as we have also seen, is the adopted designation for the political process bringing about an increase in the resulting variables of the second set of macrovariables, the participational variables, including (D) political mobilization, (E) political integration, and (F) political representation. The effect of these increments is an increasing consensuality in the political system, resulting from an increasing correspondence between individual and collective goals and individual and collective decisions, with a consequent decrease in the necessity for, and actual use of, coercive means in the polity. Increasing consensus and decreasing coercion imply an increased use of the available sources of energy and resources for the system's ends, instead of for the imposition of a fraction of the system on the rest of it, at the expense of the system as a whole.

Consensus maximizes the system's potentialities in three ways: (1) by eliminating the need to use energies and resources for internal fractional struggles with the result that they can be devoted entirely to the attendance of the general goals of the system, (2) by liberating the maximum creativity, initiative, and commitment of the system's members in a way essentially compatible with the system's collective convenience, and (3) by raising the moral standard of the system.

This last consequence has a double effect. For one thing, it increases the ethical internal level of the system, that is, puts its operation at a cybernetic level of higher information and lower resistance, with the result that the patterned interactions are less dependent on legal ruling and physical enforcement and determined more by internalized norms and freely observed rules. For another thing, it increases, within the limits allowed by the system's scientific-technological level, the compatibility of the political system and its respective society with other ones, in the sense of rendering that system and its society less dependent than it would otherwise be on low information and high resistance resources, which tend to be relatively scarce and subject to a zero—sum rule. This second effect of the polity's increasing ethical level concerns its international relations and is a corollary of the first effect. Given a certain scientific-technological level, internal ethicality liberates rationality for international relations, and the international optimization of the available scientific-technological resources of the concerned society moves that society away from more elementary forms and levels of conflict over resources. Of course, the higher the scientific-technological level of the society is, the greater the practical effects of high ethical levels will be, particularly with respect to international relations.

Further exploration of this subject would obviously take us beyond the scope of the present study. Let me just remark, however, that the social correlation between knowledge effectiveness and moral effectiveness is a general and constant one. Low cultural levels imply necessarily low ethical standards for any society, given the compulsion to maximize, at any price, precarious and scarce chances to obtain resources. Sophisticated forms (but not the rough ones) of nonethical behavior, however, are compatible, both internationally and domestically, with very high scientific-technological levels whenever political modernization in the concerned society is not balanced by corresponding forms of political institutionalization. This was the case in Nazi Germany and is typical, in general, of fascist regimes, which are characterized, precisely, by a high level of modernization and low level of institutionalization.

The last statement projects some light on the relationship between the two components of political development. Other aspects aside, the writers who have identified political development with political modernization, or considered the latter to be the core, if not the unique element, of the former, have not realized that quantitative and qualitative increments of the operational variables are compatible with very low levels of most of the participational variables. This compatibility means that very discriminative and exploitative regimes of participation can be sanctioned by highly modernized polities, with the result, apart from purely ethico-humanistic considerations, in a very poor use of the available sources of energy and resources. Furthermore, the greater the imbalance between the high level of modernization and the low level of institutionalization is, the more dependent the political system will be, internally and internationally, on the successful use of violence. This is precisely what the experience of advanced fascism has shown and what is being exhibited by the current fascist regimes of semicolonial and dependent countries (colonial fascism) as well as by the ethnic fascism of South Africa.

It is important to remark, in this respect, that the negative effects on political development do not come primarily from the use of violence as such, but from that kind of use of violence that results from, and/or is oriented toward, the maintenance of a low level of the participational variables. This is one of the reasons Almond's excessive dependence on the category of subsystem autonomy may be misleading. Establishing secularization and structural differentiation as one of the coordinates of political development and subsystem autonomy as the other one, Almond obtains, in his table of political development (see Table 29), the conclusion that radical totalitarianism (as in Soviet Russia) and conservative totalitarianism (as in Nazi Germany) are systems and regimes of very similar levels of political development. For the same reason he rates the political development of modernizing authoritarian regimes, as Castello Branco's in Brazil, relatively high, in spite of their low participational achievements. The point, however, as will be discussed later, is not primarily the extent of the violence and constraint used in a society, although this fact, by itself, is extremely important and is always followed by some necessarily negative consequences. The primary point lies in the reasons for which violence and constraint are used. Violence and constraint to put down an absolutist czar, to force, even at the price of many irrationalities and iniquities, the modernization of a traditional society, and to open and enlarge its regime of participation is just the opposite (whatever the unavoidable overt and covert social costs incurred) of the use of the same resources and methods for preserving traditional absolutism, a traditional culture, and a restrictive and discriminating regime of participation.

The writers who identify political development with political institutionalization either have an excessively large understanding of the term "institutionalization," and thus deprive it of conceptual precision and analytical validity, or are insufficiently aware of the operational conditions which a process of institutionalization depends on. The first criticism seems applicable to Huntington. (See the brief presentation of his views in Chapter 8.) Focusing more on the resulting institutions, such as politico-legal structures, than on the participational process of institutionalization, he is led to view effects that are the consequence of political modernization, such as the increase in the adaptability, complexity, and autonomy of a system, as a result of institutionalization. The variables adaptability, complexity, and autonomy, as can be seen in Table 21, are affected by the larger or smaller levels of, respectively, the system's capability for adaptive and developmental change (macrovariable C, variable 3), the system's intrasystemic structural differentiation (macrovariable B, variable 3), and the system's intrasocietal structural differentiation (macrovariable B, variable 2). Although the terminological aspects of the question are obviously conventional, in the sense that other names might also suit the same phenomena, the conceptual aspects are not. Conceptually, we have that empirical observation of political systems imposes distinct categories for the variables concerning the operational conditions of the system and those concerning its participational conditions. Primitive societies have open and egalitarian regimes of participation for their members, but they have very low operational conditions. Modern fascist societies achieve very high operational conditions but are very restrictive and discriminating in their regimes of participation. Aristocratic traditional societies have lower operational conditions than modern fascist societies, and they also have discriminating regimes of participation.

Another fallacy of the identification of political development with political institutionalization, when the latter term is used with convenient conceptual precision, consists in the emphasis on the mobilizational and participational aspects of the process without regard for its operational requirements. Although the participational variables, as we have seen above, are an indispensable component of any process of effective development, they cannot, either analytically or empirically, take place without a corresponding and supporting process of political modernization. The essential aspects of this point were touched on when we discussed the relationship between the ethical and the scientific-technological levels. The increase of the participational variables is not possible without the corresponding and supporting increase of the operational valuables of the same polity. An insufficiently modernized political system has neither the command on its environment to bear, for instance, high levels of political participation, mass-elite integration, and system legitimacy, nor the politico-juridical means for coordinating the decisions and performing and controlling the services required for such a purpose.

The three aspects of political development

The former discussion enables me to comment briefly about the fourth thesis of our theory of political development. As will be remembered, this thesis concerns the following three aspects of political development: (1) development of the capability of the political system, (2) development of the contribution of the political system to the overall development of the concerned society, and (3) development of the responsiveness of the political system. If any of these are taken alone, to the exclusion of the others, they correspond, as we have discussed, to the restrictive views on political development adopted by some writers. Taken together, as cumulative aspects of political development, they correspond to the process as a whole.

Considered as the development of the capability of the political system, political development corresponds to the effectiveness of the polity as a social subsystem. Writers who identify political modernization with political development are usually considering only that aspect of political development. This is due to the fact that the increase of the capability of the system is the end-product of its modernization. In itself, however, that aspect of political development is just a part of the process, because (1) capability is related to political modernization and political development includes political institutionalization as well, and (2) increased political capability, as an aspect and a consequence of a process of development, is always necessarily associated, in a way or another, with the second and third aspects of political development: increased political and social consensus. As we shall see, the difference between general and specific political development is expressed in terms of the larger or smaller compatibility between the first two aspects and the third aspect. General political development is oriented toward increasing social consensus and specific political development toward increasing social politicalization.

Considered as the development of the contribution of the political system to the overall development of the concerned society, political development corresponds to the development of the whole society (including the cultural, participational, and economic systems) by political means. Although that concept of political development fits most of the ten meanings in Pye's list, it has not been discussed in the specialized literature. This probably due, in large part, to the fact that modern political scientists are concerned with stressing the autonomy of the political, vis-à-vis the social system as a whole and its other subsystems. In part, also, I believe, this is due to the fact that those social scientists interested in emphasizing the interrelation among the various planes of society are usually inclined, because of Marx's influence, to look for the economic factors conditioning society rather than the political ones.[2]

The aspect we are now discussing, however, is particularly important for the general understanding of political development for two reasons. The first, of an empirical nature, results from the fact that the more recent and dramatic examples of political development, from the experiment of Soviet Russia to the recent attempts of Cuba, have been characterized by an effort to use the development of the political system as a precondition and an instrument for the overall development of the concerned society. The second reason, of a theoretical nature, concerns the relationship between the first two aspects of political development and the third aspect, a relationship which is related to the question, discussed briefly at the end of Chapter 3, of the distinction between general and specific political development.

The empirical aspect of that question concerns the various attempts at, and possibilities of, promoting social change and the overall development of a society by political means. In the next chapter we will study at length the problems related to the conditions and modalities of political development, including those concerning the aspect now under consideration.

What is relevant for our present purposes is to consider political development as the development of the whole society by political means in relation to aspects one and three of political development: (1) political development as the development of the capability of the political system and (3) political development as the development of the responsiveness of the political system.

The possibility of promoting social change and the overall development of a society by (1) changing in depth the former political system, more often than not by revolutionary means, and (2) using, in depth, the new political system for the referred purpose lies, in its most general form, in the principle of congruence. As we saw in Chapter 2, that principle, which generalizes empirically observed regularities, states that structural changes introduced in any of the subsystems of the social system will either bring about congruent changes in the other subsystems, be regressive, or cause the dissolution of the society itself. In addition to this general principle, we have that the political system, as the goal-achieving system of a society and the one that supplies enforcement, security, and order to, respectively, the cultural, participational, and economic systems, is structurally capable of performing, given appropriate conditions, social changes congruent with its own regime.

The problem of promoting the overall development of society by political means, therefore, consists, essentially, in the fulfillment of two conditions: (1) The appropriate change must be successfully introduced in the political system and it must be endurable and (2) the other relevant conditions must be such that the appropriate employment of the political system will achieve congruent changes in the other systems of the society.

Vis-à-vis the first aspect of political development, the one now under consideration is characterized by its dependence on the previous achievement of the first aspect. Whatever the form by which changes may be introduced in the political system for its subsequent use in the promotion of the overall development of society, the successful employment of the political system always depends on the previous increase in its capability, as well as on other conditions. It is because the development of the system's capability is a necessary precondition of the two other aspects of political development that it is the most general aspect of political development.

If we now consider the second aspect of political development (the development of society by political means) relative to the third one (political development as the development of political consensus and of social consensus by political ways), we find that the relationship between these two aspects can be, and often is, one of little or negative compatibility. In principle these two aspects are complementary rather than compatible. By definition, the second aspect designates a political development that aims, beyond the political system, at the overall development of society. This overall development includes the development of the participational system, with the corresponding optimization, for every member, of its regime of participation. This development is the basis of social consensus, including political consensus. The more development is achieved, the greater is the ensuing consensus.

Actually, however, little or negative compatibility can easily result when, given the former structural conditions of the society and of its political system, achieving societal development by political means implies, in the first place, making very radical or revolutionary changes in the political system and, in the second place, a no less radical use of the political system for the promotion of social change and societal development. In such a case the radicalness of the means—regardless of how necessary or justified their use may be—brings about conflict instead of consensus.

The developmental revolutions of our time have shown, as in the Soviet case, that, whatever the revolutionists' subjective goal commitment may be for arriving at a conflictless—and therefore totally consensual—society, they fail to reach this goal in a double sense. First, while the revolution is in the process of building a new political system and, subsequently, of using the new system in depth to build a new society, the revolutionary means increase the dissent of the counterrevolutionary sectors of the society, and moreover, these means never receive full support from more than a small, sometimes extremely tiny, group of militants. Second, for all sorts of reasons, including the weight of the required sacrifices, the unavoidable injustices, the ideological and policy discrepancies, and the sheer competition for power, overt or covert internal conflicts are always ravaging the revolutionists' ranks, even if and when successful leaders maintain control over these conflicts.

Furthermore, it seems that even when substantial societal development is achieved, consensus is much harder to obtain (although not necessarily unattainable) after the hard times of revolution and reconstruction because of some characteristics and effects inherent in the process of promoting societal development by radical political means.

This problem will be discussed further in the third section of Book II. Let me just say here that the tendential incompatibility between the use of radical political means for the overall development of society and the achievement of political and social consensus cannot be taken as an intrinsic inappropriateness of these political means for promoting the development of a society. That conclusion, as is well known, has been usually accepted by conservative writers. If, however, the problem is considered without ideological biases (to the extent that this is possible within the limits of political science), one has to acknowledge, in the last analysis, that promoting development by political means, including radical ones, is often, both in theoretical and in practical terms, the only remaining alternative in societies controlled by nonfunctional privileged elites, whose interests and values are incompatible with the development of the society, as a whole, and particularly, with the participation of the masses. Czarist Russia and, even more, Kuomintang China are good examples of that hypothesis. The least that can be said of such cases is that, when—and insofar as—radical political means actually bring about an overall development of society, the resulting political and social consensus, although not general, is still incomparably larger than in the times of the old regime, and most of the other societal conditions have been substantially improved.

The final point of our present discussion involves the third aspect of political development: development of political consensus and of social consensus by political means. Maximum general political development is achieved when the concerned polity, besides maximizing its capability, at the available scientific-technological level (first aspect of political development), and besides contributing to the overall development of the society (second aspect), also achieves maximum political consensus and opens the way to maximum social consensus (third aspect). This stage, which no modern political system has ever achieved and which can only be viewed as an ideal type, is the expression of the highest ideal level of general political development.

Specific political development, which could be called specialized political development, is a concentration of the first two aspects of political development to optimize the structural-functional support that the polity can give to the society under given conditions of extreme demand for political action.[3] Sparta is a classic example of this kind of political development. The Spartan political system achieved the highest possible level of specific efficiency, within the available scientific-technological conditions of the time, for providing the Spartans with an all-powerful police-military state, so apt for maintaining, internally, the serfdom of the Helots and for imposing, externally, Spartan hegemony. Similarly, the Communist states in our time (although running against the theoretical predictions and models of Marx) have become highly specialized in the promotion, by political means, of the special mix of overall societal development and ideological and bureaucratic control that has characterized the experiments of developmental socialism up to now. The extent to which the political systems of these societies are capable of attaining a really wide and manifest consensus and a correspondingly high degree of representativeness and legitimacy, once the development of the society reaches a high level and the threat of external aggression is lessened by their own military development, is something that is currently being tested. Movements and tendencies to liberalize, including the Soviet Union's de-Stalinization and the democratization of Yugoslavia and Czechoslovakia, are too obvious to be ignored or underrated. Neither can the resistance to these tendencies and the action of bureaucratic-military ruling cliques against these liberalizing movements be ignored or minimized. Whatever the final issue happens to be, it looks as if, similar to what occurs in biological evolution, the price paid by a polity for its successful specific political development is the proportional reduction of its general developmental potential.

As a concluding remark, let me just make it clear that specific political development does not only occur in, nor is its corresponding societal price only paid by, the polities that are promoting social change and overall development by radical political means. Other political models, like the various brands of fascism, also achieve a highly efficient specialization. In that case, however, the specialization is not to promote social change and development, but to prevent it, either domestically, by the police containment of the society's own masses, or internationally, by the economic-military domination of alien societies. The price paid by these societies for the imposition and preservation of the privileges of their ruling groups is not less restrictive of their further developmental potential.

NOTES

[1] Designations, in their verbal expression, are scientific conventions. Other terms besides modernization could, in principle, be used. The best scientific terminological choice, however, is always the closest to current use and practice if precise meanings can be assured. The two terms adopted in this book for the components of political development already have wide circulation. With an appropriate definition, content analysis, and identification and quantification of the concerned variables, these terms become fully suited for precise scientific use.

[2] Huntington, however, in spite of his reduction of political development to political institutionalization, has shown a sharp understanding of the overall developmental aspect of efficiently managed political development in his discussion of the experiments of Mustafa Kemal and Lenin. (See 1968, chap. 5.)

[3] There is an analogy between general and specific evolution, on the one hand, and general and specific political development, on the other hand. The latter, however, is not just a special case of the former. Biological evolution continues by other means, as has been seen in this book, in the form of sociocultural evolution. The evolving entities, however, are species in one case and societies in the other case. Political systems are not totally independent self-adjustable systems, like societies, which have, on their own, a general and a specific independent evolution. As a subsystem of a society, they are subject to general and specific evolution. Specific political development, therefore, is a manifestation not of the specific evolution of a given polity but of the specific evolution of the society of which the polity is the political subsystem.

B

Political Models

10

Representational and Operational Models

The concept of model

The use of the term "model" has been rapidly increasing in political science, economics, and other social sciences in the past few years. This is undoubtedly due, in part, to academic fashion. But academic fashions themselves are indicative of a cultural trend, and so we come to the other part of the explanation. The use and abuse of terminology and constructs referring to models express a correspondingly increasing concern with empirically founded and testable social theory and with two correlated notions. One refers to the methodological principle that empirically well-founded generalizations concerning social interactions should also be susceptible to high levels of formalization and axiomatization, permitting the expression of that form of knowledge in rigorous verbal or mathematical models. The other notion is that empirically well-founded theories in the social field should provide a guidance to action similar to the guidance provided by natural theory, permitting the building of a "social technology," equivalent, even if approximately, to physical technology.

Without trying now to assess the positive and negative consequences that the current trend toward models may bring to political science, economics, and other social sciences, one has to acknowledge, at least, that this widespread use of the term naturally tends to introduce an increasing looseness in its conceptual understanding. Since the present study, in keeping with the prevailing trend, uses the idea and the techniques of models extensively, it seems convenient to proceed to a conceptual clarification of the terms to be employed.

Three sorts of conceptual imprecisions currently occur with respect to the notion of model. The first concerns the location of that idea in a conceptual spectrum, which goes from the concept of concept to the concept of theory. The second concerns the relation between models and mathematical interpretations. The third has to do with the connection between the concept of model and the concept of structure.

The concept of model, like many other concepts, may be used in a broad or in a strict way. Broadly, the term models means images (real or ideal) of something (real or ideal), in the sense of a representation of the form, the pattern, or the structure of (a real or symbolic) object. As Karl Deutsch (1963, p. 5) observed, knowledge is a mental model. And he added, subsequently, that in various ways (alternatively or cumulatively), models perform four functions: (1) the organizing function, which expresses the broadest meaning of the concept, and consists in the ability of a model to permit discernment of form, pattern, or structure, (2) the heuristic function, which consists in the ability to lead to the discovery of new facts and new methods, (3) the predictive function, which consists in the ability to anticipate, in time or space, given events, in varying degrees of qualitative and quantitative specificity and accuracy, and (4) the measuring function, which applies to models that are related to the represented object by defined and quantified relationships (pp. 7 ff.).

Although Deutsch suggests both a broad and a strict meaning for the concept of model, other writers emphasize the coextensiveness of the concept of model and the concept of theory, stating that models provide an alternative explanation of a theory. So Richard S. Rudner (1966) understands models as isomorphic interpretations of the same calculus or reality. "A model for a theory consists of an alternative interpretation of the calculus of which the theory itself is an interpretation." Passing from the level of the philosophy of social sciences to social science theory, we have that Maurice Duverger (1964a) follows a similar line of reasoning, understanding models as partial theories, as opposed to general or "cosmogonic" theories.

The two other sorts of conceptual imprecisions, the identification of models with mathematical interpretations and with structures, are made, respectively, by H. Aujac and C. Lévy-Strauss, as well as by other writers. Aujac (1949) understands models as "a system of equations which substitute to a complex, rich and concrete universe, in its extension and its historical unfolding, a universe defined by a set of numbers and of relations among them." Claude Lévy-Strauss (1958, p. 305) emphasizes the fact that structures as such are related to the models of reality, not to reality. *"Le principe fondamental est que la notion de structure ne se rapporte pas à la réalité empirique mais aux modèles construits d'après celle-ci."*

The discussion of the distinctions or identities among the concepts of concept, model, and theory might be better understood if we accept the broad and the narrow meanings of the concept of model, as Deutsch does. In its broad meaning, as a representation of the form, pattern, or structure of an object, a model can be just a concept. Using May Brodbeck's (1959) definition of concept as "terms referring to a descriptive property or relation," we have that models performing only the organizing function (enabling the discernment of form, pattern, or structure) may be concepts or simple propositions. Theories, however, imply, much more than an image or a mere prediction, "a deductively connected set of laws," according to Brodbeck. In terms that are less rigid and more compatible with the social sciences, we can say, with Richard Rudner (1966), that a "theory is a systematically related set of statements, including some lawlike generalizations, that is empirically testable." Some models may fit this description, when they have a high level of predictability. This requirement, however, is not necessary for the strict meaning of model. Models can have an accurate representational ability, for given purposes, and still not have a high level of predictability, either because of the sort of object they represent or because of the sort of representation they are intended for. Static objects represented as such, as a land on a map or a person in a photograph, can be accurately represented without eliciting predictions concerning what will occur with that land or person. What is essential for a model, understood in the strict sense, is that it provide an *isomorphic representation of the structure of the represented object.* The isomorphic and the structural aspects are the conditions that make the representation of an object a model of it. Brodbeck and Rudner, already cited, also point out the isomorphic requirement of models. On the other hand, Jean Viet has stressed in his comprehensive analysis of the structural methods in contemporary social sciences (1967, p. 76) that what is essential for models to represent and reproduce is the structure of the represented object. Models can, therefore, be defined in a strict sense, as structural isomorphic representations of objects, or, more explicitly, as the *representation of the structure of a real or ideal object by another real or ideal object that presents an isomorphic structure.*

It is now possible to clarify the two remaining areas of conceptual indetermination, the relationship between models and mathematical interpretations and between models and structures. By now it should be clear that mathematical models, as a quantified way of representing a certain pattern of relationships, are ways of providing by symbols a structural isomorphic representation. Mathematical models are a particularly adequate form of model for performing Deutsch's fourth function, the function of measuring.

More apt to create confusion, I am afraid, is the excessive emphasis Claude Lévy-Strauss puts on the structural character of models, vis-à-vis the multiplicity of traits of allegedly astructural empirical reality. Ultimately, most modeling aims, for given purposes, at simplifying reality without deforming it, stressing only its structural features. But the isomorphic reproduction of a structure, in a model, could not be made, and could never be isomorphic, if that structure were not contained in the represented reality, in the sense of being an empirically deductible or analytically deductible form, pattern, or order constituting a property of that reality. Therefore, against Lévy-Strauss, it should be stated that structures as such are contained in reality, if in the form of the ideal arrangement of its constituting parts.

In his comparative analysis of several current structuralist views, Jean Viet (1967) gives an impressive indication of how the majority of contemporary social scientists understand structure as a *forma in rem* that can be grasped by empirical deduction, or by analytical deduction, or understood by phenomenological reduction. Writers with such different viewpoints as Radcliffe-Brown

(1952, p. 190), Georges Gurvitch (1958), S. F. Nadel (1957, p. 7), Jean Piaget (1950) and Lucien Goldmann (1969) agree, in a basic way, that structures are forms or patterns of relationship of reality.

Operational models

With the preceding clarification we can now begin our discussion of political models with the distinction between representational and operational models. Implicit in the characterization of models was the understanding of that concept, in both its broad and its strict senses, as the isomorphic representation of a given structure. The represented object may be real or ideal and so may its representation. The small-scale model of an airplane is a real or physical model. Ideal or symbolic models can be (1) graphic, as in pictures, maps, and graphs, (2) verbal, as in the expression of relationships by propositions, and (3) mathematical, when the isomorphic representation of a structure is expressed by quantitative symbols. In any of these cases, the models are representational ones, and that is the sort of model that is usually referred to when no qualifications are introduced. In addition to that kind of model there is another kind, the operational model.

The understanding of the operational models requires, first, a distinction between static and dynamic representational models. All the examples of representational models given above are of static models in which the represented structure is assumed to be an immutable one. The airplane represented by a physical small-scale model or the area represented by a map are realities whose structure is considered as unchanging, at least for the purpose of modeling. Representational models, however, can also give an isomorphic structural representation of the change in a structure, in ways that permit the forecasting and presenting of a succession of different future stages of structural change, each one bringing the succeeding one about in accordance with specified factors and conditions. Dynamic representational models can also be physical, as with the small-scale hydraulic models used for the study of the effects of tides or currents on shores. Most projections or forecasts, however, can only be expressed by symbolic models.

When one takes a dynamic model, isomorphically representing the projection or forecast of a process of structural change, and voluntarily introduces a proposed goal for that process, a goal that is inherently compatible with the process, together with the assumedly necessary conditions for reorienting the process for that goal, the model becomes an operational one. In addition to (1) the representation of the projected future sequence of stages with (2) the implied or expressed set of factors conditioning that process, which are also contained in representational models, operational models contain (3) a voluntarily proposed goal for that process together with (4) the isomorphic representation of the conditions necessary for the reorientation of that process in order to reach the assigned goal.

Operational models can be designed, in principle, to forecast any process submitted to a voluntary option whenever the fulfillment of that option is understood to depend on factors inherent in the process and susceptible, in their essential traits, to isomorphic representation. It is the latter characteristic that distinguishes operational models from simple plans of action or strategies. The difficulty of giving, even loosely, a satisfactory isomorphic representation of the inherent factors that will operate on a process, so that a voluntarily chosen goal will be achieved, has restricted the accuracy of most operational models and has restricted their use to limited purposes. In the fields of strategy and politics some interesting experiments have been done with simulation techniques in order to design operational models that will provide advantages to a party in a conflict game or situation or in an electoral campaign.[1]

The political system, as a social subsystem, and society as a whole can be represented by static and dynamic models and can be the object of operational models. The early political literature, from Aristotle onward, presents some crude examples of representational models, both static and dynamic, and even of operational models. Aristotle himself gave basic descriptions of the essential characteristics of a polity and of its corruption (considered with an ethical bias) that are crude static and dynamic representational models of the political system, in general, and of the specific polities he studied. Machiavelli's *The Prince* can be regarded as a crude (psychologistic) operational political model for obtaining and keeping power in certain settings and under certain conditions. Much more elaborately, but with other biases, Marx's theory of the great stages of historical change and of the future changes of the capitalist society represents an operational model for the understanding of these changes and the "praxis" of deliberate participation in their making.

The introduction and improvement of systems analysis in political science, as has already been discussed, provided new and much more accurate elements for building representational political models. As a further contribution to the field, the increasingly more refined understanding of political development is now permitting the elaboration of more sophisticated operational political models. Eisenstadt's (1963 and 1966) and Almond's (1966) representational models of the political system are among the best recent attempts, and Apter's (1965) operational model of and for the process of political modernization, although still in an incipient form, is an important contribution to that more complex sort of political model.

An attempt was made in Chapter 5 of this book to find the macrovariables that determine the structure of a polity (Table 20) and to establish on the basis of that structure the set of variables required for the basic representational model of any political system (Table 21). Using that basic model, I suggested (Table 22) a general typology of political systems and, after a critical discussion of Almond's and Apter's classification, presented and detailed a new taxonomic model (Tables 24, 25, and 26) for political systems and regimes. Finally, with these instruments I was able to propose a general list of political systems (Table 27).

The political representational models provided or made possible by that set of tables will be utilized in our subsequent analysis and discussion of operational political models. In addition, however, we shall have to keep the main theoretical findings or assumptions of the preceding chapters in mind. Special reference should be made to the following points: (1) the structural and dynamic conception of society discussed in Chapter 1, with an emphasis on our conclusions concerning the explanatory insufficiency of the equilibrium-functionalist and the single-factor conflict models of society and the corresponding necessity to adopt a new and more complex model, dynamic-functionalist and at the same time multifactor conflictualist, (2) the theory of structural change and of social structural change discussed in Chapter 2, and (3) the theory of the polity and of the political process discussed in Chapter 3.

As far as the analysis of the operational political models is concerned, one of the relevant consequences of the preceding discussions is the insufficient descriptive and explanatory capacity of neoliberalism and communism, as loose representational and operational macromodels. In addition to traits resulting from the historical setting or the empirical conditions in which these two macromodels have been used to explain given societies or inspire their social regimes with teleoligical orientation, the essential limitation of these models comes from, respectively, their equilibrium-functionalist and their single factor confictualist assumptions. The intrinsic limitations of these macromodels, however, should not lead us to forget that the current regimes of the United States and of Soviet Russia, inspired by them, are still proving rather satisfactory for each of these societies. Given, in the first place, the adjustments that neoliberalism has brought to laissez-faire liberalism, which was closer to an unqualified equilibrium-functionalist assumption and, in the second place, the pragmatic way in which that model is put into practice in the United States, we have that, basically, the American society is provided with the minimum amount of social regulation required by its present needs. Similarly, we have that Soviet communism also expresses the many theoretical adjustments gradually incorporated into the implied basic model by the successive generations of party leaders from Lenin to Brezhnev, as the pragmatic adjustments of Soviet policies and structures to the current requirements of Soviet society.

In spite of the theoretical and pragmatic adjustments introduced in the neoliberal and communist macromodels, however, their current satisfactory performance in the American and Soviet societies should not obscure two basic facts. The first concerns the very limited capacity, if there is any, for transference of these models to different societies, that is, to societies whose historical development has not been characterized by the dialectic interaction between the assumptions of these models in the prevailing social regime and the modifying impact, on the regime, of social forces and situations not harmonious with those assumptions. The Western European and the Chinese societies present similitudes with, respectively, the American and the Soviet societies and are allegedly submitted to similar regimes. Actually, however, in spite of several institutional and factual similitudes, the Western European societies are regulated by welfare states, which may even be, in certain respects, less efficient in some of their social services (education, for example) than the privately controlled American society, but which provide a much broader and effective frame for social macro-rationality than the American regime can afford. Similarly, because the present state of development in the Chinese society is much lower than in the Soviet one, the former has much less necessity for competitive freedom and subsystem autonomy than the latter. Moreover, the cultural revolution, whose positive and negative effects are still insufficiently clear, seems to have curtailed the tendency toward the unilinear development of an oligopoly of power which reduces the flexibility of the Soviet regime and the dependability of its subsystems. If things are thus in Europe and China, for the societies of the third world, as Irving Horowitz (1966) has well shown, whatever the rhetoric and, eventually, the aspirations of certain of their sectors, it is still more clear that they have not been able to transplant to their societal conditions either of these two macromodels and are not likely to do so in the future.

The second fact to be stressed in connection with these two macromodels is the unlikelihood of their long permanence in the American and Soviet societies. As has been observed by such analysts of the American society as Galbraith (1967) and Heilbroner (1969) as well as several others, there is an increasing necessity to submit the ever more complex American society to forms of social regulation appropriate for the enlargement of the social macro-rationality of that society. This necessity will, in a couple of decades, impose significant changes on the American social regime so that inevitably it will surpass the framework of neoliberalism. The Soviet society is changing in a similar way, although in a different direction. It is widely acknowledged by the students of Soviet society that the high level of macro-rationality provided by central planning and the socialization of the means of production is increasingly reduced by the unilinear overconcentration of power in the higher hierarchy of the party, with the resulting lack of individual freedom and creativity and of subsystem autonomy. As has been observed by Allen Kassof (1968, p. 502), the Communist party itself, in order to keep its commanding role, "will increasingly face the necessity of compromises, the cumulative results of which will greatly alter the atmosphere of daily life." Libermanism, in the economy, and the growing autonomy of the several professional corps, from the scientists to the managers, are indications of that structural trend, the result of which will inevitably surpass the single-factor conflict assumptions of the regime.

NOTES

[1] See R. Duncan Luce and H. Raiffa (1966), Martin Shubik, ed. (1964, particularly pp. 70 ff. and pp. 279 ff.), and Raymond Boudon (1967, particularly chap. 9).

11

Operational Political Models

ANALYSIS OF THE MODEL

Constituent elements

The previous discussion enables us now to give a conceptual definition of operational political models and to proceed subsequently to the analysis of the major elements of that sort of model. This will be done in the first part of this chapter. Then, a rapid critical survey will be made of the recent literature on the subject. Finally, an attempt will be made to formulate a new general classification of operational political models.

As was seen in the preceding chapter, operational models are a more complex form of model than the dynamic representational ones and are obtained by the introduction, in the latter models, of a voluntarily proposed goal, inherently compatible with the concerned process, together with the isomorphic representation of the conditions necessary for the reorientation of that process in order to reach the assigned goal. Designing an operational model involves, therefore, two sort of problems. The first concerns the choice of a goal. It must be the kind of goal that can be chosen in an election that consists in a voluntary decision, in the sense that the specific election was not deterministically contained in or prescribed by the process that it aims to orient, but it must also be the kind of goal that will be inherently compatible with that process and likely to reorient it for the attainment of the assigned goal. The second problem, once an inherently achievable goal has been chosen, consists in determining as well as possible the conditions that the reorientation of the process for the attainment of that goal depend on and in providing as accurately as possible an isomorphic representation of the main lines of these conditions, in order to make possible the appropriate political guidance of the process.

These essential aspects and characteristics of operational political models provide us with a definition for that sort of model: An operational political model is a *simplified representation of an elected achievable process of sociopolitical structural change* (usually sociopolitical development) *and of the respective most relevant conditioning factors; this simplified representation presents, with sufficient accuracy, the essential traits of an isomorphic structural representation of the main successive stages of the forecasted course of the change, including an indication of the main implementable successive conditions and means necessary for the appropriate political guidance of the process.*

The analysis of the constituent elements of operational political models, as defined above, brings out two distinct parts. These parts and their corresponding aspects can be presented schematically as follows:

1. Simplified representation of an elected achievable process of sociopolitical structural change and of the respective most relevant conditioning factors.

   1.1 Design of a sociopolitical structural change formulated as the goal elected by the prospective leaders of the project and to be achieved by the actors foreseen as carrying out its implementation.

   1.2. That design cannot be arbitrary. Rather it must be of such a kind that a theoretically legitimate assumption concerning its inherent implementability can be justified in terms of an appropriate knowledge of the concerned society and polity and their relevant environment. Inherent implementability means:

   a. The resources and forces necessary for realizing that design exist, actually or potentially but in a mobilizable form, in the concerned society and polity.

   b. The chosen design is intrinsically consistent and constitutes a sociopolitical arrangement compatible with the structure and the dynamic possibilities of the concerned society in its given environment.

   c. The design is not only theoretically implementable, but actually tends to be implemented because, as far as can be reasonably assessed, certain forces in that society, once they are properly confronted with the design, will have the propensity and the capability, driven by their own interests and values, to promote the realization of the design.

   1.3. The adopted design will usually be for the political and overall development of the concerned society. Theoretically, however, the design could be oriented toward any sort of implementable sociopolitical change, including the disruption of the society. Actually implementable sociopolitical structural changes are more likely to be the developmental ones or those that optimize for the society and polity and for their relevant members. In certain cases, however, intrasocietal and intrapolity dissention and conflict could favor the implementation of disruptive designs.

1.4. The conditions required for ascertaining, as in (1.2), the inherent implementability of the chosen design imply a causative understanding of how that sociopolitical structural change is going to take place, which permits the determination and representation of the relevant conditioning factors.

2. The simplified representation of an elected achievable process, as in (1), must present, with sufficient accuracy, the essential traits of an isomorphic structural representation of the main successive stages of the forecasted course of the change, including an indication of the main implementable successive conditions and means necessary for the appropriate political guidance of the process.

    2.1. For the attainment of the elected goal, the presentation of both that goal and the process leading to its achievement must meet two requirements:

        a. It must be sufficiently simplified to be intelligible and representable. Simplification is required for converting a multitude of traits, episodes, and factors into an intelligible and manageable projection of causally understood events. Such simplification may be validly obtained by selective abstraction.

        b. It must be a sufficiently accurate isomorphic structural representation of the process in order to achieve the descriptive, heuristic, and predictive requirements of a model, even if at only a minimally sufficient level of accuracy. Without these characteristics no model would be obtained, and as a result, it would not be possible to have reliable and sufficient knowledge of the concerned process to anticipate its occurrence and employ the appropriate political guidance.

    2.2. That sufficiently accurate isomorphic structural representation must include an indication of the main implementable successive conditions and means necessary for the appropriate political guidance of the concerned process.

The latter requirement—within the condition stated in (1.2)—is the very core of operational political models. The elements analyzed in (2.1) are the usual requirements of any dynamic model. Given a dynamic projection of a process and an elected achievable goal, what will enable the leaders of the process to orient that process toward the attainment of the goal will be (a) the anticipated reasonable knowledge of the successive stages forecasted for the process and (b) the equally anticipated knowledge of the conditions and means that, in each stage, will enable them to keep the project oriented toward the attainment of the assigned goal. Fundamentally, these conditions and means concern the creation of enough political power, convenient institutions, and adequate motivations for keeping the process oriented toward the elected goal. Because of the nature of these conditions, however, all operational political models, even when the elected goals are the most imminently achievable and the models are the most correctly designed, may be brought to complete failure by human errors of leadership in the utilization of the required means, whatever the availability of these means. Operational political models are the best possible instruments for combining the intelligent forecast of a political process with the intelligent utilization of the inherent potentialities of that process in a deliberate reorientation of the process in terms of realistically achievable elected goals. But they are not, and can never be, a totally sure ticket for success. In the first place, ultimate success always depends on how well the model was designed and the extent to which the process was inherently likely to be oriented toward the attainment of the chosen goal. In the second place, however favorable these characteristics are, success is always a work of political art and expresses the mastery with which the leaders are able to operate the model throughout the successive stages of its implementation. And in the third place, regardless of the other two conditions, actual success depends on a sizable coefficient of chance, expressing the innumerable unforeseeable aspects of any complex forecast, the more so the more complex the process and longer the projections.

Prerequisites of models

Independent of the skill with which an operational political model is implemented or, for that matter, designed, the building of the model, as a technical operation, has three major prerequisites.

The first prerequisite is a structural analysis of the concerned polity and its respective society and relevant environment. The objective of this analysis is to enable one to make a design that is as accurate as possible of the static representational model of that polity, society, and environment. As a consequence of the analysis, a typological classification of the society will be obtained. Most relevant for this classification are: (1) the determination of the social regime of the society, its major component forces and structures, and its relevant environment, (2) the determination of its major resources, and (3) the determination of the more relevant intra- and extrasocietal conditions for the utilization of the society's own resources.

The second prerequisite consists in the analysis of the probable structural trends of that society, inherent in the former model, in order to design a dynamic representational model of the concerned society that is as accurate as possible. This analysis implies the forecasting of the most probable structural transformations that will occur in that society as a result of its own functioning and of foreseeable external interrelations. The resulting projection makes possible an *assessment of the societal viability*, or depending on the case, *national viability of that society*.

The third prerequisite, whenever the operational political model to be designed is a developmental one, consists in the comparative analysis of the present and tendential degree of development of that society, using other comparable societies as a yardstick. The operation involves, fundamentally, an assessment of (1) the *present comparative level of development of that society* and its probable evolution in a foreseeable future, (2) the *inherent possibilities of development of that society, in terms of its potentiality of optimization and of its societal (national) viability,* and (3) *assuming its viability, the conditions, in principle and in abstract, that would be required for such optimization.*

If these prerequisites are adequately fulfilled, it is possible to formulate an operational political model by introducing, in the previously designed dynamic representational model, the two new elements peculiar to operational models: the elected achievable goal and the implementable conditions and means necessary for the appropriate political guidance of the process.

Actual model designing

The last part of the designing of an operational political model involves, essentially: (1) the election of the achievable goal, (2) the actual design of the model, and (3) the detailing of the plan for the political guidance of the process.

The problem of electing achievable goals—in the assumed hypothesis of a developmental purpose—consists, essentially, in determining which of the requirements for the optimization of the concerned society are most likely to be implementable by effectively mobilizable forces in that society. Whereas the desirable goals, in terms of societal optimization, can be indicated and even quantified in a fairly objective way, once the representational models and the developmental assessment have provided a reasonable picture of that society, the crucial problem consists in determining, from among the desirable goals, those *whose implementation is likely to be conveniently supported by sufficiently powerful and motivated social forces.* This marks an essential distinction between the ideological approach to societal improvement, which elects goals because of their desirability, and the model approach, which is characterized by its engineering-like selection of (admittedly desirable) goals because of their operational implementability. And it is precisely because Marx, in spite of the limitation of his single-factor representational model, was the first to understand the futility of "good" goals that are not inherently implementable that his own brand of interpreting society and his model for its change reached unprecedented success and are still stirring the imagination of men today.

The central problem concerning the actual design of the operational model consists in providing an appropriate adjustment between the "normal" trends of the process, as indicated by the dynamic representational model, and the reorienting pressures ensued by the social forces to be mobilized for the attainment of the elected goal. What one should obtain is a "corrected" forecast of the process and its successive stages, containing as clearly as possible a representation of the major factors conditioning each stage and an indication of the implementable means necessary for the appropriate political guidance of the process.

The detailing of the plan for the political guidance of the process deals, precisely, with the preceding problem. What must be determined and specified, along with the corresponding attainment strategy, is the sort of power accumulation required for that guidance, the institutions most convenient for that guidance, and the motivations, relative to the various strata and groups of the society, that must be used for obtaining the required power and channeling it to and through the convenient institutions.

Survey of the literature

The preceding analysis allows us now to proceed to the critical survey of the recent literature on the subject.

As has often been commented in this study, Marx produced the first consistent modern operational political model. Marx's model, in spite of the limitations coming from his single-factor representation of society, had the advantage of providing a complex, integrated, and macroscopic vision of the historico-social process, with a scope that no additional theory has obtained since. Because of its heuristic and explanatory capacity and its not despicable predictive possibilities, Marx's model has resisted the ideological abuses of Marxists and anti-Marxists alike and has been restored by more recent scholarship, together with the renewed interest in the writings of the young Marx, to its deserved academic importance.[1]

More recent political scientists, taking advantage of the new possibilities created by the incorporation of system analysis into the study of the polity and by the improvement in the theory of political development, have attempted, with varying degrees of explicitation and formalization, to indicate some operational political models. Almond (1966), Shils (1962), Eisenstadt (1966), Apter (1965) and the present writer (1968) are among those who have made such an attempt.

Almond's contribution to the field of political models was essentially oriented toward the formulation of representational models, as was discussed extensively earlier in this book, and only by inference can his ideas on operational models be considered. Two points concerning Almond's ideas, however, deserve to be focused on. The first concerns the implicit typology of operational models contained in his comparative discussion of modern political systems (1966 pp. 306 ff.). As can be seen there, particularly in the table on p. 308 (see Table 29 of the present book), the classification of political regimes in terms of their degrees of (1) structural differentiation and secularization and (2) subsystem autonomy implied different capabilities for modernization and/or for institutionalization. In the context of Almond's study it can be inferred that the several possible regimes—from high autonomy democracy and radical totalitarianism, which have the highest level of modernity, to premobilized democracy and premobilized authoritarianism, which have the lowest level of modernity—represent alternative models for promoting the modernization of societies with distinct conditions and degrees of development.

The second point I would like to emphasize is related to Almond's clear understanding, in the conclusion of his analysis of political development, of the fact that political science had reached the level at which it became both possible and necessary to study the operational aspects of development. In Almond's words: "It is perfectly reasonable to think of state building, nation building, participation, and distribution as problems of political development planning, or investment" (1966, p. 328). And later: "Indeed, these exercises in the analysis of political investment strategies bring us to the point where we can attempt to formulate a 'rational choice' model of political growth." Almond's ending remarks in this respect are highly suggestive: "We are confronted here with the ultimate question of the Enlightenment. Can man employ reason to understand, shape, and develop his own institutions, particularly those concerned with power and coercion, to plan political development with the least human cost and with bearable risks?" (p. 331). And finally: "The modern political scientist can no longer afford to be the disillusioned child of the Enlightenment, but must become its sober trustee" (p. 332).

Edward Shils' (1962) contribution to the formulation of operational models has been more analytic. After studying the determinants of political development, such as social structure, culture, personality, and political structure, Shils investigated the possible alternative courses of political development, both as distinct empirically occurring tendencies and as implicit operational models for political action. He pointed out six distinct alternative courses and corresponding implied models: (1) political democracy, (2) tutelary democracy, (3) modernizing oligarchies, (4) totalitarian oligarchies, (5) traditional oligarchies, and (6) traditionalistic and theocratic oligarchies. Each model has its own fundamental characteristics. The adoption and implementation of each model depends on specific conditions within the concerned society, and in terms of these conditions, each model presents certain advantages and risks and involves certain costs and commitments. Although Shils' study (originally published in 1959) suffers from the limitations of incipient research and is not altogether free from ideological biases,[2] it was the first qualified attempt to consider political regimes as operational developmental models—even if the voluntaristic dimension of these models was only implicitly indicated—the selection of which must be dictated by the conditions of the concerned society and the implementation of which must follow a certain sequence of stages in order to be successful and to release the possibilities of development that each model can afford.

Eisenstadt (1964 and 1966), like Almond, was primarily concerned with the comparative study of modernization and the deduction, from it, of representational models rather than operational ones. Besides achieving, however, a particularly clear and perceptive understanding of the processes he studied, he formulated the basic conditions that must be met by any systematic effort for development if it is to be successful. These conditions could be considered as prerequisites of any operational political model. Very briefly, these prerequisites are of two orders: One, concerning the conditions enabling the elite to lead a developmental process, is essentially related to the idea of leadership functionality, and the other, concerning the strategic goals to be achieved by the elite, is essentially related to the idea of balanced growth. The conditions enabling the elite to lead the process are that: (1) the elite must be a mixed one, containing people of diverse experience and occupations; (2) job functionality must be kept as high as possible, disciplined and not ascriptive; (3) the cadres must be kept sufficiently open; and (4) the commitments to modernization must not break completely with the past but must be able to link traditional institutions and values to the process of development. Concerning the strategic goals to be attained, Eisenstadt stresses: (1) the restructuring of the process of communication through gradual integration and cautious relative segregation of certain types and levels, for a certain length of time, (2) the widespread provision of primary education on the local level and expansion of specialized elite schools, with gradual extension of mobility between the two, (3) the promotion of social mobility in ways that (a) break the traditional patterns but (b) are realistically compatible with the expanding opportunities, (4) the maintenance of the rulers' power monopoly, but (a) supported by new symbols of legitimacy, (b) compensated by the growing importance of new technical occupations, and (c) with a minimization of ascriptive monopolization of upper positions, (5) the greatest firmness of design and purpose but within conditions preserving (a) the adjustment of the level of demands to the availability of resources and the capability of conversion, (b) the sequence of stages, inclusive of participation purposes, (c) the simultaneous development of the political, the cultural, and the economic planes, and (d) the flexibility of policies and pragmaticalness of means.

The earlier contributions of David Apter (1965) and of the present writer (1968) brought a higher degree of elaboration to the study of operational political models than the other early contributions. Both Apter's study and my former study, which were made independently of each other, stressed the double relationship existing between the process of political development and the concerned society. The process of political development is a part of the general societal processes, expresses the political aspect of the overall development of a society, and is therefore conditioned by the structural features of that society. At the same time, the process of political development has its own specificity, is a structural change of the polity, and by increasing the latter's capability, increases its capacity to introduce, by political means, corresponding changes in the society as a whole. This double relationship involves a particular sort of circular causality between society and polity and their respective development. Given the structure of a society and its typological features, only some forms of political development, if any, are able to occur in that society. If some do occur, however, the resulting process of political development will operate on that society and change it accordingly. With the appropriate political and sociological analysis one can determine, for each major class of society, the sort of operational political model most suitable for ensuing the political development of the concerned polity and for promoting the overall development of that society by political means.

For Apter the principal variables determining the typological classification of societies, as far as the possibilities of their political development is concerned, are: (1) the form of authority and (2) the prevailing associational value. As has been indicated (Chart 4 in Chapter 5), the modernization and overall development of the four major resulting classes of societies, (a) sacred collectivity, (b) secular-libertarian, (c) progressive oligarchical, and (d) theocracies, can occur with, in Apter's terminology, the mobilization system, the reconciliation system, and the modernizing autocracy, respectively.

The central findings and arguments of my former study (1968) can be reduced to three principal points. The first is that with the conditions of our time the development of an underdeveloped society can only be promoted through appropriate planning. The second concerns the problems of, and conditions for, appropriate planning, in terms of the typological characteristics of a society. Under the conditions of our time the national state is acknowledged as a necessary condition for autonomous development with the consequence that national viability is a prerequisite for any developmental model. The sort of operational political model most suitable for each (viable) society, however, is determined by the sort of elite and of elite-mass relationship existing in the concerned society. Three major classes of elites and elite-mass relationships are empirically observable in most underdeveloped countries: (1) elites under the leadership of an entrepreneurial sector of the national bourgeoisie, which has proved capable of starting some spontaneous socioeconomic development, with the additional characteristic that in such societies there are sectors in the middle class and the working class that are strongly development motivated, (2) oligarchical elites, generally constituting a landowning patriciate, controlling a basically peasant mass, in a society whose modern sector, usually consisting of part of the army and the civil bureaucracy in addition to a few foreign-owned modern businesses, is operated by a technocratic and managerial subelite of the middle class, (3) obscurantist and exploitative oligarchical elites of traditional peasant societies, in which there is practically no middle class and whose modern sector, if existing, is represented by a marginalized and oppressed intelligentsia. A variety of the latter type of elite consists in a *societas sceleris*, constituted by the coalition of a patrician rural class, a consular bourgeoisie, and co-opted sectors of the professional middle class and of the labor leaders, exploiting a coercively oppressed mass, with the marginalization and repression of the independent intelligentsia. The third point concerns the operational political models most suitable for each class of society. In terms of the preceding typology, these models are, respectively, the national capitalist, the state capitalist, and the developmental socialist.

GENERAL CLASSIFICATION

It is possible now to pass on to a general classification of operational political models. As was noted in Chapter 10, the general framework for any possible operational political model is provided by the tables presented in Chapter 5, particularly Tables 25 and 26. It will be clear by now, if we look back at those two tables, that Apter's "systems" are actually a set of classes of regimes of power. According to our tables, they represent, with reference to political superordination (variable G), the subvariables GP (the regime of power), of which there are four possible classes: (GP.1), conservation regime, (GP.2), reconciliation regime,

(GP.3), ordination regime, and (GP.4) mobilization regime. These classes indicate the type of regime of power that tends to prevail with three possible classes of social regime: (GS.1), patrimonial regime, (GS.2), civil regime, and (GS.3), totalitarian regime. These three classes of social regime express the three typical forms of relationship between the regime of participation, the regime of values, and the corresponding regime of property, that tend, empirically, to occur in societies.

The first type (GS.1, patrimonial regime) corresponds to close societies of restricted participation. The members of such societies are formally divided between active and passive members, as masters and slaves, serfs, or clients, the former having inherent rights of participation and being the full partners of the society and the latter having only some eventually conceded permissible activities, granting them, precariously, a dependent participation. The regime of values corresponding to such a regime of participation consecrates the values of the higher, fully participant, noble stratum of the society as the higher values of that society. The noble values are the values of the nobles. The corresponding regime of property concentrates, de jure and de facto all, or almost all, ownership in the hands of the high stratum.

The second type (GS.2, civil regime) corresponds to open societies, with an open regime of participation, although, de facto, various forms of ascriptive privileges tend to be observed. In such societies values are supposed to be, ultimately, independent of the society, expressing in terms of religious and ethico-philosophical beliefs a transcendent or transcendental axiological reality. The corresponding regime of property, contrary to what occurs in the previous case, establishes, at least de jure, equal right of access to property for everybody, either by granting, in principle, a free universal right of property (free capitalism) or by submitting property to varying forms of social regulation in the collective interest of all.

The third type (GS.3, totalitarian regime) corresponds to controlled societies with an open regime of participation in which all members are equal and have the same rights de jure but not de facto. The regime of values stresses open participation and a "material" or "moral" democracy as the supreme value and the development of the basic inherent human and social potentialities—or the protection of certain rights and values, in the case of ordinated capitalism—as the supreme goal of society. This regime of values leads to strict forms of collective control and, correspondingly, submits the regime of property to the control of a central agency of society.

These three classes of social regime are correlated to the four classes of regime of power. As we have seen in Chapter 1, regimes of participation and values are mutually conditioned, and for each type of relationship they tend to bring about a corresponding regime of property and to require the sanctioning of an appropriate regime of power. Table 25 indicates the classes of regime of power corresponding to the three classes of social regime.

GP.1, the conservation regime, is the regime of power corresponding to the sanctioning of patrimonial social regimes. The corresponding types of empirical regimes are precapitalist, today reduced to a few remaining primitive societies.

GP.2, the reconciliation regime, corresponding to civil social regimes, is a class with several empirical types. Some, as (G.2), free capitalism, characteristic of nineteenth-century Western Europe, have only historical significance today. The other types, from (G.3), regulated capitalism, typical of the United States today, to (G.5), welfare socialism, which does yet exist in any society but tends to be approached by Nordic socialism, are all regimes that try, in varying degrees, to conciliate personal freedom with social welfare through social regulation.

GP.3, the ordination regime, is one of the two classes of regimes of power corresponding to totalitarian regimes. There are several empirical types from (G.6), ordinated capitalism (Fascism, Falangism, and so forth), to (G.8), state capitalism. The great distinction to be found in that class results from whether the development of certain basic human and social potentialities, as in the case of (G.7), ordinated socialism, and (G.8), state capitalism, is the supreme goal ascribed to society by the regime of values or, as in the case of (G.6), ordinated capitalism, the ultimate purpose is to protect some allegedly eternal rights and values (as certain forms of private property and certain class values) and to impose social controls in the name and for the sake of a moral democracy.

GP.4, the mobilization regime, is the other class of regime of power corresponding to totalitarian regimes. Its empirical type is (G.9), developmental socialism. In principle, other forms of mobilization regimes could occur, as we can see in the sociopolitical content of the historical cases of Islam and the Anabaptists.

The relationship between these classes of regimes of power and the corresponding classes of social regimes are sufficiently self-evident. A regime of power consists essentially in the regulation of political power—including those who can accede to it; the extension, form, and purpose of its exercise; and the ways in which it can be transferred—in order to preserve the social regime. Given a certain regime of participation and a certain regime of values, which form the core of the social regime, we have as a consequence a certain type of elite and of elite-mass relationship, which the corresponding regime of power enforcedly sanctions. And given a certain type of elite and a certain type of elite-mass relationship, we also have, inherently, certain propensities toward larger or smaller degrees of modernization and institutionalization. This is the reason for the correlation, indicated in Table 26, between political superordination and development orientation. This correlation, however, implies another one: the correlation between the inherent propensities toward larger or smaller degrees of development, given by the type of elite and elite-mass relationship, and the operational political models most adequate, in each case, to optimize the existing developmental potentialities.

Table 30 expresses, in terms of the existing regime of power of a society, the implicit or explicit operational political models that have historically led or are likely, theoretically, to lead the concerned polity and society to a process of political and societal development. In addition, the table gives the conditions of suitability for each model.

As indicated in Table 30, liberal democracy, in the sense of laissez-faire capitalism, was able to promote the overall development of Great Britain and the United States in the historical conditions of the eighteenth and nineteenth centuries. This means essentially two things. The first is that liberal democracy was, although not explicitly, a very effective implicit operational political model for development in that period and for those countries. The voluntaristic element of the model was contained in the assumption that the active and rational pursuit, by each individual, of his own interests, particularly for his own enrichment, within the conditions of a contractual democracy, would lead to the general benefit of the whole society. The implied isomorphic representation of the successive stages and respective conditioning factors of the process was provided by the theories of the Enlightenment (Condorcet), of the physiocrats (Quesnay), and of the classic economists from Smith to Ricardo and Marshall. As will be discussed in the next chapter, the same assumptions have not been sufficient for the historical development of other societies, such as France and Germany; nor are they applicable to any society today.

Neoliberalism is the regulated form of liberal democracy currently applied in the United States and, under United States' economic, technological, and military control, in Canada and to a lesser extent (compensated by the remaining British influence and the local welfare state) in Australia. It can be defined as the quantum of liberal democracy necessary to maintain the economy under private control and, thus, to provide the groups controlling the economy with a commanding influence on the social regime and the regime of power, compensated by the quantum of social regulation necessary to prevent the system from suffering cyclical crises, to keep an active feeling of participation in the middle class, and to co-opt the unionized sectors of the working class through several material rewards and symbolic manipulations. Like liberal democracy, but not so much so, neoliberalism is more of an implicit than an explicit operational model. The voluntaristic element in both is the drive for self-enrichment. Unlike liberal democracy, however, neoliberalism does not believe in the spontaneous harmony between the individual and society and between the economic and the other societal planes; nor is it naïve about the extension and generality of the social optimization resulting from the operation of the system. Hence, the large and increasing manipulative element peculiar to that model. This element implies the bringing of increasing features of welfare statism, or of national capitalism in underdeveloped countries, into the model, beyond the intention of the leaders. In the course of time neoliberalism tends to be converted into a full-fledged welfare state.

National capitalism is already more of an explicit than an implicit operational model, because of the fundamental importance that national planning has in this model and the large amount of planning it tends to require. The model consists, in part, of the adaptation of several participational and value features of neoliberalism to the conditions of semideveloped, but dynamic and viable, societies. In part, it presents, in more modern conditions, some features of the modernizing elitocracy model, such as the relative closeness of the elite, and their large

Table 30 *Political superordination, developmental operational political models, and conditions of suitability*

G. Political Superordination REGIME OF POWER	TYPES OF REGIME	Developmental Operational Political Models (explicit or implicit)	Conditions of Suitability for Model
G.P.2 Reconciliation regime	G.2 Free capitalism	Liberal democracy	*Historical*: in conditions of eighteenth- and nineteenth-century Great Britain and the United States
	G.3 Regulated capitalism	Neoliberalism	*Restricted* to affluent superpower: the United States and Canada insofar as it is a United States' dependent; restricted to the current century
		National capitalism	*Restricted* to viable semideveloped dynamic societies, with entrepreneurial national bourgeoisie, development-motivated modern sectors in the middle and working classes, and a strong, socially entrenched will for national autonomy. It is the case in Latin America (combined with features of state capitalism) of Mexico, Venezuela, Colombia, Brazil, Uruguay, Argentina, and Chile
	G.4 Welfare capitalism	Welfare statism	*Restricted* to fairly well developed and integrated societies as Western European democracies and eventually Japan; suitable for a nationally independent course in Canada and Australia
	G.5 Welfare socialism	Welfare socialism	*Restricted* to highly developed and integrated societies, enjoying broad sociopolitical consensus; tends to be the case of Nordic democracies; may become suitable for Japan

G.P.3 Ordination regime	G.6 Ordinated capitalism	Modernizing autocracy	*Restricted* to autocratic traditional societies before the consolidation of a modern middle class, as Iran and Ethiopia. Occurred historically in Russia
		Modernizing elitocracy	*Historical:* Meiji Restoration, Bismarckian Germany *Restricted* currently to traditional societies without modern middle class but with all modernizing elite, as Iraq, Jordan.
	G.8 State capitalism	State capitalism	*Restricted* to societies where the dynamic groups belong to the modern sector of the middle class, mostly the armed forces; typical case: Nasser's Egypt; suitable for viable less-developed countries, as India and Pakistan; Egypt; convenient in Latin America for Ecuador, Peru, Bolivia, and Paraguay. When combined with features of national capitalism, suitable for the more advanced Latin American countries
G.P.4 Mobilization regime	G.9 Developmental socialism	Communism	*Restricted* to individually viable superpower, U.S.S.R., to continental society, China, and to Eastern European countries insofar as they are Soviet dependents
		Developmental socialism	*Restricted* to viable underdeveloped countries under an obscurantist and exploitative elite and an important functional counterelite. Suitable for Southeast Asia and Indonesia, and for India, Pakistan, and Latin America in the future, if they fail to develop in other ways

margin of autonomy. It also has some features of welfare statism, given the symbolic importance of the income reallocation actually effected. Finally, it has some characteristics of state capitalism, because of the outstanding role that the national state plays in that model, both as the most typical and powerful agency of the national society and as the representative of public interest.

Welfare statism and welfare socialism are both forms of regulating individual initiative in the collective interest of society, without suppressing individual liberty and initiative and actually enhancing the effective opportunities for the masses to enjoy personal freedom. The distinction between the two may be subtle or sharp, depending on the degree to which welfare statism remains capitalist and welfare socialism preserves individual initiative. In the current practice, Western European welfare statism still maintains a very large coefficient of ascriptive privileges, while increasing the extent and efficiency of social welfare. The Nordic democracies, however, seem to be gradually converting their private capitalism into a socially and nationally functional and effective system of production, with declining ascriptive features and an already negligible capacity for the extraeconomic manipulation of the respective society.

Modernizing autocracy has been, historically, the implicit model of such development-oriented autocrats as Peter the Great and Catherine the Great. With a lessened autocratic content but with still a minimum content of enlightenment, the model is currently a sort of loose reference for the negus of Ethiopia and, in a more modernizing fashion, for the shah of Iran.

Modernizing elitocracy has been, historically, within their distinct conditions, the implicit operational political model of the Meiji clans and of Bismarck for the development of their respective societies. Some Arab countries today, like Iraq and Jordan, are the kinds of societies in which this model would be suitable and in which it tends to attract the local elites.

State capitalism is in large part the contemporary version of modernizing elitocracy. Whereas the latter model requires societies that are still very traditional, with corresponding feelings of legitimacy, the former is applicable to societies in which there is a dynamic modern sector in the middle class, a secular view of authority, and some appreciable preexisting social complexity. Egypt (regardless of the setbacks caused by the Arab-Israeli wars, which are not, in themselves, intrinsically associated with the characteristics of the model) is the best current example of the type.

Communism and developmental socialism, as operational political models, are presented in Table 30 as two varieties of developmental socialism. The distinction between these two models, which may serve several analytical purposes, has been considered, in this table, primarily in terms of the criteria of international politics. Communism is understood both as the model and as the system of political influence in each of the two competing large socialist countries, the U.S.S.R. and China. It is in this sense that Eastern Europe, insofar as it remains dependent on the Soviet Union, is considered to be oriented by a communist model. Developmental socialism is understood as a developmental operational political model, based on the socialization by the state of the means of production, without inherently implying any dependence on, or allegiance to, either the Soviet Union or Communist China. An example is the line that Yugoslavia has been able to keep. In addition to other considerations, the importance of the distinction lies in the fact that, for better or for worse, the international situation of countries adopting one or the other of these two models varies in a decisive way, according to their geopolitical position and other circumstances, with relevant consequences for their own national viability.

NOTES

[1] Of the voluminous recent literature reappraising Marx, see the broad collection of studies by the International Social Science Council Symposium: *Marx and Contemporary Scientific Thought* The Hague: (Mouton, 1965) and the Notre Dame University Symposium, edited by Nicholas Lobkowicz (1967); see also: Jean Paul Sartre (1960), Georges Gurvitch (1961 and 1968), Roger Garaudy (1964), Louis Soubisse (1967), Louis Althusser (1967 and 1969b), Henri Lefebvre (1966), Kostas Axelos (1961), Eugene Kamenka (1962), Herbert Marcuse (1966 and 1969), Erich Fromm (1965 and, as ed., 1966), Franz Marek (1969), Nicos Poulantzas (1970), Joan Robinson (1956), Paul Baran and Paul Sweezy (1966), David Horowitz, ed. (1968), Adam Schaff (1970), and Gajo Petrovic (1967).

[2] The ideological bias consists in discriminating against the communist model, which is viewed as the product of malevolent oligarchies, and ignoring the societal conditions that might require, whatever the inherent costs and risks, that sort of model as an indispensable model for surmounting otherwise insuperable obstacles.

12

The Historical Experience

A trend toward planning

It is possible now, with the theoretical framework developed so far, to take a glance at the more significant historical examples of national development and to see how—and with what implied models—the leading developed countries of today have succeeded in reaching their present stage of modernization and institutionalization. This will bring us to a brief critical survey of the process of national development in (1) Great Britain and the United States, (2) France and Germany, (3) Japan, and (4) Soviet Russia and China.

The analysis of these cases will reveal that as we move from the conditions of the eighteenth century, it becomes increasingly necessary for the state to intervene in the guidance and promotion of the process of development, if that process is to be successful. Although the national development of Great Britain and the United States followed a spontaneous course, pushed by the drive for individual self-enrichment under the conditions of laissez-faire liberalism, the development of France and Germany was a much less casual process, with the respective national states actively pursuing conditions for the most rapid achievement of industrial growth and technological progress. In Japan we have already the reversal of the original picture. The state did not actively try to help the national entrepreneurs, but rather the state created them. National development was the primary purpose and concern of the Meiji Restoration. Finally, in Soviet Russia and China, the state, whatever the doctrinarian prescriptions of the official ideology, far from withering away, became itself the national entrepreneur so that it could concentrate all the resources and decisions necessary for achieving, in a couple of decades and against tremendous external pressure, what the previously developed countries had done in a century and under much easier international conditions.

England and the United States

The spontaneous development of Great Britain in the second half of the eighteenth century, although representing a typical example of laissez-faire success, was much more prepared and favored by state action that was acknowledged some time ago. A revision of the British case would confirm the assumption that the merchants of the eighteenth century and the inventors of mechanized techniques were the entrepreneurs and the innovators who actually promoted the growth and diversification of British economy. But it would also bring to the forefront the decisive importance that state policies, beginning with the Tudors and particularly with Cromwell, had in the promotion of the mercantile revolution, leading to the establishment of a great trade system, a corresponding naval power, and a resulting accumulation of wealth, the natural consequence of which was the laissez-faire development of the second half of the eighteenth century.[1]

In the sixteenth century British mercantilists such as Lord Burghley, secretary of state and lord treasurer for Queen Elizabeth, were already adopting the main political decisions necessary for creating a great fleet, for attracting shipbuilding and all sorts of other manufactures to England and for developing these. What is more important, these sixteenth- and seventeenth-century mercantilists, as opposed to the bullion-oriented Spaniards and Portuguese, clearly understood that precious metals are not, in themselves, ultimate wealth, but just good stable means of exchange, and that wealth, itself, consists in commodities and the capacity to produce or trade them. Such are the clear lessons of people like Thomas Mun, director of the English East India Company, William Petty and his *Political Arithmetic*, and Nicholas Barbon's discourses on trade.[2] Cromwell pushed the engagements of the state for the economic and overall development of England still further. The policy of the Navigation Acts, started by him and continued after the Restoration (Acts of 1651, 1662, 1663, and 1675), provided complete protection to the monopoly of English traders, ships, and goods, imposing heavy duties on goods not transported by English ships and obliging the colonies to import goods from the English ports and by English vessels.[3] Furthermore, political events in England—including the early centralization achieved by the Tudors, the basic uniformity of values and standards of behavior obtained by a state-supported and enforced Reformation, the prevention, with the Cromwellian protectorate, of political domination by a consumptive aristocracy (as was to occur on the Continent) by the transfer of political power to the middle class and Parliament, and the later perfection of cabinet government—created the other preconditions necessary for the vigorous economic, cultural, and sociopolitical development in the second half of the eighteenth century. The laissez-faire liberalism that some early eighteenth-century writers started to propose in exchange for the still prevailing mercantilism and that Adam Smith advocated so authoritatively in his *Wealth of Nations* was adopted by Great Britain when, because of her former highly successful state-supported mercantilism, she was already the most developed country in the world and the rules of free trade were the rules of her own hegemony.[4]

The United States provides a still better illustration of successful laissez-faire development than Great Britain, because the American society inherited from Great Britain all the developmental assets of the early eighteenth century, without several of the British liabilities, and the United States had many new important local advantages. As Louis Hartz (1964) pointed out in his theory of the societal "fragment"—an observation that even mitigates his excessive culturalism—the United States, as a transplanted fragment of middle-class seventeenth-century England, benefited, as a society, from all the conditions operating in the mother country, to the advantage of a further spontaneous development in the United States, and as a colony and later an independent nation, she enjoyed extremely favorable international conditions during her growth period.[5] In the New World the rather homogeneous and high-spirited initial settlers found an abundance of land and favorable natural conditions. There was no serious aboriginal resistance and no interference from other European powers, which were kept in check by British naval supremacy. These conditions permitted the settlers to develop an egalitarian society in New England and a prosperous slave-based plantation society in the South. The expansion to the West, spurred by massive European immigration, provided a continuous supply of new lands, assuring the undisturbed growth of the country, and the economic differentiation between the North and the South had, at least until the middle of the nineteenth century, an extremely favorable economic effect, leading to a domestic specialization that provided raw material for the northern textile industry and a growing market for the southern planters.[6] A favorable net of rivers and lakes and their optimum use, which was easily obtained with the digging of some canals, opened a very extensive system of transportation by steamboat in the first third of the nineteenth century, allowing the extensive agricultural development of the hinterland. The building in the next third of the nineteenth century of a railroad system, which gradually and advantageously displaced the steamboats, and its extraordinary expansion in the last third of that century (increasing the railway mileage from 2,800 in 1840 to 192,000 in 1900) had the cumulative advantage of uniting the country economically and of providing a continuously growing demand for heavy industry, while, at the same time, spreading occupational opportunities with the huge personnel requirements of the railroad companies. By the time of the Civil War, which led one of the few negative structural features of the early economic specialization of the South to its ultimate consequence, the United States was already a developed country, although, at that time, neither the Europeans nor even the Americans were conscious of it.[7]

Even that extraordinary spontaneous development, which brought to unparalleled limits the extension of the private sector in a society (in an excess that is responsible for several of the domestic troubles of the United States today) was not achieved with an entirely laissez-faire role on the part of the public sector. More than playing a simple police role in this fantastic process of development, the American federal and state governments performed the very essential function of keeping the supply of land constant and extremely cheap, which was probably the single most decisive economic factor in that continuous growth. After the creation of the Confederation most of the land was the property of the government. Of the 2 billion acres in the United States today, the federal government has, at one time or another, owned about 1.4 billion, that is, 70 percent of the total area.[8] The early policy of purchasing contiguous non-American territory, as Louisiana and Florida, or of conquering it, as the former northern half of Mexico, multiplied the original availability of land. The federal government, according to policies that were increasingly oriented toward granting quasi-free lands to whoever could work them, was able to assure, at the same time, the complete settlement of its territory, the useful agricultural utilization of the land, and the socially fair distribution of the land and to maintain, with the expanding frontier, a constantly open opportunity for remunerative work and the eventual enrichment of all active men.[9]

France and Germany

The development of France and Germany, compared with what occurred in Great Britain and the United States, has been a much less casual and spontaneous process and was more deeply a product of deliberate state action. Germany was not a united nation before Bismarck, and she retained several traditional traits of late medieval origin for a long time.[10] France, however, like England, had obtained the benefit of national political integration by the end of the Middle Ages and she had the additional advantage of being considerably larger in territory, population, and natural resources and therefore also in national wealth. Similar to England, she had a very active and enlightened mercantilist phase, under the direction of such great statesmen as Richelieu (1585–1642) who became the principal minister in 1624, and Colbert (1619–1683), who became state secretary in 1669, and was also oriented toward the expansion of commerce and development of manufactures[11] rather than toward bullion accumulation. Different from England, however, where Tudor centralization was eventually succeeded by the still more centralized "nationalism" and "popular democracy" of Cromwell, which led to an emphasis on Puritan sobriety and middle-class power, France was led, after the business-oriented reign of Henry IV, the state-building phase of Louis XIII and Richelieu, and of the Colbertian period of Louis XIV's reign, to his later abuse of the politics of grandeur and the aristocratic luxuries of Versailles. As a result, France lost in the eighteenth century what she had gained, economically, socially and politically, in the sixteenth and seventeenth. So, whereas the second half of the eighteenth century marked the starting of British modern development, leading to a self-sustained growth in the beginning of the nineteenth century, France suffered from relative decay in that period. Once the Napoleonic attempt to build a European empire under French hegemony was led to a costly failure, France was reduced, compared to Great Britain, to the condition of an underdeveloped country, economically as well as socially and politically.[12]

The national development of France and Germany, in the second half of the nineteenth century, instead of being the result, under a laissez-faire regime, of a preparatory phase in the eighteenth century, was a struggle against comparative backwardness, undertaken under the guidance of the French Second Empire and the Bismarckian empire. We can appraise the different levels of development of the three countries, in the beginning of the nineteenth century, by comparing their respective output in the production of pig iron, then, still more than today, the base of industrial development. In 1830 Great Britain already had an annual output of more than 635,000 tons; France was producing only 200,000, and Germany no more than 40,000 tons. Germany experienced her first economic acceleration in 1834 with the adoption of the Zollverein, or customs union, under Prussian pressure, and in the next year her production increased substantially, jumping to 144,000 tons. In 1850, on the eve of the French Second Empire and of Bismarck's rule, French and German production of pig iron was, respectively, 405,000 tons and 215,000 tons, whereas as early as 1848 Great Britain was already producing a record-breaking 2 million tons. With the developmental policies of Napoleon III and Bismarck, however, France and Germany doubled their pig iron output in five years, and in 1855, they were producing, respectively, 850,000 and 420,000 tons. By that year Great Britain had already obtained her peak production, with 3.2 million tons. France and Germany, whose respective governments remained oriented toward helping national development, maintained in that same period a fast industrial growth. French pig iron production reached 967,000 tons in 1860 and 1,226,000 tons in 1865, and Germany, in the same years, produced, respectively, 529,000 and 988,000 tons. In 1870, the year the Second Empire was defeated by the armies of Bismarck, German pig iron production surpassed French production and reached 1,390,000 tons.[13]

All the other relevant figures concerning French and German development express the same trend. Germany experienced her first acceleration and, in economic terms, was actually brought into existence with the customs union of 1834. Friedrich List, the great theoretician of national development, who, in the second decade of the nineteenth century, started his efforts to integrate Germany and to induce the German governments to take an active part in, and direct responsibility for, the promotion of economic development, published his *National System of Political Economy* in 1841. The book exerted a wide and long influence in Germany, and during Bismarck's rule it was a decisive counterweight against the influence of the laissez-faire doctrines of the classic economists.[14]

In France the developmental orientation of the Second Empire, together with the constant increase in the industrial output and the railroad expansion (from 4,000 km. in 1852 to 19,000 km. at the end of the empire), brought about the creation of the great French firms, some still operating today, in all sectors of economic activity, including industrial companies, as the Société Péchiney (1865) or Société Fives-Lille (1865), transport companies, as Compagnie Générale Transatlantique (1855), Banks, as the Crédit Lyonnais (1863), and the great department stores, as Le Louvre (1855), La Samaritaine (1869) and others. These firms were French marketing innovations at that time.[15]

Neither Bismarck nor Napoleon III were state interventionists in the sense of today. They kept accepting several liberal postulates concerning the natural harmony of the "invisible hand." Louis Napoleon had mixed ideas about economic policies and was inconsistent. Bismarck was not very interested personally in economic affairs and let his ministers take care of such matters. Both, however, had a clear understanding that their countries were relatively backward, compared with Great Britain, and that, if they were to achieve their national political objectives, they needed to stimulate vigorously their own national economies, helping the national entrepreneurs in all possible ways. That they did. And so, analyzing their policies retrospectively, more from their actual practice than from their eventual theoretical justifications, one has to acknowledge that the implicit model that they pursued was a sort of national capitalism, within the conditions, particularly in the German case, of a modernizing elitocracy. By political means Napoleon III and Bismarck created the necessary conditions to prevent class struggles from becoming socioeconomically disruptive, and by means of custom duties, fiscal incentives, and state-sponsored loans, they created the fiscal protection and the capital facilities necessary to launch and develop an independent national industry.[16]

Japan

In Japan national development required the employment of the state much more extensively and deeply than in France and Germany. In a sense, even Soviet Russia and China, in their later processes of development, were not so dependent on state policies as the Meiji development was. Russia was not so dependent because she inherited an important industrial base and decisive reforms in the countryside from the late czarist period. Even if Rostow's contention that Russia had reached a stage of self-sustained development before World War I is discounted as a partisan statement, the fact remains that Witte's policies, in the 1890s and the first years of the twentieth century, carried through a first successful stage of industrialization. China, although starting her socialist revolution from a much lower level than Russia, had passed through a period of active private initiative in the more constructive years of the Kuomintang.

Japan, however, found in the second half of the nineteenth century, that she was a feudal and quasi-medieval society in imminent danger of falling under the control of foreign Western powers. After the first menacing visit of Commodore Perry in 1853 and during the course of the next ten years, when several humiliating and noxious treaties were imposed on her, Japan had to reach a clear understanding of the gravity of the impending menace to her national independence, to grasp the ultimate causes of her weakness, and to obtain, in sufficiently large sectors of her elite, the decision to counteract and to change the country as deeply and quickly as necessary to preserve her sovereignty. This process was carried out in a sequence of stages, with the state as the prime mover and the principal mechanism of change, although, unlike in Russia and China, the state was not oriented to suppress and take the place of private initiative but, rather, to create and stimulate it under the state's ultimate guidance.[17]

Briefly, the process of Japan's national development, from the nineteenth-century response to the Western challenge to her recuperation in the period following World War II, can be understood as a sequence of seven successive stages. The first stage corresponds to the reactions caused by the imposition of the Western-dictated treaties on the *bakufu*. From 1853 to the final overthrow of the shogunate in 1868 the Japanese elite was profoundly affected by the realization of Japan's impotence and imminent domination by the West. There was, at the same time, a struggle for power between the Tokugawa clan, which controlled the *bakufu*[18] hereditarily, and the Western clans of Satsuma, Hizen, Choshu, and Tosa, whose leadership passed into the hands of radical men, who decided to suppress the Tokugawa hegemony. The restoration of the effective powers of the emperor and the elimination of the shogunate became the possible institutional solution for the two fights which were taking place. The restoration was aimed at the modernization of the country and at the centralization of power in the hands of new men from outside the framework of the *bakufu* system. The result of this struggle was the complete defeat of the shogun and the restoration, according to the charter oath of 1868, of the powers of the emperor, then the sixteen-year-old Mutsuhito, who assumed the reign name of Meiji. The effective government was controlled by the triumvirate of Okubo, Kido, and Saigo.

The second stage of the process, which took place in the next decade, corresponds to the introduction and implementation of broad and deep reforms in all fields of Japanese life. The Han feudal system was suppressed, and prefectures were organized under the control of the central government. Education was reformed, modernized, and broadened, providing the basis for a self-developing national educational system, and Western science and technology were transmitted to the young generations. Industries were promoted by the government, and at the same time a self-expanding nucleus of industrialists, managers, and technicians began to form. When the rebellion of the Satsuma samurai was put down in 1877, drawing into the tragedy the life of Saigo, the last vestiges of feudal Japan were suppressed. Gone also were the times of the first Meiji samurai, and in place of the old triumvirate new men, already reflecting the modernization of Japan, as Ito, Okuma, Yamagata, Inouye Kaoru, and Matsukata Masayoshi, were led into the government.

The third stage of the Meiji development is characterized by the ripening of the first fruits of the preceding efforts. There was an increasing formation and accumulation of capital, which was reinvested extensively in priority industrial and agricultural projects. By the end of that period, at the end of the nineteenth century, Japan was a modernized and developed country. In 1894 the total capital of Japanese companies employing over ten men was 44,590,000 yen in industry, 82,560,000 yen in communications, and 20,015,000 yen in commerce. In 1903 these figures had jumped to 170,000,000, 262,380,000, and 76,994,000, respectively. The improvement of techniques was not less spectacular than the capital growth. By 1899, 42 percent of the factories with more than ten men used power-driven machines, and 71 percent of the industrial labor force was employed in these larger factories.[19]

The fourth stage of Japanese development, which corresponds to the first three decades of the twentieth century, was a phase of consolidation, increased complexity, and broadening participation in the process of development. The party system, however, did not develop in a corresponding form, and a discrepancy developed between the high level of organization of the system's political outputs and the rudimentary form of its political inputs. In the cultural tradition of the samurai ethos, which was gradually transferred to the professional military and certain sectors of the bureaucracy, the circumstances of the fourth stage led the country to an increasing militarism, the outcome of which was the invasion of Manchuria in 1931, the war with China, and ultimately, Pearl Harbor and the disastrous confrontation with the United States. The fifth stage of Japanese development ended in the catastrophes of Hiroshima and Nagasaki and the unconditional surrender, followed in the subsequent phase, by the American occupation. Japan, however, started her postwar recuperation with her usual energy and astonishing pace (seventh phase), and ten years later was again in a cumulative process of overall development, this time supported by a more democratic political infrastructure and a well-functioning party system.

The Japanese development, considered retrospectively, was essentially a gigantic effort at modernization by means that were as compatible as possible with the main features of her national culture and tradition. Initially, that compatibility made it possible to have an almost pacific transition from the shogunate to the Meiji regime, followed by a phase in which very deep changes were received, in general, with acquiescence both by the elite and the masses. The preservation—and restoration—of relevant traditional aspects of Japanese culture made it easier to understand the urgent necessity for modernization and mobilized the national will for the enormous psychic and physical efforts required for its successful achievement. In the first decades of this century, however, these same values prevented the emergence of a democratic society and drove Japan into the deadlock of militarism.

In terms of the implied political models, the national development of Japan presents a combination of state capitalism and national capitalism, within the conditions of a modernizing elitocracy. It could be defined as the state capitalism of a modernizing elitocracy oriented toward the creation and development of a national capitalist society. The state operated as the prime mover of the whole process, having as its support a modernizing elite. The regime of power of Tokugawa Japan was completely reversed, a new regime of power was established and, based on it, a new social regime, controlled by the modernizing elite. The state was employed in depth to promote decisive changes in all relevant aspects of Japanese society: education, the economy, technology, and public administration. Once the new material, institutional, and human basis for these several subsystems of the Japanese society was created, they were given a proper and independent capacity of self-expansion and self-management, although under the supervision and orientation of the state. And so Japan was led, ultimately, to a capitalist development although rather distinct from the individualist capitalism of the West and much more submitted, both by the internalized values of the citizenry and the institutional regulations of the system, to the national interest and the social welfare of the Japanese society.

Soviet Russia and China

The national development of Russia and China was also achieved by the use, in depth, of the state, but in their case, besides playing the role of prime mover, the state also performed the function of national entrepreneur. In spite of the several important differences between their two developmental processes, which started from rather uneven levels of previous development and took place with very different paces of achievement, the two countries had two basic features in common. First, neither of them had succeeded, like France and Germany, in creating a national bourgeoisie in the transition from the eighteenth to the nineteenth century. Second, in both, the elite was a landed aristocracy, with an important bureaucratic branch, particularly in the case of China's mandarins, which, contrary to what occured in Japan, stuck to the *ancien régime* and, ultimately, forced the process of change to take a revolutionary course. In both cases, therefore, independent of other factors and conditions, national development not only had to be initiated by political means, but also implemented by political means, which necessarily expanded the action of the state to the other planes of society.[20]

Russia started her process of modernization with the enlightened despotism of the eighteenth century, with Peter the Great and Catherine the Great (modernizing autocracy), obtaining an impressive expansion of population as well as of territory and cultivated land. There was also a certain degree of industrial development in the first half of the nineteenth century.[21] A decisive social and economic reform was introduced by Alexander II, in 1861, with the liberation of the serfs and the allocation to them of parcels of land, which they could pay for in a long-term scheme. The liberation induced the nobles—who, as a direct result of the liberation, lost one-third of their land and the advantage of free workers to cultivate it—to gradually sell their land to farmers and bourgeois capitalists. Although initially all the land was owned by the nobles, by the time of World War I they had lost or sold 60 percent of it. The activation of the Russian economy, following the liberation of the serfs, brought about a large expansion of the railroad network. From 700 miles in 1860, Russian lines reached 36,000 miles by 1900. From the late 1880s to the first years of this century, Witte, as minister of finance, carried out an active and successful policy of industrial development, aimed at achieving, in the long run, industrial self-sufficiency. In the last years of the monarchy, Stolypin tried still another agrarian reform, establishing the subdivision and the enclosure of the communal lands, with the double purpose of strengthening the economic and political power of the "middle-class" farmers and improving the agricultural utilization of the lands.

These several relatively successful attempts at modernization, although enough to provide Russia, by the beginning of twentieth century, with an appreciable economic basis, were not sufficient to launch the country on a general process of national development. Briefly, it could be said that neither the czarist state nor the private entrepreneurs were willing or capable of carrying forward the minimum quantum of change and effort necessary to transform the Russian society. The crucial reason for this was the lack of appropriate social support for the promotion of substantial change. The Russian elite continued to be the nobility, with the accession of a few new capitalists, who were led to incorporate the values and life-style of the former, and that elite never became committed to a purpose of national development, much less to the sacrifices required for that development. Although all the reforms after the abolition of servitude were ultimately for the benefit of the gradually emerging bourgeoisie, that bourgeoisie never acquired the independence and self-confidence of an autonomous class, capable of formulating and achieving goals of its own. Squeezed between a closed aristocracy and the land-hungry peasants, between the fiscal-minded government officials and an increasingly restive working class, they were deprived of initiative by their dependence on the values of the elite and the policies and measures of the government, and by their fears that an excessive liberalization could release the masses from control. Furthermore, the still small Russian industrial complex had, in two relevant senses, the characteristics of an enclave. First, in the extensively rural society, most of the peasants were still consuming traditional handicrafts, and the relationship between town and countryside had not acquired a dynamic and complementary character. Second, the Russian industry was mostly represented by great factories owned, controlled, and managed by foreign groups, which were more likely to increase and expand their influence than to be absorbed by the weak local capital.

The promotion of the national development of Russia corresponds with the Soviet state, although its official philosophy was oriented toward internationalism and was militantly antinationalist, and its primary purpose was not economic development but the suppression of class exploitation and division. The stages of that extraordinary process, which led to both a profound modification of the purposes of the revolution and a no less radical transformation of the Russian society, were as is well known, marked by the transition from the "war Communism" of 1917 to 1921 to the New Economic Policy, which prevailed until the inauguration, in 1928, of the first Five-Year Plan. The New Economic Policy recovered the prewar levels of the Russian economy, and the Five-Year Plan was able to launch the Soviet economy in a process of rapid and continuous self-sustained growth. Oriented, primarily, to achieve decisive results in the field of heavy industry, so that its effect would dynamize the whole economy, the first plan tripled the outputs of the major basic items. From 1928 to 1935 Soviet production of coal increased from 35,000,000 tons to 108,900,000 tons, of pig iron, from 3,300,000 to 12,500,000, of steel, from 4,300,000 to 12,500,000, and of rolled steel from 3,400,000 to 9,400,000.

National development in China was achieved under conditions even less favorable than the Russian ones. China did not receive, like Russia, an important economic and education legacy from the *ancien régime*. In addition to starting from a much lower level, she had to pass through many more vicissitudes, from the fall of the monarchy to the successful beginning of her process of development, than Russia had to endure from the February (March in the Gregorian calendar) to the October (November) revolutions. The second fact is connected to the former. The Chinese revolution was a tragically protracted event, including Sun Yat-sen's organizing attempts in the beginning of the century, the overthrow of the monarchy in 1912, the following agonizing years of the deterioration of the republic, the Kuomintang-Communist united front in the 1920s, the first anti-Kuomintang struggle of the 1930s, the renewed united fight against the Japanese before and during World War II, and finally, the great confrontation from 1947 to the final debacle of Chiang Kai-shek in 1949. And this protracted revolution was due to the fact that China was not prepared for a decisive and centralized process of modernization. Lenin inherited, in addition to an appreciable economic basis, a centralized state and could count on a well-organized and disciplined party to meet the challenge of the civil war and foreign intervention. This party was able, in a few months, to take control of the czar's successor republican government and, in a few years, to build the organization necessary for managing Russia and expelling the foreign invaders. Sun Yat-sen, however, could rely on only a small and unorganized group of intellectuals. Far from obtaining control of the republic that succeeded the Manchu dynasty, he had to let Yüan Shih-k'ai, the former military leader of the *ancien régime*, take the government, as a compromise to advance his cause. The result was the fragmentation of power among the warlords that infested China until the consolidation of Chiang Kai-shek, who commanded the military forces of Sun Yat-sen's new revolutionary efforts in the 1920s. After the death of Sun Yat-sen in 1925, however, Chiang was increasingly driven to rightist positions. The process of the Chinese revolution was once again interrupted by a long fight between the rightists, under Chiang, and the leftists, under Mao Tse-tung, until the final victory of the latter in 1949.

An incredible development effort was then undertaken by the Chinese Communists. The first Five-Year Plan provided annual investments of more than $3 billion, representing 20 percent of the national income. Starting with practically nothing more than the Japanese-built industrial base of Manchuria, the Chinese were able, with the execution of the first plan, to complete 800 large industrial projects, with an increase in the gross capital output value of 120 percent. The production of steel was tripled, reaching 5,350,000 metric tons; the production of coal was doubled to 130,000,000 metric tons; electricity was doubled to 19.3 billion kw.; cement also doubled to 6,860,000 metric tons; and machine tools production was doubled to 28,000,000 metric tons. Whereas Russia jumped to a high level of industrialization with the successful execution of her Five-Year Plan, China was still below the Russian level of 1928. Her much greater backwardness, after having exacted a longer period of revolution, also imposed a longer period of development.[22]

When the Russian and the Chinese processes of development are compared, it is undeniable that, among their common features, the most salient is the utilization of political means—a successful mass-based and party-directed radical socialist revolution—for building a powerful state. Once the control of power by the party was consolidated, a strongly centralized bureaucratic state was established and applied, in depth, to the promotion of change in all planes of society. The political operational model implied in this process is developmental socialism.

The state is both an agency of social regulation and control and the actual performer of the major economic activities. The principal characteristics of that model, the coincidences and discrepancies manifested between practical communism and Marx's theories, as well as the main similitudes and differences between the Russian and the Chinese experiments will be considered briefly in the next chapter.[23] It is sufficient, for the present discussion, to stress that both the Russian and the Chinese revolutions, whatever their own official theories, purposes, and self-justifications, became in fact a gigantic effort at national development in which and for which the state not only established the rules and the goals, but also promoted their execution and controlled the results. That "statecracy" is also a "partycracy," because a single party channels and manipulates all the relevant political inputs. And that partycracy is an ideological-technical oligarchy, because a restricted circle of top party members, guided by certain ideological and technological assumptions, leads the party and the state and provide, through co-optation, the self-perpetuation of that leading stratum.

Critical comparison

As was advanced at the beginning of the present chapter, the comparative analysis of the processes of development in (1) Great Britain and the United States, (2) France and Germany, (3) Japan, and (4) Russia and China shows the increasingly decisive importance of political action and of the action of the state in the successful achievement of national development as we leave the eighteenth century and come nearer to the conditions of today. British laissez faire was not only possible but also convenient because of the preceding success of English mercantilism, the state actions that had formerly prompted that mercantilism, and the subsequent course that British politics followed in the eighteenth and nineteenth centuries. American laissez faire reflected, in more favorable and protected conditions, the convenience inherited from Great Britain. The cases of France and Germany were already quite different. For different reasons, these two countries did not enjoy, in the nineteenth century, a social, political, and economic legacy from the preceding century enabling them to find the advantage that Britain and the United States could find in the rules of laissez faire. On the contrary, in order to defend themselves from British predominance (which could have become plain domination) and in order, in a latter stage of history, to adjust the expectations of their masses to the ruling possibilities of their respective elite (in a relationship that could have become disruptive), France and

Germany had to adopt the authoritarian recourse of imperial rule. Therefore, they needed to use the resulting state, externally, as an agency to contain foreign competition and, internally, as an agency to make the masses and the elite compatible and to support and orient the national entrepreneurs in order to promote national development.

Japan, who started from much more backward conditions, at a later time, and was still more threatened in international terms, had to rely completely on political decisions and on their implementation by the state in order to overcome the internal and external obstacles to her national development. Japanese traditions and the Japanese elite, however, were inherently compatible with the process of modernization. Japan's problem was not to change the elite and the cultural tradition, but to change from one elite sector, the traditionalist, to another, the modernizing one, and from certain lines of her tradition to other lines. That peculiar combination of traditionalism and modernization, of conservatism and revolution, had both the advantage of making the initial transition easier and faster and the disadvantage of bringing the Japanese society to the deadlock of militarism, which she was only able to surmount at the price of a national catastrophe and military defeat.

The Russian and Chinese societies, beginning their national development still later, not only found themselves, like France and Germany, unable to operate profitably within the rules of laissez-faire liberalism, but unlike Japan, could not find the necessary compatibility between their former elites and their former cultural traditions and the minimum requirements for the successful promotion of a process of national development. New elites and new cultural traditions had to be painfully created through the process of revolution. It is clear, by now, that the Soviet society achieved, with the completion of the second Five-Year Plan, her self-sustained development and that, presently, she is entering a stage of generalized development and approaching a period of affluence. It is also clear, by now, that the Chinese revolution will be successful and that China will reach a stage of continuous development in a couple of years, with a prospect of generalized development within a couple of decades. Both countries have had to create a totalitarian state in order to succeed in their developmental efforts. Whatever the subjective intentions of the leaders—and as far as we can know Lenin and Mao were sincere humanists—the brutal fact that everything had to be rebuilt from scratch, from ideas and values to machines and organizations, required a totalistic approach, an all-embracing rule and, consequently, a totalitarian state. So Russia and China had to go still further than Japan and, as was inevitable, they transferred a heavy price to the future. This price is already visible in the Soviet case. It appears that it will be the same in the case of China, although the repercussions of the cultural revolution and its antibureaucratic drive still cannot be judged. This price is autonomy for the subsystems, effective popular participation in the relevant political inputs, the control of non-ideological thinking in cultural affairs, and, ultimately, individual freedom. The fundamental problem is whether or not the totalitarian state is capable, by itself, of becoming nontotalitarian once its totalitarian features are no longer functionally required but, on the contrary, become an increasing nuisance for the achievement of the official goals.

NOTES

[1] See Charles Wilson (1966); see also R. M. Hartwell, Introduction and chap. 3, and F. Crouzet, chap. 7 in Hartwell, ed. (1968).

[2] See Shepard B. Clough (1968, pp. 223 ff.).

[3] See Maurice Ashley (1958 and 1962).

[4] See Wilson (1966).

[5] See Louis Hartz (1964, chap. 4).

[6] On the New England settlement see J. T. Adams (1921). On southern economy see E. Q. Hawk (1934). On the expansion to the West see Harold Faulkner (1954, chaps. 5 and 6) and Turner's thesis in F. J. Turner (1961).

[7] See Lester S. Ley and Roy J. Sampson (1962) on water transportation and railroads; see also Faulkner (1954, chaps. 14 and 22) and G. R. Taylor (1951).

[8] See B. H. Hibbard (1939) and Herman E. Krooss (1966).

[9] See Faulkner (1954, chap. 10).

[10] On late medieval survivals in Germany see J. H. Clapham (1966, pp. 82 ff.).

[11] See Clough (1968, pp. 228 ff.).

[12] On the general aspects of European history from the late seventeenth century to the middle of the eighteenth century, see Philippe Sagnac and A. de Saint-Leger (1949) and Pierre Muret (1949). On the eighteenth-century French economy see Henri Sée (1969).

[13] See Witt Bowden, Michael Karpovich, and Abbot Payson Usher (1937, pp. 301 ff.).

[14] On the comparative growth of France and Germany, see Clapham (1966).

[15] See Robert Catherine and Pierre Grousset (1965, pp. 126 ff.).

[16] See Heinrich Herkner, pp. 453 ff. and 470 ff. in Walter Goetz (1950, vol. 8); see E. Eyck (1964) on Bismarck and J. J. Thompson (1955) on Louis Napoleon.

[17] On Japan's development, see George M. Beckmann (1962) and William W. Lockwood (1955 and 1964); see also E. H. Norman (1940); G. C. Allen (1951), Lawrence Olson (1963). For the general history of Japan, see George Sanson (1958–1964, particularly vol. 3) and Richard Storry (1965). On Japan's political system see Frank Langdon (1967) and Robert E. Ward (1967).

[18] Term generally used to designate the government during the Kamura and Tokugawa periods.

[19] See Beckmann (1962, pp. 338 ff).

[20] Of the voluminous literature on Soviet Russia, see: (1) on the broader historical aspects, Nicholas V. Riasanovsky (1966), R. D. Charques (1956), Leon Trotsky (1950), and Edward Hallett Carr (1951–1954), (2) on Soviet economic development, A. Baykov (1948), Maurice Dobb (1966), Anatole G. Mazour (1967), Harry Schwartz (1968), and René Dumont (1964a), (3) on the political system, Alfred G. Meyer (1965) and Frederick C. Barghoorn (1966), (4) on the Soviet model of development, Joseph Schumpeter (1950, Part I on Marx and chap. 18, item V), Irving Louis Horowitz (1966, particularly chap. 5), John H. Kautsky, pp. 57–59 in J. H. Kautsky, ed. (1965), Merle Fainsod, pp. 233–267 in Joseph La Palombara, ed. (1963), Allen Kassof, pp. 3–13, and Cyril E. Black, pp. 14–56 in Kassof, ed. (1968), and Alex Inkeles (1968, particularly Parts I and VII).

Of the many studies on China's revolution and development, see: (1) for the broad historical view, Kenneth S. Latourette (1964 and 1966), (2) on economic development, T. J. Hughes and D. E. T. Luard (1959), and Leo A. Orleans (1961), (3) on the Chinese Communist revolution and developmental model, Edgar Show (1962), George M. Beckmann (1962), Franz Schurmann (1966), Schurmann and Orville Schell (1967), Peter S. H. Tang and Joan M. Maloney (1967), Kewes S. Karol (1967), and Dennis J. Doolin and Robert C. North (1967), and (4) on the cultural revolution, Doolin (1964), Philip Bridgham and Ezra F. Vogel (1968), and the Keasing's Research Report (1967).

[21] In 1854 there were 10,000 industries with a total of 450,000 workers from a population of 67 million inhabitants.

[22] See Beckmann (1962, pp. 501 ff.).

[23] For an understanding of communism as a developmental model, see John H. Kautsky (1965, particularly chap. 3); see also Dobb's (1963) study on communism and national development and Ludovico Garruccio's (1969, chap. 6) sharp analysis of the "revolutionary alternative" for development. A bright contribution to the discussion of that question is given by Irving Horowitz's (1966) comparison of the capitalist, communist and third world developmental models.

13

Functional and
Dysfunctional Elites

THE CONCEPT OF ELITE

The problem

The analytical study of the three most usual developmental political models, which we will attempt in Chapter 15, still requires, in addition to the preceding review of the most typical historical cases of national development from eighteenth-century Great Britain to contemporary China, the discussion of a very essential question. That question concerns the nature and role of elites and the reasons why some elites are societally functional and some are not.

As was shown very clearly in our former historical survey, some elites have been able to lead their societies to national development and some have not been able to. The former were always elites who proved themselves capable of keeping or reaching high levels of societal functionality, either by gradual adjustments to the conditions and necessities of their time or by radical reforms in which a modernizing sector of the elite successfully overcame the traditional sector and then engaged in a dramatic effort to recuperate from the accumulated backwardness of their societies. The latter were dysfunctional elites, who were more interested in the preservation of their own privileges, within their societies, than in contributing to the general welfare.

Why is it so? Why are some elites functional and some dysfunctional? And, to start with, what is an elite?

The answer to these questions is indispensable, not only for an explanation of the inner mechanism of the historical cases we have discussed, but also for the analytical understanding of the process itself, of development of a society and of the reasons why, in given conditions, national development can be deliberately achieved through the correct implementation of the appropriate political model.

In the present chapter I will discuss these questions briefly, attempting first to clarify the sort of social reality that an elite is, then trying to analyze the

259

dynamics of the elite-mass relationship, and finally, endeavoring to find the reason why some elites are or become functional and some do not.

The performance view

The concept of elite, widely introduced in the social sciences by Pareto (1902, 1916 and 1966) and Mosca (1939), still requires a better analytical treatment, although there have been important gains in its understanding in the more recent literature on the subject. Since Pareto there have been three sources of confusion affecting the concept of elite. The first concerns the distinction between that concept and the concept of social class. Pareto formulated the category of elite precisely to object to Marx's theory of the class struggle, and he emphasized the nonclass nature of the concept. Although social classes would be, as we would say today, highly determined by ascriptive factors, with most people belonging to a class because they were born into it, the elite would represent a functional social stratum, founded on personal capacity. The elite condition, however, can be inherited both in the old society, as in the case of the patricians, and in the modern one, as happens with a substantial part of the economic elite. Furthermore, people can join a social class different from their parents' through upward or downward social mobility. The second usual source of confusion concerns the understanding of the elite, sometimes, as the relatively unified top stratum of a society and, sometimes, as the upper level of various groups, such as the financial elite, the artistic elite, or even the sports elite, or the movies elite. A third source of confusion concerns the identification of the elite with the political elite, and the political elite with a ruling class, as opposed to an understanding of the elite in one of the other two meanings.

The more recent literature on the subject[1] has shown a clear tendency to understand the social class as being determined by income and occupational factors, with a statistically high coefficient of ascriptivity, and the elite as being determined by a status-prestige differentiation, with a high correlation between status and personal competence. The inherited elite condition would correspond (in modern society, yes, but what about ancient society?) to inherited facilities for qualification confirmed by appropriate performance. Several elites, therefore, would coexist in a society, each corresponding to distinct kinds of performances. And the political elite, which would be one of these elites, would be differentiated from a ruling class by the fact that the latter would be mostly composed of incumbents of ascriptively conferred roles, whereas the former would be integrated by people whose political influence would competitively express their capacity for leadership.

The stratum-functional view

Although it would be beyond the scope of this book to attempt any major elaboration of the theory of elites, a succinct clarification of the question is necessary for our further analysis of the problem of functional and

and dysfunctional elites, which lies at the very core of the theory of developmental political models.

As was stressed by Pareto and has been elaborated by more recent writers, the elite-mass concept expresses a functional situational category. The understanding of that concept, however, is impossible if it is not situated in the context of a structural view of society, as briefly presented in the first chapter. As was seen then (see Table 4), a society presents, analytically, two dimensions. Horizontally, it is the interrelation of four structural planes or social subsystems: the cultural, participational, political, and economic. Vertically, it is the articulation of two levels: the situational level, where the regime of stratification of each social subsystem and of the society as a whole is analytically fixed, and the actional level, where, analytically, human interaction actually takes place. Whatever specific social form may be presented by the regime of stratification of a society, at any given time, in the form of estates, castes, classes, or status levels, that system of stratification always contains an upper, a middle, and a lower stratum.

These strata are functional categories, corresponding to fixed generic sets of performance roles for each of the social subsystems. The specific varieties and respective characteristics of these generic performance roles vary according to the type of society (see Table 27 for the various types) and from one society to another. But, as indicated in Table 4, they will always be: (1) for the cultural subsystem, the roles of (1.a) *symbol formulator* or *interpreter*, (1.b) *symbol propagator*, and (1.c) *symbol consumer*, (2) for the participational subsystem, the roles (and condition) of (2.a) *upper status*, (2.b) *middle status*, and (2.c) *lower status*, (3) for the political subsystem, the roles of (3.a) *decision maker*, (3.b) *decision implementer*, and (3.c) *the ruled*, and (4) for the economic subsystem, the roles of (4.a) *controller of the means of production*, (4.b) *manager* or *technician*, and (4.c) *worker*. These roles correspond, in each subsystem, to (a) the *elite* (and counterelite), (b) the *subelite*, and (c) the *mass*.

According to the type of society being considered, these functional roles may correspond to a certain estate, caste, or class, or they may not be specifically related to any of these. Let us consider, for instance, the elite role of the cultural subsystem: symbol formulator or interpreter. In a primitive society, before the structural specialization of functions, that role was not differentiated from the usual attributes of the adult males. The symbols of the society were understood as being immutably transmitted from the past, and nobody was supposed to formulate any, much less new ones. Interpretations of the existing cultural legacy, however, were necessary and were performed as a part of the functions of the paterfamilias. The more diversified primitive societies had hereditary wizards. Priestly functions had a caste configuration in the Hindu civilization and, in Christian Europe, were converted, at the higher level, into an estate. Higher church dignitaries in nineteenth-century Europe were members of the bourgeoisie as a class, but were more likely to be recruited from lower classes than decision makers or controllers of the means of production. In contrast to that tendency to form estates or class structures for the higher symbol formulators or interpreters, other societies, as the Greek in the sixth century B.C. or the Western society during the Renaissance and the Enlightenment, had free symbol formulators in the person of the philosopher (the scientist, the artist), whose high status and membership in the cultural elite did not depend on (with qualifications for nonfree men in Greece) estate or class.

There are, then, four types (and several subtypes) of elites, subelites, and masses in a society: the cultural, participational, political, and economic ones. The participational elite, however, has a special character unlike the others. To start with, it has two different senses: a minor and a major sense. In the minor sense there are innumerable participational elites, who perform upper status private functions within the restricted limits of specific and usually small groups: the father in the family, the leader of sport groups or clubs, and so forth. In the major sense the participational elite corresponds to those enjoying the upper status of the regime of participation, itself, of the society, such as the Spartan in Lacedaemonia, the patrician in early Republican Rome, and so on. Still more relevant than that, the participational elite, unlike the others, is inherently ascriptive whenever the regime of participation (which is legitimized by a congruent regime of values) establishes an inegalitarian participation among the upper-, middle-, and low-status members of the society. And here we have the origin of much of the confusion between elite and class, estate, and so on. As long as a society keeps an inflexible inegalitarian regime of participation, there is only one elite, the participational one, which is coextensive with the specific forms of social stratification, estate, caste, or class, existing in that society.

Inegalitarian regimes, however, may tend to become more flexible for several reasons—as has historically occurred—and in that case the other types of elite become differentiated from the participational one. Functional criteria of performance, in addition to ascriptive ones of participation, lead to the allocation of upper-stratum cultural roles to wise or cultivated men (philosophers), upper-stratum political roles to brave and capable leaders, and upper-stratum economic roles to efficient entrepreneurs. At that moment we have an elite-mass stratification distinct from the one by estates or classes. Patricians or nobles occupy, ascriptively, the percentage of elite roles that corresponds to the remaining inequality of the regime of participation, and the percentage of nonascriptive elite roles corresponds to the degree of flexibility attained by the regime.

Once the regime of participation has changed, at least in principle, to an egalitarian base, the participational elite, in the major sense, ceases to be an autonomous one, except in a residual form, and begins to express levels of prestige derived from the other social planes: political, economic, or cultural. The residual autonomous form of the participational elite is that of "the high society," which tends to incorporate, however, prestigious incumbents of the other elite roles.[2]

In non-inegalitarian societies[3] the four types of elites are integrated, more loosely or more tightly, as a function of the predominant values and interests of that society, as they are expressed in its social regime. The social regime may lead to a predominance of economic values and interests, as in democratic liberal societies, or to the superordination of the political, as in contemporary societies. Whatever the prevailing integrative principles may be, the various elites, with varying degrees of cohesion or lack of cohesion, form an upper-stratum cluster, which can be designated, in the singular, as the societal elite or as the elite *tout court*. A societal elite with enough coherence and consciousness of its basic values and interests becomes an establishment.

Confronting the elite there may be a counterelite. Counterelites express a high degree of social dissent in societies that have not remained integrated by traditional forms and have not achieved modern pluralist forms of integration, but that persist in maintaining by coercive means a social regime strongly incompatible with the ideas and values of the independent intellectuals, who tend to form an intelligentsia strongly critical of the regime and no less strongly repressed by it. Although such dissent may arise from several causes, it has tended, historically, to correspond to societies whose elites have not been able to change and to adapt to new conditions in the internal or external environment. In such cases a counterelite tends to emerge, to challenge the elite, to be subjected to severe repression, and in response, to try to promote the revolutionary rise of the masses against the elite.

Subelite and mass

In each structural plane of society, a subelite of middle-status people operates between the elites and the masses. This subelite includes symbol propagators, decision implementers, and economic managers or technicians. As occurs with the elite, in inegalitarian regimes of participation, the subelite coincides with a middle estate (French *tiers état*) or class (British middle class). In regimes of larger flexibility the subelite, like the elite, becomes a functional category of performers of middle-level roles (the real meaning of the new middle class).

In inegalitarian societies the subelite may occupy several different positions along a spectrum going from total allegiance to, to total rebellion against, the social regime. No social regime can exist without the allegiance of a sufficient sector of the subelite, which fills the indispensable roles of symbol propagators, decision implementers, and managers or technicians. In addition, the middle-status position of the subelite at the participational plane is the key position for the maintenance, in any society, of the necessary social mobility. It is from that subelite that the top roles and incumbents are promoted to higher statuses or higher roles at an elite level. And it is to the bottom roles of the subelite that the mass has an upward mobility. The blocking of this mobility, in the conditions inherent to each type of society, particularly from subelite to elite, is the main cause of social upheavals and not, as is sometimes believed, the pure oppression and exploitation of the masses. On the other hand, in inegalitarian societies in which a counterelite has come to be formed, it is the subelite that provides the roles and cadres for the revolutionary intelligentsia.

The masses at the bottom of each social plane represent very different realities, depending on whether we consider simple or complex societies and inegalitarian or noninegalitarian ones. In very primitive societies, as was discussed in Chapter 4, the elite-mass discrimination concerns, essentially, the hierarchy of family roles. Before the emergence of a larger social specialization, the sex and age groups were the main determinants of social status. In more complex inegalitarian societies, estates, castes, and classes (more often than not originally formed through the conquest of a society by another) discriminate strongly against those who are assigned a low status by the participational regime and who tend to form the mass of all the other planes and so constitute a societal mass. As the flexibility of the regime of participation increases, the mass becomes less discriminated against and less intrasystemically consistent. This means that the same incumbent can have a mass role in one or more planes but have non-mass roles in some other plane or planes. This also means that the same role can have a low status at one plane and a high status at another. An interesting example of the latter case is the position of the artist-craftsman in ancient Greece. Because his art was technically a craft, a sculptor enjoyed a low participational status as a *banaus*. At the same time, he could, like Phidias, enjoy high cultural status and be well off economically.

The case of incumbents having, cumulatively, roles of distinct statuses tends to be typical of modern egalitarian society. In a mass democracy everybody belongs, in several senses, to the mass. Top industrial managers belong to the cultural mass, as symbol consumers, and they may play a simple ruled role, politically. Workers, occupying a mass position in the economic plane, may enjoy an upper participational status as sportsmen (not to speak of union leaders). And top symbol formulators, in academic and scientific roles, may be at a low economic level and have only a middle participational status.

ELITE FUNCTIONALITY

Classical explanations

This brief clarification of the elite-mass relationship enables us now to consider the question of why some elites are functional and some are not. That question is intimately connected with the problem, treated by Aristotle, of the "sane" and the "corrupt" forms of government. Aristotle, as was discussed in Chapter 3, clearly understood that the distinction between monarchy, aristocracy, and, in our present terminology, democracy is much less relevant than the question of whether or not these types of government are sane or corrupt. What makes a government sane and another one corrupt? Or, if we give the question its broader meaning, why are some elites functional and others dysfunctional?

Several answers have been given to that question in the course of history. Fundamentally, they have varied around three basic positions. For some, as Plato, the answer is essentially moral. Corrupt governments are the governments of corrupt men. Corrupt elites are formed by corrupt people. This corruption, however, tends not to be arbitrary, but occurs because people with the wrong propensities are given undeserved leadership. According to Plato's theory of the passions, transposed to his theory of the state, corruption occurs because men who have not acquired the control of their appetitive passions and have not obtained higher levels of knowledge and wisdom are given high political functions. This sort of answer, ultimately, means that only when access to, and permanence at, the elite level is subordinated to moral and intellectual excellence can an elite be functional.[4]

The second answer basically accepts the former one, but tries to add an answer to the question of how elites can be kept excellent. This was Aristotle's main concern, and his conclusion was that the excellence of the elite depends on the excellence of the state's constitution. The chances of assuring the high quality of the incumbents in leading state roles are greater or smaller depending on the adopted rules. This is why Aristotle was so interested in the comparative study of all the known constitutions. He aimed, with that knowledge, to conceive an ideal constitution, the adoption of which, by an act of enlightened self-interest on the part of the governments and people themselves, would provide lasting political excellence for the states.[5] Like Plato's concept, Aristotle's solution had a long life. During the time of Roman expansion, political students, as Polybius,[6] saw the secret of Roman success in the excellence of the Roman constitution. The excellence of British, Prussian, and Japanese elites has been attributed to the excellence of their laws and traditions.

A third historical answer sees the secret of any good rule in a certain form of equilibrium between the ruler and the ruled. Once again Greek thinking provided, with the Sophists, the first formulation of that view, although more implicitly than explicitly, in their typical opposition between convention and nature, and might and right.[7] Bad governments are the result of unchecked power, which stimulates the ruler to indulge in an abuse of power. Balances and checks are the secret of good ruling. That view was accepted by the contractualists from the late Middle Ages to the seventeenth century and was transmitted to the liberals. It is the foundation of Montesquieu's division of powers and the basis of that masterpiece of the Enlightenment that is the American Constitution. It is also the basis of laissez-faire liberalism. Free competition among everybody, under equal subordination to the law, results in the predominance of the best in any relevant social field and is the only way of forming meritorious elites and of keeping the excellence of the elites.

A cost-benefit approach

Which of these three basic positions should be adopted? In order to answer this question we must first consider two points: the social cost of elite functions and the social conditions for "low-cost" elites.

As was clearly seen in our former analysis, elites perform societal functions: symbol formulation, decision making, commodities controlling. At the same time, they enjoy, whatever the content of ascriptivity and competitivity provided by the existing regime of participation, a corresponding control of symbols, power, money, and, either originally or derivatively, of prestige and influence. One could say, therefore, that the elite condition, at the level of each social subsystem and at the level of society as a whole, consists in a certain ratio between (1) *directional performance* and (2) *exaction enjoyment*.

In inegalitarian societies the exaction enjoyment results directly from the regime of participation. Coextensive with the foundation of that regime and, ultimately, of the social regime, is the assurance of certain prerogatives for the participational elite. This exaction enjoyment represents, in social terms, a sort of fixed cost, which is established irrespective of the social value that may result from the directional performance of that elite. In non-inegalitarian societies the exaction enjoyment is, at least in principle, considered the counterpart of social resources allocated to the elite (1) to allow, operationally, its functioning and (2) to reward its services.

Functional elites, therefore, may be considered as those whose directional performance, that is, the services rendered to the mass and the society as a whole, exceeds, fairly, their exaction enjoyment, that is, their social cost. Conversely, of course, dysfunctional elites are those whose net exaction enjoyment surpasses their directional performance.

The problem of appraising that "cost-benefit" account is obviously of the utmost complexity. How "worthy" are the services rendered by the elite in different social conditions? Who judges the account? How should it be computed? It would be beyond the purpose of the present study to consider any of the details concerning these questions. Let me just point out that, whatever its intrinsic complexity and even its relative insolubility, that problem has always been given a practical solution by history. Two aspects of the problem are, ultimately, of decisive importance. The first is the way in which the cost-benefit account is internally appraised by the several sectors of a society, whatever the effectiveness and the cost of the services rendered by the elite. Inegalitarian societies in which the prevailing regime of participation is maintained by coercion tend to present a conflictual picture. The Spartans, for instance, were absolutely aware of the fact that they were imposing on the Helots a regime of participation totally discriminative against the latter, only maintained by effective politico-military coercion. The Spartans just thought that the regime was justified because they were actually superior. But they did not obtain the allegiance of the mass. For centuries that same sense of superiority supported the privileges of Western nobility, but it started to falter during the Enlightenment, when nobles were compelled to acknowledge intellectually the arbitrariness of their privileges, whatever their personal interests.

As was precisely the case, for centuries, with the European nobility, however, inegalitarian societies can achieve a high degree of consensus, in the social regime, when the elite's privileged terms of participation are accepted by the mass as legitimate. This legitimacy, interwoven with the basic belief of the traditional culture of these societies, is an integral part of the existing regime of values. In such conditions the privileged elite enjoy a good conscience and tend to view their privileges both as being deserved because of their position in God's created order and as compelling them to render the services fitting their status, usually of a military and religious nature.

In non-inegalitarian societies, however, the elite-mass relationship tends to be viewed in terms of how much the incumbents in elite roles actually deserve their roles, rather than in terms of how justified the elite's status and exaction enjoyment are. Whatever views may be prevailing in a society about its elite-mass relationship and its directional performance–exaction enjoyment balance, what is relevant is the degree of allegiance the elite has obtained from the mass and, as a consequence, the legitimacy of the social regime. Whenever the obtained allegiance allows the maintenance of a *widely shared acknowledgment of the elite's legitimacy with an only marginal use of coercion, it can be said that, intrasocially, the elite is viewed as presenting a favorable directional performance–exaction enjoyment balance*.

The second aspect of the appraisal of the directional performance–exaction enjoyment balance of an elite is the comparative degree of development obtained by the concerned society. Mass allegiance to the elite can result from an objectively favorable balance between the elite's services and costs as well as from traditional views that present the privileges of the elite as natural or deserved. For that reason, consensus in the social regime, as formerly observed, has mainly an intrasocietal meaning. Objectively effective elites, however, are those that carry out their functions in an effective way, regardless of allegiance from the mass— and sometimes in spite of insufficient allegiance. This means not only—and even, for a certain time period, not necessarily—the maintenance of a *socially acknowledged* favorable balance between services rendered and resources used or consumed, but, ultimately, *the achievement of a real increase in the societal resources*. Development, as has been seen, consists, precisely, in a quantitative and qualitative increase of the relevant valuables of a society. This increase results from appropriate cultural, participational, political, and economic activity. It reflects, therefore, if not exclusively at least in a significant way, the objective[8] quality and cost of the services rendered to the society by the elite. Except in cases of particularly unfavorable environmental conditions, societal development is the objective indicator of the degree of functionality of the societal elite. This is also true in comparative terms. *Societies enjoying relatively similar conditions are more or less developed, compared to each other, according to the relative degree of functionality of their respective elite*.

Conditions for elite functionality

It is now possible to consider our initial question: Why are some elites functional and some not? If we apply the three historical answers to the processes of development in Great Britain and the United States, France and Germany, Japan, and Soviet Russia and China, we will observe, in the first place, how much the results achieved in these countries confirm our previous finding that the functional elites are the developmental ones. When the elites were not functional, they were either subjected to profound reforms, as was particularly the case with the *bakufu* elite in Japan, or ousted and replaced by a counterelite, as in the case of Soviet Russia and China. On the other hand, if we try to find out why the elites, their reform-oriented sectors, or in some countries, the counterelites have been functional, we have to acknowledge that there is some truth in each of the three historical answers. It is clear, for instance, in the case of Japan, who was confronted with the prospect of imminent Western domination because of her backwardness, that the reaction of the Western clans and all the subsequent course of the Meiji Restoration were predominantly determined by the internalized values of the elite. Supreme values, concerning the preservation of the national sovereignty and of the essential aspects of Japanese culture, and the personal honor of elite leaders were the motivation for profound changes, including changes in the cultural tradition and the self-renunciation of the elite's own feudal privileges. It could be said, in support of Plato, that the moral excellence of the Meiji elite led it to self-functionalization. It could also be said, in support of Aristotle, that the good norms that had been historically condensing in the British societal rules and uses were responsible for the functional elites of the British, and by inheritance and self-improvement of the Americans. And it would be equally appropriate to remember, with the supporters of the third point of view, that the initial difficulties of France and Germany and the lasting ones of Russia and China were attributable to the unchecked power of their former elites. Since they could afford a high exaction enjoyment ratio, these elites did not care to provide their countries with a better directional performance.

The analysis of these historical cases as well as the rest of the available evidence seems to indicate, ultimately, *that the occurrence and maintenance of a functional elite-mass relationship depends on a certain range of internalized elite values and on the enlightened self-interest of the elite, within the context of the available resources, means, and the conditions for their utilization and the pressures exerted by the mass of the concerned society or coming from other societies.* The paramount importance of the internalized values of the elite is exemplified in the cases of gradual societal development as well as in the cases of profound social reforms or successful revolutionary counterelites. It is illustrated by the importance several ethical or moral codes, as the Protestant ethic or the samurai honor code, have played in the processes of development. On the other hand, the role of enlightened self-interest is equally visible, both in the developmental efforts promoted on the initiative of modernizing autocrats or elites and in the reactions of certain elites who, facing the menace of their own masses or of alien groups, have been able to reach the point of giving up privileges and accepting heavy sacrifices for the mutual benefit of the elite itself and of the society as a whole. It is in that respect that the pressures of the mass are of the utmost importance. When masses are able to achieve a certain degree of intramass communication and organization beyond elite control, they impose on the elite both a more favorable participational regime, as far as the mass is concerned, and a more favorable cost-benefit balance, as far as the society as a whole is concerned. It is to keep their elite condition that pressed elites make or adopt innovations that will increase social productivity. The industrial revolution and the subsequent sociopolitical innovations in the West, including the welfare state of today, may be explained, in a sense, as creative responses on the part of the Western (renovated and self-renovating) elites to pressures from their masses. These responses were oriented so as to allow the elites to keep most of their leadership and several of their prerogatives while increasing the levels of consumption and participation, including increasing upward mobility, given to the masses.

NOTES

[1] See Harold D. Lasswell (1960), Raymond Aron (1950), C. Wright Mills (1956), Ralf Dahrendorf (1965), Suzanne Keller (1968), T. B. Bottomore (1964), and Peter Bachrach (1967).

[2] José Ortega y Gasset's concept of social example is applicable to the understanding of the nonascriptive aspects of autonomous participational elites. See Ortega y Gasset (1946–1947, vol. 3, pp. 103 ff.).

[3] I use the expression "non-inegalitarian society," rather than "egalitarian society," because no strictly egalitarian modern society has yet been formed and social equality, empirically, consists in the suppression of the principle of inequality rather than in the actual equalization of conditions.

[4] See particularly *The Republic*, IV, pp. 427–445.

[5] See *Politics*, particularly Book IV, chaps. 11–13.

[6] See *The Historics*, Book VI, pp. 11–18.

[7] See Ernest Barker (1952) particularly p. 64 ff.

[8] Objectivity, in this case, means the verifiability of the achieved results through empirical comparisons with other societies of the same time and with that same society in different times.

14

Societies and Models

Methodological questions

With the support of the historical experience discussed in Chapter 12 and the analysis of the elite-mass dynamics undertaken in Chapter 13, we can now return to the problem of the developmental operational political models treated in Chapter 11. In the analysis of these models we will have to utilize some notions concerning the basic operations involved in the execution of developmental projects, the corresponding stages in their implementation, and the operational conditions on which their successful execution depends. As far as the latter is concerned, it is indispensable to remember that there are two operational conditions that are *sine qua non* for the possibility of successful application of any of the developmental models: (1) national viability and (2) political mobilizability.

   These concepts will be discussed in the next section of this book. National viability refers to whether or not, at any given time, the human and natural resources of a society may be considered enough to assure the minimal conditions for its autonomous and endogenous growth, in terms of the technological requirements of that time and the structural conditions of the concerned society. Political mobilizability refers to whether or not a society, in terms of the structural conditions of that society at a given phase in her history, presents some politically implementable possibilities for increasing the rationality of the social system, in the sense of the existence or absence of sectors in its elite, subelite or, if any, counterelite that are actually or potentially interested in, capable of, and mobilizable for deliberately promoting political changes and societal changes by political means. In the discussion of the three basic models in Chapter 15, it is assumed that the societies to which they apply are altogether nationally viable and politically mobilizable. Societies that do not fulfill these two prerequisites simply cannot, with any predictable possibility of success, be the object of a deliberate effort for development.[1]

The present chapter is, essentially, an inquiry concerning the structural relationships between societies and models for the teleological and voluntaristic purpose of consistently using the latter to change the former. First, through the identification of the traits most relevant for the promotion of national development, we will make a structural analysis of societies conducive to the determination of a basic societal typology for development. Then, we will obtain a schematic indication of the principal characteristics of each developmental model, which will be understood as a blueprint for political action and for the promotion, by political means, of structural social change. It will then be possible to establish which models are convenient for which societies, for what reasons, and with what possibilities of success.

The problem of determining the relevant structural traits of a society for the promotion of her national development would involve long and exhaustive research if it were not possible to use the previous findings of this book, particularly those of the two preceding chapters, to follow a much shorter course. As a matter of fact, our critical survey of the more typical historical cases of national development and our analysis of elite-mass dynamics provide us with a basic criterion for approaching the organization of a societal typology for development. This criterion is our finding of a correlation, given the conditions of national viability and political mobilizability, between the degree of development of a society and the functionality of her elite. We have observed, on one hand, that the ultimate reason for the development of a society, given certain conditions, is the functionality of her elite, that is, the favorable balance between its directional performance and its exaction enjoyment. On the other hand, we have realized that what makes and keeps the functionality of elites is a certain range of internalized values combined with an enlightened self-interest in developing this functionality, as the most appropriate response to mass pressure for higher levels of consumption, participation, and social mobility, to the challenge of alien societies, or to both.

Preliminary survey

We can, therefore, assume with some security that of the wide range of societies that are considered underdeveloped, compared to their more successful contemporaries, those presenting a degree of development have an elite with some functionality. At a lower level, societies that are manifestly underdeveloped but are not subjected to an outstanding degree of coercion and do present characteristics of extreme backwardness have a nonfunctional elite but enjoy some sort of compensating factor. At the lowest level, extremely underdeveloped societies either have a manifestly dysfunctional elite or present characteristics of extreme backwardness inclusive of their elite.

If we consider the societies of the first group and use our informations from the preceding historical cases of national development, we will see that there are two distinct causes for the condition of relative but insufficient functionality on the part of the elite. One possible cause is the society's retention, in all its strata, of a traditional culture, compared to the degree of modernization in the other contemporary societies. In that case, the insufficient functionality of the elite is due primarily to its inability to make use of modes and means of action available to other societies, as was the case in Komei's Japan. Another possible cause is the existence of serious divisions and differences within the elite, which would cause the elite to have, at least tendentiously, a functional and a dysfunctional sector. It is not the lack of modernization but the lack of coherence of the elite, with institutions and policies representative of the dysfunctional sector creating obstacles to the action of the functional sector, that is responsible for the insufficient functionality of the elite as a whole and the resulting deficient development of the society. The case of France and Germany in the late eighteenth and early nineteenth century is a good example of this hypothesis.

The second group of societies are characterized by a certain disproportion between the hypothesized nonfunctionality of their elite and the fact that they are neither extremely backward nor subjected to extremes of coercion. There is in these societies a compensating factor which improves their final condition beyond the level of performance of their elite. If we remember some of our discussion in Chapter 11 and the brief indications in Table 30, we will see that the explanation consists in the fact that these societies have formed a modern and capable sector in their subelite. This sector is the compensating factor, and the not-so-unfavorable consequences of the elite's nonfunctionality are the result of this sector's actions. Pre-Nasser Egypt is one of the best illustrations of this type of society.

The third group presents two distinct pictures depending on whether the very low level of development is due to a manifestly dysfunctional elite or to extreme backwardness. In the latter case underdevelopment means, above all, the retention of a primitive or archaic culture, as occurs today in many of the new African states. In the former case, however, accentuated underdevelopment may be associated with relatively high aspects of modernization. Underdevelopment as the expression of a dysfunctional elite is essentially a deficiency of institutionalization, and is characterized by the maintenance of an inegalitarian regime of participation through the extensive use of coercion and/or fraud, either to support a regime of values whose legitimacy is rejected by the free-thinking sectors of the society, as in Russia and China in the late nineteenth and early twentieth century, or to enforce the pretense that the facade of an acceptably legitimate official regime really does correspond to the actual social regime, as in Batista's Cuba.

If we add our current knowledge of the regimes of stratification in contemporary societies to these observations, we will be able to replace the abstract functional categories of elite, subelite, and mass with the effective classes, sectors of classes, and relevant groups that are actually interacting in these societies. It is also indispensable to take into account the current forms of international domination, hegemony, and preponderance, in anticipation of the brief analysis in Chapter 18 of the international stratification prevailing among nations today. As has always occurred in history, the relationships of domination, hegemony, or preponderance among societies, although affecting the concerned societies as a whole, are actually based on, and processed through, relationships in which the elite of the dominated societies are dependent on the elite of the dominant ones. The understanding of these relations of international dominance-dependence between elites is an essential requirement for the intrasocietal analysis of the degree of functionality of any elite.

A general typology

We can now attempt to formulate a general typology and characterization of underdeveloped societies. Although the main categories of our analysis, because they are based on permanent functional traits of the elite-mass dynamics, are applicable to any society, at any time, we can concentrate on contemporary societies, which are the object of our present interest; and by so doing, we can dispense with details and qualifications that would not be relevant for the central purpose of this inquiry.

As was seen in the preceding preliminary survey, underdeveloped societies can be classified in three major types. These types include six varieties, as indicated in Chart 6.

Let us now, following Chart 6, attempt a brief typological characterization of these types of societies.

The societies of type I have in common a relative degree of development, due to a relative degree of functionality of their elites, but the two varieties are profoundly different. What is meant by relative degree of development also tends to be rather different in the two cases. The relative development, in the conditions of our time, of a traditional society (I–1) concerns primarily its degree of institutionalization. The preservation of the traditional culture brings with it the preservation of the traditional forms of legitimacy, in the context of which the directional performance–exaction enjoyment ratio of the elite tends, more often than not, to present a favorable or at least a socially unobjectionable

Chart 6 *Types and varieties of underdeveloped societies*

Type I.	*Societies with a Semifunctional Elite*
	I–1. Traditional societies
	I–2. Societies with a split elite
Type II.	*Societies with a Nonfunctional Elite*
	II. Societies sustained by the modern sector of the subelite
Type III.	*Primitive or Archaic Societies and Societies with Dysfunctional Elite*
	III–1. Primitive or archaic societies
	III–2. Coercive inegalitarian societies
	III–2.1. Societies with a rigidified aristocratic elite
	III–2.2. Societies with a *societas sceleris* elite

balance. For societies with a split elite (I-2), however, relative development means primarily their degree of modernization, although their legitimacy may be contested. It is necessary to study each case separately. Similarly, the societies of type III present three distinct varieties. The first (III-1) refers to primitive societies that have kept important remains of their former tribal organization and culture, as most of the new African states have, and to archaic societies, as some Islamic (Saudi Arabia, Iran) and Coptic (Ethiopia) societies, whose degree of comparative backwardness is of such an extent that, whatever the remaining intrasocietal legitimacy, the respective status quo cannot be maintained without an increasing dysfunctionality of the elite.[2] The two other varieties belong to the same subtype: (III-2), coercive inegalitarian societies. They are both characterized by a coercively imposed inegalitarian social regime. In societies with a rigidified aristocratic elite (III-2.1), the crisis of legitimacy results from the fact that the elite's regime of values is rejected by the modern sectors of the subelite and the free-thinking individuals, who usually form a revolutionary intelligentsia, with the consequence that the elite can only maintain the old social regime through coercive means. In societies with a *societas sceleris* elite (III-2.2), there is a lack of compatibility between the society's culture and the effective social regime, which actually provides the elite with privileges that are not in accord with the prevailing regime of values. For that reason the elite pretends to have a social regime that is different from the real one and maintains both the pretense and the regime through a combination of coercion and fraud. We will briefly examine each one of the six varieties.

(I-1) Traditional societies. The best historical example of a traditional society (see Table 27, group A.2), compared to contemporary ones, with a semifunctional elite, is Japan in the middle of the nineteenth century. The traditional culture permeated all the strata of society and all social roles. The prevailing regime of participation, in correspondence with the regime of values, was an inegalitarian one, but it was legitimized by the tradition that was accepted by both the elite and the mass, preserving among the former a strong sense of estate duty and maintaining in the latter a basic allegiance to the regime. The present examples of traditional (but not primitive) societies are much less simple and typical than nineteenth-century Japan due to the increasing worldwide penetration of Western influence since the nineteenth century and the corresponding detraditionalization of most cultures. Except in primitive and archaic societies, which in our typology belong to another group (III-1), the elite in the remaining traditional societies of our time, mostly represented by unmodernized Eastern countries, has been affected to a large extent by Western culture and does not keep a traditional outlook comparable to the one of the Japanese elite in the middle of the last century. Some Southeast Asian countries, as Laos and Cambodia, are possibly the closest contemporary examples of a remaining traditional society, but they are already in a deliberate drive for their own modernization, like Meiji Japan. India and Pakistan, with a still larger amount of Westernization of the elite, are also examples of traditional societies purposefully striving to modernize. Besides the arrested permanence of tradition and the consequent lag in modernization, the other relevant feature of such societies (for the purposes of our typology) is the preservation, together with the legitimacy of the social regime, of a sense of duty in the elite, according to the prescriptions of the tradition. It is that sense of duty that will impel a sector of the elite to adopt a modernizing posture and that will cause a large part of the elite, even at the cost of great class and personal sacrifices, to adhere to that purpose, driving the elite to self-renovation in the line of modernization and of overall national development.

(I-2) Split elite. The best historical examples of societies with a split elite (see Table 27, item 3.1.1.1) are the French and German cases of national development, under Napoleon III and Bismarck, respectively. The category also fits many of the contemporary Latin American countries. The typical feature of such societies is the actual or tendential division of the elite into a functional and a dysfunctional sector. The dysfunctional sector, usually of traditional origin (patrician landlords, consular bourgeoisie, upper-class professionals, top military), imposes the preservation of structures and policies that block the possibility of national development, essentially by maintaining a dualistic society. The extreme concentration of wealth, education, prestige, and power in the hands of the elite and the corresponding marginality of the mass prevent the social integration of the country, limit the potential of the national market and its capacity for growth, and affect in a similar way the social, cultural, and political planes of that society. The members of the functional sector of the elite (new industrial bourgeoisie, modern national entrepreneurs, top technicians, and executives), whose interests and values would be much better attended with the general expansion of the nation, are not sufficiently aware of the contradictions that oppose them to the dysfunctional elite. A loose ideological identification of the functional sector with the dysfunctional sector of the elite negatively affects not only the interests of the former but also the clarity, affirmativity and consistency of its values and behavior. The society, as a whole, is subjected to serious distortions, which substantially reduce the efficiency of the system of rewards and penalties, with the corresponding restriction of national cohesion and productivity. In such societies the opposition between functional and dysfunctional sectors is also found at the subelite and mass levels. The subelite is divided into a traditional sector, including the agrarian administrators, the conventional professionals and old-fashioned intellectuals, the semiparasitic (cartorial) public functionaries, a large sector of the military, the traditional churchmen, the traditional clerks, and the shopkeepers, and a modern sector, including the national managers and technicians of the new industries, the new professionals and modern intellectuals, the social-minded churchmen, the technocrats, the modernizing military, and the new national executives of modern businesses. The urban mass is also divided into traditional and modern sectors. The former includes either the older unionized workers, sticking to a rigidified view of the protection of labor, or the nonunionized (mostly the marginal tertiary and the lumpen proletariat) recent migrants from rural activities. The latter includes the workers of the new industries of transformation. The rural mass in such societies is still predominantly traditional and parochial.

(II) Societies sustained by the modern sector of the subelite. The best historical examples of this type of society are pre-Kemal Turkey and pre-Nasser Egypt. Bolivia before the MNR revolution of 1952 and the Ecuador of today are also representative examples of this type (see Table 27, item 3.1.2.1). Such societies are under the control of a nonfunctional elite, comprehending sectors of varying degrees of dysfunctionality; the top stratum is a patrician sector of landowners with national and foreign financial and merchant interests and associates, including the top military. The elite is always linked to, and increasingly dependent on, external business circles. The control of rural and urban property is kept in the hands of the elite, but the new modern industrial and larger commercial and financial concerns which gradually make their appearance are owned and controlled by foreign groups, although with a minor or nominal participation of the local elite. In such societies there is a clear differentiation between the traditional and the modern sector in the subelite. The former represents the typical middle sector of colonial and semicolonial societies. It is composed of the rural administrators, the shopkeepers, the traditional professionals and clerks, and the bureaucrats of the more conventional departments of the state, including the military. The modern sector, much smaller in size than the former one, includes the national technicians and managers who operate the few modern departments of the state, usually in the ministries of finance and the economy, the modern sector of the army, and the few executive functions in the modern private sector that are not directly operated by foreigners. Because of the action of that modern sector of the subelite, the final picture in that kind of society is less distressing than it would be otherwise. As long as that sector of the subelite plays its role efficiently without challenging the position of the elite and the usual expectations of the latter are satisfied, the elite's dysfunctionality is partially contained and the content of coercion necessary to preserve the social regime is moderate. The elite, however, within the limits of its capacity of enforcement, is prepared to increase its coefficient of exaction enjoyment and of coercion whenever its habitual income decreases.

(III-1) Primitive and archaic societies. The best historical examples of this group are such African countries as the Congo of Leopoldville and Ethiopia. Primitive societies (see Table 27, group A.1), however, present the widest possible range from the Australian aborigines and other groups, which are not capable of even nominal independent statehood, to the societies of many of the new African states. Archaic societies (see Table 27, subgroups 5 and 6 of group A.2), although much less numerous, have examples, in addition to Ethiopia, in the Islamic world and in Asia. The limits separating archaic societies from traditional ones are not clear when bordering cases are considered. In its typical form, a traditional society is one whose cultural system is not inherently incompatible with modernization (that is, its cultural system is not founded on a magic conception of the world) and whose social regime can, in principle, be reformed on the initiative of the modernizing sector of the elite. Conversely, archaic societies are those whose cultural system is founded on beliefs that are not compatible with higher levels of rationalization and whose social regime is too rigid to be self-reformable. Primitive societies can be understood, for the purpose of the present typology, as including all forms of nominally independent and sovereign societies that, in spite of some form of central government, have kept basic tribal features. In all of these societies when their respective elites encounter Western civilization, they have to react to the Western influence and challenge before they, themselves, can obtain a higher level of nontraditional education. Brought to the awareness of their backwardness without time or the conditions for a strategic withdrawal, the elites of these societies are compelled to achieve their own modernization by submitting to a foreign-directed and -controlled Westernization.

(III–2.1) **Societies with a rigidified aristocratic elite.** The original form of this group (see Table 27, subgroup 6 of group A.2) has mostly an historical significance today. Its typical examples disappeared with the Russian and Chinese revolutions. Such societies are characterized by what could be called a stratified traditionalism. Whereas traditional societies preserve, beyond their historical possibilities of functional survival, a cultural tradition that keeps permeating all their social strata and sectors, societies with a rigidified aristocratic elite preserve their cultural tradition as only a class or estate tradition of the elite. The modern sector of the middle class is led to an increasing rejection of that tradition, thus breaking the traditional foundations of legitimacy and imposing on the elite an increasing necessity for coercion in order to maintain the social regime. The coextensiveness of class conflict with the cultural conflict of values increases the rigidity of the elite and the rebelliousness of the intelligentsia, establishing a situation in which public order can only be kept by the permanent employment of the most violent forms of repression and in which opposition becomes necessarily of a conspiratorial and revolutionary nature. To an extent, archaic societies, as Ethiopia or Saudi Arabia, are also societies with a rigidified aristocratic elite, although in the conditions of archaic societies an intelligentsia is less likely to emerge and much less likely to have a meaningful communication with the mass.

A derivative form of that kind of society, however, is one of the two possible typological consequences of the deterioration of societies with a split elite (I–2) (see Table 27, items 3.1.3.1 and 3.2.2.1). In this case, the functional sector of the elite either is not capable of obtaining the minimum ideological consciousness necessary to identify its own basic interests and values, is prevented from taking a course of action consistent with its views because of an excessive fear of the risks involved, or looses the power contest with the dysfunctional sector of the elite. The latter then tends to drive the society to one of the two varieties of coercive inegalitarian societies. In most cases the result of the supremacy of the dysfunctional sector of the elite is the establishment of (III–2.2), a *societas sceleris* elite. In a few cases, however, the dysfunctional sector of the elite may keep a basic ideological bona fide, understanding its role, in accordance with a dogmatic regime of values that is of an archaizing nature but of modern outlook and formulation,[3] as the championship of some supreme cause, such as the defense of the "Christian Western civilization," which is understood in an archaized idealization as the absolute good, against communism, the absolute evil.

This was the case of Western fascism until its defeat in World War II, and it presently corresponds to the several varieties of colonial fascism occurring in the underdeveloped world. In such cases, the sociological equivalent of (III–2.1), a rigidified aristocratic elite, composed by the coalition of middle-class sectors, the bourgeoisie, and the remainders of the patrician landlords, form the equivalent of an *ancien régime* rigid elite. There is an important difference, however. This new elite, whatever the traditional implications of its regime of values, is basically a modern one in operational terms and is therefore much more able to impose its class interests and values than a traditional aristocracy.

(III–2.2) **Societies with a** *societas sceleris* **elite.** The best example of a society with a *societas sceleris* elite is Batista's Cuba. Most Central American countries of today keep that character (see Table 27, item 3.1.2.1). The distinction between that form of coercive inegalitarian society and the one discussed above is essentially of a subjective nature, although in terms that are sometimes empirically verifiable. This distinction consists in the rigidified elite's inner bona fide belief in its regime of values, in contrast with the naked and self-conscious exploitative opportunism of the *societas sceleris* elite. As so often occurs with distinctions of this kind, there are many intermediary cases in which the differentiation is difficult or impossible to make, and so becomes ultimately irrelevant. What is characteristic of the typical *societas sceleris* case is the formation of a coalition, centered around the elite and including the more strategic sectors and groups of the subelite, for the consolidation of the exploitation of the mass. The elite usually includes, besides a patrician agrarian sector, a consular bourgeoisie, entirely at the service of foreign interests, the upper-class professionals, equally dedicated to the interests of foreign groups and their local allies, and the military, which, in such societies, is incorporated into the higher social stratum and constitutes, in varying mixtures of a modern praetorian guard with a modern feudal nobility, the basic actual support of the regime. The co-opted sectors and groups of the subelite include the higher public functionaries, the protected sectors of private employees, the professionals, the mercenary intellectuals, the rural administrators, the noncommissioned officers, and last but not least, the union leaders. Whereas the military represents the effective base of support of the regime, maintaining the quantum of coercion and violence necessary to prevent the disaffected members of the subelite from mobilizing and organizing the exploited masses, the union leaders are the indispensable agents for mystifying the better organized sectors of the urban mass, helping to preserve a facade of social welfare and/or of populist intentions on the part of the regime or the authorities.

The operational models

The preceding classification and characterization of the types and varieties of underdeveloped societies, considered particularly in view of the contemporary picture, enables us now to analyze operational political developmental models, which will be called, for the sake of facility, "political models" or simply "models." We will concentrate on the three most widely applicable models (national capitalism, state capitalism, and developmental socialism), although, as has been observed, these three models do not exhaust the possibilities of their kind. Other models may be applicable, as indicated in Table 30, depending on the structural conditions of the concerned societies, their societal environment, and the historical period. Let me briefly review the case of the implicit models. The liberal model, in spite of its antiprogrammatic message, is nonetheless an implicit operational model, in the sense that it assumes a process of societal optimization and progress through the free interplay of self-oriented actors and that its implementation, in spite of the economics of laissez faire, depends on the installation and maintenance, by the state, of appropriate political and institutional conditions. As we saw in Chapter 12, this was the case in Great Britain and the United States. In a more explicit form the same is true of the neoliberal model.

In addition to these implicit models, there are other explicit ones (see Tables 30 and 31), as the models of modernizing autocracy (Peter the Great), modernizing elitocracy (Meiji Restoration), and the more advanced social welfare models. Furthermore, the basic political models present a wide possibility of intermediate combinations. Modernizing autocracy and modernizing elitocracy form two points of a spectrum with several intermediate positions. The same can be said of the three more relevant models, national capitalism, state capitalism, and developmental socialism. There are several possible and empirically occurring combinations between national capitalism and state capitalism and between state capitalism and developmental socialism. In fact, there may be some interesting connections between these latter more "modern" models and the more "traditional" models of modernizing autocracy and modernizing elitocracy. The Meiji modernizing elitocracy used many of the techniques of state capitalism to obtain, later, a form of national capitalism that is now evolving into a welfare capitalism. Conversely, the Soviet developmental socialism showed various important traits of an autocratic modernization during the period of Stalin. Features of autocratic modernization, moreover, also appeared in the earlier phase of Bismarck's modernizing elitocracy, which evolved, during his own time into a form of national capitalism. Table 31 presents the general picture of what has been said on this matter so far.

With this preliminary point cleared, it is necessary to stress the general meaning, effects, and implications of political models.

Essentially, as was discussed in Chapter 11, political models are designs that set goals and strategies that set conditions and means for the deliberate optimization, *in given structural conditions*, of the potential rationality (including moral rationality) contained in a given society. The question of the given structural conditions is a fundamental one for the understanding of political models. Models are not magical devices and do not create the elementary conditions, the actors, the drive for action, or the means for the implementation of action that may be required. Models are just techniques for the optimization of preexisting elements, although in a process of self-inducing growth. Some societies cannot be developed by any sort of model, either because they are not viable, as national

Table 31 *Operational political developmental models*

Traditional models	Modernizing autocracy (MA)
	Modernizing elitocracy (ME)
Implicit models	Liberalism (laissez faire) (L)
	Neoliberalism (NL)
Explicit developmental models	National capitalism (NC)
	State capitalism (SC)
	Developmental socialism (DS)
Welfare models	Welfare capitalism (WC)
	Welfare socialism (WS)

Empirically More Frequent Combinations

MA–NC	(Early Bismarckism)
MA–DS	(Stalinism)
ME–NC	(Meiji Restoration)
NC–SC	(Fit for more developed Latin American countries, for example, Brazil)
SC–DS	(Later Nasser regime and less developed Latin American countries, for example, Ecuador)

societies, or because they actually do not have, at a given stage or phase in their history, any social sector willing to, and capable of, promoting structural social changes. (The latter condition usually costs the society its own future survival.) Sometimes the conditions required for a successful innovating leadership are so exacting, in terms of the personal qualities required, the sacrifices imposed, or the initially available means for action, that nobody is willing or able to play the role—as in Paraguay since the 1940s. The operational conditions for any developmental project will be studied in Chapter 17. It is indispensable, however, to keep the following prerequisites in mind: (1) national viability, (2) political mobilizability, (3) capable leadership, (4) appropriate choice of model, (5) appropriate implementation of model, and (6) no interference from insurmountable extrasocietal obstacles (as natural cataclysms or foreign occupation).

Concerning the effects and implications of political models, as far as their successful implementation is concerned, one must realize that in politics, as in engineering, the easier the goal is to obtain, the simpler the required model is and the easier it is to reach the goal. In engineering, however, the possibility of scientific command of the subject matter is high and the possibility of accurate technological application of scientific knowledge still higher, allowing a great degree of goal attainment; whereas in politics we are confronted with a principle of declining probability of goal achievement as we increase the complexity of the models and of the requirements for their successful application.

As will be discussed later, the application of a political model involves several stages: (1) formation, which includes the choice, formulation, and politicalization of a suitable model, (2) state building, (3) nation building, and (4) consensus building. The probability that the suitable model for a given society and given conditions will be led from stage 1 to stage 2 and, successively, to stage 4 tends to be higher for more developed societies and lower for less developed ones. When the starting level of development is decreased, the complexity of the model increases accordingly, with a resulting increase in the complexity of the requirements for success and in the number of arrangements and combinations necessary, which increases correspondingly the chances of failure. As has been observed, politics is both a science and an art. As a rule, the more complex the arrangements and combinations required by a model are, the more dependent the successful implementation of the model is on the artfulness of the principal actors, the more the number of "soloists" has to be increased, and the greater are the chances of human error and distorting interference from unforeseen events. This is why so few of the countries that remained underdeveloped after the nineteenth century, as was seen in Chapter 12, have succeeded in overcoming their comparative backwardness. And, as was also discussed, this is why countries that have succeeded or are succeeding in overcoming their underdevelopment by means of a tremendous political effort, as Russia and China, are still so far from achieving a minimum of social consensus (stage 4 of the implementation of political model) comparable to that obtained by the countries whose development was achieved earlier and more effortlessly.

Essential characteristics

Before proceeding to the analysis of how our three basic models can be applied to the convenient sociopolitical cases in the societal typology previously indicated, I will summarize, in Chart 7, the essential characteristics, the main promoting actors, and the basic *modus operandi* of each of the three basic models.

Chart 7 *Characteristics of the basic models*

A. *National Capitalism (NC)*

1. ESSENTIAL CHARACTER

    Model for surmounting the obstacles to development brought about by the dysfunctional sector of the elite through the creation of conditions leading to (1) the predominance and leadership of the functional sector of that elite and (2) the nationwide mobilization of the modernizing sectors of all social classes, so that these sectors will actively support and contribute, with the necessary efforts and sacrifices, to the deliberate promotion of national development, according to a central plan formulated by the state and executed under its guidance and with its major intervention. Emphasis on the nation and its autonomy and endogeny, based on and leading to a functional nationalist ethos.

2. MAIN SOCIAL ACTORS

    Modernizing sectors of the national bourgeoisie and the middle class in alliance with the proletariat and with the support of the mobilized

Chart 7 *Characteristics of the basic models* (continued)

peasants versus traditional and consular sectors of the bourgeoisie and middle class, their foreign bosses, partners, and allies and antimodernizing rural sectors.

3. MODUS OPERANDI

Combination of state and private entrepreneurial action, under state guidance and with its major intervention, but with as much decentralization and delegation of responsibility to national private sector as is compatible with the efficient politico-economic execution of the plan. Central national planning and control, state regulation of investment-consumption ratio, massive reproductive investments, and severe but socially fair contention of consumption. State-organized or -supported corporations for infrastructural and basic industries. Highest priority for general and higher education and for research and development. Neo-Bismarckian leadership by chief of state with social arbitration of benefit reallocation among the social sectors, according to a realistic and societally functional egalitarian readjustment of the regime of participation: the new social pact. Organization of national development party for the articulation and aggregation of interests in accordance with the new social pact in a way conducive to national development. Exercise of power primarily through democratic electoral procedures with a minimum amount of strategically required authoritarian recourse. Developmental and autonomic orientation of nationalism.

B. *State Capitalism* (SC)

1. ESSENTIAL CHARACTER

Model for surmounting the obstacles to development brought about by nonfunctional elite through the creation of conditions leading to (1) the seizure of politico-economic control, (2) leadership by the modernizing sector of the subelite, and (3) the subsequent utilization, in depth, of the state, to promote societal change and national development, with active mobilization of the support of the urban and rural masses so they will endure the sacrifices and make the contribution necessary for the accelerated promotion of national development by the state. Emphasis on social reforms and national autonomous development. Based on and leading to a functional social and national reformist ethos.

2. MAIN SOCIAL ACTORS

Modernizing sector of the middle class, with full support of urban and rural masses versus traditional patrician elite and their consular allies in the bourgeoisie and middle class, particularly their foreign bosses, partners, and supporters.

3. MODUS OPERANDI

Full employment of the state as an agency of planning, entrepreneurship, and control, without suppression of private sector but with transference to state agencies and corporations of the main economic and cultural functions, with the orientation and development of possible private national entrepreneurship toward supplementary and supporting activities. Strict regulation of personal income, according to basically egalitarian criteria. Maximum, socially endurable, effort at saving in order to concentrate resources on economically and educationally strategic investments. Highest priority for general and higher education. Maximum effort for surmounting scientific-technological backwardness in the shortest possible time. Strict functional-technical criteria in personnel selection and state management, combined with strict loyalty to state and nation in strategic functions. Organization of party of revolution for active mobilization of urban and rural support for social change and national development, and resistance to foreign intervention. Conveying rewards to supporters leading struggle against reactionary forces. Exercise of power primarily by forms of authoritarian co-optation combined with mass plebiscites. Early adoption of mechanism providing for expansion of democratic participation and control as general and political development increases.

C. *Developmental Socialism* (DS)

1. ESSENTIAL CHARACTER

Model for surmounting the obstacles to development brought about by dysfunctional elite, particularly in coercive inegalitarian societies, through the revolutionary overthrow of the former elite by the counterelite, with the appropriate employment of a well-organized and disciplined party. Subsequent socialization of the means of production, through the in-depth utilization of the state, to promote revolutionary societal change and national development, with the revolutionary support of the urban and rural masses, who, within the frame and for the sake of a socialist and national society, endure the sacrifices, make the contribution necessary for the accelerated promotion of national development, and fight against foreign intervention. Emphasis on revolutionary reforms and national autonomous development based on and leading to a rationally framed social and national revolutionary ethos.

2. MAIN SOCIAL ACTORS

The intelligentsia of the counterelite organized in a revolutionary, well-disciplined party, with support of party-controlled urban and rural masses and an eventual tactical alliance with disaffected sectors of the former elite and subelite, versus the dysfunctional elite, their subelite supporters and respective repressive apparatus, and their foreign bosses, partners, and supporters.

3. MODUS OPERANDI

Revolution promoted, accelerated, and guided by the party, according to the models of the "conspiratorial revolution," the "Jacobin revolution," or the "military mass insurrection."* Once political power is conquered, all the agencies and institutions of political, cultural, economic, and social action formerly used by the dysfunctional elite are suppressed or totally readjusted to new requirements and purposes. The state, under the direction and control of the party, is employed in depth as an agency of planning, entrepreneurship, and control of all relevant societal activities, with as complete socialization as is possible, without indemnification of the means of production. Basic equalization of incomes and maximum, socially endurable, effort at saving in order to concentrate resources on economically, educationally, and

Chart 7 *Characteristics of the basic models* (continued)

defensively strategic investments. Highest priority for general and higher education. Maximum efforts for surmounting scientific-technological and defense backwardness in the shortest possible time. Nationalization of all patents and inventions. Strict functional-technical criteria in personnel selection and state management, combined with maximum party and national loyalty in strategic functions. Adjustment of revolutionary party, after conquest of power, to the function of active mobilization and politicalization of urban and rural masses in order to obtain their support of the revolution and the national development of the new regime and authorities, to obtain their high morale, to prevent and suppress counterrevolutionary attempts, and to wage a deadly fight against foreign intervention. Exercise of power by centralized democracy at party level and hierarchical decision at state level. Early adoption of mechanisms as automatic as possible, to prevent the conversion of functional centralism into bureaucratic oligarchy, providing for the adoption of democratic electoral practices as general and political development increases.

*See Chalmers Johnson (1964).

NOTES

[1] Sociohistorical facts have a large margin of unpredictability, and "nonviable" countries may be led to successful revolutionary changes against the predictable probability, as in Cuba with Fidel Castro. As will be discussed in Book III, however, the Cuban revolution did not overcome at once (and still may not overcome) the nation's problems of viability. They are being gradually surmounted because of a Soviet aid which, in its actual form (that is, without imposing Cuba's satellization), was not and could not have been foreseen by Castro.

[2] Such unavoidable dysfunctionality results, along with other reasons, because the elite, unable to withstand international pressures within the conditions of the status quo, has a tendency to preserve its elite status by becoming a satellite of a big power.

[3] Contrary to what occurs in traditional societies, where the legitimacy of the social regime is really founded on the religious values of the culture, fascist and colonial-fascist elites sustain archaized traditional religious values for what they represent as an archaized idealization and not for their actual religious content, as it is manifested in their current modern versions. For that reason the commitment for the defense of "Christian culture" is usually associated with the actual prosecution of the modern Christian churches and with militants, as occurred in Nazi Germany and has been occurring since the coup of 1964 with the manifestations of colonial-fascist tendencies in Brazil.

15

The Three Basic Models

Model fitness

We can now discuss why and how the three basic models fit the structural conditions of some of the societies considered in our former typology, in what terms are they implementable in these societies, and with what foreseeable course.

The comparative analysis of the typology of underdeveloped societies and the characteristics of the basic models presented in Chart 7 make most of the cases of model suitability rather clear. It is clear that insofar as the suitable model may be and actually is consistently implemented, the following holds true: National capitalism (NC) is the adequate model for promoting the development of societies with a split elite (I–2). State capitalism (SC) is the appropriate model for societies sustained by the modern sector of the subelite (II). And in the two cases of coercive inegalitarian societies, societies with a rigidified aristocratic elite (III–2.1) and societies with a *societas sceleris* elite (III–2.2), the suitable model is developmental socialism (DS).

The problem of model selection or implementation becomes more complicated in cases of *protracted underdevelopment* and *consolidated underdevelopment*. Protracted underdevelopment is the condition of underdeveloped societies in which consistent efforts to implant and implement the suitable model on a national scale either have not taken place or have failed, in spite of long-term and widespread acknowledgment of the situation by the society's elite and subelite, as is notably the case in Latin American societies. Consolidated underdevelopment is a case of protracted underdevelopment in which the long absence of consistent or successful attempts to introduce the required changes has given rise to a stabilized deterioration of the social fabric, maintained through the emergence of a firmly entrenched coercive inegalitarian regime, either of the colonial-fascist or of the *societas sceleris* brands. Latin America, once again, presents some of the best examples of both.

In cases of protracted underdevelopment the selection of the suitable model and the process for its implantation are rather more difficult than in cases of simple underdevelopment. More often than not, a "pure" model will not be adequate. Most of these societies are of the split elite type, but they remain in protracted underdevelopment because the functional sector of the elite either is too weak to undertake an attempt at gaining leadership (Argentina in the 1960s) or is unwilling (Brazil in the 1960s) to assume the inherent risks of such an endeavor. In such cases a special combination of models, of the NC–SC kind or, for some fewer cases (societies between types II and III–2), of the SC–DS kind, is needed. In any case, the promotion of the suitable model or model combination requires much more exigent political conditions, such as the appearance of exceptional leaders and the formation of a very strong party or political coalition.

In cases of consolidated underdevelopment, in which only a DS model or a SC–DS combination may be suitable, the problem lies in the fact that the consolidated deterioration of such societies always substantially affects their national viability and political mobilizability to the point of converting them into hopeless cases, whatever their former situation may have been. This may be the present case of Paraguay, where the military, which took over the control of the country after the Chaco War and failed in its early attempts to promote a SC solution, was led to convert the regime into a spoliative colonial praetorianism. A similar course threatens the destiny of Bolivia, which fell under the control of a praetorian military after the failure of Victor Paz Estenssoro's attempt to establish an SC regime, and once again after the failure of the new developmental efforts of Generals Ovando and Torres.

Let us now consider the more relevant structural aspects of the implantation and implementation of each of the three basic models in nationally viable and politically mobilizable societies. The following analysis will not lead to the actual formulation of any of these three models in terms of an isomorphic representation of a sociopolitical reality. To complete our theoretical understanding of the problems of model formulation, we still need to discuss some basic questions, up to now only enumerated, concerning the operational conditions and stages of model implementing. These questions will be studied in the subsequent section of this book. The theoretical discussion of a model, however, is one thing and the technical formulation of it another, for political models as well as for any model. The technical formulation of political models (see Chapter 11) requires that the concrete relevant aspects of the society for which the model is designed be duly represented. What I am going to do now, therefore, is not design concretely implementable models but rather indicate *why* and *how* the basic models that have been considered suitable for certain types of underdeveloped societies are actually so.

National capitalism (NC)

Why? NC is the suitable model for (I–2) societies with a split elite insofar as the functional sector of the elite is capable of exercising functional leadership and is willing to do so. In addition to the general precondition of national viability and political mobilizability, if the NC model is to be suitable for societies of the (I–2) type, the functional sector of the elite must be sufficiently strong and motivated to undertake the sort of societal changes the NC model is designed for. Otherwise, the result will be a case of protracted underdevelopment, for which a pure NC model will no longer be adequate and in which the conditions for implanting and implementing an NS–SC combination will be rather more complicated.

When, however, the functional sector of the elite in the (I–2) society is capable and willing to undertake the required societal changes, the NC model is the suitable one because it represents the easiest form of politico-societal development, at the lowest social cost and with the maximum of social support. And this is so because of the basic correspondence between what is good for the main social actors, who are themselves the leading sectors of the society, and for that society as a whole. This correspondence constitutes the inherent foundation for the suitability of a model and for its consequent implementability. With the NC model that correspondence lies, in the final analysis, in the fact that the functional sector of the elite needs to establish an expanding basically egalitarian social regime in order to give appropriate attendance to its own interests and values. Given the existing conditions, and whatever de jure the social regime may be, the masses are currently marginalized, both as producers and as consumers, in all the societal planes. There is, as a consequence, a vicious circular causality between the marginality of the majority (often as much as 80 percent) of the population and the general stagnation of the system. In such conditions the society can only respond, internally, to the claims and expectations of the masses through an unsustainable redistribution of the scarce supply of existing wealth (which would be suicidal even if its concentration in a few hands is a serious socioeconomic problem) or through a repression of those claims (which is what actually tends to occur). This means both that the stagnation is self-perpetuating and that the coefficient of coercion tends to increase. Externally, however, the society is increasingly incapable of surviving on its own merits, becoming necessarily a dependent client of some alien big power. The internal stagnation tends to create, in addition to an increasing incapacity for self-defense (due to the increasing economic and technological lag vis-à-vis the more developed societies), an increasing external economic dependence, because of domestic budgetary and balance-of-payment deficits. The overcoming of the dysfunctional sector of the elite, however, along with its accompanying institutions, practices, and agencies, would allow the functional sector to expand an economy and a society of which they would be the leading elite, with a more than proportional stake in the process of national development (and even a simply proportional stake would be good enough).

If the functional sector of the elite is capable and willing to introduce the required changes, the basic problem it is confronted with is whether or not the process of change can be kept in terms that are compatible with its class interests and values. That sector of the elite, as formerly discussed, is essentially composed of entrepreneurs of the national bourgeoisie. The NC model, however, involves both an alliance with the middle class and the proletariat and a considerable reinforcement and expansion of the public sector, with the submission of private business to state planning, guidance, and control. How can the national entrepreneurs be sure that they are not contributing to their future ruin, by mobilizing forces that may overpower them and by creating institutions that, under the control of other social groups, will superordinate their own firms and groups?

Here comes, obviously, the problem of the political reconciliation of conflicts, which exists, potentially, from the first moment and which will, empirically, tend to become more visible and menacing, particularly if, as occurs more often than not, the social protagonists either are not sufficiently clear about goals and means or are not sufficiently aware of the advantages of class and group self-restraint. As will be studied in Book III, this is the sort of problem that has caused the protracted underdevelopment in some Latin American countries, of which Brazil is the best example. That sort of problem can only be solved by appropriate political leadership. When the main social actors are unaware of that problem, as in the current Latin American case, the requirements for successful political leadership become more exacting. When, however, as occurred in the recent second wave of development in Germany under Adenauer and in France under de Gaulle,[1] the greater sociohistorical experience of the main social actors (entrepreneurs, technocrats, and union leaders) help them to adopt moderate demands and conciliatory lines of action, there is an enhancing of interclass cooperation and a corresponding decrease in the required level of authoritarian decisions. Historically, however, as we have seen, the overcoming of French and German underdevelopment in the middle of the nineteenth century was only possible because of the emergence of authoritarian leaders and regimes under Napoleon III and Bismarck. The national entrepreneurs, in both cases, were not the main decision makers. Decisions were made by the political leaders. The conditions for the implementation of an NC model were adopted for, but not by, the bourgeoisie.

How? Let us now see how the implementation of the NC model occurs structurally, assuming that, in the conditions of our time, past experience and a clearer theoretical and political formulation of the problems involved in implementing the model help the main social actors to be more rational and cooperative.

First, as with any of the models, the NC model is formulated, not only as an object of scientific study (as in this book) but as a political design for a specific society, by the intellectuals. Whatever their scientific understanding of the problems involved, the intellectuals will have to take the initiative in making a sociopolitical diagnosis of their society and polity and, in accordance with that diagnosis, propose the design of an appropriate solution, which will involve, with varying degrees of accuracy, an attempt at politicalizing a suitable model. Sometimes the activist intellectuals formulating the NC model are also politicians, as were Louis Napoleon and Bismarck. With some models, such as DS, the implanters and implementers must be members of an intelligentsia. With the NC model, either the model is formulated and politicized by intellectuals and later accepted, in several forms and ways, by the political leaders and the main social actors (entrepreneurs, union leaders, and so forth), which is what tends to occur in less underdeveloped countries because of their greater functional diversification, or the political leaders themselves are able to formulate and politicalize the model or obtain the advice of intellectuals for this purpose.

Once the model has achieved a sufficient level of politicalization, the NC project will soon be confronted with the first problem of its implementation: whether or not, given the experience and perceptiveness of the main social actors and the capacity of the political leadership, enough interclass confidence and cooperation will be generated, with sufficient political guidance, to lead to the formation of a great party or political coalition. The potentially and theoretically interested involved sectors and groups will represent, if they accept the project, a massive force and will tend to acquire a dominant position. They will include, in addition to the functional sector of the elite, which in itself will form only a small group, the much larger groups of the modernizing subelite and the ample groups of the urban and mobilizable rural masses. If the test of political interest aggregation is favorably passed, the NC party or coalition will tend to amass political power rather rapidly, because of its majoritarian character, and will soon have sufficient power to be entrusted with the charge of government. Otherwise, the sociopolitical deadlock will continue, which will tend to generate a state of protracted underdevelopment.

When favorable political interest aggregation is followed by the taking of governmental responsibility, the NC party or coalition will then have to overcome two other unavoidable obstacles. One, of domestic origin, occurs because there tends to be, in several forms and for several reasons, a negative imbalance between the initial resources available to the NC government and its total expenditures. This includes both the economic and the political resources. The crucial aspect of the NC model being its energetic promotion of national development, with the corresponding high level of investments and heavy demand for resources, there is a tendency to exhaust formerly accumulated capital (which in underdeveloped countries is necessarily meager) before the product of the new investments can replenish the invested funds. In a parallel way, the political capital of the NC government tends to be overtaxed in overcoming the tensions accompanying the period of maturation of the investments before the results are able to generate new support.

The second obstacle, predominantly of foreign origin, concerns the tensions rapidly generated in the relations between the NC government and some of the main foreign-interest groups, which were formerly enjoying particularly advantageous conditions, and their political supporters in their respective countries. One of the main features and requirements of the NC model is the transference of the control of the national economy to domestic groups and capital under state supervision and guidance. In the conditions of our time, particularly in underdeveloped countries, as will be discussed in Chapter 18, the so-called multinational corporations, most of them American, are rapidly taking control of the

dynamic or strategic positions of the economy in all countries that do not succeed in deliberately preventing this effect by using strong appropriate defensive
policies. Precisely because one of the fundamental aspects of the NC model consists in articulating and implementing such defensive policies, that model necessarily brings about conflict with these vested interests and their powerful home
political support. That conflict tends to result, externally, in foreign diplomatic
and financial pressures against the NC government; and, internally, strong and
often perfidious pressures exerted by the national associates and agents of these
interests, usually controlling the mass media, seriously aggravate the negative
balance of resources.

To overcome these two usually interconnected obstacles, the NC government
needs to be able to handle its deficit of material resources through compensatory
symbolic means, increasing the social commitment to national development,
activating the pride in national autonomy and the loyalty to the national government. For that purpose the government must mobilize the support of the progressive and nationalist sectors of the bourgeoisie and the middle class, the urban
masses, and as far as possible, the peasants. If, as usually occurs with the NC
model, the government is a democratically elected one, with a sound basis of
validity, the legality and legitimacy of the government, combined with the support of the national and popular forces, tend to be sufficient to enable the government to sustain its policies in the critical formative period and to generate
enough political credit to allow it to yield its first developmental results, consolidating the regime. If, however, enough support is not generated soon enough, as
has occurred in countries like Brazil and Argentina, the NC model is aborted, and
the country is driven to a situation of protracted underdevelopment.

State capitalism (SC)

Why? SC is the suitable model for (II) societies sustained by the modern sector
of the subelite, insofar as that sector is capable and willing to overcome the nonfunctional elite, take the initiative of readjusting the machine of the state, and
use it in depth to promote national development. As is similar to the case of the
NC model, the functional sociopolitical foundation of that suitability lies in the
fact that there is a basic and inherent correspondence between what suits the
interests and values of the modernizing sector of the middle class and what is
convenient for the national development of the society: the overcoming of the
dysfunctionality of the patrician-consular elite and the creation and expansion
of a modern nation through the intensive and extensive use of the only national
organization that can be adjusted to that function, the national state, under the
guidance of the subelite and with the active support of the urban and rural masses.

As with the NC model, the key initial provision is the capability and the willingness of that sector to perform the role assigned to it by the SC model. Sometimes the modernizing sector of the middle class is too small to obtain the mass
necessary for both the successful overthrow of the nonfunctional elite and the
subsequent minimally efficient management of the state machinery, which must

be deeply readjusted to perform its new role and necessarily will be heavily solicited. This may be, in part, the explanation of the difficulties in the implanting of the SC model in a country like Ecuador, in which the model would otherwise be suitable.

More often than not, however, the principal missing element is not so much the potential capability of that sector as its actual lack of willingness to take the proper measures. This unpreparedness is sometimes due to the excessive involvement of the modernizing sector of the subelite in the values of the nonfunctional elite, which imparts to the former a traditional-conservative view of society, frequently associated with a laissez-faire or neoliberal bias. The implied risk in this propensity is the final co-optation and corruption of that sector by the elite, leading to a *societas sceleris* arrangement, as occurred in Machado's and Batista's Cuba. Another common reason for this unpreparedness is the subelite's fear that the active and deep mobilization of the masses, which is an essential requirement of the SC model, will liberate forces that will subsequently escape the control of the middle-class military and the technocrats. This seems to be, to some extent, a limiting factor in the case of Peru, where the men of the military coup of 1968, although decidedly oriented toward an SC model, have been afraid to start the actual implementation of some of the participatory requirements of the model because of fear of losing the control of the masses. The implied risk in this inhibiting fear of the masses is the inevitable deterioration of the morale of the military and the technocrats, leading the society to forms of consolidated underdevelopment, as has occurred for that reason in Paraguay.

The way to overcome both forms of unpreparedness in the subelite (involvement in the elite's values and fear of the masses) is through the political education and organization of the subelite. As in the case of the preconditions of the NC model, in which the political leadership must reconcile the interests and fears of the bourgeoisie and of the masses, so in the case of the SC model, the political leaders of the subelite must bring that subelite to a sufficient level of political education and organization before it will be capable and willing to undertake its role. Given the basic inherent suitability of the SC model for the structural conditions of societies sustained by the modern sector of their subelite, the education and organization of the subelite for the performance of its social role in the SC model is perfectly feasible for a capable leadership. As has already been observed and will be discussed more fully in the next section, the leadership factor is an indispensable one. It is likely to occur when there is a pressing social demand for the action of leaders but not in any necessary or automatic form. And so leadership is sometimes missing, in which case the subelite is not led to play its potential role, and the society keeps deteriorating and declines into some form of consolidated underdevelopment.

How? If, given the appropriate political education and organization of the modernizing sector of the subelite, that sector becomes capable and willing to carry out the implantation and implementation of the SC model, the first obstacle it will have to overcome is the conquest of power. Unlike the case of NC, in which there is, at least analytically, a sufficiently clear distinction between model formulation and political aggregation, in the SC model the two phases must come together. This does not mean that the intellectuals may not, as so often they actually do, anticipate the political leaders in making the appropriate diagnosis of the problems of their society and in formulating the goals to be attained and the ways to attain them. What it does mean is that a concrete project of implanting and implementing an SC model cannot be politicalized, in a concrete society, in an uncommitted form as a free offering presented at the "political market," as may occur with the NC model. A concrete SC design is inherently conspiratorial, because it means the overthrow of the existing nonfunctional elite by means incompatible with the existing regime of power. Preparing the modernizing sector of the subelite to adopt and implement that model, therefore, is actually to prepare for a coup or even a revolution. Such a coup (or revolution) may be of various modalities but the form that is most likely to fit is that of the conspiratorial coup d'état.[2] In order to achieve both the necessary degree of preparedness for the implantation of the SC model and the necessary capability for implementing it later, the politico-military preparation of the SC model, its strategy, and its initial tactical requirements must reach a rather high level before the actual overthrowing of the *ancien régime*. That preparation presents a peculiar difficulty because what tends to be most convenient for the first step of the implementation of the model, the seizure of power by a conspiratorial coup and the overthrow of the *ancien régime*, may easily be at variance with what will be most convenient for the subsequent step of reorganizing the state, formulating completely new and rather radical policies, and starting their effective implementation. Seizing power and overthrowing the *ancien régime* by a conspirational coup tends to be most feasible, since much of the military apparatus of the country, with its preexisting system of commands, is used in the coup. Very seldom, however, if ever, is that apparatus, and particularly that system of commands, in its totality or even the larger part of it, likely to be able, or even willing, to perform the postcoup steps. In such cases, which are the most frequently occurring ones, the political leaders of the SC project have to make decisions that will enable them to maximize the possibilities of adopting the appropriate course of action after the coup without seriously endangering the chances of a successful—and as bloodless as possible—seizure of power.[3] Of the several possible ways of dealing with that problem, which include various ways of bypassing or suppressing reactionary commanders as well as various ways of neutralizing their possible future negative influence, the most usual one in historical practice has been the implantation of the model in two steps. In the first step most, eventually almost all, of the former chain of strategic commands is used to overthrow the *ancien régime*. For that a conventional but respected military boss is used by the political leaders of the coup as a front man and nominal chief of the movement, while the real leaders secure for themselves the strategically appropriate military positions in the new system of command. Once this is achieved, a second step brings the real leaders to the actual seizure of power, and the convenient implementation of the model is then rendered possible. As is well known, this is the way Nasser used Nagib's former authority in the Egyptian army to overthrow Faruk.

Once power is seized and conditions have been established for the convenient implementation of the SC model, the problems to be confronted by the new regime include (1) an aggravated version of the initial obstacles of the NC model: lack of enough resources and foreign pressure and (2) two other difficulties inherent to the SC model: the leadership's difficulty in keeping appropriate control on the implementing cadres and the main social protagonists and the difficulty of the main social protagonists and strategic cadres in keeping appropriate control on the mobilized masses.

The problem of the relative scarcity of utilizable resources, both economic and political, before the returns on the initial investments replenish the corresponding funds is dramatically aggravated in the SC model, because there is usually a poorer stock of available resources in the beginning of the process and there is only one source of resources and one entrepreneur: the state. In practice this aggravated deficit of resources takes particularly the form of a critical deficiency in managerial capability. Too many things have to be decided and done by the central administration (not for the love of a centralized bureaucracy but for lack of alternative means). The total number and quality of available agencies and actors is insufficient. Foreign pressures, which tend to take the form of diplomatic and economic harassment in the NC model, will assume, in the SC model, a much more aggressive and direct form: foreign-instigated and -supported countercoups or either covert or overt foreign-based and -equipped armed intervention.

The two other difficulties peculiar to the SC model consist in the mutually aggravating problems of control from the top to the middle level and from the middle level to the bottom. Controls at the top tend to be difficult because of the conspiratorial origin and base of the new regime. Whereas the first step of the conspiracy was founded on motives and values widely shared by all the members, the next ones necessarily involve policy and power controversies that have to be solved by a much smaller consensus, frequently by the authoritarian arbitration of the top leader against important groups and actors in the conspiratorial circle. This tends to cause disaffection and to motivate attempts at rebellious "coups within the coup" by colleagues competing with the top leader. Controls from the middle level to the bottom tend to be more or less difficult, depending on the actual extent of the success of mass mobilization. The mobilized mass creates new subleaders that were not included in the original cadres, and the relationship between these and the former may easily become difficult, whenever their co-optation either is too rapid to offer them a meaningful participation or was not preceded by a political education and organization that will keep them loyal to the cause and its leaders.

These four crucial problems, essentially of a politico-administrative nature, creating reciprocally reinforcing difficulties, would easily become unmanageable were it not for the fact that the ways to solve them also create reciprocally reinforcing facilities. In the final analysis, what occurs is that the breaking of the much more accentuated forms of underdevelopment, inherent to the type of societies under study, entails at the same time a very profound and complex mobilization of all the available remaining resources of these societies, through procedures necessarily of a rather radical character and totally alien to their former experience, in conditions of sharp conflict with superpowerful foreign interests, which have enjoyed old and consolidated local support and not less old or consolidated political support from the governments of their own nations. This task, as is easy to understand, could never be successfully undertaken if the appropriate social and political mobilization of the masses did not liberate an incalculable amount of new energy, reversing the former balance of resources. The key of the SC model, in its initial stages of implementation, consists in mobilizing these energies at the appropriate time and in the appropriate way. And the basic conditions for that consist in building a very efficient center of political power and in using, with maximum efficiency, the few strategic resources immediately under the control of that central power. Fundamentally, concerning these four crucial problems, we have that the ways for solving the last two provide the conditions for solving the first two. The essential requirements are (a) power efficiency, (b) optimum use of the strategic resources, and (c) mass mobilization.

Power Efficiency. The most important of the four problems is the one concerning the central power of the system. And it is precisely for that reason that, in the preparation of the coup, no strategic concessions can be made concerning the men and groups that will be led (initially or subsequently) to central positions of power. They must form a highly coherent group, composed of really capable men, strongly motivated to perform their historical task and presenting a high level of political education and organization. If these conditions have not been met, the SC model will hardly escape the dissolving effects of power rivalry and policy stalemate, with the resulting loss of power by the central leadership and the consequence that it will either lose the capacity or the willingness to mobilize the mass or will lose its control over the process, leading the whole experiment to final failure, as has tragically occurred with the MNR revolution in Bolivia. If the central power meets these conditions, however, it will be able to obtain a sufficient degree of power efficiency for the coherent and disciplined exercise of leadership, both at the top level and from that level to the middle one.

Optimum Use of Resources. The second fundamental requirement for success is the ability of the top leadership to use its few immediately available resources in the most efficient way. These resources, ultimately, consist of (a) a few top men and qualified cadres, (b) very modest financial means, and (c) an expandable but initially small stock of political symbols and values. The peculiar difficulty resulting from that shortage of resources is the obvious impossibility of giving attendance, even partially, to all of the innumerable important and urgent demands arising from the situation and the implementation of the model. The solution to that difficulty lies in selecting the most strategic goals for *full attainment* and just to postpone any attempt to solve *directly* any other problems. These strategic goals will naturally vary according to local conditions. They are basically related, however, to some *sine qua non* functions:[4] (1) implementation of the fundamental political and administrative decisions of the central leadership, (2) financing of the essential necessities of the central leadership, (3) formulation and propagation of the symbols and political values necessary for creating and maintaining a powerful ideological motivation among all social strata and groups, including the leaders, (4) ample and deep mobilization of the masses for the combined purpose of imparting to them an active participating solidarity with the movement and its values and goals, making them an effective contribution to the implementation of the model, in terms of work, self-organization, and spontaneous and creative cooperation, and last but not least, the formation of a high-spirited national militia prepared to repel countercoups and foreign-supported armed invasions and to defend by all means the national and popular conquests and the loyal leaders of the movement, and (5) the preparation of new conditions and the creation of new resources for the fastest possible future upgrading of the cultural, economic, political, and social levels of the concerned society.

These five strategic functions are self-explanatory and do not require more detailed elaboration. What is important to consider is that, in the hypothesized case of power efficiency at the level of the central leadership, the convenient performance of these five functions will solve the three other crucial problems. If the central leadership is able to organize an appropriate system of commands and quality cadres for the implementation of its most important decisions and has the minimal required financial means, the top leadership's control of the middle levels is assured, as well as some of the conditions for the appropriate guidance of the masses. The creation and maintenance of a powerful ideological motivation, together with mass mobilization, is the only possible alternative way of compensating for the overall deficiency of material resources. The "end of ideology" outlook is a typical effect of preaccumulated affluence and sociopolitical consensus. The need for moral incentives (for the good or the bad of mankind) decreases in proportion to the availability of material incentives. Very poor societies, confronted with the Herculean task of breaking centuries of nonfunctionality and superpowerful vested interests, mostly foreign-based and supported by still more powerful nations, can only compensate for their obvious insufficiency of resources by motivating men to overcome their current destituteness at a very high physical and psychological price, including the readiness to sacrifice their lives.

Mass Mobilization. The response of the masses to authentic and consistent ideological appeals, as can be judged by historical experience, is very great, and when it is combined with effective mass mobilization and participation, it liberates unlimited individual and social energies. This energy will compensate for the almost complete lack of resources which the new SC regime is initially confronted with. The organization of the masses in a national militia and in some other strategic task forces will provide the means for containing or overcoming attempts at counterrevolutionary coups or foreign-supported invasions, and domestically, it will be a decisive factor in preventing the military apparatus inherited from the *ancien régime* from being attracted by the prospect of praetorian adventures.

The fifth of the formerly mentioned strategic functions, the preparation of new conditions and the creation of new resources for the fastest possible national development, is both the end purpose of the model and *the* condition for the consolidation of its conquests. Crucial among the tasks to be immediately accomplished are the formation of a capable group of socioeconomic planners, with the corresponding establishment of an efficient planning system, and the formation of a capable group of educators and the corresponding establishment of an efficient educational system. In the past decades underdeveloped societies have been fatally attracted by the economic illusion of what could be called "socially unsupported industrialization." This statement certainly does not imply any underestimation of the crucial role of industrialization in the national development of many countries. It just stresses the fact that industrialization unsupported by certain indispensable social prerequisites is likely to be incomplete and in a sense abortive, as has occurred in Latin America. Among these prerequisites education, not to mention its indirect effects, is one of the most crucial, not only to secure the proper operation and management of the new equipment but also to provide a sufficiently autonomous national scientific and technological base, so that economic-technological decisions may be congruent with national means and goals.

When the SC regime successfully overcomes the four crucial problems discussed formerly, a new stage will begin in which the problems of administration and management and of scientific and technological research will become increasingly more important. The next stage will not appear as a clear-cut new phase in the implementation of the model but will gradually take shape as the most urgent problems of the preceding phase are solved. Some of these problems will be analyzed in Chapter 16, although from a different point of view. What should be indicated now is only the fact that the SC model tends to present a transitory character. Essentially this model is for overcoming the nonfunctionality of the elite in societies maintained by the modernizing sector of their subelite. Its most peculiar feature is the reconciliation of the subelite with the masses and the creation of several sorts of conditions inducing the modernizing subelite to break with the traditional society and making that process easier. Once the consolidation of the regime is achieved, the optimum utilization of the resources will tend, although not necessarily, to bring the regime to choose between an evolution oriented toward its transformation into national capitalism or one oriented toward its transformation into developmental socialism.

The former option usually corresponds to either very high or rather modest levels of success. Very high levels of success, as in the case of Meiji Japan, allow and induce an increase in individual initiative and also rapidly create the minimum amount of wealth necessary for an NC model. A rather modest success tends to rapidly undermine the power of the ideological mobilization of the masses, leading to and requiring as soon as possible, the introduction of economic incentives in order to compensate for the erosion of the moral ones, as in the case of post-Cárdenas Mexico.

The option for a developmental-socialist model usually corresponds to the intermediate cases. The symbolic means of social and national mobilization remain powerful and the level of the morale rather high, but the accumulation of wealth does not go as fast as desired and, to speed it up and eventually to provide a better response to the economic sabotage of the remaining elements of the *ancien régime* and their foreign supporters, a fully integrated socialist economy becomes more advantageous. This was the trend of Nasserism in Egypt even before the catastrophic defeat in the Six Day War, which has, moreover, imposed the adoption of still more stringent economic measures.

Developmental socialism (DS)

Why? DS is the suitable model for the two varieties of (III–2) coercive inegalitarian societies: (III–2.1), societies with a rigidified aristocratic elite, and (III–2.2), societies with a *societas sceleris* elite. The former practically disappeared in its original form after the Russian and the Chinese revolutions. There is, however, as an ideal type, a new derivative form of that variety: colonial fascism. Some of the societies whose protracted underdevelopment drives them to some form of consolidated underdevelopment tend to become colonial fascist, as may be the case in Argentina and Brazil. The *societas sceleris* kind of society is the other form of consolidated underdevelopment which societies with protracted underdevelopment, like Central America and Paraguay, may deteriorate into.

As in the case of the SC model, the DS model requires, besides the preconditions of all political models (national viability and political mobilizability), that the main social actors for the implantation and implementation of the model, the counterelite of the intelligentsia, be sufficiently capable and willing to perform their role. And as occurs with the other two models, the suitability of this model for the two types of society indicated lies in the inherent correspondence between what the revolutionary intelligentsia wants to do and is actually led to do by its political views and values and the personal commitments of the group members, and what must be done in these societies to promote their national development. With the NC model, however, and in large part with the SC model, the correspondence between what is "good" for the social actors and for the concerned society contains, as one of its essential components, some of the fundamental class interests of these actors, whereas the DS model presents quite a different picture, since the actors' class interests are in contradiction with their commitments and actions and are actually denied and surmounted by these commitments and actions. This is because the revolutionary intelligentsia is a sector of the middle class in revolt against its class. The members of that intelligentsia, given the conditions of their society, have been led to an insoluble conflict between their intellectual and moral convictions and the beliefs and/or practices characteristic of the prevailing social regime. And it is precisely because of the excruciating contradiction between the social conditions of existence within their own class that their society offers them, as members of the intelligentsia, and their own intellectual and moral beliefs that they cannot accept any possible reconciliation without betraying their own ideas and values, losing their own self-respect and the respect of their comrades. Thus, the acceptance of a revolutionary way of life becomes the ultimate alternative remaining open to them.

As in the case of the SC model, the crucial preliminary difficulty involved in the implantation of the DS model is obtaining the capability and willingness of the intelligentsia to perform its role. The capability of the intelligentsia may be maintained below a minimum critical mass because the concerned society does not provide conditions for the higher education of enough young men to allow the formation, out of their ranks, of a significant group of politically and morally motivated intellectuals, who are able to challenge the validity of the existing social regime. This is what tends to occur in countries such as Honduras, Nicaragua, or Haiti. In countries like Paraguay, although the educational situation is better, the lack of opportunities for intellectual work outside the governmental agencies, which are strictly attentive to preventing the admission of, or expelling, all nonconformists, and the most thorough repression of any form of intellectual freedom create conditions in which an intelligentsia cannot develop. In other situations the willingness of the intelligentsia to endure the hardships of permanent conspiracy for the revolution may be seriously affected by the effectiveness of the repressive measures, the poor realistic prospects of revolutionary success in a foreseeable future, and often the relative ease with which the more qualified men may find respectable and congenial academic jobs in other countries or in international institutions. The price that is paid by those societies that are able to prevent the formation or the activities of an intelligentsia is to condemn themselves, as nations and independent states, to becoming an undifferentiated part of the external proletariat of the developed world, whose inhabitants are a sort of anthropological garbage. The intelligentsia is the ultimate human resource of a society, and its revolutionary mobilization, the ultimate chance of development for countries that have fallen into consolidated underdevelopment, usually of the *societas sceleris* form. When even this recourse does not achieve momentum, nothing can save the society from historical annihilation in the course of sociocultural evolution, which benefits the fitter societies.

How? Once a revolutionary intelligentsia achieves sufficient capability and willingness to undertake its sociopolitical role, the problems with which it is confronted are still more formidable than the ones faced by the modernizing sector of the subelite in the SC model. And this is basically so because the DS model has to overcome still greater difficulties after the seizure of power, and the seizure itself is incomparably harder than in the SC case.

As we saw in the study of the preceding model, what complicates the SC process of seizing power is the fact that the necessity for securing, in anticipation, the actual politico-military conditions that will allow the convenient implementation of the model, once power is obtained, does not allow the simple use of the preexisting military apparatus and its chain of commands to overthrow the *ancien régime*. The several kinds of maneuvers thus required introduce an important complicating factor, demanding that the solution be such that the conspiratorial group neither achieves its political "purity" at the expense of its capacity to efficiently wage the military coup nor acquires military fitness at the price of a future political stalemate. With the DS model the *ancien régime* military, as a corporation and an institution, is intimately associated with the dysfunctional elite and tends, as a rule, to be the most dysfunctional sector of it, either as the main leaders and custodians of a colonial-fascist regime or as the neofeudal members of the privileged praetorian guard of a *societas sceleris* elite.

In the situation of the current world, moreover, as will be discussed in Chapter 18, the difficulty in overcoming local fascist or mercenary military is elevated to an almost unsurmountable level by the active interference of the superpowers. As we saw in the preceding cases, foreign powers exert diplomatic and financial pressure in order to prevent the NC model from securing control over the national economy. In the case of the SC model these pressures become much more serious and take the form of supporting and helping reactionary counterrevolutionaries or of armed invasions. With the DS model foreign intervention becomes the most or one of the most important elements of the picture, so much so that in the present world situation only the superpowers are able (as foreign interventionists) to participate in the game. Among the tacit rules of today's international equilibrium, one of the most scrupulously respected is the one concerning the acknowledged areas of hegemony of each of the superpowers. In these areas each superpower is free to wage whatever military intervention it may deem necessary, as the Soviet Union has in Hungary and Czechoslovakia and the United States has in Guatemala and the Dominican Republic. The perfection of the technique of military intervention has converted it into a preventive device, the use of which is planned in anticipation, reinforcing the local apparatus of coercion of satellite countries in all convenient ways, so that the satellite countries become able to detect and to smash any insurgent force before it gains momentum. In case of emergency, metropolitan troops can be sent rapidly by air transport to dangerous sites, and they will complete or even do the actual job of the local military.

Because of the complication introduced in more recent times by unchecked systematic foreign intervention in the revolutionary process of implementing the DS model, the analysis of that process requires a differentiation between the conditions prevailing since the mechanisms of foreign intervention were perfected and preassembled for preventive action or instant counteraction and the conditions existing formerly. For the United States the dividing line may be considered to be the Cuban revolution (1956–58), and for the Soviet Union, the Hungarian revolution (1956). Before these two events—and in accordance with the generalizations that can be made about past experience—it can be said that the process of revolutionary implantation of the DS model could take[5] three distinct general patterns: (1) conspiratorial revolution, (2) breakdown revolution, and (3) militarized mass insurrection.

The conspiratorial revolution is the least typical revolutionary process for the implantation of the DS model and is mentioned more for analytical purposes (because it represents a *possible* form of revolutionary process) than as an historical example. The conspiratorial revolution, as a revolutionary process, is close to the conspiratorial coup d'état, in the sense that either a critical minority of the army or a decisive part of the former government joins the conspiracy of the revolutionary party. Unlike the sheer coup d'état, however, it involves, as a process of violent political change, the direct participation of the masses. The so-called Prague coup of 1948 was actually a conspiratorial revolution in which the Communists and the left-wing socialists used their legal posts in the coalition cabinet to manipulate the police, neutralize the army, and use the Communist masses to overthrow the former government. That government, however, far from representing any of the two varieties of a coercive inegalitarian society, was the very progressive socialist-democratic government of Dr. Eduard Benes. The Bolivian MNR cadres were, in part, a revolutionary intelligentsia but also the modernizing sector of the subelite. The intended model of that revolution, however, was not developmental socialism but state capitalism. In spite of the fact that the historical precedents have not been typical of the DS model, the conspiratorial revolution, as a pattern of revolutionary process, may be used in certain conditions[6] for the implantation of that model.

The breakdown revolution is one of the two typical patterns of revolutionary implantation of the DS model. It presents two distinct varieties: (a) the Jacobin revolution and (b) the guerrilla revolution. In both varieties the revolutionary process and its final success depend on the previous or concomitant breakdown of the coercive apparatus of the state because of factors not directly determined by the revolutionaries. This can be because of military defeat in war inflicted by foreign armies, as occurred in the Russian Revolution, or because the coercive apparatus is affected by internal disintegration, as occurred in the Cuban revolution. It is in this sense that such revolutions are breakdown ones, for they operate as catalysts or as beneficiaries in the breaking down of the former coercive apparatus. What distinguishes the Jacobin variety is the fact that in that case the revolutionary mobilization of the masses, along several concomitant lines, under the loose coordination or at least the guidance of the revolutionary party, is the actual force of the revolutionary process. In the guerrilla case the participation of the mass is much more passive and only takes place when the internal disintegration of the coercive apparatus of the state allows the eruption of a final generalized upheaval. Most of the time the small guerrilla cadres lead the revolutionary process directly, in a series of actions harassing the government troops, which demoralizes rather than defeats them, combined with other actions of highly symbolic value, such as the making of partial land reforms and the taking of other revolutionary measures, which dramatize the meaning and scope of the movement, even if they are hardly implementable.

The third pattern of revolutionary implantation of the DS model, the militarized mass insurrection also involves conditions, not directly imposed by the revolutionaries, that enfeeble the repressive forces of the government. In the

Chinese revolution, the most spectacular and typical example of this pattern, these conditions were a combination of foreign-inflicted military defeat (the Japanese in Manchuria and during World War II), deficient technical facilities of the Kuomintang troops, and finally, particularly favorable geotopographic conditions for the preservation of the revolutionaries' bases, protecting them from efficient large-scale attacks while they were still building up their strength. The essential trait of this form of revolutionary process consists in a protracted conflict between the revolutionaries and the forces of the *ancien régime* in the course of which the former, because of some weaknesses in the latter not directly caused by the revolutionaries, are able to organize a mass insurrection, to form a revolutionary army, to take control of significant parts of the territory, to wage a winning symbolic political war against the validity of the government, and finally, with the gradual increase in their strength and corresponding decrease in the government's military capability and political authority, to inflict on the latter a complete political and military defeat.

The problem confronting the DS revolutionaries, once they seize power, is to keep it under extremely adverse conditions, characterized by the exhaustion of the national resources because of the civil war, the lack of effective means of administration, the sabotage of the counterrevolutionary groups, the lack of managerial and technical skills in most of their supporters, the unwillingness of the peasants to deliver their goods to the cities, and last but not least, the actual or imminent military intervention of inimical great powers. Just as the SC problems, after the seizure of power, are an aggravated form of the NC problems, the DS post-power-seizing problems are a still more aggravated form of the SC ones. The way of solving these tremendous difficulties is basically the same way that is available for the SC model: the maximization of the power efficiency of the central leadership, the optimum use of the scarce strategic resources, and the widest and deepest mobilization of the masses and of their capacity for self-help and creative cooperation.

The reason the almost desperate conditions of the new DS government can actually be surmounted, as has historically occurred, whenever enough central power is maintained and the implementation of the model is correctly performed, lies in the unlimited new energies liberated by the total mobilization of the masses. And it is because it is inherent to the DS model, when it is correctly carried out, to achieve a degree of mass mobilization and participation incomparably greater than the SC model (in which many blockages remain because of middle-class ascriptiveness) that the socialist model is able to overcome obstacles that are also incomparably larger. Thus, in terms that are magnified both for the confronting difficulties and for the released energies, the DS model has to solve the same sort of problems that the SC model does in its initial phase of implementation, and subsequently, has also to face the same kind of necessity: the shift from predominantly political to predominantly technical and managerial questions.

Besides the degree of mass mobilization, there are two other distinct features that differentiate the implementation of the DS model from that of the SC model. The first refers to the technical and managerial facilities for implementation. The second refers to the scale of foreign intervention. Concerning the technical and managerial facilities for implementation, we have that in the case of the SC model most of the capable men and groups that were formerly responsible for the operation of the *ancien régime* are people of the subelite that, directly or indirectly, took part in the SC coup and support the new regime. In the case of the DS revolution, however, most of the technicians and administrators of the concerned society were either associated somehow with the former *societas sceleris* or rigidified elite or are likely to react unfavorably to the new egalitarian trends of the new regime. Most of these men will either leave their former occupations voluntarily or be forcefully driven away from them, leaving a vacuum of skills very difficult to fill. As the historical experience has shown, the new DS government will have to rely to a large extent on improvised new incumbents, which will involve costly training on the job, and will also be forced, for more exacting functions, to use foreign advisers, who are either contracted at high prices or attracted by ideological solidarity. In the case of China the new government could benefit from the help of the Soviet Union during their initial phase of collaboration.

Concerning the formidable problem of foreign intervention, we have here a question that is less amenable to sociopolitical generalizations, since each case is conditioned by its historical context. The first Jacobin revolution, the Puritan revolution of Great Britain, enjoyed the advantages of British insularity, which prevented effective Spanish or French intervention. The French Revolution, which is already a modern example of the kind, although not socialist, brought about the direct intervention of the great European powers, who were repeled by the *levée en masse*, which was also a typical expression of the new popular participation and the new energies liberated by the revolution. The Russian Revolution enjoyed the favorable circumstances of the distraction of the great powers in World War I. The German interest in putting Russia out of the war led her, initially, to help the revolution, transporting Lenin to Russia, and later prevented her from taking a direct stand against the new regime. The Allies, unable, in the last years of the war, to remove their troops from the front, could only send a minor expeditionary force in 1917 to support and equip White Russian troops, which proved to be insufficient to overcome the fighting determination of the popular Red Army improvised by Trotsky. After the war the uncontrollable trend toward demobilization and the general weariness of war prevented the Allies from attempting a new intervention. The Chinese, under the protective umbrella of Soviet military power, could reduce the foreign intervention to the preservation of the Kuomintang troops which took refuge in Formosa. The nature of this problem has changed, however, since the Cuban revolution and, for the Soviet area of hegemony, the Hungarian revolution. And here we come to the other historical context that frames the attempts at the revolutionary implantation of the DS model, which is the current one.

The Chinese and the Cuban revolutions seem to have been the two last successful

DS revolutions of the twentieth century that were not prevented or contained by foreign intervention. The Chinese, as was mentioned above, were protected by the Soviet army. The Cuban revolution was made possible because of its original non-Communist and even nonsocialist character. Starting as a Garibaldian radical movement (not implying any irremediable danger to the large industrial interests), it took a socialist course after the consolidation of its power and was skillfully maneuvered by Castro, who imposed on the Soviets their unwished involvement in the basic defense of the regime. Even so, the Castro government had to repel a CIA-managed invasion, which could have been much more dangerous if Castro's capability and national support had not been underrated by the CIA's own ideological biases.

After these two revolutions, and following the Cuban missile crisis and the Nuclear Test Ban Treaty, the tacit recognition by each superpower of areas of unchallenged hegemony, which include most of the world, leaving out only some sites of disputed predominance, has created completely different conditions for the DS revolutionary process. These conditions will be studied in Chapter 18. What can be said in advance is that foreign military intervention became the most important single factor in a revolutionary process. Because of it most of the current clichés concerning revolution are dramatically futile. Only in the diminishing areas of the world where the superpowers have not yet clearly settled the boundaries of hegemony—such as India and Pakistan, Indonesia, and tropical Africa—is it likely that DS revolutions will not be freely prevented or contained by the locally hegemonic superpower. In the rest of the world a DS revolution, which is to be carried out against the freely operating mechanisms of superpower intervention, must accumulate an amount of social energy and affect an extent of territory of which the Vietnamese revolution is a tragic yardstick. Only at the price of the most complete convulsion of the normal conditions of life, promoted and supported by the total revolutionary mobilization of a huge population, prepared and organized to endure massive manslaughter for a very long time, and in geotopological and other conditions preventing its technical annihilation without the use of nuclear weapons, is a DS revolution likely to succeed in the areas of the world submitted to the free hegemonic control of one of the superpowers. The Vietnam hecatomb, along with so many lessons it has taught the world, has shown the basic limits beyond which a superpower will not go in order to contain the revolutionary war of liberation in an underdeveloped country. Ultimately these limits are (1) the creation of conditions necessarily leading to a direct confrontation with the other superpower (which will prevent, for instance, the use of nuclear weapons) and (2) the necessity to keep close to 1 million men in permanent mobilization and to endure several thousand casualties per year. This last condition, however, will probably tend to be less stringent, in the future, since the superpowers, driven by the implacable objective logic of imperialism, are likely to organize, in due time, "imperial" armies, recruited in the provinces and composed of professional legionnaires, whose fate will be of far less consequence to the citizens of the superpower.

NOTES

[1] In the case of France, however, the student revolt of 1968, led precisely by a social sector without the experiences conducive to social restraint, ruined a large part of the formerly accumulated success.

[2] See Chalmers Johnson (1964) on the theory of conspiratorial coups d'état and the typology of revolutions in general.

[3] The minimization of the prospects of actual fighting in an SC coup, besides being a way of reducing the chances of failure, is, essentially, a way of preventing the development of an opportunity for foreign intervention.

[4] The same set of goals and functions are applicable to the implementation of the DS model in the conditions inherent to that model.

[5] Chalmers Johnson (1964).

[6] The decisive condition is the existence of a dissident sector in the army willing to join the intelligentsia in the conspiratorial revolution, as may occur in the future in some Latin American countries.

C

The Process
of Political
Development

16

Operational Analysis

Chapters 7–15 dealt with the meaning and essential characteristics of the process of political development, considered within the general framework of the polity and the social system, and the political models by which it can be achieved. In the present section we will attempt to understand how such a process actually occurs, first, in Chapters 16 and 17, in a general analytical and functional way, and subsequently, in Chapter 18, in the concrete historical conditions of our time. This endeavor will bring us first to the general operational analysis of the operations and stages involved in the promotion of political development, which will be the subject of the present chapter. Then we will study, but still in a general way, the conditions that the successful implementation of these operations and stages depends on. Finally, Chapter 18 will be concerned with the analysis of these problems in the concrete historical conditions of our time, particularly in terms of the new emerging international system, its present features, and the likely evolutionary trends.

The idea of stages

The more recent literature on political development, as will be briefly discussed, has become sharply aware of the fact that, analytically as well as empirically, the promotion of political development involves distinct sets of operations and stages, presenting both a typical and determinable configuration and a patterned and predictable sequence, although in the view of most writers their occurrence is not subject to any deterministic fatalism.[1] In this respect, as in so many others, the study of political development has been influenced, in part, by the study of economic development and by the similar propensity to submit the study of economic development to operational analyses and to view it in terms of a succession of stages. In a deeper sense, however, regardless of the earlier influence of contemporary analysis of economic development on the analysis of political development and particularly the impact of Rostow (1964), the present trend stems from the fact that the overall societal process of development cannot be understood without the identification and explanation of its major constituent operations and the understanding and forecasting of its successive "typical phases."

Stages, in that sense, are phases of a broader social process (that is, they are structurally characteristic temporal segments of that process), differentiated from one another by a distinct type of analytical, and eventually also empirical, set of operations that follow a certain order and successiveness, due to an analytical, and eventually empirical, relationship of cause and effect.

Although the connection between the phasic view of political development and the earlier phasic understanding of economic development is widely acknowledged, the dependence of both stage views on the earlier understanding of the unfolding of history is much less perceived but not less relevant. As a matter of fact, the contemporary social scientist has inherited from the philosophy and theory of history an understanding of historical phases that is the last formulation of an age-old controversy between the cyclical and the progressive views of history, as well as the final expression, within the framework of the latter, of a gradual immanentization of the idea of divine providence. As has been particularly well discussed by J. B. Bury (1955), the idea of progress is the immanentization of the idea of divine providence, which was itself a Judeo-Christian substitute for the classical cyclical view of history. To that it should be added that our current idea of development is a second and value-free immanentization of the idea of progress.

The discussion of this fascinating topic would take us too far from our central concern. Let me just note that both the classical and the Judeo-Christian views of history implied, and actually came to be formally treated in terms of, a phasic sequence of typical stages. Plato's initial view of a world life cycle of 72,000 solar years, after which the complete decay of the world would exact its re-creation by the deity, led him to distinguish two great cycles of 36,000 of solar years each, the first corresponding to an orderly and well-functioning stage of the world, the second to its gradual decay until the final chaos that would require a new act of creation. The Greeks finally accepted a regressive three-stage life cycle: the ages of gold, silver, and iron, successively reenacted after each new re-creation.

Opposed to that cyclical view, which implies the ultimate nonexistence of a transcendent meaning for the world and man and also implies that the best times were in a mythical past, the Judeo-Christian view was progressive linear. The world and man had an absolute and nonrepeatable beginning with the creation. This irreversible and unique stage, it was understood, had been and was to be succeeded by other nonrepeatable and unique stages: the fall of man, the revelation of Christ, the (in this world) time for repentance, the advent of the anti-Christ, the end of the world, and the last judgment. Along that religious guideline, the medieval scholars conceived of a succession of four historical stages from the fall of man to the advent of the anti-Christ, each characterized by its predominant civilization: Babylonian, Persian, Macedonian, and Roman.

The great change in the Judeo-Christian conception of history, which gradually evolved from the Renaissance and received its clear formulation with Fontenelle and the Enlightenment, was the immanentization of the idea of divine providence in the idea of progress. History was no longer seen as the unfolding of a divine plan, designed before the actual beginning of the world, directed by the divine providence, and bringing the full realization of man to a trans-historical other-world. History was seen as a wordly process of gradual perfection of man through the natural and improved use of his inherent rationality. Whatever the several factors and their order of importance that the various writers have seen as conditioning that process, what is common to these writers is their understanding of that process as a natural and immanent one, ultimately determined by the fact that man, although disturbed by his own passions and prejudices and by natural and social external events, is by his own nature endowed with reason, the gradual use of which brings him to the full understanding of the world and of himself, with a corresponding enlargement of his self-control and command on nature.

Turgot's three stages (animic, abstract principles, and rational observation) clearly anticipate the future positivist idea, including Comte's law of the three stages, of a scientific progress involving a corresponding moral betterment, a conception that Condorcet brought to its most elaborate "enlightened" form. Hegel's stages of the self-realization of the spirit (subjective, objective, and absolute) is the acknowledged origin of the future historicist idea of cultural progress, which also involves moral improvement. The culmination of the idea of progress, as an immanentization of the idea of divine providence, is found in the Spencerian conception of evolutionary progress and the Marxian conception of historical materialism, which, either in a progressive linear or in a dialectical way, imply a stage-by-stage process of increasing rationality and liberty.

Currently, the social sciences have predominantly returned to a stage view of a sociocultural evolutionary development, after passing through an antievolutionist phase, which followed the metaphysical abuse of Spencerian evolutionism and the dogmatization of Marxian dialectics. That question has already been discussed in Chapter 2. The discrediting of the idea of progress in the first half of this century brought about a new form of the cyclical view of history. Spengler, Toynbee, and Sorokin are among the most preeminent new cyclical theorists. These writers made important contributions, leading to a new emphasis, as well as to other consequences, on the recurrent aspects in the development of societies. Nevertheless, the ideas, central to any cyclical view of history, of (1) a basic repetition or reiteration of the social drama and (2) the ultimate nontransmissibility and noncumulativeness of the cultural achievements of societies have been increasingly rejected by the contemporary social sciences. As was said in Chapter 2, the new cultural evolutionism, besides differentiating general from specific evolution, stresses the fact that general evolution, in itself a value-free concept, is not equal to moral progress. Moreover, as has been pointed out by Erich Kahler,[2] the continuation of biological evolution in terms of sociocultural evolution seems to be leading to developments that surpass the individual human being for the benefit of the collectivity. In the words of Kahler: "the tremendous recent expansion of human reach, and the incorporation of world contents into human consciousness, applies to man as a whole, but no longer to the human individual" (1967, p. 16).

This brief clarification of the historical origins of the concept of stages of development allows us now to discuss that problem in terms of political development.

Current literature

The views of the students of political development concerning the basic operations and stages characteristic of that process have been referred to in our former review of the literature on political development (Chapter 8). It is not necessary to return now to an extensive discussion of these views. Let me just stress that, explicitly or implicitly, all the writers think of the process of political development as presenting, both historically and analytically, a succession of identifiable typical stages. Looking, restrospectively at how the process of political development has occurred in some European countries and the United States, Huntington (1966a) differentiates three basic sets of operations, each of which has corresponded, in the countries that have successfully achieved their political development, to a distinct and successive stage of that process: (1) rationalization of authority, leading to the replacement of many local authorities by one central authority, (2) differentiation of new political functions and development of specific structures for them, and (3) increased participation, by means of the gradual incorporation of peripheral social groups and strata into the center. That process, according to Huntington, has been successful when these three basic operations have been accomplished in a successive way, each corresponding to a given stage of political development. Their overlapping, which may occur, as can be seen today in most underdeveloped countries, is a fatal obstacle to development. The required strategy for ensuring the appropriate successiveness of these stages is characterized by two essential conditions: (1) the slowing down of mobilization, to prevent people from coming from the periphery to the center before they can be duly absorbed and (2) the promotion of institution building, which is the basis of political development.

Eisenstadt (1966) also tries to understand the basic operations and stages of political development by historical analysis and deduction from past processes of some general principles applicable to any developing society. He sees the process (in its modern phase) as being essentially divided in two stages: (1) limited modernization, which historically corresponds to the eighteenth and nineteenth centuries in the West and consists in the incorporation of the middle classes into the centers of decision, combined with cultural secularization and scientific-technological development, and (2) mass modernization, which historically corresponds to the twentieth century in the West and consists in the incorporation of the masses, together with massive expansion and use of science and technology. The overlapping of the two stages, which tends to occur today in the societies that were not able to achieve the first stage in the last century, creates an excessive pressure on the political system which tends to break down, unless a particularly delicate form of regulation is appropriately adopted, combining the incorporation of the masses with their adequate socialization and the non-disrupted functioning of the overall society.[3]

Almond (1966) attempts a more analytical approach and is more specifically concerned with the political system proper. He has devised four basic operations and stages: (1) *state building,* bringing about the formation of a central authority, its penetration in the polity, and the integration of the various groups under the jurisdiction of that central authority, (2) *nation building,* creating loyalties and commitments and thus increasing the input of supports, (3) *participation,* expanding the groups and strata actively included in the political process, and (4) *distribution,* increasing, through several forms of reallocation, the access of all to the benefits of social life. Like the other writers Almond observes that these basic operations have corresponded to distinct successive stages in the societies that have successfully achieved their political development in the past and that this will have to be so for the developing societies of today. The current tendency of some or all of these stages to overlap will severely overstress the latter's political systems, bringing about disruptions.

The most complete study, up to now, of the stages of political development has been made by Organski (1965) in a very interesting and valuable book bearing the subject as its title. Organski understands political development "as increasing governmental efficiency in utilizing the human and material resources of the nation for national goals" (p. 7). On the other hand, he considers that national development, national growth, and modernization are just different expressions for indicating the same reality: increasing economic productivity, increasing geographic and social mobility, and increasing political efficiency in mobilizing the human and material resources of the nation for national goals. As can be seen, the last part of his broader concept of national development corresponds to his concept of political development.

As nations continue developing, the functions of the national government for promoting further development keep changing, according to a succession of stages of development. According to Organski these stages, although not inevitable, are empirically observable, correspond to what has actually occurred in any society so far, and represent a highly probable sequence of phases for those societies that are to succeed in promoting or continuing their development in the future. For both analytical and empirical reasons these stages are successive ones, the complete achievement of a stage being impossible if the preceding one has not been implemented. The problems peculiar to two continuous stages, however, can, in part, be overlapping, but within limits. This would mean that the preceding stage has not been completely implemented, and while that situation exists the following stage will never be successfully obtained.[4]

Organski distinguishes four basic stages of political development. The first is the *politics of primitive unification,* which consists in the building of central authority on a given territory and for a given people or group of peoples (historically, for the West, until the middle of the eighteenth century). The second is the *politics of industrialization* (for the West from mid-eighteenth century to late nineteenth century). This stage involves both the process of economic industrialization and the sociopolitical changes bringing about new classes, enlarging participation, and increasing national integration. This process has been performed historically and presents, analytically, three alternative possibilities: (a) the *bourgeois* model (distinct from modern democracy), in which capital accumulation is made by private means, at the expense of the working class, but in a covert way, with the bourgeosie overcoming the former aristocratic elite either by revolution or by gradual transitions, (b) the *Stalinist* model, with capital accumulation being ostensibly made at the expense of the working class and with the new class of bureaucrats (or their revolutionary predecessors) forcibly overcoming, through a radical revolution, the former aristocratic and bourgeois elites, and (c) the *syncretic* model, of which the typical example is Italian Fascism, where there is a compromise between the former landed elite and the bourgeoisie under the mediation of middle-class rightist radicals, leading to an authoritarian state that protects the agrarian interests, with capital accumulation being made, although at a slower speed and to a lesser extent, at the expense of the working class. The third stage is the *politics of national welfare* (for the West the first half of twentieth century). This stage consists (in reverse of stage 2, which involves capital accumulation at the expense of the masses) in protecting people from capital and involves both the massive reallocation of (highly increased) resources and mass participation (not necessarily "democratic"). Both historically and analytically there are three models for that stage: (a) *mass democracy,* combining the expansion of franchise with increasing access to consumer goods, (b) *Nazism,* combining symbolic and highly irrational forms of mass participation and gratification with an authoritarian state, and (c) *communism,* combining the requirements of the welfare state and mass symbolic participation with totalitarian rule and party dictatorship. And the fourth stage is the *politics of abundance* (just appearing in the United States). This stage is based on the super-productivity (cybernetics, scientific management, and so forth) of the economic system, with a general availability of goods for everybody, a sharp decline in the necessity for work and corresponding decrease in "productive" employment and in the strength of organized labor, a shift of social emphasis from economic to other interests (political or cultural), a fusion of economic and political elites (increasing the concentration of power), an expanded necessity for planning, and a propensity toward a sort of socialist society, either democratic or not, probably more often not.

Organski's central view concerning the succession of stages is based on his understanding of industrialization, both as an economic and as a social, cultural, and political process of (technologically supported) modernization as the crucial phase in the development of a society. Entrance into the industrialization phase corresponds to Rostow's takeoff. The great difficulties to be overcome in that phase, which are more of a political, cultural, and social nature than of an economic character, and the fact that, as time passes, these difficulties tend to increase for the latecomers have historically forced the late-developing societies to adopt models distinct from the bourgeois one. Organski expressly doubts that the bourgeois model may still be utilizable in any developing nation.

On the other hand, he stresses that the subsequent development of a nation is profoundly influenced by the way she achieves her industrialization. The models of stage 3 are predetermined, basically, by the course taken in stage 2. Stage 4, finally, is still an open question, since only now do the more developed nations seem to be achieving the preceding stage. Although the new conditions imposed by economic super-productivity, with the corresponding substantial decrease in the necessity for human labor, combined with the "super-massification" and super-urbanization of the world, and the corresponding necessity for central planning will create demands and functions that still cannot be clearly forecasted, Organski implies that even at that advanced and forthcoming stage the choices made in stage 2 will have significant influence.

Another very interesting aspect of Organski's study is his understanding of the syncretic (Fascist) and Stalinist models as alternative ways of industrialization, differentiating them from Nazism and communism, respectively, the two latter being models of national welfare. I have reservations concerning the understanding of Fascism, both in its historical Italian example and in its generalized abstract meaning, as syncretism, as an alternative model of industrialization. It was and is, certainly, an alternative model of *modernization:* what in this book has been designated as modernization without institutionalization. Precisely because industrialization, particularly at the level of a specific national society, is a process that far surpasses its economic aspects, the attempt, inherent to syncretism, to modernize a nation without affecting its former regimes of participation and of power, and to a large extent of values, is unable to generate many of the *sine qua non* conditions that a successful national industrialization depends on. Mussolini improved, in a purely (law-and-order) administrative sense, the use of the preexisting Italian industrial complex, adapting it, with some additions, to his war purposes. The Italian industrialization had been started by the bourgeoisie of the Risorgimento and was completed after World War II by the Christian Democratic regime.[5] I would also qualify Organski's view of Nazism as an alternative model of national welfare by stressing the fact that, Volkswagens and some other material or institutional devices apart, the welfare reallocations to the mass did not actually take place in a significative form, not only because of the war effort (which could be admitted as external to the model), but also because of the "Stalinist" capital accumulation aspect of Nazism, so essentially inherent to it.[6] I therefore doubt that Nazism, as an abstract general form, may be suitable as an alternative welfare model.

What is more relevant than these and similar qualifications, or "internal criticisms," of Organski's formulations is an "external criticism" of the overall pertinence of his theory. Comparing Organski's stages of political development with those presented by the other scholars, like Almond, for instance, we can see that in spite of certain similitudes (as between Almond's stage 1, state building, and Organski's stage 1, primitive unification), there is a difference in kind.

(See Table 32.) Almond has presented a series of stages of political development in the strict sense. Organski speaks of political development and certainly treats it; but his general frame of reference is the overall development of modern nations, and his stages of development refer to national development as an overall societal process. Seen in that perspective, the discussion of Organski's theory requires two approaches: one concerning the overall process of national development of a society and its respective stages and the other concerning the specific processes and stages of political development and their relationship with the former process.

As indicated in footnote 4, about Organski's theory of stages, which, as was said above, concerns the overall national development of societies, he returns to Marx's idea of "real" developmental phases, although under the assumption of a more complex system of historical causation. Seen in these terms, Organski's theory of stages is an empirically well founded and analytically pertinent typological description of the successive real phases that the Western societies have historically confronted in their process of national development since the late Middle Ages, and particularly since the Renaissance. Moreover, his theory is both empirically and analytically appropriate for the understanding of the process of attempted national formation and development in non-Western societies since the time when they were confronted with the Western commercial and industrial revolutions and the challenge of Western domination. Finally, his theory is also adequate, at least heuristically, for the forecasting of future tendencies and characteristics of the national development of societies that have successfully achieved the second stage.

Two qualifications, however, are indispensable, in my judgment. The first concerns the fact that Organski's theory presents a convenient explanation and typology for the national development of *Western modern societies* and, because of the universalization of Western influence and standards, for modern societies in general. If it were to be used for broader historical purposes, it would have to be reformulated and Organski's stages would have to be framed in a larger historical series of stages. The second qualification, more immediately relevant to the problems of political development, concerns the fact that Organski's stages are stages in the *national* development of societies, that is, in the development of self-governing societies as national ones, within the framework of the national state. This is clearly implied in his theory and has even been formally acknowledged by Organski, but he has not considered two fundamental consequences of that national requirement.

The first consequence, of a general character, concerns the fact that societies that are unable to successfully achieve their industrialization *will lose their national viability* and will tend, in the long run, to be incorporated into other social systems, under the control of centers of decision alien to them, in a process which will culminate in the suppression of their national autonomy and the dissolution of these societies as distinct, self-sustained and self-adapting systems. This problem will be treated more extensively in the next chapter, as the first condition for the possibility of any political development. The second

Table 32 *Recent typical views of the stages of political development*

Functional Approach		Real Approach
HUNTINGTON (1966)	EISENSTADT (1966)	ALMOND (1966)	ORGANSKI (1965)

HUNTINGTON (1966)	EISENSTADT (1966)	ALMOND (1966)	ORGANSKI (1965)
1. Rationalization of authority (centralization)	1. Limited modernization: incorporation of middle classes, secularization, and development of science and technology (eighteenth-nineteenth centuries for the West)	1. State building	1. Politics of primitive unification
2. Differentiation of new political functions		2. Nation building	2. Politics of industrialization.
3. Increased participation	2. Mass modernizaton: incorporation of the masses, massive expansion of science and technology (twentieth century for the West)	3. Participation	Alternative ways:
		4. Distribution	a. Bourgeois model
			b. Stalinist model
			c. Syncratic model
			3. Politics of national welfare.
			Alternative ways:
			a. Mass democracy model
			b. Nazi model
			c. Communist model
			4. Politics of abundance
Observation:	Observation:	Observation:	Observation:
Overlapping is possible but is disruptive. Preventive measures include: a. Slowing down of political mobilization b. Institution building	Overlapping is possible but is disruptive. Preventive measure is the regulated incorporation of peripheral groups into the center.	Overlapping is possible and is disruptive.	Overlapping between continuous stages is possible, but only in limited terms. The complete achievement of a stage is impossible before the preceding stage has been incorporated.

consequence, applicable to the historical conditions generated since the end of World War II, concerns the fact that the international system in which the Western nations developed and industrialized (from the late eighteenth century to World War I) and the succeeding international system (between the two world wars), in which the process of national development has been extended to the world at large, are completely different because of the emergence of the superpowers and other connected effects. As will be studied in Chapter 18, the new international system, still in the initial stages of its configuration, will be incompatible with the development of new nations and will profoundly affect the already developed ones, that is, those already in the process of entering Organski's third and fourth stages, suppressing, in different ways and to different degrees, the self-determination of those nations that do not at least achieve, in the next two or three decades, an appropriate level of "international autonomy."

The second approach to Organski's theory involves its analysis in terms of its explanatory and heuristic contribution to the understanding and forecasting of the process of political development in the strict sense. As has been already advanced, Organski's stages are immediately and properly applicable to the overall societal process of national development and not, as such, to the intrasocietal process of development of the political system. In this respect, therefore, there is a lack of correspondence, both analytically and empirically, between the theory and its overt purpose. As Almond has appropriately indicated and as will be expanded in the next chapter, the stages in a process of political development, in the strict sense, concern the typical, analytical and empirical, operations and their necessary sequence in any environmental conditions for increasing the capability of a political system (political modernization) and for increasing the serviceability of the polity for the society and for some, many, or all of its individual members (political institutionalization). The matter presents a clear analogy with the process of economic development. Savings, capital accumulation, selective investments, effective management, and increase in production and productivity are, analytically, distinct typical operations, presenting a basic sequential order that must be performed or achieved in any process of economic development, whatever the model used (capitalist or socialist, for instance), the the historical time, or the developmental stage of the concerned society. The concrete meaning of these operations, however, will vary, to a certain extent and for certain purposes, in terms of the adopted model and, to a larger extent and for other purposes, in terms of the historical time and the developmental level of the concerned society.

The mainstream of inquiry among the students of political development has been oriented toward the identification and analysis of the functional operations and stages of that development, independent of sociohistorical conditions. Organski, in his concern with real stages, has been particularly aware of these sociohistorical conditions, but has unduly assumed an identity between the real stages and the functional ones. Actually, both series, the functional one of Almond and the other writers and the real one of Organski, are necessary for the comparative study of political development.

Functional and real stages

Taking into account the above discussion of the several views on the stages of political development, we can now use the analyses and findings of the preceding chapters in an attempt to advance some steps in the theoretical understanding of the basic operations and stages involved in the process of political development. As was observed in Chapter 9, political development is political modernization plus political institutionalization. This process consists in a comparable and admeasurable increase in the set of (I) operational variables and (II) participational variables, each set containing several macrovariables whose quantitative and qualitative variations bring about an increase or decrease in certain resulting variables. (See Table 21.) Some of these resulting variables are comparable and admeasurable along a continuum, whatever the concerned society and the historical time. This is true of most of the operational variables, which are indicative of the degree of political modernization. It is true, for macrovariable (A), rational orientation, of the resulting variables secularization[7] and controllability; for macrovariable (B), structural differentiation, of the resulting variables complexity and subsystem autonomy; and for macrovariable (C), capability, of the resulting variables dependability, effectiveness, adaptability, and flexibility. Some other resulting variables express a relation between the polity and its respective society, including intrasocietal elements (social classes, groups, individuals) and extrasocietal elements (the other interacting societies) and can only be compared as sets of relationships between one polity and its society and another polity and its society. This is the case with the few remaining operational variables, all which include, for macrovariable (B), structural differentiation, the resulting variables independence (which refers to a given international system) and autonomy (which refers to a given society) and for macrovariable (C), capability, the resulting variable national viability (which refers to a relationship of self-preservation between a society and its international environment). And this is the case with all the participational variables, which are indicative of the degree of political institutionalization, because of the polity-society relationship which is inherent in their character.

Whether along a continuum, as with the first group of resulting variables, or in terms of pairs of polity-society relationships, the comparison and admeasurement of the political development of two or more political systems, of the same society in different times or of different societies in the same or in different times, present very different pictures, depending on whether or not the respective historical time is taken into account and, with it, the respective real stages of development of the overall concerned societies. Diachronic functional analyses of political development, so often performed by political scientists, are a useful and indispensable device for a better understanding of the operational and analytical aspects of the political processes of the polities under study. The sort of "absolute" standard of political development implied in such comparisons—as when, for instance, one compares the political development of Pericles' Athens with Tudor England or Louis XIV's France with the United States today—has only an analytical meaning, expressing how much and how well certain functions are performed by distinct polities. But a polity can have more effectiveness than another and in general more modernization and can also present, vis-à-vis its respective societies, a larger participation and in general more institutionalization than another, and still, that notwithstanding, that polity can be *relatively* less developed than the other one, if the respective historical time and overall societal level of development of the two polities are considered. Along with other factors affecting the direct comparability of the degree of political development of polities of distinct societies,[8] what excludes the empirical relevance of absolute diachronic admeasurements of development is a reason of historical character. This reason stems from the fact that each historical time and each real stage in the development of a society contains, both analytically and empirically, certain *limits of developmental possibilities.* When one diachronically compares stages of development without taking the involved limits of developmental possibilities into account, he is comparing coefficients of different quantities for entities of different qualities. This is why both functional and real series of stages must be used, in different combinations depending on the needs and purposes of one's analysis.

The real stages

Let us advance another step and consider the distinct typical operations, their sequential order, and the corresponding stages involved in the process of political development. Both the real and the functional approaches, for analytical as well as for empirical reasons, imply a set of basic distinct typical operations, occurring in a sequential order and corresponding to some basic stages. The basic operations and stages implied in the real approach concern, ultimately, *the process of formation and utilization of collective human power.* This process corresponds to the general sociocultural evolution of the human species: its increasing command over its human and natural environment. Empirically, that is, according to what has ultimately occurred in history, this process (if we start with already humanized man) can be divided into three macrostages: (1) *societalization* (political control over society), (2) *mechanization* (societal control over nature), and (3) *socio-organization* (societal self-control). The first stage, societalization, corresponds to the emergence and consolidation of political power through the formation of territorial societies, their expansion, and the incorporation of various formerly discrete groups into the larger society, under a central authority and rule. That long process, which continued with ups and downs and through several civilizations from prehistory (as discussed in Chapter 4) to the dynastic absolute monarchies of the eighteenth century (in the West), corresponds to Organski's stage of primitive unification. As was clearly understood by Hobbes, it is a process through which the comparative weakness of individuals and small groups is able to generate, through the division of labor and the centralization of power and authority (in *Leviathan*, the "superman" made of many men), the strength of societal power, which is many times greater than the unorganized sum total of the individual strength of the society's members. The second stage, mechanization, corresponds to the enormous multiplication of that power by the scientific and technological control of nature. This stage is Organski's stage of industrialization. The third stage, socio-organization, corresponds to the planned reorganization of society through the societally self-controlled use of the previously accumulated and ever-expanding means of control over any environment. Organski's last two stages correspond to this stage. Analytically, three distinct basic typical operations correspond to these three macrostages: (1) partial and limited control of the societal natural and human environment through centrally coordinated collective actions, (2) multifold expansion of the range and content of this control through socially articulated (by market and/or central authorities) scientific and technological action, and (3) planned employment of this expanding environmental control by socially controlled forms of societal self-control. A more detailed study of this fascinating topic[9] would take us too far from the central concern of the present book. For our present purposes it is sufficient to present the essential features of each real macrostage and the subdivisions of each macrostage. The essential features, in my view, derived from the evidence that can be deduced from the sociohistorical comparative study of societies and civilizations are given in Table 33.

Table 33 *Real stages of societal development*

Stages	*Operations (when development is successful)*
1. *Societalization*	
1.1 POLITICAL UNIFICATION Formation and development of territorial society under centralized authority	Society building and the achievement, through centrally coordinated action, of moderate control over the natural environment, based on the use of natural resources
or Collapse of centralizing rulers with societal segmentation at lower organizational level	
1.2 EXTRASOCIETAL EXPANSION Extrasocietal expansion and occupation of new lands until the sociogeographic limit of the capacity to incorporate or dominate formerly existing discrete societies is reached and a viable equilibrium with other independent societies is achieved: intersocietal balance	Intersocietal balance of power and stratification with corresponding allocation of control of accessible human and natural resources, including territory, at a low level of energy use
or	

Table 33 *Real stages of societal development* (continued)

Stages	*Operations (when development is successful)*
Collapse under external pressures and fall under alien domination or influence	
1.3 INTRASOCIETAL DIVERSIFICATION	Domestic stratification and institutionalization of corresponding social regime in terms at least minimally compatible with societal self-maintenance and continuing growth
Intrasocietal diversification, according to the social regime, and the achievement of minimally functional (usually highly ascriptive) social stratification	
or	
Disruptive social conflicts, societal segmentation, and alien domination	
2. *Mechanization*	
2.1 INDUSTRIALIZATION	Multifold expansion of range and scope of control over natural environment through socially articulated scientific and technological action
Formation and development of self-sustained industrialization, with emergence of new regimes of participation and values and corresponding new social structures and groups	
or	
Disrupting social conflicts and (1) arrestive consolidation of coercive inegualitarian society at a subindustrial level or (2) societal segmentation into units that are not self-sustainable; in both cases, fall under alien domination	
2.2 INTERNATIONAL EXPANSION	International balance of power and stratification with corresponding allocation of control on earth's human and natural resources, including territory, at a very high level of energy use
International expansion of the dominance and influence of society, based on new industrial capability and oriented toward its reinforcing such capability; further development until a self-sustained international equilibrium is reached	
or	
Contraction or collapse under stronger pressures from the international environment and fall under alien domination	

2.3 NATIONAL DIVERSIFICATION	Domestic institutionalization of social regime and corresponding social stratification in terms of increasing functionality
National structural-functional diversification with increasing control over natural environment, enlargement of domestic market, and incorporation of formerly peripheral groups into center; society reaching decreasingly ascriptive and increasingly functional forms of social stratification	

or

Arresting disruptive social conflicts, decreasing domestic cohesion and exposure to external influence until fall under alien domination

3. *Socio-organization*

3.1 GENERALIZED ORGANIZATION	Unforeseeable enlargement of former control on natural environment and its generalization to the human environment through socially controlled forms of societal self-control
Formation and development of expanding generalized environmental control through socially controlled forms of societal self-control, with emergence of new social regime and corresponding new social structures and groups	

or

Disruptive effects of socially non-regulated new capabilities, with social disintegration and fall under alien domination

3.2 INTERNATIONALIZATION	Formation and development of uni- or pluri-centered minimally functional and balanced international system
International expansion of dominance and influence of society, based on expanding and societally self-controlled generalized environmental control, until the achievement of minimally functional and balanced uni- or pluri-centered international system	

or

Self-destruction in catastrophic international conflicts

Table 33 *Real stages of societal development* (continued)

Stages	Operations *(when development is successful)*
3.3 REHUMANIZATION (OR DEHU-MANIZATION) Intrasocietal expansion through almost unlimited productive and self-regulated capability, leading to: (1) an unforeseeable extent of basically egalitarian forms of social welfare and regulated collective and individual creativity or (2) planned biopsychological differentiation, specialization, and stratification of society and individuals with unforeseeable mutations of human species or (3) suicidal extinction of species by inadequate environmental and genetic manipulations	Socially controlled formation and development of unforeseeable forms of (1) basically egalitarian collective and individual creativeness or (2) planned biopsychological human and social differentiations

The functional stages

If we now take the functional approach and analyze the process of political development (that is, of increasing political modernization and institutionalization) at any historical time for societies in any of the developmental stages referred to in Table 33, we will see that the process can be divided into four basic typical stages: (1) *model building,* (2) *state building,* (3) *nation building,* and (4) *consensus building.*

Model building. The first stage corresponds to a dialectical change (which can be obtained through incremental processes) in the regime of power. Whatever the causes of this change and the ways in which it takes place (see Chapter 5) and whether or not it is in accordance with the former political regime and its legal order, a change in the regime of power brings about, explicitly or implicitly and to a larger or a smaller extent, a new political model, with new political promises and regulations, and also involves changes in the incumbents in power and authority roles. The change in question will have developmental effects whenever it causes a positive significant increase in the resulting variables of the operational and participational macrovariables indicated in Table 21.

The first functional stage involves a sequence of four basic operations. The first is the formulation (explicit or implicit) of a new, development-oriented political design or model, implying different forms and different extents of participation and distribution and interesting new social groups or strata under a new political leadership. The formulation of this new model, addressed (alternatively or cumulatively) to new social sectors, under a new political leadership, whether or not formally compatible with the existing political regime, implies a challenge to the current authorities and the interests and values they express, creating a political confrontation between the current authorities and the new political leaders, or pretenders according to our terminology. (See Table 14.) The next basic operation in that stage includes the processes of interest articulation and interest aggregation in favor of the new political model and its leaders. These processes are usually followed by similar processes in favor of the authorities and the status quo. The pretenders' successful performance of this operation will allow them to pass on to the next operation, which consists in the politicalization of the interests they have articulated and aggregated, in accordance with their new political model. This is the crucial phase in which all the preconditions and the former operations take the ostensible political form of a bid for power, in terms of a political movement or party, which can use formerly existing institutional vehicles and channels or create its own. The fourth and last basic operation consists in the pretenders' seizure of power, legally or illegally, through their supporting political movement. If this fourth operation does not take place, the first stage is not achieved, and the whole process of political development will end abortively.

A clear-cut victory or defeat, however, is not often the result of a confrontation between the leadership of a new political movement and the status quo regime and authorities. All forms of compromise are possible and have actually occurred, in which case the crucial question is, regardless of the ostensible and nominal form of the compromise, the extent to which the new regime, its leaders, and its supporters prevail over the former ones. What is relevant is always the extent to which, in one way or another, structural changes of a developmental character are actually introduced into the former regime of power and its implied political model.

State building. The second stage, which I call "state building" to retain the current terminology (originally proposed by Almond) as much as possible, does not necessarily correspond to the building of a new state. This is one of the incorrect implications resulting from the fact that, up to now, the distinction between the real and the functional stages of developmental processes has not been made. Creation of states, properly speaking, is a process that occurs in certain historical conditions and times, with reference to societies at a given real stage of their development. As we have seen, Organski does not understand this point and places the original building of states in his primitive unification stage. According to the real-stage typology and series suggested in this book (Table 33), original state construction takes place in the stage of societalization. In the next real stage (mechanization), however, new forms of state construction takes piace when, for instance, the international expansion of an industrialized society causes her to create colonies, as in the nineteenth century, or satellites, as in current times. The subsequent real stage (socio-organization), which is only now beginning in the most developed societies of today, will also involve, in terms that cannot yet be clearly seen, the building of new forms of state.

For the purposes of our functional series the state-building stage must be understood as including all the historically possible forms, at any real developmental stage of a society, of building or rebuilding structures and functions of centrally controlled antonomous jurisdiction. This second functional stage of a process of political development is concerned, in the various sociohistorical conditions in which it can take place, with the congruent adjustment of the political regime and its legal order, including the political organization, to the new regime of power, which succeeded in prevailing in the preceding model-building stage. This congruent adjustment involves, essentially, as its basic operation, the adaptation of the structures, functions, and incumbents of the political system, particularly in its conversion and output sectors (central government and central bureaucracy), to the new regime of power and its (explicit or implicit) corresponding political model. If the new political model, which was implanted, by hypothesis, in the preceding stage, and the new leaders then brought to power and authority roles are not able to build or rebuild the state in a form congruent with the new regime of power that they represent, this regime of power will be deprived of the necessary conditions for its implementation. The result, sooner or later, will be the end of that regime of power and the implantation of another regime of power, usually with some sort of return to the former status quo. When state building is successfully achieved, within the concerned sociohistorical conditions, through the building or rebuilding of a state machinery that is adjusted and has incumbents that are adjusted to the new prevailing regime of power, it will provide the necessary implementation of that regime. This operation may be the conversion of the former aristocratic state of an agricultural society into the liberal democratic bourgeois state of an industrializing society, as in eighteenth- and nineteenth-century Europe. It may also be, as in some underdeveloped societies of today, the change of an oligarchical patrician state into a national-capitalist, state-capitalist, or developmental-socialist state, according to one of the developmental models studied in Chapter 15. Whatever the case, the successful performance of that functional stage opens the operational possibilities for the succeeding one, the nation-building stage.

Nation building. As in the case of the state-building stage, the term used here may be misleading. Historically, nation building, in its original form, was the task of the bourgeois European states that emerged from the Renaissance. In the form of absolute monarchies until the eighteenth century and subsequently in the form of democratic liberal bourgeois states, these states were the direct, although not the exclusive, agents in the transformation of their respective societies in the immediate sense of nation building.

As a functional stage, which may occur in various sociohistorical conditions, nation building means, essentially, the congruent adjustment of the regime of participation of a society and, in part, to a larger or a smaller extent, of its regimes of values and property, to the new regime of power and its political structures and functions, including the corresponding readjustment of structures, functions, and to some extent, elite incumbents of the other systems of the society (nation). The basic operation involved in this stage is the shaping or reshaping of a society by its political system. It consists, therefore, in the ultimate achievement of the social purposes explicitly or implicitly contained in the new political model. Failure on the part of the new leaders and their political model (because of an inherent or contingent incapacity), in the performing of this operation of sociopolitical engineering necessarily involves, sooner or later, the illegitimization of the new regime of power, of the new state machinery, and of the new authorities. If the ongoing process of political development is unsuccessful in becoming a general developmental process and in extending its configurative action to the other planes of the concerned society, it will create disruptive conflicts and will be arrested in the political plane. Such disruptive conflicts, which in certain conditions can provoke the segmentation of the society (as in Latin America), will in any case bring about the blockage of the developmental process and the emergence of another regime of power, with some sort of return to the former status quo.[10] If, however, the nation-building stage is carried through to its full achievement, the process of political development, which has already succeeded in shaping, or reshaping, congruent state machinery, will exert a congruent effect on all the other systems of the concerned society. The development of the political system will be consolidated, and there will be a basic congruent adjustment of the whole society to that development, at the level of possibility allowed by the model and by the historical conditions of the concerned society.

Consensus building. The fourth and last functional stage of a process of political development, consensus building, corresponds to the intrasocietal congruent readjustments that result from the achievement of the previous stage. The regimes of values and property, which were, to a larger or a smaller extent, partially adjusted to the new regime of power in the preceding stage, are now subjected (at the occurring real level of development) to a complete congruent adjustment. This general congruent adjustment of the other societal systems to the development reached by the political system—always within sociohistorical conditions of the concerned society—generates a basic consensus at the achieved level of participation. The basic operations performed in this last stage are of an integrative nature: societal (national) integration, value integration, and mass-elite integration.

In this stage as in the other stages, the occurring processes are conditioned by the real stage of development and the historical times of the concerned society. The several forms of integration and the related forms of consensus obtained in this stage, therefore, express the real sociohistorical development actually achieved by the concerned society. If the society (as Elizabethan England) is only, in real terms, in the stage of societalization, integration and consensus refer basically to the aristocracy. The agrarian mass may be peacefully submitted to a traditional conformity, but it will never manifest in political or social terms any active or intentional consensus, since whatever consensus it may express will be of a cultural-religious nature. At that sociohistorical level, there fore, the "last" stage of a process of political development, which may have started with the foundation of a national dynasty and the successful configura tion, by it, of a dynastic state and a dynastically integrated nation, will express a form of political and generalized national development that is a "final" one only in terms of the developmental possibilities presented by that polity and society at that evolutionary stage. The same is applicable, in terms of the his torical time and social conditions, to societies that have successfully achieved a process of political development in the real stage of mechanization (as Victorian England). Its forms of integration and consensus refer primarily to the bour geoisie and the reassimilated former upper class.

Table 34 gives a brief indication of the four functional stages of political devel opment, the basic operations involved in each, and the tendential effects of the successful achievement of each.

Open and cyclical processes

Whereas the real stages of development, as formerly indicated, are "open-ended" stages, preventing any anticipation of how the now just-beginning stage of socio organization will evolve, the functional stages of political development have a cyclical character. Each real stage for a developing society can contain at least one and often several full cycles of functional stages. This is due to the fact that each historical time presents a certain limited range of developmental possibilities. Within each of these historical ambits, one or more full cycles of political devel opment, with the resulting societal generalization of the development eventually achieved by the political system, can take place. Once changes of a deep nature, affecting the socioevolutionary capability of the concerned society, produce alterations in the social regime, the sort of societal equilibrium formerly achieved at a certain level and within certain conditions of consensus is led to a break down, and a new model-building stage is initiated, insofar as the society in ques tion keeps its capacity for development.

The functional stages of development, understood in accordance with this theory, are not susceptible to the overlapping, except in a limited form, of two successive stages in the process of general sociocultural evolution. The real stages do not overlap because they express distinct levels and typological structures in the process of general sociocultural evolution. The functional stages do not over lap because, both analytically and empirically, they express a sequence of typical operations in which the performance of a more advanced stage requires the pre vious performance of the operations of the preceding stages. As can be seen in the light of what has been discussed, the reason most writers have supposed that the developmental stages are susceptible to overlapping (and resulting disruptive effects) comes from the fact that they have not distinguished the functional stages from the real ones. New sociohistorical conditions disrupt a formerly obtained state of political and societal equilibrium, which involved a certain level and form of consensus. But this does not mean that a *certain level* and a *certain form* of consensus was not obtained in the preceding conditions. It just means that new levels and forms of consensus have become necessary. To obtain them, a new cycle of political development will have to take place, involving a process that will not necessarily be successful and may fail at any of its successive functional stages. The disturbances caused by participation or distribution conflicts, at a given sociohistorical stage of *real* development, however, will not prevent the subsequent achievement of a form of equilibrium and consensus compatible with the conditions of that *real* stage, whenever a successful process of political development does come to be carried out.

An often-presented example of stage overlapping is that of the troubles that assail the currently underdeveloped countries, who are confronted with participation and distribution demands before they have consolidated the political and economic systems giving them the capability to attend to such demands. What is actually occurring in this example is not, properly speaking, an overlapping of stages. Such societies, in terms of their real development, are in some early or middle phase of the stage of mechanization, in which the accumulation of resources and means of production is not compatible with the generalization of high standards of consumption. But since they are latecomers in the process of industrialization and, what is still more important, they are surrounded by an international system controlled by societies at a much more advanced real stage of development, they suffer extremely sharp demonstration effects, as for instance, Japan suffered, although in milder conditions, during the Meiji period. In political terms, they are confronted with the problem of putting into motion a process of political development, in accordance with one of the developmental models discussed in Chapter 15. If they succeed in adopting and implanting a political model that fits their structural conditions and if they succeed in implementing that model through the successive functional stages, they will successfully overcome their demonstration effects as well as their former lack of political and economic capability. Through the successful adoption and implementation of the appropriate political model, they will successfully achieve their real stage of mechanization, and so they will acquire the capability to provide much higher participation and distribution without affecting their developmental potentialities.

It is not conceptually correct, therefore, to speak of stage overlapping. Instead, one has to speak of the increasing difficulties for societies at lower real-stage levels, surrounded by an international system dominated by much more advanced societies, in successfully achieving a process of political development, particularly in the earlier functional stages of that process. As will be studied, the new international system that is emerging in the historical conditions of our time will be incompatible with new processes of national development in a couple of decades. And even those societies that have successfully achieved their real stage of mechanization will not be able to preserve their international autonomy if they do not obtain certain very exacting minimal conditions of national viability.

Table 34 *Functional stages of political development*

Stages	Operations (for achieving each stage)	Tendential Effects (of achievement of each stage)
1. Model Building		
Expresses and brings about changes in the regime of power and whether changes are in accordance with political regime and legal order or not, creates political confrontation between current authorities and the pretenders and their (explicit or implicit) political designs and models, with final transfer of power and authority to new incumbents or Failure of pretenders and maintenance of status quo	Formulation of new, development-oriented political design and (explicitly or implicitly) of corresponding new political model Articulation and aggregation of interests in favor of new political model Politicalization of these interests: formation and expansion of supporting political movement or party Final seizure of power (legally or illegally) by leaders of new movement	Increase in political mobilization, particularly more politicalization, participation, and political commitment to new political model Increase in expectations of more participation and distribution
2. State Building		
Congruent adjustment of political regime to new regime of power and corresponding reorganization of structures, functions, and incumbents of political system, particularly the conversion and output sectors (government and its bureaucracy) or If congruent adjustments are made, new change in the regime of power, usually with some sort of return to status quo	Adjustment, in congruent form, of the structures, functions, and incumbents of political system to new political model: creation of new state and government machinery or reform of former ones	Increase in rational orientation, secularity, and controllability Increase in structural differentiation Increase in capability Usually, participation, political equality, and redistribution are below the expectations, with a consequent (large or small) decrease in or diffusion of support: expectation gap. Basic political modernization achieved at the level of capability provided by model in the historical conditions of concerned society

3. Nation Building

Congruent adjustment of regimes of participation and in part of values and eventually of property to new regime of power and corresponding reorganization of structures, functions, and incumbents of the other societal systems and of nation (society) in general

or

If congruent adjustment are not made, illegitimation of regime of power and disruptive conflict between authorities and most social sectors, with blockage of developmental process, eventual societal segmentation, and emergence of another regime of power, with some sort of return to former status quo

Adjustment, in congruent form, of structures, functions, and incumbents of other societal systems to the regime of power and its corresponding political regime and legal order

Increase in operational and participational resulting variables, with reduction or practical suppression of expectation gap

Consolidation of political development and congruent adjustment to that development of the whole society, at the level of possibility provided by model in the historical conditions of concerned society

4. Consensus Building

Congruent adjustment of the whole of the social regime to new regime of power, legitimation of authorities and regime, and eventually of whole political system, at certain level of political and social consensus

or

If adjustments are not made, loss of legitimacy by authorities and eventually by regime

Adjustment, at the occurring level of participation, societal (national) integration, value integration, and mass-elite integration of political and social claims to political and social systems

Increase in legitimacy of authorities, regime, and system

Consolidation of the overall societal development, at level of possibility provided by model in the historical conditions of concerned society

NOTES

[1] They are not subject to deterministic fatalism in the sense that history is not rigidly determined by structural conditions and objective factors because of human liberty and the interference of unpredictable occurrences.

[2] See particularly his essays "Culture and Evolution" and "Science and History" in (1967b). See also his very relevant contributions in (1961) and (1964).

[3] As I understand Eisenstadt, this would include experiences, with different models and different margins of success, like Yugoslavia's regulated self-management, China's communes, and Chile's "revolution in liberty."

[4] The incomplete overlapping of stages is a concept implied in the understanding of these stages as "real" stages, not only analytically but also empirically typical, structurally differentiated from one another, and causally conditioned by the preceding stage. For the same reason Marx, who first introduced the idea of real stages, thought that a stage could not be superseded before it exhausted its inherent "productive" possibilities.

[5] The creation, however, of such entities as the IRI (founded for temporary purposes in 1933 and given permanent functions in 1937) and of several other public holdings and enterprises, although never brought to their full development by Mussolini, were decisive in the postwar industrialization of Italy. See, on the subject, Giuseppe Petrilli (1967) and Serge Hughes (1967, particularly pp. 254 ff). For a broader theoretical and historical perspective, see the excellent study of Ludovico Garruccio (1969).

[6] Central to Nazism was the project of building a new German world empire, and for this project far greater capital accumulation and industrial development was required.

[7] The secularization of distinct polities can be compared along a continuum in the sense of the secularization of their political culture. Otherwise comparisons must be made in sets of polity-society relationships.

[8] These other factors include the systemic connections between a polity and its society that can only be abstracted methodologically and for analytical purposes but which involve distinct empirical consequences, from one society to another, particularly in distinct historical times and evolutionary stages.

[9] A more detailed study would include, along with many other problems, the question of whether or not a series of real stages is an open or a closed one, which ultimately involves the question of a progressive or a cyclical view of natural and cultural evolution. In the picture presented in Table 33 the series is assumed to be an open one, since self-programmed evolution brings about unforeseeable results.

[10] Typical examples: Hungary's return to the status quo after the failure of Bela Kun; Turkey, after insufficient nation rebuilding by Mustafa Kemal; and Latin America in the current decade, after the failure of the populist democracies.

17

Operational Conditions

Conditions for political development

The preceding study of the operation and stages implied in a process of political development now requires the study of the conditions that the implementation of that process depends on. There are two distinct aspects to such an inquiry: (1) the consideration of the conditions of political development in analytical functional terms, that is, as conditions that have to be met by any society at any time[1] if a developmental process is to be successful and (2) the consideration of those conditions in concrete terms, that is, for specific societies at a given historical time and the terms of the characteristics of that historical time. In the present chapter we will proceed to a brief analysis in analytical functional terms and will then deal with the problems concerning the specific conditions of our time in the next chapter.

It is interesting to observe that although the already voluminous literature on political development has been particularly aware of the problems concerning the various typical operations and stages involved in the process, negligible attention has been paid to the question of the conditions that the successful implementation of that process depends on. At times this question has been confused with the problem of stages, a successful process being considered one that is appropriately carried out from each stage to the successive one without overlaps. Sometimes the question has been seen as being identical to the actual performance of the developmental process and the problems inherent to the several implied models and ideal types. Only Eisenstadt (1964 and 1966) and Almond (1966) have dealt more directly with the problem.

Eisenstadt tries to determine what conditions contribute to the success of certain elites and the failure of others in promoting the development of their respective societies. He concludes that successful elites meet, in general, five basic conditions: (1) *restructuring of communications*, adjusting the flux and level of communications to the conveniences and possibilities of mobilizing the masses for the developmental effort, (2) *concentration on primary and higher education*, with later attention to intermediate education, thus providing in the early phases of development sufficiently educated rank-and-file people and qualified elites, with the subsequent filling, when there are more resources and time, of the middle-level gap, (3) *controlled social mobility*, in such a way that a sufficiently large number of people from lower and peripheral sectors are mobilized for and incorporated into the new developmental activities without, however, there being an overloading of them that would disturb the elites' capacity for ruling and socializing them, (4) *functionality of power*, meaning the capacity of the elites to keep their drive for power and their use of it in terms compatible with the appropriate direction of the society, and (5) *firmness of design*, meaning, essentially, the capacity of the elites to form and maintain a clear idea of their plans, with a resulting consistency in their implementation. Conversely, according to Eisenstadt, the unsuccessful elites, besides not being able to meet these five conditions, are characterized by three typical dysfunctional features: (a) closeness of vast groups alternating with unrealistic flexibility, somehow according to a too little too much inadequate alternation, (b) tendency to indulge in *societas sceleris* practices, defrauding, for inexcusable group and individual private ends, the commond good of their own societies, against their own allegedly supported principles, and (c) ascriptiveness in the distribution of higher functions, opportunities, and rewards.

Almond singles out five conditions that make the attainment of developmental goals possible or impossible: (1) *successiveness* in the stages of development, instead of cumulative attempts to deal with problems of distinct stages at the same time, as in the case of premature participation or distribution, (2) *availability of resources*, that is, whether or not a society has access to the resources necessary for her development, (3) *congruent development of the other social subsystems*, so that the developmental requirements do not hang exclusively on the political subsystem but are sufficiently shared by the others, (4) *intrinsic sufficient capability* of the political system to meet the corresponding problems to each stage, and (5) *adequate response to challenges by the elite*, so that objective and functional solutions are given to the problems in each situation.

Although these two writers' attempts to identify the main developmental conditions seem partly appropriate to me, I believe a greater clarity concerning the distinction between stages and conditions, on the one hand, and between the developmental process itself and the conditions that make it feasible and successful or unsuccessful, on the other hand, is desirable and achievable. The sort of conditions we are trying to identify (necessary and sufficient conditions) are (1) those including the *necessary* general requirements that must be met, cumulatively, by any developmental process if it is to be successful and (2) those that are such that the fulfilling of them must be *sufficient* to assure the success of that process. These conditions, therefore, refer to the environmental requirements (including resources and the possibilities of their use), the inherent capabilities of the concerned social groups (including their aptitude for selecting realistic convenient goals), and the appropriateness of the ways in which the available resources are used for the attainment of the selected goals. Following this set of specifications, we have the conditions indicated in Chart 8.

The question of national viability

Up to now, *national viability*, the first of the conditions of political development indicated in Chart 8, has been given negligible attention. This is really a rather strange fact when one considers that this condition is not only one of the *sine qua non* requirements of any national developmental process, but is precisely the most basic and the most general one. The development of a national society

Chart 8 *Conditions of political development*

1. National viability	Existence, in terms of the technological requirements of a given time and of the available political capability of the concerned society, of sufficient human and natural resources to allow the autonomous and predominantly endogenous national development of that society
2. Political mobilizability	Existence, in that society, of social strata and groups with actually or potentially sufficient motivation and capability for introducing, by the ways that are required, development-oriented structural political changes and societal changes by political means
3. Leadership appropriateness	Timely appearance, in that society, of an individual or collective political leadership with an appropriate understanding of the means and ways required for the promotion of development-oriented structural political change and societal change by political means and with the necessary will and skill for actually carrying on the implementation of that change, including the mobilization of the necessary implementing cadres
4. Model fitness	Adoption, by the political leadership, of a developmental political model structurally fit for the concerned society
5. Consistency of model	Adjustment of adopted strategy and tactics to model requirements
6. Absence of insurmountable extrasocietal impediments, including foreign intervention	Nonoccurrence of insurmountable extrasocietal impediments, such as natural disasters and foreign intervention

consists, necessarily, in the increase of its capacity, as a nation, to ensure its autonomous and, as much as possible, endogenous, quantitative and qualitative growth. Given an international system, as the one that has gradually taken shape since the Renaissance, in which any social system (except state delegations) either forms itself as a nation, which is supposed to enjoy international self-determination, or is part of another nation, independent nations (in that technical sense of the word) are necessarily the subjects and the relatively self-contained social arenas of any possible developmental process. If this is so, it is rather obvious that a process of political development, which implies autonomous decisions concerning the polity and the use of political means to cause societal changes, cannot take place if the concerned society is not minimally endowed with the conditions necessary for preserving her nationhood and for developing herself as a national society.

It is not the purpose of this book to inquire into the causes of this strange lack of concern in the literature about the effect of the viability of nations on national development. I suggest, however, that this omission is of such a nature that it cannot be casual. It results, in my view, from the ideological conditioning, deliberate and unconscious, that has interfered so much with the scientific study of the development of societies. As was commented on in Chapter 10, the two competing ideological models of our time, the neoliberal and the communist, both assume, although for different reasons that the nation is not a relevant configurative form of society, in spite of the steady practice to the contrary of the leaders of both ideological positions. Due to Marx's well-known underestimation of the specific character of the national pattern, which he considered to be a superstructure of the bourgeois mode of production, the communist model has not been oriented toward seeing that pattern as a requirement of any autonomous societal development. Although post–World War II communism became nationalistic in practice,[2] and is now also nationalistic in theory, the analysts have not yet carried this fact to several of its ultimate consequences, including the prerequisite of national viability for any possibility of a successful developmental process. On the other hand, the neoliberal ideological model is oriented, consciously or not, toward justifying the conditions that have contributed historically and that continue to contribute today to the development of the leading Western nations, including, particularly, the exportation of capital investment and the external expansion of Western technical and managerial control. In this model there has been a consistent tendency to emphasize the absolute irrelevance[3] of the national origin, loyalty, and jurisdictional subordination of capital and technology as a factor of production. National development has therefore been considered as being equal to *territorial* development. What is important for any (native) society is that it increase its GNP and obtain more and better mines, plants, banks, and department stores, regardless of the nationality of the invested capital and technology and of the owners and the management.

Not only have *all* the successful processes of independent societal development since the Renaissance and particularly since the French Revolution until our days been national ones (that is, processes of development of national societies qua national ones), but moreover, as the more recent analysts of the nation have made clear, one of the most peculiar traits of nations, as a specific pattern or form of organization of societies, is the fact that they present, inherently (but not necessarily successfully), a propensity for societal development. It is, precisely, because nations, as an organizational form of societies, have this built-in propensity for their societal development that that specific form of societal organization has prevailed, historically, over its competing alternatives, such as the city-state (too restrictive) and the dynastic empire (too loose), not to speak of less-developed preterritorial structures.

In order to clarify this aspect of the nation before discussing the problem of national viability and its implications for political development, we will make a brief analysis of the characteristics of the national pattern.

The nation

As is well known, the understanding of the nature of the nation has been the object of a controversy for a long time between the "objectivists,"[4] who stress certain specific objective common traits shared by the members of a nation, such as territory, language, and other cultural features, and the "subjectivists,"[5] who point out that what actually shapes a nation is the common will of its members to stick together under a national form of organization. As might be expected, this controversy led to an intermediate or synthetic view, "objective subjectivism,"[6] which contends that the nation is the result of both kind of factors: The objective ones create the conditions that make "national togetherness" possible and desirable, and the subjective ones arise from those conditions and render that togetherness consciously and positively valued and normatively prescribed as a civic duty.

The more recent analysts of the nation have kept the basic framework of the objective subjectivistic approach. "The nation," says Rupert Emerson (1960, p. 95), "is a community of people who feel that they belong together in the double sense that they share deeply significant elements of a common heritage and that they have a common destiny for the future." Although, as Emerson has stressed, the European-based ideal type of nation implies the objective cultural common traits that have been traditionally mentioned in the voluminous literature on the subject, the extension of the national form of organization to non-Western societies and some of the particular conditions of the present historical time limit the applicability of the European-based ideal type to only the standard European examples. Seen in the broader and contemporary perspective, as Carl Friedrich (1966, p. 31) says, "a nation is any cohesive group possessing 'independence' within the confines of the international order as provided by the United Nations, which provides a constituency for a government effectively ruling such a group and receiving from that group the acclamation which legitimizes the government as part of the world order." The relevant new aspect in that view is the characterization of a social group as a nation, whatever its formerly shared and nonshared objective traits, whenever that group is able to generate a stable process of self-government, presenting, intrasocietally, effective ruling capacity and, intersocietally, an independence acknowledged formally by the international system. So viewed, the nation is a politically independent self-willed society.

Of the contemporary writers, Karl Deutsch (1966) has made three important contributions to the analysis of the nation. The first concerns the identification of the specific principal factor that, given certain objective conditions, and reinforcing them, creates the desirability of the feeling of togetherness. This factor is *mutually shared information.* "Membership in a people essentially consists in wide complementarity of social communication. It consists in the ability to communicate more effectively, and over a wider range of subjects, with members of one large group than with outsiders" (p. 97). And he adds, "Ethnic complementarity, the complementarity that makes a people, can be readily distinguished by its relatively wide range from the narrow vocational complementarity which exists among members of the same profession, such as doctors or mathematicians, or members of the same vocational group, such as farmers and intellectuals" (p. 98).

The second important point stressed by Deutsch is the fact that, ethnic complementarity notwithstanding, social-class divisions may be of such a nature as to affect that picture, not because the theory is wrong but because of the divisiveness of social-class differentiations. "Under such conditions [extreme social-class differentiation] men may discover more similar experiences and greater mutual understanding with their fellow workers in other countries than with their 'own' well-to-do countrymen who will see them only at the servant's entrance" (p. 98).

Deutsch's third important point is that nationality, compensating, in part, for that divisiveness and exerting on it a constraining action, forms a system of loyalties and participation that favors intrasocietal exchanges, rather than intersocietal ones and provides facilities for vertical mobility. "To the extent that the division of labor in a particular society is competitive and stratified, nationality can thus be used to hamper 'horizontal' substitution from individuals outside the group, and to facilitate 'vertical' substitution within it" (p. 103). One of the major consequences of the fact that nationality inherently makes extrasocietal horizontal pressure more difficult than intrasocietal vertical pressure is, as Deutsch observes, that the elite of a nation, when confronted with pressure from the lower strata and groups for more participation and better distribution, is led to seek a new and more stable form of equilibrium, becoming more functional and providing more advantages to the mass for the consolidation of the elite's leadership. That, as was seen in Chapter 13, is the origin of the dynamics of a developmental process. Elites that are unable or unwilling to become more functional (that is, to promote national development) face the alternatives of increasing their coefficient of coercion, being overthrown by either a new sector of the elite, subelite groups, or the counterelite, or finally falling under alien domination.

National viability

We can now return to the problem of national viability, the first and most general condition for political development. According to the definition presented in Chart 8, national viability is a relative concept expressing two variables, human and natural resources. The requirements for these variables change, essentially, according to (1) the technological requirements of a given time and (2) the available capability of the political system. What is fundamentally at stake is whether or not, given certain conditions at a certain historical time, a society has the necessary human and natural resources to assure its autonomous and predominantly endogenous national development, including its national defense, either by itself or in alliance with others. National viability means that in the existing conditions a society has enough human and natural resources to assure, in the above form, its national development. As is obvious, there is no "absolute" measure of national viability. At a certain historical level in the development of technology—for instance, the late nineteenth century—when the currently operating blast furnaces were producing ten tons of pig iron per day, "enough" natural resources and population meant something quite different from today, when blast furnaces are undersized, in comparative international terms, if they produce less than 1,000 tons of pig iron per day. The small developed European countries of today, such as Belgium, Switzerland, and the Netherlands, were able to achieve a high level of national development in a technological situation and in an international system completely different from the one that the small underdeveloped countries of today, such as the Central American countries, are confronted with. And it is precisely because, in these new conditions, even the "large" European countries have become too "small" that the Europeans have been forced to devise some form of European association, whatever their success in implementing it.

As far as the dimensions of territory, mineral deposits, agricultural land, and other natural resources, on the one hand, and populations and their principal characteristics, such as level of education and participation, on the other hand, are concerned, we have that the development of technology in the last 200 years has constantly increased the minimum resource availability necessary for a society to become capable, other conditions being equal, of undertaking an autonomous and basically endogenous development. So it becomes difficult for small societies to develop either through profitable international trade or through autonomous industrialization. The international differentiation between industrialized and nonindustrialized societies has, on the whole, severely penalized the latter and rewarded the former, bringing about, as has been exhaustively discussed by Raul Prebisch and ECLA,[7] the deterioration of the terms of trade for exporters of primary products. And as a result autonomous industrialization for societies that have become too "small," at a given historical time, is impossible because of the lack of enough natural resources to provide the inputs, and a sufficiently large domestic market to absorb the outputs of a national industrialization.

To escape permanent stagnation such societies could still try to form, in equitable conditions, a common market, such as the European one, pooling their natural and human resources. International pressures, however, have made it difficult for small underdeveloped societies to form effective common markets or equivalent arrangements in the conditions of the present international system. As the example of Central America so well illustrates, when small underdeveloped societies finally overcome the several and complex obstacles to the formation of a regional integration, they are obliged to comply with international impositions and to adjust their arrangement to the convenience of the hegemonic power they are subject to. So, for instance, the Central American Common Market had to observe a rule of free movement for international capital, when one of the rationales for the market's foundation was precisely the creation, for the concerned countries, of a larger capability for their own savings and investments. Because of the free entrance of capital from outside the market, however, the so-called industries of integration, which were to be the dynamic pole of development of the CACM, have come to be controlled by large American corporations. The result is that the Central American nations provide, in a preserved market, the consumers for the industrial goods made by nonregional companies, with nonregional capital and management; and, of course, the resulting *capital accumulation* (whatever the local benefits provided by salaries and taxes paid locally) and, still more important, the resulting *political influence* derived from the control of these locally important economic centers are kept in the hands of nonregional groups.

In addition to the minimal requirements for available natural and human resources, which vary historically according to the requirements of the technology of each time, the conditions concerning the political capability of the concerned society are equally important for the determination of its national viability. These conditions are essentially concerned with the polity's external capability for defending its society from extrasocietal pressures and with its internal capability in terms of its dependability, effectiveness, adaptability, and flexibility, as was extensively studied in Chapter 5. (See particularly Table 21.) The concept of *minimal sufficient capability* (like the concept of *minimal sufficient resources*) is a relative one. Besides varying in terms of the concerned historical time, it also varies in terms of the geopolitical situation of a country and the dimensions of its resources.

The geopolitical aspect is still of relative importance, even though its importance is tending to decline with the new emerging international system and the present conditions of technology, which have put all the sites of the world within easy reach of ICBMs and other devices. In historical terms, it is easy to see how the national development of certain countries, for instance, Poland, has been negatively affected by their geopolitical situation (for Poland the Prussian and Russian borders), whereas other countries, such as the United States in the nineteenth century, have been highly favored by their geopolitical location (for the United States the two coasts and the Canadian and Mexican borders). Nineteenth-century Uruguay was adversely affected by her borders with two local great powers, Brazil and Argentina, but in the Latin American conditions of today, that location has become one of Uruguay's assets, converting her into a sort of potential "District of Columbia" for the Latin American system. An opposite example is provided by the Central American countries, which were favored in the early nineteenth century by their location between North and South America but since the late nineteenth century have been submitted to complete and unchecked American domination because of their proximity to that country. Geopolitical location had the same negative effect on Mexico in the middle of the nineteenth century (causing her to lose more than half her territory to the United States) and still contributes, today, to the ambiguity that characterizes the Mexican attempts to attain international autonomy, causing a large gap between the nominality and the effectiveness of such attempts.

More important than the geopolitical situation of a country, particularly today, is her internal political capability. Developing the political capability of a society is a central goal for any process of political development, as was seen in Book II, Part B. It is also a self-reinforcing objective, since increased development brings increased political capability. But the initial level of political capability enjoyed by a country, when she starts a consistent effort of political development, will not only affect her chances of success, since higher starting levels of capability ensure better means of action from the beginning, but will also decisively influence her level of *resource liquidity*. The higher the political capability of a society is, the better use she will be able to make of her available human and natural resources. The determination of a country's level of national viability, therefore, is decisively influenced by her political capability. Countries with few human and natural resources, by international standards, but with a high level of political capability will rank better, in terms of national viability, than countries in the opposite situation. Japan is, perhaps, the best example of a country that has compensated for her limited resources (principally natural ones) with a total organized national commitment to development and self-determination. Brazil is an example of a country in which extremely huge natural resources have been miserably used (chiefly the human resources) because of elite dysfunctionality and the resulting lack of political capability. The case of Uruguay, vis-à-vis Central America, is also illustrative. Although the natural resources and the population of the former are close to those of the Central American countries, her superior political capability (up to recent years), expressed in terms of national integration and commitment, ensures for Uruguay, if with increasing difficulties, a national viability that the Central American countries have already lost.

Another very crucial question in the problem of national viability involves the means and ways in which the national resources are utilized. This question is essentially one of the allocation of roles, facilities, and opportunities among the individual members and groups of a nation, within the conditions allowed by the availability of natural resources and the general real level of development of the concerned society. We have just seen that the relationship between national resources and political capability ultimately determines the ratio of resource liquidity, so that some countries may be very successful and some become inviable with the same level of national resources. If we consider that matter a bit more closely, it will become apparent that to understand what is involved in such a relationship, it is not enough to refer to something which might be called the "degree of national commitment." National commitment is certainly and decisively involved, either as an empirically observable trait provided by the political culture (as in Japan) or as an also empirically observable consequence of political organization (as in Switzerland). But precisely because national commitment is not only and sometimes not primarily the result of unplanned traits of the culture of a society but, whatever the cultural basis, the consequence of policy supported by appropriate organization, we have to look more closely into what forms or reinforces it.

Based on our former discussion of the nation, we can understand national commitment, or the commitment to one's nation, as the widely spread and deeply felt positive evaluation of the nation and its political system by the respective members, generating a propensity for collective efforts aimed at preserving and enhancing the national society, its autonomy, individuality, and general development. These characteristics are closely connected with the question of elite functionality, discussed in Chapter 13. Functional elites tend to optimize the use of resources, facilities, and opportunities, including the institutionalization and social allocation of corresponding roles, for the people of their societies. Dysfunctional elites, on the contrary, are led, for several reasons, to view their interests and values in ways that are not compatible with the generalization of these interests to the society as a whole and tend, therefore, to create dualistic societies, in which elite and mass interests become submitted to zero-sum game rules.

Congruence as a requisite

The present discussion will not return to the problem of what makes some elites functional and some dysfunctional, which has already been given sufficient attention. What is relevant for the problem of national viability is to stress the extent to which elite functionality depends on the degree of congruence and complementarity existing among the four typical sets of elite roles, as well as on other factors and conditions. We have seen that each social plane and its respective social subsystem (cultural, participational, political, and economic) necessarily gives rise to an elite-subelite-mass relationship and a corresponding, more or less formal and structured, stratification. We have also seen that the four structural elites can more or less coalesce into an establishment and, on the other hand, that in pluralistic mass societies incumbents in elite roles at any one of the structural planes can fill nonelite roles at other planes. Now, we must consider the fact that elite functionality cannot be achieved and maintained without a sufficient congruence and complementarity among the four types of elites.

The ultimate reason for that fact is to be found in the inherent characteristics of the social system in general, as a sufficiently congruent system of roles. If a society lacks congruence among its major subsystems and roles, after a certain limit it will not be able to prevent its disruption, and before that limit it will not be able to provide efficient defense against any serious challenge from alien societies. That special form of societal organization that is the nation requires, as an inherent element and aspect of its pattern, a larger cohesiveness among its main subsystems, groups, and roles. That larger cohesiveness has been historically responsible for the success of the national organization over other forms of society. But it has also imposed the need for a higher minimal degree of congruence and complementarity among the elites of the four social subsystems for the satisfactory working of a nation (as compared, for example, to a dynastic organization).

The sort of congruence and complementarity among the elites of the four social subsystems that is necessary for the attainment and maintenance of a nation requires that the basic interests and values of the four elites, besides being compatible with the interests and values of the subelite and the mass of their respective social subsystems, be compatible and mutually reinforcing with each other. In other words, the basic interests and values of the cultural, social, political, and economic elite must be compatible and mutually reinforcing. This basic compatibility certainly does not exclude many mutually incompatible specific aspects. For example, in all societies, even in such highly congruent ones as post-Meiji Japan, many of the interests and values of the military clash with those of the intellectuals. Labor leaders have conflicts with employers' leaders, and so on. What is necessary is that their *basic* interests and values be congruent and mutually reinforcing. This means that, in principle, conflicts will be solved at a higher level, through mutual reduction of conflicting interests and values to higher interests and values commonly shared.

Interelite exchanges

What is relevant for the question now being discussed is the necessity for sufficiently interchangeable and mutually reinforcing basic interests and values among (1) the cultural elite (particularly the intellectuals and scientists), (2) the economic elite (particularly the entrepreneurs and top managers), (3) the political elite (the political ruling group, be they the politicians of a mass democracy, notables of an oligarchy, or leading military), and (4) the social elite (the one or several top high-status groups). This occurs when there is a sufficiently balanced flux of exchanges between the boundaries of the social subsystems, which is mutually advantageous for their respective elites. Such is the case when the symbols exchanged by the cultural elite carry scientific and technological innovations favorable to the economic elite and legitimacy for the political elite, and in exchange the cultural elite gets appropriate solvency and regulations from the economic and the political elites. Similarly, the political elite exchanges commands that enforce the property interests of the economic elite for solvency, enabling it to pay the costs of law enforcement and the undertaking of other public services. The matter has already been sufficiently discussed in Chapter 5 and graphically represented in Tables 18 and 19. To facilitate reading, a simplified version of Table 19, is presented here as Table 19a.

As Table 19a reminds us, each of the societal systems, under the control of its respective elite, supplies the other subsystems and their respective elites with some basic valuables and, in exchange, receives other valuables. Cultural elites provide (1) respectability for social elites and obtain performance (actors and spectators), (2) legitimacy for political elites and obtain enforcement, and (3) rationalization, in the sense of scientific and technological facilities, including organizational and managerial ones, for economic elites and obtain operability, in the sense of the material means for action. Social elites supply (1) performance for cultural elites and obtain respectability, (2) support for political elites and obtain security, and (3) labor facilities for economic elites and obtain means of subsistence. Political elites supply (1) enforcement for cultural elites and obtain legitimacy, (2) security for social elites and obtain support, and (3) order for economic elites and obtain solvency, in the sense of the financial means to meet political and governmental expenses. Economic elites supply (1) operability for cultural elites and obtain rationalization, (2) means of subsistence for social elites and obtain labor facilities, and (3) solvency for political elites and obtain order.

This exchange of valuables, which is as indispensable for the congruence of the elites and their respective subelites and masses as for the coherent functioning of society as a whole, can be negatively affected, to the point of disrupting the society, by factors of extra- or intrasocietal origin. It is not necessary to proceed to detailed analysis of these factors. Let us just consider them, in their most generic aspect, as factors introducing changes in the goals pursued by the elite of one of the subsystems, either (1) because that group of actors has been led to make relevant changes in its interests and values or (2) because there has been a change in the incumbents in relevant elite roles and the new actors have different interests and values. An example of the first kind of disturbance in intra-elite exchanges can be seen when new religious convictions either create a chasm among the elites, dividing them into conflicting camps in a socially self-destroying dispute, or oppose the political, intellectual, and economic elites to each other, in a no less self-destroying confrontation. The Byzantine conflict of the iconoclasts during the eighth and ninth centuries is a good example of the first case.[8]

Examples of the second case can be clearly discerned in the behavior of the Spanish and Portuguese elites since the introduction of the Inquisition in Iberian kingdoms.[9] The alienation of these elites explains in large part the resulting decadence of the Iberian nations, which were so dynamic and progressive in the fifteenth and sixteenth centuries, when they finished the expulsion of the Moors from their territories and proceeded to great maritime discoveries.

The second kind of disturbance, caused by changes in the incumbents in relevant elite roles and the fact that the new actors have interests and values that are not sufficiently congruent with those of the other elites, has become more usual in modern times, because of the acceleration of the pace of social change

Table 19a *Societal interchange of functions*

Societal Systems	Cultural	Social	Political	Economic
Cultural	X	Performance → / Respectability ←	Enforcement → / Legitimacy ←	Operability → / Rationalization ←
Social	Respectability → / Performance ←	X	Security → / Support ←	Subsistence → / Labor ←
Political	Legitimacy → / Enforcement ←	Support → / Security ←	X	Solvency → / Order ←
Economic	Rationalization → / Operability ←	Labor → / Subsistence ←	Order → / Solvency ←	X

and because of the unprecedented international expansion of the great corporations. As far as social change is concerned, the disturbance may result because the processes of social mobilization are going on much faster than the corresponding processes of socialization, as many students of political development have remarked. In such a case newly recruited elites may be unable or unwilling to supply the valuables they should to preserve a congruent interaction with other elites. Such has often been the case with "populist" political elites in underdeveloped countries, who fail to supply enforcement, security, and/or order to the other elites. Examples of that sort of dysfunctionality are abundant in Africa and Latin America, and even relatively successful varieties of populism, as Peronism and Varguism in Argentina and Brazil, respectively, have had their quota of such dysfunctionalities.

More relevant for the purpose of the present analysis, however, are the inherently dysfunctional results of the unprecedented expansion of the great corporations, now usually called, improperly, multinational corporations. These gigantic economic-technological systems have, with few exceptions, a very defined national character,[10] the great majority being American corporations and a few European. They operate, however, with varying degrees of local autonomy, in many other countries besides their native one. These macrocorporations are increasingly obtaining control of all the important foreign investments in the world, particularly in the underdeveloped countries. Moreover, they are rapidly becoming the most important industrial agencies in the countries where they open their subsidiaries. What lends a very particular relevancy to these corporations is the fact that they themselves, as business firms, and their managers, technical people, and executives, as individuals, whatever their legal nationalities may be, are actually filling, under the central coordination of the directors of these corporations, the most important roles in the economic subsystem of alien countries. The problem involved has nothing to do with the cloak-and-dagger version given by certain critics of foreign investments. The problem lies in the fact that a new economic elite is created and takes the place and the roles of the former one, providing, for all sorts of reasons, a much higher level of economic performance, but being inherently and necessarily unable to maintain a sufficiently congruent relationship with the other elites and with the recipient nation in general.[11]

Once again, this is not a question of ill will. It is just the result of the inherent impossibility of alien agencies and people filling national roles congruently. Although all the relationships these foreign enclaves have with their local parties may be (and this is often not the case) both morally and legally correct and even permeated with an enlightened good will, they cannot overcome the fundamental fact that they do not belong to the recipient social system. Much more than abstract and impersonal agents of the production of goods and services, as the classics and the neoliberals tend to view economic actors, these actors, as was formerly stated, are involved, in addition to their purely productive activities, in many sorts of relevant exchanges with the other actors of the recipient social system.

This social system, in the world of today, is a nation, usually an underdeveloped one. That nation exists because of its flux of exchanges, particularly the exchanges among the elites of each of its social subsystems. What makes that nation a nation is precisely the national character of its intrasocietal exchanges (see Deutsch, 1966) and of its outputs to other societies. And that national character is not primarily dependent on the legal nationality of the intervening actors but on their ultimate concern and allegiance. As was commented on earlier in the chapter, all the students of the nation have stressed the fact that allegiance to the nation as such, based on a strong positive evaluation of her and guided by a normative orientation toward her enhancement, autonomy, and the preservation of her individuality, is both an essential characteristic of that form of society and the reason for its peculiar strength. That national character becomes irremediably affected, to the point of total disruption of the national pattern, if one of the social subsystems lastingly loses its national congruence with the others and with the society as a whole.

It is particularly in the exchanges between the new economic elite, now mostly alien, and the cultural and political elites that the lack of basic congruence has its most dysfunctional effects. The new economic elite is not interested in or willing to accept the contributions of established rationalization that the cultural elite could provide. The new economic elite has its own scientific and technological support, admittedly much better than anything the local cultural elite might be able to supply. And the economic elite is not oriented toward exchange, except for propaganda purposes and so in rather modest and secondary forms, or toward providing the local cultural elites with costly operative facilities. Any study of the development of American business and American universities, for instance, will show the closest possible relationship between the cultural and the economic systems. Business financed the expansion of higher learning, and the latter provided the former with increasing scientific and technological support, to the point of almost complete national self-sufficiency, today. In an underdeveloped country where most of the important and modern companies are controlled by foreign groups, the relations between the economic and the cultural elites are merely ornamental. The functional relations continue to be between these foreign groups and their own national cultural elite. The local cultural elite, therefore, are restricted, on the one hand, either to forms of luxury entertainment, such as productions of folklore, or to the terminal literature of existential or political despair. On the other hand, the scientifically oriented groups, which are unable to obtain work in the local conditions, are reduced to an unending and self-aggravating dependence on the great foreign universities, to which they eventually become attached.

Likewise, in their exchanges with the political elite, the alien groups controlling the economic subsystem are inclined to contemplate certain output aspects of the political process with aversion and to distort most of the input aspects. As discussed in Chapters 5 and 13, what makes a political elite functional is the existence of a flux of exchanges between the political and the other elites and between the political elite and the mass, which is of such a nature that the political interest will basically correspond to the forms of political regulation most conducive to the national development of the concerned society. In underdeveloped countries one of the fundamental requirements for assuring the functionality of these exchanges is that strong rewards be provided for the creation of new and better conditions of education, consumption, and participation for the masses. When the economic elite is a national one, with strong commitments to the development of the nation, it not only demands formal public order from the political elite, but also a constant increase in the quality of that order. This demand—in spite of unavoidable conflicts and short-term egotistic resistance, will lend to social development, as well as political and cultural development, as a necessary counterpart of a self-centered and self-sustained economic development. Alien economic elites, however, are exclusively interested in the formal and mechanical aspects of public order. Moreover, they exercise a strong influence, which tends to be an overwhelming one in underdeveloped countries, to prevent policies considered directly or indirectly inconvenient to foreign-controlled interests, including such diverse things as trade or exchange restrictions and social- or nationalist-oriented regulations. The result of the lack of national congruence between the economic and the political elite will inevitably be a collision course. Whereas the lack of national congruence between the economic and the cultural elite produces the marginalization of the latter, that same lack of national congruence, vis-à-vis the political elite, produces conflict. That conflict, however, is inherently incompatible with being the host to foreign capital and groups. It causes, therefore, a disruptive pressure on the political system, which can lead to one of two alternatives. The political elite, supported by the mass, may keep its national character and its national ways—even if in terms of a real or apparent decline in the economy—in which case nationalistic policies will finally be adopted and the alien economic elite will be excluded or its importance substantially reduced (Cárdenas in Mexico). Or the political elite may finally be tamed, however complex and long that process may be, and converted into an instrument of the economic elite, as happens in most of the underdeveloped countries today.

Summing up our discussion of national viability, we have that this requirement is the general and basic condition for the possibility of a successful independent process of development for any society. The main points concerning national viability are: (1) It requires the availability of sufficient human and natural resources for the autonomous and predominantly endogenous development of the society (*minimal sufficient resources*), at a given level of the development of technology and of the political capability (minimal sufficient capability) of the concerned nation. (2) The concept of minimal sufficient resources is historically relative, and in the last two centuries it has tended to imply the necessity for increasingly larger populations, territory, and mineral and agricultural facilities or if possible in a given international system, the compensatory formation of equitable common markets and similar arrangements. (3) The concept of minimal sufficient capability is also a relative one, varying (a) in part, in terms of the favorability of the nation's geopolitical placement and (b) principally in terms of

the degree of organized national commitment. (4) The achievement and maintenance of a sufficient level of national commitment requires essentially: (a) functional orientation of the elites and (b) national basic congruence among the interests and values of the elites of the four societal subsystems. (5) The current
unprecedented expansion of foreign investments and the resulting predominance
of foreign-controlled interests in the economic system of many societies is
creating an alien new economic elite inherently incompatible with the maintenance of the national basic congruence of the elites of the recipient countries
and so incompatible with their national viability.

Political mobilizability

The second general condition for any process of political development is *political
mobilizability*. As defined in Chart 8, that requirement implies the actual or potential existence in a society of social strata and groups with sufficient motivation
and capability for introducing, by the ways that are required, development-
oriented structural political changes and societal changes by political means.
Many aspects of this question have already been discussed in Chapter 14. As we
observed then (see Chart 6), underdeveloped societies can be differentiated into
three major types, with several varieties and subvarieties. Some of the varieties
or subvarieties of these types can present a great stability, both intrasocietally
and intersocietally. Traditional societies, variety I–1, as well as primitive or
archaic societies, variety III–1, can be very stable when they are not submitted
to external challenges (a condition that no longer occurs today). Societies with
a *societas sceleris* elite, subvariety III.2.2, can also be rather stable once they fall,
as tends to occur today, under the protective hegemonic tutelage of one of the
superpowers. Conversely, societies with a split elite, variety I.2, and societies sustained by the modern sector of the subelite, variety II, tend to be very unstable.
Societies with a rigidified aristocratic elite, variety III.2.1, in their contemporary
form with a new establishment elite, have a similar potential for unrest and
change, but they also enjoy more available instruments of efficient repression.
    Political mobilizability expresses, as an ideal type, the potential for change
contained, in general, in the several varieties and subvarieties of underdeveloped
societies. In concrete terms, of course, only the empirical study of each particular society, in terms of the existing internal and external conditions at a given
time, will permit an estimation of its political mobilizability. The typological
characterization of the several varieties of underdeveloped societies, as attempted
in Chapter 14, provides, although in a general and abstract way, a clear view of
the possible social strata and groups that could be the agents and supporters of
change. In Chart 7 these various strata and groups were broadly indicated in
terms of the developmental model that would be typologically suitable for each
case. As an aid to the reader, a simplified version of that chart is presented here
as Chart 7a.
    The problems concerning the modes and ways of mobilizing these potential
agents of change were discussed in Chapter 15. Within the general conditions

Chart 7a *Mobilizable strata and groups in terms of the suitable developmental model*

A. *National-Capitalist model*

Modernizing sectors of the national bourgeoisie and the middle class in alliance with the proletariat and with the support of the mobilized peasants versus traditional and consular sectors of the bourgeoisie and the middle class, their foreign bosses and partners, and antimodernizing rural sectors

B. *State-Capitalist model*

Modernizing sector of the middle class, with full support of urban and rural masses versus traditional patrician elite and consular allies in the bourgeoisie and middle class, particularly their foreign bosses, partners, and supporters

C. *Developmental-Socialist model*

The intelligentsia of the counterelite organized in a revolutionary, well-disciplined party, with support of party-controlled urban and rural masses and an eventual alliance with disaffected sectors of the former elite and subelite, versus dysfunctional elite, their subelite supporters and respective repressive apparatus, and their foreign bosses, partners, and supporters

that are typical of each variety of underdeveloped societies there are, naturally, great differences, due to each society's specific sociohistorical conditions, the sort of leadership that may come to emerge, and the society's situation in the international system.

Specific conditions aside, we have that political mobilizability becomes particularly difficult in the case of protracted underdevelopment and still worse, to the point of practically disappearing, in the case of consolidated underdevelopment. As was discussed in Chapter 15, protracted underdevelopment is the case of societies whose underdevelopment is widely acknowledged by their elite and subelite (as is notably the case in the Latin American societies) without that fact bringing about consistent or at least successful attempts to promote the required changes. Consolidated underdevelopment is a case of protracted underdevelopment that, in the long absence of consistent or successful attempts at introducing the required changes, has given place to a stabilized deterioration of the social fabric, maintained by the emergence of a strongly entrenched coercive inegalitarian regime, either of the colonial-fascist or of the *societas sceleris* brands. Political mobilizability in societies with protracted underdevelopment tends to be low because, as indicated by that protractedness itself, the potentially mobilizable sectors of these societies have given signals for too long a time that they either lack the capability to change the existing social regime or lack sufficient motivation for that undertaking. The case of consolidated underdevelopment is still worse and may, in specific conditions, present an insurmountably insufficient mobilizability. Sometimes, the support given by the status quo social forces to the existing regime, combined with the preparedness and strength of the repressive apparatus, and on top of all that, the international interests vested in the maintenance of that regime are more than enough to contain any possibility of change. Sometimes, the regime's capacity for co-optation, usually in the extreme cases of *societas sceleris,* is so large that all capable people and groups become conniving with it, abandoning the masses to an irremediable destituteness.

As has often been repeated in this book, sociohistorical processes, because of the unpredictability of human liberty and of moral impact, we always reserving surprises for the social theorist. The emergence of an exceptional leader, supported by some extraordinarily dedicated immediate followers can, in certain conditions, create miracles and generate actual political mobilization when mobilizability would have been assessed as being completely insufficient. In this respect, as well as in what concerns her national viability, the extraordinary case of Cuba is an exemplary exception.

Other conditions

The four other conditions of political development can be discussed more summarily, since they are sufficiently self-explanatory or have already been appropriately dealt with in the preceding section of this book. The third condition, *leadership appropriateness,* belongs to the group of self-evident requirements. Political leaders, even more than economic entrepreneurs, are the indispensable combiners of factors for the production of political events. Moreover, given the fact that power, distinct from money, is not a physical commodity, although it depends on and is expressed by physical means, but actually consists in certain forms of human interaction and, therefore, can in a certain sense be "produced out of nothing," the political leader, much more than a combiner, is a discoverer and inventor of political factors. It is because political leaders can create, within certain limits and conditions, the actual factors of power that an exceptional political leader, in exceptional circumstances can, like Fidel Castro, overcome very precarious conditions of political mobilizability and introduce radical structural change in societies and situations that had all the objective indications of hopelessness.

Another relevant point concerning political leadership is the sociohistorical possibility of the untimely appearance of the required leader. In part as a result of Marx's influence concerning the self-configurability of structural conditions and, in part, as a resistence against hero worship and the romantic exaggeration of the godly leader, political scientists currently show a propensity to assume that, given a reasonable time, each situation will tend to generate its own leaders. That assumption has not materialized in a number of cases. Sometimes the requirements for political leadership are so exacting, in terms of the exceptional human qualities needed and/or in terms of the seemingly insurmountable difficulties to be overcome, that nobody is willing or capable enough to exert a valuable leadership. In certain cases societies have been deprived of capable and representative leaders for an impressively long time. China, from the decay of the Manchu dynasty until Sun Yat-sen and Turkey until Mustafa Kemal are typical examples. The long crisis of France until the return of De Gaulle and the consolidated forms of fascist rule, such as the ones of Salazar and Franco, which have prevented the possibility of any alternative political leadership appearing, are also good illustrations. What is particularly serious about long absences of appropriate leadership is the fact that the societies that are thereby deprived of conditions for promoting their development can be, and finally are, driven to irreversible forms of deterioration or disruption.

The fourth condition of political development, *model fitness,* was discussed extensively in Chapter 15. As we saw then, the successful promotion of political development necessarily depends on the fitness, in terms of the structural conditions of the concerned society, of the political model explicitly or implicitly adopted for the structuring of the new regime of power and corresponding political regime. Models are not intrinsically better or worse than each other, although, in principle, they imply, typologically, larger or smaller initial bases of consensus. As instruments for achieving given results in given conditions, models can only be judged by their structural fitness, and other conditions being equal, the success or failure of the model's results will be a function of that fitness.

The fifth general condition, *model consistency,* is a rather self-evident requirement. It is not enough to have opted for, and implanted, the convenient model for a given society. It is equally indispensable to implement it in a consistent way, through the adoption of the appropriate political strategy and the employment of the tactics that that strategy requires in the various situations during its execution. Lack of model consistency has been the fault most often responsible for unsuccessful attempts at political development. As will be discussed in Book III, this has been particularly true of the frustrated national-capitalist efforts undertaken by Perón and Frondizi in Argentina and by Vargas and his successors in Brazil. The same can be said of the failure of Paz Estenssoro's state capitalism in Bolivia.

The sixth and last general condition of political development, the *nonoccurence of insurmountable extrasocietal impediments,* involves two distinct orders of problems. The first, physical catastrophes, tends to become less important in terms of the huge and continuous increase in the populational, economic, and territorial dimensions of modern societies, in spite of the extent of the potential damage such disasters as earthquakes and volcanic eruptions can cause. The second, the preclusion of *international permissibility* which would allow the development of a given society, is more serious. The condition of international permissibility is steadily deteriorating in the international system that has been gradually (and is now rather quickly) replacing the European-centered system of balance of power which prevailed until World War I and, more loosely, until World War II. This matter will be specifically discussed in Chapter 18, and so does not need more than a brief comment here. What is meant by international permissibility is the extent to which, and the conditions in which, a given society in a given international system will actually be allowed to promote her national development without insurmountable intervention by one or more foreign powers.

In the past, the conditions of international permissibility were principally affected by geopolitical factors. With the balance of power peculiar, with changing variations, to the international system that prevailed, in broad terms, from the Congress of Vienna to World War II, no country or combination of countries ever achieved a status of general primacy. Among the implications of this fact, we have that many medium or small powers, protected from insurmountable challenges from any of the great powers of the day by the balance of power, could enjoy sufficient international independence to preserve their domestic autonomy and their possibilities for predominantly endogenous growth. Insufficient international permissibility, therefore, was the exception and not the rule for medium or small powers and was primarily connected with specifically unfavorable geopolitical locations. Poland, has already been noted, was particularly victimized because of her location between Prussia and Russia, although not at the cost of her national viability. Small powers, like the duchies of Schleswig and Holstein, dynastically associated with Denmark, were militarily annexed by Bismarck to Prussia, under arguments of realpolitik, because of their geopolitical importance. The same occurred, in the early phases of World War II, with the three Baltic nations of Estonia, Latvia, and Lithuania. These nations had maintained a difficult balance between German and Russian pressures and, at the outbreak of World War II, were finally occupied by the Soviet troops, as a realpolitik measure to prevent the Germans from occupying them. Geopolitical reasons, although in a rather different context, were also responsible for the first (annexation of Mexican territories) and the second (annexation of formerly Spanish colonial possessions) waves of American military expansionism. The emergence of American imperialism,[12] concomitant with the second expansionist wave, was also initially of a geopolitical character, since it then oriented its web of economic-diplomatic-military controls toward Central America and the Caribbean islands.

The problem facing small and medium-sized powers today, as will be studied in Chapter 18, lies in the fact that the negative conditions of international permissibility are no longer primarily associated with particularly unfavorable geopolitical situations, but with the actual internal structure and dynamics of the new emerging international system, which is ceasing to be inter-*national* and is becoming inter-*imperial*.

NOTES

[1] For the sake of simplicity the following inquiry will be slightly less general than the above statement implies. The general conditions that will be studied will not be considered in terms of "any possible historical time" but in terms of the broad historical period that starts with the formation of nation-states, includes the Renaissance, and brings us to the present.

[2] Stalinism was already a form of rather thorough nationalism, but it was not acknowledged as such by the Soviet Union, much less allowed by non-Russian socialist parties.

[3] In actual practice the more advanced capitalist countries have been as unfaithful to their capitalist internationalism, whenever they were themselves involved, as post–Lenin Soviet Russia has been to her socialist internationalism.

[4] See among others Rudolf Rocker (1939), Carlton J. H. Hayes (1960), and Morris Ginsberg (1961).

[5] See among others John Stuart Mill (1861), Ernest Renan (1887), G. P. Gooch (1920), and E. H. Carr (1945).

[6] See principally Frederick Hertz (1944) and Hans Kohn (1944 and 1955).

[7] Among other Prebisch–ECLA publications, see (1950, 1963a, and 1963b).

[8] See George Ostrogorsky, (1956, pp. 130–186) and J. M. Hussey (1961, pp. 28 ff.).

[9] See Friedrich Heer (1968, pp. 49 ff.). See also my study (1971).

[10] Besides the fact that the centers of decision for these corporations, wherever their nominal headquarters may be located, are in the United States (or in Europe for a few), what imprints on them a decisive American (or European) national character is that they are functionally an inseparable part of the American (or European) social system, filling the most important roles of its economic subsystem and playing major roles in all of the other three subsystems.

[11] See Frank Bonilla, "The Invisible Elites" (1970, vol. 2, chap. 9).

[12] American historians have generally considered the two expansionist movements referred to above as imperialist, but the really imperialist process, which is currently occurring, has not been acknowledged as such. See Richard Van Alstyne (1965), H. Wayne Morgan (1967), and Ernest R. May (1968), among others.

18

Present Historical Conditions

THE TECHNOLOGICAL REVOLUTION

Conditions in our time

The study of the stages and the operational conditions of political development in the two preceding chapters enables us now to deal with the last major remaining aspect of our theoretical inquiry: the historical conditions that presently configure the limits and possibilities of current processes of political development.

The question we have to analyze, continuing our former discussion about (1) the real stages of societal development and the functional stages of political development and (2) the general conditions for a process of political development, from national viability to international permissibility, is how these stages and general conditions occur and operate in the concrete historical conditions of our time. Essentially, we have to determine the limits, possibilities, and requirements of international permissibility for the societal and political development of the various countries, actually or prospectively endowed with a national state, in the conditions of our time.

Given the unparalleled complexity of the sociocultural conditions of our time, this inquiry would be impossible within the limits of the present chapter if we could not point out what may be considered, for our purposes, the two most salient aspects of the contemporary world. The first is the revolutionary development of technology, along an exponential curve of scientific discoveries and technical applications that, gaining increasing acceleration in the course of the current century, has achieved a quasi-vertical progress in the past two decades. The second, which is not unconnected with the former, is the emergence of a new international system in the aftermath of World War II.

Both features have been widely acknowledged by the students of contemporary affairs, particularly the first one. If we understand "our time," in a broad sense, as the period subsequent to World War I and, in a strict sense, as the period following World War II,[1] the technological revolution, particularly in terms of the developments brought about by cybernetics and nuclear energy, is universally understood as the most important characteristic of the contemporary world. The difference between the role of technology in the post–World War II decades and in the preceding ones, after the industrial revolution, is of a quantitative-qualitative character. Through its immense expansion, diversification, and increased complexity, technology has been converted from an instrument for the adaptation of man to nature into a man-made nature, which constitutes the new ecology of contemporary society.

The problem of technology

The voluminous literature dedicated in the 1960s to the science of technology (the invention of inventions), to the sociology of technology (the reciprocal conditioning of society and technology), to bionics (the synthesis of biology and cybernetics), and to the scientific anticipation of the probable future and its chief technological aspects (futurology) is quite indicative of the "technologicalization" of our time.[2] Although some of these studies, such as the works of Ellul (1964) and Kahn and Wiener (1967) and some others, are of extraordinary interest and are relevant to an understanding of our time, it would be beyond the purpose of our present inquiry to attempt discussion of them.

It will suffice to mention three crucial questions involved in the problem of contemporary technology. The first is the question of whether or not the creation of a technological ecology and the development of techniques rendering technological advancement a built-in process, so that technology has become a self-developing system, has introduced an irreversible cultural mutation in the evolution of mankind. Jacques Ellul (1964) powerfully contends that this has occurred, with the result that man is becoming a dependent, if not a slave, of his now autonomously growing invention. This view is opposed by other writers, but it is interesting to observe, as in the typical case of Ferkiss' (1969), that the accepted basis for man's continued control of technology (technological man in place of the former industrial man) is further technological development. That is why some other students of technology, as McHale (1969), accept technological development as the most relevant evolutionary change in the overall biocultural evolution of mankind. The fact is that, whatever one's final judgment of Ellul's views, the possible effects of such innovations as cyborgs[3] and the widespread use of psychosociological conditioning may eventually either bring about a general debasement of man or introduce irreversible qualitative inequalities among men and societies. This possible—if still rather avoidable—catastrophic consequence of the general technologicalization of our time would completely change the conditions for societal and political development discussed in this book.

The second question is whether or not, contrary to the former assumption, technological civilization could be on the threshold of a nonscientific-technological reversal. Sorokin dealt with that question in its most general form, in his monumental study (1937–1941) on social and cultural dynamics.[4] He contends, as is well known, that the analysis of the facts of civilization gives empirical evidence to a law of alternation, in the course of history, of the basic understanding of truth, giving rise to distinct and successive cyclical cosmo-visions: the *ideational,* the *idealistic* or *integrated,* and the *sensate. Sensate culture* tends to evolve into *late sensate,* in which the empirical, pragmatic, and secular tendencies of the former are brought to their most extreme forms and manifestations. The resulting intensification of the dysfunctional aspects and the internal contradictions of the sensate culture finally causes it, in its late sensate form, to lose its capacity to operate as a meaningful and useful cultural framework and pattern for social life. As a consequence, the culture loses its historical viability, and gradually, out of the disintegration of that culture, a new cultural principle, of an ideational or eventually of an idealistic character, emerges. The new cyclical view introduced by Sorokin is also supported by Quigsley (1961), although in different terms. And, of course, there are the earlier cyclical theorists, such as Spengler (1947), Berdyaev (1968), Schubart (1938), and Toynbee (1934–1961).

It would be beyond the purposes of this book to discuss Sorokin's views on the historical alternation of cosmo-visions or to discuss the general question of cyclical changes in history.[5] Whatever the general validity of Sorokin's theory, the fact remains that our scientific-technological culture is being submitted to severe challenges, precisely because of its scientific-technological character. Such a challenge is unequivocally the nature of the hippie movements and of the tendencies to follow psychedelic practices, which are still growing rapidly. Should these tendencies and their implied life-style predominate in the next decades to the point of changing the now-prevailing scientific, pragmatic, acquisitive ethos into something that is the opposite of that ethos, the resulting historical trend, still unforeseeable, would hardly be compatible with the conditions required for the deliberate promotion of the development of societies and polities. In such an eventuality, as in the opposite case of a dehumanized and self-determined totalitarianism of technology, the developmental requirements discussed in the present book would be out of place.

The third question brings us back to the general problems of modern technology and the technology-man relationship. The question is not, however, whether man's creation has become his master but whether or not man's technological aggression on his natural ecosystem is causing irreparable damage to it. This is becoming the most serious and urgent of all the problems presented by the contemporary hypertrophy of technology. And the new science of ecology, just emerging from the systems analysis of all the aspects of man's natural environment, including its technological additions, stresses alarmingly that there is already only one generation that can save mankind from ecological disaster.[6]

The ecological problem

The ecological problem stems from the fact that the combined effects of a rapidly increasing population and still more rapidly increasing consumption of raw materials and production of pollutants are far surpassing the earth's material availability and its capacity to self-regenerate the biosphere.

The sheer increase in the human population is in itself a symptom and a cause of ecological disruption. As the first and only living being that has been able to overcome practically all the factors controlling its expansion as a species, man's unchecked procreation has increased the human population of the earth from about 5 million some 8,000 years ago, to 1 billion in 1850, 2 billion in 1930, and about 3.5 billion in 1970. If the current world rate of growth of 1.9 percent per year continues, the human population will reach more than 7 billion by 2007, more than 14 billion by 2044, and the incredible figure of 25 billion by 2070. According to Barry Commoner, the earth cannot hold more than about 7 billion people under the present conditions.

The consumption of raw materials by industrial and postindustrial man is extraordinary and ever-growing. Paul Ehrlich[7] estimates that each American child is fifty times more of a burden to the environment than each Indian child. Charles F. Park, Jr., observes that it is only because two-thirds of the world remains underdeveloped that the industrialized nations can maintain their existing patterns of consumption. If, as Park has remarked, the American per capita consumption of raw materials, such as iron, copper, lead, were to be reached by the whole world—which, incidentally, is the official purpose of all policies for the promotion of international development—the annual consumption of these materials would increase twelve to sixteen times, leading to the rapid exhaustion of the world's exploitable reserves.[8] Furthermore, the industrial wastes of modern societies, even if their polluting effects should be controlled, are quickly reaching physically unmanageable proportions. California alone contributes daily twenty pounds of solid waste per capita. On a similar worldwide scale such waste would represent more than 31 million metric tons per day, which would have to be buried in landfills in order to be disposed of.

Last but not least, the chemical pollution of air and water has already surpassed in many places the critical limits for the preservation of life and the spontaneous self-maintenance of the equilibrium of the ecological system, and it is seriously affecting the ecological balance of the oceans. The problem, as ecologists are coming to see it, lies in the fact that pollution is not only the result of industrial effluents, such as smoke and fluid, which could be filtered to a large extent, even if at a high cost, but is also the result of the undesired but unavoidable effects of pesticides, fertilizers, and the other devices that modern agricultural mass production is based on.[9]

The alternatives

A discussion of the three alternative futures, although constituting a fascinating and relevant subject, which could not be discarded from any serious attempt to study the possible evolution of our time, would not fit the narrower scope of the present inquiry. Let us only keep in mind the real possibility that our time may still follow one of those trends, however improbable any of them may appear today. In such a case, the developmental era inaugurated by the Renaissance would probably be led to an end. A dehumanized, self-sustained totalitarianism of technology would increase and rigidify the inequality among the various classes of men and societies, specializing each in its respective roles and levels. And a new nonscientific civilization, which would not be capable of maintaining the present population of the world and its levels of life, would be still less qualified for, and interested in, achieving any deliberate project of societal and political development, in the sense in which these concepts have been discussed in the present book. And a serious deterioration of the biosphere, if not prevented in time, would either bring about the annihilation of the human species or involve, as a condition for survival, a great debasement of the quality of life. This alternative would also block the chances for new developments.

It is more likely, however, as Kahn (1967) has suggested in his interesting speculations about the year 2000, that our civilization will be able to absorb the various conflicting trends caused by the acceleration of the technological revolution.[10] Noteworthy is his hypothesis about the possible transformation of the present class stratifications and conflicts (which basically imply a homogeneous cultural continuum along which the different situational levels are determined by the same basic criteria of power, wealth, and competence) into a differentiated psychocultural pattern. The new classes and conflicts (before the possible later occurrence of a new cultural synthesis) would center around distinct coexisting but not internally compatible cultural systems, all of them affluently supported by a superproductive automated economy. In ecologically conscious and protective societies, new stoics, oriented toward self-disciplined action and rationality, would be, as a new leading "class," coterminus with hippies, psychedelic introspective escapists, neomystics, and new sybarities who would form controlled subordinate "classes."

THE NEW INTERNATIONAL SYSTEM

Besides the revolutionary development of technology, as was observed at the beginning of the chapter, the second salient aspect of the contemporary world, which is not unconnected with the former, is the emergence of a new international system in the aftermath of World War II.

The cold war fog

This second aspect has not been as well or as widely understood as the first because of the dimming effects, until recently, of cold war involvement. Both the Soviet Union, with her policy of building buffer states, and the United States, with her policy of communism containment (these two policies having rapidly replaced the uneasy wartime cooperation between the two powers), have been too deeply enmeshed in the biases of their own interests and values to be able to discern the actual consequence of the cold war process. To a large extent, and in the context of an ideological haze that has only recently begun to be permeated by rational criticism, the same biases have affected, in different ways, the allies of these two countries and the intellectual community of the two conflicting camps.

Essentially, until the end of the 1950s the cold war was a mixture of conflicts between the United States and the Soviet Union, involving their real interests and their supposed intentions and aggravated by the religious-like self-righteousness of the contending ideologies. The conflict of real interests consisted, essentially, in the necessity each party felt to increase its own strength and world influence and to try to reduce the power and influence of the other party, in what appeared, initially, to be a two-party zero-sum game. The conflict of supposed intentions resulted because the Soviets' primary purpose of preventing new aggression, directly or indirectly based in Germany and on German power, led the Soviet Union to use all available means to build a protective wall of buffer states along its western border, a process that included the permanent division of Germany. From the Western point of view, these moves seemed to be the initial stage in an all-out invasion and occupation of Western Europe. As a defensive measure, the United States responded with a worldwide effort to build anti-Soviet alliances for the containment of "international communism," which was conceived of as the mischievous combination of Soviet military strength and Soviet-based promotion of world revolution. The religious-like self-righteousness of the contending ideologies—democracy versus socialism—resided in the fact that each party considered its own position grounded on intrinsically excellent principles, viewing its own shortcomings of state and practice as regrettable but accidental or temporary limitations or expediencies, and considering the other party's position as inherently founded on evil principles, from which necessarily derived all defects, both visible and concealed.

Some countries and some people (Nehru being the paramount example) refused to accept a partisan view of the cold war from its earliest days. It took some time for even the first neutralists to realize, however, that, independent of any Machiavellian plans that each of the two contending superpowers might have, what was really occurring in the world was the replacement of the old balance of power in the international system with a bipolar interimperial system. As a matter of fact, until the end of the 1950s the cold war, with its emphasis on ideological issues (and in spite of the neutralists' efforts at nonalignment) obscured the fact that both the American leadership of the "free world" and the Soviet leadership of "international socialism" were de facto oriented toward the control of their respective blocs much more than toward a worldwide crusade for sociopolitical principles.

Actually, the defeat of Germany and Japan and the exhaustion of Great Britain and France after World War II promoted the United States and the Soviet Union to the level of imperial superstates. Rather than a sudden and accidental result of World War II, and independent of any ideological connotation, the emergence of these two countries as superpowers and superstates was the direct consequence of their former development. In the nineteenth century some very sharp observers already realized that the era of European supremacy was coming to an end and that America and Russia would be the superpowers of the future.[11] First the Bismarckian and then the British Empire concealed the gradual shift of world power from Europe to its two extreme offspring. World War I and its aftermath could have made it clear that the balance of world power had already changed. But the ideological curtain raised, in spite of their sincerity, by Lenin and the anti-imperialism of the Russian Revolution and, in counterattack, by Wilson and his American crusading democratic self-determination for all peoples concealed the new realities of world power between the two world wars, as has been noted by Barraclough (1967, pp. 118 ff.). In this sense, it could be appropriately said that the cold war started in 1917.

In our time, however, the deadlock of the balance of terror has imposed the rules of coexistence on the superpowers, as the Soviets were the first to acknowledge publicly; and it has gradually uncovered the fact that the alignment of allies in two blocs, in a tendentiously world-embracing division, was not determined by the defensive reasons alleged for the original formation of the alliances as much as by the subjection of the allies in each bloc, although according to different modalities, to the imperial rule of their respective bloc leaders. This situation, as is well known, far from being historically original, is one of the typical ways in which empires have been built. The Delian League originated as an effort at collective defense against the Persians. Once Greek-Persian relations stabilized, however, in the deadlock following the failure of the latter to conquer the former, the league was gradually converted into the Athenian empire, and the former allies, which had voluntarily joined the league, became the subjects of Athenian hegemony. A similar process can be observed in the formation of the Roman Empire (the alliance with and support of Greek cities against Macedonia), although in that case, instead of a protracted military deadlock, Macedonia's Philip V was defeated by the Romans.

The attributing of an imperialistic aim to the other party has been one of the most typical cold war techniques. The nonpartisan and nonpolemical acknowledgment of the imperial character of both superstates is a more recent achievement of rational analysis. On the Soviet side, the invasion of Hungary in 1956 for the military suppression of the Nagy government was the first unequivocal brute fact of realpolitik, understood as such by the world at large and by the sympathizers of the Soviet cause. It was also a dramatic demonstration of the noninterference of the superpowers in the other's area of hegemony. The invasion of Czechoslovakia in 1968 and the subsequent imposition of a pro-Russian government in that country was just further irrefutable proof of the Soviet imperial management of its own bloc. The American side, enjoying a much more flexible administration of the affairs in its camp, was able to avoid the use of direct state violence for longer. The invasion of Guatemala, in 1954, by Carlos Castillo Armas' bands and the overthrow of Jacobo Arbenz's government, although unequivocally organized and supported by the U.S. Central Intelligence Agency, was still within the limits of a nonofficial paramilitary action. The 1961 invasion of Cuba, which culminated in the Bay of Pigs disaster, was already an operation directly supported by the United States government, as was openly acknowledged by President Kennedy. President Johnson's military occupation of the Dominican Republic, in 1965, was finally an overt official act of imperial rule.

Based on this evidence a broad debate began all over the world, in the course of the 1960s, about the true nature of the two superpowers, their international role, and the new characteristics of the international system. In Soviet Russia, under a regime based on the assumption of a "scientific" official truth, the debate has been repressed, as far as Russian imperialism is concerned, although the government has not been able to silence the courageous voices of some writers and some sincere believers in international socialist solidarity.[12] Similar repressions, this time concerning references to American imperialism, have occurred in the colonial-fascist satellites of the United States in Latin America and Southeast Asia. What is particularly interesting, however, is to follow the main lines of that debate in the United States and Europe. It is not necessary, for the purpose of this book, to review or summarize the already voluminous contributions to that discussion. Suffice it to make a brief mention of some of the most typical views that have been presented so far. These views deal with the emerging American empire and its position in the world, since they are the critical views of concerned American and European analysts. We will have the occasion, further on, to compare the American imperial position with the Soviet one.

In a very succinct way it could be said that the views on the emerging American empire, understood as a post–World War II phenomenon, although directly related to the preceding American history, might be classified in three major groups. The first includes those that, in one way or another, give predominant emphasis to more or less deterministic economic causes, from classic Marxism (the Lenin thesis) to neo-Marxism and various other economic-oriented formulations. The second comprehends, in an opposite position, those that see the event as the undeliberate result of contingent policies, which have been basically due to errors of judgment, could have been different, and still could, in principle, be reversed. The third group, finally, tends to see the emergence of the American empire as an historical process which, expressing the particular traits of the American society and culture in the past, resulted from the much more favorable development of the United States vis-à-vis the rest of the world.

The economic view

Lenin, as is well known, in continuation of Hobson (1965) and Hilferding (1923), gave the decisive formulation (1941) to the thesis that imperialism is the necessary outcome of advanced capitalism, since imperialism forces an enlargement of the markets for investing surplus capital and provides a favorable control of raw materials and of the supply of finished goods, thereby preserving and increasing the real level of demand and the margins of profit and interests. Lenin's thesis has been widely discussed since its publication, either in terms of its general validity or, more recently, in relation to the extent to which it could still provide a convenient explanation for post–World War II imperialism. In a recent discussion of Lenin's thesis, D. K. Fieldhouse (in Nadel and Curtis, eds. 1964), interpreting colonialism in a strict legal sense, contends that it does not correlate with the export of surplus capital. J. Gallagher and R. Robinson (Nadel and Curtis, eds, 1964, pp. 97–111), however, stressing the necessity for understanding imperialism in a broad sense, including informal ways of dependency, give evidence of the opposite, showing that the export of surplus capital, in a circular and self-reinforcing relationship including political intervention, is visibly a way both for obtaining higher benefits and for expanding trade and influence.

The most comprehensive attempt to apply Lenin's thesis to an economic interpretation of American current affairs was undertaken by Harry Magdoff, in several essays published in 1966 and 1968 and now collected, with a new introduction, in book form (1969). Magdoff's central argument is that the usual custom of analyzing the relevancy of economic facts through comparisons with a nation's GNP has completely concealed the real significance of American foreign interests for the United States. Because American exports represent less than 5 percent of her GNP and American foreign investments much less than 10 percent, it has been widely accepted that economic imperialism *is not* at the root of United States' foreign policy, only political aims. In his studies Magdoff shows that when more appropriate yardsticks are used, it becomes clear that foreign investment is crucial for the leading corporations, whose influence is also crucial in the shaping of foreign policy. The foreign market for American-owned firms and American exports represents two-fifths of the domestic output of United States farms, factories, and mines, not including the lease of patents. Moreover, the importance of that market is constantly and rapidly increasing, at a pace much faster than the domestic one, in terms of sales as well as in terms of earnings. Comparing domestic manufactures sales with sales by American-owned foreign firms plus exports, one finds that in 1950 domestic sales were $89.8 billion and foreign sales, $15.8 billion, and in 1964 the domestic sales were $203 billion and foreign sales, $57.9 billion. Given the index of 100 for 1950, domestic sales increased to 226, whereas exports and sales by American-owned foreign companies increased to 367. Earnings also grow much faster for American-owned foreign companies than for the domestic ones. From 1950 to 1965 profits for domestic firms increased, after taxes, from $21.7 billion to $36.1 billion, which represents a growth of 66.3 percent. Profits for the foreign companies, in the same period, increased from $2.1 billion to $7.8 billion, which represents a growth of 271.4 percent. (See Magdoff, 1969, chap. 5.)

Similar basic views are held by the New Left critics. One of the most articulate intellectuals of the young generation, Carl Oglesby,[13] a former national president of S.D.S. stresses (1968) the identity between the free world and the international markets controlled by the United States. "The Free World is the world economic area in which the American businessmen enjoy freedom of commercial maneuver. . . . The Free World itself is the American Empire" (p. 73). Like many other analysts of this imperial process, Oglesby emphasizes the correlation between external imperialism and domestic Caesarism. "Whether or not Americans will choose to be free is the transcendent political question, the one question that coordinates and subsumes all the searing issues of foreign and domestic policy. If Americans choose freedom, there can be no totalitarian America. And without a totalitarian America, there can be no American Empire" (p. 111).

The understanding of American post–World War II expansion as an imperial process moved by economic causes is not, in any way, limited to Marxist and neo-Marxist writers. For instance, let us mention only two interesting studies from among others. Organski's valuable and scholarly treatise on world politics (1964) and Julien's factually rich analysis of United States foreign activities (1968) agree in their understanding of the emergence of a new American empire, founded on the necessity for the ever-increasing economic expansion of the large American corporations. Organski, considering the new Russian as well as the new American empire, says: "classical colonialism is dying, but new forms of colonialism are arising to take its place. Nations that have won their nominal political independence are not necessarily free. No one observing the present international scene can miss the extension of Russian control over the nations of Eastern Europe, nor is it possible to overlook the control exercised by the United States over large portions of Central and South America as well as various outposts in Asia such as Formosa, South Korea, and Vietnam" (1964, p. 246). Today's colonialism, suggests Organski, presents three main forms: (1) *political colonies*, remnants of the old colonialism, (2) *economic dependencies*, typical of the new colonization of the underdeveloped world, and (3) *satellites* subject to political manipulation. Economic dependencies ultimately express an alliance between the dominant foreign country, interested in controlling new markets and sources of raw materials, and the local elite, interested in preserving its privileges and for that preservation exchanging national sovereignty for foreign protection (See Organski, 1964, p. 256.)

Claude Julien (1968) stresses the fact that the American empire resulted from the necessity to expand and consolidate American economic interests all over the world, particularly to control the sources of raw materials. Different from traditional empires, which are coextensive with a precise territorial domination, the American empire is without boundaries, because it is a functional, not a territorial empire. "*C'est ainsi que, pour répondre aux besoins de l'Amérique, est né l'empire qui ne ressemble à aucun autre, l'empire sans frontière*" (p. 19).[14]

The contingency view

Quite a different view is taken by the second group of analysts of American imperial expansion. This group assumes that contingent policies, due to errors of judgment, are the cause of the current imperial career of the United States, which in principle could still be reversed. Ronald Steel (1968) is probably the most typical and articulate representative of that position. "We are a people on whom the mantle of empire fits uneasily, who are not particularly adept at running colonies. Yet, by any conventional standards for judging such things, we are indeed an imperial power, possessed of an empire on which the sun truly never sets, an empire that embraces the entire Western Hemisphere, the world's two great oceans, and virtually all of the Eurasian land mass that is not in communist hands" (p. 15). This empire, however, was built undeliberately, as a consequence of a worldwide effort to contain communism, undertaken for the protection of the world, although that effort finally led to an empire itself. Steel contends, however, that world conditions have changed since the 1940s and that today the American empire should be converted into an international system of cooperation, both to conform to the new desires of the free world and for the best interests of the United States. "The task of our diplomacy, like the task of our society, in the period that lies ahead, is not to remake the world in the American image through wars of intervention and the maintenance of a benevolent empire, but to help achieve a period of stability in which a tolerable international order may be created in cooperation with others" (p. 354).

The military critics of American militarism and of America's imperial career should also be considered in this group. They are men who have devoted their lives to the hardships of military service not for purposes of power, personal or national, but for the defense of "the American liberal tradition," to use Louis Hartz's expression. These men have become deeply concerned about the escalated use of military power for objectives increasingly less connected and compatible with the liberal values which, originally, that power was to preserve. Generals James M. Gavin and David M. Shoup are probably the most typical and articulate representatives of these liberal military men. Gavin points out (1968) that the United States has become a prisoner of rigidified cold war concepts that are no longer applicable to present conditions. A realistic understanding of the conditions of our time shows the necessity for resuming efforts for international cooperation through the United Nations. Shoup, ex-commandant of the United States Marines and a former hero of the Battle of Tarawa, denounces (1969) the new American militarism and its danger to international order and domestic democracy. "America has become a militaristic and aggressive nation. Our massive and swift invasion of the Dominican Republic in 1965, concurrent with the rapid buildup of U.S. military power in Vietnam, constituted an impressive demonstration of America's readiness to execute military contingent plans and to seek military solutions to problems of political disorder and potential communist threats in the areas of our interest" (p. 51). After analyzing the causes of militarism in the United States, including the military-industrial complex, he recommends an all-out effort to curb militarism. "Militarism in America is in full bloom and promises a future of vigorous self-pollination—unless the blight of Vietnam reveals that militarism is more a poisonous weed than a glorious blossom" (p. 56).

Another line of critics who stress that current American foreign policy is based on incorrect assumptions and should be profoundly revised includes some of the most distinguished experts on American international relations, such as Ambassador George F. Kennan, Professor Hans Morgenthau, and Senator J. William Fulbright. Both as a theorist and as the major person responsible for the orientation of American foreign affairs after World War II, Kennan was the architect of Truman's containment policy. In his influential book on American diplomacy (1951), he provided the foundations for the containment doctrine. His basic assumptions, at that time and in that book, were that the Soviet Union, because of her ideology, which was committed to world revolution, and her domestic power base, which was supported by a pretense of scientific infallibility, would be constantly engaged in every possible form of operation to expand communism and to disrupt noncommunist societies. Concerning the Soviet ideology, he said, "It means that there can never be on Moscow's side any sincere assumption of a community of aims between the Soviet Union and the powers which are regarded as capitalism" (p. 95). And concerning the Soviet power base, he remarked, "The Soviet concept of power, which permits no focal point of organization outside the Party itself, requires that the Party leadership remain in theory the sole repository of truth" (p. 96). As the only possible remedy for permanent Soviet assault, he proposed permanent containment. "In these circumstances it is clear that the main element of any United States policy toward the Soviet Union must be that of a long-term, patient but firm and vigilant containment of Russian expansive tendencies" (p. 99). Fifteen years later, however, Kennan reviewed with critical eyes the present position of American foreign policy. We cannot, in these brief comments, assess the extent to which his present positions are the expectable consequences of the containment policy formulated and proposed by Kennan himself or a result of its inappropriate implementation. In a recent book on relations with the communist countries (1964), however, Kennan warns against "viewing communism as the only serious evil in the world" (p. 6). Stressing that important changes have taken place in the last decade, both inside Russia, which has become more liberal, and in the international system, which is becoming polycentric, he criticizes the rigidity of the West and its lack of understanding of, and appropriate response to, these current changes. (See 1964, pp. 36–54.)

A similar position is held by Hans Morgenthau, who was the most illustrious academic formulator of a foreign policy of limited containment in the late 1940s and early 1950s. (See Morgenthau, 1951, 1957, and 1960). In his most recent reassessment of American foreign policy (1969), he contends that the United States retains the containment view when conditions have changed completely. "In consequence, the U.S. has taken upon itself global responsibilities which it cannot discharge with a chance of success and which, if it were to try to discharge them, would entail its ruin" (p. 10). Such global commitments involve a double weakness: "the inability to distinguish between what is desirable and what is possible, and the inability to distinguish between what is desirable and what is essential" (p. 10). Morgenthau, who still refused to acknowledge, in the third edition of his classic *Politics Among Nations* (1960), the existence of an American empire, did become deeply concerned about the expansionist performance of the Johnson administration and about its theoretical support and the overt defense of an imperial policy by such scholars as Zbigniew Brzezinski (1967).[15] "What Great Britain and Russia were doing in the nineteenth century, the United States and the Soviet Union seem to be doing today" (1969, p. 118). The world of today, however, is completely different from the Victorian world. Neither an empire building nor a confrontation with the Soviets would bring any advantage to the United States nor would they even be feasible. The American paramountcy, contrary to what is supposed by Brzezinski, is not likely to last more than one decade, in the course of which, while the nuclear balance of terror will continue, the Soviets will probably be able to substantially reduce their present inferiority in mobile tactical forces. In the meantime, the United States should use her power to stabilize the world, so that when she is superseded, the world will be firmly on the road to development and international stability. (See Morgenthau, 1969, pp. 15–29.)

The position of Senator Fulbright, chairman of the Senate Committee on Foreign Relations and America's most noble and competent liberal voice, has been an indefatigable campaign for an American-led, peaceful, and consensual effort toward international cooperation. In a bright, scholarly, and passionate series of speeches and lectures, some of which were later organized, expanded, and put into book form (see particularly 1963, 1964, and 1966), he has expressed his views on current international affairs. His central thesis could be summarized in the statement that the United States has enough power to be comfortably safe and to sincerely help the world in becoming more prosperous, democratic, and peaceful, by accepting and supporting progressive revolution and movements in the third world, and exerting a self-discipline and restraint in the use of her power, according to the best traditions of the America of Lincoln and Adlai Stevenson. There is a second America, however, the America of Theodore Roosevelt and the superpatriots, which currently tends to prevail. This America is a terrible menace to the world and to herself. It is the America that, according to the beginning statements of one of Fulbright's best-known works, "is now at that historical point at which a great nation is in danger of losing its perspective on what exactly is within the realm of its power and what is beyond it. Other great nations, reaching this critical juncture, have aspired to too much and, by overextension of effort, have declined and then fallen" (1966, p. 3). Concluding, Fulbright says: "Gradually but unmistakably America is showing signs of that arrogance of power which has afflicted, weakened, and in some cases destroyed great nations in the past. In so doing we are not living up to our capacity and promise as a civilized example for the world; the measure of our falling short is the measure of the patriot's duty of dissent" (p. 22).

The historical-evolutionary view

Let us now consider some of the most typical views of the third group of analysts of the American empire: those who see its emergence as an historical process resulting, in various ways, from the evolution of American society in the contemporary world.

It is not surprising that the first scholarly formulation of an analogy between the Roman Empire and the contemporary expansion of the United States was made by Toynbee, whose monumental *Study of History* (1934–1961) was so influenced by his deep knowledge of the classical world and his understanding of diachronic similitudes among societies. In a series of academic lectures given from 1960 to 1962 and later gathered in book form (1962), Toynbee suggested a parallelism between the expansion of Rome and that of the United States, implying similar causes and analogous development. Contrasting America's present conservatism with her revolutionary origins and past, he observes: "By contrast, America is today the leader of a worldwide anti-revolutionary movement in defense of vested interests. She now stands for what Rome stood for. Rome consistently supported the rich against the poor in all foreign communities that fell under her sway; and, since the poor, so far, have always and everywhere been far more numerous than the rich, Rome's policy made for inequality, for injustice, and for the least happiness of the greatest number" (1962, pp. 92–93). Later, he says: "What has happened? The simplest account of it is, I suppose, that America has joined the minority" (p. 93). Ultimately, Toynbee sees the central line of events, both in Rome and in America, as follows: A patrician oligarchy achieves control of its society, expands that control territorially over an ever-increasing area of hegemony, and in that process, is transformed, as the dominant class of an imperial system, into a plutocratic-military oligarchy.

The same view was later expanded by Stringfellow Barr (1967), a classic scholar whose studies of Greek (1961) and Roman (1966) civilizations led him to analyze the analogies existing between Hellenism and Europe, and Romanism and America and to draw a parallel between the formation and expansion of the Roman Empire and the present-day United States. Other scholars, such as David Horowitz (1965 and 1967) and Neal Houghton and his contributors (1968) maintain the same line of thought, although the ones mentioned here focus more on the current American reality than on the Roman precedent. Horowitz stresses that the antirevolutionary preservation of the status quo is the central motivation of present American foreign policy. Not communism itself but the emancipatory revolution of the third world is what the United States is currently trying to contain, according to the basic argument of editor Houghton and his contributors. And this is because of the conversion of American society into a corporate state, under a business-military condominium.

Amaury de Riencourt has presented the most complete version of the Roman Empire analogy in his book (1968) on the historical formation and expansion of the American imperial drive and its current process and mechanism. Like most of the writers who share that view, he does not think the United States is alone in this imperial venture but shares it, in a competitive-cooperative way, with the Soviet Union, which he views as a sort of new Sassanid empire. "Very slowly, but surely, the shadowy outline of the Great Condominium is becoming visible; the vague contours of this worldwide understanding are beginning to emerge out of the fog which is surrounding us. The Condominium will be essentially a tacit alliance between two imperial *states*, not between irreconcilable and and competing ideologies. It will be the partial conjunction of their national and imperial interests that will serve as foundation for their virtual alliance which will, in no way, put an end to their rivalry" (p. 329).

Liska's views

In this context of increasing awareness of the Roman-like character of America's imperial expansion, with its implied or explicit overtones of reprobation, the works of George Liska, of the Washington Center of Foreign Policy Research of Johns Hopkins University, occupy a singular place and mark a shift in values, from accusatory or excusatory to frank commendation. In a series of very interesting scholarly studies (1967, 1968a, and 1968b), Liska starts with the assumption that empires are necessary historical products. They emerge in given conditions and represent, once these conditions exist, an inevitable outcome, which is not intrinsically good or bad, but whose meaning and value depend on several factors, including the internal character of the imperial society and the way its leadership is exercised. Actually, Liska believes, there are only five possible types of world order (1968b, p. 5), of which *imperial order* is one. *Contest for primacy, balance of power, functionalist institutionalization,* and *no centrally ordering power* are the four other possible types. In our time, as a result of World War II and the following events, the superpowers became imperial states, but only recently, due to a series of events (including the Vietnam misadventure), have their imperial character and their interempire relations become impossible to conceal. The coexistence of a revival of nationalism, with the gradual mounting of a new interimperial order, and the spread of industrialism as a worldwide aspiration delayed "the perception of anything like a hegemonial threat from the United States to the national independence of the revived or newly-created members of the international system" (1967, p. 6). And here there is a similitude with the conflict between France and the Habsburg empire in which Charles V did not appear as the real challenge until late in the conflict.

Liska's view of the new empires is different from Lenin's, since in Liska's view political, rather than economic motives, are their driving force. "An 'empire' is a state exceeding other states in size, scope, salience, and sense of task" (1967, p. 9). The concept of empire, properly used, should mean, according to Liska, a superstate rather than a colonial power. The Roman Empire is the paradigm. America is a modern equivalent of the Roman Empire. Soviet Russia is a new Macedonia (instead of the Sassanid analogy of de Riencourt), and the Parthian equivalence is given to China. Historical, as well as present, empires have arisen for several reasons, within a limited range of typological possibilities. Whatever the cause, the imperial condition is achieved when the international order ceases to depend on the distribution of antagonistic power in a reciprocally countervailing pattern, but rests, in the final analysis, on the widely shared presumption of the ultimate controlling power of the imperial states. (See 1967, pp. 36–45.)

Liska's analysis of the main imperial traits of America today (1967), including the distinction between the imperial state, as an objective international condition, and imperialism, as a design, led him to a study of the present international system, to which his two subsequent books are devoted (1968a and 1968b). He considers it a bipolar, unifocal, and bisegmented system, evolving, uncertainly, into a multipolar one. (See 1967, p. 36 and 1968a, p. 8.) It is bipolar, in military strategic terms, because of the presently exclusive imperial features of the two superpowers and their mutual nuclear containment. It is unifocal because only the United States has become a global primary power (or empire), without, however, achieving paramountcy in all areas. It is bisegmented because of the developmental cleavage between the north and the south. And it is uncertainly evolving into multipolarity because of the capabilities for the autonomy of some countries and for their further development into local primacy, actually or potentially retained by some other international actors. Liska distinguishes two main areas: one, in which the issue of primacy is settled, comprehending the Western hemisphere and Eastern Europe and the other comprehending the areas where that issue is not yet settled. The latter should be subdivided into three sectors: (1) Western Europe, where primacy possibilities may still revert in favor of either the United States, the local powers, or the Soviet Union in an all-European framework, (2) Southeast Asia, where primacy is undecided and could be obtained by China, Japan, India, the Soviet Union, or Australia with American backing, and (3) Africa, where there is a tendency toward subregionalization of the (a) north, under the primacy of Algeria and the United Arab Republic, (b) several tropical zones, under various possible influences, and (c) south, under white South African primacy.

Liska contends that neutralism has exhausted its chance in the second area, where primacy is not settled, but that nonalignment or loose alignment has become possible in the Western hemisphere, as in the cases of France, Rumania, and Cuba. The possibilities for autonomy in the latter area are determined by the characteristics of that autonomy vis-à-vis the interests and possible action of the superpowers. "Autonomy is not hegemony; and both differ from the intermediate status of a country or region contended over by two or more outside powers" (1968a, p. 44). Autonomy, however, requires two basic conditions. Externally, the situation must be such that intervention by a third great power would require an agreement with the primary power, bringing great powers to mutual restraint. Internally, the autonomous country or system needs either to have a second-strike capability or to lack nuclear armament. Destabilizing nuclear capability would attract concerted foreign intervention. Autonomy, therefore, "requires a decent measure of self-discipline in foreign policy" (p. 45).

Liska's last book (1968b) is both a synthesis of his main views on the present international system and a strategic guide for American action, written with the same subjective perspective as Machiavelli's *The Prince*, which was intended to be a theory on the international environment of Italian Renaissance cities and a strategy for Italian unity and supremacy. Liska's central message is that the international system has become an interimperial system. Whatever the remaining possibilities in the new system for the preservation of certain areas of autonomy and local primacy, the relations between the United States and the Soviet

Union have acquired an irreversible interimperial character, in which a power vacuum is impossible. Each of the imperial states, therefore, is confronted with a double constraint. On the one hand, any decrease in either's international and overall influence, in any relevant sense, favors the expansion of the other's influence. On the other hand, each of the imperial states must contribute to the maintenance of world order (interimperial order), in a process that involves, for their respective areas of primacy, a consensual-coercive rule of the area's affairs (intraimperial order). In these conditions, the American empire, which is still an objective process, occurring without appropriate acknowledgment by the American people and, to a large extent, against their values and wishes, must become an accepted fact and, more than that, an accepted mission. The empire cannot be ruled in a casual and unconscious way (and with the employment of means of merely national scope), and it cannot be given up by the Americans without falling into inevitable decay and, ultimately, submission to foreign rule. The empire must be acknowledged as an overall historical stage and managed in the most enlightened but efficient[16] way for the mutual benefit of the American people and the whole world.

Discussing, in general, the "nation or empire" alternative for the United States and, in the process, Liska's views, Robert Tucker, also of the Washington Center of Foreign Policy Research, stresses (1968) the central point of that alternative: the relationship between national security and national purpose. Security requirements are constantly invoked for the expansion of military facilities and for the extension of the United States' capability through all forms of overseas territorial or functional control. National security, however, is a complex concept, which may be stretched from a minimum of protecting the national territory from foreign attack to the maximum of achieving the capacity to prevent the formation of, or to destroy, any potentially inimical force anywhere in the world. What limit of national security should be adopted by the United States? The answer, observes Tucker, depends on how the United States understands its national purpose. It is purpose that determines the character of the nation and the extent of its commitments, which in turn determine the requirements of national security. Starting with this basic clarification, Tucker suggests that the United States has shifted its purpose and commitment from Truman's containment to world order, moved by the very success of the former enterprise. "World order is, in practice, containment writ large" (1968, p. 149). But in American terms "world order" is an euphemism for the American empire. Imperium was not deliberately acquired by the United States, but, now that it has been acquired, it is being deliberately preserved. Among the consequences of imperium, we have that maintaining order among states requires maintaining order within, which makes Vietnams unavoidable. That consequence, however, implies an imperialism that is contrary to American feelings and to the United States' basic purpose; the universalization of the American experiment would be betrayed by imperialism. Concluding his analysis, Tucker suggests that the new American purpose (a world order that is identical to the American empire) is no longer relevant for the world which, formerly attracted by the American experiment, as the great democratic society, now repeals American imperialism. He also contends that the United States should acknowledge the internal and external contradictions presently existing between her imperial expansion and her permanent commitment to the great democratic society, and solve these contradictions by returning to the framework of the nation and reorganizing her security requirements accordingly.

A critical appraisal

An extensive discussion of the three groups interpreting the emerging American empire and of the several views on the matter would drive us too far from the central theme of this book. It will suffice to remark that the historical-evolutionary interpretation, because it understands the process in its broad historical framework, containing all the past and present factors that have brought about the current expansion of American power and influence, and compares that expansion with the volution of the other parts of the world, is consequently the most comprehensive and the one that provides the best explanation of that process. The historical explanation, however, including among its heuristic merits the analogy with the Roman Empire—provided the analogy is used in a non-mechanistic and isomorphic way—does not imply the deterministic contents introduced by some writers partaking that view, such as de Riencourt; nor does it exclude the large amount of truth contained in the two other kinds of explanation.

Liska I would suggest, is basically right in presenting the emergence of empires, including the American empire, as a process resulting from the comparative success of a society, vis-à-vis her contemporaries, in a struggle for a broader control over their respective environments, associated with several kinds of internal and external impulses for imperial expansion. He is also right in observing that many of these impulses may have dysfunctional characteristics, either with respect to the expanding society, as was the case when the Roman society became an oligarchy, or with respect to the dominant societies, as, once again, was the case in most of the Roman provinces, at least in many phases of their annexation to the empire. So, in the case of the United States, it is undeniable that economic motives, although not as exclusively as assumed by some writers, have been a determining factor in the American imperial process, including the propensity, mentioned by many, to convert communism containment into an American-controlled world order and to identify the free world with the world where American business is free from social controls.

It is also true, as pointed out by the writers holding the contingency views, that there have been many casual aspects to the building of the American empire, founded on errors of judgment. The building of the American imperium would have been impossible without the support of American public opinion. Until recently, that support has been given to it, but not in the name and for the purpose of imperium; rather it has been given in the name and for the purpose of defending liberal values and protecting the nation's security. This is so much so that, once the imperial character of present American commitments was uncovered with the Vietnam crisis, the national consensus was broken, public support withdrawn, and the imperial purpose questioned and contested by a very large plurality, if not majority, of the American people. This basic point admitted, however, it should be acknowledged that the contingent character of the American empire has been unduly stressed by most writers of that group, particularly Steel. As Tucker has pointed out, imperium, if undeliberately acquired, is being deliberately preserved. Moreover, the empire building was only accidental as far as certain specific policies are concerned. These policies could have been different if other men or groups, also belonging to the ruling circle, had been in office. Considered as a tendency and a trend, however, imperium was the necessary (not deterministically) consequence of the character (oligopolistic) and the success (through self-improving competition) of American capitalism, in particular, and in general of certain other basic traits (many expressing personal and social qualities) of American society and culture.

Contrary, therefore, to the views of most of the writers in this group and also of Tucker, the current reality of the American empire cannot be renounced merely through the adoption, in the near future, of enlightened policies by enlightened men. If we assume, for the purpose of the present discussion, (1) that the contradiction between imperium, as a contingent framework, and the great democratic society, as a permanent national goal, could be solved by returning to the framework of the nation and (2) that a corresponding reduction in the military requirements could be maintained with a comfortable margin of safety for the security of the nation, it is not true that simply more enlightened decisions could bring about that change. *The fact is that there is today—whatever the historical causes—an overall necessary interdependence between the present structure of the American society and its imperial character.* Only deep structural changes, therefore, modifying the present regimes of participation, property, values, and power in a more sweeping way than what occurred as a result, in the remote American past, of the Jacksonian revolution and, more recently, of the New Deal, could bring about that consequence. That such deep changes are not likely to occur seems to be a reasonable assumption, although they are not impossible—particularly in view of the current ethical revolution of the youth and of the emergence of new national leaders, such as McGovern.

The interimperial system

At this point what needs to be studied first is the new interimperial system, which has finally replaced the international balance-of-power system generated after the Napoleonic wars. Then what we require is an analysis of the consequences of the emerging interimperial system for the present and foreseeable possibilities of political and overall national development of the nonimperial societies.

Liska's sketch of the present world order, as previously summarized, presents, in my opinion, a convenient basis for the discussion of the emerging interimperial system. This system presents, now and for the foreseeable future, an international order of stratification in which there are four classes of societal actors.

The first class corresponds to actors of *general primacy*, which involves the inexpugnability of the concerned actor's core territory, a very broad regional paramountcy, and a general world predominance in areas or sectors that are not specifically protected. General primacy might eventually become a general paramountcy, in the unlikely case that the second level of contending powers should fail to achieve regional primacy, either because of internal disruptions or because of a technological-military gap leading to the loss of minimally sufficient second-strike capability. The second class corresponds to actors of *regional primacy*, which involves the inexpugnability of the concerned actor's core territory, a narrower regional paramountcy, and a relevant world influence. The third class corresponds to actors with *autonomy*, which involves, instead of the inexpugnability of the actor's core territory, the enjoyment of a situation in which, independent of the will of third actors, aggression against the core territory would involve very high costs to any potential aggressor. That situation is associated with conditions assuring, for the concerned actor, an autonomous capability for making domestically relevant decisions and a basic endogeny of its factors of societal development. The fourth class corresponds to actors of *dependency*, which is characterized by less than minimally sufficient enjoyment of the conditions inherent in the higher classes and a resulting internationally subordinate status and role.

This interimperial system is a dynamic one, in which the actors' positions are changeable for better or for worse, within certain limits. The foreseeable historical course for the concerned actors can be considered in three major stages: (1) the present one, which is leading to the culmination of the processes started after the World War I, (2) the end of the current century, and (3) the further future. On the basis of the structural conditions[17] of the concerned actor and its comparative position, vis-à-vis the other actors, in the present stage, the course and resulting position of each actor in the next stage can be forecasted in terms of the more probable and the less probable set of alternatives. It should be assumed, however, that, as a rule, the margin of class variation will decrease as an actor passes from the first (present) stage to the second (end of this century) and from this one to the third (beyond 2000). This is due to the fact that the distance between actors following courses of different class levels tends to increase and become unsurpassable. For all practical purposes, therefore, the stratification order that will probably be obtained in the second stage (with the exceptions of China and Western Europe, which will be discussed later) will tend to prevail in the third. For the same reason, the classification order that will probably be obtained in the third stage will tend to be coextensive with the duration of the entire interimperial system that is now emerging.

The societal actors to be considered in that system, although not necessarily excluding the possibility of future changes resulting from new societal integrations or disintegrations, will be either (1) those that are already existing as independent countries or (2) the actually or potentially integrated or coordinated groups of countries that are sufficiently unified to keep an international behavior functionally comparable to that of the independent countries. There is no point, for the purpose of the present discussion, in examining, one by one, the countries or groups of countries (such as an enlarged list of the members of the United Nations) that might be considered actors in the interimperial system today. We can, taking into account the characteristics of our four classes of international stratification, limit our consideration to the countries or groups of countries that presently present, or may present before the end of the century, a reasonable possibility of fitting the requirements of the three higher classes. For the other countries, we can reserve the generic designation the "rest of the world." Excluding these residual actors, we will be limited to nine actors. Some, such as the United States, Soviet Russia, China, Japan, India, and Indonesia, are presently single independent countries. The others, such as Western Europe, Latin America, and the Arab world (of North Africa), are groups of countries that have achieved variable degrees of integration or mutual coordination and hopefully assume that before the end of the century they will obtain a higher degree of integration, sufficient to enable them to operate as a basic unit in the international arena. In the case of these groups of countries, however, the question of whether or not they will achieve their integration as well as the exact indication of which will be the final partners in each group must be kept open. Western Europe may or may not come to form an operative union, incorporating one, some, or all the countries of the free-trade area. Although less likely it may also come to have a pan-European arrangement, including Eastern Europe and the Soviet Union, in which case, however, it would share the status of the latter, although substantially reinforcing it. The same sort of variations, within their respective conditions, apply to Latin America and the Arab world. It is necessary to stress that this picture is an approximation. A more precise classification of the actors in the system would require a discussion of the positions of such countries as Canada, Pakistan, and Australia, which have been summarily included in the residual group of the rest of the world, but have enough characteristics to be differentiated from most of the other residual actors. It would also require an analysis of the isolated chance of the survival, if a Latin American integration should fail, of a semicontinental country, like Brazil, and of the two other large countries of the region, Argentina and Mexico. Moreover, the United Nations, which may acquire more autonomy of action in the future, should also be mentioned, although it would never be an independent actor, itself.

With these explanations we can now consider the picture that would result from the adoption of our criteria and assumptions concerning the interimperial system in the three stages. As indicated in Table 35, we have that in the present situation the United States enjoys the status of general primacy and the Soviet Union of regional primacy. The third stratification class, autonomy, includes only China, Japan, and Western Europe. The fourth class, dependency, includes, in addition to the "rest of the world," Latin America, India, the Arab world, and Indonesia.

As has been observed, the next stage, corresponding to the end of the century, is likely to present a similar picture. Some possible, although less likely variations, would be: (1) Western Europe's early fall into dependency, vis-à-vis the

Table 35 *The Emerging Interimperial System*

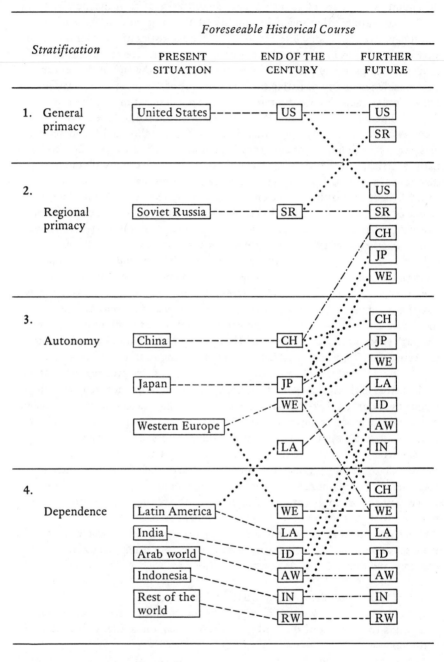

Key: — — — — — — Very probable course

    — · — · — · — Probable course or alternative

    · · · · · · · · · · Least probable alternative

United States, and Latin America's early obtention of autonomy. In both cases, the occurrence of that less probable course in the second stage would imply, in turn, a very high probability of the continuation of the new relative position in the third stage. This would mean that the early decay of Western European autonomy, now the less probable course, would very probably consolidate its dependency in the third stage. And Latin America's obtention of autonomy, again the now less probable course, would very probably consolidate her subsequent autonomy in the third stage.

The third stage of our picture, corresponding to the next century, presents a wider general possibility of change, although, with two exceptions, the highest probability is still the continuation of status. There is a wider possibility of change because the possible cumulative effects of societal development would bring certain actors, which remain in the fourth class in stage 2, up to the next higher class in stage 3. Conversely, the possibility, if smaller, of insufficient development would cause the relative position of some actors to deteriorate in stage 3.

It is interesting to observe, in terms of relative likelihood, the special cases of China and Western Europe in the transition from stage 2 to stage 3. In that transition, as in the former, most actors are likely to keep their relative positions. This is not so, however, for China and Western Europe. In the decades preceding stage 3 China is likely to accumulate enough capital, technology, and popular education to jump to the class of regional primacy in the next century. Conversely, Western Europe, whose level of integration is likely to remain low because of entrenched national parochialism, which can hardly be overcome through consensual ways, will probably not obtain the conditions necessary for attaining regional primacy. In that hypothesis, it is more likely that Western Europe will be attracted by some comfortable and dignified form of dependency[18] rather than mobilize the effort necessary to preserve her autonomy.

General consequences

The above discussion and the picture shown in Table 35 provide some indications of the consequences of the new interimperial system for the political and the overall national development of the underdeveloped countries of today.

The main general consequence resulting from the emerging interimperial system is a very severe reduction of the possibilities for free maneuvering in the international arena for all actors except, within limits, for the ones enjoying general primacy and, in a restricted way, for the ones enjoying regional primacy. The inexpugnability and the general world predominance provided by general primacy grants to the actor enjoying it a very broad ambit of choices and a very large margin of tolerance for errors, although within limits. Its capacity for imposing policies in its own area of paramountcy (Latin America for the United States) and for predominating in all areas and sectors of the world that are not specifically protected by regional primacies or consolidated autonomies gives a complete imperial character to that actor. Regional primacy, although affording only a moderate world influence (mainly derived from the actors' bargaining capacity, vis-à-vis each other and the actor enjoying general primacy), assures paramountcy in a narrower area (Eastern Europe for the Soviet Union), which is also of an imperial character. Autonomy once it is consolidated, allows a discrete world capacity for bargaining, but its main consequence is the protection of the concerned actor's core territory and, eventually, of some overseas functional sectors (such as certain branches of commerce or of cultural influence) from easy or arbitrary interference from powers enjoying regional or general primacy. Autonomy, therefore, is essentially related to domestic self-determination and to a self-sustained capability for maintaining the country's inherent national and societal identity and development. *Autonomy, therefore, in the precise sense used here, is the necessary condition for national viability in the interimperial system.*

In that situation only those actors actually or potentially enjoying conditions for autonomy are capable of deliberately carrying out their own political and societal development. For actors potentially capable of enjoying autonomy, therefore, the crucial problem is how to obtain it, and for actors already enjoying it the problem is how to maintain it. In the present concrete historical conditions, these two problems concern the seven actors in the third and fourth classes in Table 35. In order of stratification they are China, Japan, and Western Europe, on the one hand, and Latin America, India, the Arab world, and Indonesia, on the other hand. The former face the problem of maintaining and consolidating their present autonomy. The latter face the problem of converting their potential autonomy into an actual one while they still enjoy that possibility. The next three decades are widely accepted by most writers as the time period in which these problems will have to be solved.[19]

It would be interesting, but too far from the central purpose of this book, to examine, one by one, the main problems confronted by each of these seven actors. We will have the opportunity, in the final part of this book, to discuss more closely the problems of Latin America. Let us now just consider, in a general way, the autonomy problem of these seven actors. That problem could be summarized as follows: Domestically, all of these actors, within their peculiar conditions, are confronted with the necessity for performing the policies necessary to assure the minimal pace of societal integration and development to maintain, if they belong to the third class, or to achieve, if they belong to the fourth class, their own self-sustained autonomous and basically endogenous national development. Internationally, they have to maneuver in a way that will enlarge or maintain their respective margin of international permissibility, which is a necessary requirement for their autonomous development. There is a circular causation between autonomous development and sufficient international permissibility. The former creates domestic conditions for the latter, which, in turn, is a prerequisite of the former.

The trouble with this self-reinforcing circular causality is that those actors that are actually or potentially autonomous are submitted to strong pressures from the actors enjoying general and regional primacy, and they have to take these pressures into account, to varying extents, both for external and for domestic reasons. In a sense China and Indonesia represent extreme cases. In China the internal political success of Mao and his followers required the adoption of ideological positions and policies that have driven the country to the extreme limits of her (rather wide) international permissibility, particularly vis-à-vis the Soviet Union. The impending danger of preemptive Soviet action (with or without United States' agreement), aimed at the early elimination of China's incipient nuclear capability, represents a serious constraint on her capacity for autonomous development. In Indonesia, at the opposite end of the spectrum, the current military government has been so dependent on American support and assistance that in order to prevent the impending seizure of central power by the Communist party the government renounced the country's former neutralist autonomy, in conditions that may preclude its future reassumption.

Japan and Western Europe are confronted with particular difficulties involving the reconciliation of their autonomy with their tight economic relationship with the United States. Japan succeeded admirably in getting rid of the internal control of her economy by American business, after the period of military occupation, but she depends on the American market—and so on the conditions of access to it—for an increasing part of her production. Western Europe is freer in terms of international trade, but is less capable of achieving her own domestic autonomy, because of the inextricable intimate (and dependent) association between her and the American business system.

India is enjoying a substantially broad margin of international permissibility but, domestically, seems quite unable to overcome her underdevelopment problems. In addition to the tremendous complexity of those problems, India's deficient level of political integration, both horizontally and vertically, does not allow the central government to concentrate as much power and to adopt as thorough a policy as would be minimally required for the successful promotion of her development.

The Arab world also enjoys a large margin of international permissibility, as far as the two superpowers are directly concerned, because of its frontier position in relation to both; but it has been stopped, internally, by its difficulties in achieving a minimally sufficient horizontal integration among the concerned countries, and vertical integration of the several layers in their respective populations. Compounding these difficulties, to an extent that seems close to the point of insolubility, the Arab world has been driven (by its own lack of vertical integration) to a suicidal confrontation with Israel.[20] In that process, the Arab countries are exhausting all their national energies and resources, increasing their dependency on the Soviet Union, and becoming, at the probable cost of their historical survival, a mere instrument and arena for an indirect limited confrontation of power and influence between the United States and the Soviet Union.

The case of Latin America

Latin America enjoys the advantage of being the most developed of the underdeveloped areas, but the problems of her autonomous development combine, in a sense, the several shortcomings experienced by the previously mentioned actors. Like Western Europe, but in far worse conditions, she suffers the paralyzing effects resulting from the internal control of her economic system by American business. Like India, she does not seem to have succeeded in accumulating enough central power and political commitment to meet the problems of her underdevelopment. Like the Arab world, the horizontal integration among the Latin American countries and the vertical integration of their own populations are well below the minimum level required for efficient action. And like Indonesia, she buys American support (with the possibly extendible exception of Peru) for her military regimes at the price of renouncing her possible margin of international autonomy.

This last aspect of the Latin American situation deserves a brief additional comment. One of the peculiar distinctions between the characteristics of the paramountcy of the United States and that of the Soviet Union, vis-à-vis their respective areas of unchecked hegemony (Latin America and Eastern Europe), is the fact that the former is all-pervasive but not monolithic, whereas the latter is monolithic but sectorally restricted. Because of the pluralistic character of the American society and the multilinear relationships existing among its subsystems and their integrating social groups, the American hegemony over the Latin American countries tends to be very broad, all-pervasive, internally co-opted by several domestic groups, but no externally unified, except in moments of crisis or over issues concerning very relevant strategic interests. Conversely, Soviet hegemony over Eastern Europe is monolithic, in the sense of being externally unified and exercised in a basically coherent form, through tight and concentrated lines of command from government to government, and official party to official party. The extent of Soviet internal control, however, over the nonpolitical subsystems and groups of the dominated countries is very small or nonexistent and effectively contained by deliberate nationalist resistance.

The consequence of this difference in control is that in Latin America the internal propensities for the actual exercise of autonomy are small, inconsistent, and sporadic, although the potential margin of international permissibility is sufficiently broad; and in Eastern Europe the internal propensities for the actual exercise of autonomy are large, consistent, and continuous, although the potential margin of international permissibility is the smallest enjoyed today by any large group of countries in the world. The question remains open, without doubt, concerning the extent to which a substantial change in the internal conditions in Latin America would bring about a corresponding tightening of its potential margin of international permissibility. That problem will be dealt with in the next and final part of this book. The fact remains, however, that the inherent character of the American society and of its domination over the Latin American countries involves a minimum content of pluralism and contradictions that tends to keep open a margin of international permissibility, which would probably be sufficient, in the next decades, to let Latin America achieve an autonomous development, within limits and under certain conditions. The problem facing the Latin American countries, however, given the existing relationship between their societies and the American one, lies in their particular difficulty in concentrating enough political power and determination to undertake substantial changes.

Should the concentration of that political power and determination be achieved—as occurred for a while in Argentina and Brazil and has occurred in Peru and Chile—Latin America's potential margin of international permissibility would probably prove sufficient, in spite of American regional paramountcy, to allow an autonomous development of the area and its integrating countries. Given the nonmonolithic character of the American society and, as a consequence, of the American empire, its tolerance of (not deliberate openness to) the existence of areas of autonomy within the empire can be obtained through the use of appropriate policies on the part of some (not all and not even many) of the intraimperial countries. The crucial factor in that respect—besides the existence of a better-than-critical potential international permissibility—is the unequivocal adoption and consistent maintenance on the part of the concerned country of some basic strategic distinctions between American economic and military interests. American military and economic interests cannot be challenged simultaneously in the areas of the empire's paramountcy, such as Latin America. Any such challenge would ultimately be met, if need be, by military intervention. But American internal economic control can be challenged (within limits) and overcome, particularly by gradual forms of nationalization, whenever the autonomy thereby obtained is clearly not used to reinforce the influence of other superpowers or, in general, in ways implying politico-military risks to the United States. In some cases, nationalization that excludes politico-military risks to the United States can be procured in pure legal and economic terms, such as the disappropriation of concerns or their legal restriction to national firms. In other cases, alternative forms of access to particularly relevant raw materials, installations, or sites will have to be provided through complementary arrangements with the United States. Finally, in some cases, reliable political assurances will have to be given to the United States to prevent consequential loss of American influence in the international arena or to compensate the United States for her economic interests. The nonmonolithic character of the American empire, compared to the Soviet (and for that matter to the Roman Empire), allows more room for strategically well-balanced autonomistic policies. Moreover, for the time being and the near future, since the American empire is not yet acknowledged or accepted by the American people and, consequently, is not yet managed with subjective understanding and a deliberate imperial purpose supported by appropriate imperial instruments, the possibility for autonomistic policies are particularly enhanced.

It is essential to consider the time factor and the resulting problem of the historical deadline, insofar as they concern the remaining room for international permissibility allowing intraimperial countries to achieve an autonomous development and also allowing some presently autonomous international actors to preserve their autonomy. Generally, when it is applied to processes of national development, the time factor represents the basic period necessary for achieving significant structural changes. So, for instance, in the historical cases of successful processes of development, formerly discussed in Chapter 12, overall significant changes have been achieved, as a rule, in a period of about three decades. Significant intermediate changes are observable in smaller periods of ten or five years. These intervals correspond, in the decision-making phase, to the periods of time necessary, in political, economic, and scientific and technological terms, to assess the problems involved, study alternative solutions, and make decisions; in the subsequent phase, they correspond to the time period necessary to implement the decisions in organizational and material terms.[21] For developmental processes, however, the time factor also represents the basic time limits, or deadlines, after which tasks that could have been accomplished formerly become practically or totally unfeasible, due to structural changes in the relevant conditions.

Conditions for an action may change in various ways and for various reasons. When such changes substantially affect the motivation of the concerned actors, their means of action, or the circumstances under which that action would have been possible, the possibility of performing that action may be severely impaired or altogether prevented. The occurrence of such changes represents the advent of a deadline, after which the concerned action is no longer realizable.

There are very clear indications that if the Latin American countries (that is, the countries in the group with critical masses, Brazil, Argentina, and Mexico) do not succeed in achieving their autonomous development in the course of the next three decades, the conditions for that achievement will rapidly decline and disappear. The first essential condition that is likely to disappear, if autonomous development is not reached by the end of the current century, is the motivation of the elite. The crucial problem in Latin America, as will be studied in Book III, is the weakness of Latin American elite in performing its elite functions: leadership and excellence of performance. As autonomous development is delayed, the Latin American elites try to compensate for the inconveniences of underdevelopment by multiplying, more by their own pull than by American pressure, all sorts of dependent links with the United States. If that process continues for another thirty-year period, all the relevant centers of decision and performance, as well as all the relevant factors of action and production, will be located in or dependent on the United States. This will involve the suppression of the second essential condition. Whatever the eventually surviving aspirations for autonomy, all the necessary means for its achievement will have become unavailable. And although in that picture, as will be later discussed in this book, the conditions for a revolutionary mass insurrection, under the leadership of the Latin American counterelite, will be extremely enhanced, the possibilities of achieving autonomous development through a Chinese-like revolution may have to be considered very cautiously, given the incredible means of mass control that will tend to be available, in the future, for the preservation of the status quo within the frontiers of the new emerging empires.

Forms and consequences of dependence

A final point, which needs to be examined, in connection with the current and foreseeable historical conditions for the promotion of national development, concerns the consequences of the failure to achieve it before the precluding deadlines. What is wrong with dependency, in the new conditions of the world? Can it not be assumed that the new empires, once consolidated within their own boundaries and more or less settled in their interimperial relations, might be very livable systems, similar to the Roman Empire from Augustus to Marcus Aurelius?

There are obvious limits to the scientific use of historical analogies and in the predictive possibilities of futurology. Nobody can really state what life is likely to be like in the empires of the twenty-first century. A new social humanism, supported by fabulous technological means, as has been discussed, is one of the possibilities of the future, as well as its Ellulian reverse. The analogy with the golden days of the Roman Empire should call our attention to the fact that those days were golden for a small minority of urban middle-class people, who were surrounded by the miserable plebs and millions of working slaves. Insofar as dependency in the next century is concerned, two basic remarks can be made about what dependency is in the present and has been in the recent past and about what the process of rapid modernization has represented for the unskilled sectors of dependent populations.

Very briefly, it can be said that today we can see four kinds of dependency, in international terms.[22] The first is *colonial* dependency, which represents a remainder of the European mercantile expansion, which began with the Renaissance and has almost disappeared since World War II. The second is *neocolonial* dependency, which is characterized by a shift from formal to informal dependency and a change in emphasis from legal and institutional forms of dependency to economic and technological ones. The third is *satellite* dependency, which is characterized by informal but actual political subordination to a superpower, within the framework of the emerging intraimperial order. The fourth, finally, is *provincial* dependency, which still does not exist, in its modern version, but which appears to be the last phase in the evolution of the current forms of satellitism and is likely to be the future intraimperial form of dependency.

What is particularly interesting about these four forms of dependency is the fact that they present clear characteristics of inherent successiveness. As a matter of fact, dependency has historically begun in the colonial form. The Iberian countries in the fifteenth century, followed by the Low Countries, England, and France, established, both with force and without, colonies in the Americas, Africa, and Asia. These colonies continued to serve the interests of the metropolitan countries after the industrail revolution, following the classic pattern of supplying raw materials and importing finished industrial goods. Unlike the independence of the American colonies, which was won in the eighteenth and early nineteenth centuries through effective military victories, most of the European ex-colonies in Africa and Asia have recently been granted independence.

Far from expressing a process of decolonization, as has been so prematurely advanced, that independence only characterizes a change in the ways of exploitation. Classic colonialism involves unnecessary administrative expenses and responsibilities, which in recent times have tended to outweigh the advantages of strict colonial control. That is why the jailed leaders of the nationalist movements were suddenly called by the colonial powers to take over the political control of their countries. Neocolonialism, as the ex-colonies were soon to learn, took the place of the former colonialism. This meant that all the administrative expenses and responsibilities, formerly borne by the metropolitan countries, were now carried by the ex-colonies, but the basic colonial relationship—the exchange of low-priced primary products and services for high-priced industrial goods and technical services—was maintained and enhanced.

The trouble with neocolonialism, as is well known in the Latin American countries—which fell into it in the last century for reasons of their own, even though their independence was not granted to them but was won through military victories—is that it is a self-exhausting system. Neocolonialism, as well as classic colonialism, is a form of primary dependency. The latter ceases when its administrative costs become too high; the former ceases when its exploitative possibilities are led to exhaustion. This exhaustion is due to the effect of neocolonialism on the balance of payments in the dependent country. Because the essence of the system consists in an unbalanced exchange which consistently favors the metropolitan partner, the dependent country is finally led to a complete incapacity to import, thus exhausting the possibilities of the system. At that moment a spontaneous process of industrialization tends to take place in order to replace imports, as is well known in the Latin American countries. That process runs against the current wishes and the apparent interests of the former metropolitan country and her associate partners in the elite of the dependent country. After some time, however—unless the local elite decides to choose autonomous development, is capable of managing it, and is willing to contribute the necessary efforts and sacrifices (Meiji Japan)—it becomes clear that the new process induces only a change from neocolonial to satellite dependency. That change involves, in the first place, a shift from dependency on the former European metropolises to dependency on a superpower, that is, in the present situation of the Western hemisphere, on the United States. In the second place, it involves a change in the inherent nature of the dependency. It is no longer, basically, an unbalanced exchange of low-priced primary goods and high-priced industrial and technical goods and services. It is, essentially, a financial, cultural, and political dependency. It consists in the growing flux of capital and technology from the new metropolis to the satellite, together with politico-military guardianship that maintains both the internal predominance of the local elite over its own mass and the intraimperial dependence of the satellite on the metropolis. The new "foreign" investments and some other imperial forms of aid redress the satellite's balance of payment, keeping it even enough to enable the process to keep going for a long time, in a way that both perpetuates the status quo and aggravates the dependency.

The problem with satellitism, however, as the Latin American countries are beginning to realize in the current decade, is that, like neocolonialism, *it is also a self-exhausting process,* although in different and more subtle ways. As is understandable, in general terms of systems analysis, all unbalanced input-output processes are necessarily unstable. In the case of neocolonialism, the final breaking point is the exhaustion of the dependent country's import capacity. In the case of *satellitism,* the final breaking point *is the exhaustion of the metropolis' free-floating funds for subsidizing the satellite.* Satellite growth is necessarily uneven, implying the increasing marginalization of the large masses, mostly rural, and creating deficiencies in the domestic structure of the supply of food and, still more, of the demand for industrial goods. Industry, therefore, keeps operat- . ing at very high costs, releases insufficient surpluses, and generates insufficient revenue for the satellite state. There is a lack of employment, even at the level of the urban middle class, which increases the propensity for counterelite revolutionary movements. In order to control these movements, increasingly coercive methods, military dictatorships, and fascist regimes are required. And these methods require, economically and politically, more free-floating funds from the metropolis than even a superstate like the United States is able and willing to supply, in the current conditions. (See Chapter 24.) The crisis of the satellite form of dependency, however, can only be solved by one of two opposite methods. Either the satellite must change the regime, take the way leading to autonomous development, and make the necessary efforts, or she must find a more balanced form of dependency. That more balanced form of dependency, as far as we can judge from a considerable mass of sociohistorical inferences, is provincial dependency.

Provincial dependency, in the sense in which that form may fit the new requirements of the intraimperial system, consists in a way of optimizing, in terms of the metropolis, the rational use and management of the resources of the "provinces." That optimization has to follow an appropriate cost-benefit pattern, so that inflows to the provinces from the metropolis and outputs from them remain balanced, in order to prevent the necessity for costly subsidies to keep the provincial affairs running, as well as to prevent the risk of hard-to-repress rebellions. In historical practice, of which the Roman Empire offers the best, but not the exclusive, example, that pattern has been obtained by the final suppression of the satellite elite and its replacement with a "Romanized" local middle-class bureaucracy, under the direct rule and supervision of the metropolis' authority. In the new emerging class of international "executives," who are coming to be recruited from the local middle class of countries under United States hegemony, through a previous educational and training program that makes their standards of work and behavior conform to the American executive pattern, we can see something equivalent to the Roman class of equites, who were also, after some time, recruited from the provincial middle classes through a previous process of Romanization. The new equites are likely to form a dependable, efficient, and honest bureaucracy, much better qualified to manage the provincial affairs than the relatively inept local elites, who were led to choose the dependent way because of their own incapacity for autonomous development. The provincial form of dependency would, therefore, improve both the self-support of provinces and their dependence on the metropolis, enlarging, along the way, the employment conditions for the local middle class, to which the new international executive careers would be opened. The extent to which a universalization of the "Roman" citizenship would occur in that process is open to speculation.

One thing, however—and this is the second remark to be made on the subject— can be anticipated. All available evidence, from both historical and current practices, indicates that the process of incorporation of dependent peoples into a more powerful and culturally advanced society is made at the expense of the great unskilled masses of the former. In ancient times they were enslaved and provided the manpower for the painful jobs of mining and metal working. In a cybernetic society, where unskilled labor is almost unnecessary and where the cost of education is so high (and the United States will have to cope with her own large ghetto population), it is likely that the great "demographic surpluses" of the provinces will be condemned to gradual extermination. How painful that process will be is an open question. There are many indications that the huge marginal tertiary which is being rapidly formed in the semistagnating cities of the third world, formed by the migrants of a fully stagnating subsistence agriculture, is flooding those cities and ruining their precarious public services and feeding facilities. The provincial administrations of the near future will probably be led to establish internal controls for population movement, obliging the rural masses to remain in the countryside, and thereby create a sort of reserve of natives, whose admission to the modern sectors of their countries will be contingent upon the real increase in the demand for labor in the cities. Malnutrition and the lack of appropriate sanitary conditions and medical care will gradually reduce these populations. An additional outlet, of a certain importance, may come to be the recruitment of provincial masses for the professional military service of the empire, whose intraimperial police operations, as has been clearly shown by the Vietnamese case, cannot be performed by American citizens. The practice of using Romanized barbarians in the army was an early one in Rome, where they were employed in legions stationed outside their native countries.

Concluding remarks

As a conclusion to the preceding analysis of the new emerging interimperial system, the seven following points could be stressed. (1) Capitalist-democratic America and socialist Russia, independent of their sociopolitical regimes, ideological commitments, and any Machiavellian plans for world domination, have become, in the aftermath of World War II, two imperial states, enjoying, respectively, general and regional primacy. (2) As stressed by most of the writers aware of the emergence of the American empire, the imperial condition, which implies, objectively, various forms of national and international oppression and requires, subjectively, an imperialist design for the appropriate management of the empire, contradicts the American liberal tradition and the national purpose of building the Great Society. (3) Although the American and the Soviet empires are not deterministic, they are not casual either, and they express both the comparatively more successful evolution of the American and Soviet societies, in the past, and their present structural characteristics. The imperial condition of the United States could not be renounced just by the adoption of enlightened policies by enlightened men. A return to a mere national framework could be possible, in terms of national security, but it would involve changes in the American social regime deeper than any that have ever occurred in American history, and for that reason they are unlikely to take place, in spite of the new trends among the American youth. (4) Although the imperial framework involves, domestically and externally, a large extent of structural oppression and injustice, it can be managed in more or less enlightened ways. American liberalism, rather than renouncing the new imperial system, is more likely to be reoriented toward a more enlightened administration of it. (5) The new interimperial system has severely reduced the possibilities for the autonomous development of the non-imperial actors, but has not suppressed the possibilities altogether. Seven countries or regional systems of countries do still actually or potentially enjoy the possibility of autonomous development: China, Japan, and Western Europe, on the one hand, Latin America, India, the Arab world, and Indonesia, on the other. Basically, they will have to consolidate or achieve their autonomous development by the end of this century or face the preclusion of their chances for national viability and, as a result, their submission to permanent structural dependency. (6) Dependency presents four major typical forms—colonial, neocolonial, satellite, and provincial—which tend to be successive. Provincial dependency, still not existing in the emerging interimperial system, is likely to be a more stable form, insofar as we can judge from historical inference. It will be characterized by the suppression of the former local elites and direct rule by representatives of the metropolitan authority, supported by a new Romanized bureaucracy recruited from the provincial middle classes. (7) Whatever the future evolution of the conditions of life in the new emerging empires, and whatever the ways in which imperial citizenship may be gradually extended to the provincials, it can be assumed that, if autonomous development fails, the large unskilled provincial masses will hardly be incorporated into the modern sector and the higher levels of their respective systems. More likely, these masses will be driven to gradual extermination, through controls containing them in the hinterlands as a sort of native reserve of labor, only utilizable in accordance with the real increase in the manpower demand. An additional outlet for some sectors of these provincial masses is likely to be their recruitment into the professional military service of the empire.

NOTES

[1] Geoffrey Barraclough, in his well-known study of contemporary history (1967), accepts

the inauguration of Kennedy as a convenient mark for the beginning of contemporary "worldwide history."

[2] See, for instance, on technology and the technological problem, Peter F. Drucker (1957 and 1969), Raymond Aron, ed. (1963), Jacques Ellul, (1964), Nigel Calder, ed. (1965), Daniel Bell, ed. (1967), Herman Kahn and Anthony J. Wiener (1967), Stuart Chase (1968), Victor C. Ferkiss (1969), and John McHale (1969). On the ecological problem see particularly Eugene P. Odum (1959), René J. Dubos (1965), Barry Commoner (1966), Paul R. Ehrlich (1969), La Mont C. Cole (1968), and Francois de Closets (1970).

[3] Cyborgs are biological forms that incorporate man with computers and other technical devices in order to expand man's natural powers. They were imagined by Arthur C. Clarke in a well-known science-fiction book (1964).

[4] See Pitirim Sorokin's more recent, revised and abridged, version of that book (1957), as well as his study on the basic trends of our time (1964).

[5] The view assumed in this book is that the sociocultural development of man has been linear, although not continuous, as was discussed in Chapter 10. See Table 33 on the real stages.

[6] See Commoner's views (1970).

[7] See Time (February 2, 1970, p. 59).

[8] See Charles F. Park, Jr. (1969). See also McHale (1969, pp. 231–237).

[9] See R. Carson, (1962) and P. De Bach, (1969). For studies on the general problem of the dangers to man's ecology, see the bibliographic list at the end of this book.

[10] This is particularly likely if we introduce an assumption missing in Kahn's forecasts, concerning ecological awareness and a corresponding technical-organizational ability to preserve the ecological balance.

[11] See Alexis de Tocqueville (1951) and Sir John Seeley (1919).

[12] See the typical case of André D. Sakharov and his study on coexistence and freedom (1968); his case is, in a general way, the same as that of a large group of dissenting Russian intellectuals, such as Sinyavsky, Daniel and his wife, Svinsburg, Bulovski, Litvinov, Brodski, and Odnnopozov. See, on the subject, James N. Billington, "The Intellectuals," in Allen Kassof, ed. (1968a, pp. 449–472); see also the special issue of Esprit (No. 386, November, 1969, pp. 633 ff.).

[13] See Carl Oglesby, ed. (1969).

[14] "Thus, to respond to America's needs, there is an empire which does not resemble any other, the empire without frontiers."

[15] George Liska's works on the subject were probably not known to Morgenthau when he wrote his 1969 book.

[16] Among the basic requirements for efficiency and even for imperial survival, Liska points out the necessity for organizing a professional international army to replace the present citizens' army, which is unfit for keeping extrametropolitan imperial order.

[17] These conditions include, as main variables, the major quantitative and qualitative aspects of the population and of the societal subsystems and, for smaller actors, the geopolitical situation.

[18] That dependency would be a sort of neo-Hellenistic dependency on a new "Roman Empire."

[19] Thirty years represent one biological generation and two sociological generations. It has been, in the more recent historical experience, the time lapse usually taken, on an average, to achieve substantial societal changes, as in the case of Bismarck's Germany, Meiji Japan, and Soviet Russia. (See Chapter 12 of this book.)

[20] Deficient vertical integration has subjected the most capable Arab leaders, such as Nasser and the Syrian Ba'athists, to populist pressures for a holy war against Israel, depriving them of a political margin for intelligent compromises.

[21] Implicit in these considerations are certain assumptions about the historical period in

question and the average social, cultural, and technological speed of its development. The aforementioned thirty-year period, for instance, is good for the modern history of Western civilization, but could not be applied to ancient Egypt.

[22] On this subject, see Organski (1964, pp. 256 ff.), who was discussed earlier in this chapter.

Book III
A LATIN AMERICAN CASE STUDY

A

The Main Structural Characteristics of Contemporary Latin America

19

General Description and Typology

The Latin American countries

In the last part of this book an attempt will be made to apply the theories and hypotheses that have been formulated and discussed up to now to Latin American societies and political systems. The purpose in view is to provide both an illustration and an empirical application of that theorical framework as well as to provide a clearer and deeper understanding of the problems concerning the national development of these societies and the reason for their continued failure, up to now, in achieving that aim.

This Latin American case study will be based, in a succinct way, on three central points. The first point concerns the main structural characteristics of contemporary Latin America. A brief attempt will be made to present a meaningful general description of the Latin American societies, their typological characterization, and an analysis of their most relevant structural features. The second point concerns the historical causes of Latin America's underdevelopment. An effort will be made to understand the reasons for its persistent underdevelopment, in terms of the major characteristics of the Iberian conquest, settlement, and colonization and in terms of the subsequent historical course of these countries after their independence in the early nineteenth century. The third point concerns the alternatives and prospects with which Latin America is presently faced. Confronted, as we have seen in the preceding chapter, with the alternative of achieving an autonomous development, by urgently undertaking and implementing the appropriate measures, or of becoming a dependency, in one of various possible forms, of the rising American empire, the Latin American countries will live, in the course of the 1970s, the most decisive and dramatic period of their historical existence.

The origin of the expression "Latin America" is alien to Latin America itself and comes from the United States' ethnically centered desire to differentiate their own America from their southern neighbors. Until the aftermath of World War II the Latin American countries had not experienced, except in a vague geo-cultural sense, their regional unity. Formerly, they had been separated into two rival blocs, with the Spanish and the Portuguese empires opposing each other. Their distinct identities and rivalry did not diminish even during the reunion of the two crowns (1580–1640) under Philip II and Philip III. After their independence, the Latin American countries became still more separated from one another, due to the breakup of Spanish America into many different, competing, and often fighting independent countries. The Latin American countries tended to relate individually with such Western countries as England (commercially) and France (culturally) and later with the United States, without keeping, in any effective way, a particular bond among themselves.[1]

That state of affairs has changed profoundly since the crisis of 1930 and particularly since World War II. The Latin American countries were compelled by the Great Depression to live on their own and were led, by an increasing understanding of their common features and fate, notably enhanced by the work of the United Nations Economic Commission for Latin America (better known by its Spanish and Portuguese initials, CEPAL), to attempt common policies and integrative efforts. As a result, they came to think of themselves as forming a basic common system, and they have been obtaining an increasing unity of purpose and action.

Consolidated now by the acknowledgment on the part of the concerned peoples of their common condition, Latin America, as the expression is usually employed, refers to the twenty independent republics occupying the southern part of the North American continent and Central America, including the Caribbean, and South America. Geographically, however, that area includes many other small societies, most of which are still under colonial rule, although a few are now attaining independence. These are, in alphabetical order: the Bahamas, British Honduras, the Dutch Antilles, French Guiana, Guadalupe, Guyana (former British Guiana), Jamaica, the Leeward Islands, Martinique, Surinam, Tobago and Trinidad, the (American and British) Virgin Islands, and the Windward Islands.[2] These small societies, many of which will probably tend in the future to have close associations with the Latin American countries and even to join the Latin American system, have not had any relevant relationship with the region in the past and still do not in the present.

A distinct case is presented, in a sense, by French Canada and, still more pertinently, by Puerto Rico. French Canada has not had, historically, any connection with the Latin American countries, from which it was separated by the English colonization of the northern part of the Americas. Its internal socio-cultural characteristics, however, present many traits similar to those of the Latin American countries, thus emphasizing the importance of the colonial legacy and of the transfer of the mother country's "fragment," as observed by Louis Hartz (1964). Puerto Rico, on the other hand, is sociohistorically an integral part of Latin America, annexed to the United States only after the Spanish-American War (1898), and constitutes a very interesting example of how a small (2.5 million inhabitants in 1965) Latin American society tends to act and react under North American institutionalized control. The present study, however, will be concerned only with Latin America in the strict sense.

The expression Latin America also gives an exaggerated emphasis to the original Spanish and Portuguese (and minute French) stock of the population of the region, in the same way that the expression "Anglo America" would overrate the quota of British ascendancy in the population of the United States. Both Americas have had, in a later period, a massive immigration from other countries besides their mother countries and, in an earlier phase, a large importation of African slaves. Several Latin American countries, moreover, such as Mexico, Central America, and the Andean countries, were the site of highly developed Indian civilizations when the Europeans arrived and have kept a very substantial number, in most cases a majority, of peoples of pure or mixed Indian descent in their population.

Besides their ethnic diversity, the Latin American countries present a still greater differentiation in the size of their territory and population and also a considerable unevenness in their levels of development. Table 36 presents some basic data in connection with these aspects.

General traits

The general traits of Latin American societies, some of which are apparent in Table 36, combine the characteristics of underdevelopment (average per capita GDP of $512) with those of social dualism, together with the fact that the population is heavily concentrated along the coastal strips, and the hinterland, particularly the immense Amazon basin, is practically uninhabited. Letting the structural analysis of these traits go for a moment, we can get some indication now of the social stratification in Latin American countries. As should be expected from the diversity of sizes and incomes shown in Table 36, that social stratification also varies considerably, according to the overall level of development, the larger or smaller social homogeneity of the concerned countries, and so on. In a general way, however, *the region is characterized by a dualist society*, which involves a very great concentration of wealth, education, and influence in the top 5 percent of the population, partially enjoyed by the next 15 percent, and the complete or almost complete destituteness of the rest of the population, particularly the 50 percent constituting its lowest strata. Such stratification expresses a profound class differentiation and cleavage.

The Latin American societies today are clearly divided between an upper- and middle-class cluster, forming the new Establishment, and the rest of the population, forming the mass. The upper class, understood in a broad sense, represents, on an average, about 5 percent of the population and includes, in forms that vary according to the levels of development and complexity of the country: (1) the remainder of the former agrarian patriciate, (2) the higher (commercial and industrial) bourgeoisie, and (3) the upper professional middle class. The middle class, representing about 15 percent of the population, presents a

Table 36 *Territory, population, and development indicators of Latin America*

Country	Area (thousands of miles)	Population (thousand inhabitants 1970 estimate)	GDP — Per Capita for 1969 (dollars of 1960)
NORTH AMERICA			
Mexico	760.4	50,670	677
CENTRAL AMERICA			
Guatemala	42.0	5,276	359
Honduras	43.3	2,603	247
El Salvador	8.2	3,441	349
Nicaragua	57.1	2,024	344
Costa Rica	19.6	1,809	570
Panama	28.7	1,410	740
CARIBBEAN			
Cuba	44.2	8,341	431
Dominican Republic	19.6	4,277	233
Haiti	10.7	5,255	85
SOUTH AMERICA			
Venezuela	352.1	10,399	878
Colombia	439.8	20,875	367
Ecuador	104.5	6,093	323
Peru	496.2	13,586	450
Bolivia	424.1	4,658	203
Chile	286.4	9,969	671
Brazil	3,287.2	93,292	379
Paraguay	157.0	2,379	272
Uruguay	72.2	2,886	710
Argentina	1,072.7	24,050	950
LATIN AMERICA	7,764.0	273,293	512

SOURCES: Area: Robert C. Kingsbury and Ronald M. Schneider, eds., *An Atlas of Latin American Affairs* (New York: Praeger, 1966), 24 pp.
Population and GDP: CEPAL, *Estudio Económico de América Latina*, 1968 (E/CN.12/825), March 1969, Tables 1.2 and 1.6.
GDP: The per capita income of Cuba refers to the year 1957. See Bruce M. Russett *et al.*, eds, *World Handbook of Political and Social Indicators* (New Haven, Conn.: Yale University Press, 1964), Table 43.

Urbanization (2000 and more) of Total Population	Initial Registration, As Percentage of Corresponding School-age Population		
	PRIMARY	SECONDARY	SUPERIOR
51	56.7	3.8	1.2
31	29.6	5.9	0.8
31	30.9	2.6	0.6
39	48.2	3.6	0.6
34	35.3	3.3	1.1
35	73.8	6.4	1.9
42	81.1	20.0	2.2
55	45.9	8.1	3.2
31	59.9	5.2	1.0
13	22.6	0.4	0.3
63	61.6	5.6	0.8
46	48.4	5.7	0.9
35	60.4	7.8	1.4
47	79.6	8.2	3.0
30	35.8	5.0	4.9
67	78.5	14.1	9.5
45	49.6	6.0	1.0
36	79.0	6.8	1.3
82	89.5	13.2	—
68	81.8	20.0	5.5
46	57.0	7.3	1.8

Urbanization and School Registration: Centro Latinoamericano de Pesquisas en Ciencias Sociais, *Situação Social da América Latina* (Rio de Janeiro, 1965); for urbanization, graphic V, p. 53 (data for 1960) and for school registration, Table 41 (data for 1950).

traditional sector, including larger or smaller numbers of liberal professionals, the civil servants, the military and the lower bourgeoisie, and a modern sector, which includes the technical and managerial professionals, some of them in the military. The rest of the population is distributed among (1) the lower middle class, mostly represented by the urban lower echelons of the bureaucracy and the lower white-collar workers, and (2) most of the working class, including the urban unemployed groups and the peasants.

The extent of income concentration created by this stratification can be seen in Table 37. As can be seen in the table, groups I, II, and III, forming the mass and representing 80 percent of the total population, have access to only 39.4 percent of the national income, and groups IV and V, forming the new Establishment and representing 20 percent of the population, control more than 60 percent of the national income. This stratification, which represents the regional average, is less accentuated in a few cases, as in Argentina, and significantly worse in many other countries, as in Central America and the less-developed countries of South America: Bolivia, Ecuador, Paraguay, and Peru.

Typological classification

Recently, the identification of the structural characteristics of the Latin American countries and the admeasurement of several of them have made an attempt at a typological classification of these countries possible. I have already dealt with that problem to some extent elsewhere[3] and will present here only some basic considerations on the subject. The essential question concerning Latin America, as with any typological classification, is the choice of the most relevant

Table 37 *Income distribution and concentration in Latin America (values for 1965, expressed in U.S. dollars of 1960)*

Income Groups	Participation in Total Income (%)		Index of Income, National Average = 100	Per Capita Average ($)
I. The lowest 20 percent	3.5		18	68
II. The 30 percent below the median	10.5		35	133
III. The 30 percent above the median	25.4	39.4	85	322
IV. The 15 percent below the highest	29.1		194	740
V. The highest 5 percent	31.5	60.6	629	2,400

SOURCE: CEPAL, *Estudio Económico de América Latina*, 1968 (E/CN.12/825), March 1969, Table 1.8.

variables with which to build the typology. Previous attempts have usually centered around certain sets of indicators of economic, social, cultural and political development. That method is certainly appropriate, since the main purpose of such typologies is to permit meaningful analyses of national development, both for comparing the countries of the area to each other and to other countries and for admeasuring advancement or regression in the course of time. It is indispensable, however, as I have pointed out in former studies, to take objectively into account each country's potential for national viability. Many comparative analyses of countries are incomplete because that fundamental aspect has not been taken into account. So some people will compare the growth rates of Hong Kong with mainland China (usually to show how well the former is progressing, because of its free enterprise system, vis-à-vis Communist China) as if Hong Kong could exist, in any meaningful sense, as a national society. The same thing occurs in the case of Latin America when one compares a Central American state or a nominally independent Caribbean island with Argentina or Brazil, without taking the question of national viability into account.

Enough has been said in this book (see Chapters 17 and 18) and in my preceding book (1968, pp. 35 ff.) about the problem of national viability to demand further elaboration. Let us remember that the concept of national viability is a relative one, which varies according to certain conditions, notably the historical level of technology and the level of societal integration. In terms of these conditions, national viability indicates sufficient availability of human and natural resources and of societal autonomy for their use.

Given the present conditions of international permissibility, in terms of the new emerging international stratification, the assessment of the national viability of the Latin American countries presents a continuum between two extreme possibilities. One extreme manifests the fact that, for all practical purposes, some countries do not have now, and will not have in the near future (in historical terms, say, ten years), either a national viability of their own or even an autonomous access to any form of *collective viability*. The other extreme indicates that some few countries have actually attained or can potentially attain, in the near future, the condition of national viability, either by acquiring and developing it *individually* or, at least, by playing the role of an autonomous pole of integration in a system of collective viability. For the sake of simplicity the first extreme will be called *nonviability*, the opposite of *relative individual viability*.[4] A third position, in between the other two, will be called *minimal collective viability*.

Nonviability is the condition of a country, usually a nominally independent state, which, at a given historical time (the current one for the purpose of the present analysis), does not have enough human and natural resources, in terms of the technological level of the time and of her own level of societal integration, to provide, individually or collectively, for her autonomous and predominantly endogenous development and survival. This is also the definition of structural external dependency. A relevant distinction must be made between individual and collective viability. Few countries, today, enjoy even a relative individual viability. Not enjoying collective viability, however, means that, for different reasons, a country has not even an autonomous access to the possibility of actually joining other countries in mutually convenient (self-controllable) institutional arrangements (such as common markets) capable of compensating for their respective individual shortcomings. In Latin America, this is the case of the Central American countries[5] and the Caribbean islands; Cuba has a special position in that group.[6]

Complete individual viability, as discussed in Chapter 18, implies general or regional primacy. No Latin American country will enjoy that condition, now or in the near future. *Relative individual viability*, however, involving only consolidated autonomy, should be acknowledged at least potentially and for the near future as an achievable status for Mexico and Argentina and particularly for Brazil. The latter enjoys, because of its continental characteristics—even if substantially affected by her current low level of societal integration—the possibility of acquiring and developing national viability by herself. Mexico and Argentina probably do not meet the requirements for a purely isolated achievement of national viability, but certainly they qualify to become integrative poles around which two subregional integrations could be built.

The other South American countries can potentially achieve, today and in the near future, the intermediate position of *collective viability*, centered around some possible poles of integration. A first possible subregional integration, already in an advanced stage of preparation, is the Andean subsystem, centered around Chile and Peru and including the other Andean countries.

In addition to national viability, the usual sets of economic, social, cultural, and political indicators are also relevant parameters for a typological classification of the Latin American countries. In spite of the merits presented by some of the more elaborate typologies, such as Vekemans' (1962), I have suggested in a former study (1968) that it would be advantageous to adopt a simpler classification, differentiating only the less-developed from the more-developed countries in the group of viable Latin American countries. The typological grouping based on these two parameters is presented in Table 38.

If we now remember Chart 6, presented in Chapter 14, we will see, as has been anticipated, that there is a significant relationship between the suggested typological grouping of the Latin American countries and the three basic types of underdevelopment. To aid the reader that chart is reproduced here as Chart 6a.

The countries in boxes A–I and A–II of Table 38 are also those of the I–2 group of Chart 6a, that is, countries with a split elite. The countries in box B–II are those of the II group of Chart 6a, that is, societies sustained by the modern sector of their subelite. The countries of box B–III correspond to the III–2 group, that is, coercive inegalitarian societies, mostly of the *societas sceleris* kind. The Latin American countries do not constitute an exception to the theory of operational political models. We will see that, in accordance with the hypotheses discussed in Chapter 14, the basic models suitable for these three groups of countries are, respectively, national capitalism (with elements of state capitalism), state capitalism, and developmental socialism. With respect

Table 38 *Typological grouping of Latin American countries*

| *National Viability* | (−) Relative Level of Societal Development (+) | |
	B LESS-DEVELOPED COUNTRIES	A MORE-DEVELOPED COUNTRIES
I Relative individual viability		Brazil Mexico Argentina
II Collective viability	Peru Ecuador Bolivia Paraguay	Venezuela Colombia Chile Uruguay
III Nonviability	Guatemala Nicaragua Honduras Dominican Republic Salvador Haiti	Cuba Costa Rica Panama

Chart 6a *Types and varieties of underdeveloped societies*

Type I. *Societies with a Semifunctional Elite*

    I-1.   Traditional societies
    I-2.   Societies with a split elite

Type II. *Societies with a Nonfunctional Elite*

    II.   Societies sustained by the modern sector of the subelite

Type III. *Primitive or Archaic Societies and Societies with a Dysfunctional Elite*

    III-1.   Primitive or archaic societies
    III-2.   Coercive inegalitarian societies
        III-2.1.   Societies with a rigidified aristocratic elite
        III-2.2   Societies with a *societas sceleris* elite

to the latter model, however, the nonviability of the concerned countries, due as much to their own deficient resources as to their geopolitical location, precludes the applicability of that model. As has already been discussed, Cuba is likely to be the only possible experiment for that model for a long time.

NOTES

[1] Closer relations, however, have been maintained among members of subregional systems, such as Central America, Great Colombia, Peru and Bolivia, and in a sense Argentina, Uruguay, and Brazil.

[2] Robert C. Kingsbury and Ronald M. Schneider, eds. (1966).

[3] See Helio Jaguaribe (1968, pp. 66–67). See also Roger Vekemans and J. L. Segundo (1962).

[4] Nonrelative individual viability, in the present international system, as formerly discussed in this book, requires general or regional primacy.

[5] The Central American Common Market is not an instrument for the collective viability of the member countries because it is based on the principle of free movement of private capital. As a result the American corporations control the so-called industries of integration, and the corresponding processes of capital accumulation, technological development, and political influence are completely alien to the Central Americans.

[6] Cuba is a borderline case as far as her natural and human resources are concerned. Because of her geopolitical situation, however, Cuba is confronted with a dilemma. In order to overcome her socioeconomic underdevelopment, she has had to adopt a developmental-socialist model, which has brought about the systematic hostility of the United States, forcing Cuba to depend on the protection of the Soviet Union. Her national viability, therefore, is precarious, affected by political dependency on the Soviet Union and on an unstable Soviet-American modus vivendi.

20

A Structural Analysis

Structural characteristics

From CEPAL's earliest studies on the structural characteristics of Latin America, in the late 1940s and early 1950s, to the analyses of today, there is an unchanged consensus among the students of the region about the fact that *underdevelopment* is the most general and salient of the structural characteristics. The fact that the situation has remained the same for twenty years is in itself highly significant and reveals, at least, another important structural feature of the region: the *stagnating character of its underdevelopment*.

As seen by CEPAL, Latin American underdevelopment was the result of, along with other interfering but less relevant factors, the combination of (1) an inherent deficiency in domestic capital formation and (2) a continued insufficiency in the external supply of foreign capital.[1] One of the most original contributions of Raul Prebisch and CEPAL to the analysis of Latin American underdevelopment was the identification and theoretical explanation of that inherent deficiency in internal capital formation.

Under Prebisch's leadership, CEPAL pointed out that that deficiency has been due to a secular deterioration of the terms of trade between Latin America and the developed countries, resulting from the peculiar way in which the region has taken part in the process of the industrial revolution, as a supplier of primary goods and an importer of finished industrial products. For several reasons, indicated by CEPAL, the prices of the primary agricultural and mineral commodities that Latin America exported tended to fall per unit of weight or volume, vis-à-vis the prices of the manufactured goods that the region imported. As a consequence, Latin America has had to increase constantly the amount of its exports, with a corresponding increase in the investment of man-hours, in order to keep importing the same amount of goods, creating the condition of a steadily decreasing capital-product ratio. Internal capital formation, therefore, has been strained by that process, preventing the region from accumulating enough capital for its development. External supply of foreign capital could, in a way, compensate for that deficiency. In the long run, however, the net inflow of foreign capital has been smaller than the losses caused by the deterioration of the terms of trade. In more recent years, moreover, the ever-increasing interest payments for ever-growing compensatory foreign loans ahve outbalanced the inflow of foreign capital and have turned Latin America into a net exporter (more than $501 million in 1967) of capital,[2] definitively aggravating the insufficiency of internal capital formation.

Although these views retain their validity today, in spite of some controversies over the historical fluctuations of the terms of trade, both CEPAL and other students of Latin America have shifted the main focus of their attention to other aspects. The terms-of-trade explanation was particularly relevant for the nineteenth and early twentieth centuries, when the Latin American economy was an export-oriented one. Since the Depression of the 1930s and, particularly, since the development impulse of the 1950s, the region—notably the larger and more developed countries—has become inward-oriented. The coefficient of importation on the GDP for these countries has become rather small: 7.8 percent for Mexico, 6.6 percent for Argentina, 5.6 percent for Brazil, and 9.9 percent for Latin America as a whole.[3] Notwithstanding the remaining importance of CEPAL's earlier theory and its relevance for an understanding of the historical deficiency in internal capital formation in Latin America, other hypotheses are required for an explanation of the current persistence of Latin America's underdevelopment.

Students of the area are reaching a new consensus concerning structural characteristics of the region that are presently more salient and an explanation derived from these characteristics for the persistence of the underdevelopment of the region. The new view stresses the mutually reinforcing circular relationship between *stagnation* and *marginality*, which is connected with an increasing process of *denationalization*. I have already discussed these three major present structural characteristics of Latin America elsewhere.[4] In view of their relevancy, however, I will present a succinct analysis of them.

Latin American stagnation

As a current main structural characteristic of the region Latin American *stagnation* is, in economic terms, the result of the exhaustion of the import-replacement drive without the achievement of a general process of self-sustained growth. The term could also be used in a broader sense to point out a corresponding lack of self-sustained processes of cultural, social, and political development in the other societal structural planes. For a global structural analysis of Latin American societies, it would be extremely important to study the main noneconomic features of that general stagnation and their interrelations. Such a study, however, would expand the ambit of the present inquiry way beyond its intended scope. For the purposes of this book it will be enough to present some basic indications concerning the Latin American economic stagnation.

Briefly, that stagnation can be characterized by the fact that the region's GNP is not increasing enough, given its high population growth (about 3 percent per year), to approach the present per capita level of the developed countries within a reasonable period of time, say, by the end of the century. The gap now separating Latin America from the developed countries is continuously increasing and will be much larger in the future, if dramatic increases in growth, requiring very broad and deep structural changes, are not quickly achieved. Table 39 gives a picture of Latin American growth since 1950. What aggravates that picture is the fact that such strategic countries as Argentina and Brazil are among those that have had a low rate of growth in the last decade, except for 1967–1968, as can be seen in Table 40.

Based on past development and probable future variations due to developmental changes, such as increasing urbanization, industrialization, education, and so forth, Herman Kahn and Anthony Wiener (1967, chap. 3) have projected demographic growth rates for several areas of the world for three successive periods, 1965–1975, 1975–1985, and 1985–2000. For Latin America and the OECD and the Warsaw Pact countries, they obtained the population projections given in Table 41. Because of the high rate of population growth in Latin America, compared to the growth rates in the OECD and the Warsaw Pact countries, the former would require an extremely high yearly increase in its domestic product in order to gradually catch up with the latter. As formerly seen, however, this is not the case. Table 42 presents Kahn and Wiener's extrapolations in terms of total and per capita GNP for the same time periods and the same areas.

If we compare the relation between the Latin American per capita product in 1965 and the per capita products of the OECD and Warsaw Pact countries, we will see that the OECD was 5.3 times and the Warsaw Pact 3.3 times larger. If

Table 39 *Total and per capita growth of the Latin American GDP*

	Percentage GDP Growth	
Period	TOTAL	PER CAPITA
1950–1955	5.1	2.2
1955–1960	4.7	1.7
1960–1965	4.5	1.5
1965–1966	3.0	0
1966–1967	4.5	1.5
1967–1968	5.4	2.4

SOURCES: CEPAL, *La Evolución Económica de la América Latina en los Últimos Años* (E/CN.12/696) July 1964, and *Estudio Económico de América Latina, 1968* (E/CN.12/825) May 1969.

Table 40 *Percentage growth of Argentine and Brazilian GDP*

Period	Argentina		Brazil	
	TOTAL	PER CAPITA	TOTAL	PER CAPITA
1950–1955	3.2	1.0	5.7	2.9
1955–1960	2.7	0.9	5.9	2.9
1960–1965	2.8	1.3	4.9	1.8
1965–1966	2.6	1.1	3.8	0.7
1966–1967	2.0	0.5	4.9	2.0
1967–1968	4.5	3.0	6.0	3.2

SOURCE: CEPAL, *Estudio Económico de América Latina, 1963* (E/CN.12/696), 1964, *Estudio Económico de América Latina, 1965*, and *Estudio Económico de América Latina, 1968* (E/CN.12/825) March 1969.

we take Kahn's projections for the year 2000 and compare them, as in Table 42, we will see that these differences rise from 5.3 times to 11 times for the OECD countries, and from 3.3 times to 7.1 times for the Warsaw Pact bloc. The fact that some of these figures may be, in one way or another, debatable is practically irrelevant as far as the growth trends and the proportions between Latin American figures and those of the developed capitalist and socialist blocs are concerned.[5]

Why does the Latin American economy suffer from structural stagnation? In a deeper sense the explanation of such structural characteristics requires a broader framework and a sociohistorical analysis of the whole social system. A brief discussion of that question will be attempted in Chapters 21 and 22. It is possible, however, to give a satisfactory partial explanation of Latin American

Table 41 *Projection of population and population growth rate: 1965–2000 (total in millions)*

Areas	1965		1975		1985		2000
	TOTAL	GROWTH (%)	TOTAL	GROWTH (%)	TOTAL	GROWTH (%)	TOTAL
Latin America	233	2.9	313	2.8	417	2.6	615
OECD	686	1.0	756	1.0	833	0.9	1,160
Warsaw Pact	333	1.1	370	1.1	415	1.0	482

SOURCE: Herman Kahn and Anthony Wiener, *The Year 2000* (New York: Macmillan, 1967), p. 151, Table 9.

Table 42 *Comparative projections of GNP (totals in billions, 1965 U.S. dollars)*

Areas	1965			1975			1985			2000	
	TOTAL	PER CAPITA	*Growth Rate*	TOTAL	PER CAPITA	*Growth Rate*	TOTAL	PER CAPITA	*Growth Rate*	TOTAL	PER CAPITA
Latin America	86.6	371	4.2	131	419	4.4	202	485	4.6	396	646
OECD	1,348.2	1,966	4.6	2,122	2,808	4.7	3,362	4,039	4.8	6,823	7,120
Warsaw Pact	409.1	1,230	5.0	666	1,800	5.0	1,085	2,626	5.0	2,256	4,679

SOURCE: Herman Kahn and Anthony Wiener, *The Year 2000* (New York: Macmillan, 1967), Tables 10 and 11.

structural stagnation in more restricted economic terms. As a matter of fact, such an explanation has already been suggested by some students of Latin American affairs and by the later works of CEPAL.[6]

In a few words, it can be said that Latin American stagnation is the result of the insufficient demand of the Latin American markets. On the one hand, the Latin American economies are not able to use their idle productive capacity for exports,[7] and on the other hand, the Latin American governments are unwilling or incapable of compensating for the insufficiency of the spontaneous demand of the domestic markets by means of a centrally planned expansion of the economy. Concentrating on the problem of the domestic markets, which is and will always be, by far, the most important problem, we can start by observing what has occurred in the import-replacement process. As is well known, with the Depression of the 1930s the Latin American economies could no longer import the commodities required for their consumption, and therefore started to produce these commodities domestically in a process of import substitution which was accelerated after World War II. The process began spontaneously. It was after World War II that it became the object of deliberate policies adopted by most Latin American governments. These policies created all sorts of credit, fiscal, and exchange incentives for the industrialization of the Latin American countries. In adopting these policies, however—with the short-lived exceptions of Perón's first Five-Year Plan and Vargas' second government (1950–1954)— the Latin American governments always assumed that private initiative should be the primary agent of their country's economic development, reserving for the state a subsidiary role. The Latin American markets, however, suffer from a double limitation. For most countries the market is too small, in absolute terms (see Table 36), and so unable to provide the level of demand required, in the conditions of modern technology, for an integrated industrialization. Moreover, with the exception of Argentina and Uruguay (whose populations are small or very small), the Latin American countries suffer from a very high rate of marginality, which neutralizes from 30 percent to 80 percent of their population. This is the case with the two largest countries, Brazil and Mexico, whose populations would, in principle, be sufficient to sustain a well-advanced level of industrialization. In these countries, however, most of the peasants, representing, respectively, 55 percent and 50 percent of the population in 1960, live in a quasi-natural economy, at a subsistence level and have no acquisitive power for industrial goods, except for a few very cheap clothes. In the urban population, on the other hand, about 50 percent live at the level of minimum wage, just earning enough for basic food, and so are also kept outside the stream of industrial consumption. Reduced to about 20 percent of their population (see Table 37 on income distribution) (and because of the interference of other factors), Brazil and Mexico have also proved unable to bring their process of import replacement to the point of self-sustained economic growth.

Confronted with the insufficient pull of their markets, the Latin American governments have been unwilling or unable to transfer the main responsibility for economic development to the public sector. Some of these governments, such as Kubitschek's in Brazil, actually tried to do so. Kubitschek, however, never received enough external support from the international and American financing agencies, and domestically never obtained congressional support so that he could increase taxes. As a consequence, he was obliged to accept short-term foreign suppliers' credit, at higher interest rates, in order to finance the external payments of his program of development. And internally, he was forced to resort to inflationary procedures to produce the required financial means.[8] Predictably, the rising external debt and the domestic inflationary spiral prevented the continuation of Kubitschek's development methods by the succeeding governments. Brazil was brought to the very threshold of self-sustained development at the end of the 1950s, only to be forced backward in the 1960s.

Marginality

Marginality, the second structural characteristic presently under our scrutiny, has already been mentioned in our analysis. As was observed, the Latin American markets, even in the large countries such as Brazil and Mexico, are actually reduced to about 20 percent of their size by the marginal condition of most of the population.

We can speak of marginality in Latin America in three different senses. First and basically, it expresses the fact that the great majority of the Latin American populations are marginal people in terms of their economic, social, cultural, and political participation, both as producers and as consumers. Second, it expresses the fact that, due to the geographic concentration of the modern and more prosperous areas in every Latin American country, most of their territorial regions are marginal, vis-à-vis a privileged region or, in the case of Brazil, a privileged central-southern coastal strip. Third, marginality also expresses the fact that the intraregional gap between most of the Latin American countries, vis-à-vis the few more-developed ones, and the interregional gap between Latin America as a whole and the northern hemisphere are constantly increasing, with the resulting marginalization of the Latin American countries.

For the purpose of this study, it will be sufficient to consider only, and in a succinct way, the first and basic sense of marginality. We have already presented some of the main data about it. As can be seen in Table 36, Latin America is still very rural[9] and, what is worse, very uneducated. Only 57 percent of the population of the proper school age (5 to 14 years) had registered in the initial grade of the primary schools in 1950. Initial registration had improved by 37.7 percent in 1960 and probably by more in later years. Most of the children, however, still fail to go beyond the two first years, and very few are able to complete primary school. This is why, in addition to other reasons, only 7.3 percent of the children of the proper school age (15 to 19 years) had registered in the initial grade of secondary school in 1950.[10] Furthermore, as indicated in Table 37, 80 percent of the Latin American population receives only 39.4 percent of the region's income, most of this group living on per capita incomes of about $100 a year.

The picture of Latin American marginality can be characterized, in a general way, by the following main traits (estimates for 1969): (1) extremely low general level of productivity and/or income for about 80 percent of the total population (see Table 37), (2) very high rate of rural unemployment and under-employment, estimated at about 32.6 percent of the agricultural labor force, which represents 42.2 percent of the working population, (3) relatively high rates of unemployment in the sectors of mining (19 percent), manufacture (16.7 percent), and trade and financing (19 percent), (4) very high rate of unemployment in the sector of general urban services (35.7 percent), (5) practically total unemployment of the urban marginal sector, representing 5.6 percent of the total active population, and (6) very high overall rate of unemployment for the total population, representing 30.4 percent of it.[11]

These figures express, ultimately, an economic structure characterized (1) by its very low agricultural productivity and its incapacity to provide employment for one-third of the rural labor force and (2) by the fact that industry and the more productive urban services are not able to generate enough jobs for the urban population and to receive the unemployed surplus of the agricultural sector. In 1950 agriculture represented 53.4 percent of the active population, and the production of nonagricultural basic goods and services occupied 23.5 percent of that population. The estimates for 1969 (CEPAL, 1969a, Table I.21) indicate a reduction of the agricultural population to 42.2 percent, whereas the production of nonagricultural basic goods and services remained almost un-changed, representing only 24.8 percent.

The result of that situation is a rapid increase in urban marginality and flood-ing of Latin American capitals and big cities with an unskilled jobless population, living on the assistance of the public services and from eventual marginal occupa-tions of the boot-shining kind. Strict urban marginality, which represented 2.3 percent of the active population in 1950 increased in 1969 to 5.6 percent—that is, it more than doubled.

As becomes clear from the combined analysis of stagnation and marginality in Latin America, the two phenomena are mutually reinforcing in a process of cir-cular causation. In the conditions of a market economy, marginality prevents or limits, and distorts, industrial expansion, because of the insufficient demand, and contributes in various ways to the increase in the operating costs of the economy and to the decrease in its productivity. The resulting stagnation, perpetuating the conditions of underdevelopment, prevents a significant in-crease in the domestic formation of capital and in educational efforts, which, along with other factors, operates to maintain or aggravate the rate of marginality.

Denationalization

The third major structural characteristic of Latin American countries, *denational-ization*, expresses, within the international conditions inherent to our time, a consequence that is closely related to the stagnation-marginality complex. I will attempt, as with the other characteristics, to present a succinct analysis of denationalization.

As occurs with stagnation, the process of denationalization affects the whole fabric of the Latin American societies. There is, as well as an economic denationalization, a cultural denationalization and a politico-military one. With respect to denationalization, however, we cannot include its other aspects, even for simplicity's sake, in the economic one, as we did in our brief study of the problem of stagnation. Stagnation may be predominantly viewed as an economic process, but the three aspects of denationalization must be analyzed, if briefly, for their own characteristics.

Generically speaking and insofar as a national state is concerned, the process of denationalization, in any of its three main varieties, consists in the actual transference of control over relevant decisions or factors, and conditions affecting them, from actors loyal or favorable to a nation to actors loyal or favorable to another nation. It is not relevant for the process of denationalization whether the processes occur de jure and in an official way (as in the cases of legal transference of control) or as a de facto situation, either in a deliberate or in a spontaneous way. Neither is it important whether the agents obtaining control are formally nationals of another country. What is essential is, on the one hand, the effective exercise of control, whatever its form, of societally relevant decisions and, on the other hand, the fact that the agents of control, independent of other considerations, are loyal to another nation and/or proceed in a way that actually tends to favor that nation.

The theorical and general aspects of that question were discussed sufficiently in Chapter 17. Let us just review two of our conclusions concerning the conditions for national viability, which, in turn, is the basic requirement for any successful process of political and societal development. The first of the conclusions that now needs to be stressed is that national viability, in addition to being determined by the level of available natural and human resources, is also a function of the political capability of the concerned society. That political capability involves the degree of the society's national commitment and is related to the extent of the elite's functionality, which is ultimately dependent on the degree of congruence and complementary occurring among the four sets (cultural, social, political, and economic) of elite roles. The second conclusion to be recalled is that the basic congruence among the interests and values of the four sets of elites requires their national allegiance and, therefore, is not compatible with any process of denationalization affecting in a significant way any of these elites.

As can be seen, the problem of denationalization is of the utmost importance for the future possibilities of development of the Latin American countries. According to the extent to which denationalization affects the Latin American elites and is or is not containable and reversible, the national viability of those countries will be correspondingly affected and, with it, the possibility of their national development.

As has already been mentioned, the process of denationalization presents three distinct varieties (economic, cultural, and politico-military), each of which has to be specifically considered. Let us briefly discuss each of them.

Economic denationalization

Until recently, economic denationalization has been ignored or avoided by most scholars and public officials, and relegated to treatment by radical polemists. Only the aspects of economic denationalization related to foreign indebtedness were recorded and discussed, and even so in terms of pure financial accounting, with careful avoidance of its political implications. As far as the growing control of the more strategic and dynamic sectors of the Latin American economies by the so-called multinational corporations was concerned, there was, until a few years ago, a persistent silence. Neither the Latin American countries, nor even such specialized agencies as CEPAL and ILPES, have records or data concerning the extent of foreign control of relevant economic activities and firms in the region. The available information, mainly supplied by American sources, concern the investment of private American capital, in addition to public and private loans, in the recipient countries, without indication of the relative importance of these investments in the corresponding sectors.

The first aspects of the process of economic denationalization to come to the attention of the students of Latin America, as was formerly noted, has been the growing foreign indebtedness of the region. And even if that matter has been kept strictly within the pure limits of balance-of-payment considerations, the size of the involved amounts as well as their rate of growth have caused increasing concern. As we can see from CEPAL's studies, the accumulated amount of long-term financing in the period from 1951 to 1955 amounted to $597.3 million. Adding to that the value of direct foreign investment for the same period, which was $1,715.5 million, we have a total of $2,312.8 million.[12] In the period from 1955 to 1966 the amount of Latin American indebtedness for long-term loans increased to $24,840 million, and the value of direct investment went up to $6,668.4 million, presenting a total of $31,507.4 million.

As a result, the percentage of Latin American credits from exports and services involved in servicing foreign capital and loan amortization rose from 20.7 percent in 1955 to 35 percent in 1966. In 1968, out of a total of $18 billion in credits from exports and services, $8 billion were used for the service of the foreign debt.[13]

Although less spectacularly than the long-term loans, the values of direct American investments in Latin America has grown very fast and reached impressive figures, both absolutely and comparatively. American private investment in Latin American manufacturing industries, which amounted to $780 million in 1950, increased to $3,077 million in 1966. The figures for overall American direct private investment in the region in 1966 are presented in Table 43.

In that year the total amount of American direct private investment in underdeveloped regions amounted to $15,781 million, of which $2,028 million were invested in Africa (including South Africa) and $3,891 in Asia. Latin America,

Table 43 *American direct investment in Latin America (estimates for 1966, in millions of dollars)*

Countries	Total	Mining and Smelting	Petrol- eum	Manufac- turing	Other Industries
Latin America	9,854	1,117	2,959	3,077	2,701
Mexico	1,244	108	42	797	297
Argentina	1,031	*	*	652	379
Brazil	1,246	58	69	846	273
Chile	844	494	*	51	299
Colombia	576	*	277	194	105
Peru	518	262	29	93	135
Venezuela	2,678	*	1,922	293	462
Other countries	1,716	66	413	151	1,087

*Combined in "other industries."

SOURCE: U.S. Department of Commerce, *Statistical Abstract of the United States*, September 1968, Table 1202.

alone, represented about two-thirds of those investments. In spite of these important figures, however, the relative significance of American investments in Latin America has tended to be grossly underrated, until very recently, because of the practice of evaluating them in terms of the GNP yardstick. Compared to the region's GDP of about $134.3 billion (in dollars of 1960) at the end of the decade of the 1960s, these investments do not appear so decisive. It occurs, however, that these investments are highly concentrated in the local branches of a few supercorporations and are preferently applied in the most dynamic industries, where these concerns play the leading and controlling roles.

The study of the relative position of American capital in Latin American industry is still rather incipient and is only now beginning to be pursued systematically. As has been stated, the existing statistical data do not differentiate between national and foreign investments, as far as ownership and control are concerned. And foreign business tends to protect itself with a cloak of elusiveness.

These difficulties notwithstanding, some surveys of the three most important host countries for foreign investments in Latin America confirm the supposition that the dynamic sectors and firms of the region's industry are already controlled by foreign, mostly American, supercorporations.

In Mexico, in spite of the long prevailing official nationalist policy, a study of the largest industrial corporations by José Luis Ceceña, referred to by Pablo González Casanova, showed that most of these corporations are foreign-controlled.[14] In the study the corporations were considered in four groups, comprehending the 100, the 200, the 300, and the 400 largest ones. In each case the foreign firms represented more than 50 percent of the group. The figures for the largest group are shown in Table 44.

In Brazil a research team led by sociologist Mauricio Vinhas de Queiroz, in 1962, studied "multibillionaire" and "billionaire" private groups—so classified according to whether their capital and reserves, in cruzeiros of that year,[15] were larger than 4 billion cruzeiros (about $10 million by the exchange rate of 1962) or between 1 and 4 billion cruzeiros, respectively. This team reached conclusions similar to Ceceña's, as can be seen from Table 45. Of the fifty-five groups comprehended in the multibillionaire level thirty-one groups (controlling 234 firms) and representing 56.4 percent of that universe were foreign or mixed. The foreign groups were heavily concentrated in industry, particularly in the more dynamic sectors of durable goods and basic industry. Moreover, it was found out that 62 percent of the Brazilian groups of that category have foreign participation and licences and interlocked directorates.

In Argentina, a survey led by Julián Delgado in 1964,[16] of the fifty largest industrial corporations of the country, classified by the value of their production, showed that the Argentine companies, accountable for sales totaling 579 million pesos, represented 49 percent of the grand total. Of these national firms, the private ones, with total sales of 183 million pesos, represented only 15 percent, and the public firms, with total sales of 396 million pesos, constituted 34 percent. The foreign companies, with total sales of 604 million pesos, represented 51 percent of the grand total.

There can be little doubt that this trend is typical for the whole region and is showing a tendency to increase fast, with the corresponding denationalization

Table 44 *Control of the 400 largest industrial companies in Mexico*

Nationality	Number		Sales in Thousand Pesos	%	
Foreign					
Foreign control	161		15,788	36.20	
Strong foreign participation	71		7,796	17.86	
		232			54.06
Mexican					
Private	132		9,215	21.09	
Public	36		10,844	24.85	
		168			45.94
		400			100.00

SOURCE: Pablo González Casanova, *La Democracia en México* (Ediciones Era, Mexico City 1965), Table XVIII; based on data of José Luis Ceceña, *Los Monopolios en México* (Mexico, 1952).

Table 45   *Brazilian multibillionaire groups in 1962*

	Brazilian		Foreign		Mixed
	TOTAL	%	TOTAL	%	
Nonindustrial					
Export-import, banking, insurance, investments, and industrial services	8	33.4	6	21.8	1
Industrial					
a. Nondurable consumer goods	8	33.2	5	17.2	
b. Durable consumer goods	1	4.2	7	24.1	
c. Heavy machinery	1	4.2	4	13.8	
d. Basic industry	6	25.0	7	24.1	1
Subtotal	16	66.6	23	79.1	1
TOTAL	24	100.0	29	100.0	2

SOURCE: Mauricio Vinhas de Queiroz *et. al., Economic Groups* (Rio de Janeiro: Revista do Instituto de Ciencias Sociais, (December 1965), vol. 2. no. 1, p. 43 ff.; *apud* Luciano Martins, *Industrialização, Burguesia Nacional e Desenvolvimento* (Rio de Janeiro: Ed. Saga, 1968).

of the strategic sectors of the Latin American economy. The predominance of foreign companies is still more salient if one takes into account, on the one hand, the relative unimportance of the private firms compared to the national ones and, on the other hand, the special position of the public firms. As a matter of fact, the trend in Latin America in the last decade has been to restrict public firms—with the exception of a few important state monopolies, such as oil in Mexico and Brazil or electric power in Mexico—to basic industry, operating with a regime of rather low profits, and to industrial services, such as railways, more often than not operating in nonprofit terms. This means, in other words, that the most important fraction of the national firms, the public ones, has been oriented toward operating as a mechanism of indirect transfer of income to the private sector, where the predominance of the foreign groups is still larger. Still more important, this also means that the *national mechanisms for generating free-floating resources have been practically suffocated in Latin America, with the transference of their role to nonnational agents, and the consequent nonnational orientation of that process.*

We are confronted, here, with one of the most crucial problems of modern mass societies, which is at the very root of the problem of economic denationalization, but has not yet been given appropriate attention: *the mechanisms for forming free-floating resources* and the ways in which such resources *are subsequently channeled to promote and support relevant social and political inputs.*

It would be impossible, in the present context, to elaborate more extensively this fascinating subject, which was considered at a higher level of abstraction in Chapter 17. Let me just indicate, in a schematic form, what I consider to be the essential aspect of the subject. It consists, ultimately, in the fact that the modern mass society, different from the traditional society of the *ancien régime* or from the restricted society of the liberal bourgeois state, is not guided by its traditions, like the former, and does not possess, like the latter, a small class of rich and educated men who have both the inclination and the resources to dedicate themselves to the government of their polity, whatever the class bias they may carry to that government. In the modern mass society the function of creating, elaborating, and diffusing social and political expectations and orientations, which will become the most relevant and configurative factor in the inputs that will feed the several bureaucracies and their decision-making processes, is not specifically ascribed to anybody. Such expectations and orientations tend to result, mainly although not exclusively, from the uses given to the free-floating resources generated in that society. These free-floating resources are principally generated by business firms (either private or public) and are represented, in market economies, by the funds that can be used by the managers under the general labels of advertising and promotion. The use and orientation given, explicitly or implicitly, with varying degrees of consciousness and purposefulness, to these funds convey, in many ways, through the mass media, through the activities of intellectuals and politicians, and through the working of all sorts of agencies, all kinds of inputs into the social system, creating expectations, demands, and orientations that condition the decision-making centers, particularly the political ones.

The process by which the free-floating resources generated by business firms are finally converted into political decisions is very complex and usually far from direct and unilinear, as we saw in Chapter 5. In that process, however, particularly in market economies, the economic agents who generate these resources play a very important role, whatever the complicating factors intervening between their intents and the produced results. It is because of this that the economic elite is so important and the degree of its congruence with the other elites so relevant. Hence, from the point of view of national self-preservation and development, the corresponding importance of the economic elite's national commitment.

Regulation of the free-floating resources generated by public firms has been a very complicated matter for modern states. In totalitarian or strongly centralized states the ruling political group, either as bosses of the official party, as incumbents of governmental roles, or as top military chiefs, tend to appropriate these funds and to manipulate them to secure for themselves, as much as possible, the monopoly on relevant input making, thus increasing their autonomy in output decisions. In market-oriented societies, even if authoritarian, as the Latin American ones are basically today, the tendency—insofar as it is not distorted by clientele politics or corruption—is to treat, bureaucratically, the free-floating resources generated by public firms as public revenues to be reinvested in these firms or elsewhere, and thus to neutralize these firms as sources of political inputs. The leading groups in the Latin American states, in spite of the usual strongly authoritarian character of their rule, prefer to increase their autonomy of decision by gross elimination of political competition and free discussion, rather than by the more sophisticated manipulation of relevant inputs through the appropriate use of the free-floating resources available to them.

As a consequence of the substantial reduction in the importance of the private national firms and the neutralization of the capacity of the public firms to generate political inputs, the fact that private foreign firms have a majority and a controlling position in the more strategic industries of Latin America gives them almost exclusive control of the political use of the free-floating resources generated in the area. And this is one of the key consequences of economic denationalization and to a large extent an explanation of how that process is a self-reinforced one.

Cultural denationalization

The second variety of denationalization in Latin America concerns its culture, particularly in terms of science and technology. That aspect of denationalization represents one of the original structural characteristics of the region, which has always tended to be culturally dependent, and can be considered coextensive with its underdevelopment.

As is well known, the development of science and technology in a society involves two distinct conditions: (1) the existence in its culture of ideas and motivations conducive to a scientific view of the world and to its technical manipulation and (2) the existence in that society of institutional conditions allowing and stimulating scientific research and its profitable technological application. That the Latin American societies have exhibited little of these two conditions in their past is hardly a disputable assertion. The reasons for this will be discussed briefly in Chapters 21 and 22. What is relevant now is that the changes introduced in Latin America since the crisis of 1930 have altered that state of affairs and created new intellectual and practical possibilities and demands for science and technology. The very suddenness of that change, however, and of the urgency that has characterized the emerging demand for technology in Latin America has led Latin America to be satisfied with the importation of ready-made technology from the developed countries, in the form of ready-to-use equipment, patents, designs, and formulas, as well as foreign experts. The same situation has led the Latin American youth to search in foreign universities for the know-how and the status that the local ones cannot give them.

What has proved to be particularly serious, in these conditions, is the fact that the importation of know-how, both in terms of equipment and formulas and in terms of foreign education, has become repetitive and self-aggravating. The Latin American countries, unlike Meiji Japan, Soviet Russia in the 1920s and

1930s, and, currently, China, have not been able up to now to bring to their own lands a self-expanding capability for scientific and technological generation. As a consequence of the way in which the process of import replacement was carried out, in conditions of dependence on foreign firms resulting from the denationalization of the economic elite and the lack of a proper orientation on the part of the political elite, Latin American scientific and technological dependency is growing fast, instead of being superseded.

Of the many relevant consequences of cultural denationalization in the scientific-technological sphere, one of the most negative for the concerned society is the gradual loss of functionality, which affects its cultural elite as a national group. The basic functional role of cultural elites—*the formulation and interpretation of the beliefs of their culture, according to the requirements of the time and the necessities of the concerned society*—presents different forms in different sociohistorical conditions. For a primitive society that function involves essentially the magic incantations that preserve the physical and moral order and the actual survival of the society. For a modern society that function contains all sorts of scientific and technological implications. Once the demands of economic rationalization are only marginally addressed to the national elite, because the fundamental scientific and technological know-how and expertise are supplied from abroad, the cultural elite loses its economic functionality. This brings about the deterioration of its other roles (see Table 19a in Chapter 17) such as the formulation and administration, in the political plane, of the criteria of legitimacy, and in the social plane, of the criteria of respectability.

There is a deep and necessary interrelation, as was stressed in Chapter 17, between the elites of each of the four societal subsystems and their basic functions. A cultural denationalization (circularly reinforced by economic denationalization) that deprives the national cultural elite of its economic serviceability and ultimately of its general meaningfulness also deprives the political elite of its criteria of legitimacy, making its rule increasingly dependent on coercive means. This process also tends to affect, independent of other factors, the national orientation of the political elite, generating many concomitant dysfunctional consequences. And so we have in Latin America reciprocally aggravating processes of denationalization and loss of elite functionality. These processes are reflected in the fact that economic elite roles are increasingly played by foreign businesses, cultural elite roles by the more prestigious foreign universities, and political elite roles by the military.

Politico-military denationalization

The last form of denationalization that we have to study concerns its politico-military dimension. We have already seen that the three varieties of denationalization are interrelated and mutually reinforcing. That notwithstanding, each of these three varieties has its own specifications, and the politico-military one is no exception.

To speak of Latin American politico-military denationalization is to refer to a double process: (1) the process that has led most of the Latin American armed forces, particularly the local armies, to seize and control the government of their countries through military force and (2) the process that has led the Latin American military, with few exceptions, to depend on the United States and to follow, in its main lines, the policies and recommendations of the American defense establishment. These two processes are interrelated. The ability of the Latin American military forces to seize and keep power in their own countries is significantly enhanced by the facilities and support provided to them by the American defense system, and, at the same time, the advantage for that system in having control of or influence on the Latin American military is significantly enlarged by the military's seizure of the local governments.

The politico-military denationalization of Latin America has been studied still less than either of the other two forms of denationalization. The wall of secrecy usually surrounding military affairs makes it very difficult for outsiders to study the internal aspects of such processes as military denationalization; and the fact that military denationalization is not yet a completely realized occurrence, as far as the Latin American military itself is concerned, prevents its internal study by the military itself. Whether they like it or not, Latin American businessmen are not ignorant of the fact that they have become dependent on American business and that American corporations, capital, technology, and experts have a controlling influence on Latin American economies. The intellectuals in Latin America are the first to acknowledge the overwhelming foreign cultural influence on their countries and the extent to which they are dependent on foreign science and technology. The Latin American military, however, professionally committed to the idea of patriotism, national defense, and national security, and considering itself the specific guarantor of these values, does not, in any way, see its activities as involving any denationalizing effect. The military acknowledges, of course, the existence of many objective links of dependence between the national defense systems in Latin America and the American defense system. These links, however, euphemistically called links of interdependence, are considered by the military as a useful way of reinforcing the defense capabilities of the Latin American countries. The military's fundamental assumption is that the two Americas have a basic common interest, much more important than their eventual points of conflict, and that they are equally engaged in a life-and-death struggle against the same enemy, international communism, both as an external military danger and as an internal subversive risk.

Whatever the difficulties in obtaining certain specific data, the understanding of these two interconnected aspects of Latin American politico-military denationalization (control of the national governments by the military and of the military by the United States) requires the understanding of two distinct but interconnected aspects of Latin American politics: (1) the reasons why, with few exceptions,[17] the Latin American military forces, particularly in the course of the last decade, were led to, and were successful in, taking control of their governments and of practically the whole political system of their countries and (2) the reasons why, with still fewer exceptions (Peru), having achieved that result, they were led to adopt the orientation and the policies that they have actually followed. The discussion of these two questions—which I have already treated briefly in another study[18]—would require a much wider and more complex approach than is possible in the context of the present topic.

The first question concerns the whole political process of the Latin American countries in our time and is intimately connected with the whole history of the region. A succinct attempt to analyze its more relevant aspects will be made in Chapters 21 and 22. The second question, in many ways related to the first, requires the understanding of the ideology and of the corporate interests of the Latin American military, which will be presented briefly below. Further treatment of that question would require a much more extensive study, taking into account the internal complexities of each of the military establishments and the national differences among them.

The seizure of most Latin American governments by the military is essentially related to the failure of the Latin American societies, in the course of their current process of modernization, to build a viable political system. That failure, in turn, has resulted from the excessive incompatible demands that the Latin American polities have had to process, in conditions that have prevented the possibility of forming a sufficiently broad social consensus. In the resulting crisis of power and legitimacy, particularly sharp in the 1960s, the military came to be the only social group with wide national organization, cohesion, and the strength to impose its rule. And because the military had in general enjoyed, at least initially, the allegiance of most of the middle class (which is currently the leading political force of the new Establishment) and the middle class formed the widest ruling strata of those societies, military rule could be imposed and exerted with minimal violence and few changes in the status quo.

Once complete control of the national governments and political systems was achieved, the Latin American military, with few exceptions, adopted a political orientation that implied and resulted in severe sacrifices for the national autonomy and endogeny of the respective countries. The reasons for that fact can only be understood in light of the ideological tendency of the Latin American middle class, which has been aggravated by the military version of that ideology and by the corporate interests of the Latin American military establishments.

The Latin American armies—whatever their connections in the remote past with the landed patriciate—have been a typical, although peculiar, middle sector of the urban middle class for many decades, and, since the radical movements of the late nineteenth and early twentieth centuries, have always played the role of an ultimate agency for middle-class interests and values.[19] These interests and values, particularly in their military version, are deeply connected with the idea of preserving (since the middle-class revolutions) the existing social order, which is identified both with the legitimate order and with the general requirements of military discipline and conventional security (law and order).

The ideological expression of these interests and values is a compound of moralism, ascriptive authoritarian progressivism, and militant anticommunism. The fascist proclivity of that ideology is quite manifest. It was acknowledged and even proclaimed in the fascist era, as in the cases of Uriburu or Farrell, in the Argentina of the 1930s and early 1940s, or in Vargas' *Estado Novo*, in the Brazil of the late 1930s. It has been disavowed since fascism became unacceptable as a label and an overt ideology. Overtly or covertly, however, and in larger or smaller doses, the fascist components of the Latin American middle-class ideology, particularly in its military version, have played and keep playing the role lucidly analyzed by Organski (1965, chap. 5) and already discussed in Chapter 16. It is an ideology of modernization with contained development, of economic development with minimal social change, of social change without risk to the new Establishment, and of societal mobilization without popular participation.

In the current Latin American conditions, the result of that ideology, in proportion to its fascist content and to the extent of the military control of the political system, is a more- or less-accentuated colonial fascism, in which two traits are particularly relevant for the purposes of our present analysis. The first trait is the peculiar and current (with a few exceptions) Latin American combination of economic liberalism and political authoritarianism. The second is the no less peculiar and current (with still fewer exceptions) Latin American militant anticommunism.

It would be extremely interesting, but too long for the scope of the present analysis, to study in some detail the various aspects of Latin American colonial fascism, particularly these two traits. Let us limit the discussion, however, to our present purpose: the understanding of the current politico-military denationalization in Latin America. The two traits in question provide the most important contribution to that effect. The first trait, the peculiarly Latin American combination of economic liberalism and political authoritarianism, creates the precise conditions for the increasing economic predominance of the large international supercorporations, already discussed in this chapter. The second trait, militant anticommunism, provides the conditions for the faithful acceptance by the Latin American military of the policies and instructions given to them by the American defense system, in the name and for the purpose of the world crusade against international communism.

In the conditions of Latin America, economic liberalism combined with, and supported by, political authoritarianism, if not absolutism, is the specific condition for the uncontrollable expansion of the economic predominance of the international supercorporations, with the results presented earlier in this chapter. The extent to which this is true is practically self-evident. As is rather obvious, the liberal and neoliberal rule of equal treatment for all economic actors, whatever their nationality and strength, in conditions in which the international supercorporations have infinitely better capital, technology, organization, and command or markets than the national firms, would necessarily bring about the complete control of the economy by those supercorporations. If, in addition to these conditions, the national entrepreneurs, fearful of popular pressure against the existing regime of property, prefer to be dependent partners of the international supercorporation, rather than to face the risks of a more social and public-oriented national capitalism, the only possible remaining agency able to prevent the complete domination of the national economy by the international supercorporations is the national state. The submission of the national state to an authoritarian or absolutist regime committed to the enforcement, by all means, of economic liberalism suppresses that last possible barrier to complete economic domination.

Militant anticommunism, on the other hand, based on the view that the Latin American countries are full partners in the free world and that that world is externally and internally menaced by international communism, makes the strict adjustment of each country's national policies mandatory, so that these policies meet the strategic requirements, including a loyal allegiance to the leader of the free-world bloc, for defense against that all-pervasive and terrible enemy.

A relevant aspect of these strategic requirements for the world containment of international communism, as was mentioned in Chapter 18, is the international division of labor between the American defense system and the defense systems of the less-developed "partners" of the free world. To the United States goes the task of general deterrence and containment of the military strength of international communism—which includes, in an unclear way, the combined power of the Soviet Union, Eastern Europe, and China. To such defense systems as the Latin American ones goes the task of preventing the subversive action of agents, who are supposed to be constantly infiltrating from the areas of international communism, now particularly from Cuba. External defense in the case of the former and internal defense in the case of the latter—such are the basic assignments of the central and the peripheral "partners" in the free world. The Rockefeller report, at the end of 1969, gave a new emphasis to these views, which were originally formulated in the first years of the cold war. With few exceptions, the Latin American military have doggedly maintained these views throughout the last quarter of a century, in spite of the changes in opinion and strategy that occurred in the United States during Kennedy's administration.

The ideological motivations of the Latin American middle class and the military version of that ideology, including its militant anticommunism, are quite understandable in the sociocultural context of Latin American societies, as will be discussed briefly in Chapter 22. What is much more intriguing is the dogged adherence, by most of the Latin American military establishments, to the myth of international communism and its supposed unity of purpose and action and, to a smaller extent, to the myth of the free world and the supposed unity of its condition and interests.

In the conditions of the late 1940s and early 1950s, as was discussed in Chapter 18, it was perfectly understandable for countries preserving a market economy and interested in keeping close connections with the more developed capitalist countries to accept the American view of the cold war. The liberal behavior of the United States, vis-à-vis the defeated countries, and the enlightened policies of the Marshall Plan and the Point Four program, on the one hand, and the ruthless rule of Stalin and Soviet Russia's politico-military domination of Eastern Europe. in a movement that appeared to aim at the total conquest of Europe, on the other hand, were more than sufficient justification of the American theses. There was, under Soviet leadership, an international communist system, supported by terrific military strength and by a fanatic international subversive movement, which constituted a very serious menace to the free world, provisionally defined as the loose system of noncommunist countries willing to preserve their own institutions, acknowledged to be actually or tendentiously oriented toward democratic principles. That the defense of the free world would require, for the benefit of all partners, a common strategy, under the guidance of the United States as the leading power of the bloc, and that that strategy would involve a division of labor between the central and the peripheral powers, as formerly indicated, could hardly have been opposed in the conditions of that time.

What is so intriguing, as already observed, is the fact that most of the Latin American military establishments kept doggedly clinging to that view of the world even after the United States herself, under Kennedy, acknowledged the complete difference in conditions and interests that separated the developed from the underdeveloped countries in the free world. What is still less understandable is how most of the Latin American military could retain the idea of international communism as an operational concept, in view of the notorious and deadly conflicts opposing China to the Soviet Union and separating the latter from her Eastern European satellites.

A full discussion of that question would require more information than is available about the internal opinions of the military and would also demand a more extensive treatment than can be afforded here. I would suggest, in accordance with the analysis presented up to here of the process of Latin American politico-military denationalization, that the retention, by most of the Latin American military establishments, of the increasingly outdated American theses of the late 1940s and early 1950s is due to the combined effects of their ideology, the internal conditions of their rule, and their new corporate interests.

To the Latin American military leaders of the late 1940s and early 1950s those theses would have seemed rather unobjectionable. They were, besides, in complete accordance with the ideological tendencies of the military leaders. The fact that those ideological tendencies have not changed and that the new generations of officers have kept the same ideological outlook, if not a magnified version, has been primarily responsible for the preservation of cold war doctrines during the following twenty-five years. Moreover, the men who have committed themselves to these doctrines have also been, as a rule, important institution builders and as such have acquired a longer-lasting capacity for remaining influential. After World War II higher war schools were created throughout Latin America, with American help. The American military books and texts, with their inherent views on the containment of international communism for the defense of the free world, were converted into the main literature of the new military schools. Without any Machiavellian plot on the part of the American military, its motivations and views were incorporated by the Latin American military and preserved way beyond the time when they were reasonably meaningful. Only later, during the Kennedy administration, did the United States military system and, through it, the United States government come to realize the fabulous capacity they had undeliberately acquired to manipulate politically the Latin American military establishments and, through them, the Latin American governments. The struggle, during the Kennedy administration, between the military and those who thought such an important instrument of power should be preserved and enhanced, and the enlightened reformers, including Kennedy himself, who considered it a precarious advantage based on misunderstandings that would sooner or later be displaced by the Latin Americans and who, therefore, wanted a more endurable and mutually satisfactory basis for their Latin American policy, was finally won, after the Kennedy days, by the short-term realists. And so the spontaneous alienation of the Latin American military, preserved and cultivated by the higher military schools, has been deliberately manipulated by the United States defense system since the Johnson administration.

This external aspect of the matter relates it to the corporate interests of the Latin American military establishments. The adherence to cold war doctrines beyond the time of their reasonable credibility cannot be ascribed only to ideological blindness. What has occurred, as a matter of fact, is that the military, as an institutionalized group of professionals, has become increasingly dependent on the preservation of these doctrines for its collective and individual corporate interests. In such a complex matter, full of subtle implications, it is enough to stress three major points. The first refers to the increasing—and in some cases complete—dependence of the Latin American military systems on equipment, instruction, and facilities provided by the United States military system, with the resulting institutionalization of their condition as satellite appendages of the latter. The subtle—and sometimes not so subtle—manipulation of ancient classic rivalries among the Latin American military establishments (if A has so many planes B must keep the balance) is an important additional institutional motivation to keep them duly aligned with the United States.

The second point, also of a general institutional character, concerns the extent to which the cultivation of the old cold war doctrines represents a very important rationalization, in the sense of Mannheim, for the interference of the military in the domestic political affairs of the country. Once military rule became widespread, its justification and maintenance reinforced the necessity for keeping the free world defense system in constant alertness against an all-pervasive international communist infiltration. The fact that real native guerrillas, in addition to the mythical ones, have made their appearance in Latin America in the last decade—to a large extent as the result of the suppression of any nonconspiratorial form of political opposition—was a most welcome confirmation of how serious the menace of infiltrated subversion was.

The third point is the increasing—in some cases complete—dependence of a successful military career on the blessings of the United States military system. The official acceptance by the Latin American military of the old theses that the free world is confronted with a constant imminent menace from international communism and that the military's job is to fight, under United States guidance, the subversive maneuvers of infiltrated agents has created the necessity for a sort of American clearance for promotions to the higher military echelons. And the fact that the domestic military systems are entirely organized in terms of these cold war theses naturally requires an internal correspondence between these views and the criteria for assessing the merits and qualities of the officers, particularly for their promotion. And so a closed and self-reinforcing complex of ideological motivations, rationalization of interests, and internal co-optation has been formed and consolidated, objectively functioning as a factor in and a framework for the politico-military denationalization of the Latin American countries.

NOTES

[1] See United Nations, *The Economic Development of Latin America and Its Principal Problems*, 1950, and *International Cooperation in Latin American Development Policy* (E/CN.12/359).

[2] See CEPAL, *Integración, Sector Externo y Desarrolo Económico de América Latina*, 1966; see also CEPAL (1969a, chap. 3, particularly Tables I.53, I.54 and I.55).

[3] See CEPAL (1969a, Table I.16). That coefficient is a good indicator of the achieved extent of industrialization.

[4] See Helio Jaguaribe (1969a).

[5] The same trend can be observed in the past. By 1850 the developed countries of today had per capita incomes of about $150 (dollars of 1952–1954), and the underdeveloped ones had incomes of about $100. That is a relation of 1.5 to 1. See Osvaldo Sunkel, (1970b, p. 44). See also C. Bettelheim (1970, particularly chaps. 3 and 4) and S. Amin (1970) for a dialectical view of underdevelopment.

[6] See Maria da Conceição Tavares (1964, pp. 1–62). See also Aldo Ferrer (1963), Celso Furtado (1969), and Sunkel (1970a).

[7] The insufficiencies of Latin American exports can be summarized as resulting from: (1) the small increase in the international demand for its traditional commodities, aggravated by the unfavorable trend in the terms of trade, and (2) lack of competitive conditions enabling Latin America to obtain a larger participation in the international trade of industrial commodities. This last aspect is the consequence of many factors, including such different things as, in some cases, the comparatively higher cost and lower quality of the regions' industrial products, and in a general way, the restrictive practices adopted by the developed countries, including governmental regulation or manipulation of foreign trade and the policies of the head offices of the great corporations of the United States or Europe, vis-à-vis their Latin American branches.

[8] On Kubitschek's Target Plan, see Jaguaribe (1968, chaps. 11 and 12). See also Celso Lafer's doctoral thesis presented to Cornell's Graduate School of Political Science (1970).

[9] The figures in Table 36 correspond to 1960. For 1968, CEPAL estimates that the rural population is 45.8 percent of the total. See CEPAL (1969a, Table I.20).

[10] See Centro Latinoamericano de Pesquisas en Ciencias Sociais, *Situação Social da América Latina* (Rio de Janeiro, 1965), chap. 2.

[11] See CEPAL (1969a, pp. 52 ff., particularly Table I.24, based in ILPES study INST/5.5/6.3, particularly its Table I.20).

[12] See CEPAL (1963b, vol. 2, p. 1, Table 76).

[13] See CEPAL (1969a, vol. 1, pp. 172 and 173).

[14] See also F. Carmona, *et al.* (1970, pp. 70 ff.).

[15] Figures are in old cruzeiros. The new cruzeiro, adopted in 1967, is worth 1,000 old cruzeiros.

[16] See Julián Delgado, "El Desafío a la Argentina," in *Primera Plana*, (Buenos Aires, September 3, 1964), no. 297, pp. 35 ff.

[17] The most important and neat exception is Chile. Uruguay comes close to Chile, and Venezuela, in spite of the partial veto power of her military, is still an exception. Other exceptions are Costa Rica, which has no army, and Cuba, where the army is under the political control of the socialist government. In Mexico, where military political interference is officially denied, the military has fused with the ruling bureaucracy and has as such a decisive influence and the usual veto power.

[18] See Jaguaribe, *Political Obstacles to National Development in Latin America*, (Mexico: Center for the Study of Democratic Institutions, 1969), mimeographed.

[19] See J. Nun (1968).

426   *Book III: A Latin American Case Study*

B

Causes of Latin American Underdevelopment

21

The Dualistic Society

Two basic questions

In Chapters 19 and 20 we had an opportunity to consider a brief description and analysis of the main structural characteristics of Latin American societies, as they can be currently observed. As we have seen, the central characteristic of the countries of the region, although to different degrees and in different conditions, is their general underdevelopment, particularly as national societies. Furthermore, they are characterized by a triple process of denationalization.

In the course of that description some of the factors and conditions contributing directly to those characteristics were indicated or discussed. In the present section an attempt will be made to formulate, as succinctly and precisely as possible, some general explanations of them.

Although providing a large and worthy amount of data, categories, and interpretative constructs, the already voluminous literature on Latin American underdevelopment,[1] whether considering it in the framework of a global sociohistorical process or focusing on particular countries, periods, social sectors, or issues, has not yet provided a succinct and coherent set of sufficiently rigorous and verifiable propositions, or a theorylike set of interrelated explanatory hypotheses. Earlier attempts at a synthetic view of the region's underdevelopment have been spoiled by the adoption of fallacious single-factor explanations, such as the supposed inherent racial inferiority of mestizos or the supposed unviability of civilization in the tropics. In more recent times a legitimate concern for empirical research and factual details has discouraged most scholars from attempting to reach a valuable and confirmable general theoretical explanation for Latin American underdevelopment. It is such an attempt that will be made in the present section. The attempted explanation has been conceived to fill two basic requirements, one concerning the form and kind of explanation and the other concerning the presentation of the sociohistorical process whose characteristics are to be explained.

The first requirement, concerning the form and kind of explanation to be given for the characteristics under our scrutiny, is to build a few precise hypotheses (actually, two) at a sufficiently broad and high level of generality to fit the region as a whole, notwithstanding national diversities, and to allow a rigorous propositional formulation, without losing the concrete sociohistorical meaning of the characteristics. The second requirement is to preserve the historicity of the sociohistorical process to be explained within the framework of these hypotheses. What is involved is the well-known problem of combining the here-and-now character of an historical process with the universality of social science generalizations. The way to solve that problem, in my opinion, is to incorporate the lawlike theories of sociopolitical explanation into the descriptive historical narrative, in the way suggested by Gallie (1968).

In the present section the historical narrative—or more properly, argument—considers two phases of uneven length. The first includes the preindustrial period in Latin America, from the conquest to the crisis of the early 1930s. The second includes the subsequent three decades and the region's still-unfinished transition to the structure, or at least to many of the features, of an industrial society. Ultimately, for the purposes of the present study, these two periods present two successive basic questions: (1) *Why didn't the Latin American societies achieve national development between the time of their independence and the first third of the twentieth century?* (2) *Why, after more than twenty years of deliberate commitments for achieving a self-sustained national development, haven't the Latin American countries been able to reach that goal since the end of the second world war?*

To answer these two questions, within the requirements formerly indicated, I will formulate two successive hypotheses, trying with each to present, in a very succinct way, a comprehensive explanation for one of these questions. The first will be presented in this chapter; the second in Chapter 22.

The first hypothesis, concerning Latin American underdevelopment until the 1930s, will be in the form of an adjustment of a general theory—*Dysfunctional elites historically bring about the underdevelopment of their societies*—to the particular case of Latin American underdevelopment. For that purpose an initial reference will be made to the theory of elite functionality and dysfunctionality discussed in Chapter 13, and to the earlier discussion of the historical illustration of that thesis presented in Chapter 12. Then a succinct analysis will point out the most salient aspects of the historical dysfunctionality of the Latin American elites and show how that dysfunctionality, in accordance with the theoretical assumptions formerly considered, has brought about the underdevelopment of the Latin American societies.

The second hypothesis, concerning the failure of the Latin American societies to achieve their self-sustained development in the last three last decades, will be in the form of two subhypotheses covering the initial period of spontaneous import substitution and the subsequent period of deliberate state-supported efforts to promote national development. For the first period, the explanation will be given in the form of a socioeconomic generalization: *"Small" national markets do not have enough pull, in present conditions, to induce a spontaneous self-sustained development.* Then the discussion will show how and why Latin American domestic markets are "small" or operate as such and, therefore, how the Latin American case fits that generalization. The explanation for the second period will follow a similar course, showing how the general sociopolitical conditions (including relevant decisions concerning the redistribution of wealth and power and their management) for a state-promoted effort at national development have not been obtained in the Latin American societies.

The first hypothesis

Latin American societies remained underdeveloped from their independence to the first decades of the twentieth century because they became dualistic societies in which the optimization of the elite's aims was not compatible with the basic interests of the mass, thus preventing the social integration of the concerned countries and establishing in them a social regime (that is, a combined regime of values, participation, power, and property) that was not amenable to their national development.

As discussed in Chapters 7–15, national development is the development, as a whole, of a national society qua national. It depends, in economic terms, on successfully achieving a self-sustained economic growth, based on an increasingly better utilization of the means of production through better technology and organization. In order to be self-sustained, it requires a high level of autonomy of decisions and endogeny of growth. But it also requires cultural, social, and political development.

Cultural development involves, essentially, the functional adjustment of the information system and the regime of values of a society in order to provide that society (1) with efficient means to control its environment and to adapt itself to that environment and (2) with values, norms, and life-styles conducive to social cohesiveness and to the prevalence of rational and dependable behaviors. Since the eighteenth century these requirements have involved (1) the development and diffusion of science and technology and the emergence of social conditions conducive to their appropriate use, preferably, within a humanistic framework, and (2) a clear predominance of egalitarian values.

Social development consists, essentially, in the functional adjustment of the regime of participation prevailing in a society in order to minimize ascriptive privileges and forms of authority and to maximize competitive and egalitarian access to all opportunities and roles.

Political development consists, essentially, in the modernization and institutionalization of the political system, increasing its rational orientation, structural functional differentiation, capability, political mobilization, political integration, and political representativeness.

The understanding of national development as the overall development of a national society (that is, as the functional aggregation of cultural, social, political, and economic development) leads, ultimately, to the understanding of the development of a society, whenever its environmental conditions are not particularly unfavorable, *as the result of a functional relationship between the elite and the mass*. (See Chapter 13.) That functional relationship, as we have seen, consists ultimately in an elite-mass rapport according to which: (1) the services that the elite renders to the mass and to the society as a whole, including political, economic, cultural, and participational leadership, entrepreneurship, and excellence of exemplarity in the performance of societally required functions, are substantially greater than the various kinds of resources that the elite exacts from the mass and the society as a whole for its own consumption and operation—that is, the elite's social cost–benefit account manifests a fairly favorable balance; and (2) social mobility is sufficient to allow capable men from the mass access to elite roles and replacement of less capable incumbents in elite roles with more capable men—that is, the circulation of elites keeps the elite open, flexible, and competent.

Empirically, the occurrence and maintenance of a functional elite-mass relationship has proved to depend on a certain range of internalized elite values and enlightened self-interest, within the context of the available resources, the means and conditions for their use, and the pressures exerted by the mass of that society or by other societies. (See Chapter 13.) The internalized values of the elite, as has been seen, are a fundamental aspect of the relationship and may, in certain conditions, represent the major favorable or unfavorable factor for a functional elite-mass relationship. Values orienting the elite toward a militant responsibility for its own society and toward rational and dependable behavior tend—whatever the original class differentiations and elite feelings of superiority—to favor in the long run a functional elite-mass relationship: the Protestant ethic, the samurai honor, and so on. Enlightened self-interest may bring the elite to accept sacrifices or to give up privileges for the mutual benefit of the elite itself and the society as a whole. In that last respect the pressures of the masses, as has been discussed, are of the utmost importance. When the masses are able to achieve a certain degree of communication and organization, outside of elite control, they impose on the elite both a redistribution scheme that is more favorable for the mass and a cost-benefit balance that is more favorable for the society as a whole. It is to sustain their elite level that pressed elites make or adopt innovations that will increase social productivity. The industrial revolution and the subsequent sociopolitical innovations in the West, including the welfare state of today, may, in a sense, be explained, as we have seen, as the creative response of the Western (renovated and self-renovating) elites to pressures from their masses. That response was oriented so as to allow the elites to keep most of their leadership and advantages while increasing mobility.

As was extensively analyzed in Chapter 12, all the historical cases of development since the development of Great Britain in the second half of the eighteenth century have resulted from a more functional elite-mass relationship. In some cases, as in Great Britain and the United States, that more functional relationship was achieved through the gradual adjustment of the elite, in terms of both its internalized values and its enlightened understanding of its own self-interest to the necessities of the time. In the case of Japan, as was seen, the functional readjustment of the elite, under the pressure of imminent seizure of control by the Western powers, led to a reform movement. The bakufu elite was superseded by the Western clans, and through the device of restoring the powers of the emperor and eliminating the shogunate, part of the tradition was used to change the other part and to promote, with the rapid modernization of Japan, a much better utilization of the national resources and capabilities. France and Germany, under the empires of Napoleon III and Bismarck, presented an intermediate case between the British gradualism and the radical reformism of the Japanese. When the former elites of the *ancien régime* in France and Germany lost their capacity to lead, the emerging elite of the bourgeoisie had not obtained the self-confidence and social prestige acquired earlier by the English bourgeoisie. The device of the French and Prussian-German empires served to reshape the elites of these countries, bringing about a combination of the old and the new in conditions of much higher functionality. With Russia and China, also formerly discussed, we have an example that is the opposite of Great Britain. An elite that was not susceptible to adaptation and renovation was finally ousted by a violent revolution, and an able counterelite took control and achieved rapid modernization.

In spite of the complexity of the factors and conditions that have enabled certain elites to gradually adjust and change, have caused others to split so that a modernizing sector has replaced the traditionalist one, and have rendered some elites incapable of changing so that in the end they have either been subdued by a counterelite or led their societies to ultimate failure, it has been suggested (in Chapter 13) that, in all cases, a basic explanation can be found in (1) the sort of internalized values that the elites have and (2) the capacity of the masses to exert pressure. The village culture of the Middle Ages, the free boroughs and the emergence in the Renaissance of a new strata of men who were independent of the nobles, the religious mobilization carried out during the Reformation, bringing men from humble origin to positions of influence which the former church hierarchy would not have allowed, and the general educational facilities provided by the Enlightenment in the eighteenth and early nineteenth century—all these factors, as we have seen, contributed profoundly in Western Europe (except in Spain and Portugal) to making the elite more flexible and to the opening of elite roles. These events oriented the elites toward values that were socially more functional and, at the same time, increased the efficiency of the corrective and redistributive pressures exerted by the masses. In Russia and China, however, as was formerly discussed, the absence of most of these events in conditions including a great abundance of servile labor, contributed to the rigidification of the elite and the impotence of the mass. As will be seen, the Latin American case is much more similar to the Russian and Chinese cases than to the North Atlantic one.

Latin American dualism

An appropriate analysis of the origins of Latin American dualism would require a comprehensive study of the social, economic, cultural, and political characteristics of Spain and Portugal in their Renaissance period and of the consequences of these traits in the subsequent history of these two countries and their colonies through the seventeenth and eighteenth centuries. Such a study, however, would not be compatible with the limited scope of the present chapter. Let me only point out two of the most relevant sociocultural aspects of these two countries in the Renaissance period. These two characteristics particularly differentiated Spain and Portugal from the other Western European societies of that time and proved to be a decisive influence in the shaping of their subsequent futures.

The first concerns the social structure of the Iberian countries and consists in the abortive development of their medieval *tiers état*, particularly of the intermediate urban social strata living in the free boroughs and comprehending a mixture of independent artisans and merchants. An adequate explanation of the unsuccessful development of the earlier Spanish and Portuguese bourgeoisie would be, by itself, a complex subject, which has not yet been sufficiently studied. I will just mention that recent evidence (see Wiznitzer, 1960) suggests the existence of a close correlation between the Iberian borough dwellers and the Jews. The expulsion of the Jews by the Iberian kings, first in Spain and subsequently in Portugal, for a variety of reasons, ranging from alleged religious motives to complex economic-political factors, seems to have deprived these countries of most of their skilled and entrepreneurial middle class. As a consequence, the promising late medieval *tiers état* of Spain and Portugal was led to an abortive outcome in the fifteenth and sixteenth centuries. Whereas in the rest of Western Europe the Renaissance unleashed the creative potential of the emerging bourgeoisie, forming strong and permanent intermediate strata between the bottom level of the social stratification, including the peasants and the lower sectors of the urban manual laborers, and the upper levels, including the clergy and the nobility, the Iberian countries were led to a new simplification of their social structure, which was divided between the low strata of peasants and workers and the high strata of nobles, clergy, and an ever-growing bureaucratic sector of military and civil servants of the crown.[2] Several circumstances have made this basic dualism less sharp in metropolitan Spain and Portugal, but it has been accentuated in the Latin American colonies, particularly because of the abundance of servile labor.

The second of the Iberian characteristics requiring special attention, which is not unconnected with the sociocultural conditions that led to the expulsion of the Jews, is the conservative resistance to the new scientific spirit that emerged from the empirically oriented physics of the Renaissance. The Iberian countries were open to the artistic and literary revolutions of the Italian and Flemish quattrocento and cinquecento, but not to the inductive orientation of the new science or to the philosophical and theological challenges of the sixteenth century. The conservative preservation of the Scholastic forms of culture, in socioeconomic conditions in which an aristocratic-bureaucratic society had prematurely suffocated its private initiative, led to the development of values and the consolidation of a social structure that were neither conducive to democratic

and egalitarian trends nor conducive to modern ideas and scientific and technological views and practices.[3]

These two characteristics, along with others, profoundly influenced the way
in which the Iberian countries approached the settlement, colonization, and
expansion of their American possessions. Comparing the colonization of the
two Americas, we can see how they reflected the conditions and contrasts of
their respective mother countries. The settlement of Anglo-America was essentially a middle-class venture, based on the free initiative of independent groups,
whereas the occupation and colonization of Latin America was the enterprise of
an elite minority directly influenced, from the beginning or soon after, by the
Iberian crowns.

The fact that Spain's original conquistadores were not from the elite but were
exceptionally enterprising common adventurers is irrelevant. They were immediately promoted to the higher ranks of the elite, and their successors were, by
birth or function, given elite status. In both Spanish and Portuguese America
the sort of society that took form in the sixteenth century was characterized by
a sharp division between an elite of landowners and officials, with a tiny incorporated segment of merchants, and the great mass of servile peasants. These
were either the local Indians, whose civilization was rapidly destroyed, or imported African slaves.

Thus, the first important characteristic of that society was its strong dualistic
nature, which opposed, more sharply than in Spain and Portugal, masters and
servants, those who had inherent rights and those who were only given the per-
mission to exist as a labor force. This opposition did not involve an unbridgeable
gap between elite and mass levels. On the contrary, the colonial society was
much more open to new talents and individual success than the European one,
and was not particularly race-discriminating. The opposition meant that, whatever the origin of the incumbents in elite roles, these roles as such, not the incumbents' qualifications, granted them privileges, whereas mass roles were
inherently underprivileged.[4]

The excess of labor

The second essential characteristic of Latin American societies from the late
sixteenth century until today, with the relative exceptions of Argentina, Uruguay,
and Chile, has been the immense abundance of labor. Only part of the Indian
population was ever actively used. African slave trade was soon brought to very
high proportions, constituting one of the greatest businesses of the world in the
seventeenth century. The historical consequence of that enormous abundance
of labor, which persists today, has been to depress the conditions of the Latin
American masses profoundly. It was responsible for keeping peasant slavery
through the middle of the nineteenth century and, in the case of Brazil, until the
end of that century, maintaining, after the abolition, a de facto complete dependence of the peasants on the landowners. In modern times it has affected the
conditions of the working class, whose unions were granted by the governments,

rather than being built from the bottom, and whose capacity for bargaining has so often been curtailed by the immense availability of unemployed labor.[5]

The result of the master-servant relationship in conditions of enormous labor surplus, with an elite whose values were oriented toward self-magnification and high levels of consumption, was a social regime that was not amenable to the social integration and the national development of the Latin American countries. After independence, the Latin American elites, although keeping most of the characteristics inherited from their Iberian culture and their colonial past, withdrew their allegiance to the former mother countries and identified with those selected aspects of French and English culture that were a part of the Latin American image of these two societies. Their feeling of belonging to a Western European elite, conditioned by French literature and the French view of the world and associated with some traits of the English gentleman ideal, increased the alienation of the Latin American elites vis-à-vis their own masses and societies. To the elite, the Latin American masses became the equivalent of an alien colonial people, very much as if two distinct nations were in a relationship of domination and subordination. And the ethnic differentiation usually separating the predominantly Caucasian elites from predominantly Indian, mestizo, Negro, and mulatto masses has strongly reinforced that dualism, even though racism, as an ideology, has been alien to Latin American tradition.[6]

It is interesting to note that Argentina, Uruguay, and Chile, which did not have that excess of dependent labor through their colonial period and until the last third of the nineteenth century, have presented distinct traits in their national formation, in spite of the similitude of their other conditions. The case of Chile is the clearest because she did not suffer, like Uruguay, from the pressure and interference of two overwhelmingly superior, but happily competing, neighbors. Also she did not have the peculiar conflict of Argentina between the port city and the provinces, which so paralyzed that country's development. Chile, therefore, was able to organize a national society and a national state early and to aggressively and successfully expand her territory and resources to the north, at the expense of Bolivia and Peru, and to the south, at the expense of the Araucanian Indians. And she was able, in terms of a successful agricultural and extractive society, to reach a high level of political and cultural development in the second half of the nineteenth century. Chile's trouble, from 1930 onward, when external and internal conditions required her industrialization, was not so much the difficulty of surmounting her own social constraints, which were moderate, as the limitation of her population and market for an autonomous and endogenous industrialization.[7]

Like Chile, Argentina and Uruguay did not enjoy an excess of labor until the great immigration of the last quarter of the nineteenth century. Nineteenth-century Uruguay, however, because the split between the Colorados and the Blancos was successfully used by Argentina and Brazil to interfere in her domestic affairs, remained in a state of quasi-permanent civil war. In spite of that, however, she was able to achieve a high level of social (not political) integration and also to obtain a substantial agricultural growth. As soon as the suicidal party conflict was mediated by a man of political genius (Battle y Ordóñez) in the first years of this century, the way was open for rapid progress.

In Argentina the conflict between the port city and the provinces was more significant than the opposition of liberals and conservatives and more important than even the conflict between the civilized *porteños* and the barbarian gauchos, as Sarmiento saw it. The conflict between the port city and the provinces was a confrontation between two ideal forms for organizing the country: the city-state and the nation. The fact that for so long those with the capacity to organize the nation were committed to a city-state loyalty and those with an allegiance to the nation were hindered by their rural background was responsible for the delay of Argentina's growth until the last third of the nineteenth century.

The private appropriation of land

A third characteristic of Latin American societies, which became important in the last third of the nineteenth century, for Argentina, Uruguay, and Chile as well as for the other countries, was the complete private appropriation of land, in anticipation of its useful cultivation. One of the most important factors in the development of the United States, as can be seen now in retrospect, was that about 70 percent of American land was owned at one time by the federal government, which could, through appropriate legislation, of which the Homestead Act is best known, distribute the land for its effective occupation and cultivation. So it was possible both to attract active people to the frontier, expanding the occupation of the territory, and to provide very cheap land to whoever wanted to work it, maintaining the full employment of the population, restricting speculation, and preventing an excessive pressure from labor in demand of jobs.[8] This last fact, in spite of the maintenance of slavery in the southern states, created two of the fundamental conditions for the industrialization of the North: the existence of a rather large acquisitive market and sufficient advantages in the mechanization of production.

The private appropriation of land by the Latin American elite, before it was usefully occupied by the migrants of the last third of the nineteenth century, helped to maintain the features of the dualistic societies where they already existed, or to strengthen these features, particularly in Argentina. The massive immigration of landless Europeans to the *pampa gringa*, where they could have become the equivalent of the midwestern American farmer but were compelled to be dependent tenants, gave to the Argentine elite, in support of the traits resulting from their former values, the new economic support necessary to consolidate them into a landed oligarchy, transforming Argentina into a dualistic society.[9]

As a very successful dualistic society, Latin America was able to maintain a highly profitable specialized trade with Europe during the several stages of her colonial and postcolonial history. The productive capacity of Latin America, with almost limitless availability of land and labor, was also almost limitless, being contained only by the ceiling on European demand. From the second half of the nineteenth century until the Great Depression of the 1930s, the industrial revolution provided a growing demand for Latin American products, while Latin America imported the industrial goods for its consumption from Europe at relatively cheap prices. The enormous wealth produced by that specialization—in which the plantations, the great haciendas, and the mines supplied the primary goods in exchange for which the elites obtained their luxury articles and also provided for most of the daily needs of the masses—assured the stability of the system, keeping the rural masses under the complete domination of the landed oligarchy. While that system kept expanding, the emerging and growing urban middle class could easily be co-opted by a politics of clientele, through the "cartorial" state, for more or less idle public jobs in exchange for political support and good social behavior.[10]

In spite of its stability and wealth, however, that system was inherently incapable of bringing the Latin American countries to social integration and national development. The very foundation of the system was its dualism. The rural masses had to be kept dependent, landless, and unorganized so that cheap labor would be available Industrialization could not take place because the effective purchasing market was very small, and given the low prices of the imported goods and the low cost of labor, it was always an economically better alternative to invest in the expansion of the primary sector.

This system was brought to a rapid and irreparable disruption when two eliminatory conditions developed. One, internal, consisted in the growing unrest of the middle class. As time passed, that class became less amenable to the passive role assigned to it by the elite. It became a cultivated class of liberal professionals or a powerful group of military officers, which was moved by new ideas and aspirations to exact an increasing participation in the higher level of decisions. Finally, with the emergence of the radical parties, that class brought the dualistic structure of societies that had, at last, become socially modern to a social and political crisis. The second condition that destroyed the semicolonial system of Latin America and its dualistic foundation was external to the region: the world depression of the 1930s. Suddenly it became impossible to provide for all the domestic needs of the Latin American countries just by importing finished goods from Europe and the United States, because Latin American exports were brought, quantitatively and in terms of price, to a drastic reduction by the crisis. The cumulation of these two conditions destroyed the supports for Latin American dualism and caused a rapid and profound change in the region in the course of the 1930s and 1940s, something we have to keep in mind when we consider its picture after World War II.

NOTES

[1] See the bibliography at the end of the book.

[2] For the class relationships arising from the emergence of the Renaissance bourgeoisie, see particularly the brilliant study of Alfred von Martin (1946); see also Henri Pirenne (1947, chap. 7) and Pierre Jeannin (1969). For the case of the Iberian countries see Sergio Bagu

(1949, chap. 2) and J. H. Elliott (1966, particularly chaps. 3 and 6); for the cultural aspects of the process see Friedrich Heer (1968, vol. 2, chap. 14). For the particular case of Portugal, see Joaquim Pedro de Oliveira Martins (1968, book 5).

[3] See Heer (1968); see also Helio Jaguaribe (1971).

[4] See Jorge Abelardo Ramos (1968b, particularly chaps. 3–5), and Bagu (1940, chap. 5).

[5] See Bagu (1949, chaps. 3 and 4), Celso Furtado (1969, chap. 2), and Alonso Aguilar Monteverde (1967, pp. 28 ff.).

[6] On Latin American Dualism see Aguilar Monteverde (1967, chaps. 1–3), L. A. Costa Pinto (1963, particularly chaps. 3, 6, and 10), and Furtado (1969, chaps. 4, 7, and 8). On Mexico see Pablo González Casanova (1965, chaps. 5–7), Jesús Silva Herzog (1960, vol. 1, chaps. 1 and 2), and Fernando Carmona, in Fernando Carmona et al. (1970, pp. 13–102). On Brazil see Ignacio Rangel (1957a, particularly pp. 19–44), Alberto Guerreiro Ramos (1960, chaps. 4–6), José Honorio Rodrigues (1965, part 1), N. Werneck Sodré (1965a), and Alberto Passos Guimarães (1968). On Argentina see Jorge Abelardo Ramos (1957, chaps. 1–3), Fermin Chávez (1965), Alberto J. Pla, in Alberto Ciria et al. (1969).

[7] See Anibal Pinto (1964).

[8] See Frederick J. Turner (1961) and H. U. Faulkner (1954, chap. 10).

[9] See Aldo Ferrer (1963, chap. 10).

[10] See Furtado (1969, chaps. 4 and 5) and Osvaldo Sunkel (1970a, chap. 2).

22

The Obstacles of the
Dualistic Inheritance

The second hypothesis

I will now proceed to formulate, as succinctly and precisely as possible, the second hypothesis, in an attempt to explain the failure of the Latin American countries to reach their goal of self-sustained national development in the last three decades. I will then try to justify that hypothesis, splitting it into two subhypotheses covering first the initial phase of spontaneous import replacement and then the subsequent phase of deliberate state-supported efforts to promote national development.

The second hypothesis can be formulated as follows: *The Latin American drive for national development has not reached a self-sustained level in the last three decades because (1) when the process was spontaneously induced by the domestic demand, the national markets proved to be too small and (2) when it was promoted by deliberate efforts on the part of the national governments, the cost of incorporating the masses into the centers of participation and higher consumption proved to be substantially higher than the limits consensually accepted by the new Establishment, which successfully used the military to interrupt the process of change and to keep or reestablish a dualistic society.*

This hypothesis is based on two contentions. The first is that the process of national development, propelled by the spontaneous process of import replacement that was generated by the crisis of the 1930s, was accelerated from the end of World War II through the early 1950s, but that it has been prevented from achieving, even in the largest of the concerned countries, a level of self-sustained growth by the structural limitations of the Latin American domestic markets. The second contention is that the Latin American governments of that time, especially of the 1950s and particularly in the larger and more developed countries of the region, deliberately tried to stimulate and reinforce the process of national development, in conditions that can be generically described as populist development and populist democracy. These governments failed, how-ever, to obtain their goals because they lacked appropriate political and economic support, both domestically and internationally and their own policies and man-agement were deficient; and they were finally overthrown, in the late 1950s and the 1960s, by military movements, which have reestablished or consolidated a new form of dualistic society.

In the Latin American conditions, populism may be generally described as a political movement characterized by a direct appeal from a charismatic leader to the urban masses. That appeal is made more by his personal actions than through the mediation of a party, and it conveys to the masses that they can have strong hopes for the relatively fast improvement of their condition if that leader can obtain enough power to carry out important socioeconomic reforms, promote the national development of the country (checking the abusive influ-ence of foreign groups), and undertake welfare programs and substantial redis-tributive measures. According to that definition, Perón (1946–1955) in Argentina and Vargas in Brazil (last two years of the *Estado Novo*, 1944–1945, and again in 1950–1954) were the two paradigmatic cases of populism. In different conditions and to different degrees, Cárdenas (1934–1940) and, to an extent, López Mateos (1958–1964) in Mexico, Rómulo Betancourt (the junta phase, 1945–1947) in Venezuela, Rojas Pinilla (1950–1957) in Colombia, Ibáñez (1952–1958) in Chile, Kubitschek (1955–1960) and Goulart (1961–1964) in Brazil, and Frondizi (1958–1962) in Argentina led populist governments. As far as the expression "populist democracy" is concerned, it should be observed that, more often than not, electoral mechanisms were preserved, that the populist leaders commanded effectively wide mass support—and reflected that support—and that the political participation of the masses was substantially enlarged, although often through nonliberal means. Liberal values and practices, however, were severely curtailed, particularly for the middle classes. See Table 46 on Latin American populism.

The failure of spontaneous development

The process of spontaneous development generated by the crisis of the 1930s and the final exhaustion of the growth inducements of the process of import replacement have been widely studied by CEPAL economists and other students of Latin America.[1] That process, which was increasingly influenced and sup-ported by state intervention in the course of the 1950s, originated because of the pressing demands of the domestic market once the crisis of the Great De-pression had irremediably affected the region's capacity to import. This situa-tion altered the former basic conditions of the Latin American economy. The external crisis, depressing the prices of the export goods and the quantum of their demand, reduced the capacity of the Latin American countries to import goods by more than 50 percent. This compelled the Latin American countries to produce, domestically, the articles formerly imported as much as they could. Furthermore, the comparative advantages that formerly favored the production of primary goods changed so that the production of industrial consumer goods

Table 46 *Latin American populism from the 1940s to the 1960s*

Period	Country and Leader	Essential Features
1940s I	Mexico, Cárdenas 1934–1940	More organic and leftist than the typical populism of the 1950s; state-capitalist orientation
	Brazil, Vargas 1937–1945	Protofascist *Estado Novo* developed in last two years (1944–1945) into syndicalist populism; overthrown by military coup
II	Colombia, Gaitán 1948	Opposition radical populism; leader's assassination generated *bogotazo* of 1948
	Venezuela, Betancourt 1945–1947	Association, in governing junta, of *Acción Democrática* and young military; nationalist populism but with a strong party base; successor (Gallegos) overthrown by military coup
	Argentina, Perón 1946–1955	National-developmentalist government based on strong unions and the military, with supporting Peronist party and discretionary control of electorally conquered government
1950s I	Colombia, Pinilla 1950–1957	Poor military copy of Peronism without fundamental union basis and with insufficient military support; overthrown by revolution
	Brazil, Vargas 1950–1954	National-developmentalist, elected, and democratic government, supported by loose coalition (PSD*–PTB)**; loose organization of supporting unions; insufficient party (PTB) strength and discipline; military opposition; Vargas committed suicide in protest against military deposition
	Argentina, Perón 1946–1955	Continuation from the 1940s; last years weaker; compromises with conservative forces; overthrown by military coup
	Chile, Ibáñez 1952–1958	Nationalist populism; charismatic leader who could obtain power through election better than he could use it
II	Brazil, Kubitschek 1955–1960	Developmentalist populism; elected democratic government, socially moderate, supported by loose progressive coalition (PSD–PTB)

Period	Country and Leader	Essential Features
1950s II	Argentina, Frondizi 1958–1962	Progressive-developmentalist, elected, democratic government, with initial loose populist support and overtones; rapid loss of popular basis and military acquiescence; overthrown by military coup
1960s I	Mexico, López Mateos 1958–1964	Progressive-developmentalist government supported by the official party (PRI)***; tried to revive Mexican revolution and some of Cárdenas' policies; afraid of radical *Fidelista* response of the masses; returned to conventional line, weakening his political authority
	Brazil, Goulart 1961–1964	Syndicalist and nationalist populism, supported by unions and loose progressive coalition (PTB–PSD), within democratic institutional framework; opposed by the new Establishment; overthrown by military coup
II	Colombia, Lleras Restreppo 1964–1970	Progressive-developmentalist, liberal government supported by the liberal-conservative *Frente Nacional*, with mild populist overtones; loose support of unions
	Chile, Frei 1964–1970	Christian-democratic, national-developmentalist, elected government with support of progressive sectors; strong social commitments with middle populist overtones, but most unions communist-socialist oriented

*PSD—*Partido Social Democratico* (Social Democratic Party)—unrelated to its German homonym, was a party with conservative tendencies in the countryside, but supporting urban industrialization.

**PTB—*Partido Trabalhista Brasilire* (Brazilian Labor Party)—unrelated to its English homonym, was a unionist party entrenched in the machinery of the Labor Ministry.

***PRI—*Partido Revolucionario Institucional* (Institutional Revolutionary Party)—the last form taken by the Mexican revolution movement, strongly entrenched in the state machinery.

was more favorable. That process has become known as industrialization through import replacement.

After a longer or shorter time, however, depending on the economic capacity of the concerned countries, the limits for import substitution were reached. Most countries that experienced the process could achieve a relatively high level of production of nondurable consumer goods. Some could go as far as achieving a large production of durable consumer goods. Only Mexico, Brazil, and Argentina, the three largest countries of the region, reached a higher level and started the production of capital goods and intermediate goods. At that point, however, which was very close to the level of industrial autonomy, even these countries suffered from the restriction of their limited markets, and they could not succeed in becoming large exporters of such products before they were capable of mastering all the technological requirements for that kind of production.

Even with her large population of more than 90 million inhabitants, Brazil, the largest of the Latin American countries and the one that has gone furthest in the way of industrialization, was confronted, in the early 1960s, with the limitations of her market. This is because the active Brazilian consumers constitute about 25 percent of the total population, which is an inheritance from her recent dualistic past. Fifty percent of the population is composed of peasants, who are living at a subsistence level and so are practically out of the market. Half of the 50 percent that constitutes the urban population is composed of unemployed or very poorly paid people, earning at best a minimum wage which is strictly enough to buy basic food and does not allow the acquisition of durable goods. The resulting actual market proved to be insufficient to maintain the spontaneous development of the economy.

The alternative outlet, exportation of other than the traditional goods, has been barred to Brazil, as well as to the other Latin American countries. Often their industrial production has not reached a level of international competition. In addition, several intricate factors conspire against the exportation of industrial goods by these countries: tariff barriers or other forms of preference adopted by the developed countries, their own deficiencies in shipping, marketing, and merchandising, their inability to grant customers competitive forms of credit, and, last but not least, the fact that most of their modern industry is owned by large international corporations, which reserve the international trade for their home plants and companies.

The failure of state-oriented development

The obstacles hindering the spontaneous development of the Latin American countries led their governments, sooner or later and in one way or another, to interfere in the economic sphere with the purpose of promoting their countries' national development. It was particularly a financial crisis that initiated the systematic practice of state intervention in economic affairs. That crisis was the shortage of foreign currencies experienced by most Latin American countries sometime after the end of World War II—caused by their thoughtless waste of the reserves accumulated during wartime in nonpriority applications. Whatever the forms and origins of that intervention, it assumed, in the late 1950s, and for the most advanced countries of the region, the character of a deliberate and programmed effort to promote national development. (See Table 46.)

In spite of some valuable contributions,[2] the analysis of the Latin American experiment in state-oriented development is still rather insufficient, particularly as far as the intimate relationship between the economic and the sociopolitical aspects is concerned. It would obviously be impossible to attempt such an analysis in the restricted limits of this topic. For our present purpose, it will be enough to stress two fundamental characteristics of that experiment. The first consists in the inability of the Latin American governments of the time to define consistently the purpose, basic conditions, and limits of the economic scope that they proposed for the national state, combined with their inability to appropriately implement their economic policies, whatever the defects in the conception of these policies. The second characteristic consists in the political inability of these governments either to attract to their side sufficient sectors of the elite and subelite to neutralize the antipopulist, antiprogressive conspiracies of the reactionary forces,[3] or to face these forces and subdue them. Both cases involve specific weaknesses of the Latin American populist democracies in the middle of the century, which ultimately caused their ruin.

Failures of conception and of implementation

Three particularly relevant aspects of the first characteristic of the Latin American populist governments, their failures in the conception and implementation of their economic policies, should be stressed. The first is related to the ambiguity and vagueness of Latin American populism. As a loose association between a charismatic leader, such as Perón, Vargas, Ibáñez, or in earlier and different conditions, Cárdenas, and a heterogeneous cluster of followers, combining a large working-class support with a smaller support from middle-class and bourgeois sectors, populism was different things to different groups, and a basic articulation of its political philosophy and socioeconomic goals was never obtained—even in the better integrated attempt of Perón's *justicialismo*.

The rich and fascinating theme of Latin American populism presents many important facets that deserve analysis and elaboration, but they cannot be treated in the present context.[4] (See Table 46.) It is essential only to remark, insofar as the leadership of the populist movements is concerned, that the leaders' lack of a sufficiently clear political philosophy, associated with a tactical propensity to please too many diverse sectors, prevented these leaders from reasonably defining their economic policy. They were always, in a general way, favorable to economic development, which they understood in a nationalist form and in predominantly industrial terms, and they were oriented toward a social redistribution of wealth and opportunities. But they were never able to delineate, even roughly, their proposed boundaries between the sectors to be predominantly or exclusively reserved for the initiative of the state and those to be kept open for private initiative, or to subdiscriminate between those for foreign capital and those for national capital. Moreover, in spite of the populist inclination for state planning and state intervention in the economic sphere, the populist leaders, with the possible exception of Perón during his first years of government, were firm believers in development through private initiative, considering that the state's role as investor and entrepreneur should be only subsidiary and complementary to the private sector. Hence the lack of a reasonably clear definition of the roles to be assigned to the state and the private firms, or to national and foreign entrepreneurs, which one observes in Perón's (1946–1955) Argentina as well as in the Brazil of Vargas (particularly his second government, 1950–1954).[5]

A still less clear picture can be noted in the governments of less defined or less markedly populist leaders, such as Frondizi (1958–1962) in Argentina, Kubitschek (1955–1960) and Goulart (1961–1964) in Brazil, López Mateos (1958–1964) in Mexico, Rojas Pinilla (1950–1957) and Lleras Restreppo (1966–1970) in Colombia, Rómulo Betancourt (junta phase 1945–1947) in Venezuela, and Ibáñez (1952–1958) and Frei (1964–1970) in Chile. That ambiguity in their conceptions, due in part to tactical reasons, as formerly remarked, yielded some advantages to those leaders in that it usually helped them to play a much more radical role before the masses than their actual performances could support. That same ambiguity, however, produced the reverse result vis-à-vis the powerful and well-organized conservative elites of these countries, who were led to believe they were confronted with far more radical policies and prospects than the populist governments ever intended. That double distortion of the political image of the populist governments was, ultimately, much more detrimental than beneficial to them, because it contributed to the weakening of the political drive of the masses and to the increasing resistance of most of the new Establishment, depriving the populist democracies of the cooperation of valuable sectors and finally dooming them to ruin.

The second and third aspects to be discussed briefly concern the failures of the populist movements in implementing their socioeconomic policies. Briefly, these aspects are related to deficiencies in the financing of the populists' projects and deficiencies in their management. Let us have a very quick look at each of these two aspects.

Financial deficiencies were a constant in most Latin American projects in the phase of populist development. To start with, the ambiguity of the economic policies of the populist governments was an initial obstacle to clear and realistic budgeting. To make their projects more acceptable, those governments, as a rule, were inclined to underrate their costs and to overrate the ease with which they could be implemented. The real difficulty, however, was the domestic and international hostility surrounding these governments.

Domestically, their formal political situation varied from country to country. At one extreme we have the situation of Perón, who acquired and kept for many years the complete control of the basic and the formal agencies of power in Argentina: on the one hand, the labor unions, the army, and the Peronist party, and, on the other hand, as a reflex of his control of the infrastructures of power, the executive government (where ministers were mere executors of his orders), the legislature (which was reduced to the passive role of rubber-stamping the wishes of the executive), and the judiciary (which was cleared by purges and subjected to the will of the president). At the opposite extreme we have the position of Vargas, who was elected by an heterogeneous coalition of parties and had to bargain all his decisions with Congress and to carefully maneuver the military in order to preserve their loyalty (which he finally lost).

Whatever the extent of their control over their political systems, however, the populist governments were always particularly helpless vis-à-vis the economic elite of their countries. It is not possible to analyze here the complex problem of the relationship between the populist governments and the economic elite in Latin America.[6] Some further comments will be made later in the chapter. Now, it suffices to stress that Latin American populism, in spite of certain socialistic appearances and slogans, was a form of private capitalism, in the realities of power as well as in the intentions of the leaders, although it was oriented toward a radical reformism. (See Chapter 6.) The economic elite, in spite of the support given to populist development by some industrial and technical sectors, was on the whole hostile to the populist regimes, because of their reform-minded tendencies. That elite kept playing a biased game with the populist governments, in the old tradition of the Latin American elites that Celso Furtado once defined as the "privatization of benefits and socialization of costs." In practice, the economic elite, in defense of its class interests, was able, in one way or another, to prevent significant increases in taxation and other methods of increasing the revenues of the populist governments. This forced those governments to resort to monetary issues and other inflationary devices as the only available alternative for financing, in local currency, their developmental projects.

Externally, Latin American populist development was surrounded by an ill-concealed hostility from the United States and the international financial agencies under her influence, such as the World Bank.[7] Once again, a discussion of this issue would be too long and complex to be presented here. I would suggest that the causes of that hostility were a particular combination of pragmatic motives and ideological biases. In pragmatic terms populist development was running against short-range American economic interests. The acceleration, as well as the dramatization, of the import-replacement process was negatively affecting several traditional lines of American exports to Latin America, particularly durable consumer goods (such as house appliances). These goods had started to be produced locally and were supported by conditions prohibitive to external competition. Although in fact many of the opportunities for foreign investment remained and new ones, such as in the automobile industry, were created, the emphasis on economic autonomy and nationalism scared the American business community and induced its members to believe, in a phase when the supercorporations were beginning to become increasingly oriented toward world expansion, that the Latin American markets would be closed to them and kept under the control of local public corporations. Ideologically, populist development appeared to be financially unsound, because of its inflationary implications (which were actually aggravated by the behavior of the financial community), and politically dangerous, because of the increased interference of the state in economic affairs. All these views and feelings led the United States and the international financial agencies to deny long-term credit to the populist governments, even for some of their soundest projects, such as the Brazilian steel industry.[8] Confronted with that financial obstacle, the populist governments were compelled to accept European short-term suppliers' credits in order to carry on their projects, in conditions that soon became unbearably heavy for their balance of payments, with equally negative effects on their domestic cash flow. (See Chapter 20.)

The combination of domestic inflationary means and external short-term indebtedness brought populist development to a deadlock, eventually forcing the Latin American countries, either still under populist regimes or already under military regimes (which as a rule have succeeded the populist regimes), to adopt sterile programs of financial austerity, putting a premature end to their developmental efforts.[9]

The third aspect formerly mentioned, also concerning the implementation of the populist projects, is related to the poor management of most of the newly created public corporations. The public or mixed corporation, in which the state keeps a controlling majority, was one of the typical features of populist development in Latin America. This did not result from capricious decisions or from any doctrinaire propensity, as can be inferred from what has already been said, but simply from the fact that, given the overall insufficiency of private capital and the latter's natural preference for investments of earlier maturation and higher profits rather than those in basic and infrastructural sectors, the sectors demanding high capital could only be developed, in national terms, by public or mixed corporations. While entering into such ventures, however, the Latin American states were plagued by their political dependence on clientele politics (including clientelistic populism) and by the almost insoluble problem of middle-class unemployment. The combination of these two factors led to the forcing on the public corporations of an excess of personnel that had to be employed somewhere. It also often hindered the choice of managers for these corporations. And in general, it subjected the public corporations to political pressures that always tended to affect their efficiency negatively.

The ultimate consequence of these conditions was an increase in the cost of populist development, reducing its benefits and providing easy targets and arguments for the reactionary sectors[10] eager to stop, while they still had time, a process of social, economic, and political change that came very close to being irreversible. As a matter of fact, that process has, in any case, decisively affected these countries; they will never return to what they were before their populist experiments.

Growth and participation

The second characteristic of the populist experiment, which was formerly mentioned and requires a brief analysis, is the incapacity manifested by these governments in the peculiar condition of populist development either to attract to their side sufficient sectors of the elite and subelite to neutralize the conspiracies of the reactionary forces, or to face those forces and smash them. The understanding of this problem requires the basic understanding of the relationship, in the process of populist development, between the mobilization of the masses and the improvement of their conditions of life, on the one hand, and the situation and interests of the bourgeoisie and the middle class, on the other hand.

Whatever may have been the subjective intentions of the populist leaders and the extent of their awareness of the social, economic, and political problems of their countries, the fact is that populism always brought about, and depended on, a wide mobilization of the urban masses, orienting them, in the framework of the national state and of private capitalism, to higher levels of economic and political participation. In its roots, as will be remembered, populism was a response, through political means, to the insufficient conditions in the Latin American markets for spontaneous economic growth. Fixing, through political decisions, higher economic targets than those that were likely to result from the free play of the forces of the market, the populist governments were relying on the mobilization of the masses to accumulate enough power to choose and to obtain these targets.

At the same time, however, these economic goals, within the limits of the national state and the capitalist regime, were embedded in the wider framework of a welfare system, oriented toward improving the living conditions of the masses, in a more direct response to their expectations. At its roots—it should also be remembered—populism was also a political victory of the masses. It was not a political victory in the sense of eliminating the economic and political power of the old ruling classes, but in the sense of forcing them, electorally and otherwise, to hear the claims of the masses, to attend to several of these claims, and to enlarge the participation of the masses in the economic and political systems.[11] In that sense populism represented for the lower urban strata in the middle of this century what radicalism represented for the middle class in the late nineteenth and early twentieth centuries: a forced enlargement of the political system. Unlike radicalism, however, which imposed a redistribution of power on the patriciate without changing the underlying economic structure, the populist revolution, in its ascending phase, caused both an expansion of the economic system and an acceleration of the industrialization of the concerned countries.

Because of that dual dependence on general economic development and on the attendance to certain claims of the masses, the generation of a dialectic relationship between the overall growth of the economy and the increasing participation of the masses in the economic-political process was a peculiar feature of populist development. While the whole system kept growing, a minimal, if unbalanced, compatibility existed between the two major elements of the process, that is, between (1) the increase in the economy, which was provided by the initiative of the state and generated new means for social assistance, and (2) the increasing participation of the masses. In the course of that process, many social sectors, in spite of their potential or actual conflicts of interests, were favored, although in uneven terms, by the general growth in the production and supply of commodities and the increasing expansion of their demand.

The populist governments, to be sure, were led into such a dialectic system more by expediency than by a clear understanding of its underlying mechanisms. In part because of that, in part because the inflationary distortions—which were initially incurred as a calculated risk but finally went out of control—those governments were sooner or later confronted with the negative side of that dialectic system, without being prepared to face it. In other words, when the distorting effects of excessive inflation, along with other factors, led to the disruption of the minimal compatibility between the two elements of the system (growth of the economy and increasing participation of the masses), the process could no longer be maintained without the sacrifice of certain sectors. Either the richer classes had to contribute much more heavily toward the formation of a national surplus with which to finance the developmental efforts and the social improvements for the masses; or (which is what came to prevail) the balance between demand and supply of commodities and between investments and social benefits, on the one hand, and the national formation of surpluses, on the other, had to be obtained by the compression of the level of consumption among the masses and by the general adjustment of investments to the availability, if any, of the national surplus.

Behavior of the Establishment

As would be expected, the reaction of the several bourgeois and middle-class sectors forming the new Establishment of the Latin American countries varied according to whether the populist experiments were in their ascending or descending phases. Although the general trend could hardly have been altered by the populist governments, it seems, in retrospect, that those governments could have played their cards much more advantageously in their phase of growth in order to assure their later survival in the more difficult phase. For that, however, those governments needed an understanding of the inherent process of populist development that they were actually promoting, and none of them ever achieved that understanding.

Briefly, it can be said that the peculiar weakness of populism, as a sociopolitical movement, was precisely its inability to obtain a critical understanding of its real social meaning. Populism was essentially an objective process, in which the main leaders—mostly typical middle-class members—were themselves the victims of populist slogans and imagery, which referred to a more nominal than real transference of power from the old ruling classes to the masses. And that self-obfuscation prevented them from conveying to the sectors of the elite and subelite that would be most effectively favored by populist development (the industrialists and the technical sectors of the middle class) the full awareness of that fact and, therefore, from capturing their conscious allegiance and support.

While populist development was in its ascending course, industrialists and technocrats were divided in their feelings vis-à-vis the populist governments. As a rule, they did not fail to realize the extent to which these governments were bringing significant advantages to them, in the form of fast-expanding businesses or in terms of more and better technical and managerial jobs. They were, however, more often than not, affected by the ideological counter-propaganda diffused by foreign and domestic speakers of so-called orthodox economic views, which were based on all sorts of monetary and laissez-faire biases and fallacies. Moreover, they were frightened, in their conscious and unconscious class feelings, by the ascent of the masses, which actually tended to loom much larger in the propaganda of both the government and the opposition than in actual fact. And finally, what was worst, they did not understand the intimate connections between the general expansion of the national product, the active interference of the state in the economic sphere, and the increased participation of the masses, functioning both as the political supporter of such policies and (within limits) as a sustaining feedback for the economic expansion.

In general, as a result of these mixed feelings and misconceptions, industrialists and technocrats, although more favored than most of the other sectors by populist development, were reticent followers of the process. They never gave their full allegiance to the populist governments and never seriously offered their talents for improving the ongoing policies from within. One of the curious aspects of populist development, seen in retrospect, is how few men of high quality were actually fullheartedly engaged in its planning and execution. The elite and subelite sectors that were gratified by populism graciously indulged in accepting its benefits, in spite of their supposedly nonimpeachable origins, when the process was in a positive progression. As soon as the difficulties began to be felt, and the process of economic growth was arrested, these sectors were easily driven to join the right-wing opposition.

Position of the national bourgeoisie

It is noteworthy that in the phase of crisis for populism the national bourgeoisie, which was ultimately an offspring of the populist development, was rapidly confronted with the alternative of opting for its bourgeois interests, at the expense of its national values, or of following a nationalist course, at a certain price in terms of class and individual interests. That dilemma, which was so quickly sensed by the national bourgeoisie of the different Latin American countries in different periods (the last years of Perón in Argentina, the last months of Goulart in Brazil) is connected with two important features of populist development.

The first and most visible of these features was the propensity, manifested by all populist regimes, to become more radical when the former basic compatibility between overall economic growth and increased mass participation was interrupted. Confronted with this problem, all populist regimes, whatever their actual future performance (which was always moderate), indicated the intention of increasing the extent of state control on the economy (to include control of profits, rents, and so forth), of expanding the area of the public sector (to include electric power, telephone service, and so on), of adopting more extreme social legislation (such as agrarian reform), and of using similar measures. These prospects—independent of their intrinsic socioeconomic merits—would probably have led to a clearer differentiation between the roles of the state and those of the private sector. As far as it can be inferred from the available evidence, these policies were never intended, in any Latin American populist regime, to suppress or even to substantially curtail the private sector,[12] but they were always and everywhere understood by the new Establishment as implying an imminent risk of overall socialization of the economy. The double image of populism and the fact that the national bourgeoisie's involvement in the process of populist development was superficial and opportunistic explain why their contingent cooperation with the populist regimes was easily broken and changed into positions of fear and hostility in the time of crisis.

The second feature connected with the dilemma of the Latin American national bourgeoisie concerns the international position of these bourgeoisie. In the conditions of Latin America, the term national bourgeoisie, as it is now widely used, means that sector of the bourgeoisie—coming partly from earlier commercial sectors, partly from the former agrarian patriciate, and partly from immigration—that was led by the process of import replacement to produce and market, domestically, industrial goods that were formerly imported. Although some manifestations of native industry can be observed in Latin America in the middle of the nineteenth century (Brazil's Viscount Mauá) or even earlier, and although an initial broader process of industrialization took place in the late nineteenth century and was stimulated by World War I, it was, undoubtedly, the Depression of the 1930s that launched Latin American industrialization. The later years of that period (the 1950s), corresponding to the phase of deliberate state-supported industrialization, strongly reinforced the trend and converted the national bourgeoisie into the leading sector of the Latin American bourgeoisie and, ultimately, into the leading sector of Latin America's ruling cluster.

Unlike what has occurred in the purely colonial areas of the third world, where industrialization started as a foreign venture, the Latin American industrial bourgeoisie, in the course of the 1950s, particularly in the larger countries such as Brazil and Mexico, was predominantly formed by national groups, although with many international links. Populist development gave these groups the opportunity to establish profitable connections and arrangements with the large international corporations, without releasing the control and leadership of their businesses. At the same time, however, the great international corporations, mostly American-owned and -controlled, started their accelerated course toward a worldwide control of markets and raw materials, in the form of the so-called multinational corporation. There was, therefore, a more than potential trend toward conflict between the rapidly growing new Latin American native industrial bourgeoisie and the still more rapidly expanding multinational supercorporations. Some populist governments, although without continuity, understood in time that a conflict between the emerging Latin American native capitalism and the supercorporations would be inevitable and would require, in defense of the former, a deliberate intervention on the part of the Latin American states.[13] Before that conflict reached more serious proportions, however, the Latin American national bourgeoisie was confronted with the crisis of populism. As formerly described, they experienced the contradictions between their class and individual interests and their national values. With few exceptions, they followed the course of their interests, rather than of their values. It was in this conjuncture that the potential conflict between the Latin American native bourgeoisie and the multinational supercorporation was brought to a solution. Adhering to the supercorporations became, for the Latin American national bourgeoisie, the easiest and surest way of escaping the risk they felt (and grossly overestimated) of an impending general socialization. As a rule, arrangements of incorporation and association were made in such a way that, ultimately, the larger Latin American industrialists became, with varying degrees of local autonomy, minor partners of the great American-controlled international capitalist system. (See Chapter 20.)

Populist indecision

The populist governments, confronted with the lack of effective allegiance of the national bourgeoisie in their phase of development and with the bourgeoisie's hostility in the phase of crisis, were not able to bring them to a more consistent cooperation in the first case or to fight and subdue them in the second. The explanation for that double inability has already been advanced to a large extent in the preceding lines. As already said, Latin American populism was a form, although socially and nationally oriented, of private capitalism. Populist governments were concerned with planning national development, increasing the participation of the masses, and supplementing, with state instruments, the action of the national bourgeoisie. They never seriously considered the possibility of imposing upon the national entrepreneurs a more severe discipline than a loose adjustment of their activities to the targets of the national plans. And they never went beyond mild forms of social control of the private firms, in spite of not infrequent bombastic proclamations to the contrary, uttered especially in the phase of crisis. In these conditions the populist governments failed, in fact, to exert more than an effort to persuade the national entrepreneurs and, for the matter, the whole private sector. Even concerning foreign groups the actual restrictions imposed by populist governments were very few, and were ultimately limited to the nationalization of some public utilities and the adoption of state monopolies for certain infrastructural industries, such as oil.

In their phase of crisis, when a life-and-death confrontation occurred, as with Vargas in 1954, Perón in 1955, and Goulart in 1964, to mention only the most typical populist leaders and their most dramatic ordeals, the populist leaders consistently refused to defend their cause by nonconventional means. If Perón's and Goulart's cases are considered in a bit more detail (Vargas, in his older years, was more concerned with the preservation of national harmony than with the victory of his own cause, and so preferred to commit suicide rather than to provoke a civil war), it can be seen that both Perón and Goulart could have tried, with a good possibility of success, to mobilize the workers in defense of the regime. The only thing that would have been necessary, ultimately, would have been to let the unions arm themselves. But this is precisely the solution they deliberately refused to adopt, because they knew that that solution, if successful, would necessarily carry populism beyond its capitalist boundaries. And they remained until the end, and at the cost of their own regimes, strictly confined within the limits of private capitalism, whatever their social and national qualifications of capitalism, on the one hand, and their rhetoric for popular consumption, on the other hand.[14]

The Latin American patriciate in the late nineteenth and early twentieth centuries, under the victorious pressure of radicalism, was forced to accept the enlargement of the old Establishment and finally incorporated, at its lower echelons, the emerging middle class. The cost of that process, as a whole, was covered, on one hand, by higher and greater taxation, since the incorporation of the middle class was done mostly through the enlargement of public services. On the other hand, these costs were more than matched by the continued expansion of the traditional economy up to the crisis of the 1930s and, later, by the initial phase of spontaneous industrialization through import replacement.

The populist revolution from the 1940s to the 1960s, expressing the increased number and strength of the urban masses as one of the consequences of the rapid industrialization of Latin America, imposed upon the new Establishment, by political means, a larger economic and political participation of the masses. It also provided, at the same time, a new expansion of the economy through the active interference of the populist governments in the later stages of the process of industrialization. Unlike what had formerly occurred in the relations between the old patriciate and the middle class, however, the leading sectors of the masses were not incorporated into the new Establishment. As soon as the process of economic growth was arrested in the late 1950s and early 1960s, the new Establishment (including the sectors that had been most favored by populist development), afraid of a new intensification of class struggles and the apparently impending risk of socialization, refused to bear the sacrifices necessary to maintain a nationally and socially oriented process of development.

The populist governments were systematically overthrown throughout Latin America by right-wing military coups, assisted or supported, in one way or another, by the United States. With the exception of few countries,[15] the consumption by the masses was severely curtailed. Economic development was subjected to the constraints of financial and social equilibrium, with the resulting stagnation described in Chapter 20, and the former national and social orientation of the Latin American governments was shifted, under the euphemistic label of "interdependence," to a general position of dependence, vis-à-vis the United States economic and defense systems.[16]

The legacy of dualism

There can be no doubt that the populist governments committed, and paid a heavy price for, serious mistakes that could, in principle, have been avoided. To avoid these mistakes, however, as has been discussed, they would have needed a critical understanding of their own social meaning, which they were never able to obtain. Populism was always an objective process with little capacity for self-consciousness.

The crucial question, therefore, was the legacy of the former Latin American dualism. Whatever the distances that separated the Latin American patriciate, in the times of its maximum strength and self-righteousness, from the emerging middle class, the differences between these two classes were more of degree than of quality. Once the middle class, continuously growing in numbers and influence through the last decades of the nineteenth century and the first decades of the twentieth century, finally won its struggle for recognition and participation and was incorporated at the bottom of the new Establishment, what made that incorporation easier was the basic psychocultural compatibility between these two classes. The traditional dualism inherent in Latin American societies since their origins had worked to orient the middle class toward the values and life-styles of the upper class. The real and deep social cleavage in Latin America passes below the middle class and separates it and the upper class from the masses, manifesting the hugest material and cultural inequalities in most countries, as in the typical cases of Brazil or Mexico, or an engrained psychological hostility, as in the case of Argentina.

Populism proved that the overcoming of that dualistic legacy cannot be consensually accepted by the middle and upper classes if they have to bear the cost of it and have the means to impose alternative solutions, even at the price of the liberal content of some of their beliefs. This is precisely the meaning of the second hypothesis formulated in the present section of this book, which I have tried to demonstrate in the preceding lines.

NOTES

[1] See CEPAL (1968), (1964), (1969a), and (1969b). See also Maria Conceição Tavares (1964, pp. 1–60); Osvaldo Sunkel (1967b, pp. 43–75), Celso Furtado (1968a) and (1969), and Andrés Bianchi et al., (1969).

[2] See CEPAL (1963), Albert Hirschman (1963), and Anibal Pinto (1968); see also Helio Jaguaribe (1968). For the Brazilian case particularly, see Octavio Ianni (1965b), Luciano Martins (1968), and L. C. Bresser Pereira (1968).

[3] These forces, in the Latin American conditions of the 1950s and 1960s, were represented by an alliance between more conservative sectors of the higher and middle strata—such as the remainder of the rural patriciate, the consular bourgeoisie, and the traditional sectors of the middle class, including most of the military, which formed the bulk of the old right—and the small but dynamic groups of the new right, comprehending some modern entrepreneurs and executives, oriented toward a dependent association with the multinational supercorporations, and including a larger fraction of neoliberal technocrats, some of them military, also oriented toward a dependent association with the American techno-economic and defense systems.

[4] See Torcuato Di Tella (1965a, pp. 47–74) and Fernando Henrique Cardoso (1969). For populism in Argentina see Di Tella (1964), Jorge Abelardo Ramos (1965), Carlos S. Fayt (1967), Gonzalo Cárdenas et al. (1969), and Rodolfo Puiggrós (1969). For populism in Brazil see Ianni (1965b and 1968), Ianni et al. (1965a), Thomas Skidmore (1967), Jaguaribe (1968, chaps. 11–14), Luciano Martins (1968), and Bresser Pereira (1968).

[5] On Perón's failures in conceiving and implementing his policies, see Jorge Abelardo Ramos, (1965, pp. 633–658). On the failures of Vargas see Ianni (1968, pp. 53–70 and 123–136) and Skidmore (1967, pp. 93–142).

[6] See Di Tella (1965a, pp. 47–74).

[7] See Pinto (1965, pp. 35 ff.).

[8] Such was the case with Cosipa, USIMINAS, and Ferro e Aço de Vitoria.

[9] See Furtado (1969, chap. 16) and A. Aguilar Monteverde (1967, pp. 136 ff.).

[10] Such an argument is the usual slogan that the "state is a bad manager." Of course, the real conditions of the concerned society are omitted, and the "state" is assumed to be a reality endowed with immutable properties, independent of the society of which it is a part.

[11] The process, however, was basically limited to the urban masses and, among them, to the unionized and better-organized groups.

[12] On Argentina see Alberto Ciria (1968, chap. 8); on Brazil see Martins (1968, chap. 4).

[13] Such was the case of Perón's first Five-Year Plan and of certain Santiago policies in the Goulart government.

[14] On Perón see Jorge Abelardo Ramos (1965, pp. 643 ff.). On Goulart see Skidmore (1967, chap. 7) and Ianni (1968, chap. 8).

[15] Chile is the first example, but she is not without serious problems and is still capable of unpredictable courses. Progressive trends have also been preserved in Venezuela, in Uruguay, and to an extent, in Colombia. Peru, after passing through a phase of crisis, seems to have found a new national-developmentalist orientation under military government.

[16] See Martins (1968, chap. 1) and Jaguaribe et al. (1969a).

C
Alternatives and Prospects

23

The Basic Alternatives

Trends

The present and last section of this book is an attempt to discuss the current and foreseeable trends and alternatives in the Latin American societies. It will take into account the main structural characteristics analyzed in Chapters 19 and 20, considered in the light of the explanatory hypotheses proposed in Chapters 21 and 22 and of the whole theoretical framework discussed in this book, particularly in Chapters 16–18. I have already dealt with the subject of the present section in an earlier study,[1] in which, as I previously noted, I also discussed several of the problems considered in Chapters 19 and 20. As then I will try now to treat the subject in a succinct way, reproducing, when convenient, part of the text from my former study.

The discussion of the trends and alternatives of a sociohistorical process involves, essentially, two distinct kinds of analyses. One consists in the determination, based on an assessment of a society's main structural characteristics, its environment, and its intrasocietal and intersocietal processes, of the tendencies that express general and endurable trends and thus are most likely to configurate those processes, and the determination of which of those trends are most likely to exert a conditioning effect on the other trends. The second kind of analysis consists in determining the basic alternatives, as ideal types, that are involved in the foreseeable development of these central trends and, therefore, the alternative trends that the central trends will probably be confronted with.

In the case of Latin America, as was seen in Chapters 19 and 20, the crucial issues are (1) the interrelation, which is a reciprocally conditioning circular process, between the stagnating underdevelopment of the concerned countries and their own social marginality and (2) largely as a consequence of that circular process, a rapidly growing process of economic, cultural, and politico-military denationalization in these countries. That process consolidates the nonviability of the countries already affected—given the general conditions of our time, their own internal political conditions, and their geopolitical location—by insufficient human and natural resources, such as the Central American and the Caribbean countries. And the process of denationalization seriously imperils the national structures of the other Latin American countries and the commitment of their elites to their own nation.

If we consider only the viable Latin American countries, then we have that stagnating underdevelopment and social marginality, as a mutually conditioning circular process, are largely contributing to the triple process of economic, cultural, and politico-military denationalization. That syndrome, as we saw in Chapters 21 and 22, has been caused by historical dualism, with its resulting cleavage separating the helpless Latin American masses from the middle class and the bourgeoisie, which have come to form a self-protecting new Establishment. In Latin America promoting national development has come to mean bridging the cleavage between the masses and the new Establishment through the incorporation of the former into higher levels of participation. The material and psychocultural costs required for that incorporation, however, which would have to be borne by the new Establishment, have proved to be considerably higher than the concerned sectors are consensually prepared to accept. As a consequence, the syndrome follows a self-aggravating course, in which increasing dependency is required in order to balance an increasing internal deficit of resources and of consensus in the Latin American societies. There can be no doubt, as the former analysis indicates (according to what has been discussed and established in the two preceding sections of Book III) that the central trends of the Latin American society, currently and for the foreseeable future, are characterized by the double interrelation between stagnating underdevelopment and social marginality, on one hand, and the process of economic, cultural, and politico-military denationalization, on the other hand.

As was clearly seen in our discussion of the emerging interimperial system (see Chapter 18), there also can be no doubt about the strongly expansive characteristics of the American business system, supported by an also expansive defense system. In this sense, the Latin American societies would undoubtedly have been submitted to hard American pressures, in the international conditions resulting from World War II, regardless of their internal characteristics. It is due to the internal conditions of these societies, however, that these pressures have so successfully and steadily led to the process of denationalization. Even discounting her particularly favorable geopolitical location, vis-à-vis the American empire, Japan, submitted to unconditional surrender and full military occupation, was able, nevertheless, to resist American pressures and, far from succumbing to any denationalization process, managed to achieve, in two decades, a consolidated internal and international autonomy. In the conditions of the Latin American societies, however, the external pressures from the United States, instead of being resisted, were actively supported and even demanded by the local elites, configurating what should be called a "pull" imperialism, in opposition to the forms of "push" imperialism forcefully imposed from outside.

Of the several possible alternatives with which the two interrelated central trends of the Latin American societies are confronted, the determining one, both analytically and empirically, is the alternative between dependency and autonomy. What renders this alternative the determining one is the fact that it operates as an independent variable, vis-à-vis the others. Indeed, confronted with the dependency-autonomy alternative, the other alternatives, such as stagnation-development and dualism-integration, either operate as simple requirements for the consolidation of Latin American autonomy, if that is the course that is taken, or cease to be alternatives at all, because if the road ahead for Latin America leads to dependency, Latin American societies will no longer be self-steering and thus will not have to face alternatives. The course of dependency, once it becomes irreversible, involves the also irreversible transference of decision making to the ruling society, which becomes the one that can face alternatives and whose choices determine the subsequent fate of the dependent society.

As can be inferred from the two preceding sections of this book and as will be discussed further in the next chapter, the Latin American countries, considered as a whole, are currently moving toward the alternative of dependency, whatever the extent to which this is deliberate or acknowledged. The present Latin American status quo unquestionably shows a predominant, although seldom clearly acknowledged, propensity for the dependent alternative. That implied option of the governments and the ruling strata in most of the Latin American countries has been, in a few cases, overtly manifested by the official ideology, as in Brazil during the Castello Branco government, in the name of a united front against international communism. A few other Latin American countries, however, (not to mention the official Mexican rhetoric) have in certain periods, such as Chile under Frei, or Peru and Bolivia under the Velasco and Torres military regimes, expressed a clear option for the alternative of autonomy. Because of their relatively small influence on the general Latin American picture, however, these exceptions, which are not being joined by other countries, are not changing the current dependent trend. Not making a choice, therefore, currently implies for Latin America, as a whole, the following of the alternative of dependency.

As discussed in the last part of Chapter 18, dependency presents four distinct types, which tend to occur in successive order: colonial, neocolonial, satellite, and provincial. We will analyze that matter, as it concerns the Latin American countries, in more detail in the next chapter. For now it suffices to keep in mind that each of these types of dependency expresses a certain kind of structural relationship between the concerned societies, and each implies distinct sociopolitical models for the dependent country.[2]

Although, as was seen in Chapter 18, the alternative of autonomy also presents different types, internationally, such as absolute individual autonomy (United States, Soviet Union), relative individual autonomy (Japan), or collective autonomy (Western Europe), it is not submitted to any principle of successiveness. For given empirical cases, however, such as the current Latin American one, the alternative of autonomy, in addition to presenting a limited range of typological possibilities (collective autonomy for most of the Latin American countries, possible relative individual autonomy for Brazil), also presents alternative ways and implied sociopolitical models for its eventual adoption and implementation. The alternative ways are the reformist and the revolutionary ones. And, as we saw in Chapters 14 and 15, the implied model for the reformist way is *state capitalism* or a mixture of state capitalism and national capitalism, depending on the conditions of the concerned society. The only possible model for the revolutionary way is developmental socialism.

The historical deadline

As we saw in Chapter 18, historical processes are submitted to positive and negative prescriptions, although without the neatness of natural or legal deadlines. Once deadlines are reached, however, certain situations and tendencies become irreversible, positively or negatively. Because of that, there are configurative periods with broad limits of historical deadlines, in the course of which certain situations and decisions have the ability to privilege certain social forces and actors, in a way that renders increasingly unlikely the possibility of other competing social forces and actors coming later to prevail over the former ones.

In the case of Latin America, as was formerly seen, certain conflicts in the present status quo are likely to find a solution in the course of no more than approximately three decades. That deadline operates as a prescriptive limit for Latin America's attainment of consolidated autonomy, at a sufficient level for self-sustained development. Otherwise, the chances of the Latin American countries ever obtaining an autonomous development will sharply decrease and will finally disappear altogether. This being so, the configurative period in which Latin America, through some of its strategically more important countries, can make the decisions and organize the conditions that will make a successful process of autonomous development possible is not likely to last more than one decade—the decade of the 1970s.

Historical deadlines result, as was discussed in Chapters 2 and 18, because historical periods, more than being a simple methodological expediency for the understanding of the historical process, express macrostructural changes in that process. These changes, modifying systems of belief, technology, power, and economic capability, make certain things possible and other things impossible, opening new and closing old situations. It is in this sense that there are positive prescriptions, such, for instance, as the possibility opened by the industrial revolution for the mechanization of societies and the corresponding change in their economic, political, and social institutions from their formerly rural to new industrial bases. Those societies that succeeded in mechanizing and making that change within a certain time period, in this case by the second third of the nineteenth century, have persisted as developed societies in improved conditions (England, France) or have become developed societies (Germany). The societies that did not mechanize and make the appropriate changes, such as the non-Western countries or, in the West, the Iberian countries (which were vanguard societies from the end of the Middle Ages to the first half of the seventeenth century) have declined from their absolute and relative positions and become underdeveloped countries. The same occurs with negative prescriptions. The European societies that were not able to complete their liberal democratic revolution in due time, in this case in the period corresponding to the European balance of power under European hegemony, or by the end of World War I, lost their chance for performing such a revolution in the bourgeois democratic framework and had to readjust the sociopolitical structures of the *ancien régime* in the framework of a mass social revolution, as occurred in Russia.

Let me note, concerning the question of historical deadlines, that the possibility of obtaining reasonably objective and verifiable knowledge of an historical deadline before it is reached and of analyzing it ex post depends on two conditions: (1) the sophistication of the social theory available to the observer and (2) the extent to which the concerned macrosocial changes are determined by observable current processes. Thucydides and some other Greek analysts understood perfectly the crisis of the polis and its probable effects long before the consolidation of the Macedonian empire. Marx understood the conditions of Manchestrian capitalism long before the Russian Revolution or the Great Depression. In these examples contemporary social science had reached a sufficient degree of objectivity and verifiability. Unlike these examples, however, some social transformations are shaped in a barely observable way, as occurred with the upsurge of the great revealed religions. Tacitus and the Roman writers of the second century did not guess the importance that Christianity would come to have. Muhammad unexpectedly changed the world in only thirty years of preaching. And it would not be impossible, although it cannot be currently forecasted, for the romantic humanistic mood presently affecting the West's young generation, of which the hippie phenomenon is one manifestation, to bring about a new ethicoreligious attitude that could profoundly change the world in some decades.[3] It remains true, however, in spite of such cases, that most macrosocial changes have resulted from processes perfectly observable by those equipped with the required criteria and analytical instruments. And in this sense, one cannot fail to observe that in our time new forms of power concentration are cumulatively taking place, which are similar, if on the much larger scale inherent to our time, to the processes that brought about, in sociopolitical terms, the formation of the Roman Empire and, in economic-technological terms, the first industrial revolution.

The question concerning the observability of historical deadlines is not only relevant from a theoretical point of view, as something that analysts can and must be aware of. It is still more relevant in that it is currently interfering with the historical process itself. The concerned actors' awareness or lack of awareness of the available time for them to achieve certain goals and the extent to which they think they are or are not in the process of achieving those goals are reoperating on the whole picture. People are constantly readjusting their own goals and plans to prevailing conditions, as they see them. Changes in these conditions and in the prevailing views about them induce people to make corresponding changes in their final goals and in their plans for achieving them. In Latin America, for instance, the feeling that autonomous development is in progress brings people to aim at goals implying that development—inducing them to invest their savings in industries producing for the domestic market, or to buy shares in public corporations, to send their children to local universities so that they get acquainted with the local ways of doing things, to make local friends, and so forth. All these actions, taken in order to benefit from a foreseen situation of autonomous development, actually contribute to its emergence and consolidation. Expectations concerning a future situation of dependency bring people to protect their savings by investing abroad, to send their children to study in the universities of the dominant country so that in the future they will be incorporated into the winning side more easily,[4] and so on. And in this example also, all these actions actually help to reinforce the trends bringing about the kind of future people had anticipated.

These considerations, concerning the well-known correlation between the historical process and the social forecasts about it, carry a very special weight as far as the future of Latin America and its time limits for achieving an autonomous self-sustained development are concerned. This is so for two reasons. The first concerns the fact that, with the exception of some countries, the dependent alternative is the one that is currently being followed, even if it is seldom officially acknowledged, and that the Latin American elites are becoming increasingly aware of that situation and are moving increasingly to adjust their behavior accordingly. So, as we have seen, there is a growing feedback reinforcement of the dependent trend. The second reason concerns the time limit and is related to the fact that the Latin American countries became aware, in the decade of the 1950s, of their own underdevelopment, although at that time the external limitations and the problems of dependency were not yet understood.

That earlier awareness of Latin American underdevelopment, promoted by CEPAL and spread throughout the various countries by the progressive sectors of the intelligentsia, provided in one way or another the support for the populist movements. The diffusion of that awareness, however, was limited by two important obstacles. The first is that the understanding of the problems of Latin American underdevelopment on the part of the populist movements and of the political forces in general was mechanical and in a sense marginal to their central concern, which was more directly oriented toward mass mobilization (or the prevention of it) and its political requirements. As a consequence, the developmental policies of the populist governments were negatively affected by their insufficient understanding of the problems involved, as we have seen in Chapter 22, in a way that contributed significantly to their becoming relatively helpless targets for the reactionary forces. The second obstacle, which contributed directly and decisively to the overthrow of the populist governments by the military, was the fact that the earlier awareness of the underdevelopment of these countries did not penetrate, except very marginally, the military establishment. They were left aside both by the intellectuals, who tended to underrate their significance, assuming that the populist era had superseded the times of barracks coups, and by the populist leaders, who overrated their own political strength, because of their mass support.

Latin America, therefore, has already experienced frustration in the promotion of her autonomous development. That fact brings additional limitations to the time available for the formulation of another project of autonomous development in the current decade. In these conditions, the suggested deadline of thirty years, which corresponds to one biological and two sociological generations, seems to be the maximum possible limit for the achievement of that goal. Insofar as a cumulative process of autonomous development does not take shape in the course of that time limit, the social forces will be brought, through the constant readjustment of their interests to the prevailing conditions, to situations that are only compatible with the alternative of dependency, or some other sectors will be brought to very radical forms of opposition to the status quo, which will only be compatible with the revolutionary way. In both cases the achievement of autonomous development in Latin America by reformist ways would be rendered impossible.

Latin American integration

A final point that must be considered, concerning the central trends and alternatives of Latin America, is related to the integration of the region. The integration of Latin America, as an operational idea, has been CEPAL's last contribution up to now. After diagnosing Latin American underdevelopment and presenting their theory of the deterioration of the terms of trade in the late 1940s, and after endorsing, in the early 1950s, central economic planning as a sine qua non condition for overcoming that state of underdevelopment, Prebisch and his staff acknowledged that the relative smallness of Latin American markets, as discussed in Chapters 21 and 22, could only be compensated for by the regional integration of the Latin American countries. Felipe Herrera and the staff of the Inter-American Development Bank have championed the thesis of Latin American integration since the early 1960s and have tried, by all means, to put it to practice.

We have already discussed the main general problems related to Latin American integration. As will be remembered, they concern two facts particularly. One involves the problem of national viability. The Central American and the insular Caribbean countries, because of their insufficient human and natural resources and their extremely unfavorable geopolitical location, suffer from critical problems of national viability. Other Latin American countries, such as Ecuador, Bolivia, Paraguay, and Uruguay, in distinct situations of development and national integration, are also negatively affected by their insufficient human and natural resources. Only Mexico, Brazil, and Argentina (particularly the first two) have the conditions for individual national viability. The second fact involves the problem of international autonomy. Related to the former, that problem concerns the extent to which collective or relative individual autonomy is achievable by the Latin American countries, such autonomy being a necessary requirement for the promotion of autonomous development. In both cases it becomes clear that the Latin American countries, with the possible exception of Brazil, need to achieve some sort of regional integration in order to achieve or consolidate their national viability and their collective autonomy. The question that now requires a brief elucidation concerns the ways and modes by which Latin American integration can be practically achieved.

The practical efforts at Latin American integration may be roughly divided into three partially overlapping phases. The first attempts were oriented toward the organization of a broad Latin American free-trade area and led to the signature of the Montevideo Treaty in 1960. Mexico, Peru, Chile, Paraguay, Brazil, Uruguay, and Argentina were the initial signatories of the treaty, later followed by Colombia, Ecuador, Venezuela, and Bolivia. By 1968 the Montevideo Treaty included all the South American countries plus Mexico. In a similar fashion, in 1958, the Central American countries, including Guatemala, Honduras, El Salvador, and later Nicaragua and Costa Rica, signed the Central American Multilateral Treaty of Free Trade and Economic Integration. Whereas the Central American free-trade area was rapidly transformed into a comprehensive economic integration, with the Treaty of Economic Association of 1960, between Guatemala, Honduras, and El Salvador, and later joined, in 1962, by Nicaragua and Costa Rica, the Mexican–South American association, called the Latin American Free Trade Association (known by its Spanish and Portuguese initials, ALALC), has retained its original limited purposes. The Montevideo Treaty, expressing, as formerly said, the first phase of Latin American practical integrative efforts, was deliberately conceived in restricted terms. It was then thought that the national development of the concerned countries required only an enlargement of their markets' possibilities and that that enlargement should be made within cautious limits in order to prevent disruptive unbalances, which were feared as a possible consequence of uneven levels of productivity among the countries and the larger firms of the area. The basic method employed by the signatories of the Montevideo Treaty to open their national markets to each other is an annual agreement on national lists of goods, under the form of new reciprocal concessions. As could have been foreseen, the adopted system leveled off rapidly after an initial important increase in the intrazonal trade and finally became practically irrelevant as an instrument of national development. This can be seen if we compare the previous exchanges among the earlier signatories of the treaty (Mexico and the South American countries with the exception of Bolivia and Venezuela) with their later exchanges. In 1959–1961 the FOB value of those exchanges was $321 million. In 1965 their value rose to $635 million. But in 1966 it increased to only $675 million and in 1967 decreased to $614 million.[5]

As a reaction to the poor results and development of ALALC, many people in Latin America, particularly economic experts of the several countries and of the Inter-American Development Bank, under the leadership of Felipe Herrera, former president of that bank, tried to go a step further, introducing the notion of a planned sectoral integration in addition to ALALC's commercial liberalization. The Inter-American Bank created a special institution, the Institute for the

Integration of Latin America (INTAL, by its Spanish and Portuguese initials), with headquarters in Buenos Aires, for undertaking studies and promoting measures oriented toward the economic integration of Latin America.[6] The central idea suggested in that second phase was the adoption, through a grand political decision on the part of each of the Latin American countries, of an integrating master plan, which would be approved by a general treaty and operated by appropriate common institutions. That plan would provide, particularly, for the creation and development of some key joint supercorporations in the industrial, commercial, financial, transport, and educational sectors, which would open new frontiers and dimensions to the area without the disruptive risks of unchecked free competition. The book *Factores para la Integración Latinoamericana* (1966), organized by Felipe Herrera and containing contributions from a group of Latin American social scientists and experts, expresses the plan in a systematic form. The idea got a warm reception from Latin American experts and intellectuals and from President Frei of Chile,[7] but failed to motivate the other governments, particularly the Brazilian and Argentine governments,[8] which showed less interest in creating inter-Latin American ties.

At the same time, a new awareness emerged in Latin America about the grave risks involved in the rapid expansion of the so-called multinational corporations, mostly American-controlled. It became clear that if the Latin American countries would not make a collective decision to define and regulate the role and the limits of foreign capital and, moreover, would not make the decision to create Latin American supercorporations, the creation of an integrated Latin American economic community would mean only the organizing of the Latin American countries as compulsory consumers of the goods produced there by the great international corporations.[9] The example of the industries of integration of the Central American Common Market, where economic integration was not supported by protective measures against the great international corporations showed that that kind of integration only packed the Central American countries together as compulsory consumers of goods produced by nonregional groups. And the fact that such an economically and technically powerful association as the ECC fell under the predominance of American supercorporations for the same reasons, as Servan-Schreiber (1967) dramatically indicated, was a decisive confirmation of the inevitability of that consequence in the absence of appropriate protective measures.

It was, then, at the end of the 1960s that a third phase started in the history of Latin American integration, without interrupting the former trends. That phase was marked by subregional forms of integration. The initiative for that move was once again taken by Chile, as soon as the Frei administration came to the conclusion that they would have to wait too long for the more desirable planned integration of the general region. The Bogotá Declaration of 1966, signed by the presidents of Chile, Colombia, and Venezuela and representatives of Peru and Ecuador, joined in the following year by Bolivia, and later formalized by the Bogotá Convention of 1969, created the Andean group, with the purpose of achieving, within the general framework of ALALC, the subregional economic integration of the concerned parties.[10] The Andean group is a tighter and more complex system than ALALC. Unlike the former, it provides automatic deadlines for the suppression of customs' barriers; it is operated by a supranational three-man permanent executive committee and has a common investment agency, the Andean Corporation of Development, for financing and creating joint enterprises and projects. The Andean group, moreover, is likely to proceed, at the request of the Chilean and Peruvian governments, with protective regulations concerning nonregional capital, although that matter has some complicated aspects which contributed to preventing Venezuela from signing the convention.

Considered in subregional terms Latin American integration seems to be more feasible, at least as a first stage. This is because (1) the need for integration is not equally urgent or, to an extent, equally indispensable for all the Latin American countries and (2) their facilities for integration are considerably greater, in an initial phase, if the integration is to be subregional, centered around certain poles or axes of integration, than if the region as a whole were to be integrated. As far as the first aspect is concerned, the situation of the Central American countries, as a group, and of the Andean countries, as another group, is undoubtedly different from the situation of the three larger countries of the area— Mexico, Brazil, and Argentina. As far as the second aspect is concerned, it can also be contended that a process of subregional integration, centered around certain poles or axes of integration, corresponds more immediately to the interests and possibilities of the concerned parties.

Insofar as urgency and necessity are concerned the Central American countries, with their tiny populations and resources, are obviously those more immediately in need of pooling their resources, which explains why their free-trade area has envolved into an integrated economic community.[11] The countries of the Andean group are also more immediately under the constraint of their limited human and natural resources. By getting together they reach a total area of more than 1.7 million square miles (compared to less than 500,000 square miles for the largest of them, Peru) and a total population (1970) of more than 55 million inhabitants (compared to less than 21 million for the most populous of them, Colombia).

In addition to the Andean group, along the Chilean-Colombian axis, two other subregional integrations could be formed to tighten general Latin American integration. The second axis of integration is the Brazilian-Argentine one, along which an Atlantic group could be formed, including Paraguay and Uruguay. This would represent a subregional area of more than 4.5 million square miles with a total population (1970) of more than 122 million inhabitants. Finally, Mexico is a third pole of integration, around which the Central American and the insular Caribbean countries could get together, forming a subregional area of more than 1 million square miles, with a population (1970) of more than 84 million inhabitants.

Another remaining possibility is the eventual independent course of Brazil. Because of her continental proportions (more than 3.2 million square miles and, in 1970, 93 million inhabitants), the distinctness resulting from her Portuguese culture, and the fact that she is a single unified (if underintegrated) state, Brazil has both the capacity and some propensity to follow an independent course, at least in terms of subregional integration. Should Brazil be uninterested in forming an Atlantic group, Argentina would probably be attracted to the Andean group, bringing Paraguay, Uruguay, and Venezuela with her. This would increase the Andian group area to more than 3.3 million square miles and its population (1970) to more than 94 million inhabitants, rendering it the most important subregion of Latin America, in the hypothesis that the Atlantic group is not formed.

With the exception of the Andean group—itself still in a preliminary stage—the possible subregional integrations are still no more than projects proposed by experts and international technical agencies, which may never materialize. It is likely, however, that a positive development of the Andean group will either induce Brazil and Argentina to form the Atlantic group or persuade Argentina to join the Andean group, which would very probably welcome her. The discussion in the following chapters of the Latin American alternatives indicated here—dependency or autonomy—requires, particularly in the case of the latter, that subregional integration be kept in mind.

NOTES

[1] See Helio Jaguaribe (1969a, pp. 1–86).

[2] For the ruling country the influence of the type of dependency is not symmetrical but also not irrelevant. Becoming the center of an empire, as was seen in Chapter 18, requires purposeful imperialism, with its internal Caesarean implications.

[3] See Edgar Morin (1970, pp. 515–548).

[4] That example actually portrays the currently prevailing behavior of the Latin American elites, reflecting the extent to which they expect a dependent future for their countries. It also reveals the uselessness of discouraging that trend by legal means if the overall official policies remain oriented toward that dependency.

[5] See Celso Furtado (1969, chap. 21 and Table I-21).

[6] See the studies under the editorship of Gustavo Lagos, first president of INTAL (1965).

[7] See *Hacia la Integración Acelerada de América Latina*, prepared by CEPAL (Mexico, 1965). See also Aldo Ferrer "Integración Latinoamericana y Desarrollo Nacional" in *Comercio Exterior*, vol. 17, (March 1967).

[8] In Argentina, along with other factors contributing to her cautious approach to the idea of Latin American integration, there is a view, supported by some sectors and formulated by Rogelio Frigerio, contending that national integration must precede, in the national interest, regional integration. See Rogelio Frigerio (1968). Less explicitly, the same view seems to influence some Brazilian sectors.

[9] See Inter-American Development Bank (1968); see also Stephen Hymer (1967), Arpad von Lazar (1969a), Jaguaribe (1965), and Jaguaribe *et al.* (1969a).

[10] See Carlos F. Díaz Alejandro (1968).

[11] The fact that the Central American Economic Community has not been enough to render those countries nationally viable does not diminish their urgent need for that kind of association.

24

The Alternative of Dependence

We saw in the preceding chapter that the Latin American countries are currently confronted with the basic alternative of dependence or autonomy, each presenting certain typological characteristics, ways of implementation, and implied sociopolitical models. We then considered, briefly, the main characteristics, ways, and models and saw that the whole process and the possibilities of choice involved in it are subject to certain historical deadlines. The alternative of dependence reflects the current prevailing trends and implied choices of the Latin American elites, and, as was stressed, if those trends continue, they will lead, independent of any dramatic or ostensible option, to irreversible forms of dependence. The adoption and implementation of the alternative of autonomy, however, which is still available for a limited time, will require some deliberate and radical changes in the current trends. Finally, we reviewed the question of Latin American integration, which constitutes a prerequisite for any autonomous development of the region, with a few possible exceptions.

   The purpose of the present chapter is to analyze the alternative of dependence, its consequences, and its conditions. For that we will attempt, initially, to study the characteristics, causes, and implied models of that alternative more closely. We will then proceed to a brief discussion of the dialectics of dependence for the concerned countries and the implied colonial-fascist model.

Dependence and its implied model

As was discussed in Chapter 18, the process of dependence presents four typical structural forms, which tend to occur in succession: colonial, neocolonial, satellite, and provincial. In the case of Latin America (see Chapters 19–22), colonial dependence on the Iberian countries changed into neocolonial dependence on Great Britain in the nineteenth century and shifted to neocolonial dependence on the United States in the first decades of this century. Then the crisis of the

1930s disrupted the semicolonial system. The succeeding period was one of relative autonomous development, propelled by the process of import substitution, which came to be deliberately promoted by the populist governments. The crisis of the import-substitution process and of populist development, discussed in Chapter 22, led the new Establishment in Latin America to increasing forms of satellite dependence on the United States, and thus became, in the course of the 1960s, the current situation and trend for the Latin American countries, with a few exceptions (Chile and Peru).

What is peculiar to the present satellite dependence is that it configurates a situation that is not viewed as such and not even willed as such by the dominating country. Outside of a limited academic group nobody in the United States contemplates the question of Latin American dependence with the conceptual neatness with which it is being treated here. From the Latin American side as well, the social forces that have implicitly opted for that alternative do not view it with clarity. The alternative of satellite dependence, therefore, is, first of all, an objective historical tendency, which results from the societal conditions prevailing in Latin America, within the general framework of the interimperial system that has emerged since World War II. In addition to that, however, the alternative of dependence, even if conceived in terms of false consciousness—which disguises and adulterates reality, making it sweeter—is to a certain extent a purposeful design, although not very consistently formulated and carried out, on the part of certain sectors, both in the United States and in Latin America.

In the United States these sectors are represented by the multinational super-corporations and the business community in general and by the military establishment. In Latin America these sectors include: (1) some middle-class groups and working-class sectors that have been engulfed (such as the automotive complex) by the economy of dependence, (2) the sectors of the former national bourgeoisie that, with varying degrees of self-awareness, have come to the conclusion that, actually or potentially, very serious conflicts exist between the development, in national terms, of the Latin American countries and the full maintenance of a regime of private capitalism and have chosen, against their national values, in favor of their class and corporate interests, opting for the position of "branch" bourgeoisie, (3) the consular bourgeoisie, which has remained linked to the old semicolonial structure and thinks (without realizing the irreversible successiveness of the forms of dependence) that satellite dependence will retain or restore the old semicolonial conditions, (4) the military groups that are victims of an ideological alienation based on systematic anticommunism, and (5) the praetorian military groups that have been converted into foreign legionnaires of an American-centered military system.

An analysis of each of these groups would be too long for the purposes of the present chapter. I will just mention the two major ideological justifications that, although in terms of false consciousness (sweetening self-protective adulteration of reality), try to give a rationale to satellite dependence. The first of these justifications, which has been already discussed in Chapter 20, includes systematic anticommunism and its correlates—moralism, the primacy of order, and authoritarianism. The second of these justifications, fashionable in bourgeois circles and among the pro-satellite intelligentsia, is the theory of dependent development, usually phrased as "interdependent" development and presented, in terms of its idealized example, as the "Canadian model."

The Canadian model

The "Canadian model," of which Roberto Campos has been the most competent and militant proponent, is characterized by three main assumptions:[1] (1) Under-developed countries, precisely because they are underdeveloped, cannot, without intolerable sacrifices, generate domestically the investment resources they need. It rests, therefore, with foreign capital to play the role of the dynamic factor in the economic development of the concerned countries. That role, because of the natural propensity of those with free capital to look for the best international opportunities for investment, will always tend to be filled when the governments of the host countries fill their own role in the game: the maintenance of public and financial order and adoption of a regime of protection and attraction of foreign capital. (2) The economic development that will be achieved thereby will radiate from the economic plane to the other societal planes, thus promoting the balanced overall development of that society. (3) There is a basic harmonic interdependence between the countries with raw materials and large investment opportunities and those with export capital and technology. Due to that harmonic interdependence the gradual development of the former countries will, in each stage of the process, lead to new and higher forms of cooperation with the latter countries until the concerned partners reach an association of basic parity, which will include similar levels of development. The example of Canada is then given as an illustration of the validity of that model and its assumptions.

Several of the aspects involved in the Canadian model have already been discussed in this book. I will therefore limit the following comments to what I consider its main fallacy, which represents a typical expression of "idealist economism." It is interesting to observe that the conception of the Canadian model, in the ideological framework of capitalism, presents a position that is symmetrical, in the opposite camp, with Menshevism, in the ideological framework of socialism. It consists, in a way, in a "capitalist Menshevism." Indeed, in the last analysis Menshevism supposed that the free forces of the economy in the capitalist regime would, on the one hand, produce the economic development of the bourgeois society and, on the other hand, generate in that society the contradiction that would give birth to the socialist society. The idealist economism of the satellite conception implies, in the first place, that the economic process and its agents, in a free economy regime, spontaneously generate economic development in a neutral political, cultural, and social situation. In the second place that conception implies that because of a sort of preestablished harmony, the economic development of a society always brings about, internally, its cultural, social, and political development—whatever the prerequisites for the latter—carrying out, at the same time, a spontaneous mutually beneficial readjustment of the relations between the host country and those supplying the former with capital and technology.

As can be seen immediately, all the criticisms, in the economic field, of the laissez-faire conception of spontaneous economic equilibrium and development and, in the broader field of social theory, all the criticism of economism, in the sense of an understanding of the economic process as a determining independent variable among all other societal variables, are fully applicable to the so-called Canadian model. Without elaborating on the criticisms of laissez-faire liberalism and of economism, I will just mention two points. The arguments demonstrating the fallacies involved in the theories of spontaneous growth have followed two basic lines: The first and most comprehensive was formulated by Marx and has been elaborated, in different forms, by scholars of Marxian persuasion,[2] the second, more strictly related to the thinking on business cycles and anti-recession policies, has been given its best recent formulation by Keynes and has been treated in various ways by the theorists of economic planning.[3] The recent thinking on the criticisms and overcoming of economism has returned, with new perspectives, to a global approach to the process of societal development, understanding it as necessarily involving a structural interrelation between the cultural, participational, political, and economic planes.[4] See Chapters 1 and 2.

As a matter of fact, it is not true that the economic process spontaneously leads a society to economic development. As discussed in Chapter 12, spontaneous economic development has only occurred in Great Britain and some of her ex-colonies, and even then because of some fundamental previous or concomitant noneconomic conditions. As one gets further from the eighteenth-century process of development in Great Britain, one sees that latecomers had to pay the price of increasing state interference if they wanted to succeed in their developmental efforts. As the process of development becomes more dependent on state action, the capacity for autonomous decisions on the part of the principal strategic actor, the national government, becomes increasingly more relevant than the availability of resources outside the control of the national state. This is still more so if the concerned resources are submitted to investment policies and to a management oriented toward the maximization of private profit in terms of foreign firms rather than for the domestic development of the host society. That notwithstanding, the availability of resources retains, of course, its fundamental importance, conditioning the limits of national viability, as has already been discussed.

Nor is it true, as we have seen in Chapter 2, that economic development, when it is promoted, automatically produces the development of the other systems of a society. The principle of congruence, regulating intrasocietal structural relations, only leads to the congruent development of the other systems when the respective corresponding conditions are also matched. When, as in the Latin American case, national development is prevented by structural dualism, resulting from specific social and cultural conditions, preserved and reinforced by a certain regime of power, as has been discussed in Chapters 19–22, only the change of those conditions, brought about or supported by a new appropriate regime of power, can overcome that dualism. In international terms, as well, the existence and strengthening of relations of economic and technological dependence of a society vis-à-vis another one does not, in any way, lead the former to parity relations with the latter or favor harmonious relations between them.[5]

The propensity to colonial fascism

As a matter of fact, as was indicated in Chapter 20, the alternative of dependence is characterized not only by the process of denationalization, which is inherent to it, but also by the circular and mutually reinforcing processes of stagnation and marginality, which usually lie behind the former and to a large extent determine it. There is, therefore, at another level, another circular process of causation between the stagnation-marginality syndrome and the alternative of dependence. Once certain cultural, social, economic, and political conditions and features that have prevented Latin American elites from socially functional behavior (those originating in the colonial system) came to prevail in the recent past, the system resulting after the collapse of populism required the coercive repression of the expectations of the masses for the maintenance of its equilibrium. But both the stagnation inherent to that situation and the repression required for the maintenance of the system render its equilibrium increasingly dependent on external conditions. Exporter of agricultural and mineral primary products, subject to the deterioration of its terms of exchange, and unable to complete its process of industrialization, as discussed in Chapter 22, the system lends itself not only to internal disequilibrium (compensated for by repression) but also to external disequilibrium, which results in the deficits in its balance of payment. These deficits can be compensated for by foreign loans, which is what usually occurs, as we saw in Chapter 20. But these loans, given the structural character of those deficits, only aggravate the inherent disequilibrium of the system, constantly increasing its state of indebtedness.

The system's dependence on constant and cumulative external inputs, moreover, involves much more than balance-of-payment compensatory loans. Because the system is not capable of generating, internally, enough capital to meet its current needs (including those for its frustrated developmental attempts) and is still less capable of scientific and technological self-sufficiency, capital for various domestic purposes and all sorts of scientific-technological contributions must come permanently from abroad. Furthermore, on the top of all that, the system, at least in the least-developed Latin American countries, also depends on foreign aid in order to increase its internal capacity for repression so that that capacity will not be inferior to the increase in the pressure from the masses.

The conjunction, in the sociopolitical model implied in the system of dependence, of external dependence—economic, scientific-technological, and military—with the domestic repression of the masses, makes that model, politically, a special variant of fascism, as has already been seen in Chapter 14. What distinguishes that variety of fascism from its pre–World War II European model is the fact that its dynamic center is not internal but external. In both cases we find some of the features that are characteristic of fascism: domination of the polity by a self-appointed ruling elite, consisting of sectors of the middle class associated with the bourgeoisie, that is not traditional and does not have power founded on any sort of effective popular delegation, and that uses discretionary processes of control in order to retain self-granted power and to reconcile policies of economic modernization with the preservation of the socioeconomic status quo. The distinction between these two kinds of fascism consists in the fact that the European one was autonomous and endogenous, whereas the Latin American variant is dependent and exogenous. For that Latin American variant, therefore, as has already been suggested, the designation of colonial fascism is fitting.

The experience of the last decade has confirmed the propensity of the Latin American dependent regimes to assume forms increasingly closer to the colonial-fascist model. In some cases, as in Brazil and Argentina, the military establishments that support their respective regimes have not yet fully realized their true nature. They remain subjectively involved, to a large extent, because of the biases of the ideology of systematic anticommunism and its correlated beliefs and their mistaken identification of legitimate order with enforced order, the national security of their own countries with the interests of the American military establishment, and the defense of Western civilization (assuming they could actually help it) with a policy of dependence on the United States. In these same countries, however, and particularly in Brazil, the actual incapacity shown by the model to overcome the supposedly provisional phase of corrective repression and to really start a comprehensive process of self-sustained development is leading increasingly larger sectors of the military establishment to a deep uncertainty about the fitness of the model and about the governing ability of their present leaders.

In other countries, as in the group of nonviable Latin American countries or in the borderline case of Paraguay (see Chapter 14), the respective military establishments, led to cynicism by the acknowledgment of the nonviability of an autonomous-national project and led to corruption by the unchecked exercise of irresponsible power, have been converted into praetorian forces in *societas sceleris* regimes, which are hardly corrigible from within the system. These regimes, as has been seen, can be appropriately designated as colonial praetorianism.

The dialectics of dependence

The central problem involved in the process of dependence has already been mentioned: the relation of circular causation between stagnation, marginalization of the masses, and the system's efforts to maintain equilibrium internally by increasing the degree of coercion and externally by increasing the extent of dependence. That spiral of deterioration, however, cannot go on forever. The process involves an increasing degree of denationalization and of popular repression which, after a certain point, will be incompatible with the maintenance of the national structures and of relations of minimal solidarity between the masses and the elites. Once that critical point is reached (and rather than of a point, one should speak of a critical strip, which is narrower or wider depending on local conditions), the system is confronted with a set of alternatives in which one of the possibilities is revolution and the other is the stabilization of dependence. These alternatives may remain in confrontation for a long time, overtly or latently, before one of them comes to prevail irreversibly. Revolution will be discussed in the next chapter. Let us now consider the stabilization of dependence.

Unlike Marx's idea, expressed in his theory of increasing pauperization, in the sense that the marginalization of the masses caused by the capitalist mode of production would necessarily bring about the revolutionary overthrow of the regime, it happens that stagnation and dependence may persist for a very long time. What causes revolutions, as has been seen (see the end of Chapter 17), if other circumstances do not interfere, is not the marginalization of the masses, but that of sectors of the subelite and of groups of the elite, in conditions in which the masses are disaffected. Abandoned to their own marginality, the masses do not have, by themselves, the ability to organize and the techniques necessary for undertaking a revolution with a reasonable margin of success. The masses can mutiny spontaneously and succeed in seizing the eventual control of important areas of a country. And they can aggravate and precipitate contradictions already existing at the level of the elite and subelite. But they cannot obtain the strategic and tactical capacity required for overcoming the repressive apparatus of a political system without the participation of organized and organizing cadres, particularly if that apparatus has not been seriously hurt beforehand by other confrontations, such as external or internal-sectoral conflicts.

The grave problem presented by the colonial-fascist model, for the Latin American systems, is that it also tends to create the marginalization and the disaffection of middle-class sectors (that is, sectors of the subelite) and of groups of the bourgeoisie. That fact has a double origin. First, and in predominantly economic terms, it results because the stagnation inherent to the model also affects the creation of new jobs for the middle class. Since the lack of economic expansion prevents the creation of the new productive jobs, the colonial-fascist state is compelled to maintain its *cartorial*[6] characteristics, forging parasitic public jobs to accommodate the middle class. That system, however, rapidly exhausts the fiscal possibilities of the state, forcing it to adopt inflationary expediencies without economic growth and leading to a decrease in the real income of the middle class. Since that process cannot be mended within the model, either the hegemonic foreign power interferes in a compensatory way, subsidizing the system, or the system loses its capacity to keep the allegiance of its own subelite, giving birth to the conditions that tend to arouse the revolutionary mobilization of the mass.

The second origin of the crisis to which the colonial-fascist model tends to be brought is of a predominantly cultural character. With its increasing denationalization, the system tends to lose, along with its capacity for self-determination, its ability to mobilize with a minimum amount of efficiency those symbols actually capable of awaking responses of national solidarity and self-sacrifice. It becomes increasingly manifest that the system as such is a despoiling one for the benefit of the ruling elite and the hegemonic power, and that, therefore, it retains a meaning only for those who derive some gain from it. Whatever the system's capability for minimizing, through coercive and terrorizing methods, some of its direct operating costs, the passive resistance of all those who do not feel in partnership with the regime constantly increases its indirect costs and lowers its level of efficiency. Thus, for that order of reasons, the system requires compensatory subsidies from the hegemonic power.

The distinctive characteristic of the dialectics of the colonial-fascist regimes, considered as an ideal type, is the final exhaustion of their capacity to sustain themselves with their own resources, even when they are enjoying conditions allowing the unrestricted use of the utmost forms of repression. It thus results, in the final analysis, that the sustainment of the model, in its typical form, depends on the resources and policies of the hegemonic power. Otherwise, the model will change, either through an increase in its capacity to incorporate the marginal masses, with the correlated increase in its capacity for development, in which case the model would change into some superior sociopolitical form, or through a simplification of the structure of the society, converting the model into a more rudimentary form, such as that of colonial praetorianism.

Should the hegemonic power be willing and capable of bearing the costs required for subsidizing the system, at least at the minimum level necessary to maintain its viability, particularly by providing the middle class with a level of employment sufficient to prevent serious disaffection among the subelite, the model of satellite dependence could last indefinitely. Since the critical sociopolitical aspect of the model is not the misery and discontent of the masses, which are controllable by repressive means, but the disaffection of significant sectors of the subelite and elite groups, the former may be kept submissive by appropriate measures as long the latter retain their allegiance to the regime. Such measures would include, in case of need, and in addition to the general coercive forms of maintenance of the public order, the adoption of means for reducing the demographic pressure and of other means associated with territorial allocation and containment. In Latin America, for instance, it is already evident that in a not-too-distant future, if the present model of dependence is maintained, the rural masses will no longer be allowed to emigrate to the cities. A sort of apartheid regime, as we saw in Chapter 18, is likely to be imposed, keeping the unemployed rural masses in the Latin American hinterland, as a kind of superreserve of natives, in order to prevent an increase in urban marginality from rendering the cities unmanageable, excessively increasing crime, clogging the services for public assistance, and in this way, making the living conditions of the middle class and of the usefully employed sectors of the masses intolerable.

The limits of subsidization

The crucial question, therefore, as has already been advanced in Chapter 18, is the possibility of the hegemonic power's subsidizing its dependent systems. As large as the free resources of the hegemonic power may be, she will not be willing to waste them; nor will she be capable of using them beyond their availability. With respect to this last aspect, it can be stated, in relation to the United States and her area of hegemony, that American free resources—understood as those that could be withdrawn from their present applications without negatively affecting the current operation and development of the American economy, including its own domestic subsidies—would not be enough to directly subsidize all the American dependent systems.[7] Within the existing conditions, the superpowers and the Great Powers only dispose, at their respective scale of capability, of limited margins of free resources for the *selective* financing of some of their dependent systems. In the case of the United States this is currently applied to areas of imperial confrontation with other superpowers, such as certain countries in Southeast Asia (South Vietnam, South Korea) and some relevant outposts (Taiwan, Turkey). In the case of the Soviet Union, which has a similar general conception, countries like Cuba, which is both a showcase and an outpost, receive particular support.

The limits of deterioration

A brief final comment on the alternative of dependence is still pertinent, with respect to the possible changes in the typological characteristics of the system and the corresponding changes in its implied model. As we have seen, if external compensatory assistance is not forwarded by the hegemonic power and a provincial model is not adopted in time, the troubles brought about by colonial-fascist dependence may lead to the gradual or sudden transformation of some of the essential characteristics of the system. In other words, the structure of the system and its model, as an ideal type, may change into some distinct configuration. Should the changes be of a favorable character—in conditions that would allow favorable changes—involving an increase in mass participation and a correlate tendency toward socioeconomic development, former trends toward dependence would be replaced by new trends toward autonomy. The models for autonomous development have already been studied extensively in this book (see particularly Chapters 14 and 15), and the problems of autonomy, as a basic alternative, including the conditions for its possibility, will be discussed in the next two chapters. What we have to consider now, very briefly, is the opposite possibility: the deterioration of the structure of a society—because of the dysfunctional effects of colonial fascism, without compensatory interference from the hegemonic power—leading that society to more elementary forms of despoliation and dependence, of which the usual typical model is colonial praetorianism.

As has been seen, colonial praetorianism is a simplified version of colonial fascism, characterized by a regressive dichotomization of the societal structures, not in terms of former traditional values, but in terms of a *societas sceleris* polarization, opposing those who have power, wealth, and culture and who form a spoliatory ruling strata led and supported by the praetorian military, and those who are deprived of everything and who form a plundered and dominated strata comprehending the peasantry, most of the working class, and the lowest echelons of the bureaucracy. The political culture of colonial praetorianism is also a simplified version of colonial fascism. In the latter model, the new rigidified elite tends to develop an irrational restoration of an ethos of class superiority, expressing idealized forms of bourgeois middle-class values, with varying degrees of patrician overtones. Colonial praetorianism, however, is ideologically cynical and hypocritical, pretending to express national and social ideals that have no connection with the real practice of the regime and are not actually supposed by anybody to have the slightest application.

We have already discussed the societal characteristics of the colonial-praetorian model. (See Chapter 14.) Now we can add one more observation concerning the relationship between that model and the societies that might come to be regulated by it. As we have seen (see Chapter 14, Chart 6), the colonial-praetorian model usually corresponds to societies with a *societas sceleris* elite. That type of society is a subgroup of the coercive inegalitarian society, which, in turn, is a subdivision (Type III) of the underdeveloped society with a dysfunctional elite. This means that societies that are likely to be submitted to colonial praetorianism are usually simple societies with small populations and territories, like the Central American countries and Paraguay. In large and complex countries like Mexico, Brazil, or Argentina, colonial praetorianism would be incompatible with the preservation of their national structure, present complexity, and, of course, level of development. Such large and complex countries can follow the alternative of dependence and come to be regulated by a colonial-fascist model, which is the current tendency—although still reversible—in these three countries. The deterioration of their structures and social fabric, in the hypothesis of a long submission to dependence and colonial fascism, would not, however, lead them directly to a colonial-praetorian model. First, they would have to undergo severe disruptive processes, involving their national unity and the structure of their social and economic systems. Only if they should not be able to shift their satellite dependence to a provincial dependence or to overcome, through revolution or reform, their former dependent status and colonial-fascist model and head in the direction of autonomous development, would they be led to formal or informal processes of national and intrasocietal segmentation, with the resulting conversion of segments to colonial-praetorian configurations. It is very likely, however, that the hegemonic power, given her important vested interest in that sort of satellite, would interfere in time to prevent such disruptions. In principle the best solution for the hegemonic country, as we have already seen in Chapter 18, would be to reorganize the ailing dependency according to the provincial model.

NOTES

[1] Roberto Campos, one of the most distinguished Brazilian economists and former planning minister of the Castelo Branco regime, has published abundantly in support of the Canadian model.

[2] Concerning Marx see, in particular, his criticism of Say's law in *Das Kapital*, vol. 1, chap. 3, and his discussion of the contradiction between the micro-rationality of the firm and the macro-irrationality of the laissez-faire economic system in *Das Kapital*, vol. 3, chap. 5; see also Marx's earlier sociopolitical writings, particularly *Division of Labor* and *The Communist Manifesto*. Among recent scholars of Marxian persuasion see Henri Bartoli (1950, part 2, particularly chaps. 1–3), Jean Marchall (1955, particularly pp. 198 ff.), Paul Baran (1957, particularly chap. 11), Joan Robinson (1956, particularly chaps. 8 and 9), John Strachey (1956, particularly chaps. 3, 5, 11, and 13), Maurice Dobb, (1962, particularly chaps. 5 and 6, and 1967, particularly chaps. 2 and 3), C. Wright Mills (1963a, particularly chap. 6), Oscar Lange (1963, particularly chap. 5), Paul Baran and Paul Sweezy (1966, particularly chap. 11), and David Horowitz, ed. (1968, particularly articles by Joan Robinson, pp. 103–116, J. Steindl, pp. 244–269, James F. Becker, pp. 270–290, and Paul Baran and Paul Sweezy, pp. 291–311). See also Joseph Schumpeter (1950, part 2).

[3] Concerning Keynes and the theorists of planning, see John Maynard Keynes (1936) and Schumpeter's comments (1954, part 5, chap. 5, pp. 1170–1184); see also Emile James (1955, vol. 1, chap. 5, sect. 3), Abba Lerner (1944, particularly chaps. 1, 2, and 23), Carl Landauer (1945, particularly chap. 1), W. Arthur Lewis (1955), ILPES (1966). See also, on contemporary capitalism, François Perroux (1964, particularly Introduction and parts 1 and 5), John K. Galbraith (1962 and 1967b, particularly chaps. 3, 4, 6, 20, 22, 31, and 35), Andrew Shonfield (1965, particularly chaps. 1, 4, and 13), and Robert Heilbroner (1966).

[4] Concerning the recent sociological and global approaches to national development, see Bert F. Hoselitz (1960), David Novack and Robert Lekachman, eds. (1964), Jagdish Bhagwati (1966, particularly part 2), Eugene Staley (1961, particularly chap. 1, pp. 201–227), Dobb (1963, particularly chap. 2), and Heilbroner (1963). See also Helio Jaguaribe (1968).

[5] This analysis of the fallacies of the Canadian model make it clear that the historical case of Canada, itself, does not fit the model supposedly deduced from it. The empirical process of Canadian development, although undoubtedly expressing the consequences—both for the good and for the bad—of massive dominating American investments, has presented a final overall positive character because of certain decisive cultural-ethnic and geopolitical features that are peculiar to American-Canadian relations. Being culturally and ethnically a simple continuation of the United States, territorially an extension of it, and politically a system of the same origin and tradition with the same basic international interests, Canada is for most purposes an inner part of the American social system. In fact, Canada is closer to that social system than two formal American states, Hawaii and Alaska, and one formally associated state, Puerto Rico. These common traits have certainly created serious problems for the Canadian national identity, but in exchange, it has rendered the Canadian development a particular variant of the general American development, as a sort of independent super-Alaska.

[6] The expression "cartorial state" is a now widely used to designate the kind of state, common in Latin America, in which the public bureaucracy is oriented less toward the effective performance of public service than toward the provision of parasitic jobs for the political clientele of the ruling sectors, in exchange for their political support. The expression "cartorial," originally coined by me in a study called *Politics of Clientele and Ideological Politics*, comes from the colonial public notaries in Latin America, whose role and status were incomparably superior to those in the British tradition.

[7] For any country the capacity to mobilize free resources, in the conditions mentioned, is necessarily limited to a small percentage of her former personal consumption expenditures,

which would be collected through some form of additional taxation. It must be assumed that to impose that additional fiscal sacrifice on the public with the corresponding reduction of its consumption capacity, that reduction has to be very small—let us say, no more than 10 percent of the personal consumption expenditures—and the motivation for it rather high. If the American people should be willing, in order to finance the country's alien dependencies, to allocate as much as 50 percent of the total currently granted for domestic welfare subsidies ($100,239 million in 1967), the public would have to accept a reduction of 10 percent of its current personal expenditure capacity, which amounted to $491,700 million in 1967. This would yield about $50 billion, which would be about 10 times the current American foreign aid ($5,101 million in 1967). It is very unlikely that such a huge effort would ever be acceptable to the American people. Even if it were, the resulting amount would still be insufficient for the purpose indicated.

25

The Alternative of Autonomy:
The Revolutionary Way

Purpose of the present analysis

We will proceed here and in the following chapter to the study of the second alternative, as discussed in Chapter 23, with which the Latin American countries are confronted: the alternative of autonomy. The purpose in view is to discuss the two basic ways in which that autonomy can be achieved: the revolutionary and the reformist ways. What we have in mind is to obtain valuable generalizations, as much as possible with predictive significance, about the possibilities and conditions for autonomous development in Latin America. We are, therefore, concerned with the study of certain relevant historical cases, such as the Cuban revolution, the progressive reformism of the Chilean Christian Democrats, and the reformist military governments of Velasco's Peru and Ovando's Bolivia, only insofar as the analysis of these cases provide us with empirical data for our theorizing attempt. The analysis of those cases for their own sake, although indispensable for the understanding of the current sociohistorical process in the concerned countries and of contemporary Latin America in general, would go beyond the scope of our present study.[1]

The dichotomy between revolution and reform as ways for achieving autonomy, is not aribtrary or due to casual circumstances, but a result of the structural characteristics of Latin American underdevelopment. As we have seen, Latin America's underdevelopment, which already presents the characteristics of protracted underdevelopment, is ultimately the consequence of the historical and current dysfunctionality of its elites. In some cases, that dysfunctionality is not generalized and has not yet brought about a state of consolidated underdevelopment. Chile and, to an extent, Venezuela, provide examples of relative elite functionality. Mexico, Brazil, and Argentina, in spite of a very serious and currently prevailing propensity for a colonial-fascist consolidation of the dysfunctional sectors of their new Establishment, still have large functional groups in their elite and important functional sectors in their subelite. In other words, a reformist way is still open, if for a limited time, in those and in some other Latin American countries. At the same time, a revolutionary way, independent of these considerations and viewed by its proponents in different terms, is currently being attempted in practically all the Latin American countries. We know, moreover, from what has been studied in Chapter 14, that, independent of ideological preferences, the revolutionary way and the developmental-socialist model present the only possible solution for some cases of underdevelopment. This applies to several Latin American countries, such as the Central American and Caribbean ones and Paraguay, to the extent that changes in the overall conditions relating Latin America to the United States should enlarge the present international permissibility of such countries in particular and of Latin America in general.

The Marxist-Leninist orientation

Revolution, both as a political means of change and as the content of a deep and large social transformation of society, is a widespread aim in Latin America. The revolutionary way has been successfully carried out in Cuba, with a profound structural change in Cuban society. In practically all the other Latin American countries several groups are continuously, if up to now rather unsuccessfully, attempting also to achieve the conquest of power and radical social changes through revolution. Although differences in strategy and in tactics, and to an extent in theory, exist among these various groups, they have several things in common: They have a Marxist representational model of society and of revolutionary change; they acknowledgedly adopt Lenin's operational model for the implantation of revolutionary socialism; and although without acknowledging it, they share some of the basic views and purposes of the developmental-socialist model, as formerly discussed in this book. These points require a brief clarification.

The common Marxist view of society and revolution on the part of the various Latin American revolutionary groups hardly needs elaboration. Former non-Marxist revolutionary ideas, such as the several modalities of French and English socialism (Proudhon, Owen, and so forth), anarchism, and anarcho-syndicalism, have definitively become things of the past in Latin America, at least since World War II.[2] Revolutionary populism, which some Peronist groups once favored, and other Latin American native revolutionary political ideas, such as APRA in the 1930s, have either lost all revolutionary content or ceased to exist. Marxism became the central theoretical framework for all Latin American militant revolutionary groups. In the course of the 1960s, however, that basic Marxist framework became increasingly independent of the orthodox Communist parties, both in terms of theoretical influence and in terms of actual organization, as far as effective revolutionary militancy was concerned. Rather than being channeled through the orthodox (that is, Moscow-oriented) Communist parties, theoretical influence has come from very distinct sources: Among the more radical militant sectors from Castro and Maoism, among the radical leftist catholics from Christian Marxism, and, more diffusely, among the intellectual circles from the several neo-Marxian formulations of contemporary philosophers such as Marcuse, Adorno, Garaudy, or Sartre. In terms of practical action, the orthodox Communist parties—following what seems to be a lasting propensity of Western Communist parties to become a new form of labor party, with an implicit theoretical tendency, if still strongly denied and resented, toward neo-Bernsteinism—have de facto abandoned the revolutionary way and shifted, in spite of the persisting rhetoric, to a reformist way. But the militant revolutionary groups stress, the voluntaristic aspects of the revolutionary praxis even more than Lenin did and, in overt opposition to the orthodox Communist parties, either follow a Chinese line or, as with the several *Izquierdas Revolucionarias*, are committed to Cuban-inspired guerrilla warfare. The Cuban Communist party, because of its current governmental responsibilities and the peculiar relationship that it maintains with the Soviet Union, follows a distinct organizational line, although in any sense quite different from the line adopted by the orthodox Latin American Communist parties.

Although Marxism, with various new influences, supplied the Latin American revolutionary groups with their basic representational model of society and revolution, their operational model for the seizure of power and its subsequent exercise is basically Leninist. That Leninism, however, presents two important qualifications. One, consciously and overtly acknowledged by the concerned groups, concerns the strategic and tactical contributions of the two more recent successful Marxist experiences: the Chinese and the Cuban revolutions. The other, still not acknowledged by those groups, concerns the new assumptions and purposes that the historical experience of the last three decades has imposed on revolutionary ideas and practices. These new assumptions and purposes were referred to in the discussion of the development-socialist model.

It is not within the scope of the present analysis to elaborate on the extent to which Lenin's operational views of the process of revolution were or were not fully consistent with Marx's theory of revolutionary change. I personally think that although Lenin's views can be perfectly compatible with certain writings of the younger Marx of the time of the German revolution, which bear a significant Blanquist voluntarism, they vary from the central trend of Marx's thought, which rejects any macro-voluntaristic view of history and stresses the limiting effect of structural conditions.[3] What is relevant for the point in discussion, however, is the fact that current revolutionary groups in Latin America have not only adopted all the Leninist propensities for revolutionary voluntarism but also emphasize the additional voluntaristic elements of Castro and Maoism. As we will see in the subsequent discussion, the two proposed revolutionary strategies for Latin America, the Cuban and the Chinese, share the assumption that the objective conditions for revolutionary change already exist throughout Latin America and that only direct revolutionary action can improve these conditions and introduce new changes, in a dialectic process that will lead to the final victory of the revolutionary forces in the near future, if they fight properly and determinedly.

The second qualification deserves some attention. It was stated that the historical experience of the last three decades has imposed new assumptions and purposes on revolutionary ideas, along the lines already analyzed in the former discussion of the developmental-socialist model. It was also pointed out that that qualification, although conditioning the actual pursuit of the revolutionary way, is not yet consciously acknowledged by militant revolutionists. Essentially the qualification includes two points. The first is the fact that, even when orthodox Marxist views are maintained with respect to the contradictions of capitalism, the inherent impotence of capitalism in its advanced stages to salvage the capitalist relations of production, and the impending outcome of a socialist revolution, in the more developed capitalist societies, operational ideas and practices are oriented *as if* the socialist revolution, rather than following the degree of maturity of capitalist societies, *would, on the contrary, take place in the underdeveloped world*. The second point concerns the actual purpose of the socialist revolution. Although all the conceptions concerning the classless society are retained, operational ideas and practices are oriented *as if* the socialist revolution *would have as its first and necessary goal the building of national autonomous development*. These are precisely the basic assumption and purpose of developmental socialism, as a political operational model. The fact that militant revolutionists do not yet realize (and may eventually refuse to acknowledge) that they have been compelled, by historical practice, independent of theoretical awareness and elaboration, to adjust their ideological thinking to the pragmatic requirements of political development is just another confirmation of the objective constraints imposed on political action by societal needs.

A final comment should be made about the militant revolutionary groups and the DS model. Because the adjustment of the former to the basic assumptions and strategies of the latter is the effect of an objective and pragmatic process of adaptation to social realities that is not supported by a critical understanding of the involved problems, the explanatory and predictive possibilities of the DS model (and of political models in general) are not consciously used by such groups. Of the many consequences of the misuse and lack of use of the DS model, the most relevant is the fact that the model's conditions of applicability are not taken into account by these groups. This being so, Latin American militant revolutionists are led to a serious contradiction between their theoretical and their practical views. Their theoretical views are based on a Marxist understanding of society and revolution, unqualified by a theory of political models, such as the one discussed earlier in this book. According to these views, the socialist revolution is the outcome of the internal contradictions and crises of capitalism, which tend to increase in proportion to the inherent development of the capitalist process. But the practical views of the militant revolutionists are determined by the historical experience of the last decades, which has objectively shown—in accordance with the assumptions of the DS model—that socialist revolutions are revolutions for national autonomous development, occurring in those countries where, along with other conditions, the former elite is brought to consolidated forms of dysfunctionality, and a functional counterelite succeeds in neutralizing or defeating the subsystem of coercion of that former elite. These two views, as can be seen immediately, do not agree on the objective preconditions for a socialist revolution, which would be capitalist ripeness in Marx's terms and capitalist failure in practical terms. Confronted with these contradictory views, the Latin American revolutionary groups—contrary to the trend followed by the orthodox Communist parties—practically ignore the problems concerning objective preconditions and place all their emphasis on the subjective and voluntaristic aspects of revolutionary action. Wage guerrilla warfare, and the revolutions will be made—that is the final conclusion of the theorists of the new revolutionary militancy.[4]

The two models of revolution

Two strategies or models (using the term model in a loose and broad sense) are currently proposed for undertaking the revolution: the Cuban and the Chinese models. Both constructs attempt to express what is thought to be of general and permanent value in the experience of the Cuban and Chinese revolutions. They can be very briefly described as operational revolutionary schemes for the defeat of the repressive apparatus of the elite in two typical situations.

The Cuban model, which is by far the most widely accepted among Latin American militant revolutionary groups, is essentially oriented for situations in which an initially very small group of militants has to face a relatively large and strong army. In that sense, the typical situation and conditions assumed by the model are supposed to fit, to a smaller or larger extent, all the Latin American countries. The essential assumptions of the Cuban model are (1) that the small initial group of militants will be able to successfully challenge, through guerrilla action, the authority of the government and its army, while skillfully escaping the attempts for their capture and (2) that this group *will rapidly acquire the support of the peasants* for many purposes, including their voluntary help in feeding and sheltering the guerrillas, their willingness to guide the guerrillas through unknown lands and to refrain from giving any voluntary help to the government and its army. Some recruiting of new militants from among the peasants is also expected, although in a limited way. The most important sources for new recruits are supposed to be the urban underground of the radical intelligentsia and of former party and labor militants. The basic strategy of the Cuban model consists (1) in creating conditions, through a war of attrition, urban activism, and political propaganda, for the internal demoralization of the government and its army, the creation of internal conflicts among them, and between them and the population at large, and (2) finally, in neutralizing and practically suppressing the fighting capability of the government, by depriving its causes of any kind of social support, until the army itself is so internally divided and devoid of morale and any resolve to fight that the governmental system collapses almost by itself. In that crucial moment the control of key centers is seized through the combined action of an expanded guerrilla force and urban underground activities, and the revolution is won.[5]

The Chinese model is favored mostly by splinter sections of former orthodox Communist parties, which took the Peking militant revolutionary line. It also appeals to revolutionists who are more conscious of the international implications of radical revolutions and/or who are aware of the extent to which the Cuban model is limited to the peculiar conditions of Cuba. Unlike the Cuban model, which has actually been tried in several Latin American countries, notably Mexico, Guatemala, Venezuela, Colombia, Bolivia, and Brazil, the Chinese model is still primarily a matter of speculation and discussion among militant radical groups. To an extent, it could be said that the former attempts to create peasants' republics in Colombia were inspired by the Chinese model, and that certain revolutionary militants in Brazil, even if they eventually collaborate with the actions of urban and rural guerrillas, are oriented by the Chinese model and are trying to create the conditions for its subsequent application.

The differences in the Chinese and the Cuban models express the distinct features of the two revolutionary experiences. Essentially, the Chinese model differs from the Cuban one in that its basic assumption is not that the rural masses can and will, if properly dealt with, give their collaboration and help to vanguard guerrilla groups. Rather, its basic assumption is that the rural masses can and will, if properly educated and mobilized, *supply the actual body of the revolutionary liberation army.* The Chinese model, therefore, is oriented toward obtaining the conditions required for the mass education of the peasantry and the revolutionary armed mobilization of the peasants for the final surrounding and assault of the cities and their armies, with the help of the urban underground activists. The basic strategy of that model, therefore, is not oriented toward the defeat of the government and its army by means of its internal demoralization and an ensuing self-collapse, but toward its final military defeat, once the governmental armies are duly isolated from the rural and urban masses.[6]

More recently, with the increasing awareness of the current international conditions, notably in Latin America, and the extent to which unchecked American military intervention would change the assumptions of each of these models, revolutionists have tended to fuse these two models into a sort of mixed model, incorporating the idea of several simultaneous "Vietnams."[7] According to the multiple Vietnams scheme, a movement of guerrilla warfare, of the Cuban brand, would start simultaneously in several Latin American countries, creating conditions, through their proliferation and the resulting generalization of the field of action, for a Chinese-like mass insurrection in the whole of Latin America, which would bring both Washington and the Latin American governments to impotence.

The crucial trouble with the revolutionary way, as it is currently proposed for Latin America, both in the Cuban and in the Chinese models, is the voluntaristic ignorance of the objective preconditions necessary for any revolutionary movement. As has often been noted in this book, Marx, in spite of his deep and inflexible commitment to the revolutionary change of the world, constantly emphasized that a social system could not be changed just because it was inherently unjust for most people and some well-meaning men were heroically prepared to undergo all risks in order to force its change, as in the classic case of Spartacus' revolt. Social and revolutionary change, according to Marx, is the result of human action and resolve, but it can only be successfully carried out when the internal contradictions of a system render the maintenance of its social regime actually inviable.[8] In the Latin American conditions of today and of the foreseeable future, insurmountable crises of viability of the prevailing social regimes are only occurring in those countries that are, in addition, affected by their own lack of national viability, such as the Central American and the Caribbean countries and probably Paraguay. In these countries, however, precisely because of their lack of national viability, radical internal changes cannot be promoted from inside by domestic actors. First there must be appropriate changes in their international environment, so that they acquire larger international permissibility and with it the possibility of an advantageous integration into a wider and more viable system. This matter has already been discussed in Chapter 23. As we have seen, radical internal change in nonviable nations is submitted to external conditions, and so, although in different terms, we are also remitted in their case to the question of objective preconditions.

Considering the Latin American countries that are not immediately affected by critical problems of national viability (see Table 38), we have that, as far as the objective preconditions are concerned, they do not, currently or for the foreseeable future, present a sociopolitical picture in which a revolutionary outcome is likely to occur. As was seen in the discussion of the structural relationship between societal structures and fitting political models (see Chapter 14), revolutions, in the sense considered here, require not only, and not even primarily, the contradiction between the marginalization and pauperization of the masses and the overconcentration of wealth and privileges in a tiny elite, but also, and essentially, the combination of the consolidated dysfunctionality of the elite and the marginalization and disaffection of relevant sectors of the subelite. What is currently characteristic of Latin America, as was discussed in Chapters 19–22, is the existence of two typical situations of underdevelopment: (1) the situation in which there is a protracted split between a prevailing dysfunctional sector and an important remaining functional sector of the elite, with a corresponding division of the subelite, as in Mexico, Brazil, and Argentina, and (2) the situation in which there is a contrast and potential conflict, as in Ecuador, between a ruling parasitic elite, of a patrician-consular character, and a modern and productive sector of the subelite, represented by the technical and managerial groups of the middle class, particularly inclusive of its military branch. If the present precarious equilibrium of the Latin American political systems, essentially dependent on the coercive capability of the ruling elite, eventually breaks down, under the accumulating pressure of the societal dysfunctionality of these countries, what is likely to occur is not a socialist revolution under the control of the counterelite, but movements oriented according to several combinations of the state-capitalist and national-capitalist models. We will return to that question in the discussion of the reformist way.

Unfitness of the Cuban model

In addition to their lack of objective preconditions, the two proposed schemes for the revolutionary way in Latin America are irremediably affected by the fact that their strategic assumptions and requirements do not fit the conditions of Latin America, currently or for the foreseeable future. Very briefly, the assumptions and basic strategy of the Cuban model, as formerly indicated, require conditions that were peculiar to Cuba at the time of Castro's action and *cannot be repeated elsewhere in Latin America*. Essentially, these conditions can be reduced to two cumulative points, if we set aside other decisive intervening factors, such as the extraordinary personalities of men like Fidel Castro and Che Guevara, in contrast to the vile and opportunistic character of Batista, and the sheer good fortune of the physical survival of the guerrillas, particularly in the beginning. The first and more general point is that it was possible for the Cuban guerrillas to inflict irremediable damage on the Cuban government and army merely by challenging them from Sierra Maestra and resisting for two years their continuous attempts to smash the rebellion. The second point is that it was possible for Castro's movement to be carried out without international interference; it did not become a premature issue in the cold war confrontation, and it did not attract the unilateral preventive intervention of the United States. These two cumulative conditions cannot be repeated.

The crucial aspect of the first condition was the vulnerability of the Batista regime and its forces to guerrillas' war of attrition. That vulnerability, in itself a complex matter, was essentially due to three elements: (1) the smallness of the Cuban territory and, to an extent, its insular condition and (2) the *societas sceleris* nature of the Batista government, characterized by the exceptionally high opportunism of Batista and his inner circle, associated with (3) the socio-political naïveté of its wider peripheral circle of support.

Because Cuba is a small island the effect of rural guerrillas on the vital centers of the country was very great. Similar attempts in large countries, such as Mexico and Brazil, would remain unnoticed for a very long time, more than would probably be required for an efficient governmental action to find and destroy the guerrillas. And whatever the fate of such guerrillas, their effect on the vital centers of these countries would lack practical relevancy. This is actually what is indicated by some precedents in these two countries. The famous *coluna Prestes*, in the Brazil of the early 1920s, when conditions were quickly ripening for the revolutionary overthrow of the old republic—which finally fell in 1930— was only able to create a legend of romantic heroism. It never really challenged the power of the central government, even though the Prestes column was never militarily defeated. As with any new guerrilla movement in such countries, the Prestes column had to remain in the deep jungle in order to resist the forces of the government, just as Castro hid out in his Sierra Maestra. Unlike Cuba, however, the relation between the deep hinterland and Brazil's vital centers is extremely remote; after a time the Prestes column realized the inherent futility of its efforts and decided to take asylum in Bolivia. More recent attempts at guerrilla warfare in Mexico, during the government of López Mateos, and, on a smaller scale, in Brazil, in the *serra dos Caparaós* episode, proved equally ineffective as far as the vital centers of these countries were concerned, although, this time, the guerrillas were suppressed with relative ease in Mexico and very easily in Brazil.

The second and third elements, concerning the inner and the peripheral circles of the Batista regime, are equally important. Few Latin American governments, after the death of Somoza and Trujillo—with the possible exception of Duvalier, in a country whose culture, however, is not actually Latin American—could be compared to the private gangster-like character of Batista and his inner circle. Having amassed an enormous fortune, these people were not willing to face high risks once they felt the symptoms of deep demoralization among their forces; they preferred to enjoy the advantages of a timely flight, rather than to keep fighting up to their last possibilities. What is still more relevant, however, is that the peripheral circle of Batista's supporters, including the military as a corporation, the Havana bourgeoisie and upper middle class, the larger farmers, and the leaders of the pro-Batista unions, fooled by the liberal appearances and appeals of the guerrillas, thought that what was essentially at stake was the destiny of a tyrant and his immediate followers. They did not realize that the whole regime they were associated with would be liquidated, in a very deep and radical way, bringing most of them down in its fall and, in any case, rendering completely impossible the basic conditions of life that they were used to and that they would have fought for if they had been aware of what a future with Castro's government would mean for them.

The combination of these three elements can hardly be repeated in Latin America. The larger territories of Mexico and of most of the South American countries, together with the different sociopolitical conditions of their societies, do not offer realistic conditions for the success of the Cuban model. It is true that the model would be fitting in the Central American and Caribbean countries for territorial and other reasons, and that in these countries most of the present governments are of the *societas sceleris* kind, if not so paradigmatically as Batista's. The wider peripheral circles that support the current status quo in these countries, however, are certainly not likely to forget the Cuban lesson. Revolutions not only teach prospective new revolutionists how to reach their goals better but also teach supporters of the status quo how to better avoid similar revolutions. Precisely because the Cuban model is essentially a strategy for bringing about the self-collapse of the regime in power, it fundamentally depends on the behavior of the larger peripheral groups of supporters of the status quo. If, as occurred in Cuba, these groups disengage themselves from the government and are willing to offer the tyrant's head in exchange for the expected goodwill of the new guerrilla rulers, the Cuban model could work again, if the other essential conditions are also matched. If, however, one of the critical lessons that the Cuban revolution taught these groups is that their fate, independent of their cooperation with the guerrillas and perhaps even of the individual will of the new leaders, is inextricably associated with the former regime—although not necessarily with the individual destiny of the former tyrant—the behavior of these groups will be radically different. The alternative scenario resulting from that awareness, should a Cuban-like situation develop in some Central American or Caribbean country, would probably be the overthrow of the government, at the beginning of a real crisis, by "progressive" sectors of the military and the bourgeoisie, in the name of the same liberal proposals and goals as the guerrilla propaganda. A new "democratic" government would be formed; free elections would be held or promised; and the guerrilla group would either be invited to join the new regime as a minor partner or else converted into the marginalized position of untreatable extremists or political adventurers, who would lose practically all of their former explicit and implicit bases of support.

The second condition inherent to the Cuban model, which could not be repeated, is the absence of international interference. Given the external and internal Latin American conditions, that interference could not be avoided, particularly in the form of American military intervention, either unilaterally or under the cover of the OAS. The Cuban revolution was unique in that sense because of the neo-Garibaldian appearance of Fidel Castro's rebellion. The extent to which Castro was already a Marxist at the time of Sierra Maestra is irrelevant for the point under discussion. In spite of some of his official declarations on that subject, he has acknowledged, in less formal exchanges of views,[9] that his Marxist education, as one would expect, was a gradual one, which started with the usual Marxist *influence* during his university years and continued, through his own experience and study, throughout his revolutionary years. What is important to consider is that the anti-Batista guerrillas had a strong liberal flavor, were totally motivated by libertarian ideals, and had a wide political base. Initially that base excluded the Cuban Communist party (then illegal and called Partido Socialista Popular), which later joined the anti-Batista coalition under Castro's leadership, but only as a minor partner. In the current Latin American conditions, it would be practically impossible for any new guerrilla movement to be or to pretend to be of a sheer liberal character. But regardless of the labels and intentions, real or pretended, of any new armed revolutionary movement, the United States' defense system *gave the clearest indications after the Cuban experience, both directly and through its Latin American agents, that it would act as if any such movements in Latin America, whatever their origins, alleged goals, and any other characteristics, would necessarily bring about a socialist revolution.* Implicit in the assumption of the United States' defense system is the belief that pro-capitalist and pro-American positions in Latin America are extremely artificial, completely lacking any real popular support, and entirely dependent on the maintenance of politico-military control by the dysfunctional sectors of the elite. As a corollary, the United States' counterinsurgency doctrine is based on the assumption that Latin American popular armed movements, if they succeed in defeating the coercive apparatus of the former ruling elites, will be led, whatever their previous declarations and intentions, to establish some form of revolutionary socialism. The same doctrine, moreover, although for ill-founded reasons, supposes that all such popular movements will also be led to a militant alignment with the Soviet Union, rather than to neutralism. For all these reasons the United States' counterinsurgency policy, vis-à-vis the areas of direct and unchecked American hegemony such as Latin America, is oriented in principle—and only limited by its own available means and its calculations as to the involved international risks—toward intervention, to the extent and on the scale deemed necessary, whenever a local satellite government is likely to be overthrown by armed popular insurrections, whether or not that government requests such intervention.[10]

Inapplicability of the Chinese model

The Chinese model, different from the Cuban model, has the advantage, as far as the present conditions in Latin America are concerned, of proposing a strategy that is fitting for large countries (without being inherently inadequate, as far as the geographic aspect is concerned, for the small ones) and that is sociopolitically realistic. If the revolutionary forces are able to successfully educate the peasants politically, on a sufficiently large scale, and to mobilize them militarily against the central government, its armies, and its urban supporters, many of the weaknesses of the Cuban model are, by hypothesis, overcome. The Chinese model overcomes, particularly, the practical irrelevancy of remote rural guerrilla forces as far as the vital urban centers of large countries are concerned; the probability that the status quo governments will show a greater determination to fight; and finally, the probable decision of the peripheral circle of supporters of the status quo not to surrender the government to the revolutionists, even at the cost of ousting the incumbents themselves. These points are self-evident and do not need any elaboration. Confronted with a highly motivated and powerful armed military insurrection, the status quo government and its supporting circles would necessarily be at the mercy of the revolutionists if militarily defeated by them. The trouble with the Chinese model is of a practical nature and consists in the conditions necessary for the revolutionary leaders to educate the peasants politically and to mobilize them militarily on a sufficiently large scale. Furthermore, of course, the success of the model requires the military victory of its armies, which does not necessarily follow from the former successful education and mobilization of the peasants. But let us set aside the decisive questions concerning military victory and assume that it could be obtained by highly motivated and sufficiently strong revolutionary troops. The question about educating, forming, and mobilizing such troops again puts into focus the hardly repeatable conditions of a given historical experience, such as the Chinese revolution.

If, once again, we speak very briefly and put aside many important intervening factors, such as the general sociocultural conditions of China, the more immediate consequences of the previous republican revolution, Sun Yat-sen's action, and the revolutionary propaganda of the first decades of the century, we have that four particular cumulative circumstances, the functional equivalents of which are hardly repeatable, were decisive in Mao's success. First, the Kuomintang army was not efficient enough to retain continued control of the whole of China's territory or even to have access to certain areas. Second, the Kuomintang's general lack of efficiency was made even worse by the efforts required for, and the losses inflicted by, the conflict with the Japanese during Japan's occupation of Manchuria in the early 1930s and, later and still more severely, during the general war with Japan from 1935 to 1945. Third, in addition to the historical episodes preceding and following the republican revolution, the Communist party, notably in 1935, became the most militant and prominent patriotic agency in the fight against the Japanese and acquired in that struggle a national legitimacy that even Chiang Kai-shek was forced to acknowledge, although he was aware of the risks involved for his leadership and regime. Fourth, at the end of World War II and during its aftermath the United States government was neither able nor willing to assume the cost and risks of massive military intervention in China.[11]

These four circumstances are sufficiently self-evident to practically dispense with further elaboration. Because of their technical and organizational insufficiencies, which were compounded by the diversion of forces imposed by the Manchurian war, the armies of Chiang Kai-shek failed in their four initial attempts, from the end of 1930 to the end of 1934, to seize the Communist stronghold of the province of Kiangsi. And even when the Kiangsi Soviet was finally overrun in 1934, the Kuomintang army could not prevent important Communist forces from moving, in the "long march," to the borders of Tibet and north to Shensi province. There, helped by much more favorable topographical conditions and the additional diversion of Kuomintang forces imposed by the war with Japan, the Communist party was able to stabilize and to expand its rule over "liberated areas." The war with Japan provided the Communist party with invaluable help, both by diverting and weakening the Kuomintang forces and by allowing the party to play the patriotic role of major defender of the fatherland, thereby imposing its politico-military legitimacy. Moreover, the end of the war with Japan gave the Communist forces the opportunity, which proved to be a decisive factor in Mao's victory, to seize Manchuria and many other areas formerly occupied by the Japanese, with all their human, material, and military resources, including Japanese equipment. And finally we have the circumstances that prevented American intervention during World War II, such as the desire to retain all possible allies, notably the Communists, in order to defeat the Axis. Subsequently, in the politico-psychological conditions of the first postwar years, which were characterized by expectations of a durable peace and the general acceptance by the Great Powers of all nations' right to self-determination, it became impossible for the United States' government to assume the cost and risks of a major military intervention in China, including a highly probable clash with the Soviet Union, in order to take sides in an internal political struggle.

It is easy to see how these conditions are inapplicable to the current Latin American situation and, considered as a whole, could not presently be repeated. So although it is true that as far as the territorial aspect is concerned the Chinese model is better suited than the Cuban one for the large Latin American countries, such as Brazil or Mexico, and might be usable elsewhere, it is also undeniable that the control of the armies in the large Latin American countries over their own territory and their access to all of its areas are incomparably better than they were for the Kuomintang troops. The present technological and organizational level of the Brazilian, Argentine, and Mexican armies, and of some other Latin American armies is clearly sufficient to render it completely impossible, without other intervening factors, for any revolutionary leadership to maintain its rule over a meaningful area and there to organize a peasant army capable of confronting the official troops. Small guerrilla groups may survive in the deep hinterland, because of their virtual invulnerability, but they will not have any relevant impact on the vital centers of the large countries. Militant and powerful peasant armies could, once fully organized, trained, and equipped, challenge and eventually defeat the official armies, but the official armies have all the previous conditions necessary to forcefully prevent the formation, training, and mobilization of such peasant armies.

Furthermore, the hypothesis of non-American intervention would not prevail in the present Latin American conditions, even, in several cases, regardless of whether or not the local concerned governments would accept help. In the case of the larger countries, such as Brazil, Argentina, and Mexico, where *unrequired* United States' military intervention would be less likely—and would provoke strong nationalist reactions among the military—there can be no doubt that the presently existing regimes would call for all the United States' military help they deemed necessary, inclusive of the direct sending of troops. As was observed in Chapter 18, only a few very large countries, such as India, Pakistan, and eventually Indonesia, which are not yet definitively included in the boundaries of any of the new empires, would presently be capable of carrying out a Chinese-like revolution. Their present armies might not be able to prevent the formation of an insurrectionary peasant army, given some initial conditions of support, and the superpowers might mutually neutralize each other's intervention. These conditions, however, are conspicuously absent in Latin America, both now and for the foreseeable future.

Concluding remarks

Two basic conclusions can be drawn from what has been discussed with respect to the revolutionary way in Latin America. The first is that the objective preconditions for a radical revolution in Latin America, currently or in the foreseeable future, do not exist in most countries. Where these conditions seem to be occurring, as in Central America and the Caribbean countries, the lack of national viability of the concerned countries, within the tacit division of areas of hegemony between the two imperial systems, renders a revolution unfeasible for external reasons. In these circumstances, neither the strategic assumptions and requirements of the Cuban model nor those of the Chinese model, as revolutionary schemes, fit the present internal and external conditions in Latin America.

The second conclusion, however, is that this state of revolutionary inviability will not remain unchanged for too long a time. The problem of Latin American deadlines has already been discussed extensively (see Chapter 23), and we have seen that the present status quo in Latin America is very unlikely to continue for more than two or three decades. If in the course of this period a process of autonomous development is not successfully carried out through a reformist way, in conditions that will be subsequently studied, or alternatively, if, as has already been discussed, the dominant hegemonic power is not able to change the form of dependence from an inherently unstable satellite form to a stable provincial one, the now missing prerevolutionary conditions will quickly and cumulatively arise. It is in that sense, provided that the time of action is displaced from now to the decades of the 1980s or 1990s, that the model of the multiple Vietnams is both representationally and operationally correct. Fundamentally, as has been stressed, the deadlock of Latin American stagnation, marginality, and denationalization, temporarily containable by colonial-fascist and colonial-praetorian regimes, will lead to an inescapable and uncontrollable explosion whenever the critical level of marginalization and disaffection of sufficiently large sectors of the subelite and groups of the elite is surpassed. In that case, as foreseen by the multiple Vietnams scheme, simultaneous guerrilla movements in several strategic Latin American countries, very probably centered in Brazil, are likely to unleash terrible social forces, including relevant sectors of the Latin American armies, creating a massive generalized insurrection that no organized power in the world will be able to contain.

NOTES

[1] For studies of recent events in Peru, Bolivia, and Chile, see the bibliography at the end of this book.

[2] See Helio Jaguaribe (1967a, pp. 83–126).

[3] See Jaguaribe (1967a).

[4] See Regis Debray (1967).

[5] See Ernesto Che Guevara (1968, chap. 21); see also Robert Taber (1967) and Peter Paret and John W. Shy (1966).

[6] See Lin Piao (1966). On the Chinese model for revolutionary development and the content of that model, see also S. Prybyla, in Harry G. Shaffer and Jan Prybyla, eds. (1961).

[7] See OLAS (Organizacion Latinoamericana de Solidaridad) theses, particularly Che Guevara's "Message to the Tricontinental" (1968, chap. 35).

[8] See particularly Marx's *Preface to the Critique of Political Economy.*

[9] See Lee Lockwood (1967, pp. 138 ff.).

[10] See Willard F. Barber and C. Neale Ronning (1966). See also The Rockefeller Report (1969).

[11] See Peter S. H. Tang and Joan M. Maloney (1967). See also Franz Schurmann and Orville Schell (1967) and George M. Beckmann (1962).

26

The Alternative of Autonomy:
The Reformist Way

Purpose of the present analysis

The second possible way for the Latin American countries to achieve autonomous development is the reformist way. As was discussed in Chapter 6, it is necessary to distinguish reform and revolution, as means of political change, from these two terms as they apply to the social nature of the content of a given change. What is to be discussed primarily in the present chapter (as in the case of revolution in the preceding chapter) is the reformist way of change.

The changes that would be required for the promotion of autonomous development in Latin America have already been widely discussed in this book. (See Book II and Sections A and B of Book III.) Both the general problem of political and national development and the particular conditions inherent to Latin America have been discussed. That matter, therefore, will only be referred to incidentally in the present chapter. Let us just remember that, in addition to what is generically inherent to any developmental process, there are three kinds of structural changes that necessarily have to be achieved in the particular Latin American conditions. They correspond to the overcoming of the three basic structural characteristics of Latin American underdevelopment analyzed in Chapter 20: (1) stagnation, (2) marginality, and (3) denationalization. If, therefore, Latin American autonomous development is to be achieved by a reformist way, that way must be capable of putting into practice policies and measures necessary and sufficient for overcoming each of these three kinds of structural constraints.

The purpose of the present chapter is to study the feasibility of a reformist way for the promotion of Latin American autonomous development. That study can ultimately be reduced to the fundamental question of whether or not, and to what extent, the social nature of the content of the changes that would be required for the autonomous development of Latin America is compatible, in the current and foreseeable conditions of the region, with the possibility of change through a reformist way.

This fundamental question involves essentially two aspects. The first and most general aspect is the determination of what kind of reformist way, if any, is compatible, in general, with the social nature of the content of the changes required for Latin America. The second aspect, if we assume the first can be given a positive answer, is the determination of whether or not the kind of reformist way necessary, in general, for implementing those required changes is actually compatible with the specific reformist possibilities of the Latin American societies, as those possibilities may be assessed in the current conditions and in the foreseeable future.

The problem of feasibility

Basically, the first aspect of our question has been dealt with in Chapter 6 and in Chapters 19–23. Let us briefly review the fundamental conclusions of those chapters.

As we saw in Chapter 6, reform, as a political means of change, is a reorientation of policies affecting the regime of participation of a society, fundamentally in the sense of enlarging it, through a decision on the part of the ruler or of prevailing members of the ruling group. That decision is based on the regime of power and is in basic accordance with the political regime. As has been seen, the three following features are peculiar to the reformist way of change: (1) Reformist changes modify policies but do not substantially change the composition of the incumbent authorities, because reforms express the decisions of these authorities. (2) These changes eventually affect the regime of participation in a deep way, but not, at least directly or initially, the regime of power and the political regime, because reforms are based on the former and their enforcement is in fundamental accordance with the latter. (3) Finally, changes in the regime of participation are always in the sense of enlarging it, not of restricting it, precisely because reforms do not significantly alter the regime of power or the political regime.

Reform, therefore, always consists in an act of enlightened liberality, whatever the extent of ultimate self-interest on the part of the ruling circle and ruling class. As such, and still viewing reform as a means of political change, there are four modalities of reform: autocratic, oligarchic, radical, and progressive. The first is only of historical interest today. The last two are currently the most important modalities. What distinguishes radical reforms from progressive reforms, as ways of change, is the fact that the former are proposed and pressed forward on the initiative of an intelligentsia admitted to the ruling circle but coming from and representing the rising new class, which demands equality of rights with the ruling class, whereas progressive reforms are proposed by an intelligentsia belonging to the ruling strata but advocating and representing the position of the lower strata and pressing for the extension to these strata of some of the rights of the ruling strata. In both cases reforms reflect the work of an enlightened intelligentsia, acting as an interclass broker through an effort of intellectual and emotional persuasion oriented toward introducing nontrivial changes in the participational subsystem.

We also saw in Chapter 6 that, in terms of the social nature of their content (that is, in terms of the relevancy of the changes introduced in the participational subsystem), reforms can present three levels of depth. At the deepest level, they substantially change the regime of participation, although not immediately and directly changing the social regime as a whole. In that case, in terms of the social nature of their content, we have reforms of a revolutionary character.[1] At a less deep level of depth, reforms can change the basic structures of the participational subsystem without fundamentally changing the regime of participation, with eventual concomitant changes in other social subsystems or in the whole social system. In that case we have reforms of a radical character. Finally, at an even less deep level of depth, reforms can change the mode of operation of the basic structures of the participational subsystem without fundamentally changing those structures, with eventual concomitant changes in the mode of operation of the basic structures of other social subsystems or of the whole social system. In that case we have reforms of a progressive character.

We have also seen that the social nature of the content of a reform and the modality of the way in which that reform is adopted do not necessarily present a strict interdependence. Progressive reforms can have a radical character, such as Fabianism, or even a revolutionary character, as occurred with the abolition of serfdom or of slavery in several countries. Although there is not a strict interdependence, however, there is a statistically observable propensity for a positive correlation between the degree of radicality of the way in which reforms are adopted and the degree of radicality of their character.

The question of content

Let us look now at the other side of the problem, the content of the changes required for the autonomous development of Latin America, which has already been treated extensively in Chapters 19–22. I suggest that such changes, considered in principle, are analytically compatible with the kind of changes that can be achieved through reformist ways. Essentially, as was noted at the beginning of the chapter, any modality of Latin American autonomous development consists—in addition to the general requirements of a developmental process—in overcoming a situation characterized by the circular and self-reinforcing process of structural stagnation, marginality, and denationalization. Any endeavor to overcome that circular process must (1) change the basic conditions of participation, in order to enlarge the producing and consuming capabilities of the Latin American societies and to reduce their rate of social marginality, and (2) change the orientation of the decision-making processes and the character of the main strategic factors from their present alien reference and control to a national reference and control. Changes of that kind do not necessarily, analytically speaking, have to be adopted and implemented in a revolutionary way. In other words, changes of that kind, considered, at a categorical level, in terms (1) of the abstract characteristics of the involved contents (what have to be changed) and (2) of the foreseen means for achieving these changes (reform), do not imply any incompability. And this is so because the two crucial elements involved in the required changes (enlargement of the regime of participation and the changing of the center of reference and control from alien groups and factors to national ones) represent precisely the kinds of change for which, in principle, a reorientation of policies is needed, without, necessarily, a substantial change in the incumbent authorities of the regime of power and its corresponding political regime. Reforms of a radical and even of a revolutionary character, according to the conditions of each case, would be required, but such reforms can be perfectly sufficient for the obtention of those changes, without, in principle, requiring a political revolution. Only by examining the concrete specific conditions in which those reforms will have to be carried out, therefore, is it possible to determine whether or not the possibility, in principle, of achieving the desired changes through reformist ways actually exists in the current empirical conditions of the Latin American countries.

This second part of our question would have been more difficult to discuss some years ago, during the period of the crisis of populism in Latin America, because populism, as was indicated in Chapter 22, was a typical experiment of reformism in Latin America, which finally failed. The final failure of the populist regimes does not necessarily imply the practical impossibility of any successful reformism in Latin America, as was made analytically patent in Chapter 22. After the failure of populism, however, doubts about the practical possibility of a successful reformism in the current conditions of that region could not be erased, except by the occurrence of some other successful experiments.

Without elaborating further on the analytical distinction between the failure of populism and the remaining practical possibility of successful reform oriented toward the autonomous development of Latin America, let us just review the main conclusions of our former discussion of the subject. Ultimately, as was seen, Latin American populism presented two principal limitations: (1) a deficiency in the conception and implementation of many of its policies because of the lack of clear goals and consistent purposes and (2) an inability to command enough support from among those sectors of the elite and subelite that would benefit most directly from populism because of the lack of a critical understanding of its real social meaning. The latter brought the populist movements to an unsustainable position, because they could neither attract the allegiance of the Latin American armies nor neutralize them through appropriate countervailing power or compelling moral authority. Nor could the populists destroy the armies, which would, of course, imply a shift from reform to revolution.

If we compare the unsuccessful reformism of populism to the historical cases of successful radical reformism, such as Brazilian republicanism (1889–1894) and Argentine radicalism (1916–1930), or the cases of contemporary successful progressive reformism, such as Chile's Christian Democrats, we will see the difference. Radical reformism gained the allegiance of the armies; progressive reformism neutralized military resistance by keeping the armed forces out of politics and under the moral authority of the legitimate government. The armed forces were either incorporated into the reformist movement or kept outside the political controversy, instead of being challenged by forces unable to control them.

In order to establish the actual possibility of new reformist movements in the current Latin American conditions, it is not enough, as has already been noted, to observe that the failure of populism was due to contingent circumstances and that failure is not inherently inevitable for any reformist endeavor. It is still necessary to find empirical evidence of the actual possibility of successful modalities of reformism. This evidence exists and is currently provided, in Latin America, by two distinct kinds of reformist experiments: the progressive reformism of a few well-organized Latin American parties and the radical reformism of the military establishment of Peru.

Progressive reformism

The best example of successful progressive reformism by means of party organization in Latin America is given by Chile, first with Eduardo Frei and his Partido Demócrata Cristano (from 1964 to 1970) and subsequently, and with a shift to radicalism, with Salvador Allende and his Unidad Popular leftist coalition. The Allende government, in spite of the rhetoric implying revolutionary procedures that the candidate used in his propaganda, remains, as far as can be assessed early in 1972, a typical (if radical in content) reformist government. The fact that possible future events may create conditions forcing or inducing the Allende government to adopt revolutionary means does not alter its original reformist character.

A second good example is provided, in Venezuela, by the basically uninterrupted succession of progressive reformism from the Acción Democrática administrations of Rómulo Betancourt (1959–1964) and Raúl Leoni (1964–1969) to President Rafael Caldera's COPEI since 1969.

It would be extremely interesting to submit the Chilean and Venezuelan cases to a comprehensive critical and comparative analysis, in order to determine the factors and conditions that have brought about the appreciable extent of success of these reformist experiments. Such an attempt, however, would extend the present chapter way beyond its intended limits. It will be sufficient to stress two major points concerning these reformist experiences. The first refers to the character of the reforms achieved in Chile and Venezuela. The second is related to the main conditions in which these reforms have been carried out.

Fundamentally, as is well known, the Chilean and the Venezuelan experiments, irrespective of their specific differences, have been oriented toward achieving four principal goals: (1) maintenance or consolidation of political democracy, including an increasing political participation of the masses, (2) promotion and acceleration of economic development, (3) nationalist reorientation of the economy and of the whole society in general, and (4) enlargement of the extent of socioeconomic participation of the rural masses, particularly through comprehensive agrarian reform, and of the urban masses, particularly through a combination of more and better urban employment with several welfare measures.[2]

In very succinct terms, it can be said that these four goals have been approached either well or at least satisfactorily in both countries. The political systems of Chile and Venezuela have developed democratic procedures and content, with a broad and well-organized participation of the masses. This has been particularly important in Venezuela, which did not have, like Chile, a former tradition of democracy and constitutional rule and where, that notwithstanding, power was scrupulously transmitted to COPEI from Acción Democrática, after the latter's defeat in 1969. COPEI, moreover, within its own programmatic line, has basically continued the reformist policies of the former regimes. In the case of Chile the peaceful and constitutional transition from the Christian Democrats to a Socialist coalition overtly manifesting a Marxist orientation was not a minor feat. Both Chile under Frei and Venezuela obtained either satisfactory or very good results with their reformist governments.[3]

The case of Chile is the more difficult to analyze, because of the low productivity of Chilean agriculture and the long years of stagnation preceding Frei's government. From 1955 to 1960 the average annual growth rate of the GDP was negative: –1 percent. From 1961 to 1964 it was poor or bad, except in 1962.[4] From 1964 to 1968 the Frei administration had two brilliant years (4.1 percent in 1965 and 5.5 percent in 1966) followed by two poor years (2.0 percent in 1967 and 2.1 percent in 1968). Venezuela, with a better agriculture and a faster-expanding industry, had an annual average increase of 5.1 percent from 1960 to 1966. In 1967 and 1968 the rate was still higher: 6.0 percent and 5.5 percent, respectively.

The policy of nationalist reorientation of the major factors of production has been successfully accomplished in Chile with the agreements concerning the "Chileanization" of the copper mines, transferring the controlling majority of those mines to the state. That policy received a still larger priority and emphasis with the Allende government. The government made a commitment to nationalize all the major foreign concerns, although without predefining the way in which that policy would be implemented. In Venezuela, the state-owned Corporación Venezolana de Petróleo has been given, through a combination of legal and administrative measures, the future control of oil exploitation, which is to be achieved by the end of the 1980s, with the transference to that corporation of the now foreign-controlled oil fields and reserves upon the expiration of the present concessions.

Finally, to obtain the fourth goal, the enlargement of participation, both countries have adopted decisive agrarian reforms and important measures for the social welfare of the urban masses. The Chilean agrarian reform, after a naturally difficult legislative debate and some complex preparatory administrative measures, was put into effect in 1965, with some additional legislation approved in 1967. The adopted plan foresaw the distribution of land to 40,000 families by 1970 (and many more thereafter), through a system in which an initial three-year joint exploitation by the peasants and the Corporación de Reforma Agraria (CORA), in *asentamientos*, gave the new farmers the necessary training and technico-economic means for their subsequent autonomous exploitation of the farms, as family or cooperative units. From 1965 to 1968 about 15,000 families were granted land in the *asentamientos*, totaling more than 1.3 million hectares. The Allende government committed itself to a much broader and deeper agrarian reform. Jacques Chonchol, the former director of CORA—who quit the Frei government because he considered its reform pace too mild and slow—has been appointed minister of agriculture by Allende. The purpose of the new Chilean government is to suppress all forms of latifundia and to provide access to land for all peasants. In Venezuela, the agrarian reform, started in 1959, aims at the distribution of idle or badly exploited lands to landless peasants in the form of family farms. By 1968 more than 3.8 million hectares had been distributed to more than 145,000 families. Urban welfare measures in these two countries, involving housing facilities (more than 45,000 new houses per year in Chile and 37,000 in Venezuela), medical care, and other social benefits, have significantly improved the conditions of their poorer urban populations.

The second major point in our assessment of the importance and meaning of the Chilean and Venezuelan reformist experiments concerns the main conditions in which these reforms have been and are being carried out. These main conditions can be considered in terms of two basic characteristics. The first concerns the typological structure of the concerned society. As can be seen from Table 36, Chile and Venezuela are among the Latin American countries with the highest GDP per capita ($671 and $878, respectively, in 1969), with the greatest urbanization (67 percent and 63 percent, respectively), with the best level of popular education (primary enrollment of 78.5 percent and 61.6 percent, respectively, of the school age population), and so on with the other relevant indicators. Both have small populations (less than 10 million) and sufficiently large territories (286,000 and 352,000 square miles, respectively). In other words, both countries, in terms of their populations, are favorably endowed with natural resources, have relatively developed and efficient economies, and are well-functioning societies, which are not afflicted by too severe conflicts and unmanageable problems.

The second basic characteristic concerns the political system of these countries. In both cases political conflicts are not totally insoluble, which reflects the basic consensuality of the respective societies. Chile has the best Latin American tradition of institutional settlement of sociopolitical conflicts. The transfer of power to President Salvador Allende in 1970—in spite of sporadic acts of violence, such as the assassination of General Schneider by right-wing extremists—has represented, even by Chilean standards, an exceptionally high mark of constitutional behavior. Few fully developed democratic countries in the world would have been capable of a similar performance. As a matter of fact, none, up to now, has passed through a similar experience under the same conditions (English socialism being, actually, a form of welfare capitalism).

Venezuela had a very poor political past and was the stage, during the second

Betancourt administration (1959–1964), of urban and rural guerrilla warfare. That violence, however, was very strictly limited to a small, militant revolutionary sector of the intelligentsia (the Fuerzas Armadas de la Liberación Nacional—FALN) with some support from among certain economically marginal and politically militant sectors of the urban mass, but representing only a rather small fraction of the proletariat. In contrast with those focuses of violence, the great majority of the urban masses, practically all the peasants, the middle class, including the military, and the bourgeoisie fully supported the political system (as it was rebuilt after the downfall of the Jiménez dictatorship in 1958) and, basically, the political regime, channeling their differences and conflicts, concerning the government, the authorities, and their policies, mostly through the political parties.[5]

And here we have the second relevant distinctive trait of the Chilean and Venezuelan political systems. More than comprehensive and basically consensual systems, these political systems are characterized by the importance and meaningfulness of their principal political parties. This characteristic of the Chilean and Venezuelan political systems puts Chile and Venezuela in a singular position in Latin America. Chile and Venezuela, together with Mexico, Brazil, and Argentina, present higher levels of economic development and national success than the other Latin American countries. Unlike Mexico and Brazil, whose societies are still very poorly integrated, with a huge marginal peasantry and low national averages of social and cultural development, Chile and Venezuela, as has been observed, are, together with Argentina and Uruguay, much better integrated and socially developed societies, unaffected by too severe social contradictions. Unlike Uruguay—and setting aside the latter's deficiencies in national viability—the Chilean and Venezuelan parties are well-functioning input agencies. And unlike Argentina, where the political system has not been able to institutionalize the sociopolitical conflicts and where, because of that, political parties are not meaningful and important, the Chilean and Venezuelan parties are representative of the broad sociopolitical expectations of the country and are convenient instruments for their political expression.

Applicability of the Chilean and Venezuelan experiments

It is convenient now, before we discuss the applicability of the Chilean and Venezuelan experiments to the rest of Latin America, to summarize the main findings of our brief analysis. In both cases the way of change is a progressive modality of reformism,[6] adopted by the enlightened action of progressive political parties through electoral and congressional procedures. In Venezuela and in Chile with Frei, the social nature of the content of the reforms is of a progressive character, strongly opposed by the radical left in Chile and militantly contested by the FALN in Venezuela, on the grounds that only revolutionary changes would be satisfactory. In both countries, therefore, and even in Chile with Allende, the sociopolitical conflict concerning the reforms is not a two-party struggle between reformers and conservatives, but a four-party struggle between

(1) reformers, (2) conservatives, and (3) radicals within the system, and (4) a small antisystem revolutionary group. Finally, in both countries the modality and character of the reform has been made possible by two sets of circumstances: (1) The concerned societies are well-integrated, sufficiently developed ones, without too severe and unmanageable conflicts, and (2) the political systems of these countries are basically consensual[7] and are operated by meaningful and well-organized competing political parties, which are able to express most of the sociopolitical expectations of these societies and to process the attendance to these expectations through electoral and congressional ways.

Taking these findings into account, let us now return to the second aspect of our basic question about the feasibility of reform in Latin America: To what extent, if any, is the kind of reformist way necessary for implementing the changes required for Latin American autonomous development actually compatible with the specific reformist possibilities of the Latin American societies, as they may be assessed in the current conditions and in the foreseeable future?

When we are confronted with that question, the Chilean and Venezuelan reformist experiments, given the two sets of circumstances rendering them possible, seem to have little applicability to the other Latin American countries. As a matter of fact, the first set of circumstances—the existence of a high level of social integration, based on a considerable degree of development, without too severe and unmanageable conflicts—drastically reduces the applicability of the Chilean and Venezuelan experiments to the rest of Latin America. To start with, neither the nonviable countries of Central America and the Caribbean nor the less-developed countries of South America would be eligible. Of the remaining countries—Mexico, Colombia, Brazil, Uruguay, and Argentina—the first three would not meet the requirement for enough social integration and, as a consequence, would present more profound and irreducible conflicts than would be compatible with the requisites of the Chilean and Venezuelan cases.[8]

If we consider the two remaining countries, Uruguay and Argentina (setting aside Uruguay's severe problems of national viability), we find that these two countries do not meet the other requirement of the Chilean-Venezuelan case: the existence of meaningful, well-organized, and competing, but reciprocally compatible, political parties, which are able to give, through electoral and congressional ways, attendance to most of the sociopolitical demands of their society. In Uruguay, where the Colorado and Blanco parties have a very long history, including a long period in the first half of this century of good and stable functioning, the problem consists in the present meaninglessness of these parties, which is a consequence of a mutual clientele arrangement. Today, they no longer express, as political parties, distinct alternatives of policies, in terms of distinct relevant social interests, but rather represent one and the same political class, sharing among its members and clientele the spoils of government in a cooperative venture. The main social demands, therefore, are no longer expressed by these parties; nor are they attended to in electoral and congressional ways. On the contrary, they are conveyed directly, through several means, to the governmental bureaucracy, which operates both as an agency of interest aggregation and as an agency of political conversion and output. A considerable range of sociopolitical demands does not find any institutional way of expressing through official agencies, and this has led to a radical rejection of the system. The Tupamaros movement is the most radical and active form of that rejection and is committed to revolutionary change by means of urban guerrilla warfare.

In Argentina the conflictual legacy of Peronism—opposing in an uncomprising way the unions and the armed forces, as agencies of political aggregation, recip-rocally aspiring to political supremacy, and behind them opposing labor and middle-class interests and values—has rendered the party system inoperable, be-cause of the lack of a minimal underlying regulative consensus. Since the down-fall of Ongania in 1970, however, a new consensus has appeared in Argentina, concerning the necessity for reestablishing democratic procedures and institu-tions. That consensus presents features that are likely, in the long run, to surpass the incompability of the Peronistas and the middle class. Argentina is still a long way, however, from the formation of meaningful political parties, such as those in Chile.

It is true that, under closer comparative analysis, one will find that the inap-plicability of the Chilean-Venezuelan experiment to the rest of the Latin Amer-ican countries presents important differences in degree. The nonviable and less-developed nations of the region do not present any possibility of approach-ing the necessary requisites for eligibility, but it is arguable that Mexico, Colom-bia, and Brazil might eventually come to attain those requisites. Their poor social integration and the grave latent and manifest conflicts resulting therefrom do not, necessarily, impose a zero-sum political process on these countries. An inspired and skillful political leader might be able to mobilize enough support, from among both the marginal mass and the privileged sectors, to carry out the sort of reforms required for the autonomous development of these countries. This is actually what was achieved in Brazil in the best phases of populism, with Vargas in the early 1950s and with Kubitschek (1955–1960). It was tried with partial success by the reform-minded López Mateos (1958–1964) in Mexico and is being tried again by Echeverria. Lleras Restreppo, in Columbia, although kept within modest limits by the conservative character of the Frente Nacional, was able to follow a line of progressive reformism in his administration (1966–1970). The problem in these countries, as far as the eventual applicability of the Chilean-Venezuelan model of reformism is concerned, is that, besides their lack of suffi-cient social integration, and largely because of that, they have not been able to develop the kind of political parties required for stable progressive reformism. This is why, in the past, their successful forms of reformism have been of a pop-ulist kind, not of a congressional character. And this is why they have finally succumbed to compact forms of bureaucratic or military authoritarianism.[9]

A still different case, as far as the applicability of the Chilean-Venezuelan ex-periment is concerned, is the one of Uruguay and Argentina. There is no inherent impossibility, in either of these countries, for surmounting the present crisis of their political systems. As a matter of fact, as far as Uruguay is concerned, the irremediable exhaustion of the old clientele system is pressing the political class to new efforts of innovation. The reestablishment of the presidential office in 1967, in place of the collegiate system, is a first step in that direction. It is not impossible that, in the near future, popular pressure and compelling problems will induce the parties to follow a more programmatic behavior. In Argentina the conversion of Peronism into a kind of multiclassist labor party is an ongoing process likely to be accelerated after the death of Perón. That trend is already forcing the military, under the pressure of other broad social interests, which operate inside the military establishment, to reopen the political process and let a new party system be formed. The ousting of Levingston by Lanusse, in 1971, although containing the nationalist proclivities of the Levingston government, led to a regime of a still more transitional character. Efforts are being made to reach a new broad national compromise in which, with the exclusion of the radical left, the political parties would be reactivated and the political system would move in an electoral-congressional direction.

Both Uruguay and Argentina, therefore, are nearer the possibility of attaining the Chilean-Venezuelan requirements than the rest of the Latin American countries. That consideration, however, should not conceal the fact that, in the currently existing conditions, even these two countries do not satisfy the requirements necessary for applying the same kind of reformist experiment that has been followed by Chile and Venezuela.

General features of military reformism

In view of the preceding conclusions, we can now proceed to the analysis of whether or not the second kind of reformist experiment that has recently taken place in Latin America, the radical reformism of the military establishment of Peru, is applicable to other countries of the region. In order to make the comparison between the two kinds of reformism (Chilean-Venezuelan and Peruvian) clearer, let us follow the same analytical framework used previously. That is, let us consider two basic points: (1) the most relevant characteristics of the Peruvian case, as a type of reform oriented toward autonomous national development and (2) the main conditions in which these reforms have been and are being carried out. This being done, we will be able to find out whether or not, and to what extent, these experiments are applicable to other Latin American countries, given their main characteristics and the conditions of their implementation.

The more relevant characteristics of the Peruvian experiment can be reduced to six major features: (1) the corporate character of the political interference of the armed forces, (2) the nationalist, (3) developmentalist, and (4) social-reform concerns and purposes of the radical reformism of the military, (5) the monopoly of political decision by the armed forces, and (6) an ideology of military radical reformism that associates certain traits common to most Latin American military, such as moralism, anticommunism, authoritarianism, with other traits inherent to, or more explicit in, the Peruvian military, such as nationalism, developmentalism, and social reformism.

Any analysis of the main characteristics of the Peruvian case must start by taking into account that this country is submitted to a military regime that did not obtain political power through reformist ways (that is, through an act of enlightened liberality on the part of the former rulers) but, on the contrary, that has forcefully displaced and subdued the former rulers by a successful military coup. Coups d'état, however, as political means for seizing power, are neutral as far as the purposes for which that power will be used are concerned, as we saw in Chapter 6. The main characteristics of the Peruvian reformism, therefore, although instrumentally dependent on the way (military coup) in which power was acquired, are not explained by the coup as such. What is particularly relevant in the military origin and character of the Peruvian experiment is the fact that, in a general way, the coup d'état and the exercise of government as well as the engagement of the new government in policies of radical reformism *are the collective decision and responsibility of the armed forces*. It is true that this collective commitment does not involve a complete or even deep unity of views among the services, in the first place, and among the more influential groups of the leading service—the army—in the second place. There are very important differences, in general, between the navy, which is basically conservative, the air force, which is less "intellectual" and has particular attachments to the United States, and the army, which has a progressive or radical proclivity and a prevailing deep nationalist orientation. That notwithstanding, the armed forces have been able to operate in a corporative way in Peru in part because of the military supremacy of the army and in part because of the profound commitment of the officers of the three services to the preservation of the basic unity of the armed forces—usually strengthened by diplomatic and conciliatory measures taken by the army.[10] Furthermore, as far as the more influential cliques and groups within the dominant service, the army, are concerned, similar rules of military discipline and preservation of unity have maintained the corporate integrity of the military establishment.[11] More than a military coup and a military government, therefore, the Peruvian experiment is basically a corporate commitment of the armed forces, led by the army, to introduce radical developmental reforms.

In addition to that internal aspect, which gives a corporate character to the political activities of the armed forces, a still more relevant feature of their interference in political affairs, as a corporation, is the high level of subsystem autonomy with which they play their corporate role. It is certain that that autonomy should not be considered as unconditioned and unconditional. Whatever the extent to which corporate motivations and loyalty among the military may supersede any other attachment (a premise that would already require several qualifications), the armed forces are, undoubtedly, immersed in a social environment—of their own nation first, but also, in varying degrees of influence, of other societies—that conditions them in every respect. It is ultimately from this larger social environment that they receive their basic value system, whatever the extent to which it is subsequently reshaped by intramilitary socialization. The point in question, therefore, is not the lack of extramilitary conditioning. It is rather the crucial fact that, insofar as organized political action is concerned, the military corporation of Peru through its internal structural configuration—the three services and their coordinating agencies and rules—has acquired and developed the capability to act by self-decision, with its own means, and eventually, if necessary, against the opposition of any other organization or sector of its national society. The requirements for putting that capability into action, through an autonomous decision cutting its legal subordination to its government and driving it to move against that government, include two requisites that will be discussed later: the existence of a *basic predisposition* toward a given political interference and of a *catalyzing circumstance* rendering that interference feasible at a given moment.

The analysis of why that capability came to exist in Peru (and in Bolivia for a certain time) and for that matter, as will be seen, in most Latin American countries—is of utmost theoretical importance but, unfortunately, would extend the present topic much beyond its permissible limits. I will only suggest that, ultimately, the corporate autonomous capability of the armed forces in Latin America is a consequence of social dualism. It expresses the fact that, in conditions of deep social dualism, the organized existence of the society and of its subsystems —because of the resulting lack of a minimum underlying regulative consensus— *is only possible through an implicit operational superordination of the political system over the whole of society and an operational, but also structured, superordination of the coercive subsystem, that is, the military as a corporation, over the political system.*

Military national developmentalism

The second relevant characteristic of the Peruvian experiment is its developmental nationalism. That nationalism is neither a simple superaffectation of the usual patriotism of the officer corps nor, at least in its deeper meaning, an antiforeigner resentment or a folkloric parochialism. That nationalism, in its deeper meaning, expresses both a view and a commitment about its own society. It expresses the view—already discussed in this book—that societies are self-directed systems that can only perform their internal function and optimize their adaptability to their environment, thereby attending to the collective needs of their members, if the main societal agencies and actors are oriented toward the preservation and development of the society as a whole, with as much control as possible over the society's own human and natural resources. And it manifests, as a commitment, the attribution of the highest value to its own society and its preservation and development as a self-directed system.

These ideas and feelings have been expressed by the speakers of the Peruvian reform movements, although, of course, in their own terms and style, as military men and leaders engaged in the practical job of mobilizing the country for national development. Since their first declarations, after the coups of October 3, 1968, the military government has stressed the nationalist commitments of its regime and the character of that nationalism as a condition and instrument for achieving the national development and the national dignity of the country.[12]

Following these declarations the military put their nationalist views into practice with a set of basically integrated policies and acts.

Briefly, these policies and acts may be classified in two groups. One group includes specific measures of very great economic and political importance for the country and its international relations, most of which were rapidly adopted. The other group includes decisions of a general character, aimed at establishing long-term policies.

In Peru the most dramatic of the specific measures was the expropriation and immediate seizure of the Brea y Pariñas oil complex, exploited by the International Petroleum Company, seven days after the coup. In a typical expression of the mixture of economic and moral motivations of that kind of nationalism, the day of the expropriation, October 10, 1968, was declared, by decree, the "Day of National Dignity." It has taken the revolutionary government in Peru much more time to reach internal consensus concerning the nationalist decisions of more general scope. Two of these decisions have great importance: the nationalization of the commercialization of mineral exports and the adoption of a new regime for foreign investments. The first measure was enacted to assure the optimization of prices in the exportation of minerals by preventing the exporters, who are also the importers, from depressing export prices in order to make their profits in the latter capacity. The new policy on foreign investments, adopted in 1970, follows basically a policy recommended for Latin America by some distinguished reform-minded economists, such as Osvaldo Sunkel of Chile, Paul Rosenstein-Rodan from M.I.T., and Albert Hirschman from Harvard.[13] It consists in establishing a system by which major foreign investments are processed in accordance with a detailed agreement between the investor and the government of the host country, concerning not only the technical and economic aspects of the project but also its regime of amortization. A given time period is agreed on for the repatriation of the investment in successive installments and of an agreed amount of profits, with the final transfer of the assets to the property of, and exploitation by, the host country. Provisions are made for the appropriate maintenance and renewal of equipment, technological transfer, training of national personnel, and so on, so that the enterprises are continuously kept in optimum working condition.

Although the Bolivian experiment in military radical reformism, under generals Ovando and Torres, was never quite successful and led to final disaster, in August, 1971, it is important to study its main aspects, which are basically similar to the Peruvian case. There was also an important initial specific measure in Bolivia: the prompt revocation of the Oil Code of 1956 and, some weeks later, the expropriation of the Bolivian Gulf Oil Company, with the immediate seizure of the installations. As in the case of Peru, that decision was determined by a mixture of economic and moral reasons. In a dramatic speech to the nation, in the evening of the day of expropriation, October 17, 1969, General Alfredo Ovando Candia, president of the revolutionary government, stressed not only the legal and economic reasons for the decision, but also that to return to public control an oil concession obtained and kept in violation of Bolivian national interest was to put an end to the time of contempt for the country.

The Gulf expropriation led to the subsequent crisis of the Ovando government. Pressed by a clique of right-wing officers, led by General Miranda, Ovando thought he could prevent a division within the army and a direct confrontation with Miranda by accepting Miranda's demands for a reversal in the oil policy. Compensation began to be paid to Gulf, and nationalist measures were discontinued. As it turned out, Ovando's concessions only caused his final ruin, facilitating the conditions for a successful rightist coup, under Miranda's leadership, in October 1970. The timely and victorious reaction of General Torres, however, supported by workers and students, brought the final defeat of Miranda and the reestablishment, under Torres' presidency, of another national-developmentalist government.

In terms of long-range nationalist policies the two Bolivian nationalist governments were confronted with a situation completely different from that of Peru, because of the former Bolivian revolution of 1952. Eighty percent of the non-agricultural production of the country was already performed by public enterprises, including the exploitation by the Corporación Minera Boliviana (COMIBOL) of the tin mines, the most important item in Bolivia's economy. The long-range nationalist measures of the Bolivian government, therefore, rather than introducing a national orientation in the country's economy, because it existed already, were intended to rationalize the system, particularly to correct the inefficiency of the public corporations.

The third major characteristic of Peruvian reformism, intimately connected with its nationalist philosophy, is its orientation as far as economic development is concerned. Economic development is approached, on the one hand, in terms of *national* development—in opposition to the abstract neoliberal concept of *market* development—and, on the other hand, as a dimension of the overall development of the society.[14]

In Peru, after about one year of internal discussions among the leading groups in the army and the government, General Velasco and the radicals obtained approval for a developmental policy that is basically a form of state capitalism. It involves the creation and expansion of key public enterprises, with the subsidiary contribution of the private sector, supported by the expected results of regulated foreign capital and of the agrarian reform.

Bolivia adopted a similar position in the first days of the Ovando government and again under Torres. In her case, as has been mentioned, state capitalism had already been implanted and (although not very efficiently) implemented by the MNR, with the revolution of 1952. What had to be done, in part, was to suppress some attempts to change or distort the state-capitalist model stemming from the Barrientos counterrevolutionary period (1964–1969). For the most part the problems consisted in reorganizing and operating more efficiently the already existing system of public enterprises. The Bolivian experiment of Ovando and Torres was never administered successfully and collapsed in 1971. More time is needed for an assessment of the extent to which the Peruvian National-developmentalist policies and measures will be implemented and crowned with success.

Military social reformism

The fourth relevant trait of the Peruvian experiment is its commitment, both ideologically and practically, to a profound social reform, directed at the effective and fast incorporation of the masses, particularly the rural ones, into the national life, granting them conditions for higher levels of socioeconomic participation. The country, as is well known (see Table 36), is among the Latin American societies with the deepest forms of dualism. She presents, in the first place, a sharp contrast between the huge rural masses, living at subsistence levels and practically outside the national system, and the comparatively privileged smaller urban population. In the second place, she presents another equally sharp contrast between the upper middle-class ruling cluster and the large urban masses, also living at subsistence levels in the *barriadas*. The Peruvian social reforms are primarily directed toward the rural masses, aiming, ultimately, at three main objectives: (1) the incorporation of the Indian into the national society, transforming him into a Peruvian citizen by educating him and providing him with appropriate socioeconomic conditions, (2) a substantial increase in the productive and consumptive capacity of the peasants, through an agrarian reform combining the distribution of land, or the assurance of stable working conditions for the landless peasants and *minifundistas* (small land holders), with the technical, economic, and organizational improvement of the exploitation of the land, and (3) the creation and improvement of external economies in the countryside for the integration of the countryside into the national market, combined with new facilities for marketing the agricultural production and for protecting the prices paid to the farmers.

The way in which and the extent to which the country has succeeded up to now in reaching its goals for the rural masses requires some examination. Until the coup of 1968, Peru had basically retained her semicolonial rural structure, based on the large plantation farms on the coast and the more troubled and archaic exploitation of the Indians on the latifundia of the *altiplano*. The agrarian reform was started in a very moderate and limited way in 1968 with the expropriation, against cash payment, of the agricultural lands of the Cerro de Pasco Corporation, a mining enterprise which extended its activities to large farming. In the following year, however, after overcoming the resistance of the more conservative members of the army and the government, President Velasco was able to sanction a broad agrarian reform act on June 24, 1969. That act regulates the expropriation of the coastal plantations and the Andean latifundia, with most of the compensation being paid in the form of public bonds, and it provides for the organization of state farms, cooperatives, community farms, and family farms. Complementary measures are rapidly being undertaken by the Peruvi_n government to provide efficient management for the new farmers, educational and technical assistance for the Indian communities, improvement of transportation and marketing facilities, and so forth. The prompt seizure of the expropriated lands by agents of the government and their uninterrupted exploitation were crucial in the initial success of the reform.

In Bolivia, during her aborted experiment in military reformism, the problems were completely different because a broad agrarian reform had already been decreed in the revolution of 1952, but the MNR government was not able to control its execution. Instead, the peasants just took possession of the land where they were working or living, creating a system of small properties, exploited in very primitive conditions and still deprived of external economies and marketing facilities. The Bolivian government wanted to organize these small farms into large cooperatives and to help them with technical, financial, transportation and marketing facilities. Because of the very poor functioning of the governmental machinery, the direct assistance of the army was considered, but not actually attempted.

Once again the efficiency of the implementation and the extent of final success of the Peruvian agrarian policies cannot be judged without more time. The programs concerning urban social development are being given lower priority because the current resources and management capacity of the country would be manifestly insufficient for the simultaneous undertaking of rural and urban reforms.

The fifth main characteristic of the Peruvian experiment, also related to the field of popular participation, concerns the question of popular political participation. In Peru, as a matter of fact, the people's political participation remains very small, more nominal than real, more supportive than determinative and with no choices and checks concerning their leaders. The situation of Bolivia, under Ovando and Torres, has been different. The Bolivian regime officially claimed the inheritance, with corrections and improvements, of the message and goals of the revolution of 1952, which was essentially participatory and democratic. In practice, the Bolivian governments brought to office by successful military coups were the projection of an alliance between a left-wing military faction in favor of national development led by Generals Ovando and Torres, who held the reins of power, and a group of intellectuals, who provided ideological and technical support. Although a sort of democratic centralism presided over the internal decision-making process of the leading military-civil group, there was no institutional way in which the people at large and even the sectors more effectively politicized could participate in the political process. In a noninstitutional way there were several pressure groups of varying influence: the main factions of the armed forces, including the specific influence of the commanders of the various military units; the managers of the public enterprises; the several institutional or political groups in the public bureaucracy; the unions, with the great strength of the miners, coordinated by the powerful Central Obrera Boliviana; the peasant leaders; the church; the larger private entrepreneurs, notably the medium-sized miners, and so on. The Bolivian leftist military governments, however, with their attachment to the revolutionary tradition of 1952 and their large dependence on public support (because of their limited autonomous political and managerial capability) were interested in organizing, in association with the armed forces, a large national party of the revolution, which could command wide popular support and provide an electoral base for its reform programs.

In the Peruvian regime, however, there is a great deal of resistance to opening the political process to popular participation, even if under certain regulative controls. Some more conservative sectors fear that such a move would excessively increase the radical content of the current reforms, or even convert the military reformism of today into a popular revolution. Other groups are afraid that a widening of political participation would displace certain leaders, or most of them, or would reduce or suppress the control of the army over the political system. On the other hand, General Velasco and the more consistent reformists in the army acknowledge the necessity for active, even militant, popular support in order to mobilize enough strength to undertake and endure the heavy task of national development and to resist external pressure and conspiratorial machinations. The way in which that contradiction may come to be solved is not yet clear, but it will be decisive for the future of the Peruvian regime and its reforms.

The ideology of the military reformers

Finally, the sixth relevant feature of the Peruvian experiment is the ideology of the radical military reformists who undertook that experiment. Basically, their ideology is a combination of the views and feelings shared by most Latin American military officers with a deep concern for the national development of their country and the understanding that its underdevelopment, derived from the historical formation of a dualistic society, is maintained by the vested interests of the oligarchy and its associates to preserve their privileges, articulated with the foreign supercorporations' extractive and enclave policies. Like most Latin American officers, the Peruvian military officers profess a moralist, authoritarian, anticommunist ideology. They have been led, however, because of the conditions resulting from the course of events in Peru in the last decades, to revise the traditional position of the armed forces as simple guardians of the status quo. Instead of the formal law-and-order ideology, still prevailing in the other Latin American (and also non-Latin American) military establishments, the Peruvian armed forces have achieved a deeper understanding and feeling of their societies. They became committed not to any order or to any legal system, particularly not to the order of underdevelopment and the legal system that maintains it, but to a new order, oriented toward the national development of their societies, and to the laws required for promoting and protecting that national development. And so they were led to radical reformist aspirations and ideas, which they are now trying to put into practice.

With this brief analysis of the most relevant characteristics of the Peruvian experiment we can now consider, very succinctly, the main conditions in which these reforms have been and are being carried out. Those conditions led to the fulfillment of the two requisites necessary for putting into motion the capability of the armed forces for autonomous decision. With this new analysis, we will be able, in conclusion, to assess the extent to which the Peruvian kind of reformism is applicable, with any adjustments that may be required, to the other Latin American countries. For the same purpose we will also briefly survey the

Bolivian abortive case, during the regimes of Generals Ovando and Torres, from September 1969 to August 1971.

The Peruvian case

Fundamentally, to analyze the conditions in which Peruvian reformism became a sufficiently widespread and compelling expectation on the part of the military of that country, it is necessary to distinguish the conditions in which the *basic predisposition* for such military reformism was created from the specific conditions that, in a given moment, united and motivated them to take action. The latter may be called the *catalyzing circumstance.*[15]

In the case of Peru the basic predisposition is related to the whole politico-military history of the country in the last four decades. If we reduce a long and complex history to very brief terms, it can be said that in the last four decades the Peruvian army has undergone two distinct changes. One was its conversion into a modern professional army, for which recruitment is increasingly from the provincial lower middle class or else inbred from among military families. The second concerns the dialectical rapport that came to take place between the army and Alianza Popular Revolucionaria Americana (APRA), the party founded by Victor Raúl Haya de la Torre in the late 1920s.

Originally conceived as a revolutionary party with a strong Marxist influence, although adapted to what Haya considered the conditions of "Indian America," APRA soon entered into violent conflict with the Peruvian army. That conflict acquired, in the course of time, the character of an institutional war between APRA and the army. It led to a permanent veto, by the military, of any of the ways in which APRA tried to obtain power. In the course of the last four decades, APRA has been able to command popular support, but has been unable to defeat or to neutralize the army. In this long and agonizing struggle, a fascinating phenomenon occurred, a comprehensive analysis of which could not be done within the limits of the present chapter. Essentially, that phenomenon consisted in the propensity, on the part of each of the contending parties, to invert their original political position and meaning. APRA started as a revolutionary party, a sort of "Marxism of the Indian peasants," and the army started as a conservative supporter of law and order and the status quo of a semicolonial agrarian society under the control of a patrician landed oligarchy. Moved by the tactical necessity for obtaining the support of the upper class as a countervailing power against the army and increasingly led, as he became older, to very conservative views, including a systematic anticommunism, Haya de la Torre gradually converted his party into a rural-based conservative force, allied to the patriciate and the high bourgeoisie. The opposite occurred with the army, which became increasingly concerned with economic and social development, increasingly hostile to the patrician-bourgeois upper stratum, coming to view it as being responsible for the underdevelopment of the country and the preservation of that underdevelopment, in the egotistic class interest of its members. The new generations of the military, whose social and economic status has been ever more dramatically at variance with the Peruvian upper class, started to study, in addition to their conventional military subjects, the problems of national development. Centro de Altos Estudios Militares (CAEM), created on the independent initiative of the army, has given an institutional framework to such concerns in the last years, contributing in an important way to the configuration of a military doctrine of national development. Unlike what happened in other Latin American armies— where higher war schools, founded under American supervision after World War II, were oriented toward a partisan propaganda of the American cold war view of the late 1940s, which involved a Manichaean division of the world between international communism, as absolute evil, and the free world, as absolute good— the Peruvian Center of High Military Studies was not controlled by alien influences and was able, through its free researches, to obtain a higher level of understanding of the Peruvian reality. It was in such conditions that in 1962 the army once again prevented Haya de la Torre, who had won that year's elections by a small margin of votes against his main challenger, Fernando Belaúnde Terry, from taking the presidential office. The next year Belaúnde was elected, as the leader of a new middle-class and development-oriented party, Acción Popular, and was invested by the military junta with the presidential office.

The fact that Belaúnde, for reasons that cannot be analyzed here, was ultimately led to a position of dependence vis-à-vis the interests of the large American corporations and their Peruvian oligarchical allies, and so disenchanted the hopes of the reformists, was a decisive factor for the increasing discredit, both popularly and among the military, of the last years of his government. But, given this background and the formation, in the army, of the basic predisposition for radical reformism, the catalytic circumstance that provoked the military coup of 1968 was the action taken by Belaúnde in the old Brea y Pariñas case, culminating in his frustrated attempt to settle the affair by the so-called Acta de Talara.

Once again it would be impossible, within the limits of the present chapter, to give a complete explanation of the long debates involved in that case. The whole affair is linked to the fraud involved in the original concession of the Brea and Pariñas oil fields to their first (1890) concessionaries, the English firm London and Pacific Petroleum Co. The fraud concerned the false measurement of the fields, which were supposed to have an area of about 40 square kilometers and actually had an area of 1.644 square kilometers. From this large difference of area arose a very long dispute between the Peruvian offices of oil supervision and both the original concessionaries and their successors, the International Petroleum Co., which included Peruvian claims for unpaid fees on the additional area and its production and correlated taxes, fines, and other charges. The long controversy was complicated still further when, in 1922, the Leguia government, bending to international pressures signed an agreement with the company yielding to practically all its demands, in violation of the former Peruvian law of 1918, which had submitted the case to Swiss arbitration. Peruvian nationalist public opinion did not accept the Leguia solution, and so the matter was kept alive in spite of the protocol of 1922. In his electoral campaign, Belaúnde made an issue of this old affair, promising to solve it in a few months. Instead, after five years of negotiation and indecision, and after ignoring a formal recommendation from the army for the annulment of the concession, Belaúnde signed another agreement, the Talara Protocol, on August 13, 1968. In that agreement, under the cover of compensating the company for the devolution to the government of the surface property of Brea y Pariñas (the subsoil property has always been inalienable under Peruvian law), Belaúnde granted the company the pardon of its fiscal debt (estimated at $144 million) and of its obligation to refund the value of the oil illegally extracted ($80 million), along with other advantages. This agreement, repelled by the nationalist sectors of the public opinion, was considered inacceptable by the military, because of its being highly noxious to the national interest. And so was formed the catalyzing circumstance for the coup and with it for military radical reformism. Less than two months later, Belaúnde was deposed by the military, under the command of General Velasco, commander in chief of the army, with the active and decisive intervention of a group of radical reformist colonels.

The Bolivian case

In Bolivia the formation of a basic predisposition for radical reformism among the military followed a completely different course, because of the revolution of 1952 and the counterrevolutionary coup of 1964. Again very briefly, it should be noted that military radical reformism in Bolivia appeared historically as a reaction to the defeat of the country in the Chaco War (1932–1936) with Paraguay. The first reformist attempt was successively carried out under Colonels David Toro and Germán Busch from 1936 to 1939. A second attempt brought to power, through a successful coup in 1945, a more articulated reformist movement, based on the alliance of young reform-minded military, under the leadership of Major Gualberto Villaroel, and the young intellectuals of the MNR (Movimiento Nacionalista Revolucionario), under the leadership of Victor Paz Estenssoro. The Villaroel government, in which Paz Estenssoro was finance minister, was violently deposed by a reactionary coup in 1946.

Working in the underground, the MNR expanded its membership, mobilized the mine workers, and organized combat groups, thereby building its strength for a return to power. After the denial of Victor Paz Estenssoro's electoral victory of 1951, the MNR prepared for a revolutionary insurrection, which was unleashed and won in 1952. The miners and other MNR militants, with the help of a small section of the police forces, inflicted a complete military defeat on the Bolivian army. The old army was disbanded, and only some reform-minded offers were retained to form a small new army, under the guidance of the MNR.

It is not possible to summarize here the purposes and achievements of the MNR during the successive presidencies of Paz Estenssoro (1952–1956), Siles Suazo (1956–1960), and again Paz Estenssoro (1960–1964). Let me only say that, although basically they reached most of their goals, from the nationalization of the large tin mines to agrarian reform, the MNR governments were rather less successful in efficiently implementing and managing their programs. As formerly observed, they lost control of the agrarian reform with the peasants' direct seizure of the land. The management of the mines was poor; the public corporations were run in deficit; the inflation rate increased sharply; the country became increasingly dependent on American help.[16]

In this critical process the second Paz Estenssoro government, weakened by internal factional struggles, was led to expand and reequip the army with American help, to use the army to curb the power of the miners—who were following Paz's rival, Lechin—and to discipline them with military force. Once this had been achieved, however, a counterrevolutionary military group, under the leadership of air force General René Barrientos and supported by a broad anti-MNR conservative coalition, realized that Victor Paz Estenssoro was then at the mercy of the army and staged a successful coup against him in 1964.

The Barrientos government, until his death in a plane crash in the beginning of 1969, although unable to introduce important structural changes in the socioeconomic organization built by the MNR, was essentially oriented toward conservative solutions and characterized by a total and undiscriminating alignment with the United States. This was a period of reflection and revision of ideas for many Bolivian officers, who had been concerned with the deterioration of the administrative capability of the last years of the MNR regime, but became still more concerned with the reactionary and antinational proclivity of the Barrientos government. Leading the group of new reformists, General Ovando, who had played a complex and unclear role in the days preceding and following the fall of Victor Paz Estenssoro,[17] preferred not to interfere in political affairs during Barrientos government, in order to preserve the unity of the armed forces. The basic predisposition, however, for a new radical reformism, this time under military sponsorship, already existed among a majority of the officers in the army by the end of 1963. The catalyzing circumstance that created the opportunity for action was the death of Barrientos and the succession of civil Vice-President Siles Salina. At that moment, it became possible to prepare a military coup with radical reformist purposes, without risking a division and internal conflict within the armed forces. Once again in Bolivian history a young group of intellectuals, this time under the leadership of José Ortiz Mercado, Marcelo Quiroga Santa Cruz, José Luis Roca García, and some others, associated themselves with radical reformist military leaders, such as General Ovando, General Juan José Torres González, and others, and prepared the coup that successfully took control of the government on September 26, 1969. The pro-Barrientos sectors of the armed forces, considerable particularly in the air force, were mostly people without a clear ideological orientation, whose association with the former government was based more on considerations of personal advantages and clique alignment than on programmatic commitments. They represented, however, a sizable minority in the armed forces, and the Ovando government tried to attract them to the new regime, initially with success, by cautiously avoiding criticisms of Barrientos and using the cover device of charging the few months of the Siles Salina government with all the errors of the preceding regime.

The crucial issues with which the Ovando government was confronted, such as the expropriation of Gulf assets, however, had a divisive effect among the military groups, according to their ideological proclivities. In that issue, as in some others, Ovando's lack of boldness and his attempts to prevent conflicts by increasing appeasement finally caused his ruin. The right-wing sector of the military, under the leadership of General Rogelio Miranda, after succeeding in removing General Torres from the command of the armed forces, launched, with initial success, a coup against Ovando, who was forced to resign on October 5, 1970. A military junta, without the direct participation of General Miranda, but loyal to him, was then placed in the government.

The prompt reaction of General Torres, however, who succeeded in mobilizing the nationalist military against the junta, with the support of workers, peasants, and students, put in motion a victorious countercoup. In 48 hours the junta was defeated, and Torres was able, on October 7, 1970, to organize a new left-of-center and more consistent and homogeneous national-developmentalist government under his presidency. Torres' new attempt to promote and consolidate a policy of deep reforms, however, has not been successful. Led by the ever-increasing radical demands of the workers, under Lechin's leadership, to a revolutionary leftist rhetoric, Torres aroused the fear, among his former military followers, that he would lose the control of power to the left-wing unions and was finally overthrown by a conservative coup in August, 1971.

Applicability of the Peruvian experiment

Having briefly analyzed the characteristics of the Peruvian military reformist experiment and of the Bolivian unsuccessful attempt, including the conditions under which such experiments have been carried out, we can now try to assess the extent to which such reformism is applicable to other Latin American countries, with whatever adjustments may be required in each particular case. The problem we are confronted with is to determine whether or not the reforms necessary for the promotion of the autonomous development of these countries can be undertaken in any of them—in accordance with the Peruvian model—on the initiative and under the responsibility of the armed forces, given the characteristics of the other Latin American armed forces and the main conditions to which their possibilities for political action are currently subjected.

Before we start the discussion of this question, it seems advisable to limit the field of inquiry to the Latin American countries that are not affected by critical problems of national viability. As was analyzed in Chapters 17 and 19, although the assessment of the relative national viability of a society, in a given historico-technological situation, is an extremely complex operation, subject to the possibility of unforeseeable change, it can be assumed, as far as Latin American development is concerned, that the Central American and Caribbean countries (with the exception of the particular and practically nonrepeatable case of Cuba) do not enjoy the conditions for autonomous development, at least before that process is well advanced in the rest of Latin America. In that case, there is no use in exploring the current possibilities for the autonomous development of these countries by the reformist way. And in Cuba, the reformist hypothesis has been, at least in the current and foreseeable conditions, superseded by the actual course of the historical events, since the revolutionary way has already been chosen and is in full application.

What we must consider, therefore, is whether or not, and to what extent, the Peruvian experiment of military reformism is applicable to the rest of Latin America. The answer to that question involves, essentially, a critical comparison (1) between the fundamental characteristics of this experiment and the chief characteristics of the concerned Latin American armed forces and (2) between the conditions in which that experiment has been carried out—giving attention to the requisites (basic predisposition and catalyzing circumstance) in terms of which the Peruvian armed forces were led to political action—and the current and foreseeable conditions predominantly influencing the corporate behavior of the Latin American armed forces in political affairs.

The first fundamental characteristic of the Peruvian experiment, as we have seen, is that, started by a military coup, it has been and is being carried out by the corporate action of the armed forces. That corporate action presents, in turn, as we have also seen, two aspects. One, internal to the military subsystem, concerns the fact that the officers of the three services have been led to attach the utmost importance to the preservation of their unity of action and the internal cohesion and discipline of the armed forces and are prepared to exert a great effort of loyalty and dedication for that purpose. As a consequence, the Peruvian armed forces are operating in a corporate way in political affairs and are accepting, in such activities, the supremacy and leadership of the army, which practically controls—although skillfully and within certain rules of the game—the political action of the armed forces. The other aspect, concerning the relationship of the armed forces with the national society and its other subsystems and sectors, is the high degree of subsystem autonomy of these armed forces, which are able to play a political role by their own internal decision, eventually against any other opposing subsystem or sector, including the legal government of the country, provided that two kinds of requisites are met: (1) the existence among the military of a basic predisposition for the political action in question and (2) the occurrence of a catalyzing circumstance rendering that action feasible at a given moment.

If we consider the other Latin American armed forces within our field of inquiry in terms of that first characteristic, we will see that, to a larger or smaller extent, most of them present similar corporate features. As far as the internal aspect of that corporate character is concerned, however, the Mexican armed forces manifest a distinctive trait. Their intramilitary corporate loyalty and feelings are extensively fused, particularly at the level of the top commanders, with a corporate loyalty to the subsystem of political domination, which is usually identified as being the official party, the PRI. Actually, in the current situation, the PRI is only the overt party facade of a subsystem of political domination that, under the institutional leadership of the president (whose individual autonomy of decision may be small), includes, in addition to the party leaders, the top military administration and the civil government, including certain high-ranking administrators and technocrats. That power system, which in pure functional terms is very similar to the Soviet one, substantially reduces the pure intramilitary corporate allegiance of the higher echelons, particularly among the leading commanders, since their share of power is not operationally self-sustained by their military service and unit, but by an interrelation between their military and their relative political positions and clique alliances.

In addition to the Mexican exception, a distinction should also be made, although in different terms, for the Chilean and for the Uruguay military, within their particular situations[18] and, in a less and still incipient form, for the Venezuelan military. They are not, like the Mexican military, involved in a broader corporate loyalty to a subsystem of political domination. They are, however, in an unorganized way, and within limits that vary in each country in terms of the concerned military units and individuals, committed to a constitutional rule that superordinates, if loosely, the military rules. Thus, they are exceptions more in terms of the extramilitary corporate behavior of the armed forces than in terms of intramilitary corporate behavior.

In terms of the interrelationship of the armed forces with the national societies and their other subsystems and sectors, we will see that, similar to the Peruvian armed forces, most Latin American military establishments present an extremely high degree of autonomous capability for the reasons that have been already suggested. Exceptions to that norm—if we keep the Mexican armed forces out of the comparative analysis because of their peculiar fusion with the subsystem of political domination—are the Chilean and, to a lesser degree, the Uruguayan and Venezuelan armed forces. This is not only due to the fact, already pointed out, that the military of these countries, in varying forms, keep an allegiance to constitutional rule that superordinates, if loosely, their intramilitary corporate loyalty. It is also due to the fact, clearer and more consolidated in Chile but also occurring in Venezuela and, in its own conditions, in Uruguay, that in those societies other subsystems have a life of their own and share, with the military corporation, the participation and the resulting loyalty of the citizens, including the military. In other words, these societies have not become deeply dualistic societies, like the other Latin American countries, and have actually been able to develop a pluralistic social structure, supported by a minimum of underlying consensus. This is also the reason why Chile and Venezuela have become successful examples of progressive reformism, performed by electoral-congressional ways. Uruguay, now particularly affected by problems of national viability, was also an example of progressive reformism in less troubled times.

Unlike these exceptions, the Brazilian and, to a lesser degree, the Argentine armed forces[19] match perfectly well the two aspects of the corporate character of the Peruvian military establishment. And compared to Bolivia, whether during or after its abortive experiment in military reformism, they present an intramilitary corporate loyalty and an extramilitary corporate autonomous capability that is manifestly superior to those of the Bolivian armed forces.

In Paraguay these corporate characteristics have been led to such an extreme that it is more accurate to say that the Paraguayan armed forces own a nation than to say that the Paraguayan nation has armed forces. This extreme situation creates all sorts of societal problems, including an inherent propensity for a *societas sceleris* regime, and renders particularly aleatory the possibility of the armed forces ever coming to play a reformist role. Unlike either the Paraguayan or the Chilean extremes, the armed forces of Ecuador and Colombia have enough internal corporate cohesion and external autonomous capability to fit, in a general way, the corporate characteristics of the Peruvian case.

In conclusion, then, we have that the Brazilian and the Argentine armed forces, followed by the Ecuadorian and the Colombian ones, basically match the first fundamental characteristic of the Peruvian experiment.

The second fundamental trait to be comparatively examined is nationalism. Here we find the crucial point in the applicability of the Peruvian experiment to the rest of Latin America. This is because the rest of the Latin American armed forces are not, as a corporation, oriented toward a nationalist understanding of their national development or committed to the implementation of that view, in the way that has been indicated for the case of Peru. In all Latin American armed forces there is an important nationalist sector. Limiting our analysis to the military corporations that fit the first characteristic of the Peruvian experiment (Brazilian, Argentine, Ecuadorian, and Colombian), we find that, in addition to greater or smaller internal pressures in the direction of nationalism, there are also strong internal factors in these military establishments that contain the nationalist propensity.

Ultimately, these factors can be reduced to two sorts of ideological constraints. The first and most general is intimately associated with the prevailing anticommunist feelings of most Latin American military and to the Manichaean view, largely derived from such feelings, that divides the world between evil, represented by international communism, and good, represented by the free world. These feelings and views, which have already been discussed in this book, imply the necessity for supporting the unity of the Western camp, under the natural and irreplaceable leadership of the United States, against divisive national particularisms. They also include suspicions that all nationalist formulations are leftist. That kind of constraint is particularly strong in certain sectors and among the senior officers of the Colombian and Ecuadorian armed forces, is widespread among the Brazilian military, particularly in the navy and the air force, and is less important, but still observable, in the Argentine armed forces, particularly in the navy. The second ideological constraint against nationalist propensities in these military establishments is economic liberalism. Either in terms of laissez faire or neoliberal emphasis on the free enterprise (a view particularly strong in Argentina and Colombia) or in terms of a technocratic emphasis on efficiency (widespread in Brazil and leading to the fear of the allegedly inherent inefficiency of the public corporations), that constraint prevails, unlike the other one, among some of the intellectually more sophisticated military.

Given those and some other factors that contain the nationalist view in the armed forces of the four mentioned countries, they currently fail, as corporations, to match that fundamental characteristic required for the possible application of the Peruvian experiment. That circumstance, however, should not be considered as a permanent disqualification. The Peruvian armed forces in general and the army in particular, as has been seen, were still not under the prevailing influence of the nationalist and reformist military just a few years ago. Similarly, the armed forces of Brazil, Argentina, Ecuador, and Colombia are currently submitted to strong nationalist pressures, which may come to prevail much sooner than is usually expected. The problem of nationalism, therefore, must be considered in dynamic terms. It tends to be the central issue, if the nationalist view comes to prevail, in the formation of the basic predisposition that induces the armed forces to take a corporate responsibility in introducing developmental reforms in their respective countries.

The other four main characteristics of the Peruvian experiment (developmentalism, social reformism, military monopoly of power, and a synchretic ideology) may be considered more schematically for the sake of brevity. Two of these characteristics, the developmental and the social-reform orientation, constitute, together with nationalism, the essential content of any reformism capable of promoting autonomous development. Of the other two characteristics—military monopoly of power and an ideological orientation combining reformist traits with the usual content of military ideology—it can be said that they are either of a consequential character, as the latter one, or they represent features peculiar to authoritarian organizations, such as the armed forces, whose propensity to monopolize power is proportional to their autonomous capability. This last characteristic, however, is not, except transitorily, an inherent functional requirement of reformism. On the contrary, it can easily become a distorting factor. For our analysis, therefore, it suffices to see how the four Latin American armed forces under our examination fit the first two of these remaining characteristics: developmentalism and social reformism.

Developmentalism is always a declared aim of technocrats, which the modern Latin American military tend to be, particularly in Brazil and Argentina. The crucial question about technocracy, however, is the extent to which, as has been discussed earlier in this book, it consists in a trend to modernization only with the basic preservation of the social status quo. This is precisely the tendency that has been manifested by the Brazilian and the Argentine military since they seized the political control of their respective countries in 1964 and 1966. That technocratic modernization, which its proponents like to clothe with the labels of revolutionary (being essentially antirevolutionary), democratic (being discretionarily authoritarian), and developmental (being merely modernizing), is just a modern military expression of cameralism, as has been discussed in this book.

In spite of that, however, the developmental potential of the current Brazilian and Argentine military regimes should not be underrated. There is, to start with, a distance, which may be extraordinary, between what the officer corps thinks it stands for and are helping to do, without a clear formulation of its aims, and what these regimes actually do (in Argentina's case before Ongania's ouster), under the control, at the top, of conservative old generals and neoliberal technocrats, deeply indoctrinated with the views and values of international capitalism. Even with all the distortion resulting from that "conservativism at the top," the Brazilian and Argentine military regimes have made important developmental efforts in their countries' economic infrastructures, such as power, roads, and communications. But above all, they have succeeded in building a powerful and efficient state machinery, with a level of political and administrative capability never reached before. What gives particular relevance to that achievement *is the fact that, with just a few adjustments, that same machinery, if reoriented toward social and national developmental goals, mobilized by a new reformist spirit, and supported by popular participation, could become a decisive instrument for the promotion of the autonomous national development of these countries.*

In terms of social reformism, as with nationalism, the military establishments of Brazil, Argentina, Ecuador, and Colombia are divided between the reformist feelings of the brighter and younger officers and a conservative sector, mostly formed by old generals and members, whose views prevail at the top commands. The same uncritical fear of international communism, combined with nineteenth-century laissez-faire prejudices and with various forms of association with national and international big business, leads these people to a conspiratorial view of society.[20] Given the authoritarian and disciplinarian character of the armed forces and the particular conditions in Latin America, which have converted the armed services into inward-oriented systems for the preservation of the social order, it is relatively simple for conservative military commanders to neutralize the reformist feelings in the armed forces for the sake of antisubversive and counterinsurgency policies.

As a summary of the findings of our inquiry concerning the extent to which the fundamental characteristics of Peruvian military reformism are matched by the main characteristics of the armed forces of the other viable Latin American nations, the following points can be stressed: (1) Because of the way in which their respective armed forces are interrelated with their national society, its other subsystems, and the prevailing political culture, Mexico, Chile, Uruguay and Venezuela (to a lesser extent), and (in distinct conditions) Paraguay do not appropriately fit the Peruvian experiment. (2) The armed forces of Brazil and Argentina and of Ecuador and Colombia are very close to the Peruvian type as far as their internal characteristics and the position and role they play in their national societies are concerned. Currently, however, they lack enough nationalist and social-reformist orientation to engage in similar reformist experiments. (3) In the Brazilian, Argentine, Ecuadorian, and Colombian armed forces, the current discussion and revision of the now-prevailing positions concerning the issues of nationalism and social reformism and the best orientation and policies to deal with them, along with other relevant factors, keep open the possibility of deep changes in these prevailing positions. The more recent events in Argentina, however, since the ousting of General Levingston, have reinforced the tendency for a return to electoral-partisan forms of government.

The requisites for military political interference

In order to finish our inquiry on the feasibility of the reformist way by the Peruvian line, it is necessary to consider briefly the conditions decisively influencing the political behavior of those Latin American armed forces that are eventually amenable to that kind of reformism. As we have seen, these conditions include two distinct orders of requisites: (1) those that contribute to the formation, among the military, of a consensual or prevailing basic predisposition for a certain course of political action and (2) those that, given that predisposition, constitute a catalyzing circumstance that actually moves the military into action. A basic predisposition for reformism, among the military of the four concerned countries, ultimately depends, in the present situation, on the enlargement of nationalism and social-reformist views and commitments within the armed forces, particularly the army. That occurrence, in turn, depends essentially on two other conditions. The first is related, in the concerned governments (of which the Brazilian, Argentinean, and Ecuatorian are already directly controlled by the military), to the extent to which the current policies and measures, which are qualified formulations of a neoliberal view, are successful or unsuccessful. The second condition concerns the extent to which the speakers for nationalist development and social reformism, confronted with these policies and measures, are able—and allowed—to consistently formulate alternative policy proposals and to persuade the military, and the public in general, that their alternative policies should be promptly adopted.

The first question is related to our earlier discussions concerning national development, the political models for its deliberate promotion, the structural characteristics of Latin America, its basic alternatives, and the negative effects of dependence for the Latin American countries. According to our findings and conclusions, there can be no doubts about the impossibility, in the long run, of success for the neoliberal model in the Latin American conditions. Two kinds of distinctions, however, have to be made concerning the necessarily negative effects of neoliberal policies in Latin America. The first is related to the typological characteristics of the concerned countries. Neoliberal policies will have very different sorts of negative long-range effects, depending on whether the concerned country is a well-integrated one, with a high level of social development and not too large a population, such as Argentina, or a deeply dualistic one, with a poor average social level of development, immense sectoral and regional differences, and a very large population, such as Brazil. In the first case, the historical penalty for submission to neoliberalism and its implied dependence on the United States may be limited to the loss of national self-determination. In the second case, in addition to the former, other very severe, probably catastrophic, penalties will be suffered, such as structural stagnation—with the exception of some privileged sectors or enclaves—massive unemployment and marginality, and consequentially, structural instability, lack of consensus, and permanent subjection to coercive regimes.

The second kind of distinction to be made refers to the behavior of the hegemonic country, in this case the United States, in relation to the negative effects of neoliberalism in Latin America. That behavior can be an active interference or simply remote manipulation and can vary from the most enlightened to the most short-sighted positions. This matter will be discussed briefly in Chapter 27 and does not need further elaboration here.

It suffices to point out that only Argentina, because of her characteristics, could endure a lasting submission to neoliberalism without catastrophic effects—even so, at the expense of her national autonomy. Of the four countries in question (and in general of all the Latin American nations), Brazil would be the society in which lasting neoliberalism would have the most catastrophic effects. It is interesting to note that although the conditions in Brazil are less compatible with the neoliberal model than in Argentina, it is in the latter country that the neoliberal model first came to be challenged in recent times, by Aldo Ferrer's interesting, if short-lived, national-developmentalist policies.

If such is the predictable consequence of lasting neoliberalism in the case of our four countries (as it is in general for the whole of Latin America), what is likely to be, to answer our second question, the evolution of the nationalist and social-reformist tendencies in the armed forces? A complete answer to that question (even if we put aside the margin of unpredictability contained in any question concerning the future state of a society) would require more elements than those presently considered—notably the possible alternative policies on the part of the United States. That matter, therefore, will be reconsidered in Chapter 27, which will treat such problems. For the purposes of the present analysis, it is sufficient to observe that, as long as a free discussion on the crucial issues and policies at stake is allowed to continue in the armed forces, particularly in the army, it is rather probable that the nationalist and social-reformist views will come to prevail in the military establishments of those countries in a couple of years.

The events in Argentina and Brazil, at the end of 1970 and the beginning of 1971, were already indicative of that trend, although in different ways. When a change in the technocratic leadership in Argentina, where the nationalist section of the military is relatively weak, enabled national-developmentalist experts to control the economic administration, the government began to lean in that direction, in anticipation of a corresponding decision among the military factions. That fact contributed significantly to the conditions necessary for General Lanusse to oust General Levingston and replace him. The reorientation of the economic policy in a more neoliberal direction, however, has also brought about a reinforcement of the trend toward a civil, electoral-partisan form of government.

In Brazil the Medici government has succeeded in curbing the nationalist faction in the army,[21] but not at the price of shifting to civil, electoral-partisan forms of government (a fake version of which was already in existence). Rather, it has been done by incorporating several of the nationalist claims and slogans in the government's policies.

Conclusions

We can now summarize the main findings and conclusions of our inquiry on the possibility of promoting the autonomous development of the Latin American countries, in present conditions, by a reformist way. These conclusions can be reduced to seven major points:

(1) Considered in principle, the social nature of the content of the changes required for the autonomous development of Latin America, including the specific necessity for overcoming the region's structural stagnation, marginality, and denationalization, is not, in analytical terms, incompatible with the kind of changes that can be carried out through reformist ways. The fact, however, that populism, which was the typical experiment of Latin American reformism from the mid-1940s to the early 1960s, ended everywhere in ultimate failure, although not excluding, analytically, the possibility of other successful modalities of reformism in the region, has raised doubts about the feasibility of such reformism that can only be fully answered if empirical evidence is produced on the actual possibility of some successful modality of reformism in Latin America.

(2) That empirical evidence has been provided by the margin of success already achieved by two still ongoing reformist experiments: the progressive, electoral-congressional reformism of Chile and Venezuela and the radical military reformism of Peru. When the main characteristics and involved conditions of these two models (using the latter term in its broad and looser meaning) of reformism are compared with the main characteristics and involved conditions of the other Latin American countries, the following three conclusions can be reached:

(3) The Central American and Caribbean countries, because of their current lack of national viability, and, for reasons of her own, Paraguay, are not suited for either of these models and do not qualify, in general, for a reformist solution, as far as their autonomous national development is concerned.

(4) The Chilean-Venezuelan model is of little applicability to other Latin American countries because most of them lack the necessary degree of social integration and development, and none of them enjoys a political system that is sufficiently stable and developed to process reforms, on the initiative of meaningful political parties, through electoral-congressional competitive procedures. Uruguay and Argentina, however, are closer than the rest of the Latin American countries to meeting the requirements of the Chilean-Venezuelan model and may eventually come to do so in the future.

(5) The Peruvian model which was temporarily successful in Bolivia is not immediately applicable to any of the other Latin American countries, because of the current lack of the required basic predisposition in their respective armed forces. The Brazilian and Argentinean and the Ecuadorian and Colombian armed forces, because of their main characteristics and conditions for political action, are the closest to qualifying for that model. Given the internal process of free discussion and revision of crucial issues and policies that is currently taking place in these armed forces, they are likely to obtain the basic predisposition necessary

for promoting the adoption of the concerned model in a few years, as long as that process of revision is not successfully contained.

(6) Mexico, because of the particular features of her political system, resulting from the Mexican revolution, does not qualify for either of these two models, but she will retain, for a certain time, characteristics and conditions compatible with, and partially favoring, the renaissance of progressive reformism within her subsystem of political domination, as it is being currently attempted by President Luis Echeverria.

(7) With the exception of the Central American and Caribbean countries and of Paraguay, the Latin American countries will enjoy, for a certain time, the possibility, in analytical terms, of following other modalities of reformist experiments, but the likelihood of their occurrence seems to be extremely small.

NOTES

[1] Unlike revolutions, revolutionary reforms do not change, at least directly and immediately, the regime of power and the political regime.

[2] In Chile's second reform experiment under Allende, the emphasis was shifted from point 4 to point 1. But (at least early in 1972) the same four basic goals have been retained.

[3] For the statistical data, see CEPAL, *Economic Study of Latin America, 1968* (1969a) and Inter-American Development Bank, *Economic and Social Progress in Latin America,* eighth Annual Report, 1968.

[4] According to CEPAL, the annual rate of increase of Chile's GDP for these years was: 1961, 2.1 percent; 1962, 4.1 percent; 1963, 0.2 percent; and 1964, 1.4 percent.

[5] See F. Bonilla and J. A. Silva Michelena, eds. (1967, particularly chaps. 3 and 4 by the latter and chap. 7 by the former).

[6] In the case of Chile its reformist process, with the Allende government, shifted to radicalism, both in content and in form.

[7] Although consensuality has substantially dropped in Chile, with Allende, it remains at a basic level, concerning the preservation of the democratic regime.

[8] It is because of that lack of social integration and the deep latent conflicts resulting from it that the Mexican political system and its official party, the PRI, became a conservative-coercive system for the preservation of a profoundly inegalitarian social regime, once the drive of the revolution and of Cárdenas' reformism was exhausted.

[9] This is the case with Mexico and Brazil but not, properly, with Colombia, which retains oligarchical features of pre-populist character.

[10] The tendency of the armed forces in Latin America to stress their unity and to successfully operate in politics, in a corporate way, is very general. Such has occurred with left-of-center reformist movements, as in Peru and Bolivia in the time of Ovando and Torres, as well as with rightist movements, as in Argentina and Brazil. In Argentina, however, a serious break of unity resulted after the coup ousting Frondizi. In 1967 there was a violent confrontation between the moderate *azules,* mostly of the army, under Ongania's command, and the extreme rightist *colorados,* mostly of the navy, who were completely defeated. New divisions within the military took place as a result of General Lanusse's successful coup against Ongania in 1970.

[11] Once again, in this respect, the form of consensus building and decision making, in political affairs, adopted by the Peruvian army (and the Bolivian army in the governments of Ovando and Torres), is similar to that of the other Latin American armies. It consists, basically, in an extension and adaptation of the military technique of command: staff, high command, line of commands. Technical staffs collect data, survey the prevailing opinions

of the officer corps or of experts, and formulate a policy proposal, usually containing some alternatives for action and comparing them critically. The high command studies the data and the proposed alternatives and formulates, by majority or plurality of votes, a recommendation for the top chief, who makes the final decision, usually in accordance with the high command. Then the ultimate decision is transmitted from top to bottom through the chain of commanders. The crucial questions in this process are usually: (1) How much of the prevailing opinion of the officer corps and experts is considered by the staff? (2) Who is admitted to the high command "senate" to vote (for example, only four-star generals, most of the generals, some influential colonels)? (3) What extent of autonomy of decision, vis-à-vis the recommendations of the high command, is given to, and accepted from, the supreme commander?

[12] See the manifesto of the revolutionary government of Peru of October 3, 1968. See, also, the manifesto of the Bolivian armed forces of September 26, 1969, and of General Torres of October 7, 1970. Torres' movement has turned out to be a leftist nationalist countercoup successfully aimed at the removal of General Miranda, who ousted the Ovando regime in a briefly successful right-wing military coup. Torres, in his turn, was later overthrown by a rightist military coup.

[13] See Osvaldo Sunkel (1967b, pp. 43–75, particularly 62 ff.), Paul Rosenstein-Rodan, in Inter-American Development Bank (1968). See also Albert Hirschman (1969).

[14] See on the subject the already mentioned initial declarations of the three governments.

[15] On the necessity for catalyzing circumstances in order to unleash revolutions and coups, see Chalmers Johnson (1964 and 1966).

[16] In spite of the Bolivian left-of-center program, the United States government decided to support the MNR, considering it the best solution, in Bolivian conditions, and granted to the government about $100 million per year in aid. To a large extent, that aid conditioned Paz Estenssoro's policies, particularly in his second government.

[17] As chief of the armed forces, although not able to prevent the 1964 coup, he was urged by President Paz Estenssoro to assume the command of the military junta, as a way of preserving the political orientation of the 1952 revolution. Ovando, however, was not able to supersede Barrientos and later decided to limit himself to his military functions.

[18] The peculiar situation of Uruguay is characterized by the fact that although the country achieved a very large and stabilizing progressive social reform early in this century, she currently has problems of national viability that require a more productive and investment-oriented society.

[19] In Argentina the subsystem autonomy of the armed forces is substantially checked by the independent and well-organized power of the unions.

[20] The ousting of General Levingston by General Lanusse in 1971 (after the present book was already written) introduced two interrelated changes in the political orientation formerly attempted by the Levingston government. One is a shift from economic nationalism to what could be called "regulated neoliberalism." The other is a stronger and more effective endeavor to reestablish democratic procedures and party life. This means, in terms of the analysis being carried out in this study, that Argentina's compatibility with the electoral-congressional model (in the Venezuelan rather than in the Chilean pattern) has been enhanced.

[21] The leader of the nationalist faction in the Brazilian armed forces, General Albuquerque Lima, who had more than one opportunity to try to stage a nationalist coup from 1969 to 1970, preferred to remain loyal to the military hierarchy, under the implied assumption that he would have a timely promotion to four-star general. As a four-star general he would be a member of the armed forces high command and better able to induce his colleagues to follow a nationalist line. On the proper occasion, however, at the end of 1970, President Medici failed to promote General Albuquerque Lima, who was not able to induce any opposing reaction, with a consequent loss of influence for the nationalists in the army, and for his leadership of the nationalists.

27

Trends and Prospects

TRENDS IN LATIN AMERICA

Summary of previous conclusions

In order to draw some tentative conclusions from the preceding discussion of the basic alternatives with which Latin America is currently confronted, we must make an additional effort to assess what is likely to occur finally and what the more probable course of the events is. That assessment will have to consist, ultimately, in a critical comparison of the more probable trends in both Latin America and the United States (in her capacity as the superpower with general primacy and regional paramountcy), followed by an attempt to forecast the effects that are most likely to result from the interaction of these two sets of trends.

For the reader's convenience, we will briefly review the main findings and conclusions of the preceding chapters in this section. They can be summarily enumerated as follows:

(1) Latin America is currently confronted with the basic alternatives of dependence or autonomy and will have to follow one or the other in the next decades.

(2) Dependence is the currently prevailing trend, although it is not yet supported by a deliberate, conscious effort, on the side of both the United States and Latin America. So far it is not an irreversible tendency.

(3) Satellite dependence, which is the form of dependence toward which the Latin American countries are currently moving, requires a colonial-fascist model in more advanced societies. That model, however, is inherently unstable because it tends to generate fewer resources and less consensus than the concerned societies require, and so it depends, externally, on continuous and tendentiously increasing foreign aid to cover the deficit of resources and, internally, on continuous and tendentiously increasing coercion (with foreign support) to cover the deficit of consensus.

(4) In theory, stable forms of dependence for complex societies can be achieved by the conversion of satellite dependence into provincial dependence. That change, however, requires, on the part of the United States, an imperial purpose and preparedness that she does not currently possess.

(5) The alternative of autonomy, although more difficult to follow and so statistically less probable, will continue to be possible as long as dependence does not become irreversible. This involves, both in theory and in the empirical conditions of Latin America, the problem of historical deadlines. Historical deadlines are objective characteristics of historical processes that, in certain conditions, can be predicted as reasonable approximations. In the case of Latin America a deadline of thirty years may reasonably be considered as the time limit within which the larger and strategically more important countries of Latin America can achieve their autonomous and self-sustained national development and achieve a viable system of regional integration. This implies a shorter deadline, of about ten years—the decade of the 1970s—for such countries to adopt the more important measures and policies necessary for the appropriate subsequent execution of their developmental plans.

(6) The failure of populism and the resulting emergence, in the 1960s, of reactionary tendencies throughout Latin America has in turn aroused in some sectors, mostly among the youth, widespread expectations of, and attempts at, change by revolutionary ways. Currently and in the foreseeable future, however, revolutions based on the Cuban, Chinese, or other models are not viable, due to the societal conditions still prevailing in Latin America, the present counterinsurgency capability of the more important Latin American armed forces, and the United States' readiness to support the latter or to intervene directly. If the present status quo, however, is not changed by reformist ways or by the establishment of stable provincial forms of dependence, revolutions will tend to become uncontrollable in the long run, maybe not within the next ten years, but hardly for longer than thirty years.

(7) Reformist ways are currently being attempted, with success, in three Latin American countries. These attempts follow two models: the progressive, electoral-congressional model of the Chilean and Venezuelan experiments and the radical military model of the Peruvian experiment.

(8) The Chilean-Venezuelan model, given its characteristics and requirements, is of little applicability elsewhere in Latin America, although it may, eventually, be applicable in Uruguay and Argentina.

(9) Neither is the Peruvian model, given its characteristics and requirements, immediately applicable to other Latin American countries, but it may become applicable in such countries as Brazil, Argentina, Ecuador, and Colombia (and eventually again in Bolivia), if tendencies toward national-developmentalist reforms, which already have many supporters in the armed forces, are not prevented from developing.

Most of the aspects concerning the main trends in Latin America have already been discussed. For the purpose of our present assessment, we will add certain clarification and attempt to reach a general conclusion.

Essentially, as we have seen, with the exception of the three countries currently undertaking, rather successfully, a reformist experiment, Latin America is objectively following, although still without a conscious purpose, the alternative of dependence. For the more complex and developed of these societies, satellite dependence involves the adoption of the colonial-fascist model. None of these countries, however, has reached a complete and consolidated form of colonial fascism. The process is still incipient, and other adverse forces in these societies prevent that propensity from crystalizing. Basically, that notwithstanding, there is a trend toward combining military authoritarianism with economic neoliberalism, under tight technocratic management. In Brazil, where this type of regime has hitherto been carried furthest, and where military rule is most complete and overt, there is a discernible official tendency to follow a pattern similar to Franco's Spain. Similar to the first phase of *Franquismo* although less clearly than in Spain, the Brazilian military regime showed an initial propensity for some sort of combination including a corporative sociopolitical regime, under military control and with Falangist proclivities, and a technocratically regulated neoliberal economy. Subsequently, from 1970 onward, it shifted, similar to the second phase of *Franquismo*, to a tendency toward a sort of *Opus Dei* technocratic regulated neoliberalism, within the framework of an authoritarian, quasi-absolutist, paternalist, and modernizing military regime.[1]

The trouble with the colonial-fascist model for the larger and less socially integrated Latin American countries, such as Brazil, Mexico, and Colombia, consists in the fact—aggravated by the regime's sociopolitical traits—that the neoliberal model is inherently unable to generate the conditions necessary for the incorporation of the huge masses into forms and levels of minimally acceptable participation in the national systems. From this inability results the deficits of resources and consensus that sustain a social state of permanent instability and tension and that compel the regime to maintain itself through processes of continuous internal coercion and external dependence, which cannot continue forever.

For demographically smaller and socially better-integrated countries, such as Argentina, the problem created by the colonial-fascist model is not so much of a socioeconomic character as it is of a political nature. The model imposes, on the one hand, the penalty of increasing denationalization, which not only affects in the long run the historical chances for the country, reducing her future prospects, but immediately narrows the internal occupational and role-performing possibilities, in direct detriment to the middle class. Furthermore, by establishing in a well-educated and well-integrated society a discretionary political system, which is unaccountable to the citizens and expresses only the views of small military and business circles and their leading cliques, colonial fascism introduces an increasing deterioration in the social fabric and creates by political means all sorts of counterdevelopmental effects, reducing the overall development of the society.

The three ideological lines of thought

Confronted with the present problems of their countries, including those raised by their rule, the military in Brazil and Argentina currently tend to split along three main ideological and programmatic lines. One stresses the necessity for the military to return the direction of the political process to "acceptable" civil leaders, within the framework of a militarily supervised democracy. The armed forces would retain a political supervisory role, as the supposed embodiment of the nation (idealistically differentiated from the society), and as such would fix the basic rules of the political game, would exercise a continuous veto power on unacceptable political groups, leaders, issues, and policies, regarded by them to be contrary to the national security, and under those conditions, would let the political process be decided by electoral means. The proponents of this solution believe that it has the advantage of combining their democratic aspirations with their feeling that the armed forces should retain a top regulative role. This line, which might be called "supervisory liberalism," is particularly appealing to former classic liberals, who dream of a generalized laissez-faire system in the new conditions of Latin America, if tempered by military political supervision. In Brazil that line is supported by most of the former close supporters of the Castelo Branco regime, such as Generals Golbery do Costa e Silva, Cordeiro de Farias, and Juarez Tavora. In Argentina it was held by the late General Pedro Aramburu and his supporters, such as General Julio Alzogoray, and among the present military leaders, by General Alejandro Lanusse before he succeeded General Levingston in the presidency. As president, however, he has substantially adjusted his neoliberal views to a more pragmatic line.

The second line, more overtly oriented toward a colonial-fascist model, presents a subdivision between those directly attached to certain traits of "classic fascism," particularly the corporative view of the state, and those more interested in neoliberal forms of technocratic management. With the caution always necessary in the employment of historical examples and analogies for analytical purposes, I would suggest that we use Franco's regime as a pattern of reference for these two varieties of military views. The first variety, which tended to be first chronologically, but still exists as an ideological group in the Brazilian and Argentine armed forces, could be called "Falangist." General Torranzo Montero in Argentina and, in different conditions, General Jayme Portella in Brazil during the Costa e Silva government, together with all the remaining former *integralistas* provide typical examples of the Falangist line. That line stresses the necessity of direct and tough military rule, having mainly moralistic and anticommunist purposes, as well as a wish—at least as a reference goal—to organize society along corporative lines.

The Falangists (as occurred in Spain) were overcome, both in Brazil and Argentina, by a much more sophisticated variety of colonial fascism, which could be called, following the Spanish analogy, *Opus Dei* technocratic neoliberalism. Like the supervisory liberals, they stress a private enterprise market economy, although they are no longer laissez-faire liberals, as many of the others still are, but Keynesian neoliberals, strongly committed to the technocratic management and manipulation of the economy. On the other hand, they do not believe in the possibility of a well-functioning supervised democracy, because of the immanent conflict between the two terms of such a regime. They prefer a military-based authoritarian technocratic regime—oriented by middle-class traditional Christian values—enjoying in principle absolute power but using it as moderately as possible, in a paternalist, welfare-oriented, and modernizing version of the eighteenth-century cameralists. They suppose that the cumulative success of that model, if it is well implemented, will gradually reduce the initial tensions formed by real or supposed conflicts of interest, and that successful technocracy, manipulating, as an instrument of efficiency, foreign capital, private firms, and fiscal incentives, will rapidly advance in the direction of overall development and reach Daniel Bell's state of "the end of ideology." The Medici government in Brazil (although incorporating several nationalist traits) and the former Ongania government in Argentina, are examples of this *Opus Dei* technocratic neoliberalism.

The third line of military thought is the nationalist. The nationalists fully realize the distinction between *national* and merely *territorial* development and strongly favor the first form. They understand, therefore, the extent to which all liberal and neoliberal economic models, in the present conditions of the world, have a denationalizing effect. They are becoming, moreover, increasingly conscious of the interrelation between the circular process of Latin American structural stagnation and marginality, with its ultimate denationalizing results. To reverse that trend they favor a normative central-planning system, committed to national and social development, particularly based on public enterprises and supported by broad social measures, such as agrarian reform. They acknowledge, however, that public enterprises have often been badly and inefficiently managed in Latin America and that in order to assure their appropriate operation, in addition to scientific management, a great discipline and austerity is required in the whole society and particularly in the public sector. They have been militant supporters of antisubversive repressive measures, but although retaining a traditional anticommunist stand, they have in general shifted their emphasis from repressive counterinsurgency to active social reform. They have come to understand that the answer to insurgency lies less in the repression of rebel leaders than in the promotion of radical and honest social reforms, which will eliminate the causes of social marginality and incorporate the masses into the national system by substantially increasing their levels of production and consumption. In Brazil General Albuquerque Lima was acknowledged in the late 1960s as the leader of the military nationalists, who represent a very large sector in the armed forces, although not at the level of top command. In Argentina the nationalist sector of the armed forces has been particularly identified with the group of the National Security Council, of which General Osiris Villegas was the head until recently, and where there seems to be now a tendency to follow General Pasquer Cambrai. Because the influence of laissez-faire views is significantly stronger in Argentina, the relative strength of the nationalists in the Argentine armed forces is probably smaller than in Brazil, although the available empirical information on the subject is poor.

These three basic ideological and programmatic military positions have similar equivalents in Colombia and Ecuador, although they are less clear because of different conditions, including the present covert forms of political interference of the armed forces. In Ecuador the military junta that ruled the country from 1963 to 1966, under the presidency of navy Captain Ramón Castro Jijon, had a frank nationalist and social-reformist orientation and was forced to resign by the joint pressures of the Guayaquil merchants and the supervisory liberals in the armed forces. The new military junta who seized power again, in 1972, over-throwing President Velasco Ibarra, is more ambiguous about the issue. In Colombia military nationalism and social reformism have been steadily growing, particularly since the mid-1960s, under the leadership of General Alberto Ruiz Novoa, now retired. Symptomatic of the expanding influence of nationalism and social reformism, both in the armed forces and in Colombian society at large, is the success that has been obtained in a crude populist version of these views, by ex-dictator General Rojas Pinilla, who has returned to public life. Founding a new party, the Alianza Nacional Popular (ANAPO), he started to seriously defy the Frente Nacional in 1966, and lost the presidential election of 1970 by a very small margin of votes. Subsequently, Rojas Pinilla made a very poor show in the 1972 congressional elections, losing a great deal of his former impact. The na-tionalist trends, however, did not seem to have been affected by Rojas' declining appeal, but have been reoriented again toward Lleras Restreppo and his sector of the Liberal Party.

The conditioning factors

The evolution of these three ideological lines within the armed forces of these countries seems, from the current developments, to have been predominantly influenced by the interplay of four main factors: (1) the exposure of the mili-tary to a free internal debate concerning these three ideological and program-matic positions, and the different reactions to them, (2) the interaction between these military lines, the various social strata, and the different tendencies, (3) the policies and measures adopted by the governments of the concerned countries and their results, and (4) the course of events followed in international affairs, particularly as far as the development of the cold war and the relations between Latin America and the United States are concerned.

A comprehensive analysis of the interplay of these four factors would be ex-tremely important for an understanding of the current foreseeable ideological development of the armed forces of the concerned countries, which will config-urate the tendency of their political action in the near future. Such an analysis, however, would not be compatible with the limits of the present chapter. I will, therefore, restrict myself to the more crucial aspects of that complex process, concentrating on the case of Brazil, because it is the country where both the autonomous capability of the armed forces is greatest and a change in govern-mental policies would have the most decisive influence in Latin America.

Ultimately, the most important aspects of the process of that interplay may be reduced to three points. The first is that the free discussion of the confronting views within the armed forces, particularly in the army, seems to clearly favor the nationalist line. Empirical evidence on that is difficult to obtain because of the armed forces' policy of preventing the divulgence of that sort of information, in the interest of maintaining military unity. But what can be obtained from personal information and available inferences frankly indicates the above.

The second point concerns the estimates, among the military, of the feasibility of a new nationalist and social-reformist policy compared to the current form of technocratically managed neoliberalism. That concern, to start with, manifests the realistic and critical approach that is beginning to prevail among the new military, which is increasingly influenced by a scientific-technological outlook. It is once again, for the same reasons, difficult to gather enough and appropriate information on that subject, although in the case of Brazil articles in the *Military Club Journal* provide some indications, in addition to those obtainable from personal sources. My own impression on this subject is that the armed forces, increasingly inclined to a nationalist and social-reformist view, are trying to assess the feasibility of a new policy expressing that view. They are concerned, on the one hand, with the possibility of combining, theoretically and practically, the involved values and desired goals with sound financial and managerial practices, and on the other hand, with the sociopolitical conditions for, and consequences of, such a new policy. Military nationalists and social reformists in Brazil, as well as in Argentina—unlike what may still occur in Colombia and Ecuador—are concerned with avoiding another populist experiment. They want, therefore, before putting their present ideological views into practice, to be sure that they have technically sound operational procedures and that these procedures can be implemented in acceptable sociopolitical conditions, both domestically and internationally. The extent to which the military will come to conclude that these two conditions of feasibility may be attained is still difficult to forecast. Their conclusions are likely to be strongly influenced by whether or not the reformist intelligentsia, in countries such as Brazil and Argentina, are able to present sound formulations of such a new policy and to advise appropriate forms to assure that its implementation will not cause sociopolitical disruptions, either domestically or internationally. To facilitate a comparison between the forces, models, conditions, and probable results of (1) a nationalist and social-reformist policy oriented toward autonomous national development, (2) a policy of technocratic neoliberalism, allegedly oriented toward "interdependence," but actually, as formerly seen, oriented toward satellite dependence, and (3) a revolutionary way of achieving autonomous national development, I have attempted to present the principal elements involved in Table 47.

The third point concerning the interplay of factors currently shaping the predominant political orientation of the armed forces, particularly in Brazil and Argentina, is related to the many facets of internal military politics and the military's relations with external actors and conditions, such as, particularly, the composition and orientation of the national government, the main social strata and groups in these countries, and the course of international affairs. In that respect some alternatives are extremely important. One alternative concerns the

Table 47 *Dependence and autonomy in Latin America: forces, models, conditions, and probable results*

Alternatives — Factors and conditions	Dependence (Based on present regime of participation. Strategic decisions and factors are U.S.-controlled or oriented.)	Autonomy (Strategic decisions and factors are Latin American-controlled or oriented.) REFORMIST WAY	Autonomy REVOLUTIONARY WAY
Leading forces	Consular and foreign bourgeoisies plus conservative armed forces plus conservative civil middle class	Nationalist military (or progressive parties) plus intelligentsia, national bourgeoisie, progressive middle class, and masses	Revolutionary intelligentsia plus radical military groups and popular forces
Economic model a. / Key instrument b.	a. Technocratic neoliberalism b. U.S.-controlled multinational corporations	a. National developmentalism with regional integration b. Public enterprise, national and regional	a. Developmental socialism b. Public corporation
Sociopolitical conditions	Alliance of business and military, supported by conservative middle class; repression of intelligentsia and masses; reasonable economic growth	Prevalence of nationalists in armed forces (or electoral prevalence of progressives), supported by leading forces listed above	Precondition: general Latin American social disruption caused by continuous aggravation of present status quo for more than ten years
Political model	Colonial fascism	Varying combinations of national capitalism and state capitalism	Developmental socialism
Probable results	a. Satellite and provincial development or b. Disruptive aggravation caused by dualism; tendency toward revolution	a. National and regional autonomous development or b. Disruptions caused by conflicting parochialism and tendency toward dependence	a. No U.S. intervention: neutral socialism or b. U.S. intervention: Chinese-like revolution or multiple Vietnams constituting popular liberation wars

position that the nationalist members of the military, in such countries as Brazil and Argentina, may come to have within their respective armed forces, if the formerly hypothesized tendency in favor of nationalism and social reformism continues. That position may vary from a loose and unorganized ideological sympathy to a massive, organized, and militant support. Another and crucial alterna ive involves the way in which the military nationalists come to relate to their government. That relationship can be one of collaboration and support, insofar as these governments decide to accept a nationalist and social-reformist orientation (as it is increasingly occurring in Brazil with Medici, since the second half of 1971), or it can be one of incompatibility and struggle. In the first case radical changes in policy could be made in reformist ways. In the second case a coup would be necessary for these changes. A third alternative concerns the course of international affairs. The extent to which the former ideological aspects of the cold war become increasingly a conflict-cooperation process of interimperial adjustments or, conversely, return to a quasi-religious opposition will discredit or reconfirm the international outlook of the supervisory liberals. And the extent to which Latin American integration does or does not become more or less effective will tend to reinforce the assumptions of the nationalists or of the technocratic neoliberals, respectively.

It would be of little scientific value to try to explore the possible course of military trends beyond this point. As can be observed from the preceding discussion, nationalism and social reformism, as ideological and programmatic lines, seem to be gaining increasing support in the armed forces, particularly in the army, of such countries as Brazil and Argentina, Ecuador and Colombia. Furthermore, in Brazil and Argentina military nationalists and reformists are seriously concerned with sound financial and managerial practices, nondisruptive sociopolitical effects, avoiding adventuristic risks, and so on. We are confronted, therefore, with an open process, which presents some indications that nationalism is likely to become a predominant view in the armed forces of the concerned countries. The conversion of that view into actual governmental policies, however, may be a long way away. Nationalists may not coalesce into a sufficiently strong and predominant group in the armed forces for political action; appropriate correspondence between the nationalist view and its militants and a specific set of policies and measures may also fail to materialize, because of deficiencies in formulation or the successful mystification of nationalists by skilled neoliberal technocrats; the nationalist military may also conclude that many of their policies and desired goals would create, in their opinion, unacceptable sociopolitical conflicts, domestically or internationally.

Although a specific conclusion concerning such an open process would not be warranted by the evidence, it seems possible to state that military nationalism and social reformism tend to become the central issues in the political orientation of the armed forces of these countries. That fact is likely to reduce the Supervisory Liberals to a secondary position in the case of Brazil and possibly also of Argentina; is still likely to contribute to the final discredit in these countries of the Falangist variety of colonial fascism. Nationalist reformism and the

Opus Dei style of technocratic regulated neoliberalism, as well as their possible blends, appear therefore as the two most probable ideological and programmatic contending lines in the armed forces of Brazil, Argentina, Ecuador, and Colombia. These lines will orient the armed forces and the concerned countries to either autonomous national development or forms of so-called interdependence with the United States, which will actually result in dependence, as formerly discussed in Chapter 24.

TRENDS IN THE UNITED STATES

Basic alternatives

Shifting our analysis now to the other side of the picture, let us try to assess briefly the principal tendencies that are likely to characterize the United States in the coming years, largely in terms of the main processes that are currently taking place in American society and in terms of her interrelationships with the world.

The determination of tendencies and trends in such a complex society as the United States, in which no single institution or group can claim anything approaching the extent of autonomous capability that the armed forces presently enjoy in many Latin American countries, presents a great problem, both in terms of the appropriate methodology for the attempt and in terms of the treatment of the involved facts and variables. An analytical approach considering, at each of the four structural planes of the American society, which tendencies and groups are currently competing to shape what sort of main social, cultural, economic, and political trends, although perfectly legitimate, would obviously be incompatible with the dimensions of the present topic. That limitation could be an insuperable impediment to the attainment of our purpose in other moments in American history. Presently, however, the American society, in spite of the immense and tragic confusion that has come to prevail in all its sectors and that might appear to render impossible the indication of any general trend, is, very much to the contrary, confronted as a whole with two interrelated alternatives, which are of the widest scope and consequences. It is precisely because of the conflicts generated by these two alternatives (which even include their actual formulation and the clear acknowledgment of what is really at stake) that the American society is currently so agitated. The fact that these two alternatives are so comprehensive and decisive, however, as far as the future development of the American society and the world at large is concerned, permits an assessment of the society's main tendencies and trends in terms of these alternatives.

The first alternative consists in the opposition, in the present conditions of the world, between two forms for the internal and international organization of the American society: empire and commonwealth. The second alternative, interrelated with the first but standing on its own terms, consists in the opposition in the American society but, tendentiously, in the whole world, of two forms of ethics: the ethics of duty and the ethics of liberty.

These two alternatives are interrelated in at least two principal ways. First they are interrelated in that the prospect of an empire, which is currently confronting the American society, is the consequence of a long and complex historical process in which the prevalence, up to our time, of an ethic of duty in the United States has played a fundamental role. Second, they are interrelated because the choice between the two terms of the organizational dilemma is and will be strongly influenced, although not isolatedly determined, by the choice between those two competing ethics. That interrelationship, however, does not go as far as being a strict interdependence. The two alternatives are, in many senses, of two different kinds. The empire-commonwealth alternative tends to be objectively imposed on the American society, which will be led to follow one of the two terms, whether or not the choice becomes a conscious and deliberate one. The choice between the two ethics, however, although representing something that is objectively proposed to every individual by the sociocultural development of the American society and as such subjects everybody to sociocultural constraints, will have to be an individual decision on the part of each concerned person, whatever the influences exerted by sociocultural constraints. Furthermore, the second alternative does not involve a global "either–or" outcome. The American society is more likely to become divided between these two ethics, with predominance oscillating between them, than it is to be led to massively follow either of them. That ethical alternative, moreover, is not exhaustive in terms of ethical possibilities, leaving open various other possible types of ethical choices. And, as was formerly said, it is not a choice that only Americans are being, or will be, confronted with; it tends to be faced, although reflecting distinct traditions, by all modern societies as they come to have sociocultural conditions comparable to the present American ones.

The ethical alternative

What is immediately relevant for our present study is the first alternative, which involves an overall political choice, conscious or not, that, along with other consequences, will directly interfere with the possibilities and trends concerning the autonomous development of Latin America. The second alternative, however, cannot be omitted from our picture because of its interrelationship with the first. It would not be possible, within the inherent limits of this study, to explore succinctly the complex problems involved in the present ethical alternative of the American society. An analysis of these problems would require a broad historical and sociocultural study of the evolution of that society and of the Western world, which would be alien to the purposes of this book. What we do need, for the brief analysis of the first alternative, is to understand that the new complexities of post–World War II America, the unprecedented extent of her international involvement, and the not less unprecedented expansion of her rate of higher education have both shaken the basis of the traditional American ethic of duty and created or socialized new values and expectations, which require new ethical approaches, such as the ethics of liberty.

Reducing that complex situation to its fundamental traits, we can say that in the process of its secularization, and practical application, the traditional American ethic of duty has been increasingly confronted, in recent times, with a crisis of legitimacy and a crisis of relevancy. The American ethic of duty is a secularized expression of the Protestant ethic, which is oriented toward "justification through faith"[2] by a voluntaristic decision to accept the message of the Christian revelation and abide by it. In the historical process of its secularization, from colonial times to the conditions of the mid-twentieth century, the religious and transcendent nucleus of that ethical outlook, around which a code and a style of behavior was shaped, became increasingly more remote. It became a mere principle of reference still accepted for logical, metaphysical, or simply traditional reasons, but no longer the actual sustaining foundation of the ethic. The code of behavior and style, however, largely enriched by the input of values and norms of social and civic character, became the standard of correct behavior for every respectable and self-respecting man. That ethic was an ethic of duty, in its original sense, because it reflected the "Protestant principle," which stresses grace and the will of God, instead of inherently good human values, and which accordingly leads to ethical standards of an operational rather than of a content character. And that ethic became an ethic of duty in its modern and contemporary social form because it established certain patterns of legitimacy and behavior that everyone should follow, including private secularized moral prescriptions derived from traditionally accepted versions of the Protestant revelation and a set of normative responsibilities concerning sociopolitical affairs derived from the American communitarian and civic tradition. The increasing bureaucratization and regimentation of contemporary American life created the necessity for regulating the behavior of people accordingly. Interim instances and agencies of legitimacy and prescriptiveness were provided—such as the norms and instructions of the federal government and the far-reaching management decisions of the great corporations—all inserted into the general corpus of the current American ethic of duty. Inherent to that ethical corpus was the assumption of a basic compatibility and complementarity between (1) Christian ethics (implicitly identified with its Protestant version), (2) the American tradition and way of life (seen in an idealized way), and (3) the United States and her major aims and acts, as constitutionally formulated and decided by the three federal branches (idealistically differentiated from mere partisan politics).

The crisis confronted by that ethic of duty resulted from the rapid appearance, in recent times, of deep and widespread doubts concerning the actual legitimacy of many of its instructions and norms (from segregation to the Vietnam War), of the authorities issuing these instructions (alleged undemocratic electoral and administrative procedures), and, ultimately, of the whole axiological and conceptual system related to that ethical outlook. At the same time, new values and expectations were created, or at least widely socialized, all of which related to a new existential view of man and his liberty, as the ultimate source and object of all values.[3] These new expectations and values, which were alien to the American ethical tradition and hardly adjustable to it, also had a different, remote origin: classic humanism. More recently, they have become a tributary to Continental existentialism and to the present revival of young Marx and of humanistic socialism, associated, mostly for the young generation, with a desperate neoromantic search for interpersonal communication, subjectivization of all value patterns, sexual freedom, and unbound hedonistic exploration of all sensorial possibilities.

The two ethics represent both a generational conflict and a deeper conflict concerning how to deal with, and what to do in, the new world created by the continuous and self-sustained expansion of technology. As has already been advanced in this book (see the initial part of Chapter 18), one of the crucial problems presented by the complete technologicalization of man's environment consists in the fact that the former behaviors derived from certain natural constraints and scarcities no longer make sense (if the available technological possibilities are actually and rationally used); and yet man's contingency cannot be overcome in many essential respects, and hyperaffluence does not suppress the necessity for, and the problems of, political decisions and their implementation.

The consequences of these two aspects of the modern world, for the ethical alternative in discussion, are far reaching and cannot be analyzed here. They concern, in one respect, the inherent social validity of the two conflicting ethics, as they are currently formulated and practiced. Insofar as the current ethic of duty does not solve its crisis of legitimacy and relevancy—which would require new foundations and new values and therefore a new ethical outlook—that ethic tends to become an ideological rationalization of particular (class, group, or generation) interests, only socially enforceable by coercive means. Insofar as the emerging ethic of liberty proceeds along certain of its currently salient terms—which cannot provide a general pattern for socially dependable and functional forms of human interaction, particularly in the conditions of the contemporary world—that ethic tends to lead either to general social disruption or to a self-invalidating restriction of its applicability to only socially secluded minorities.

In another respect, the fact that hyperaffluence does not suppress human contingency and the need for political rule, interrelates the ethical alternative with the empire-commonwealth alternative. An international communitarian commonwealth can be attained and maintained (the other necessary conditions being given) by nonascriptive and humanistically oriented forms of an ethic of duty—as in the case of the Stoic ethic—as well as by forms of an ethic of liberty inherently conducive to dependable patterns of functional sociability. Contrarily, ascriptive and potentially antihumanist forms of an ethic of duty, with its crisis of legitimacy and relevancy, can only lead to an empire. Forms of an ethic of liberty that are not socially dependable and functional could only lead to social self-destruction in the purely theoretical hypothesis of its generalization, or, in actual practice, will tend to lead to restrictive sect behavior in the wider context of a prevailing ascriptive ethic of duty.

This brief analysis of the problems related to the ethical alternative confronting American society today and, tendentiously, the world at large enables us to examine the other alternative, which so immediately concerns our present inquiry: the alternative between empire and commonwealth.

Empire or commonwealth

The alternative between empire and commonwealth, as has been noted, is objectively imposed on American society by the course of history, and the United States will be forced to follow one of the two terms of that alternative, whether she does so in a conscious way or not. As was examined in Chapter 18, in the conditions following World War II, the United States became a superpower endowed with general world primacy and Western Paramountcy. It was, de facto, converted into a world empire, even though that result was not deliberately planned and is not being currently acknowledged by the American people, in general, including most of their leaders, with the exception of some experts and the young intelligentsia.

At the present stage in the development of the American empire, however, the moment is coming, for internal as well as for external reasons, when the gap between the fact of imperium and the lack of its acknowledgment, particularly by the ruling circle, will create rapidly increasing difficulties for the management of American interests and, ultimately, for the very existence and survival of the American society. Not acknowledging the American empire does not imply that the American people are opting for the other term of the alternative, the establishment of a communitarian international commonwealth. On the contrary, it just keeps the empire going, given the empire's inherent expansive propensities, but at the same time, it implies random forms of rule and management, which will soon overtax the empire's huge but not unlimited resources and so lead the whole system, including its core part, the American society, to inescapable disaster.

It is highly improbable, however, that widespread unawareness of the United States' imperial condition will continue for long, even if, for cultural or tactical reasons, the facts may continue to be officially denied and some of the terminological aspects of that awareness may come to be systematically repressed by certain circles. Full and sophisticated understanding of the empire has already been expressed by modern scholarship, inside and outside the United States, and it has also been expressed, with vehement condemnation, by the students and anti-imperialist leaders. And the trend is to make the study of the new empires and of interimperial and intraimperial relations the main subject of the field of international relations. Even if traditional and certain tactical reasons would conspire against an open way of dealing with the imperial fact, the issues and problems related to it and the necessity for their rational treatment are, altogether, so vital that an objective and scientific approach to the imperial question is quickly becoming an uncontainable exigency of the American society.

It is clear, therefore, that now and in the next few years, the American empire, as a state of fact, either will be submitted to increasingly costly contingencies, due to the lack of a rational and systematic acknowledgment and treatment of its problems by the American ruling circle, or will be the object of a deliberate option. Continued official refusal to acknowledge the imperial reality and to deal with it in a rational and purposeful way, if highly improbable in the long run, would simply mean an objective option in favor of the empire, although in the described disastrous form. Facing the facts in a rational and deliberate way, however, would open to the United States the alternative of either accepting the imperial condition, for whatever reasons, with the possibility of managing it as deemed best, or rejecting it and choosing, in its place, another form of organization for the American society and its international relations. That other form, as an ideal type, is an international communitarian commonwealth.

The two terms of this alternative must be understood as ideal types, admitting many possible empirical varieties along a spectrum. Essential to the idea of empire—along with other conditions concerning its world status--is the fact that a given society exerts power and authority, by its own strength, as the ruling or hegemonic society over other distinct societies that are dependent, even if unwillingly, on the former.[4] That power and authority may be accepted and even welcomed by any of the dependent societies or their members, but are independent of that acceptance and can be autonomously enforced in any of the dependent societies by the ruling or hegemonic one. As the opposite term we have, in the contemporary conditions of the world, the ideal type of an international communitarian commonwealth. Essential to this idea (along with other conditions concerning its world status) is the fact that several distinct societies, independent of their relative strength and level of development, maintain, in an institutional and endurable way and by their own original decision, a supranational organization. That organization is based on egalitarian principles concerning the regime of participation of each society and its respective members in that organization, and it is endowed with sufficient power and authority for self-government or for the rule and management of some relevant common interests.

The two terms of this alternative, as previously said, admit many empirical varieties. As a result, the distinction between them, although always preserving an essential differentiation between the inegalitarian and the egalitarian basis, may come, in practice, to be small. This is because an enlightened way of ruling and managing an empire may, for a given time, deny any practical significance to the privileges of the ruling society and its members, vis-à-vis the dependent societies and their members, by granting de facto egalitarian and fair conditions of participation. On the other hand, a communitarian international commonwealth, in spite of its institutional provisions and even without their actual violation, in any legal sense, may be ruled and managed in such a way that the stronger society and its members are de facto privileged. The Roman Empire, for example, in spite of the full preservation of the imperium of the Roman people over the subject societies and peoples, was ruled and managed in an enlightened way under Augustus or under the Antonines, providing basically fair and egalitarian conditions for all free men of the empire, particularly in the higher classes. Conversely, the recent international commonwealth established by Egypt and Syria, with the institution of the United Arab Republic, was resented by the latter because it privileged the former, leading Syria to unilaterally secede from the organization.[5]

Whether with more or less enlightened views and purposes, the fact remains that the American society will have to follow one of the two terms of the empire-commonwealth alternative, in one way or another. As has been reiterated, making no option and maintaining the status quo would simply mean following the imperial path, which is the current one. In an equivalent way for the Latin American societies, as has been seen, making no formal option and keeping the status quo simply means following the alternative of dependence, which is their current course.

From the Latin American side, we have seen how autonomy is achievable, in principle, through a revolutionary and through a reformist way, although in the current conditions and those of the foreseeable future, the reformist way is the only feasible one. We have also seen that, of the possible models of reformism, military developmental nationalism and social reformism constitute the one most likely to be applicable in such key countries as Brazil and Argentina, in addition to its current experiment in Peru. Is it possible to discern some trends and implied models concerning the American alternative between empire and commonwealth?

Shift in the focus of the discussion

With the caution so often reiterated in this book, because of the essential openness of historical developments, I suggest that some forecasts can be advanced in answer to the above question with a reasonable margin of probability.

The first point that needs to be clarified concerns the evolving characteristics of the debate about the American empire, currently taking place in American society. That debate does not directly and inherently concern the alternative that we are discussing (empire-commonwealth) but rather its first term only. One side of the debate is represented by those who identify and describe the facts that necessarily prove the existence of the American empire and reveal its characteristics and, based on them, vehemently denounce that empire as inherently evil, from a predominantly ethical point of view. Most of them are humanist and radical intellectuals and students, whose views and motivations reflect the new ethics of liberty. The other side basically denies the imperial fact, attempting to contend either that the alleged facts are not duly proved or that they do not have the imperial meaning alleged by the other camp. This side, however, does not dare to challenge the inherently evil character that an American empire would have if it actually existed. Most of the people on this side are conservative members of the ruling circle, who reflect the traditional ethic of duty. As the debate goes on, and is interwoven with it, the scholarly study of that question, as has been said, clearly tends to acknowledge the imperial conditions of the United States, although not necessarily in the same way that the anti-imperialists do. It seems likely that the subjective conviction of those denying the imperial fact will rapidly decline. As a matter of fact, it is clearer every day that those opposing the anti-imperialist camp are doing so not because they ignore the factual evidence of the American empire, but because they ultimately do not agree that such an empire is necessarily inherently evil, although they are not yet prepared to admit its existence and to justify it.

Since the debate about the American empire has arrived at that point, it seems inevitable that its appraisal will shift from its present pseudofactual level, centered around the empire's existence or nonexistence, to a different level, concerning whether or not that empire could be disposed of and what better international arrangement could be assured for the United States—which, ultimately, involves the alternative between empire and commonwealth.

As was discussed in Chapter 18, of the analysts of the present interimperial system, George Liska has presented the best formulation concerning two crucial aspects of it. First, he has sustained that, in the conditions following World War II, the transformation of the international system brought about by that war and reflecting earlier developments rendered inevitable the emergence of the American and the Soviet empires. Second, he has contended that, in these conditions, an American empire would be a decisively positive contribution to the world. It would establish and maintain a world order that would not be possible without it, and because of the cultural, social, political, and economic characteristics of American society, that order would be assured in the most favorable conditions for the world at large and particularly for the peoples subject to the American area of hegemony. Liska's views have already been discussed in Chapter 18, and there is no need to review them again. It suffices to mention that, even if we admit the national bias and the idealistic fallacies of Liska's justification of the American empire, the direction opened by his analysis provides a sound way for a sociopolitical argument in favor of such an empire without gross factual distortions, hypocritical pretenses, or cynical Machiavellianism.

It should also be noted that in addition to the international conditions that have favored the rise and expansion of the American empire, it is also the necessary and direct consequence of the form of development and resulting internal stratification of the American society. I will not elaborate on that fascinating question, which would require a complex analysis, but it should be pointed out that the particular combination of democracy and oligarchy that has come to characterize contemporary American society (presenting important analogies with the Roman society at the end of the republic) has exerted a decisive pressure for imperial expansion. A democracy of private rights, including very fair chances for ascent by merit, combined with a very stable oligarchy at the level of relevant decision making, assured by the oligopolization of wealth and economic control (long concealed by the myth of free competition), and the oligopolization of power (still concealed by electoral-congressional procedures), that society needed imperial expansion for the reasons already indicated in Chapter 18. Along with many other important functions, the empire is, economically, an outlet for capital surpluses, an instrument for preventing scarcities or price rises in raw materials, a favored market for finished goods, and, for these reasons, a decisive factor in the socioeconomic stability at home.

If we take that aspect into account, plus those indicated by Liska, the criticism of the empire becomes a much more complex matter. If the cultural revolution now agitating the American campuses and the new ethics of liberty should come to change, in a sufficiently deep and general way, the prevailing patterns motivating the American society, the imperial question would, of course, not escape these revolutionary changes. That hypothesis, however, is a very remote one. The ethical changes pressed by the young generation are not likely to spread much beyond the very particular conditions of the campus life of most of their present militants—not even to the future behavior of these militants as mature men. And ethical changes, alone, have not been sufficient historically for the complete modification of the social regime, as was discussed in Chapter 2. In order for changes in the regime of values to affect congruently the other societal regimes, they have to meet certain basic requirements inherent to each social subsystem. In other words, in order for the American society to shift from its present imperial course to one of a communitarian commonwealth more than good intentions would be required. Important structural changes concerning the use and control of wealth and power, that is, *changes in the American social regime*, would be necessary.*

At this new point in our discussion, it becomes clear that, whatever the intrinsic importance of the ethical standards and motivations of the contending camps, what gives the empire-commonwealth alternative its particular relevancy is the fact that (more than a conflict of values or of organizational forms for the interrelation between the United States and the rest of the world) what is at stake is the American social regime itself and, along with that, the question of who will control the American wealth and power, and how.

The problems of the American democracy

Considered in this new light, the cause of the commonwealth would not seem, in principle, to be so hard to promote that it would require a previous ethical revolution in the American society. What is at stake, after all, is the extension of American democracy from the field of private rights, of fair conditions for personal advancement, of welfare services, and of other areas concerning what could be called *democracy of consumption* to the field concerning the formation, use, and control of wealth and power, making it a democracy that could be called *democracy of allocation*. Such a democracy would interest the great majority of the American people, who would obtain an effective voice in what should be done with the resources and means of their society, and who would achieve a much better distribution of its benefits—reinforcing and consolidating their democracy of consumption. This is ultimately what has been, to a large extent, achieved by the Scandinavian democracies and, to a smaller extent, by the British democracy. Why not in the United States?

As occurs so often with the subjects treated in this book, a complete discussion of this question would transcend the limits of this study. It would be extremely interesting, in itself, and instructive for our present inquiry to try to determine

*George McGovern realized what these requirements were and ran for President advocating some of these changes.

why the American democracy has reached a high level of development in what I have called democracy of consumption, directly involving the individual as such and as an identifiable member of small groups, such as family and neighborhood, while it has been much more ritualistic than effective as a democracy of allocations, involving the large organizations and society as a whole, whose control has been subject to an increasing process of oligopolization.[6] This problem involves the patterns of development of the Anglo-American culture, with its contractual individualism and private orientation (which sees organizations as a contractual plurality of subjects rather than, as on the Continent, an emergent new subject of an institutional nature) and involves as well the patterns of development of the socioeconomic organization of American society (in which private corporations perform public roles and have inherently public faculties, contrary to the Continental tendency, where public institutions, besides exclusive obtention of public functions and faculties, also perform private roles). However, it cannot be more than mentioned here.

What has to be considered, here, is just the fact that American party politics has been traditionally concerned with the problems of the democracy of consumption, which has tended to be gradually enlarged, overcoming conservative resistance, while it has been practically unaware of many of the relevant problems concerning the democracy of allocation. In a sense the present crisis of the American party system expresses the fact that the same new forces that are striving for a new ethical outlook are also concerned with a new approach to the questions related to the formation, use, and control of wealth and power—and have come to lose faith in the possibility of orienting either of the two major parties to really care about these problems. To what extent would these forces, if they should become tired of following the dead-ended way of out-of-the-system protests and confrontation (which could only succeed in the unlikely hypothesis of a victorious revolutionary upsurge) take the initiative of creating a distinct political force, compatible with the sociopolitical system but oriented toward its change? To what extent would that new political force, either as a third party or as an influential group—probably within the Democratic party—be able to convince the average middle- and working-class American that he needs a democracy of allocation and might attain it through organized political action?[7]

By the simple enunciation of these questions and the difficult and time-consuming tasks that their attendance would involve, one sees how improbable it is that an influential political force, committed to a commonwealth view of American society, will come to be formed and to play a timely role in the empire-commonwealth alternative.* If, however, one looks at the possibilities presented by a more intelligent and competent approach to the imperial way, in the conditions of the American society and its world situation, currently and in the foreseeable future, one will have to acknowledge that they are incomparably better.

The current imperial crisis

It is important, in that respect, not to overrate, like many analysts, both inside

*McGovern's candidacy, which took place after this book was completed, may eventually introduce, even if he loses, that new political force and tendency in the American political arena.

and particularly outside the United States, the difficulties that the American empire is currently experiencing. These analysts believe that the empire, still in the initial phase of its expansion and structuring, has been mortally wounded, externally, by the heroic resistance of the Vietnamese and by the international consequences, for the American Goliath, of its inability to subdue that Asiatic David. And they think that, domestically, the rebellion of the blacks and of the youth will prevent the indispensable normal operation of the American society, seriously imperiling her social and economic functioning, and directly hindering her military capability, by depriving the officer corps of the necessary cooperation and loyalty from the drafted privates.[8]

There can be no doubt, of course, about the serious external and domestic difficulties, blows, and setbacks that the United States has been experiencing almost continuously, precisely in terms of her imperial career, since the assassination of President Kennedy. I suggest, however, that these problems, contrary to the catastrophic interpretations that see them as accumulating indications of the impending doom of the American empire, are much more in the nature of birth pains than of a death agony, as far as the empire is concerned. Very briefly and reducing that complex matter to its most essential features, I suggest, on the one hand, that the present American problems manifest the insurmountable limitations of the conventional approaches attempted first by the Johnson administration and, currently, by the Nixon administration in dealing with the imperial question. On the other hand, I would contend that the possibility for successfully overcoming those difficulties and many new ones, in terms of the consolidation and expansion of the American empire, can be clearly discerned, analytically as well as empirically, in the analysis of the current events. I will try to discuss this question as briefly as possible, analyzing it around three main points.

The failure of Johnson's approach

The first point concerns the reasons for the failure of Johnson's approach. President Johnson represented the United States, in her current domestic and international situation, as a peace-loving, democratic, anti-imperialist country, interested first in building, domestically, the Great Society and, as much as possible, in generously transferring to the world at large, by consensual ways, its benefits, with the ultimate goal of helping the whole world to become a super Great Society. Given, however, the existence of Soviet duplicity and of forces in the world, vaguely supposed to be supported by Communist China, that were interested in imposing their interests and views, essentially committed to anti-democratic forms of life, through the use of violence, military aggression, and subversive infiltration, the United States, in defense of her legitimate domestic and international interests as well as her desire to help friendly peoples who were more directly menaced by such forms of violence, had to accept the responsibility of a worldwide action to contain and repress those aggressive forces.

As can be easily seen, in view of the preceding discussion, Johnson's picture of the United States' position in the world and the policies that he tried to carry out in terms of that picture were a complete and typical expression of the radical denial of the existence of the imperial fact. That picture and those policies, however, were proposed in conditions in which both the credibility of the basic thesis and the feasibility of ruling and managing the empire without acknowledging it were historically exhausted. The time of exhaustion was the Truman-Eisenhower period. Kennedy had already inaugurated a new and different approach, implying the empire without mentioning its ascriptive and imperial features but taking into account its real needs. That approach stressed the domestic and international benefits that would result from an enlightened, social, and humanist-oriented Pax Americana.

The errors in Johnson's approach might not have cost him the intolerable price he had to pay had it not been for the fact that the extraordinary and historically unparalleled determination of the Vietnamese people not to be incorporated into the American empire made more than a simple frontier police action necessary. As soon as the drainage of American resources, particularly in terms of human lives, reached a socially noticeable level and started to affect, both personally and morally, the students, who constitute the core group of the anti-imperial camp, the demythologization of Johnson's theses and the criticism of, and opposition to, his policies inflicted irreparable damage on them. But this was, essentially, because major political actions cannot be undertaken without a sufficiently convincing ideological support. As soon as discussion of the American position and goals became a serious matter, rather than partisan rhetoric, for large sections of the American people and of the world at large, the manifest ineptitude of Johnson's representation ruined the credibility of his statements.

In spite of all these troubles, however, the Johnson administration still could have succeeded in confronting its challenges if at least Johnson and his aides, and the main leaders supporting him, had had an intelligent and competent understanding of the events for their own use. They seem, however, to have been victims of their own views. To the end they tried to promote the empire and to fight for it as if it did not exist. They attempted, ultimately, to make imperial policies with nationalist means. And so they were necessarily condemned to inescapable failure. If, in fact, the United States had not been that huge imperial system that Johnson pretended it was not, the price for his failure would have been much more serious for the American people.

Nixon's approach

The second point concerns the approach of the Nixon administration to the same crisis. Confronted with the preceding approach, the Nixon administration has, to its advantage, a nondoctrinarian and purely pragmatic position, which gives it much greater flexibility in decisions and maneuvers. To its disadvantage, however, it is guided by an implied view of the world that is still more inaccurate than Johnson's.

President Nixon is not committed to the Great Society and the ideology of its domestic and international implementation. He was elected because of the failure of the implementation of that grand design. He proposed that the American people adopt more modest collective goals and that an expedient way be found to pull the American troops out of Vietnam, letting the Vietnamese take care of their (allegedly) own affairs. He demands only not to be domestically pressed in that withdrawal, so that American interests can be better protected in Vietnam and, as a result of the example, in the rest of the world.

Behind these proposals and the policies for their execution, however, there is, as in the case of Johnson, but in a still more mistaken form, a completely inaccurate view of the United States and of the world. That view, which is currently typical of the Republican party, consists in considering the various societies and the world at large (except where totalitarian communism interferes with human liberty) as the area of action for private business concerns, which in their own interest, competitively and improvingly, meet the material needs of mankind. The role of the state is to provide the necessary legal framework and administrative facilities for such activities, to protect their legitimate interests and to prevent, through certain measures of social or economic character, some undesirable marginal effects of the free-market system, such as recessions or unemployment, and, within limits, to provide welfare services for the poorer sectors of the population.

Seen in that perspective, the world is not the arena for competing societies, some few of which tend to dominate most of the others. The world—with the exception of the Communist countries, subject to totalitarian tyranny—is the arena for competing corporations, for which the democratic states are principally the legal-administrative territorial supervisory agencies. That view, therefore, not only denies the existence of the American empire but, ultimately, does not even categorially admit its possibility. By definition, only Communist states can be imperialists. Confronted with the problems created by the American empire and its Vietnam crisis, the Nixon administration reduces the whole problem to a special relationship between two law-enforcing governments, the American and the Saigon governments. The former, having overcommitted itself essentially to help the latter in its fight against Communist aggression, and having so overtaxed its own resources, particularly in terms of American lives, must now find a morally and materially acceptable way of withdrawing. That way has been found: to gradually transfer the task of law enforcement in South Vietnam to the Saigon government and army, by reinforcing their capabilities through material and technical help and progressively replacing the American soldiers with Saigon's reinforced troops.

It is not the purpose of this brief comment on the views and policies of the Nixon administration to submit them to a general appraisal. Our central interest is in their adequacy in terms of the problems of the American empire. In that respect, the inadequacy of these views and policies is manifest.

It is important to consider, however, that because Nixon's views and policies, which look and are, theoretically, so unsophisticated, are ultimately commanded by a purely pragmatic approach, these views and policies could be completely transformed, in their practice, without giving the administration major trouble. The policy of withdrawal from Vietnam is a good example. As long as the administration really thinks that its purpose of Vietnamization of the war can be achieved by massive supply of materiel to the government of Saigon, the failure of that policy seems to be inevitable. As observed by Liska, Vietnam is a typical frontier action of the empire, which cannot be fought, under any pretext, by anybody except the empire, whatever the nationality of the individual soldiers operating there. Transferring to Saigon the responsibility of fighting that war will inevitably imply either the necessity of continuously reengaging American forces in combat, as in the case of the invasion of Cambodia, or the United States' acceptance of Saigon's ultimate defeat. If, however, "Vietnamization of the war" becomes a cover name for the policy of waging, in the name of Saigon but under direct American command and responsibility, an imperial frontier military action, using—to spare American lives and minimize home protest—non-American mercenary soldiers, who would have to be recruited not only locally but wherever convenient and possible, then the Vietnam issue might (although not necessarily)[9] become quite different. But the involved policy would also be quite different: It would consist, precisely, if implicitly, in recognizing the existence of the American empire and in using imperial means for imperial purposes.

It is now an open question whether or not Nixon's pragmatism will finally lead him (as is likely to occur) to the second form of Vietnamization, in the specific case of Vietnam.[10] Whatever his final decision on that matter may be, the problem of appropriately ruling and managing the American empire cannot be solved, in the long run, by purely pragmatic case-by-case decisions. As has been observed, it is not possible to rule and manage the empire appropriately without, on the one hand, acknowledging its objective existence and problems and, on the other hand, a legitimizing imperial ideology, capable of minimizing resistance, motivating support, and rationalizing the whole system, administratively, legally, and axiologically. In that sense Nixon's approach, at its best, may be an interim solution, which will pragmatically salvage, for a relatively short time, the basic interests of the empire. At its worst, confronted with such critical issues as Vietnam, it will have to either stick to the imperial purpose, resuming and increasing massive American involvement—with an ideological justification still less credible and motivating than Johnson's—or give up Vietnam, without harvesting the benefits of a deliberate commonwealth policy.

Enlightened populist imperialism

The third and last point I would like to present, also in a very brief form, concerns the fact that the essential inadequacy of both Johnson's and Nixon's approaches to the imperial question does not mean that that question is insoluble. As I have suggested, the consolidation and expansion of the American empire can be, analytically as well as empirically, clearly discerned in the analysis of the current events. And it is for that reason that the imperial solution (independent of one's evaluation of it and of its alternative possibility, the international communitarian commonwealth) is the one that actually tends to prevail.

Ultimately, as can be deduced from the preceding discussion, a rational option for the empire must conciliate the relevant interests of the most important sectors of the American society with the imperial solution, in conditions ethically inspiring, or at least acceptable, for most of the involved sectors; and, at the same time, that solution must optimize the use and management of the imperial resources. The way to achieve these results is to adopt an enlightened approach to *populist imperialism*. This is, in the last analysis, the way in which Caesar, who was confronted with similar problems in the Roman Republic, gave a lasting solution to them. Although populist imperialism was the model for ruling the Roman Empire up to Diocletian, the enlightened approach to that model and the wise management of imperial affairs was the distinct trait of the great emperors from Augustus to Marcus Aurelius.

Considered as a model of empire, the essence of populist imperialism consists in conciliating the democracy of consumption with the oligarchy of allocation, within the ethical framework of a humanist, paternalist, and welfare-oriented ethic of duty. In the case of the Roman Empire from the Punic Wars to the reign of the Antonines, that conciliation was achieved in two successive different ways. The first, from the end of third century B.C. to Caesar, involved a policy of external plundering, through which the wealth and power of the Roman ruling class increased immensely, while, at the same time, various consumption facilities (*panem et circenses*) were gradually extended to the plebe. After the exhaustion of the dependent areas (by such practices as Cicero's speech against Verres illustrates) made plundering less profitable, the second way was adopted. That way, from Caesar's time onward, consisted in a transfer of emphasis from crude appropriation to the efficient use and management of the provincial resources, in a process that required the centralized administration of the imperial system, under the supervision of the emperors.

For the American society an enlightened populist imperialism, in the conditions of the contemporary world, would essentially imply, both domestically and internationally, a more social orientation, under central planning and supervision, of the large American-controlled multinational corporation. That arrangement would preserve and enhance the power of the American oligarchy and, at the same time, provide the American masses and the middle classes of the provinces of the empire with the benefits of an expanding democracy of consumption. That design, in several of its fundamental aspects was already understood and sketched by John F. Kennedy, whose New Frontier conception was nothing else than an American empire of the West, under enlightened American control, militarily invulnerable to external aggression, ruled by a meritocratic oligarchy for the benefit of the American masses and, as soon as feasible, of the "Romanized" sectors of the provinces. In ethical terms populist imperialism may also provide the possibility of conciliating the discipline and effectiveness of an ethic of duty with the meaningful content of the values of a socially oriented humanism, in a sort of contemporary neo-Stoicism.[11]

Populist imperialism, as an ideal type, either in its original Caesarean conception (more ecumenical and cosmopolitan), in its Octavian implementation (more Mediterranean and Roman-centered), or otherwise in its possible contemporary American modalities (likely to be of Octavian style), tends to supersede, in practical terms, the class struggle in the metropolitan areas, by creating new conditions for interclass solidarity. This is particularly true for its contemporary form, which is based on technology instead of on slavery, and therefore excludes crude plundering from the beginning, and will tend to move very quickly toward the stage of global scientific management of the empire's resources.[12] With populist imperialism, the oligarchy loses its former "Republican" or "pre-Caesarean" uncontrolled expansiveness and becomes disciplined through central planning and supervision, but, in exchange, gets stability and legitimacy in all the areas of the empire. The metropolitan mass, in exchange for its practical marginalization from nonlocal politics and loss of former greater bargaining power for collective labor contracts, receives ever-increasing private benefits, such as increasing salaries, fewer working hours, more leisure, along with improved facilities for social promotion through education or through the empire's voluntary military service. The middle class, in both the metropolitan and the Romanized sectors of the provinces, in exchange for its former actual or pretended political freedom and partisan activities, obtains access for far-reaching careers in a huge worldwide civil and military technocratic bureaucracy. As was advanced in Chapter 18, only the large but defenseless unskilled masses of the provinces, given the empire's excessive availability of, and little need for, unqualified labor, will tend to have much more to lose than to gain with populist imperialism, and even they will have a means of escape and ascent in the imperial military service.

This last aspect of the model of populist imperialism, the empire's military service, deserves a little more attention. As was formerly seen, protest against increased drafting, for the fighting of imperial frontier police actions unconvincingly disguised as patriotic wars, was a major cause of the failure of Johnson's approach and is currently haunting the schemes of the Nixon administration. The imperial alternative, particularly in its populist modality, provides a practical solution to that problem. Compulsory military mobilization of citizens is likely to be reduced to certain emergencies involving interimperial confrontations. Most of the current military service and practically all its extrametropolitan and frontier activities would be carried out by a body of professional career officers, commanding mercenary volunteers from the provinces and the poorer strata of the population of the empire.

Concluding this analysis of the principal domestic and international tendencies of the American society, we can acknowledge that, except in the improbable case that the current ethico-cultural crisis brings about changes of a deep and general character in the prevailing American motivations, the ongoing trend toward the imperial alternative may come to consolidate and to expand. That result is not likely to exclude ethical and political forms of internal opposition to the acceptance of the imperial option by the American society, particularly in the earlier phase of deliberate imperial rule and management. But once again, if one looks to history in order to draw, from former examples, some applicable guidelines for contemporary analogous processes, one has to acknowledge that ethical and political domestic opposition to empires that were successfully formed and consolidated rapidly vanished, as opposition became futile and the concerned events became irreversible. In exchange, however, anti-imperialist radical and liberal forces, confronted with that irreversibility, tend to shift their struggle from opposition to the imperial condition to active propaganda and support of liberal rules and enlightened management of the empire. This is likely to occur with the present American anti-imperialist liberals and, to a great extent, with the radicals.

CONCLUDING REMARKS

At this final stage of our comparative analysis of trends and alternatives in Latin America and the United States, it seems possible, with the constantly reiterated caution required by historical forecasts, to present some concluding remarks.

Ultimately, as we have seen, the progressive reformist way of the Chilean-Venezuelan experiments (probably restricted to these two countries) as well as the radical military way of the Peruvian experiment (likely to be followed, in their own conditions, by Brazil and Argentina, Ecuador and Colombia) may possibly lead Latin America, or some of its key countries, to reorient their tendency and to make a deliberate option in favor of the alternative of autonomy. The United States, currently following a still predominantly undeliberate imperial course, confronted with the necessity of making an articulate option between empire or commonwealth (in conditions in which not choosing involves the worst possible way of proceeding in the imperial alternative) is likely to find the form for consolidating and expanding its present way in the model of populist imperialism.

Various possible consequences may result from the interaction of these two opposing propensities. If we assume that the present American-Soviet equilibrium of mutual deterrence will continue, keeping the Soviets from trying to interfere substantially, then it seems that, of the many conditions that will affect the outcome of these opposing tendencies, the results will be particularly determined by the way in which the two tendencies come to be expressed and managed in the circumstances then prevailing. Such circumstances, although involving many different elements, will tend to be primarily affected, at any given moment, by three main variables: (1) the extent and intensity of American control over the rest of the areas under her influence and, in consequence, the marginal importance of control over Latin America, (2) the domestic conditions in the United States, including such aspects as the estimated importance given by government and other influential agencies to the conservation of control over Latin America as well as the estimated facilities for, and risks involved in, the process, and, in consequence, the greater or smaller extent and intensity of American resolve to preserve that control, and (3) the conditions prevailing in Latin America, including such aspects as the greater or smaller extent and intensity of determination of the concerned governments and other agencies to preserve their autonomy, as well as their estimates of the facilities for, and risks involved in, the process. As is obvious, the greater or smaller extent and intensity of the resolve of each of the two parties at a given moment will vary according to these circumstances.

There are two orders of considerations which are particularly relevant, concerning the way in which the two tendencies may come to be expressed and managed. The first concerns the way in which Latin American policies of autonomy may have been conceived. If these policies make appropriate differentiation between American business and American defense interests, and give basic attendance to the latter, eliminating or compensating possible American fears of reinforcement from the Soviet (in the future also Chinese) camp, business interests may be submitted to rational discipline by legitimate Latin American interests. Even so, however, conflict may not be avoided if the circumstances should contribute to a very aggressive American stand. The second order of considerations concerns the way in which American imperial policies may have been conceived. If these policies are to contain the Latin American position by the menace of severe punishment without any flexibility, and the circumstances drive the Latin Americans to a hard stand, conflict may also become unavoidable.

A situation of conflict in which the Latin American governments would be driven to become irreversibly involved would tend to generate wide and strong mass support in Latin America, with the tendency to convert formerly progressive or radical movements into revolutionary ones, liberating unlimited social energies for the struggle. Latin American revolutionary sectors would try their best to lead the events to that point. Conversely, cautious policies on the part of the United States would tend to induce cautious moves in Latin America also and to contribute to patent or latent divisions of opinions in the ruling groups and circles, reducing the effective strength of the concerned governments and countries.

Ultimately, it can be said that, in the present and foreseeable future, the best possible interrelation between the American and the Latin American societies— if the alternative of an international communitarian commonwealth does not come (as it probably will not) to prevail—is an enlightened rule and management by the United States of her imperium, giving possibilities for enlightened forms of radical or progressive reformism in Latin America, along the lines formerly discussed. The economic, technological, and military advantages already accumulated by the United States, vis-à-vis Latin America, are of such a nature that, even within the framework of an empire, the autonomous development of Latin America—after a period of difficulties of about three decades—would be a factor for the future substantial improvement, including all sorts of benefits, in the relations between the two areas. Moreover, given the present general primacy of the United States and the fact that the most successful level that Latin America could achieve, in the three next decades, would be one of simple international autonomy, the relative strength of the former would remain untouched.

Conversely, once a real process for achieving autonomous development has effectively started in strategic Latin American countries, aggressive attempts by the United States to prevent that development—although effective with current satellite governments—would probably convert reformist movements into revolutionary ones rather than compel them to withdraw and return to the status quo of well-accepted satellitism. In that case, Ernesto Che Guevara's strategy of the multiple Vietnams would create the greatest challenge to the American empire, only soluble by withdrawal or by unimaginable genocidal methods.

NOTES

[1] That shift of tendency, however, has been associated, as formerly mentioned, with the incorporation of several nationalist features, substantially reducing the "colonial" traits of the model and correspondingly enhancing its viability.

[2] On this theme see Paul Tillich (1957). See also his (1967, particularly vol. 3, Part 4).

[3] See T. Roszak (1969).

[4] Concerning the meaning of what a society is and how distinctive societies differ from each other, see Chapter 2.

[5] The modern form of the British Commonwealth is a good example of a successful egalitarian international organization of societies and peoples of the most diverse levels of power and development. In that case, however, the common interests ruled and managed by the organization are rather limited and of restricted relevance.

[6] As was discussed in Chapter 3, Mitchel has given undue extension to his law of power oligopolization, because of his confusion between the pyramidal structure of authority and the accountability of power. Democracy of allocation, therefore, is neither analytically incompatible with the elite, subelite, mass functional articulation of the social system nor empirically inviable, as shown by the examples of classic antiquity and modern Scandinavian democracy.

[7] See Barrington Moore (1970).

[8] In addition to the pertinent literature discussed or mentioned in Chapter 18, see, on the subject, such typical European analyses as Ernest Mandel's (1970). For a more economic view of the internal crisis of the imperial system see Pierre Jalée (1969).

[9] If North Vietnamese resources become exhausted, Chinese "volunteers" are likely to intervene to continue a war of attrition indefinitely.

[10] The massive bombing of North Vietnam and mining of its ports, in May 1972, as a means to save Saigon from imminent military defeat, was a decisive indication of such pragmatic views.

[11] On this subject see the initial part of Chapter 18. See also the discussion of Kahn's (1967, chap. 4) "psychological classes."

[12] Exclusion of crude plundering does not exclude its less crude forms, such as terms-of-trade advantages and the appropriation of natural resources, as shown by current conditions in the third world. Moreover, global scientific management, as a rational potential propensity of the empire, cannot be generalized in the empire's current "Republican" stage and requires the previous building of centralized imperial power, that is, the "Caesarean" revolution toward imperial authority.

Bibliography

Adams, J. T.
   1921   *The Founding of New England*. Boston: Little, Brown.
Aguilar Monteverde, Alonso
   1967   *Teoría y Política del Desarrollo Latinoamericano*. Mexico City: Univ. Aut. de Mexico.
Ahumada, Jorge
   1966   *La Crisis Integral de Chile*. Santiago: Edit. Universitaria.
   1967   *En Vez de la Miseria*. 6th ed. Santiago: Edit. del Pacifico; first published, 1958.
Allen, G. C.
   1951   *A Short Economic History of Modern Japan: 1867-1937*. London: Allen & Unwin.
Allen, J. W.
   1960   *A History of Political Thought in the Sixteenth Century*. New York: Barnes & Noble; first published, London: Methuen, 1928.
Almond, Gabriel
   1965   with Sidney Verba. *Civic Culture*. Boston: Little, Brown; first published, Princeton, N.J.: Princeton University Press, 1963.
   1966   with G. Bingham Powell, Jr. *Comparative Politics—A Development Approach*. Boston: Little, Brown.
Alstyne, Richard Van
   1965   *The Rising American Empire*. Chicago: Quadrangle Books; first published, 1960.
Althusser, Louis
   1967   *Pour Marx*. Paris: Maspero.
   1969a   *Lénine et la Philosophie*. Paris: Maspero.
   1969b   *Lire le Capital*. 2 vols. Paris: Maspero.
Amin, Samir
   1970   *L'Accumulation à l'Échelle Mondiale*. Paris: Anthropos.
   1971   *L'Afrique de L'Ouest Bloquée—Economie Politique de la Colonisation: 1880-1920*. Paris: Ed. de Minuit.
Apter, David E.
   1963   *Ghana in Transition*. New York: Atheneum; first published, Princeton, N.J.: Princeton University Press, 1955.
   1964   Ed., *Ideology and Discontent*. New York: Free Press.
   1965   *The Politics of Modernization*. Chicago: University of Chicago Press.
Arendt, Hannah
   1959   *The Human Condition*. New York: Anchor Books; first published, Chicago: University of Chicago Press, 1958.

1963 *On Revolution.* New York: Viking Press.

1968a *Between Past and Future.* Cleveland: Meridian Books; 5th print., first published, 1954.

1968b *The Origins of Totalitarianism.* 2nd enlarg. ed. Cleveland: Meridian Books, 12th print.; first published, 1951.

Aristotle

1823 *La Morale et la Politique.* Text established and translated by M. Thurot. 2 vols. Paris: Firmin-Didot.

1968 *The Basic Works of Aristotle.* Edited by Richard McKeen. New York: Random House.

Aron, Raymond

1948 *Introduction à la Philosophie de l'Histoire.* Paris: Gallimard.

1950 "Social Structure and the Ruling Class." *Journal of Sociology* 1: 1–16.

1961 Ed. *L'Histoire et ses Interprétations—Entretiens autour de* Arnold Toynbee. The Hague: Mouton.

1963 Ed. *World Technology and Human Destiny.* Ann Arbor: University of Michigan Press.

1965a *Dimensions de la Conscience Historique.* Paris: Union Gen. d'Edit.; first published, 1938.

1965b *Essai sur les Libertés.* Paris: Calman-Lévy.

1966 *Trois Essais sur l'Age Industriel.* Paris: Plon.

1969 *Les Désillusions du Progrès—Essai sur la Dialectique de la Modernité.* Enlarged text. Paris: Calmann-Lévy; first written for *The Encyclopaedia Britannica,* 1964–1965.

Ashley, Maurice

1958 *Oliver Cromwell and The Puritain Revolution.* London: English University Press.

1962 *Financial and Commercial Policy Under the Cromwellian Protectorate.* 2nd ed. London: English University Press.

Aujac, H.

1949 "Les Modèles Mathématiques Macrodynamiques et le Cycle." *Economie Appliquée* 2: 496–592.

Axelos, Kostas

1961 *Marx, Penseur de la Téchnique: l'Aliénation de l'Homme à la Conquête du Monde.* Paris: Ed. de Minuit.

Bachrach, Peter

1967 *The Theory of Democratic Elitism.* Boston: Little, Brown.

Bagby, Philip

1963 *Culture and History.* Berkeley: University of California Press, 2nd print.; first published, London: Longmans, Green, 1958.

Bagu, Sergio

1949 *Economia de la Sociedad Colonial.* Buenos Aires: El Ateneu.

1961 *La Realidad Argentina en el Siglo XX.* Mexico City: Fondo de Cultura Económica.

1970 *Tiempo, Realidad Social y Conocimiento.* Mexico City: Siglo XXI.

Baran, Paul

1957 *The Political Economy of Growth.* New York: Monthly Review Press.

1961 "The Commitment of the Intellectual." *Monthly Review* 13.

1966 with Paul M. Sweezy. *Monopoly Capital.* New York: Monthly Review Press.

Barber, Bernard

1957 *Social Stratification.* New York: Harcourt, Brace & Co.

Barber, Willard F. and C. Neale Ronning

1966 *Internal Security and Military Power.* Columbus: Ohio State University Press.

Barghoorn, Frederick

1966 *Politics in the USSR.* Boston: Little, Brown.

Barker, Sir Ernest

1946 Tr. and ed. *The Politics of Aristotle.* New York: Oxford University Press, 9th print; first published, London.

1952 *Greek Political Theory—Plato and His Predecessors.* 4th ed. London: Methuen, reprint; first published, 1918.

1961   *Social and Political Thought in Byzantium.* London: Oxford University Press;
        first published, 1957.
Barr, Stringfellow
    1961   *The Will of Zeus.* New York: Dell.
    1966   *The Mask of Jove.* Philadelphia: J. B. Lippincott.
    1967   "Consulting the Romans." Santa Barbara, Calif. The Center for the Study of
            Democratic Institutions. Occasional paper.
Barraclough, Geoffrey
    1955   *History in a Changing World.* Norman: University of Oklahoma Press.
    1967   *An Introduction to Contemporary History.* Baltimore: Penguin Books; first
            published, 1964.
Bartoli, Henri
    1950   *La Doctrine Économique et Sociale de Karl Marx.* Paris: Ed. du Seuil.
Bastide, Roger
    1962   Ed. *Sens et Usages du Terme Structure dans les Sciences Humaines et Sociales.*
            The Hague: Mouton.
Bauer, Wilhelm
    1957   *Introducción al Estudio de la Historia.* 3rd ed. Barcelona: Casa Edit. Bosch.
Baykov, A.
    1948   *Historia de la Economía Soviética.* Mexico City: Fondo de Cultura Económica;
            English original, *The Development of the Soviet Economic System.* London:
            Cambridge University Press, 1946.
Beaujouan, Guy
    1961   "Le Temps Historique." In *L'Histoire et ses Méthodes,* edited by Charles
            Samaran, pp. 52–67. *Encyclopédie de la Pléiade,* Paris: Gallimard.
Beckmann, George M.
    1962   *The Modernization of China and Japan.* New York: Harper & Row.
    1964   "Economic and Political Modernization—Japan." In *Political Modernization
            of Japan and Turkey,* edited by Robert E. Ward and Dankwart E. Rustow.
            Studies in Political Development, vol. 3. Princeton, N.J.: Princeton University
            Press.
Bell, Daniel
    1962   *The End of Ideology.* Rev. ed. New York: Collier Books; first published, New
            York: Free Press, 1960.
    1967   Ed. *Toward the Year 2000.* New York: Macmillan.
Bellah, Robert N.
    1965   Ed. *Religion and Progress in Modern Asia.* New York: Free Press.
Bendix, Reinhard
    1962   *Max Weber, An Intellectual Portrait.* New York: Doubleday.
    1964   *Nation-Building and Citizenship.* New York: John Wiley.
Benoist-Méchin
    1954   *Le Loup et le Léopard: Mustapha Kémal.* Paris: Ed. Albin Michel.
Berdyaev, Nicholas
    1968   *The Meaning of History.* Cleveland: Meridian Books; first English translation,
            London: Geoffrey Bles, 1936.
Bernstein, Eduard
    1963   *Evolutionary Socialism.* New York: Schocken Books; German original, *Die
            Voraussetzungen des Sozialismus und die Aufgaben der Sozialdemokratie.*
            Stuttgart: J. H. W. Dietz, 1899.
Bettelheim, Charles
    1970   *Planification et Croissance Accélérée.* Paris: Maspero; first published,
            1964.
Bhagwati, Jagdish
    1966   *The Economics of Underdeveloped Countries.* New York: McGraw-Hill.
Bianchi, Andrés
    1969   *et al. América Latina: Ensayos de Interpretación Económica.* Santiago: Edit.
            Universitaria.
Black, Cyril E.
    1968   "A Comparative View." In *Prospects for Soviet Society,* edited by Allen Kassof,
            pp. 3–13. New York: Praeger.

Bonilla, Frank
    1967   with José A. Silva Michelena. *The Politics of Change in Venezuela.* vol. 1,
                A Strategy for Research on Social Policy. Cambridge, Mass.: M.I.T. Press.
    1970   *The Politics of Change in Venezuela.* vol. 2, *The Failure of Elites.* Cambridge,
                Mass.: M.I.T. Press.
Bottomore, T. B.
    1964   *Elites and Society.* London: C. A. Watts.
    1966   *Classes in Modern Society.* New York: Vintage Books; first published, London:
                Allen & Unwin, 1965.
Boudon, Raymond
    1967   *L'Analyse Mathématique des Faits Sociaux.* Paris: Plon.
Bowden, Witt; Karpovich, Michael; and Usher, Abbot Payson
    1937   *An Economic History of Europe Since 1750.* New York: American Book.
Brandt, William J.
    1966   *The Shape of Medieval History—Studies in Modes of Perception.* New Haven,
                Conn.: Yale University Press.
Bresser Pereira, L. C.
    1968   *Desenvolvimento e Crise no Brasil: 1930-1967.* Rio de Janeiro: Zahar Edit.
Bridgham, Philip, and Vogel, Ezra F.
    1968   *La Revolución Cultural de Mao Tse Tung.* Buenos Aires: Paidos; English origi-
                nal, P. Bridgham, "Mao's Cultural Revolution," and E. Vogel, "From Revolution-
                ary to Semi-Bureaucrat." *The China Quarterly* (1967).
Brinton, Crane
    1965   *The Anatomy of Revolution.* Rev. and expanded. New York: Vintage Books;
                first published, Prentice-Hall, 1938.
Brockelmann, Carl
    1960   *History of the Islamic Peoples.* New York: Capricorn Books, 3rd print., first
                published, 1944; German original, *Geschichte der Islamischen Völker und
                Staaten.* Munich: R. Oldenbourg, 1939.
Brodbeck, May
    1959   "Models, Meaning and Theories." In *Symposium on Sociological Theory,* edited
                by Llewellyn Gross, pp. 373-406. New York: Harper & Row.
Brzezinski, Zbigniew
    1967   "Address to the Foreign Service Association." *U.S. Department of State
                Bulletin,* July 3.
Bühler, Johannes
    1946   *Vida y Cultura en la Edad Media.* Mexico City: Fondo de Cultura Económica;
                German original, 1931.
Bury, J. B.
    1944   *A History of Greece.* New York: Random House; first published, 1900.
    1955   *The Idea of Progress.* New York: Dover Publications; first published, 1932.

Calder, Nigel
    1965   Ed. *The World in 1984.* Baltimore: Penguin Books.
Cardenas, Gonzalo
    1969   with Angel Cairo, Pedro Geltman, Ernesto Goldar, Alejandro A. Peyron, and
                Ernesto F. Villannova. *El Peronismo.* Buenos Aires: Edit. Carlos Pérez.
Cardoso, Fernando Henrique
    1964   *Empresário Industrial e Desenvolvimento Econômico no Brasil.* São Paulo:
                Difusão Europ. do Livro.
    1969   *Mudanças Sociais na América Latina.* São Paulo: Difusão Europ. do Livro.
Carmona, Fernando
    1970   with Guillermo Montaño, Jorge Carrion, and Alonso Aguillar, M. *El Milagro
                Mexicano.* Mexico City: Edit. Nuestro Tiempo.
Carr, Edward Hallett
    1945   *Nationalism and After.* New York: Macmillan.
    1946   *The Twenty Years' Crisis, 1919-1939—An Introduction to the Study of*

International Relations. New York: Harper Torchbooks; first published, London: Macmillan, 1939.

1950   *Studies in Revolution.* London: Macmillan.
1951   *The New Society.* London: Macmillan.
1951–1954   *A History of Soviet Russia.* 4 vols. London: Macmillan.
1963   *What Is History?* New York: Knopf, 4th print.; first published, 1962.

Carrera Damas, Germán
1968   *Temas de Historia Social y de las Ideas.* Caracas: Universitaria Central de Venezuela.

Carson, Rachel
1962   *Silent Spring.* Boston: Houghton Mifflin.

Cassirer, Ernst
1943   *Filosofía de la Ilustración.* Mexico City: Fondo de Cultura Económica; German original, *Die Philosophie der Aufklärung.* Tübingen: Mohr, 1932.
1946   *Language and Myth.* New York: Harper & Brothers; German original, *Sprache und Mythos.* Leipzig: B. G. Teubner, 1925.
1948   *Kant—Vida y Doctrina.* Mexico City: Fondo de Cultura Económica; German original, *Kants Leben und Lehre.* Berlin: Bruno Cassirer, 1918.
1951   *Individuo y Cosmos en la Filosofía del Renacimiento.* Buenos Aires: Edit. Emece; German original, *Individuum und Kosmos in der Philosophie der Renaissance.* Leipzig: B. G. Teubner, 1927.
1953a   *Substance and Function.* New York: Dover Publications, 1953; German original, *Substanzbegriff und Funkionsbegriff.* Berlin: Bruno Cassirer, 1910.
1953b   *Einstein's Theory of Relativity.* English translation appears in Cassirer, *Substance and Function*; German original, *Zur Einsteinschen Relativitätstheorie.* Berlin: Bruno Cassirer, 1921.
1953–1956   *El Problema del Conocimiento en la Filosofía y en la Ciencia Moderna.* 2 vols. Mexico City: Fondo de Cultura Económica; German original, *Das Erkenntnisproblem in der Philosophie und Wissenschaft der Neueren Zeit.* 2 vols. Berlin: Bruno Cassirer, 1906–1907 (3rd vol. published posthumously).
1953–1957   *The Philosophy of Symbolic Forms.* 3 vols. New Haven, Conn.: Yale University Press; German original, *Philosophie der Symbolischen Formen.* 3 vols. Berlin: Bruno Cassirer, 1923–1929.
1963   *The Question of Jean-Jacques Rousseau.* Bloomington: Indiana University Press; German original, "Das Problem J. J. Rousseau." *Archiv für Geschichte der Philosophie* 41 (1932): 177–213, 479–513.
1966a   *An Essay on Man.* New Haven, Conn.: Yale University Press; first published, 1944.
1966b   *Determinism and Indeterminism in Modern Physics.* New Haven, Conn.: Yale University Press, 2nd print.; first published, 1956; German original, *Determinismus und Indeterminismus in der Modernen Physik*, Part. 3, vol. 42, *Götesborgs Hügskolas Arsskriff*, Göteborg, 1936.
1966c   *The Logic of the Humanities.* New Haven, Conn.: Yale University Press, 2nd print; first published, 1960; German original, *Zur Logik der Kulturwissenschaften, Göteborg Högskolas Arsskrift*, vol. 47, Göteborg, 1942.

Posthumous Publications
1945   *Rousseau, Kant and Goethe.* Princeton, N.J.: Princeton University Press; Harper Torchbook edition, 1963.
1946   *The Myth of the State.* New Haven, Conn.: Yale University Press.
1948   *Das Erkenntnisproblem in der Philosophie und Wissenschaft der Neueren Zeit: von Hegels Tode bis zur Gegenwart (1832–1932)*; Spanish translation, *El Problema del Concimiento en la Filosofia y en la Ciencia Modernas—De la Muerte de Hegel a Nuestros Dias (1832–1932).* Mexico City: Fondo de Cultura Económica, 1948.

Catherine, Robert, and Grousset, Pierre
1965   *L'Etat et L'Essor Industriel.* Paris: Berger-Levrault.

Ceceña, José Luis
1970   *México en la Orbita Imperial.* Mexico City: E. El Cabalito.

Centre International de Synthèse
1957   *Notion de Structure et Structure de la Connaissance.* Paris: Albin Michel.

CEPAL (Comisión Económica para América Latina; also ECLA, Economic Commission for Latin America)

    1963a *El Desarrollo de América Latina en la Posguerra* (E/CN.12/659).

    1963b *Toward a Dynamic Development Policy for Latin America* (E/CN.12/680).

    1964   *Estudio Económico de América Latina 1963* (E/CN.12/696).

    1969a *Estudio Económico de América Latina, 1968. Primera Parte: Algunos Aspectos de la Economía Latinoamericana Hacia Fines de la Decada 60* (E/CN.12/825).

    1969b *El Segundo Decenio de las Naciones Unidas para el Desarrollo: Aspectos Basicos de la Estrategia del Desarrollo de América Latina* (E/CN.12/836).

Charques, R. D.

    1956   *A Short History of Russia.* New York: Dutton.

Chase, Stuart

    1968   *The Most Probable World.* Baltimore: Penguin Books.

Chavez, Fermin

    1965   *Civilización y Barbarie en la Historia de la Cultura Argentina.* Buenos Aires: Edit. Theoria.

Che Guevara, Ernesto

    1964   *Guerrilla Warfare: A Method.* Peking: Foreign Languages Press; Spanish original published in *Cuba Socialista,* no. 25 (September 1963).

    1968   *Venceremos!—The Speeches and Writings of Ernesto Che Guevara.* Edited by John Gerassi. New York: Clarion Books.

Childe, V. Gordon

    1951   *Man Makes Himself.* New York: Mentor Books, 11th print.; first published in England, 1936.

    1953   *Social Evolution.* Cleveland: Meridian Books; first published, London: C. A. Watts, 1951.

    1957   *The Dawn of European Civilization.* 6th ed., rev. New York: Vintage Books; first published, 1925.

    1964   *What Happened in History.* Baltimore: Penguin Books; first published, 1942.

    1969   *New Light on the Most Ancient East.* New York: Norton; first published as *The Most Ancient East,* 1928, rewritten in 1952.

Ciria, Alberto

    1968   *Partidos y Poder en la Argentina Moderna: 1930-1946.* 2nd ed., rev. Buenos Aires: Jorge Alvarez, Edit.; first published, 1964.

    1969   *La Decada Infame.* Buenos Aires: Carlos Pérez Edit.

Clapham, J. H.

    1966   *Economic Development of France and Germany: 1815-1914.* Cambridge, Eng.: Cambridge University Press.

Clarke, Arthur C.

    1964   *Profiles of the Future.* New York: Bantam Books; first published, 1958.

Clough, Shepard B.

    1967   *The Rise and Fall of Civilization.* New York: Columbia University Press, 4th print.; first published, New York: McGraw-Hill, 1951.

    1968   *European Economic History: The Economic Development of Western Civilization.* 2nd ed. New York: McGraw-Hill; first published as *The Economic Development of Western Civilization,* 1959.

Cochrane, Charles Norris

    1949   *Christianity and Classical Culture.* London: Oxford University Press; Spanish translation, *Christianismo y Cultura Clásica.* Mexico City: Fondo de Cultura Económica.

Cole, La Mont C.

    1968   "Can the World Be Saved?" *New York Times Magazine,* March 31, pp. 35 ff.

Cole, Margaret

    1964   *The Story of Fabian Socialism.* New York: John Wiley; first published, Stanford, Calif.: Stanford University Press, 1961.

Coleman, James S.

    1965   Ed. *Education and Political Development.* Studies in Political Development, vol. 4. Princeton, N.J.: Princeton University Press.

Collingwood, R. G.
  1944   *The New Leviathan—Or Man, Society, Civilization and Barbarism.* London: Oxford University Press; first published, 1942.
  1965   *Essays in the Philosophy of History.* Selection of essays published in the 1920s, edited by W. Debbins. New York: McGraw-Hill.
  Posthumous Publications
  1946   *The Idea of History.* London: Oxford University Press; written in 1936.
  1950   *Idea de la Naturaleza.* Mexico City: Fondo de Cultura Económica; English original, *The Idea of Nature.* Written in 1924; first published: London: Oxford University Press, 1945.
Commoner, Barry
  1966   *Science and Survival.* New York: Viking Press; 7th print.; first published, 1961.
  1970   Interview in *Time*, February 2, pp. 52 ff.
Cooley, Charles
  1909   *Social Organization.* New York.
Corbisier, Roland
  1950   *Consciencia e Nação.* São Paulo: Colégio.
  1952   "Situação e Problemas da Pedagogia." *Revista Brasileira de Filosofia* 2: 219–235.
  1960   *Brasília e o Desenvolvimento Nacional.* Rio de Janeiro: ISEB.
  1968   *Reforma ou Revolução?* Rio de Janeiro: Edit. Civilização Brasileira.
Cordoliani, Alfred
  1961   "Comput, Chronologie, Calendriers." In *L'Histoire et ses Méthodes*, edited by Charles Samaran, pp. 37–51. *Encyclopédie de la Pléiade*, Paris: Gallimard.
Coser, Lewis A., and Rosenberg, Bernard
  1964   Eds. *Sociological Theory.* A book of readings. New York: Macmillan.
Coser, Lewis A.
  1966   *The Functions of Social Conflict.* New York: Free Press; 3rd print.; first published, 1956.
Costa Pinto, L. A.
  1963   *Sociologia e Desenvolvimento.* Rio de Janeiro: Edit. Civilização Brasileira.
Cotler, Julio
  1969   "El Populismo Militar como Modelo de Desarrollo Nacional: El Caso Peruano." Mimeographed. Rio de Janeiro: IUPERJ.
Coswell, F. R.
  1952   *History, Civilization and Culture—An Introduction to the Historical and Social Philosophy of Pitirim Sorokin.* London: Thame & Hudson.
Curtis, Perry
  1964   with George H. Nadel, eds. *Imperialism and Colonialism.* New York: Macmillan.

Dahl, Robert A.
  1963   *Modern Political Analysis.* Foundations of Modern Political Science Series. Englewood Cliffs, N.J.: Prentice-Hall, 11th print.
  1964   *A Preface to Democratic Theory.* Chicago: Phoenix Books; 6th print.; first published, 1956.
Dahrendorf, Ralf
  1965   *Class and Class Conflict in Industrial Society.* Stanford, Calif.: Stanford University Press; original English edition published, 1959; German original, *Klasse und Klassenkonflict in der industriellen Gesellschaft*, 1957.
  1969   *Homo Sociologicus.* Rio de Janeiro: Tempo Brasileiro; German original, "Homo Sociologiens: Versuch zur Geschichte, Bedentung und Kritik der Kategorie der Sozialen Rolle." In *Pfade aus Utopia—Arbeiten zur Theorie und Methode der Soziologie*, Munich: R. Piper Verlag, 1969.
Davis, Kingsley
  1949   *Human Society.* New York: Macmillan.
Dawson, Christopher
  1958   *Religion and the Rise of Western Culture.* New York: Doubleday.

1960   *The Making of Europe.* Cleveland: Meridian Books, 8th print.; first published, New York: Sheed and Ward, 1932.

1962   *The Dynamics of World History.* New York: New American Library; first published, New York: Sheed and Ward, 1956.

De Bach, P.
1969   *Biological Control of Insects, Pests and Weeds.* New York: Reinhold.

Debray, Regis
1967   *Revolución en la Revolución?* Havana: Casa.

Debrun, Michel
1959   *Ideología e Realidade.* Rio de Janeiro: ISEB.

1964   "Nationalisme et Politiques du Développement au Brésil." *Sociologie du Travail,* no. 3 (July-September), pp. 235-278 and no. 4 (October-December), pp. 351-380.

de Closets, François
1970   *En Danger de Progrès.* Paris: Ed. Denoël.

de Riencourt, Amaury
1968   *The American Empire.* New York: Dial Press.

de Tocqueville, Alexis
1951   *De la Démocratie en Amérique.* 2 vols. Paris: M. T. Genin; original French edition in 4 vols. published by Gosselin, 1835-1840.

1953   *L'Ancien Régime et la Révolution.* 10th ed. Paris: Gallimard; first published by Michel Lévy, 1856-1863, 2 vols. published with posthumous notes; English translation, *The Old Regime and the Revolution.* New York: Doubleday, 1955.

Deutsch, Karl W.
1961   "Social Mobilization and Political Development." *American Political Science Review* 55: 493-514.

1963   *The Nerves of Government.* New York: Free Press.

1966   *Nationalism and Social Communication.* 2nd ed. Cambridge, Mass.: M.I.T. Press; first published, 1953.

1968   *The Analysis of International Relations.* Foundations of Modern Political Science Series. Englewood Cliffs, N.J.: Prentice-Hall.

1970   *Politics and Government.* Boston: Houghton Mifflin.

Deutscher, Isaac
1960   *Stalin—A Political Biography.* New York: Vintage Books; first published, 1949.

1965a   *The Prophet Armed—Trotsky: 1879-1921.* vol. 1. New York: Vintage Books; first published, 1954.

1965b   *The Prophet Unarmed—Trotsky: 1921-1929.* vol. 2. New York: Vintage Books; first published, 1959.

1965c   *The Prophet Outcast—Trotsky: 1929-1940.* vol. 3. New York: Vintage Books; first published, 1963.

1969   *The Unfinished Revolution—Russia 1917-1967.* London: Oxford University Press; first published, 1967.

Diamant, Alfred
1964   "The Nature of Political Development." In *Political Development and Social Change,* edited by Jason L. Finkle and Richard W. Gable, pp. 91-95. New York: John Wiley, 1966.

Dias Carneiro, O. A.
1961a   *Movimentos Internacionais de Capital e Desenvolvimento Econômico.* Recife: Comissão de Desenv. Econ. de Pernambuco.

1961b   *Noções da Teoria da Renda.* Recife: Comissão de Desenv. Econ. de Pernambuco.

1961c   *Dois Ensáios sóbre Economia Internacional.* Recife: Comissão de Desenv. Econ. de Pernambuco.

1966   *Past Trends of Structural Relationships in the Economic Evolution of Brazil: 1920-1965.* Mimeographed. Cambridge, Mass.: Center for International Affairs, Harvard University.

Diaz Alejandro, Carlos F.
1968   "El Grupo Andino en el Proceso de Integración Latinoamericana." *Estudios Internacionales* 2, no. 2: 242-257.

Dilthey, Wilhelm
    1944–1945   *Works of Dilthey.* 8 vols. Organized and translated by Eugenio Imaz.
        Mexico City: Fondo de Cultura Económica; German original, *Gesammelte*
        Schriften, vols. I–IX in 11 vols; first published, 1833–1933.
Di Tella, Torcuato
    1964   *El Sistema Político Argentino y la Clase Obrera.* Buenos Aires: EUDEBA.
    1965a   "Populism and Reform in Latin America." In *Obstacles to Change in Latin*
        America, edited by Claudio Veliz. London: Oxford University Press.
    1965b   *Socialismo en la Argentina?* Buenos Aires: Edit. Jorge Alvarez.
    1965c   with Gino Germani, Jorge Graciarena *et al. Argentina, Sociedad de Masas.*
        Buenos Aires: EUDEBA.
    1970   *Hacia una Política Latinoamericana.* Buenos Aires: Arca.
Dobb, Maurice
    1962   *Capitalism Yesterday and Today.* New York: Monthly Review Press.
    1963   *Economic Growth and Underdeveloped Countries.* New York: International
        Publishers.
    1966   *Soviet Economic Development.* Rev. enlarg. ed. New York: International
        Publishers; first published, 1948.
    1967   *Papers on Capitalism Development and Planning.* New York: International
        Publishers.
Dobzhansky, Theodosius
    1951   *Genetics and the Origin of Species.* New York: Columbia University Press.
    1965a   *The Biological Basis of Human Freedom.* New York: Columbia University
        Press; 5th print.; first published, 1956.
    1965b   *Mankind Evolving—The Evolution of the Human Species.* New Haven, Conn.:
        Yale University Press; 7th print.; first published, 1962.
    1967   *The Biology of Ultimate Concern.* New York: New American Library.
Doolin, Dennis J., and North, Robert C.
    1967   *The Chinese People's Republic.* Stanford, Calif.: Hoover Institution Press;
        first published, 1966.
Dray, William H.
    1966   Ed. *Philosophical Analysis and History.* New York: Harper & Row.
Drucker, Peter F.
    1957   *Landmarks of Tomorrow.* New York: Harper & Row.
    1969   *The Age of Discontinuity.* New York: Harper & Row; first published, 1968.
Dubos, René J.
    1965   *Man Adapting.* New Haven, Conn.: Yale University Press.
Dumont, René
    1964a   *Sovkhoz, Kolkhoz, ou le Problématique Communisme.* Paris: Ed. du Seuil.
    1964b   *Cuba—Socialisme et Développement.* Paris: Ed. du Seuil.
    1970   *Cuba est-il Socialiste?* Paris: Ed. du Seuil.
Durkheim, Émile
    1897   *Le Suicide.* New ed. Paris: Presses Universitaires de France.
    1967   *Les Règles de la Méthode Sociologique.* 16th ed. Paris: Presses Universitaires
        de France; first published, 1895.
Duverger, Maurice
    1951   *Les Partis Politiques.* Paris: Armand Colin.
    1953   *Droit Constitutionnel et Institutions Politiques.* Paris: Presses Universitaires
        de France.
    1964a   *An Introduction to the Social Sciences.* New York: Praeger; French original,
        Méthodes des Sciences Sociales. Paris: Presses Universitaires de France, 1961.
    1964b   *Introduction à la Politique.* Paris: Gallimard.

Easton, David
    1953   *The Political System.* New York: Knopf.
    1965a   *A Framework for Political Analysis.* Englewood Cliffs, N.J.: Prentice-Hall.
    1965b   *A Systems Analysis of Political Life.* New York: John Wiley.
    1966   Ed. *Varieties of Political Theory.* Englewood Cliffs, N.J.: Prentice-Hall.
Ehrlich, Paul R.
    1969   *The Population Bomb.* New York: Ballantine Books.

Eisenstadt, S. N.
    1963   *The Political Systems of Empires.* New York: Free Press.
    1964   "Breakdown and Modernization." *Economic Development and Cultural Change,* July 12, 1964, pp. 345–367.
    1965   *Essays on Comparative Institutions.* New York: John Wiley.
    1966   *Modernization: Protest and Change.* Englewood Cliffs, N.J.: Prentice-Hall.
    1967   Ed. *The Decline of Empire.* Englewood Cliffs, N.J.: Prentice-Hall.
Elliott, J. H.
    1966   *Imperial Spain: 1469–1716.* New York: Mentor Books; first published, 1963.
Ellul, Jacques
    1964   *The Technological Society.* New York: Vintage Books; French original, *La Technique ou l'Enjeu du Siècle.* Paris: Armand Colin, 1954.
Emerson, Robert
    1960   *From Empire to Nation.* Boston: Beacon Press.
Engels, Friedrich
    1933   *Origen de la Familia, de la Propriedad Privada y del Estado.* Barcelona, 1933; German original, *Der Ursprung der Familie, des Privateigentums und des Staates.* Zurich: Hohingen, 1884.
    1950a   *Dialectique de la Nature.* Paris: Libraire Marcel Rivière; German original, *Naturdialektik,* written in 1870–1882, first published in *Marx-Engels Archiv,* vol. 2. Frankfort, 1927.
    1950b   *Ludwig Feuerbach and the End of Classical German Philosophy.* Moscow: Foreign Language Publishing House; German original, *Ludwig Feuerbach und der Ausgang der Klassischen Philosophie in Deutschland,* Stuttgart, 1888.
    1851–1852   *Germany: Revolution and Counter Revolution.* First published in the name of Marx in the *New York Daily Tribune,* October 25, 1851, to December 22, 1852.
    1958   *The Condition of the Working Class in England.* English translation edited by W. O. Henderson and W. H. Chaloner. London: Basil Blackwell; German original, *Die Lage der Arbeitenden Klassen in England,* 1845. MEGA, Part I, vol. 4, pp. 5–282.
    1959   *Anti-Duhring.* Moscow: Foreign Language Publishing House; German original first published in *Vorwärts,* 1878.
    1968   *The Role of Force in History.* New York: International Publishers; German original written in 1887–1888, edited by Eduard Bernstein; first published in *Neue Zeit,* vols. I and XIV.
Eyck, Erich
    1964   *Bismarck and the German Empire.* New York: W. W. Norton; first published, London: Allen & Unwin, 1950.

Fainsod, Merle
    1963   "Bureaucracy and Modernization: The Russian and Soviet Case." In *Bureaucracy and Political Development,* edited by Joseph La Palombara, pp. 233–267. Studies in Political Development, vol. 2. Princeton, N.J.: Princeton University Press.
Faulkner, Harold U.
    1954   *American Economic History.* New York: Harper & Brothers; first published, 1924.
Fayt, Carlos S.
    1967   *La Naturaleza del Peronismo.* Buenos Aires: Viracocha.
Ferkiss, Victor C.
    1969   *Technological Man.* New York: Braziller.
Ferrer, Aldo
    1963   *La Economia Argentina.* Mexico City: Fondo de Cultura Económica; English translation, *The Argentinean Economy.* Berkeley: University of California Press, 1967.
    1969   Et al. *Los Planes de Estabilizacion en la Argentina.* Buenos Aires: Paidos.

Fichtenau, Heinrich
1964 *The Carolingian Empire—The Age of Charlemagne.* New York: Harper Torch-
       books; German original, *Das Karolingische Imperium—Soziale und geistige
       Problematik eines Grossreiches.* Zurich: Fretz & Warmuth Verlag, 1949.
Fieldhouse, D. K.
1964 "The New Imperialism: The Hobson-Lenin Thesis Revised." In *Imperialism and
       Colonialism,* edited by George H. Nadel and Perry Curtis, pp. 74–96. New York:
       Macmillan.
Finkle, Jason L., and Garle, Richard W.
1966 Eds. *Political Development and Social Change.* New York: John Wiley.
Frank, André Gunder
1967 *Capitalism and Underdevelopment in Latin America—Historical Studies of Chile
       and Brazil.* New York: Monthly Review Press.
1971 *Le Développement du Sous-Développement.* Paris: Maspero.
Frankfort, Henri
1956 "Myth and Reality." In *Before Philosophy,* Henri Frankfort *et al.* Baltimore:
       Penguin Books; first published as *The Intellectual Adventure of Ancient Man.*
       Chicago: University of Chicago Press, 1946.
1961 *Ancient Egyptian Religion.* New York: Harper Torchbooks, reprint; first
       published, New York: Columbia University Press, 1948.
Friedrich, Carl Joachim
1963a *Man and His Government.* New York: McGraw-Hill.
1963b *The Philosophy of Law in Historical Perspective.* 2nd ed. Chicago: Phoenix
       Books; first published, 1958.
1965a *The Age of the Baroque: 1610–1660.* New York: Harper Torchbooks; 4th
       print., first published, 1952.
1966 "Nation-Building?" In *Nation-Building,* edited by Karl W. Deutsch and
       William J. Foltz, pp. 27–32. New York: Atherton Press, 1966.
Frigerio, Rogelio
1968 *La Integración Regional, Instrumento del Monopolio.* Buenos Aires: Edit.
       Hernandez.
Fromm, Erich
1941 *Escape from Freedom.* New York: Holt, Rinehart and Winston.
1955 *The Sane Society.* New York: Holt, Rinehart and Winston.
1960 *You Shall Be As Gods.* New York: Holt, Rinehart and Winston.
1962 *Beyond the Chains of Illusion.* New York: Simon and Schuster.
1964 *The Heart of Man.* New York: Harper & Row.
1965 *Marx's Concept of Man.* New York: Frederick Ungar; first published, 1961.
1966 Ed. *Socialist Humanism.* New York: Doubleday.
1967 *Man for Himself.* New York: Fawcett; first published, Holt, Rinehart and
       Winston, 1947.
Fulbright, Senator J. W.
1963 *Prospect for the West.* Cambridge, Mass.: Harvard University Press.
1964 *Old Myths and New Realities.* New York: Random House.
1966 *The Arrogance of Power.* New York: Vintage Books.
Furtado, Celso
1954 *A Economia Brasileira.* Rio de Janeiro: Edit. A. Noite.
1958 *Perspectivas da Economia Brasileira.* Rio de Janeiro: ISEB.
1959a *A Operação Nordeste.* Rio de Janeiro: ISEB.
1959b *Formação Econômica do Brasil.* Rio de Janeiro: Fundo de Cultura.
1962a "Subdesenvolvimento e Estado Democrático." Recife: Comissão de Desenv.
       Econ. de Pernambuco.
1962b *A Pré-Revolução Brasileira.* Rio de Janeiro: Fundo de Cultura.
1964 *Dialética do Desenvolvimento.* Rio de Janeiro: Fundo de Cultura.
1967 "De l'Oligarchie à l'Etat Militaire." *Temps Modernes,* no. 257: 578–601.
1968a *Sub-Desenvolvimento e Estagnação na América Latina.* Rio de Janeiro:
       Civilização Brasileira.
1968b *Um Projeto para o Brasil.* Rio de Janeiro: Saga.
1969 *La Economía Latinoamericana desde la Conquista Ibérica hasta la Revolución
       Cubana.* Santiago: Edit. Universitaria; Portuguese original, 1969.

1971   *Teoria e Política do Desenvolvimento Economico.* 4th ed. rev. and enlarg. São Paulo: Cia. Edit. Nacional; originally published as *Desenvolvimento e Subdesenvolvimento.* Rio de Janeiro: Fundo de Cultura.

Gabrieli, Francesco
    1968   *Muhammad and the Conquest of Islam.* London: Weidenfeld and Nicolson; Italian original, 1968.
Galbraith, John K.
    1958   *The Affluent Society.* Boston: Houghton Mifflin.
    1962   *American Capitalism.* Boston: Houghton Mifflin; first published, 1952.
    1967a   *Economic Development.* Cambridge, Mass.: Harvard University Press; 3rd print.; first published, 1964.
    1967b   *The New Industrial State.* Boston: Houghton Mifflin.
Gallie, W. B.
    1968   *Philosophy and the Historical Understanding.* New York: Schocken Books; first published, 1964.
Ganshof, F. L.
    1961   *Feudalism.* New York: Harper & Row; first English edition published, New York: Longmans, Green, 1957; French original, *Qu'est-ce que la Féodalité?* Brussels: Collection Lebèque, Office de la Publicité, 1944.
Garaudy, Roger
    1961   *Perspectives de L'Homme.* Paris: Presses Universitaires de France.
    1964   *Karl Marx.* Paris: Seghers.
Gardiner, Patrick
    1964   Ed. *Theories of History.* New York: Free Press; first printing, 1959.
Garruccio, Ludovico
    1968   *Spagna Senza Miti.* Milan: Mursia.
    1969   *L'Industrializzazione tra Nazionalismo e Rivoluzione—Le Ideologie Politiche dei Paesi in Via di Sviluppo.* Bologna: Il Mulino.
    1971   "Le Tre Età del Facismo." *Il Mulino,* January-February, pp. 53–73.
Gavin, General James M.
    1968   *Crisis Now.* New York: Vintage Books.
Gay, Peter
    1962   *The Dilemma of Democratic Socialism.* New York: Collier Books; first published, Columbia University Press, 1952.
    1966-1969   *The Enlightenment: An Interpretation.* 2 vols. New York: Knopf.
    1968   *Weimar Culture—The Outsider As Insider.* New York: Harper & Row.
Gilbert, Felix
    1970   *The End of the European Era: 1890 to the Present.* New York: Norton.
Ginsberg, Morris
    1961   *Nationalism—A Reappraisal.* Leeds: Leeds University Press.
Glotz, Gustave
    1968   *La Cité Grecque.* Paris: Ed. Albin Michel; first published, Paris: La Renaissance du Livre, 1928.
Goetz, Walter
    1950   Ed. *Historia Universal.* 10 vols. Madrid: Espasa-Calpe; German original, *Propyläen Weltgeschichte.*
Goldmann, Lucien
    1969   *The Human Sciences and Philosophy.* London: Jonathan Cape; French original, *Sciences Humaines et Philosophie.* Paris: Ed. Southier, 1966.
González Casanova, Pablo
    1965   *La Democracia en México.* Mexico City: Edit. Era.
    1967   *Las Categorias del Desarrollo Económico y la Investigación en Ciencias Sociales.* Mexico City: Instituto de Investigaciones Sociales.
Gooch, G. P.
    1920   *Nationalism.* London: Swarthmore Press.
Grenier, Albert
    1969   *Le Génie Romain dans la Réligion, la Pensée et l'Art.* Paris: Ed. Albin Michel; first published, Paris: La Renaissance du Livre, 1925.
Groethuysen, Bernhard
    1943   *La Formación de la Conciencia Burguesa en Francia durante el Siglo XVIII.*

Mexico City: Fondo de Cultura Económica; German original, *Die Entstebung der bürgerlichen Welt und Lebensanschauung in Frankreich*, 1927.

Gross, Llewellyn
    1959   Ed. *Symposium on Sociological Theory*. New York: Harper & Row.
Grunwald, Joseph
    1972   with Miguel Wionczek and Martin Carnoy. *Latin American Integration and U.S. Policy*. Washington: The Brookings Institution.
Guerreiro Ramos, Alberto
    1950   *Uma Introdução à História da Organização Racional do Trabalho*. Rio de Janeiro: Dept. de Imp. Nacional.
    1952   *A Sociologia Industrial*. Rio de Janeiro: published by the Author.
    1954   *Cartilha Brasileira do Aprendiz de Sociólogo*. Rio de Janeiro: Edit. Andes.
    1957a   "Condições Sociais do Poder Nacional." Rio de Janeiro: ISEB.
    1957b   "Ideologias e Segurança Nacional." Rio de Janeiro: ISEB.
    1957c   *Introdução Crítica à Sociologia Brasileira*. Rio de Janeiro: Edit. Andes.
    1958   *A Redução Sociológica*. Rio de Janeiro: ISEB.
    1960   *O Problema Nacional do Brasil*. Rio de Janeiro: Edit. Saga.
    1961   *A Crise do Poder no Brasil*. Rio de Janeiro: Zahar Edit.
    1963   *Mito e Verdade da Revolução Brasileira*. Rio de Janeiro: Zahar Edit.
    1966   *Administração e Estratégia do Desenvolvimento*. Rio de Janeiro: Fundação Getúlio Vargas.
Gurvitch, Georges
    1941   *Las Formas de la Sociabilidad*. Buenos Aires: Edit. Losada; French original, *Essais de Sociologie*. Paris: Libraire du Recueil Sirey, 1939.
    1947   with Wilbert E. Moore; eds. *La Sociologie au XXe Siècle*. 2 vols. Paris: Presses Universitaires de France.
    1950   *La Vocation Actuelle de la Sociologie*. vol. 1, *Vers une Sociologie Différentielle*. 3rd ed. Paris: Presses Universitaires de France, 1963.
    1954   *Déterminismes Sociaux et Liberté Humaine*. Paris: Presses Universitaires de France; 2nd ed., 1963.
    1957   *La Vocation Actuelle de la Sociologie*. vol. 2, *Antécédents et Perspectives*. Paris: Presses Universitaires de France.
    1958   Ed. *Traité de Sociologie*. 2 vols. Paris: Presses Universitaires de France.
    1961   *La Sociologie de Karl Marx*. Paris: Centre de Doc. Univ.
    1962   *Dialectique et Sociologie*. Paris: Flammarion.
    1968   *Études sur les Classes Sociales*. Paris: Ed. Gonthier.

Haebel, E. Adamson
    1967   *The Law of Primitive Man*. Cambridge, Mass.: Harvard University Press; first published, 1954.
Halphen, Louis, and Sagnac, Philippe
    1950   Eds. *Peuples et Civilisations*. 2nd ed. 20 vols. Paris: Presses Universitaires de France; first published, 1926.
Hart, H. L. A.
    1965   *The Concept of Law*. London: Oxford University Press; first published, 1961.
Hartwell, R. M.
    1968   Ed. *The Causes of the Industrial Revolution in England*. London: Methuen; 2nd print.; first published, 1967.
Hartz, Louis
    1955   *The Liberal Tradition in America*. New York: Harcourt, Brace & World.
    1964   *The Founding of New Societies*. New York: Harcourt, Brace & World.
Hawk, E. Q.
    1934   *Economic History of the South*. Englewood Cliffs, N.J.: Prentice-Hall.
Hawkes, Jacquetta
    1963   "Prehistory." In *Prehistory and the Beginning of Civilization*, edited by Jacquetta Hawkes and Sir Leonard Wooley. UNESCO, History of Mankind, vol. 1. New York: Harper & Row.
Hayes, Carlton J. H.
    1960   *Nationalism: A Religion*. New York: Macmillan.
Hazard, Paul
    1946   *La Pensée Européenne au XVIII Siècle*. 2 vols. Paris: Boivin et Cie.

Heer, Friedrich
  1968   *The Intellectual History of Europe.* 2 vols. New York: Doubleday; German original, Stuttgart: W. Kohlhammer Verlag.
Heilbroner, Robert L.
  1963   *The Great Ascent.* New York: Harper Torchbooks.
  1968   *The Future As History.* New York: Harper Torchbooks; first published, 1959.
  1969   *The Limits of American Capitalism.* New York: Harper Torchbooks; first published, 1965.
Herkner, Heinrich
  1952   "La Economía y el Movimiento Obrero (1850–1880)." In vol. 8 of *Historia Universal*, edited by Walter Goetz. 10 vols. Madrid: Espasa Calpe; German original *Propyläen Weltgeschichte*. Leipzig: Propyläen, 1931.
Herrera, Felipe
  1964   *América Latina Integrada.* Buenos Aires: Edit. Losada.
  1965   "Perspectives de l'Integration Latino-americaine." *Tiers-Monde* 7: 757–776. Special issue on Latin American integration, edited by Gustavo Lagos.
  1966   Organizer: *Factores para la Integración Latinoamericana.* Mexico City: Fondo de Cultura Económica.
Hertz, Frederick
  1944   *Nationality in History and Politics.* New York: Oxford University Press.
Hibbard, B. H.
  1939   *A History of the Public Law Policies.* Gloucester, Mass.: Peter Smith.
Hilferding, Rudolf
  1923   *Das Finanzkapital.* Vienna: Wiener Volksbuchandlung; first published, 1910.
Hirschman, Albert
  1958   *The Strategy of Economic Development.* New Haven, Conn.: Yale University Press.
  1961   Ed. *Latin American Issues.* New York: Twentieth Century Fund.
  1963   *Journeys Toward Progress—Studies of Economic Policy-Making in Latin America.* New York: Twentieth Century Fund.
  1964   "The Stability of Neutralism: A Geometrical Note." *The Journal of the American Economic Association*, no. 2, pp. 94–100.
  1967   *Development Projects Observed.* Washington, D.C.: Brookings Institution.
  1968a   "Foreign Aid—A Critique and a Proposal." *Essays in International Finance*, no. 69. Princeton, N.J.: Princeton University Press.
  1968b   "Underdevelopment, Obstacles to the Perception of Change, and Leadership." *Daedalus* 97, no. 3: 925–937.
  1969   "How to Divest in Latin America and Why." *Essays in International Finance*, no. 76. Princeton, N.J.: Princeton University Press.
  1970   *Exit, Voice and Loyalty.* Cambridge, Mass.: Harvard University Press.
Hobson, J. A.
  1965   *Imperialism.* Ann Arbor: University of Michigan Press; first published, 1902.
Horowitz, David
  1965   *The Free World Colossus.* New York: Hill and Wang.
  1967   Ed. *Containment and Revolution.* Boston: Beacon Press.
  1968   Ed. *Marx and Modern Economics.* New York: Modern Reader; paperback edition, Monthly Review Press.
Horowitz, Irving Louis
  1957   *The Idea of War and Peace in Contemporary Philosophy.* New York: Paine Whitman.
  1961a   *The Social Theories of Georges Sorel.* London: Routledge and Kegan Paul.
  1961b   *Philosophy, Science and the Sociology of Knowledge.* Springfield, Ill.: Charles C. Thomas.
  1965   Ed. *The New Sociology.* New York: Oxford University Press; first published, 1964.
  1966   *Three Worlds of Development.* New York: Oxford University Press.
  1969a   with Josué de Castro and John Gerassi, eds. *Latin American Radicalism.* New York: Vintage Books.
  1969b   "The Norm of Illegitimacy: The Political Sociology of Latin America." In

    Latin American Radicalism, edited by Horowitz, de Castro, and Gerassi.
    pp. 3–28.
Hoselitz, Bert F.
    1960   *Sociological Aspects of Economic Growth.* New York: Free Press.
Houghton, Neal D.
    1968   Ed. *Struggle Against History.* New York: Simon and Schuster.
Hughes, Serge
    1967   *The Fall and Rise of Modern Italy.* New York: Minerva Press.
Hughes, T. J., and Luard, D. E. T.
    1959   *The Economic Development of Communist China: 1949–1958.* London:
            Oxford University Press.
Huizinga, Jan
    1945   *El Otoño de la Edad Media.* Madrid: Revista de Occidente; Dutch original,
            Herfsttig der Middeleenen. Haarlem, 1923.
    1946   *El Concepto da Historia y otros Ensayos.* Mexico City: Fondo de Cultura
            Económica; several essays published separately in the 1920s.
    1951   *Entre las Sombras del Mañana—Diagnostico de la Enfermidad Cultural de Nuestro*
            Tiempo. 2nd ed. Madrid: Revista de Occidente; Dutch original, *In Schatten von*
            Morgen: Eine Diagnose der Kulturellen Leiden unserer Zeit. Leiden, 1935.
Huntington, Samuel A.
    1964   *The Soldier and the State—The Theory and Politics of Civil-Military Relations.*
            New York: Vintage Books.
    1965   "Political Development and Political Decay." *World Politics* 17: 386–430.
    1966a "Political Modernization of America and Europe." *World Politics* 18: 376–414.
    1966b "The Political Modernization of Traditional Monarchies." *Daedalus* 95, no. 3.
    1968   *Political Order in Changing Societies.* New Haven, Conn.: Yale University Press.
    1969   "The Defense Establishment: Vested Interests and the Public Interest." In
            The Military-Industrial Complex and U.S. Foreign Policy. Detroit: Wayne State
            University Press.
    1970   "Social and Institutional Dynamics of One-Party Systems." In *Authoritarian*
            Politics in Modern Society—The Dynamics of Established One-Party Systems,
            edited by Samuel Huntington and Clement H. Moore. New York: Basic Books.
Hussey, J. M.
    1961   *The Byzantine World.* New York: Harper Torchbooks; first published, London:
            Hutchinson University Library, 1957.
Hymer, Stephen
    1967   *Direct Foreign Investment and the National Economic Interest.* New Haven,
            Conn.: Yale University, Economic Center. Center paper no. 108.

Ianni, Octavio
    1965a with Paulo Singer, Gabriel Cohn, and Francisco Weffort. *Política e Revolução*
            Social no Brasil. Rio de Janeiro: Edit. Civilização Brasileira.
    1965b *Estado e Capitalismo—Estrutura Social e Industrialização no Brasil.* Rio de
            Janeiro. Edit. Civilização Brasileira.
    1968   *O Colapso do Populismo no Brasil.* Rio de Janeiro: Edit. Civilização Brasileira.
Inkeles, Alex
    1956   *What Is Sociology? An Introduction to the Discipline and Profession.* Founda-
            tions of Modern Social Sciences Series. Englewood Cliffs, N.J.: Prentice-Hall.
    1968   *Social Change in Soviet Russia.* Cambridge, Mass.: Harvard University Press.
Inter-American Development Bank
    1968   Organizer; *Las Inversiones Multinacionales en el Desarrollo y la Integración de*
            América Latina. Bogotá: I.D.B.
Instituto Latinoamericano de Planificación Económica y Social (ILPES)
    1966   *Discusiones sobre Planificación.* Mexico City: Siglo XXI.

Jacobsen, Thorkild
    1966   "Mesopotamia." In *Before Philosophy,* edited by H. Frankfort, pp. 137–236.
            Baltimore: Pelican Books; first published as *The Intellectual Adventure of*
            Ancient Man. Chicago: University of Chicago Press, 1946.

Jaeger, Werner
    1945   *Paidea: The Ideals of Greek Culture.* 2nd ed. 3 vols. New York: Oxford University Press; German original published, 1933.
    1946   *Aristoteles.* Mexico City: Fondo de Cultura Económica; German original, *Aristoteles—Grundlegung einer Geschichte Seiner Entwicklung.* Berlin: Weidmannsche Buchanlung, 1923.
    1947   *The Theology of the Early Greek Philosophers.* London: Oxford University Press.
    1965   *Early Christianity and Greek Paidea.* Cambridge, Mass.: Harvard University Press; 2nd print.; first published, 1961.
Jaguaribe, Helio
    1953-1956   Ed. *Cadernos do Nosso Tempo.* N 1 to 5. Rio de Janeiro.
    1958   *O Nacionalismo na Atualidade Brasileira.* Rio de Janeiro: ISEB.
    1965   "A Brazilian View." In *How Latin America Views the U.S. Investor,* edited by Raymond Vernon. New York: Praeger.
    1967a   "El Impacto de Marx." *El Trimestre Económico* 39, no. 133: 83–176; partial English translation in *Marx and the Western World,* edited by Nicholas Lobkowicz. Notre Dame, Ind.: University of Notre Dame Press, 1967.
    1967b   *Problemas do Desenvolvimento Latino-Americano.* Rio de Janeiro: Edit. Civilização Brasileira.
    1968   *Economic and Political Development.* Rev. ed. Cambridge, Mass.: Harvard University Press; Portuguese original, *Desenvolvimento Economico e Desenvolvimento Político.* Rio de Janeiro: Fundo de Cultura, 1962.
    1969a   "Dependencia y Autonomía en América Latina." In *La Dependencia Político-Económica de América Latina,* edited by Helio Jaguaribe *et al.,* pp. 1–86. Mexico City: Siglo XXI.
    1969b   "Political Strategies of National Development in Brazil." In *Latin American Radicalism,* edited by I. L. Horowitz *et al.,* pp. 390–339. New York: Vintage Books.
    1971   "Ciencia y Tecnologia en el Quadro Socio-Politico de América Latina." *El Trimestre Económico* 38, no. 150.
Jalée, Pierre
    1969   *L'Impérialisme en 1970.* Paris: Maspero.
James, Émile
    1955   *Histoire de la Pensée Économique.* Paris: Presses Universitaires de France.
Jeannin, Pierre
    1969   *Les Marchands du XVI Siècle.* Paris: Ed. du Seuil; first published, 1957.
Johnson, Chalmers
    1964   *Revolution and the Social System.* Stanford, Calif.: Hoover Institution Press.
    1966   *Revolutionary Change.* Boston: Little, Brown.
Johnson, John J.
    1964   Ed. *Continuity and Change in Latin America.* Stanford, Calif.: Stanford University Press.
    1965a   *Political Change in Latin America—The Emergence of the Middle Sectors.* Stanford, Calif.: Stanford University Press; first published, 1958.
    1965b   *The Military and Society in Latin America.* Stanford, Calif.: Stanford University Press; first published, 1965.
    1968   with the collaboration of Doris M. Ladd. *Simon Bolivar and Spanish American Independence: 1783–1830.* New York: Van Nostrand.
Joll, James
    1966   *The Second International: 1889–1914.* New York: Harper & Row.
Jouvenel, Bertrand de
    1963   *De la Politique Pure.* Paris: Calmann-Lévy; English original, *The Pure Theory of Politics.* New Haven, Conn.: Yale University Press.
    1964   *L'Art de la Conjecture—Futuribles.* Monaco: Ed. du Rocher.
Julien, Claude
    1968   *L'Empire Américain.* Paris: Ed. Bernard Grasset.

Kahler, Erich
    1961   *Man, the Measure—A new Approach to History.* New York: Braziller; 2nd print.; first published, 1943
    1964   *The Meaning of History.* New York: Braziller.

1967a *The Jews Among the Nations.* New York: Frederick Ungar.
1967b *Out of the Labyrinth.* New York: Braziller.
1967c *The Tower and the Abyss—An Inquiry into the Transformation of Man.* New York: Viking Press; first published, New York: Braziller, 1957.

Kahn, Herman
1961 *On Thermonuclear War.* Princeton, N.J.: Princeton University Press.
1962 *Thinking About the Unthinkable.* New York: Avon Books.
1965 *On Escalation: Metaphors and Scenarios.* Washington: Hudson Institute.
1967 with Anthony J. Wiener. *The Year 2000.* New York: Macmillan.

Kamenka, Eugene
1962 *The Ethical Foundations of Marxism.* London: Routledge and Kegan Paul.

Kaplan, Abraham
1952 with Harold Lasswell. *Power and Society—A Framework for Political Inquiry.* London: Routledge and Kegan Paul.

Kaplan, Marcos
1972 *Aspectos Politicos de la Planiticacion en America Latina.* Montevideu: Biblioteca Cientifica.

Karol, Kewes S.
1967 *China, el Otro Comunismo.* Mexico City: Siglo XXI; French original, *La Chine de Mao: l'Autre Communisme.* Paris: Robert Laffont, 1966.

Kassof, Allen
1968a Ed. *Prospects for Soviet Society.* New York: Praeger.
1968b "The Future of Soviet Society." In *Prospects for Soviet Society,* edited by Kassof, pp. 497-506.
1968c "Persistence and Change." In *Prospects for Soviet Society,* edited by Kassof, pp. 3-13.

Kautsky, John H.
1965 "An Essay on the Politics of Development." In *Political Change in Under-Developed Countries,* edited by John H. Kautsky. New York: John Wiley; 4th print.; first published, 1962.

Kautsky, Karl
1964 *The Dictatorship of the Proletariat.* Ann Arbor: University of Michigan Press; Russian original, 1918.

Keesing's Research Report
1967 *The Cultural Revolution in China.* New York: Charles Scribner's Sons.

Keller, Suzanne
1968 *Beyond the Ruling Class.* New York: Random House; first published, 1963.

Kennan, George F.
1951 *American Diplomacy.* New York: Mentor Books, 2nd print.; first published, Chicago: University of Chicago Press, 1951.
1964 *On Dealing with the Communist World.* New York: Harper & Row.
1966 *Realities of American Foreign Policy.* New York: Norton; first published, Princeton, N.J.: Princeton University Press, 1954.

Keynes, John Maynard
1936 *General Theory of Employment: Interest and Money.* New York: Macmillan.

Kingsbury, Robert C., and Schneider, Ronald M.
1966 Eds. *An Atlas of Latin American Affairs.* New York: Praeger; 2nd print.; first published, 1965.

Kohn, Hans
1944 *The Idea of Nationalism.* New York: Macmillan.
1955 *Nationalism: Its Meaning and History.* New York: Van Nostrand.

Kroeber, Alfred L.
1945 *Anthropology.* Spanish translation, *Antropología General.* Mexico City: Fondo de Cultura Económica.
1962 *A Roster of Civilizations and Culture.* Chicago: Aldine Publishing.
1963a *Configurations of Culture Growth.* Berkeley: University of California Press; 2nd print.; first published, 1944.
1963b and Clyde Kluckhohn. *Culture—A Critical Review of Concepts and Definitions.* New York: Vintage Books; first published, Cambridge, Mass.: Harvard University Press. Papers of the Peabody Museum of American Archeology and Ethnology, vol. 47, no. 1, 1952.

1963c   *Style and Civilizations.* Berkeley: University of California Press, 2nd print.; first published, Ithaca, N.Y.: Cornell University Press, 1957.

1966   *An Anthropologist Looks at History.* Berkeley: University of California Press; 2nd print.; first published, 1963.

1968   *The Nature of Culture.* Chicago: University of Chicago Press; first published, 1952.

Krooss, Herman E.

1966   *American Economic Development.* Englewood Cliffs, N.J.: Prentice-Hall; first published, 1955.

Labedz, Leopold

1962   Ed. *Revisionism.* London: Allen & Unwin.

Lafer, Celso

1963   *O Judeu em Gil Vicente.* São Paulo: Cons. Estad. de Cultura.

1965   "O Problema dos Valores n'Os Lusíadas—Subsídios para o Estudo da Cultura Portuguêsa do Século XVI." *Revista Camoniana* 2: 72–108.

1969   "Una Interpretación del Sistema de las Relaciones Internacionales del Brasil." *Foro Internacional,* January-March, pp. 298–318.

1970   *The Planning Process and the Political System in Brazil: A Study of Kubitschek's Target Plan—1956-1961.* Ph.D. Thesis, Cornell University.

Lagos, Gustavo

1965   "L'Intégration de l'Amérique Latine et le Système des Relations Internationales." *Tiers-Monde* 6: 743–756. Special issue on Latin American integration, edited by Gustavo Lagos.

Laistner, M. L. W.

1967   *Christianity and Pagan Culture in the Later Roman Empire.* Ithaca, N.Y.: Cornell University Press.

Landauer, Carl

1945   *Teoría de la Planificación Económica.* Mexico City: Fondo de Cultura Económica.

Langdon, Frank

1967   *Politics in Japan.* Boston: Little, Brown.

Lange, Oscar

1963   *Moderna Economia Política.* Rio de Janeiro: Fundo de Cultura; Polish original, 1962.

La Palombara, Joseph

1963   Ed. *Bureaucracy and Political Development.* Studies in Political Development, vol. 2. Princeton, N.J.: Princeton University Press.

1966   with Myron Weiner, eds. *Political Parties and Political Development.* Studies in Political Development, vol. 6. Princeton, N.J.: Princeton University Press.

Lapierre, Jean-William

1968   *Essai sur le Fondement du Pouvoir Politique.* Aix-en-Provence: Ed. Ophrys.

Laski, Harold

1946   *Reflections on the Revolution of Our Time.* London: Allen & Unwin; 4th print.; first published, 1943.

1950   *Trade Unions in the New Society.* London: Allen & Unwin.

1951   *A Grammar of Politics.* 4th ed. London: Allen & Unwin, reprint.; first published, 1925.

1952a   *The American Presidency.* London: Allen & Unwin; 3rd print.; first published, 1940.

1952b   *The Dilemma of Our Time.* London: Allen & Unwin.

1952c   *Parliamentary Government in England.* London: Allen & Unwin; 5th print.; first published, 1938.

1953   *The American Democracy.* London: Allen & Unwin; 2nd print.; first published, 1949.

Lasswell, Harold D.

1952   with Abraham Kaplan. *Power and Society—A Framework for Political Inquiry.* London: Routledge and Kegan Paul.

1960   *Politics—Who Gets What, When, How.* Cleveland: Meridian Books; 3rd print.; first published, 1936.

Latourette, Kenneth S.
1964   *China.* Englewood Cliffs, N.J.: Prentice-Hall.
1966   *The Chinese—Their History and Culture.* New York: Macmillan; 4th print.; first published, 1934.
Leclerc, Ivor
1958   *Whitehead's Metaphysics.* London: Allen & Unwin.
Lefebvre, Henri
1963   *Problèmes Actuels du Marxisme.* Paris: Presses Universitaires de France.
1966   *The Sociology of Marx.* New York: Vintage Books; French original, *Sociologie de Marx.* Paris: Presses Universitaires de France, 1966.
1971   *Le Matérialisme Dialectique.* Paris: Presses Universitaires de France.
Lenin, Vladimir Ilyitch Ulyanov
1941   *Obras Escogidas.* 3 vols. Moscow: Marx-Engels-Lenin Institute, and Buenos Aires: Edit. Problemas.
1959   *Oeuvres.* 40 vols. Moscow: Marx-Engels-Lenin Institute and Ed. en Langues Étrangères, and Paris: Ed. Sociales.
Lerner, Abba P.
1944   *The Economics of Control.* New York: Macmillan.
Lévy-Bruhl, Lucien
1921   *La Mentalité Primitive.* Paris.
Lévy-Strauss, Claude
1949   *Les Structures Élémentaires de la Parenté.* Paris: Presses Universitaires de France.
1958   *Anthropologie Structurale.* Paris: Plon.
1962   *La Pensée Sauvage.* Paris: Plon.
Lewis, W. Arthur
1955   *The Theory of Economic Growth.* London: Allen & Unwin.
Ley, Lester S., and Sampson, Roy J.
1962   *American Economic Development.* Boston: Allyn and Bacon.
Liska, George
1967   *Imperial America.* Baltimore: Johns Hopkins Press.
1968a   *Alliances and the Third World.* Baltimore: Johns Hopkins Press.
1968b   *War and Order.* Baltimore: Johns Hopkins Press.
Lobkowicz, Nicholas
1967   Ed. *Marx and the Western World.* Notre Dame, Ind.: University of Notre Dame Press.
Lockwood, Lee
1967   *Castro's Cuba, Cuba's Fidel.* New York: Macmillan.
Lockwood, William W.
1955   *The Economic Development of Japan.* London: Oxford University Press.
1964   "Economic and Political Modernization—Japan." In *Political Modernization of Japan and Turkey,* edited by Robert E. Ward and Dankwart A. Rustow, pp. 117–145. *Studies in Political Development,* vol. 3. Princeton, N.J.: Princeton University Press.
Loewenstein, Karl
1966   *Max Weber's Political Ideas in the Perspective of Our Time.* Amherst: University of Massachusetts Press; German original, Frankfort: Athenäum Verlag, 1965.
Luce, R. Duncan, and Raiffa, Howard
1966   *Games and Decisions—Introduction and Critical Survey.* New York: John Wiley; first published, 1957.
Lundberg, George A.
1939   *Foundations of Sociology.* New York: Macmillan; rev. and abridg. ed., New York: David McKay, 1964.
Luttwak, Edward
1969   *Coup d'État—A Practical Handbook.* New York: Knopf; first published, 1968.
Luxemburg, Rosa
1922   *Die Russische Revolution.* Berlin; edited by Paul Levi, from a copy of the 1918 text.
1970   *Reform or Revolution.* New York: Pathfinder Press; German original, 1908.

MacIver, Robert M.
   1942   *Social Causation.* Boston: Athenaeum Press.
   1949   *The Web of Government.* New York: Macmillan; first published, 1947.
   1962   and Charles H. Page. *Society: An Introductory Analysis.* Rev. New York:
           Holt, Rinehart and Winston; original edition by MacIver only, first published,
           1937.
Magdoff, Harry
   1969   *The Age of Imperialism.* New York: Monthly Review Press.
Maine, Henry
   1861   *Ancient Law.* London.
Mair, Lucy
   1966   *Primitive Government.* Baltimore: Penguin Books; reprint, first published,
           1962.
Malaparte, Curzio
   1948   *Technique du Coup d'État.* Rev. French Edit. Paris: Ed. Bernard Grasset;
           Italian original, 1931.
Mandel, Ernest
   1970   *La Résponse Socialiste au Défi Américain.* Paris: Maspero; German original,
           Europäische Verlagsanstalt, 1968.
Marchall, Jean
   1955   *Deux Essais sur le Marxisme.* Paris: Ed. Génin.
Marcuse, Herbert
   1955   *Eros and Civilization—A Philosophic Inquiry into Freud.* New York: Vintage
           Books.
   1960   *Reason and Revolution—Hegel and the Rise of Social Theory.* Boston: Beacon
           Press; first published, New York: Oxford University Press, 1941.
   1961   *Soviet Marxism.* New York: Vintage Books; first published, New York:
           Columbia University Press, 1958.
   1966   *One-Dimensional Man.* Boston: Beacon Press; first published, 1964.
   1968   *Materialismo Histórico e Existência.* Rio de Janeiro: Tempo Brasileiro,
           Portuguese translation of two essays; German originals, *Beitraege zu einer
           Phaenomenologie des Historischen Materialismus,* 1928, and *Neue Guellen zur
           Grundlegung des Historschen Materialismus,* 1932.
   1969   *An Essay on Liberation.* Boston: Beacon Press.
Marek, Franz
   1969   *Philosophy and World Revolution.* New York: International Publishers; German
           original, *Philosophie der Weltrevolution.* Vienna: Europa Verlag, 1966.
Martindale, Don
   1960   *The Nature and Types of Sociological Theory.* Boston: Houghton Mifflin.
   1962   *Social Life and Cultural Change.* New York: Van Nostrand.
   1963   *Community, Character and Civilization.* New York: Free Press.
   1965   "Limits of and Alternatives to Functionalism in Sociology." In *Functionalism
           in the Social Sciences,* edited by Don Martindale, pp. 144–162. Philadelphia:
           The American Academy of Political and Social Science. Monograph no. 5.
Martins, Luciano
   1968   *Industrialização, Burguesia Nacional e Desenvolvimento.* Rio de Janeiro:
           Edit. Saga.
Marx, Karl
   1948a   *Les Luttes de Classes en France: 1848–1850.* Paris: Ed. Sociales; German
           original, *Die Klassenkämpfe in Frankreich: 1848–1850,* first published in *Neue
           Rheinische Zeitung,* 1850.
   1948b   *Le 18 Brumaire de Louis Bonaparte.* Paris: Ed. Sociales; German original,
           Der Achtzchute Brumaire des Louis Bonaparte. In *Die Revolution,* edited by
           J. Weydemeyer. New York, 1852.
   1963–1968 *Oeuvres—Economie.* vols. 1 and 2. Edited by Maximilien Rubel. Paris:
           Bibliothèque de la Pléiade. (Vol. 3 forthcoming; will contain Marx's political
           writings.)
   1965   with Friedrich Engels. *The German Ideology.* New York: International
           Publishers, 4th print.; first published, 1947; German original, *Die Deutsche
           Ideologie,* first published, 1932.

Matos Mar, José
    1963   "Diagnostico del Peru—Cambios en la Sociedad Peruana." *Revista del Museo Nacional* 22: 293–306.
    1970   with Julio Cotler, Jorge Bravo Bresani, Augusto Salazar Bondy, and Felipe Portocarrero. *El Perú Actual—Sociedad y Política.* Mexico City: Instituto de Investigaciones Sociales.
May, Ernest R.
    1968   *American Imperialism.* New York: Atheneum; first published, 1967.
Mazour, Anatole G.
    1967   *Soviet Economic Development.* New York: Van Nostrand.
McHale, John
    1969   *The Future of the Future.* New York: Braziller.
    1970   *The Ecological Context.* New York: Braziller.
Mendes, Candido
    1954   "Possibilidade da Sociologia Política." Rio de Janeiro: Artes Gráficas C. Mendes Jr.
    1960   "Perspectiva Atual da América Latina." Rio de Janeiro: ISEB.
    1963   *Nacionalismo e Desenvolvimento.* Rio de Janeiro: IBEA.
    1966a *Memento dos Vivos—A Esquerda Católica no Brasil.* Rio de Janeiro: Tempo Brasileiro.
    1966b "Sistemas Políticos e Modelos de Poder no Brasil." *Dados,* no. 1, pp. 7–41.
    1967   "O Governo Castelo Branco: Paradigma e Prognose." *Dados,* no. 2–3, pp. 63–111.
    1968   "Perspectiva do Comportamento Ideológico: o Processo de Reflexão na Crise do Desenvolvimento." *Dados,* no. 4, pp. 95–132.
    1969   "Elite de Poder, Democracia e Desenvolvimento." *Dados,* no. 6, pp. 57–90.
    1970   "Nation-Building in Southern Latin America." Mimeographed. Rio de Janeiro: IUPERJ.
Meyer, Alfred G.
    1965   *The Soviet Political System.* New York: Random House.
Mill, John Stuart
    1861   *Representative Government.* London.
Mills, C. Wright
    1956   *The Power Elite.* New York: Oxford University Press.
    1958   with H. H. Gerth, eds. *From Max Weber: Essays in Sociology.* New York: Oxford University Press; first published, 1946.
    1959   *The Sociological Imagination.* New York: Oxford University Press.
    1963a *The Marxists.* New York: Dell; 2nd print.; first published, 1962.
    1963b *Power, Politics and People.* Collected essays edited by I. L. Horowitz. New York: Ballantine Books.
    1964   with Hans Gerth. *Character and Social Structure.* New York: Harcourt, Brace & World.
Moore, Barrington
    1962   *Political Power and Social Theory.* New York: Harper Torchbooks; first published, Cambridge, Mass.: Harvard University Press, 1958.
    1968   *Social Origin of Dictatorship and Democracy—Lord and Peasant in the Modern World.* Boston: Beacon Press; 3rd print.; first published, 1966.
    1970   "Révolution en Amérique?" *Esprit,* no. 396, pp. 583–597.
Morgan, H. Wayne
    1967   *America's Road to Empire.* New York: John Wiley; first published, 1965.
Morgenthau, Hans
    1951   *In Defense of the National Interest.* New York: Knopf.
    1957   *The Purpose of American Policy.* New York: Knopf.
    1960   *Politics Among Nations.* New York: Knopf; first published, 1948.
    1969   *A New Foreign Policy for the United States.* New York: Praeger.
Morin, Edgar
    1970   "La Mutation Occidentale." *Esprit,* no. 396, pp. 515–548.
Mosca, Gaetano
    1939   *The Ruling Class.* English translation by Hannah D. Kahn; edited by Arthur Livingston. New York: Italian original, *Elementi di Scienza Politica.* Turin, 1895.

Muret, Pierre
    1949   *La Prépondérance Anglaise.* Peuples et Civilisations, edited by Louis Halphen
            and Philippe Sagnac, vol. 11. Paris: Presses Universitaires de France.

Nadel, George H., and Curtis, Perry
    1964   Eds. *Imperialism and Colonialism.* New York: Macmillan.
Nadel, S. F.
    1957   *The Theory of Social Structure.* London: Cohen & West.
Nash, Ronald H.
    1969   Ed. *Ideas of History.* 2 vols. New York: Dutton.
Nock, A. D.
    1963   *Conversion.* London: Oxford University Press; first published, 1953.
Norman, E. H.
    1940   *Japan's Emergence as a Modern State.* New York: Institute of Pacific
            Relations.
Novack, David, and Lekachman, Robert
    1964   Eds. *Development and Society: The Dynamics of Economic Change.* New
            York: St. Martin's Press.
Novack, George
    1966   *Uneven and Combined Development in History.* 3rd ed. New York: Merit
            Publishers; first published in *Labor Review* (1957).
Nun, José
    1968   "A Latin American Phenomenon: The Middle Class Military Coup." In *Latin
            America: Reform or Revolution?* edited by James Petras and Maurice Zeitlin,
            pp. 145–185. New York: Fawcett.

Odum, Eugene P.
    1959   *Fundamentals of Ecology.* Philadelphia: Saunders.
Oglesby, Carl
    1968   "An Essay on the Meaning of the Cold War." In *Containment and Change,*
            edited by Carl Oglesby and Richard Shaull. New York: Macmillan; 3rd print.;
            first published, 1967.
    1969   Ed. *The New Left Reader.* New York: Grove Press.
Oliveira Martins, Joaquim Pedro de
    1968   *História de Portugal.* 15th ed. Lisbon: Guimarães Edit.; first published, 1879.
Olson, Lawrence
    1963   "The Elite, Industrialization and Nationalism." In *Expectant Peoples,* edited by
            K. N. Silvert, pp. 398–429. New York: Random House.
Organski, A. F. K.
    1964   *World Politics.* New York: Knopf; first published, 1958.
    1965   *The Stages of Political Development.* New York: Knopf.
Orleans, Leo A.
    1961   *Professional Manpower and Education in Communist China.* Washington, D. C.:
            Government Printing Office.
Ortega y Gasset, José
    1923–1936   Ed. *Revista de Occidente.* Madrid.
    1946–1947   *Obras Completas.* 6 vols. In *Revista de Occidente.* Madrid, first
            published, 1902–1946.
    Posthumous Publications
    1957   *El Hombre y la Gente.* In *Revista de Occidente.* Madrid.
    1959   *Una Interpretación de la Historia Universal.* In *Revista de Occidente.* Madrid.
Ostrogorsky, George
    1956   *History of the Byzantine State.* Oxford: Basil Blackwell; German original,
            1940.

Packenham, Robert A.
    1966a   "Political Development Doctrine in the American Foreign Aid Program." *World
            Politics* 18: 194–235.
    1966b   "The Theory and Practice of Political Development." Mimeographed paper.
            Stanford: Stanford University.

Paret, Peter, and John W. Shy
    1966   *Guerrillas in the 1960's.* Rev., 5th ed. New York: Frederick Praeger; first published, 1962.
Pareto, Vilfredo
    1902   *Les Systèmes Socialistes.* 2 vols. Paris: Marcel Giard.
    1916   *Trattato di Sociologia Generale.* 3 vols. Florence.
    1966   *Sociological Writings.* Selected and introduced by S. E. Finer; English translation by Derick Mirfin; New York: Praeger.
Park, Charles F., Jr.
    1969   "Affluence in Jeopardy." *Focus,* June.
Parsons, Talcott
    Books
    1949a   *The Structure of Social Action.* New York: Free Press; first published, New York: McGraw-Hill, 1937.
    1949b   *Essays in Sociological Theory Pure and Applied.* Rev. ed. New York: Free Press.
    1951a   *The Social System.* New York: Free Press; paperback edition, 1964.
    1951b   with Edward Shils, eds. *Toward a General Theory of Action.* Cambridge, Mass.: Harvard University Press; Harper Torchbook edition, 1962.
    1953   with Edward Shils and R. F. Bales. *Working Papers on the Theory of Action.* New York: Free Press; rev. ed., 1954.
    1956   with Neil J. Smelser. *Economy and Society.* New York: Free Press.
    1960   *Structure and Process in Modern Society.* New York: Free Press.
    1961   with Edward Shils; K. Naegele; and J. Pitts, eds. *Theories of Society.* 2 vols. New York: Free Press; 1-vol. ed., 1965.
    1966   *Societies: Evolutionary and Comparative Perspectives.* Englewood Cliffs, N.J.: Prentice-Hall.
    Articles
    1956   "Suggestions for a Sociological Approach to the Theory of Organizations." In *Social Change,* edited by Amitai Etzioni, pp. 33–47. New York: Basic Books, 1964.
    1959   "General Theory in Sociology." In *Sociology Today,* edited by R. K. Merton *et al.,* pp. 3–38. New York: Harper Torchbooks.
    1961a   "The Point of View of the Author." In *The Social Theories of Talcott Parsons,* edited by Max Black, pp. 311–363, Englewood Cliffs, N.J.: Prentice–Hall.
    1961b   "A Functional Theory of Change." In *Social Change,* edited by Amitai Etzioni, pp. 83–89. New York: Basic Books.
    1961c   with Winston White. "The Link Between Character and Society." In *Culture and Society,* edited by S. M. Lipset and Leo Lowenthal. New York: Free Press.
    1963a   "On the Concept of Influence." *Public Opinion Quarterly* 27: 37–62.
    1963b   "On the Concept of Political Power." *Proceedings of the American Philosophical Society* 107, no. 3.
    1964a   "Some Reflections on the Place of Force in Social Process." In *Internal War,* edited by Harry Eckstein, pp. 33–70. New York: Free Press.
    1964b   "Evolutionary Universes in Society." *American Sociological Review* 29: 339–357.
    1965   "Value Objectivity in Social Science: an Interpretation of Max Weber's Contribution." Max Weber Centennial in *International Social Science Journal* 27.
    1966   "The Political Aspect of Social Structure and Process." In *Varieties of Political Theory,* edited by David Easton, pp. 71–112. Englewood Cliffs, N.J.: Prentice-Hall.
Passos Guimarães, Alberto
    1968   *Quatro Séculos de Latifúndio.* Rio de Janeiro: Paz e Terra.
Paz, Octavio
    1969   *El Laberinto de la Soledad.* 7th ed. Mexico City: Fondo de Cultura Económica; first published in *Cuadernos Americanos,* 1950.
Perroux, François
    1960   *La Coexistencia Pacifica.* Mexico City: Fondo de Cultura Económica; French original, *La Coexistence Pacifique.* Paris: Presses Universitaires de France, 1958.

1963   Économie et Societé—Contrainte, Échange, Don. Paris: Presses Universitaires de France.
1964   L'Économie du XX Siècle. 2nd ed. Paris: Presses Universitaires de France; first published, 1961.
1969   "Indépendance" de l'Économie Nationale et Indépendance des Nations. Paris: Aubier Montaigne.
Petras, James, and Zeitlin, Maurice
1968   Eds. Latin America: Reform or Revolution? New York: Fawcett.
Petrilli, Giuseppe
1967   Lo Stato Imprenditore. Capelli Edit.
Petrović, Gajo
1967   Marx in the Mid-Twentieth Century. New York: Doubleday; Yugoslavian original, Zagreb, 1965.
Piaget, Jean
1949   Traité de Logique. Paris: Armand Colin.
1950   Introduction à l'Epistémologie Génétique. Paris: Presses Universitaires de France.
1967   Biologie et Connaissance. Paris: Gallimard.
1968   Sagesse et Illusions de la Philosophie. Paris: Presses Universitaires de France.
Piao, Lin
1966   "Long Live the Victory of the People's War." 2nd ed. Peking: Foreign Language Press; originally published in Renmin Ribao (People's Daily), September 3, 1965.
Pinto, Anibal
1964   Chile, Una Economía Difícil. Mexico City: Fondo de Cultura Económica.
1965   "Political Aspects of Economic Development." In Obstacles to Change in Latin America, edited by Claudio Veliz, pp. 9–46. London: Oxford University Press.
1968   Política y Desarrollo. Santiago: Edit. Universitaria.
1970   with Sergio Aranda, Alberto Martinez, Orlando Caputo, Roberto Pizarro, Enzo Faletto, Eduardo Ruiz, Jacques Chonchol, Victor Brodersohn, Tomás Vasconi, Inés Reca, and Ariel Dorfman Chile, Hoy. Mexico City: Siglo XXI.
Pirenne, Henri
1947   Historia Económica y Social de la Edad Media. 4th ed. Mexico City: Fondo de Cultura Económica; French original, 1933.
1956   Historia de Europa, desde las Invasiones hasta el Siglo XVI. 2nd ed. Mexico City: Fondo de Cultura Económica; French original, Histoire de l'Europe des Invasions au XVIe Siècle. 1936.
Plekhanov, G. V.
1922-1927   A Year in the Homeland. 24 vols. Moscow: Marx-Engels Institute; first published, 1918.
1940a   The Materialist Conception of History. New York: International Publishers; Russian original published in Novoye Slovo, September 1897.
1940b   The Role of the Individual in History. New York: International Publishers; Russian original published in Nauchnoye Obozrenic, 1898.
1945   Cuestiones Fundamentales del Marxisms. Mexico City: Endiciones Frente Cultural; Russian original, 1908.
1956   Essai sur le Développement de la Conception Moniste de l'Histoire. Moscow: Ed. en Langues Étrangères; Russian original, 1895.
Poulantzas, Nicos
1970   Pouvoir Politique et Classes Sociales. Paris: Maspero.
Prebisch, Raul
1950   The Economic Development of Latin America and Its Principal Problems. CEPAL.
1963a   "Stabilizing the Terms of Trade of Underdeveloped Countries." Economic Bulletin for Latin America 8, no. 1. CEPAL.
1963b   Towards Dynamic Development for Latin America. CEPAL (C/CN.12/16).
1970   Transformacion y Desarrollo—La Gran Tarea de América Latina. Report to the Inter-American Development Bank.
Puiggros, Rodolfo
1969   Historia Crítica de los Partidos Políticos Argentinos. 5 vols. Buenos Aires: Jorge Alvarez Edit.

Pumaruna-Letts, Ricardo
    1971   *Peru: Révolution Socialiste ou Caricature de Révolution?* Paris: Maspero.
Pye, Lucian W.
    1963   Ed. *Communications and Political Development.* Studies in Political Development, vol. 1. Princeton, N.J.: Princeton University Press.
    1965   with Sidney Verba, eds. *Political Culture and Political Development.* Studies in Political Development, vol. 5. Princeton, N.J.: Princeton University Press.
    1966a *Politics, Personality and Nation Building—Burma's Search for Identity.* New Haven, Conn.: Yale University Press; first published, Cambridge, Mass.: M.I.T. Press, 1962.
    1966b *Aspects of Political Development.* Boston: Little, Brown.

Quigley, Carroll
    1961   *The Evolution of Civilizations.* New York: Macmillan.
    1968   *The World Since 1939—A History.* New York: Collier Books; originally published as Part 2 of *Tragedy and Hope,* 1966.

Radcliffe-Brown, Alfred Reginald
    1952   *Structure and Function in Primitive Society.* London: Cohen & West.
Ramos, Jorge Abelardo
    1949   *América Latina: Un País.* Buenos Aires: Edit. Octubre.
    1957   *Revolución y Contrarevolución en la Argentina—Las Masas en Nuestra Historia.* Buenos Aires: Edit. Amerindia.
    1959   *Historia Politica del Ejército Argentino.* Buenos Aires: Peña Lillo Edit.
    1961   *Manuel Ugarte y la Revolución Latinoamericana.* Buenos Aires: Edit. Coyoacan.
    1965   *Revolución y Contrarrevolución en la Argentina.* vol. 2, *Historia de la Argentina en el Siglo XX.* Buenos Aires: Plus Ultra.
    1968a *Ejército y Semi-Colonia.* Buenos Aires: Edit. Sudestada.
    1968b *Historia de la Nacion Latinoamericana.* Buenos Aires: Peña Lillo Edit.
Rangel, Ignacio
    1957a *Dualidade Básica da Economia Brasileira.* Rio de Janeiro: ISEB.
    1957b *Introdução ao Estudo do Desenvolvimento Econômico Brasileiro.* Rio de Janeiro: Liv. Progresso Edit.
    1960   *Recursos Ociosos na Economia Nacional.* Rio de Janeiro: ISEB.
    1963   *A Inflação Brasileira.* Rio de Janeiro: Tempo Brasileiro.
Reinach, Salomon
    1960   *Orpheus—A History of Religion.* Rev. and enlarg. London: Peter Owen; French original, 1924.
Renan, Ernest
    1887   "Qu'est-ce qu'une Nation?" Paris.
Rex, John
    1961   *Key Problems of Sociological Theory.* London: Routledge and Kegan Paul.
Riasanovsky, Nicholas V.
    1966   *A History of Russia.* 2nd ed. New York: Oxford University Press; first published, 1963.
Ribeiro, Darcy
    1968   *Estudos de Antropologia da Civilização.* vol. 1, *O Processo Civilizatório.* Rio de Janeiro: Edit. Civilização Brasileira.
    1970   *Estudos de Antropologia da Civilização.* vol. 2, *As Américas e a Civilização.* Rio de Janeiro: Edit. Civilização Brasileira.
Robinson, Joan
    1956   *An Essay on Marxian Economics.* London: Macmillan.
Rocker, Rudolf
    1939   *Nationalism and Culture.* Los Angeles: Rocker Publ. Committee.
Rodrigues, José Honorio
    1957   *Teoria da História do Brasil.* 2nd ed. 2 vols. São Paulo: Cia. Edit. Nacional; first published, 1949.
    1965   *Conciliação e Reforma no Brasil.* Rio de Janeiro: Edit. Civilização Brasileira.
    1966   *Vida e História.* Rio de Janeiro: Edit. Civilização Brasileira.

1970   *Aspirações Nacionais.* 4th ed. Rio de Janeiro: Edit. Civilização Brasileira; first published, 1963.

Rostovzeff, Mikhail
1926   *Social and Economic History of the Roman Empire.* Spanish translation, *Historia Social y Económica del Imperio Romano,* 2 vols. Madrid: Espasa Calpe, 1957.
1926–1928   *A History of the Ancient World,* 2 vols. London: Oxford University Press.
1959   *The Social and Economic History of the Hellenistic World.* London; first published, 1941.
1960   *Rome.* London: Oxford University Press. From vol. 2 of *A History of the Ancient World.*
1963   *Greece.* London: Oxford University Press. From vol. 1 of *A History of the Ancient World.*

Roszak, Theodor
1969   *The Making of a Counterculture.* New York: Anchor Books.

Rudner, Richard S.
1966   *Philosophy of Social Science.* Englewood Cliffs, N.J.: Prentice-Hall.

Rustow, Dankwart
1964   with Robert E. Ward, eds. *Political Modernization in Japan and Turkey.* Studies in Political Development, vol. 3. Princeton, N.J.: Princeton University Press.

Sagnac, Philippe, and de Saint-Leger, A.
1949   *Louis XIV.* Peuples et Civilisations, edited by Louis Halphen and Philippe Sagnac, vol. 10. Paris: Presses Universitaires de France.

Sahlins, Marshall, and Service, Elman R.
1965   Eds. *Evolution and Culture.* Ann Arbor: University of Michigan Press; 3rd print.; first published, 1960.

Sakharov, André D.
1968   *Progress, Coexistence and Intellectual Freedom.* Translated by *The New York Times.* New York: Norton.

Salomon, Albert
1963   *In Praise of Enlightenment.* New York: Meridian Books.

Samaran, Charles
1961   Ed. *L'Histoire et ses Méthodes. Encyclopédie de la Pléiade.* Paris: Gallimard.

Sanson, George
1958–1964   *A History of Japan.* 3 vols. London: Cresset Press.

San Tiago Dantas, F. C.
1962   *Política Externa Independente.* Rio de Janeiro: Edit. Civilização Brasileira.
1964   *Dom Quixote—Um Apólogo da Alma Ocidental.* 2nd ed. Rio de Janeiro: Tempo Brasileiro; first published, 1947.

Sartre, Jean-Paul
1940   *L'Imaginaire.* Paris: Gallimard.
1943   *L'Être et le Néant.* Paris: Gallimard.
1946   *L'Existentialisme est un Humanisme.* Paris: Nagel.
1948–1968   *Situations I to V.* Paris: Gallimard.
1949   with David Rousser and Gérard Rosenthal. *Entretiens sur la Politique.* Paris: Gallimard.
1960   *Critique de la Raison Dialectique.* Paris: Gallimard.
1961   *Cuba.* New York: Ballantine Books.

Schaff, Adam
1963   *A Philosophy of Man.* New York: Delta Books; Polish original, *Filosofia Czlowieka,* 1961.
1970   *Marxism and the Human Individual.* New York: McGraw-Hill; Polish original, *Marksizm, Jednostka.* Warsaw: Panstwowe Wydawnictwo Naukowe.
1971   *Histoire et Verité.* Paris: Anthropos.

Schapera, I.
1967   *Government and Politics in Tribal Societies.* New York: Schocken Books; first published, 1956.

Schilpp, Paul Arthur
1949   Ed. *The Philosophy of Ernst Cassirer.* New York: Tudor Publishing Co.

Schmitter, Philippe
1971   *Interest Conflict and Political Change in Brazil.* Stanford, Calif.: Stanford
        University Press.
Schneider, Ronald M.
1965   *Brazil-Election Factbook,* no. 2. Institute for Comparative Study of Political
        Systems, Operation and Policy Research, Inc.
1966a   with Robert C. Kingsbury. *An Atlas of Latin American Affairs.* New York:
        Praeger; 2nd print.; first published, 1965.
1966b   *Supplement to Brazil-Election Factbook,* no. 2. Institute for Comparative
        Study of Political Systems, Operation and Policy Research, Inc.
1971   *The Political System of Brazil—Emergence of a Modernizing Authoritarian
        Regime, 1964–70.* New York: Columbia University Press.
Schubart, Walter
1938   *Europa und die Seele des Ostens.* Lucerne.
Schumpeter, Joseph A.
1944   *Teoría del Desenvolvimiento Económico.* Mexico City: Fondo de Cultura
        Económica; German original, *Theorie der Wirtschaftlichen Entwicklung,* 1911.
1950   *Capitalism, Socialism and Democracy.* London: Allen & Unwin; first pub-
        lished, 1943.
1954a   *Economic Doctrine and Method.* London: Allen & Unwin; German original,
        Epochen der Dogmen-und Methodengeschichte. Tübingen: Mohr, 1912.
1954b   *History of Economic Analysis.* Edited from manuscript by Elizabeth Boody
        Schumpeter. New York: Oxford University Press.
1966   *Imperialism.* Cleveland: Meridian Books, 9th print.; first published in English,
        1951; German original published in *Archiv für Sozialwissenschaft und Sozial-
        politik* 46 (1919) and 57 (1927).
Schurmann, Franz
1966   *Ideology and Organization in Communist China.* Berkeley: University of
        California Press.
1967   with Orville Schell, eds. *The China Reader.* 3 vols. New York: Vintage Books;
        first published, 1966.
Schwartz, Harry
1968   *An Introduction to Soviet Economy.* Columbus, Ohio: Charles E. Merrill.
Sée, Henri
1969   *La France Économique et Sociale au XVIII Siècle.* Rev. ed. Paris: Armand Colin.
Seeley, Sir John
1919   *The Expansion of England.* 2nd ed. London; first published, 1883.
Servan-Schreiber, Jean-Jacques
1967   *Le Défit Américain.* Paris: Ed. Denoël.
Service, Elman R.
1967   *Primitive Social Organization—An Evolutionary Perspective.* New York:
        Random House; 6th print.; first published, 1962.
Shaffer, Harry G., and Prybyla, Jan
1961   Eds. *From Underdevelopment to Affluence.* New York: Appleton-Century-
        Crofts.
Shaw, Bernard
1948   *Fabian Essays.* London: Allen & Unwin; first published, 1889.
Shils, Edward
1962   *Political Development in the New States.* The Hague: Mouton; first published
        in *Comparative Studies in Society and History* 2 (1959–1960).
Shonfield, Andrew
1965   *Modern Capitalism.* New York: Oxford University Press.
Shoup, General David M.
1969   "The New American Militarism." *The Atlantic,* April, pp. 51–56.
Shubik, Martin
1964   Ed. *Game Theory and Related Approaches to Social Behaviors.* New York:
        John Wiley.
Silva Herzog, Jesús
1960   *Breve Historia de la Revolución Mexicana.* 2 vols. Mexico City: Fondo de
        Cultura Económica.

Silva Michelena, José A.
    1967   with Frank Bonilla. *The Politics of Change in Venezuela.* vol. 1, *A Strategy for Research on Social Policy.* Cambridge, Mass.: M.I.T. Press.
Skidmore, Thomas
    1967   *Politics in Brazil: 1930-1964.* New York: Oxford University Press.
Snow, Edgar
    1962   *The Other Side of the River: Red China Today.* New York: Random House; first published, 1961.
Sombart, Werner
    1946   *El Apogeu del Capitalism.* 2 vols. Mexico City: Fondo de Cultura Económica; German original, *Der Modern Kapitalismus.* 6 vols. Leipzig, 1902.
    1951   *Lujo y Capitalismo.* 2nd ed. Madrid: Revista de Occidente; German original, *Luxus und Kapitalismus.* 1912.
Sorokin, Pitirim
    1937-1941   *Social and Cultural Dynamics.* 4 vols. New York: Bedminister Press.
    1945   *A Crise do Nosso Tempo.* São Paulo: Edit. Universit.; English original, *The Crisis of Our Age.* New York: Dutton, 1941.
    1957   *Social and Cultural Dynamics.* revis. and abridg. ed., Boston: Porter Sargent.
    1963   *Modern Historical and Social Philosophies.* New York: Dover Publications; first published as *Social Philosophies of an Age of Crises,* Boston: Beacon Press, 1950.
    1964   *The Basic Trends of Our Time.* New Haven, Conn.: Yale University Press.
    1965   *Fads and Foibles in Modern Sociology.* Chicago: Henry Regnery; first published, 1956.
Soubisse, Louis
    1967   *Le Marxisme Après Marx.* Paris: Aubier Montaigne.
Spengler, Oswald
    1947   *La Decadencia de Occidente.* 4 vols. Translated by Manuel Garcia Morente. Madrid: Espasa Calpe; German original, *Der Untergang des Abendlandes.* 2 vols. Munich: Beck, 1918-1922.
Staley, Eugene
    1961   *The Future of Underdeveloped Countries.* New York: Praeger.
Stalin, Josef V.
    1946-1951   *Sochineniya (Works).* 13 vols. Moscow.
    1945   *Problems of Leninism.* English translation from 11th Russian ed.
Steel, Ronald
    1968   *Pax Americana.* New York: Viking; first published, 1967.
Storry, Richard
    1965   *A History of Modern Japan.* Baltimore: Penguin Books; first published, 1960.
Strachey, John
    1956   *Contemporary Capitalism.* London: Victor Gollancz.
Sunkel, Osvaldo
    1967a   "El Transfondo Estructural de los Problemas del Desarrollo Latinoamericano." *El Trimestre Económico,* no. 3.
    1967b   "Política Nacional de Desarrollo y Dependencia Externa." *Estudios Internacionales* 1, no. 1: 43-75.
    1969   "La Tarea Política y Teórica del Planificador en América Latina." *Estudios Internacionales* 2, no. 4: 519-529.
    1970a   with the collaboration of Pedro Paz. *El Subdesarrollo Latinoamericano y la Teoría del Desarrollo.* Mexico City: Siglo XXI.
    1970b   Ed. *Integración Política y Económica: la Experiencia Europeia y el Proceso Latinoamericano.* Santiago: Edit. Universitaria.
    1971   "Capitalismo Transnacional y Desintegracion Nacional en la América Latina." *El Trimestre Económico* 38, no. 2: 571-628.
Sweezy, Paul M.
    1956   *The Theory of Capitalism Development.* New York: Monthly Review Press.
    1966   with Paul Baran. *Monopoly Capital.* New York: Monthly Review Press.

Taber, Robert
    1967   *La Guerra de la Pulga.* Mexico City: Edit. Era. English original, *The War of the Flea.* New York: Lyle Stuart, 1965.

Tang, Peter S. H., and Maloney, Joan M.
  1967   *Communist China: The Domestic Scene—1949-1967*. South Orange, N.J.:
          Seton Hall University Press.
Tavares, Maria da Conceição
  1964   "Auge y Declinio del Proceso de Substitución de Importaciones en el Brasil."
          Boletín Económico de América Latina 9, no. 1: 1-60. CEPAL.
Taylor, G. R.
  1951   *The Transportation Revolution*. New York: Rinehart & Co.
Taylor, Henry Osborn
  1958   *The Emergence of the Christian Culture in the West*. New York: Harper &
          Brothers.
Thompson, J. M.
  1955   *Louis Napoleon and the Second Empire*. New York.
Tillich, Paul
  1957   *The Protestant Era*. Abridg. ed. Chicago: University of Chicago Press; first
          published, 1948.
  1964a   *Biblical Religion and the Search for Ultimate Reality*. Chicago: University of
          Chicago Press; first published, 1955.
  1964b   *The Theology of Culture*. New York: Oxford University Press; first
          published, 1959.
  1967   *Systematic Theology*. 1-vol. ed. Chicago: University of Chicago Press; first
          published in 3 vols., 1951-1963.
  1968   *The Courage to Be*. New Haven, Conn.: Yale University Press, first published,
          1952.
Tönnies, Ferdinand
  1933   *Desarrollo de la Cuestión Social*. 2nd ed. Barcelona: Edit. Labor; German
          original, *Entwicklung der Sozialen Frage*. 1927.
  1946   *Principios de Sociologia*. 2nd ed. Mexico City: Fondo de Cultura Económica;
          German original, *Einführung in die Soziologia*. Stuttgart, 1931.
  1947   *Comunidad y Sociedad*. Buenos Aires: Edit. Losada; German original,
          Gemeinschaft Und Gesellschaft. Leipzig, 1887.
Toynbee, Arnold
  1934-1961   *A Study of History*. 12 vols. London: Oxford University Press.
  1946-1957   *A Study of History*. 2 vols. Abridged by D. C. Somervell. London:
               Oxford University Press.
  1952   *The World and the West*. London: Oxford University Press.
  1956   *An Historian's Approach to Religion*. London: Oxford University Press.
  1962   *America and the World Revolution*. New York: Oxford University Press.
Trotsky, Leon
  1946   *Mi Vida—Ensayo Autobiografico*. 2 vols. Mexico City: Editorial Colon;
          Russian original, Berlin, 1929.
  1950   *Histoire de la Révolution Russe*. 2 vols. Paris: Ed. du Seuil, Russian original,
          1932-1933.
  1962   *Lenin*. New York: Capricorn Books; Russian original, Moscow, 1924.
  1965   *The Revolution Betrayed*. New York: Merit Publishers; first published, London,
          1937.
Tucker, Robert
  1968   *Nation or Empire? The Debate Over American Foreign Policy*. Baltimore: Johns
          Hopkins Press.
Turner, Frederick J.
  1961   *Frontier and Section*. Selected Essays of Frederick J. Turner. Englewood Cliffs,
          N.J.: Prentice-Hall.

Vekemans, Roger
  1962   with J. L. Segundo. "Ensaio de Tipologia Socio-Econômica de los Países
          Latinoamericanos." In *Aspectos Sociales del Desarrollo Económico en América
          Latina*, vol. 1, edited by Egbert de Vries and José Medina Echavarria, pp. 72-
          100. UNESCO. Liège.
Veliz, Claudio
  1965   Ed. *Obstacles to Change in Latin America*. London: Oxford University Press.

1967   Ed. *The Politics of Conformity in Latin America.* London: Oxford University Press.
1969   "Centralismo, Nacionalismo e Integración." *Estudios Internacionales* 3, no. 1: 3–22.
Vernon, Raymond
1963   *The Dilemma of Mexico's Development—The Roles of the Private and Public Sectors.* Cambridge, Mass.: Harvard University Press.
1966   Ed. *How Latin America Views the U.S. Investor.* New York: Praeger.
Vieira Pinto, Alvaro
1960   *Consciência e Realidade Nacional.* 2 vols. Rio de Janeiro: ISEB.
Viet, Jean
1967   *Les Méthodes Structuralistes dans les Sciences Sociales.* 2nd ed. Paris: Mounton; first published, 1965.
Vita, Luis Washington
1950   *A Filosofia no Brasil.* São Paulo: Martins.
1965   *Introdução à Filosofia.* 2nd ed. São Paulo: Edit. Melhoramentos; first published, 1964.
1968   *Antologia do Pensamento Social e Político no Brasil.* São Paulo: Edit. Grijalbo.
Von Lazar, Arpad
1969a   "Multi-National Enterprise and Latin American Integration: a Political View." *Journal of Inter-American Studies* 11.
1969b   with Robert R. Kaufman, eds. *Reform and Revolution—Readings in Latin American Politics.* Boston: Allyn and Bacon.
Von Martin, Alfred
1946   *Sociología del Renacimiento.* Mexico City: Fondo de Cultura Económica; German original, *Soziologie der Renaissance.* Stuttgart, 1932.

Ward, Robert E.
1964   with Dankwart Rustow, eds. *Political Modernization in Japan and Turkey.* Studies in Political Development, vol. 3. Princeton, N.J.: Princeton University Press.
1967   *Japan's Political System.* Englewood Cliffs, N.J.: Prentice-Hall.
Weber, Alfred
1932   *La Crisis de la Idea Moderna del Estado en Europa.* Spanish translation by J. Perez Banuc. Madrid: Revista de Occidente; German original, *Die Krise des Modernen Staatsgedankens in Europa.* Heidelberg, 1924.
1943   *Historia de la Cultura.* Mexico City: Fondo de Cultura Económica; German original, *Kulturgeschichte als Kultursoziologie.* Leiden, Holland, 1935.
Weber, Max
1920–1921 *Gesammelte Aufsätze zur Religionssoziologie.* 3 vols. Tübingen: Mohr.
vol. 1 includes:
1950   *The Protestant Ethic and the Spirit of Capitalism.* London: Allen & Unwin; 3rd print.; first published, 1930.
1962a   "The Protestant Sects and the Spirit of Capitalism." In *From Max Weber,* edited by Gerth and Mills, pp. 302–322. New York: Oxford University Press; 5th print.; first published, 1946.
1962b   "Die Wirtschaftsethik der Weltreligionen—Einleitung." Introduction translated as "The Social Psychology of the World Religions." In *From Max Weber,* edited by Gerth and Mills, pp. 267–301.
1962c   "Zwichenbetrachtung: Theorie der Stufen und Richtungen religiöser Weltablehnung." Translated as "Religious Rejections of the World and Their Directions." In *From Max Weber,* edited by Gerth and Mills, pp. 323–362.
1964   "Konfuzianismus und Taoismus." Translated as *The Religion of China: Confucianism and Taoism.* New York: Macmillan; first published, 1951.
vol. 2 includes:
1967   "Die Wirtschaftsethik der Weltreligionen—II, Hinduismus und Buddhismus." Partially translated as *The Religion of India.* New York: Free Press; first published, 1958.
vol. 3 includes:
1921   *Gesammelte Politische Schriften.* Munich: Drei Masken Verlag.

1922   *Gesammelte Aufsätze zur Wissenchaftslehre.* Edited by Marianne Weber. Tübingen: Mohr.

1944   *Wirtschaft und Gesellschaft.* Edited by Marianne Weber. Tübingen: Mohr; Spanish translation, *Economia y Sociedad.* 4 vols. Mexico City: Fondo de Cultura Económica.

1949   *The Methodology of the Social Sciences.* New York: Free Press. Partial translation.

1962   "Politik als Beruf." Translated as "Politics As a Vocation." In *From Max Weber,* edited by Gerth and Mills, pp. 77–128.

1967   "Die Wirtschaftsethik der Weltreligionen—III, Das antike Jundentum." Translated as *Ancient Judaism.* New York: Free Press; first published, 1952.

Weiner, Myron

1965   "Political Integration and Political Development." *Annals* 358: 52–64.

Welch, Claude E., Jr.

1967   *Political Modernization—A Reader in Comparative Political Change.* Belmont, Calif.: Wadsworth Publishing.

Werneck Sodré, Nelson

1963   *Introdução à Revolução Brasileira.* 2nd ed. Rio de Janeiro: Edit. Civilização Brasileira; first published, 1958.

1965a *A Ideologia do Colonialismo.* 2nd ed. Rio de Janeiro: Edit. Civilização Brasileira; first published, 1961.

1965b *História Militar do Brasil.* Rio de Janeiro: Edit. Civilização Brasileira.

1965c *História da Burguesia Brasileira.* 2nd ed. Rio de Janeiro: Edit. Civilização Brasileira; first published, 1964.

White, Leslie A.

1949   *The Science of Culture.* New York: Grove Press.

1959   *The Evolution of Culture—The Development of Civilization to the Fall of Rome.* New York: McGraw-Hill.

Whitehead, Alfred North

1929   *Process and Reality.* Cambridge, Eng.: Cambridge University Press.

1933   *Adventures of Ideas.* Cambridge, Eng.: Cambridge University Press.

1938   *Modes of Thought.* Cambridge, Eng.: Cambridge University Press.

Wilson, Charles

1966   *England's Apprenticeship, 1603–1763.* London.

Wiznitzer, Arnold

1960   *Jews in Colonial Brazil.* New York: Columbia University Press.

Wolf, Kurt, and Moore, Barrington

1968   Eds. *The Critical Spirit—Essays in Honor of Herbert Marcuse.* Boston: Beacon Press; first published, 1967.

Wraith, Ronald, and Simpkins, Edgar

1964   *Corruption in Developing Countries.* New York: Norton; first published, 1963.

Indexes

Name Index

Adorno, 484
Alessandri, Jorge, 37
Alexander II of Russia, 182, 252
Allende, Salvador, 500-503
Almond, Gabriel, 126, 138-146, 158,
    160-161, 191-192, 198-200, 204,
    208-209, 212, 225, 233, 311, 313-
    316, 331, quoted, 233-234
Alzogoray, General Julio, 532
Apter, David, 160-162, 198, 203-
    205, 209, 225, 233, 235-236
Aramburu, General Pedro, 532
Arbenz, Jacobo, 359
Aristotle, 85, 158, 160, 171, 225,
    264-265
Armas, Carlos Castillo, 359
Aujac, H., 222

Barbon, Nicholas, 245
Barr, Stringfellow, 366
Barraclough, Geoffrey, 359
Barrientos, General René, 517
Batista, 272, 278, 291, 489-490
Belaúnde Terry, Fernando, 515-516
Bell, Daniel, 533
Bendix, Reinhard, 196, 198
Benes, Eduard, 300

Berdyaev, Nicholas, 355
Bernstein, Eduard, 178
Betancourt, Rómolo, 441-442,
    446, 500, 503
Bismarck, 248-249, 275, 279,
    288, 433
Blanco, 436, 504
Bodin, 80
Branco, Castello, 83, 212, 461
Brezhnev, 226
Brinton, Crane, 89
Brodbeck, May, 222, quoted, 222-
    223
Brzezinski, Zbigniew, 364-365
Bury, J.B., 308
Busch, Colonel Germán, 516

Caesar, 39
Caldero, Rafael, 500
Calles, 37
Cambrai, General Pasquer, 533
Campos, Roberto, 472
Candia, General Alfredo Ovando, 509
Cárdenas, 37, 346, 441-442, 445
Casanova, Pablo Gonzáles,
    413-414
Castro, Fidel, 303, 349, 484, 489-491

Catherine II, 173–174, 176, 242, 252
Ceceña, José Luis, 413–414
Charles V, 367
Charles III of Spain, 176
Chiang Kai-shek, 254, 493
Childe, V. Gordon, 51, 114, 116
Choncholl, Jacques, 502
Chosu clan, 250
Cleisthenes, 177, 182, 461
Colbert, 247
Colorado, 436, 504
Comte, 10, 309
Condorcet, 179, 239, 309
Cooley, Charles H., 103
Costa e Silva, General Arthur da, 532
Cromwell, 245, 247

Dahl, Robert, 83, 100
Davis, Kingsley, 15, 18, 103, 109
De Gaulle, 288, 350
Delgado, Julián, 414
Deutsch, Karl, 80, 198, 201, 203,
    222–223, 345, quoted, 336
Diamant, Alfred, 198, 203
Disraeli, 175, 183
Dobzhansky, Theodosius, 113
Durkheim, Emile, 103
Duvalier, 490
Duverger, Maurice, 81, 222

Easton, David, 80, 126, 128, 132,
    135, 137–144, 191, 199
Echeverria, 505
Ehrlich, Paul, 356
Eisenhower, President, 549
Eisenstadt, S.N., 146, 192, 198, 209,
    225, 233–235, 310, 331
Elizabeth I, Queen, 245
Ellul, Jacques, 354
Emerson, Rupert, quoted, 335

Fainsod, Merle, 140
Farias, General Cordeiro, 532
Farrell, 421
Ferkiss, Victor C., 354

Ferrer, Aldo, 525
Fieldhouse, D.K., 361
Fontenelle, 309
Franco, 83, 350
Frankfurt, Henri, 122
Frederick II of Prussia, 176
Frei, Eduardo, 37, 443, 446, 467,
    500–501, 503
Freud, 24
Friedrich, Carl, 81–82, quoted, 335
Frondizi, Arturo, 89, 350, 441,
    443, 446
Fulbright, J. William, 363, quoted,
    365
Furtado, Celso, 447

Gaitán, 442
Galbraith, J.K., 227
Gallagher, J., 361
Gallie, W.B., 430
Garaudy, Roger, 484
Garcia, José Luis Roca, 517
Gavin, General James M., 363
Goldmann, Lucien, 224
González, General Juan José, 517
Goulart, 441, 443, 446, 453
Guevara, Ernesto Che, 489, 556
Gurvitch, Georges, 21, 103, 105, 224
Gustavus III of Sweden, 176

Hapsburgs, the, 48
Hart, H.L.A., 82–83
Hartz, Louis, 246, 394
Haya de la Torre, Victor Raúl,
    514–515
Hegel, 14, 63, 309
Heilbroner, Robert L., 227
Henry IV of France, 247
Herrera, Felipe, 465–467
Hilferding, Rudolf, 360
Hirschman, Albert, 509
Hizen clan, 250
Hobbes, 63, 80, 318
Hobson, J.A., 360
Horowitz, David, 366

Horowitz, Irving, 198, 204, 227
Houghton, Neal, 366
Hume, 63, 80
Huntington, Samuel, 195, 198, 201–
202, 209, 310
Huxley, 53

Ibáñez, 441–442, 445–446
Ibarra, Velasco, 534
Ito, 250
Izabel, Princess, 182

Jijon, Captain Ramón Castro, 534
Jiménez, 503
John of Salisbury, 63
Johnson, Chalmers, 172, 176
Johnson, President Lyndon, 360,
548–551, 553
Johnson administration, 424, 548
Joseph I of Portugal, 176
Joseph II of Austria, 176
Julian, Emperor, 44
Julien, Claude, quoted, 362
Juvenel, 81

Kahler, Erich, quoted, 309–310
Kahn, Herman, 354, 357, 405–406
Kant, 63, 80
Kaoru, Inouye, 250
Kaplan, Marcos, 80
Kassof, Allen, 227
Kautsky, Karl, 45
Kemal, Mustafa, 47–48, 349
Kennan, George F., 363–364, quoted,
364
Kennedy, President, 360, 548–549, 552
Kennedy administration, 422–424
Keynes, John Maynard, 473
Kido, 250
Komei, 272
Kubitschek, 409, 441–442, 446, 505

Lanusse, General Alejandro, 506, 525,
535
Lasswell, Harold D., 80

Lechin, 517–518
Lenin, 37, 45, 47, 226, 254, 256,
302, 360–361, 483–484
Leoni, Raúl, 500
Leopold II of Austria, 176
Levingston, General, 506, 523,
525, 532
Lévy-Bruhl, Lucien, 122
Lévy-Strauss, Claude, 222–223
Lima, General Albuquerque, 533
Liska, George, 367–370, 545–546,
551, quoted, 367–368
List, Friedrich, 248
Lleras, 443
Locke, 63, 80, 179
Lotka, 53
Louis XIV, 247
Louis Napoleon, 249, 288
Louis XIII, 247
Lundberg, George A., 21
Luxemburg, Rosa, 45

McGovern, George, 371
Machado, 291
McHale, John, 354
Machiavelli, 69, 80, 225, 368
MacIver, Robert, 103, 112
Magdoff, Harry, 361
Maine, Sir Henry, 112
Mannheim, 424
Mao, 256, 377, 492–493
Marcuse, Herbert, 484
Marshall, 239
Martindale, Don, 9, 56
Marx, 20, 24, 37, 39, 45, 63, 69, 95,
171, 181, 214, 217, 225, 232–233,
255, 260, 334, 349, 463, 473, 476,
484, 486–488
Masayoshi, Matsukata, 250
Mateos, López, 441, 443, 446, 490,
505
Mauá, Viscount, 452
Medici, 525
Meiji, the, 174–175, 197, 244, 249–
251, 268, 274, 279, 327, 382, 417

Mercado, José Ortiz, 517
Mill, John Stuart, 179
Millikan, 197
Miranda, General Rogelio, 510, 518
Mohammed Riza Pahlavi, Shah, 176
Montero, General Torranzo, 532
Montesquieu, 177, 179, 265
Morgenthau, Hans, 363, quoted, 364–365
Mosca, Gaetano, 260
Mossadegh, 181
Muhammad, 43–44, 463
Mun, Thomas, 245
Mussolini, 313
Mutsuhito, Emperor, 250

Nadel, S. F., 224
Nagy, 359
Napoleon, 39, 87–88, 178
Napoleon III, 248–249, 275, 288, 433
Nasser, 159
Nehru, 358
Nixon, President, 549–551
Nixon administration, 548–550
Novoa, General Alberto Ruiz, 534

Oglesby, Carl, quoted, 361–362
Okubo, 250
Okuma, 250
Ongania, 83, 505, 522, 533
Organski, 198, 203, 311–316, 318–319, 323, 421, quoted, 362
Ovando, General, 286, 482, 509–510, 512, 514, 517–518
Owen, 483

Packenham, Robert A., 198
Page, Charles, 103
Pareto, Vilfredo, 260–261
Park, Charles F., Jr., 356
Parsons, Talcott, 11–13, 15, 17, 19, 21, 32, 80, 84, 100, 109, 126, 128–129, 132, 138, 191, 209
Paz Estenssoro, Victor, 286, 350, 516–517

Perón, Juan, 350, 408, 441–442, 445–446, 451, 453, 506
Perry, Commodore, 249
Peter the Great, 173, 242, 252, 279
Petty, William, 245
Philip V of Macedonia, 359
Philip II and Philip III of Spain, 394
Piaget, Jean, 224
Pinilla, General Rojas, 441–442, 446
Plato, 80, 85, 264–265, 308
Plekhanov, G. V., 45
Polybius, 265
Portella, General Jayme, 532
Powell, G. B., Jr., 126, 138, 140, 142, 145
Prebisch, Raul, 337, 403, 465
Proudhon, 483
Pye, Lucian, 196–198, 201, 203–204, 214

Queiroz, Mauricio Vinhas de, 414–415
Quesnay, 239

Radcliffe-Brown, Alfred R., 223
Restreppo, Lleras, 446, 505, 534
Rex, John, 20
Ricardo, 239
Richelieu, 247
Riencourt, Amaury de, 366
Riza Shah Pahlavi, 176
Robinson, R., 361
Rosenstein-Rodan, Paul, 509
Rostow, 249, 308, 312
Rousseau, 80, 177, 179
Rudner, Richard S., 222, quoted, 223

Sahlins, Marshall D., 55–56, 190
Saigo, 250
Salazar, 350
Salina, Siles, 517
Santa Cruz, Marcelo Quiroga, 517
Sarmiento, 437
Sartre, Jean-Paul, 484
Satsuma clan, 250

Schneider, General, 502
Schubart, Walter, 355
Servan-Schreiber, Jean-Jacques, 467
Service, Elman R., 55–56, 113, 115, 190
Shils, Edward, 233–234
Shoup, General David M., quoted, 363
Silvert, Kalman, 197
Smith, Adam, 239, 245
Socrates, 81
Solon, 177, 182
Somozo, 490
Sorokin, Pitirim, 309, 354–355
Spencer, 52
Spengler, Oswald, 309, 355
Stalin, 37, 45, 422
Stammler, 82
Steel, Ronald, 371, quoted, 362–363
Stolypin, 252
Suazo, Siles, 516
Suleiman, 46
Sulla, 181
Sun Yat-sen, 254, 349, 492
Sunkel, Osvaldo, 509

Tacitus, 463
Tavora, General Juarez, 532
Thomas Aquinas, Saint, 63
Tokugawa clan, 250–251
Tönnies, Ferdinand, 103
Toro, Colonel David, 516

Torres, General, 286, 509–510, 512, 514, 518
Tosa clan, 250
Toynbee, Arnold, 309, 355, quoted, 366
Trotsky, 55, 302
Trujillo, 490
Truman, President, 364, 369, 549
Tucker, Robert, 369, 371
Tudors, the, 245
Turgot, 309
Tylor, 52

Uriburu, 421

Vargas, 421, 441, 445–446, 453, 505
Vekemans, Roger, 400
Velasco, General, 482, 510–511, 513, 516
Viet, Jean, 223
Villaroel, Major Gualberto, 516
Villegas, General Osiris, 533

Weber, Max, 33, 80, 138
Weiner, Myron, 198, 204, 354
White, Leslie, 209
Wiener, Anthony, 405
William IV, King, 174
Witte, 252
Wiznitzer, Arnold, 434

Yamagata, 250

Subject Index

Chilean experiment, the, 500–504
Chinese model for Latin America, 492–494
Chinese process of development, 252–255
Civil regime, 237
Cold war fog, 357–360
Colombia, 468
Colonial fascism, 532–533
  propensity for, in Latin America, 474–475
Colonial praetorianism in Latin America, 478–479
Communism, 242
  as a macromodel, 226–227
Community and society, 103
Comparative politics
  basic model for, 141–153
  general presentation of, 139–169
  typology of systems and regimes in, 153–169
Congruence. See Principle of congruence
Consensus building, 325–326, 329
Conservation regime, 237
Consumption, democracy of, 546
Counterelite, concept of, 263
Counterrevolution, 181
Credit, political, social, and cultural, 127–128
Cuba, 400–402
Cuban model for Latin America, 489–492

Democracy
  of allocation, 546
  of consumption, 546
Denationalization in Latin America
  cultural, 417–418
  economic, 412–417
  general discussion of, 410–412
  politico-military, 418–425
Dependence
  autonomy and, 461–462
    model for, 536

forms and consequences of, 381–384
  in Latin America, 470–472
Development processes
  Chinese, 252–255
  English, 245–246
  French, 247–249
  German, 247–249
  historical and critical comparison of, 255–257
  Japanese, 249–252
  Russian, 252–256
Developmental socialism, 242, 283–284
  how? 298–303
  why? 297–298
Dualism in Latin America, 395–398, 433–435
  legacy of, 454–455

Ecology, problem of, 355–356
Elite, the
  concept of, 259–264
  directional performance by, 266
  exaction enjoyment by, 266
  views of, performance, 260
    stratum-functional, 260–263
Elite functionality
  achievement in development of, 267
  classical explanations of, 264–265
  conditions for, 267–269
  cost-benefit approach to, 265–267
  and enlightened self-interest, 268
  general discussion of, 264–269
  good rules view of, 265
  internalized values and, 268
  and mass pressure, 268–269
  moral view of, 264–265
  social acknowledgment of, 267
Empire or commonwealth, 538–539, 542–544
English process of development, 245–246

Nationalism, military, 533
Neoliberalism, 239
  as a macromodel, 226–229

Open and cyclical processes, 326–329
Operational models, 224–227
  general discussion of, 278–284
Operational political models
  actual designing of, 232–233
  constituent elements of, 228–231
  general analysis of, 228–232
  general classification of, 236–243
  limits of efficiency of, 231
  prerequisites of, 231–232
  survey of literature on, 233–236
Opus dei, 532
Ordinated socialism, 238
Ordination regime, 238

Paraguay, 465–466, 469, 475
Patrimonial regimes, 237
Peru, 466–467
Peruvian experiment, the, 514–516
  applicability of model, 518–523
Planning, as an historical trend, 244
Political, the
  basic concepts of, 63–67
  comparative analysis of, 69–83
  general discussion of, 63–67
  major implications of, 67–69
Political action, 83–91
Political change
  content variables of, 179–181
  general discussion of, 170–179
  means and contents for, 170–171
  as radical and progressive reformism,
    177–179
  reform as way of, 173–175
  reforms, modalities, and, 176–177
  revolution as way of, 171–173
  revolutionary, radical, and progres-
    sive, 181–183
Political development
  classification of views on, 195–196
  conditions for, 331–333

as contribution to overall develop-
    ment of society, 203, 215–
    216
as development of the capability of
    the political system, 213–214
as development of consensus, 217
political capability and, 203
as a political direction, 207, 209
as political institutionalization,
    201–202
as political modernization, 196–201
  plus political institutionalization,
    204–205
as political responsiveness, 203
as a process, 207, 209–210
stages of, 310–316
  Almond's view of, 311
  Eisenstadt's view of, 310
  Huntington's view of, 310
  Osganski's view of, 311–314, 316
variables in, 207–208
Political external discreteness, 86–91
Political goal
  as inherently achievable, 229–230,
    232–233
  as isomorphically represented, 230–
    231
Political internal unity, 83–85
Political mobilizability, 347–349
Political modernization plus political
    institutionalization, 210–213
Political plane, the
  general discussion of, 91–101
  horizontal dimension of, 91–93
  vertical dimension of, 93–94
Political process, the, 85–91
Political regime, 95–96
Political system, the
  Almond's views on, 138–141
  classification of, 140–154
  critical discussion of, 141–145
  Easton's views on, 135–138
  general discussions of, 129–139
Politics
  of abundance, 312

Politics (*Continued*)
comparative, 139–165
of industrialization, 311–312
three models of, 312
of national welfare, 312
"nonpolitical," 83–85
of primitive unification, 311
Polity
formation of, 115–118
founding beliefs of, 122–125
Populism in Latin America
ambiguity and vagueness of, 445–446
behavior of establishment vis-à-vis, 450–451
failure of implementation and conception of, 445–448
financial deficiencies of, 446–448
inability to attract elite support for, 445
inability to define purpose of, 445
incapacity of self-defense against, 448–450
leaders of, 442–443
national bourgeoisie and, 451–453
poor management of, 448
and populist indecision, 453–454
Power
authority and, 94–100
uses of, 95–96
validity and, 63–66
Primitive authority
and formation of the polity, 115–118
and formation of the tribe, 112–115
general discussion of, 109–118
Primitive or archaic societies, 272
Principle of congruence
changes starting at the cultural plane, 38–43
changes starting at the participations plane, 43–45
changes starting at the political plane, 45–49
definition of, 43
general discussion of, 41–49

and noncongruent changes, disruptive cases of, 48–49
regressive cases of, 46–48
Progressivism, 182

Radicalism, 182
Reactionary change, 182
Real stages, 318–322
Reality
general framework of, 9–11
Parson's conception of, 11–12
criticism of, 12–14
Reconciliation regime, 238
Reform
as a content of change, 173–175
in Latin America, content requirement of, 498–500
feasibility of, 497–498
general conclusions on, 526–527
and progressive reformism, 500–503
as a way of change, 173–175
Regimes
civil, 237
conservation, 237
mobilization, 238
ordination, 238
patrimonial, 237
political, 95–96
of power, 96–97
reconciliation, 238
totalitarian, 237
Regressive change, 182–183
Revolution
as a content of change, 181–182
as a way of change, 171–173
Russian process of development, 252–256

Self-validating commands, 124
Social change
evolution and, 52–56
historical change and, 49–52
Social group, the
authority as role in, 109

72 73 74 75 76 9 8 7 6 5 4 3 2 1